Marketing research
Text and cases

Marketing research
Text and cases

HARPER W. BOYD, Jr., Ph.D.
Donaghey Distinguished Professor
of Business Administration
University of Arkansas at Little Rock

RALPH WESTFALL, Ph.D.
Dean, College of Business Administration
University of Illinois at Chicago Circle

STANLEY F. STASCH, Ph.D.
Charles H. Kellstadt Professor of Marketing
Loyola University of Chicago

Fifth Edition   1981

RICHARD D. IRWIN, INC.   Homewood, Illinois   60430
Irwin-Dorsey Limited   Georgetown, Ontario   L7G 4B3

ISBN 0-256-02530-4
Library of Congress Catalog Card No. 80–84593

Printed in the United States of America

1 2 3 4 5 6 7 8 9 0 K 8 7 6 5 4 3 2 1

To
L. B. B.,
C. E. W.,
and
J. M. S.

Preface

In the 25 years since the first edition of this book was published, marketing research has grown tremendously. There has been a continued growth in the sophistication of the statistical methods used, focus group interviews and other relatively unstructured techniques have had a resurgence, psychographic methods in market segmentation studies have grown more popular, and simulated sales models are now being used in new product development work. On the other hand, personal interviews in the home, long the backbone of marketing research, have declined in importance to be replaced by shopping center interviews and telephone surveys.

The format and general organization of this edition are still essentially the same as those of the first edition. The rationale for this is that the research process has not changed: It was and will continue to be a logical series of interrelated steps, each of which anticipates those which follow.

In recent years, substantial changes have occurred within the various steps, and we have attempted to incorporate those appropriate to a beginning research book. Because of the growing use of focus group interviews, telephone surveys, and shopping center interviews, these methods are treated in greater detail in the discussions on exploratory research, basic methods of data collection, attitude measurement, sampling applications, and fieldwork. Due to the widespread availability of computers in academic environments, this edition includes a simple SPSS computer program which can be easily adapted for the tabulation of data collected by students in a class project. The previous edition included for the first time an entire chapter devoted to tests of significance, and a full discussion of simple and multiple regression analysis. In this edition, two new chapters are concerned with multivariate data analysis. These present detailed descriptions in nontechnical language of linear discriminant analysis, automatic interaction detector, cluster analysis, factor analysis, and conjoint analysis. To help students understand these methods, each is introduced with a discussion of these questions: What is the typical problem or situation which can be studied with the method? What does the method do? What types of variables can be analyzed? In addition, the chapters on market segmentation, product research, and advertising research have all been updated to reflect the new developments which have occurred in those areas.

There are now 22 chapters instead of 20. Two of the chapters are completely new, and 11 have been revised significantly. The other nine chapters have been updated to include the latest materials.

The list of cases in this edition has changed substantially; 21 of the 41 cases are new. We continue to believe that cases should provide students with current, real-life problems in research procedures, and furnish them with a means of becoming involved in the materials they are studying. The cases presented in this edition are in keeping with this belief, and with the quality of the cases included in previous editions.

In this revision we have received help from many associates in both the business and academic fields. Many of these we must leave unmentioned. For this fifth edition, William D. Barclay of Foote, Cone & Belding has revised the materials he prepared for the chapters on sampling in the previous editions. John Romza, of the Loyola University Computer Center, contributed greatly to the SPSS computer program included in this edition. To those companies that have released case material to us, we can but say "thanks," since most wish to remain anonymous. We are grateful to Thelma Sims, Karen Mollitor, and Roberta Moore for their skill and patience in helping prepare the manuscript.

Despite all this good and well-qualified help, it is quite possible that some errors have occurred. It goes without saying that these are the responsibility of the authors.

HARPER W. BOYD, JR.
RALPH WESTFALL
STANLEY F. STASCH

Contents

theoretical base. Time factors. Cost of experimentation. Administrative problems of experimentation. Conclusions on experimental research.

4.   Basic methods of collecting data   96

General accuracy of data collected. Questionnaire method: *Advantages of questionnaire method. Disadvantages of questionnaire method.* Questionnaire studies classified by structure and disguise. Questionnaire studies classified by methods of communication: *Telephone interviews. Personal interviews. Mail surveys. Selection of method to use.* Observational method: *Advantages and disadvantages of observation. Methods of observation.*

5.   Secondary data   137

Using secondary data: *Advantages of secondary data. Drawbacks of secondary data. Evaluating secondary data.* Types of secondary data: *Census and registration data. Publicly circulated reports of individual projects. General guides. Guides to books, monographs, bulletins, and reports. Guides to periodicals. Commercial information. Other commercial research services. Data banks. Guides to information banks. Miscellaneous secondary data.*

6.   Decision trees and Bayesian analysis   173

Decision trees: *Evaluating the need for research. Uncertainty and the need for research. Decision tree analysis to determine the need for research.* Bayesian analysis.

PART III
The marketing research process

7.   The marketing research process: Planning the research project   201

Sources of error. Initial steps in designing a research project: *Formulating the study. Preparing a list of needed information. Designing the data col-*

lection project. Other steps in designing a research project: *Selecting a sample type. Determining sample size. Organizing the fieldwork. Analyzing the collected data and reporting the findings.* Interrelating the steps: An illustration.

8. Data collection I: Basic forms   219

Importance of questionnaire. Questionnaire construction procedure: *Determine what information is wanted. Determine the type of questionnaire to be used. Determine the content of individual questions. Determine the type of question to use. Decide on wording of questions. Decide on question sequence. Decide on layout and reproduction. Pretest. Revision and final draft.* Forms for observational studies.

9. Data collection II: Attitude measurement   259

Attitudes and scaling. General methods of collecting attitude data: *Questionnaire methods. Observation methods.* Specific methods of measuring attitudes: *Nondisguised, nonstructured techniques. Disguised, nonstructured techniques. Disguised, structured techniques. Structured, nondisguised techniques.* Multidimensional scaling.

10. Introduction to sampling   298

Confusion between sampling errors and data collection errors. Basic sampling problems: *Definition of the universe being studied. Definition of the variables being studied. Sample design.* Simple random sampling—sample selection: *What is a simple random sample? The use of tables of random numbers.* Estimation and the construction of confidence limits: *Sample values as estimates of universe values. Interval estimation. Construction and interpretation of a confidence interval estimate for the universe mean.* Estimation of sample necessary for specified reliability: *Determining sample size when estimating a percentage. Additional remarks on the determination of sample size.* Practical problems in using simple random sampling: *Cost. Availability of a current listing of population elements. Statistical efficiency. Administrative difficulties. Simple random sampling occasionally a feasible method.*

11. Application of sampling methods to marketing problems   330

Stratified random sampling: *Reasons for stratification. Estimation of the universe mean, with a stratified random sample. Interval estimation with stratified random samples. Issues in the selection of stratified random samples. Bases of stratification. Number of strata. Sample sizes within strata.* Cluster sampling: *Relative efficiency of simple one-stage cluster sampling and simple random sampling. Relative net efficiency. Systematic sampling. Area sampling. Concluding comments on area sampling.* Nonprobability sampling: *Convenience sampling. Judgment sampling. Quota sampling. Special forms of nonprobability sampling. Choice of sample design in practice. Compromise solutions: Probability sampling adaptations.*

12. Data collection and the field force   365

Fieldwork procedure. Errors in fieldwork: *Respondent selection errors. Errors in stimulating responses. Errors in interpreting and recording answers. Cheating.* Minimizing fieldwork errors: *Administrative control of projects in the field. Quality and cost control. Evaluation of interviewers.*

13. Tabulation of collected data   396

Preparing raw data: *Editing and coding. Establishing categories. Coding individual responses. Key punching.* Tabulating the data: *Using summary statistics. Percentages. Sorting and counting the data. Univariate tabulation. Bivariate and multivariate tabulation.*

14. Data analysis I: Tests of significance—Sampling statistics, Chi-Square, and analysis of variance   424

Categorical and continuous variables. Sampling statistics: *Using sampling statistics when the samples are small.* Differences between sets of data: *Chi-square analysis: Testing differences between two sets of data. Analysis of variance: Analyzing a large set of experimental data.*

15. Data analysis II: Explaining observed differences—Cross-tabulation, correlation, and regression   454

Assumptions. Explaining variation with dependent and independent variables. Methods of analysis. Cross-tabulation: *Concluding comments on cross-tabulation.* Correlation and regression analysis: *Correlation. Regression analysis.*

16.   Data analysis III: Explaining observed differences—Linear discriminant analysis and automatic interaction detector   488

Linear discriminant analysis (LDA). Automatic interaction detector (AID).

17.   Data analysis IV: Identifying interdependencies—Cluster analysis, factor analysis, and conjoint analysis   507

Cluster analysis. Factor analysis. Conjoint analysis. Proceed with caution.

18.   Research presentation and research process evaluation   545

Written research report: *Adhere to the study objectives. Be selective. Be objective. Have a purposeful organization. Write clearly. The report format.* Evaluation of the research procedure.

PART IV
Selected applications of marketing research

19.   Identifying market segments   557

Two general approaches. A priori segmentation: *Demographic measures. Usage rate measures.* Cluster based segmentation. Segmentation and the research process. Industrial buyer behavior and market segmentation.

20.   Product research   584

Developing product specifications: *What attributes are important. Relative importance of individual attributes.* Product testing: *Paired comparison placement tests.* Test marketing: *Pre-test-market research. Developing the test market plan and sample designs. Test market data. Repeat purchasing.*

PART **I**

INTRODUCTION TO MARKETING RESEARCH

This book is divided into four parts. Part I has only one chapter. This chapter is designed to introduce the student to marketing research as an important tool of marketing management. The subject is defined and a number of examples are given which illustrate major uses of marketing research. Management's need for an information system is identified, and the role of marketing research in the system is discussed. In Part I the point of view is that of marketing management; whereas, in the rest of the book the point of view is that of the research director.

1

Introduction

When Philip Morris, Inc. acquired the Miller Brewing Company in the early 1970s, they completely changed the character of beer marketing. By introducing Miller's Lite beer, and creating a new image for regular Miller beer, the company moved from seventh in the beer industry to second in only a few years. In 1978 Philip Morris bought the Seven-Up Company, which was third in the soft drink industry, well behind both Coca-Cola and Pepsi-Cola. What could Philip Morris do to transform 7-Up into a stronger competitor in the already competitive soft drink industry? Could they repeat the Miller success story with 7-Up? If so, how?

In the mid-1970s, Ford of Europe was a strong competitor in northern Europe with its compact cars (Escort, Cortina, Consul), but was a weaker competitor in southern Europe where subcompact cars were in greater demand. Ford did not have a subcompact car which could compete with the Fiat 127, Renault 5, Honda Civic and Volkswagen Rabbit, which were growing in popularity. It was apparent that Ford of Europe would lose market share in the long run if it did not manufacture a subcompact car. Because Ford would be a latecomer in the subcompact car category, it knew that its new car would have to be considered superior to the competitors' by large numbers of consumers. Could such a car be marketed profitably? What would be its design features? What would it look like?

In the early 1970s, the Quaker Oats Company was considering the development of a ready-to-eat cereal that would appeal to people who were interested in health foods and natural foods without arti-

*ficial additives. Company officials had observed that there was a grow-
ing consumer interest in health foods, and that such a product category
might be appropriate for Quaker Oats. However, the company knew
very little about health foods and those interested in them. Nor did
it know what kinds of cereal products would appeal to health-
conscious consumers.*

*When the Hanes Company introduced L'eggs hosiery in 1970, it
was an innovative product in a number of ways: it was to be sold in
supermarkets rather than in department and specialty stores; it was
attractively priced and packaged to sell in supermarkets; and one size
was expected to fit some 70 to 80 percent of the adult female population. Since both the product and its distribution were quite different
from anything Hanes had done in the past, company officials were
not confident that they could select the best possible marketing program using only their past experience. Traditionally, hosiery was
marketed with personal selling by a sales clerk, but Hanes knew that
a product in a supermarket received little or no personal selling; it
had to be presold through advertising. The question was, how much
advertising would be needed to presell L'eggs?*

All of the above situations occurred in the decade of the 1970s. They
represent situations requiring substantial capital investment and/or marketing expenditures. At the same time, a great deal of uncertainty—and hence
risk—was associated with them. It was not easy for the managers of these
firms to arrive at the best possible marketing decisions.

Most managers are far removed from their customers—the individuals
who in the final analysis determine success or failure. A complicated system
of branch offices, wholesalers, and retailers intervenes between managers and
their widely scattered customers. Yet managers must know who their customers are, what they want, and what competitors are doing to serve those
wants, if the managers are to make sound decisions. Often executives rely
on their sales representatives and dealers for information, but increasingly
the final link in the communication channel through which consumers communicate with the company is marketing research.

The managers in the companies mentioned above made extensive use
of marketing research to reduce the uncertainty inherent in the situations
they faced. Some of that research is described in the following sections
of this chapter. However, in order to gain maximum benefit from those
descriptions, readers should be familiar with the definition of marketing
research.

Definition of marketing research

The American Marketing Association defines marketing research as:
"The systematic gathering, recording, and analyzing of data about problems

relating to the marketing of goods and services."[1] This is a broad definition stating, in effect, that marketing research includes investigations of market segments, product designs, channel relationships, effectiveness of sales representatives and advertisements, pricing practices, and so forth. The point is that marketing research applies to any phase of marketing and is not restricted to any given type of marketing problem. *The essential purpose of marketing research is to provide information which will facilitate the identification of an opportunity or problem situation and to assist managers in arriving at the best possible decisions when such situations are encountered.*

But a definition of marketing research must also stress *how* the data are obtained and evaluated. At first glance, obtaining marketing information may appear simple. Why should marketing managers, for example, not base their decisions on "informal" talks with several consumers? It is unfortunate, but the consumers they select might not be typical of *all* consumers; and even if they select a group of typical consumers, they would still face the problems of obtaining accurate information and interpreting it properly. Thus, objectivity and accuracy are essential and require the use of special techniques. Experience has shown that great care must be used in gathering data or they will be misleading. How much do consumers remember of their past actions? Do they understand their buying motives? If they do not know the answer to a question, will they say so, or will they give a socially acceptable answer? These questions suggest some of the problems encountered in collecting data. They also suggest that managers should have an understanding of when and where marketing research can be used, as well as how the research process results in relevant and reliable data.

MANAGEMENT USES OF MARKETING RESEARCH

When do managers use marketing research? One way to answer this question is to look at the different kinds of marketing research companies say they do.

Research activities undertaken by companies

The American Marketing Association has used periodic surveys to investigate the marketing research being done by companies. In its 1978 survey, 386 industrial and consumer companies reported doing research in five major areas: (1) advertising, (2) business and corporate economics, (3) corporate responsibility, (4) product research, and (5) sales and market research.[2] The percentage of companies doing research in each of these

---

[1] Committee on Definitions of the American Marketing Association, *Marketing Definitions* (Chicago: American Marketing Association, 1960).

[2] Dik W. Twedt, ed., *1978 Survey of Marketing Research* (Chicago: American Marketing Association, 1978), pp. 41–44.

areas is shown in Table 1–1. Almost all companies do research on products, market potential, market share, sales analysis, and forecasting. However, industrial companies appear to do more business trend studies and ecological impact studies than consumer companies, while the latter tend to do more research on advertising, test markets, promotions, and consumer panel operations.

TABLE 1–1. Percentage of industrial and consumer companies doing specific types of research

	Industrial companies (200)	Consumer companies (186)
Advertising research		
A. Motivation research	26	67
B. Copy research	37	76
C. Media research	43	69
D. Studies of ad effectiveness	47	85
Business economics and corporate research		
A. Short-range forecasting (up to 1 year)	98	90
B. Long-range forecasting (over 1 year)	96	87
C. Studies of business trends	97	79
D. Pricing studies	93	88
E. Plant and warehouse location studies	84	76
Corporate responsibility research		
A. Consumers' "right-to-know" studies	21	32
B. Ecological impact studies	52	40
C. Studies of legal constraints on advertising and promotion	60	64
D. Social values and policies studies	40	43
Product research		
A. New product acceptance and potential	93	94
B. Competitive product studies	95	93
C. Testing of existing products	84	95
D. Packaging research: design or physical characteristics	65	83
Sales and market research		
A. Measurement of market potentials	97	97
B. Market share analysis	97	96
C. Determination of market characteristics	97	92
D. Sales analysis	97	96
E. Establishment of sales quotas, territories	95	91
F. Distribution channel studies	87	86
G. Test markets, store audits	43	83
H. Consumer panel operations	30	80
I. Sales compensation studies	79	78
J. Promotional studies of premiums, coupons, sampling, deals, and so on	32	73

Source: Dik W. Twedt, ed., *1978 Survey of Marketing Research* (Chicago: American Marketing Association, 1978), pp. 41–44.

The administrative process and management information systems

A second way to learn about management's use of marketing research is to reflect on those things that most managers do and then to indicate what types of marketing research can be of assistance to them. Perhaps, what is most common to the management profession is the phenomenon referred to as the administrative process, which consists of setting goals and establishing strategies, developing a best plan, putting the plan into action, and devising the necessary control and reappraisal procedures.[3]

By viewing management in terms of the administrative process, it is possible to visualize ahead of time those things with which management will be concerned. Initially, they will be involved with setting goals. If brought onto the scene early enough, marketing researchers can gather valuable information which will enable managers to set more precise and attainable goals. Clearly, if this is not done, the remaining steps in the administrative process will suffer. The same reasoning can and should be applied to the other major steps in the administrative process.

Table 1–2 attempts to illustrate some of management's more common information needs in the different phases of the administrative process. The table implies that, throughout this process, most of management's information needs can be identified in advance, and hence can be planned for in advance. Consequently, they can be thought of as constituting the individual component parts of a management information system. Table 1–2 also shows that some of management's information needs might not be identifiable in advance, particularly in the action and reappraisal phases of the administrative process. Such information needs tend to be filled by ad hoc research projects which, frequently, must be completed in a hurry.

When viewed in this way, management's information needs can be identified in terms of the four phases of the administrative process. Additionally, these information needs can be classified as definable in advance, or as unknown due to the unpredictable nature of the contingencies likely to give rise to the need for some kind of information. This classification scheme is useful for identifying many of management's uses of marketing research information. Examples of marketing research which can be applied during the different phases of the administrative process are discussed in the following sections.

Research during the goal- and strategy-setting phase.   In early 1979, Seven-Up revealed its new advertising strategy when it launched into its "America's turning 7-Up" campaign. What kinds of marketing research were used to help the company arrive at its new strategy?

---

[3] For an interesting discussion on this subject see Harper W. Boyd, Jr. and Steuart Henderson Britt, "Making Marketing Research More Effective by Using the Administrative Process," *Journal of Marketing Research* (February 1965):13–19.

TABLE 1–2. Some management information needs in different phases of the administrative process

Management's information needs	Setting goals and establishing strategies	Developing a plan	Putting the plan into action	Devising control and reappraisal procedures
Can be identified in advance	Regular research monitoring* Dissatisfactions and needs in relevant market segments Demand size and trend Industry/market structure and composition, competition, market shares and profitability Technological and materials innovations Supply conditions and prices Distribution, environmental and legal developments	Regular research* Identifying key market segments by product category Identifying market segment attitudes toward present products, promotions, and advertising Testing the appeal of potential product attributes Testing the effectiveness of advertising and promotion Evaluating the needs and attitudes of channel members	Regular research monitoring* Total industry and product class sales Firm's sales, by product and market Product availability in retail stores, shelf space, retailer support, and so on The costs and effectiveness of the firm's marketing efforts, by product and market, and by advertising, promotion, and so on Awareness and trial in relevant market segments Changes in competitive spending levels and strategies, including price, package, promotion, and so on	End of period compilation and aggregation of operating data to present an accurate picture of performance. Also, summary of survey findings on consumer awareness, trial, attitudes, preferences, repurchase rates, and so on*
Can not be identified in advance	Occasional ad hoc research projects; for example, when a new opportunity suddenly arises	Occasional ad hoc research projects; for example, a promising alternative plan is suggested	Ad hoc research projects to learn more when unforeseen events occur	Ad hoc follow-up research projects as needed

* This is a part of management's regular information system.

The company's advertising agency undertook five studies designed to reveal the strengths and weaknesses of 7-Up.[4] In comparison taste tests of Coke, Pepsi, Dr. Pepper, Sprite, and 7-Up, where all brands were disguised, more consumers said they preferred 7-Up than any other brand. In another study, consumers were asked to rate 7-Up against two colas on the attributes of: contains unhealthy ingredients; tastes too syrupy; tastes too sweet; leaves an aftertaste; too heavy or filling after exercise; and not in tune with the light way people were eating and drinking. The colas made a poorer showing than 7-Up on all of the attributes. Another study—a user-profile study—showed that 7-Up was perceived as a drink for women and white-collar workers. It became clear that there was nothing wrong with the product, but its image was not acceptable to younger, heavier consumers of soft drinks, and so would have to be changed.

The advertising agency then tested five potential advertising themes in a series of small group studies, to see which would be most effective in changing 7-Up's image. The theme of "active lifestyle" was clearly the most preferred. Still another series of small group studies confirmed that 7-Up fitted the active lifestyle theme better than either of the colas. Based on these marketing research findings, advertising agency copywriters then transformed the theme into "America's turning 7-Up."

Research during this first phase of the administrative process is often directed at identifying the dissatisfactions and needs of certain consumer groups. The introduction by Procter & Gamble of its Pringles "new-fangled potato chips" in the early 1970s represented an attempt to turn to advantage the three inherent problem characteristics of regular potato chips—they break easily, become stale, and require a large package for a small quantity. Over the years research had shown that consumers considered these to be problem areas, but little was done to eliminate the problems. By bringing together a consumer dissatisfaction and a change in process technology, Procter & Gamble was able to establish a successful strategy for entering the potato chip market.

Research during the planning phase.   In general, when planning products, advertising or promotions, marketing research can help define the market in terms of customer types, the needs that customers have regarding the product, how satisfied they are with currently available products, what product attributes are important, and how consumers use and evaluate the product.

For example, when Ford of Europe was planning the new subcompact car that was eventually to become the Ford Fiesta, the company spent over $1 million on marketing research projects.[5] Some of the more notable of these projects are described below.

---

4 See Philip Taubman, "The Great Soft-Drink Shoot-Out," *Esquire* (March 27, 1979):33–37.

5 See Edouard Seidler, *Let's Call It Fiesta* (Lausanne, Switzerland; Patrick Stephens Limited with Edita, 1976).

In one of the first market studies, 100 potential subcompact buyers were recruited in each of Germany, England, France, Italy, and Spain, and flown to Lausanne, Switzerland, where each group was shown seven unidentified, white, subcompact cars—four competitive cars which were already on the market, and three Ford preprototype models with different stylings. The potential buyers were asked to rate the seven cars on a number of aesthetic and functional characteristics. Because one objective was to make the new subcompact a "world-car" if possible, the same study was repeated in California with 200 foreign car owners and 200 owners of U.S. subcompacts. The study was repeated once again in Brazil with one group of Brazilians and another of Argentinians.

From these studies Ford learned the strengths and weaknesses of their three alternate designs, and used that knowledge to improve the design. As design changes were made, still other potential subcompact car buyers from four or five European countries were brought to a central location to view and rate the newer Ford designs in comparison with one or more competitive subcompacts, all unidentified and painted white. Overall, there were seven such studies carried out over a period of 28 months. In addition to these studies, 7,000 potential buyers in five European countries were interviewed in their homes in order to estimate the potential sales volume for the new subcompact, and the percentage of those sales which would be new customers for Ford of Europe. Still another study was undertaken to assess the attractiveness of different names which might be given to the new car.

When the Quaker Oats Company was planning and developing the ready-to-eat cereal that would become "100% Natural Cereal," they employed 12 separate research projects.[6] Among others, these included a small group study of consumers' ideas about health foods, and a series of small group interviews to measure consumer reaction to the concept of a natural or health food cereal. Three small samples of homemakers then taste-tested four different kinds of cereal formulations. This was followed by three separate studies involving in-home comparison taste tests of the new cereal against a number of well-known brands. Two other projects were undertaken to assist in the development of the packaging to be used, and another project screened potential names for the new cereal. Two introductory advertisements—one a print advertisement and the other a television commercial—were evaluated in two separate tests.

Research while the plan is being put into action. When a plan is put into action, management must monitor the results of the plan to see if it is achieving its objectives. This is likely to involve measuring the firm's sales and total industry sales in different geographic areas and by appropriate

---

[6] See "The Quaker Oats Company: 100% Natural Cereal (A)," copyright © 1976, by the Sponsors of the Colgate Darden Graduate School of Business Administration, The University of Virginia. ICH case number UVa: M–150.

market segments. Management also will want to know (1) if the plan is achieving the desired level of retail availability, (2) if the target market segments are seeing the advertisements, (3) if the copy is communicating the intended message, (4) if the promotions are achieving the desired trial rates, (5) how much consumers are using, and (6) the proportion of buyers who repurchase.

An interesting example of research designed to measure effectiveness of a new marketing program was that carried out by the Hanes Company when L'eggs hosiery were introduced in 1970. Hanes used two sets of test markets, with one set receiving twice as much advertising as the other. Five consumer studies were conducted in all of the test markets—6, 13, 18, 26, and 43 weeks after advertising had begun. Some of the information obtained during the studies was brand and advertising awareness, trial and repeat purchase rates, the average number of units bought per purchaser, and the average number of units bought per capita. Unit sales in each market were obtained from data on store deliveries and from audits by the A. C. Nielsen Company. All information was equally available from both high and low advertising markets.

This research program provided Hanes' management with a complete time series history of the new product introduction program under two different levels of advertising intensity. These histories showed that all aspects of the introductory program were successful, but the program was more successful in the markets subjected to heavy advertising. This evidence also indicated that the incremental revenue generated by the heavy advertising program more than offset the incremental cost of the heavy program. As a result, Hanes decided to use the higher advertising level when they began moving the product into additional markets. Sales results in the new markets were similar to the test market results, with L'eggs typically capturing about 30 percent of hosiery sales made through food and drugstores in each city.[7]

During the action phase, management will want also to monitor closely competition and other aspects of the environment in order to detect as early as possible any developments which may affect the plan. These developments may range from the case where a competitor seems to be taking effective counteraction to the case where the product seems to be appealing to a market segment other than that toward which it was targeted. Such contingencies are likely to be accompanied by a management request for an ad hoc marketing research study which will shed light on what is really happening in the marketplace. Depending upon the outcome of the research, management may or may not make changes in the marketing program.

Research for reappraising the plan effectiveness.   At the end of the operating period management will want to reappraise the plan and compare

---

[7] Babette Jackson, "The More L'eggs the Better," in the *Proceedings from the 1972 Annual Conference of the Advertising Research Foundation,* pp. 40–44.

results with the objectives. Such a reappraisal will involve an aggregation and compilation of most of the information obtained during the planning and action phases, with a special emphasis on sales, market share, marketing costs, and contribution to profit. It will also measure brand awareness, trial rates, repeat purchase rates, preferred brands, and other measures of marketing results.

An example of information needed for reappraisal is shown in Table 1–3. In this case, the plan being reappraised is the marketing expenditures plan for a product. Gross margin, marketing expenditures, and contribution to earnings are recorded for each market area and also totally. This information is also shown for each market (1) as a percentage of the total for all markets and (2) as the dollar amount of change, this year compared with last year. Additionally, the total industry sales in dollars, the firm's market share, the percentage of retail distribution achieved for the product, and television media costs are also shown for each market, both for this year and last. With these data, management can observe changes in demand (as reflected in total industry sales); changes in sales, costs, and earnings; changes in competition (as reflected in market share and retail distribution percentages); and, changes in advertising costs (as reflected in television media costs). This information is available by market and for all markets. With such information management can reappraise a product's marketing expenditures plan, as well as the effectiveness of the advertising-sales promotion mix used.

If an end-of-period reappraisal shows objectives not being met, it may be due to some unforeseen and unmeasured contingency. In such a case, management might use marketing research to investigate the causes of the poor performance and to obtain the information needed to take proper corrective action. Thus, in this phase as in the action phase, unforeseen developments may lead management to request that marketing research initiate one or more ad hoc research projects to supplement the previously obtained information.

Concluding comments.   In review of management's use of marketing research, the reader should note particularly:

1.   Different types of research projects are applicable in different phases of the administrative process.
2.   In each phase of the administrative process a "program" of regularly scheduled research projects is needed to gather the information which can be identified in advance.
3.   These programs of regularly scheduled research projects constitute the marketing manager's information system.
4.   Part of the information system is a regular monitoring of the environment in order to assure early detection of unexpected problems or opportunities.
5.   Ad hoc research projects are used to investigate unexpected developments when they arise.

TABLE 1–3. Market area summaries ($000 except where noted)

	Area A	Area B	Area C	Area D	Area E	U.S. total
Gross margin	$360	$770	$620	$850	$680	$8,210
Advertising	42	203	165	290	276	1,683
Sales promotion	58	172	130	191	124	1,507
Contribution to earnings	$260	$395	$325	$369	$280	$5,020
Financial analysis						
Percent of total gross margin	4.4	9.4	7.6	10.4	8.4	100.0
Percent advertising and sales promotion	3.1	11.5	9.2	15.0	12.4	100.0
Incremental gross margin, this year versus last (loss)	($53)	($50)	($75)	$115	$25	$744
Incremental advertising and sales promotion, this year versus last	($20)	($85)	$10	$165	$100	$354
Incremental contribution to earnings	($33)	$35	($85)	($50)	($75)	$390

	Area A		Area B		Area C		Area D		Area E		U.S. Total	
Market research data	This year	Last year	This year	Last year	This year	Last year	This year	Last year	This year	Last year	This year	Last year
Total dollar retail market	$1,790	$1,810	$6,150	$6,175	$2,590	$2,680	$7,525	$7,395	$5,900	$4,950	$54,650	$56,000
Percent share of retail market	50.2	51.9	35.6	36.1	48.6	50.3	38.7	32.4	42.9	46.1	45.8	44.6
Percent distribution	88.3	88.2	96.2	96.2	97.9	98.1	98.1	97.9	96.4	96.6	96.2	96.2
Media efficiencies:												
Television Cost per 1,000 homes*	$2.02	$2.11	$2.15	$2.12	$3.95	$2.50	$1.75	$1.75	$1.95	$1.96	$1.95	$1.93
Cost per 1,000 prime prospects*	$3.10	$3.26	$2.65	$2.70	$4.67	$3.10	$1.92	$2.03	$2.15	$2.30	$2.30	$2.27

* Figures in dollars (not $000).

Source: Adapted from Richard A. Feder, "How To Measure Marketing Performance," *Harvard Business Review* 43 (May–June 1965):137.

SOURCES OF INFORMATION

Where can managers get the information they need? This is always a problem because much marketing information is difficult to obtain, or is just not available. It is worthwhile, therefore, for managers to have some knowledge about sources of information and their accuracy. Most marketing information can be classified as coming from one of the three data sources suggested in Table 1–4.

Table 1–4. Sources of information

Internal to firm	*External to firm*

Sales and costs broken down by products, markets, and types of marketing activities (advertising, promotion, personal selling, etc.)	Secondary sources
	  Government publications
	  Trade association publications
	  Commercial services
	  Other publications
	Primary sources
	  Research projects

Some sources are *internal* to the firm, such as that information which is generated by the marketing, accounting, and production departments. Their normal operating responsibilities require that they compile some of the sales and cost data needed by management. There are also data sources which are *external* to the firm, and these can be further classified as primary or secondary data sources.

Secondary data are those which have been collected by other organizations; for example, government agencies such as the Commerce and Labor departments of the federal government, financial organizations such as Dun & Bradstreet's and Poor's, newspapers and magazines such as the *Chicago Tribune* and *Fortune,* trade associations such as the Supermarket Institute and the National Association of Manufacturers, and commercial marketing research services like the A. C. Nielsen Company. Data from these sources are called secondary because these organizations collect original data, analyze and tabulate the data, but then publish only summary tables and charts. Users of such data are limited to what is presented in the summary tables and charts; the original data are not available to them. In essence, secondary data are secondary because some intervening party is positioned between the raw data and the managers who need the data. Since these data typically are compiled for some general audience, and not just for a specific manager, it is unlikely that their form and content will perfectly satisfy a specific manager's information needs.

Primary data are those which are collected specifically by, or for, the data users. There is no intervening party which summarizes the original data. Since the original data from each unit or respondent are available, they can be retabulated or reanalyzed in as many different ways as managers choose. Most important, however, is the fact that the data collected are specified in advance by managers who will use the data; this assures managers that the data will be tailored to their needs.

The subject matter of this book

A major portion of this book is concerned with information which must be obtained from sources external to the firm—either primary or secondary. If managers wish to obtain primary information, consideration must be given to such things as what information they need and from what sources, how it will be collected, what kind and how large a sample to use, and how the data are to be tabulated, analyzed, and presented. If managers are considering the purchase of data from a secondary source of information, they should ask such questions as what information does the secondary source provide, how does it collect the data, what kind and how large a sample does it use, and how does it tabulate and analyze the data. Thus, managers must ask essentially the same types of questions when considering the purchase of information, regardless of whether the information is primary or secondary. This commonalty permits the book's contents to be oriented toward *both primary and secondary* information sources external to the firm. The rationale for such an orientation derives from the fact that managers are turning more and more to commercial services and other secondary sources to satisfy their information needs.

Frequently, managers' needs will result in the use of information from both *external* and *internal* sources. For example, in the reappraisal phase of the administrative process, managers may use information similar to that in Table 1–3. The top portion of that table is derived from internal data, while the "total dollar retail market" and "media efficiencies" are from secondary sources. The "share of market" and "percent distribution" may be derived from either primary or secondary sources. In addition, if both brand awareness and attitude and preference data are used, they will be primary data. In short, much of management's information needs can only be satisfied by a systematic integration of external primary and secondary data with the firm's internal data. While most of this book is oriented toward the gathering of external primary and secondary data, the reader should not lose sight of the fact that a systematic integration of all three data sources is necessary if the managers' information needs—as suggested by Table 1–2—are to be satisfied.

MANAGEMENT-MARKETING RESEARCH INTERACTION

Although earlier discussion has made frequent reference to both management and marketing research, it has not mentioned the relationship between them. The reader may have gained the impression that marketing research is a smoothly functioning activity and that managers encounter no problems when they are in need of research. In fact, it is increasingly evident that misunderstandings often exist at the management-marketing research interface. In some cases, it affects the quality of research undertaken and causes managers not to employ research in decision situations in which it is needed.

While the causes of this friction have not been clearly defined, evidence suggests that both parties lack a good understanding of the role and needs of the other party. Such management complaints as the following are common:[8]

1. Research is not problem oriented. It tends to provide a plethora of facts, not actionable results.
2. Researchers are too involved with techniques, and they appear to be reluctant to get involved in management "problems."
3. Research is slow, vague, and of questionable validity.
4. Researchers can not communicate, they do not understand, and they do not talk the language of management.

Researchers have their complaints about management:

1. Management does not include research in discussions of basic problems. Management tends to ask only for specific information about parts of problems.
2. Management pays no more than lip service to research and does not really understand or appreciate its value.
3. Management does not allow enough time for research. They draw preliminary conclusions based on early or incomplete results.
4. Management relies more on intuition and judgment than on research. Research is used as a crutch, not a tool.

These are not isolated complaints. A number of interested parties report that the relationship between management and marketing research is not as smooth as it might be.[9] This suggests that some of the millions of dollars being spent annually on marketing research represent expenditures which could have been more effectively employed in helping management resolve major problems.

MANAGER AND RESEARCHER RESPONSIBILITY AND INVOLVEMENT

The key issues underlying the difficulties existing between managers and marketing researchers seem to be the responsibility and involvement *of both*

---

[8] The following eight complaints are reported in "Communication Gap Hinders Proper Use of Market Research," *Marketing Insights* (February 19, 1968):7.

[9] See James R. Krum, "B For Marketing Research Departments," *Journal of Marketing* (October 1978):8–12; Roman R. Andrus and James E. Reinmuth, "Avoiding Research Myopia in Marketing Analysis," *Business Horizons* (June 1979):55–58; Danny N. Bellenger, "The Marketing Manager's View of Marketing Research," *Business Horizons* (June 1979):59–65.

parties. For the most part, this book is written with the *researcher as the focal point*. To be effective, however, the researcher must understand, and be sympathetic to, the needs and views of the manager—the buyer and user of research. On the other hand, if managers are to make the most effective use of marketing research, they should understand the process of research, as well as their involvement with it and responsibility to it.

The following discussion of the manager's responsibility and involvement in marketing research is addressed to "the manager" for two reasons. First, many readers of this book aspire to management rather than research careers. Second, since most of the book is addressed to "the researcher," it is appropriate somewhere to point out the role managers play in obtaining and using research. If the reader is interested in a research career, the following discussion serves as a guide to those things which a marketing researcher should thoroughly discuss with management to assure the latter's understanding of, and involvement in, the marketing research process.

There are five occasions when managers should contribute inputs to the marketing research process or participate in decisions relating to marketing research.

1. Initiate research projects.   Occasionally marketing researchers may be privy to information which will lead them to propose specific research projects to management for approval. However, since individual researchers are not likely to have all of the information available to managers, they cannot be expected to know all the problems managers face. One of the manager's responsibilities is to initiate marketing research when it is needed, and to do so at the earliest possible point in time.

When initiating market research, a manager should prepare a written statement of the problem and the alternative courses of action being considered. Such a statement can then serve as the basis for discussions which can help overcome two inherent problems. Frequently managers expect more than marketing research can deliver, and marketing researchers frequently reinterpret or modify a management problem in order to make it researchable. Each party unintentionally focuses on its own problems— managers are concerned with "the management problem" and may not be aware that it presents several "research problems" to the researcher. Similarly, researchers may reshape, or even distort, "the management problem" in order to minimize the "research problem." Discussions between the two help managers avoid overconfidence in what marketing research can deliver and help researchers focus on the manager's problem.

The scope of the manager's problem will be made more explicit if the problem statement includes the various courses of action being considered to solve the problem. It is one thing for a manager to say to a researcher, "Look into the causes of the sales downturn in the western region." It is quite another thing if the manager actually expects a marketing research report to tell which of the currently employed marketing mix elements— product characteristics, advertising theme, promotions, price and so on—

should be changed, by how much, and in which direction. The former problem statement suggests little more than an exploratory study while the latter would require a full-blown research program, probably consisting of a number of individual projects. If the researcher accepts the former problem interpretation, but the manager intends the latter, the end result will be less than satisfactory. The manager should attempt to avoid ineffective communication by clearly identifying in the problem statement the specific alternative courses of action being considered.

2. *Specify information needed for decision-making.* In designing the project, researchers must draw heavily on the information they believe management will need. In the sales downturn example mentioned above, researchers would know only that the project should investigate the effects of product quality, advertising themes, promotions, and price. This information is useful to them, but they still do not know what specific information managers need in order to make the decision to change product quality, what information they need in order to make the decision to change the advertising theme, and so on for the other alternatives. In their written problem statements, managers should include detailed descriptions of the information they need to make a decision on each of the alternatives being considered.

These detailed descriptions of needed information can form a basis for further discussion between managers and researchers, where the latter will have the opportunity to ask questions which will lead to a more complete picture of the information required by managers. The final version of the research project will be much more useful to managers if, in the early stages of the project's design, the managers and researchers get together and develop a clear understanding of the information the managers expect from the research and how it can lead to a decision. In this way managers can provide the inputs which researchers need in order to design a useful research project.

3. *Evaluate proposed research projects.* Typically, research studies are authorized only after a study proposal has been approved by management. In order to avoid misunderstanding or poor communications, a manager should require a written proposal and carefully evaluate it prior to approving it. A manager should ask key questions and suggest changes, if needed, *prior* to approving the proposal, not after the study is underway or after the findings have been reported.

4. *Evaluate commercial research services.* Today a firm can purchase a wide variety of commercial research services. Although marketing research personnel will take the major responsibility in evaluating which service to purchase, the marketing manager should be involved. In order to make an evaluation, the manager should first specify information needs (as in 1 and 2 above) and then compare them with the information which can be obtained from the commercial service.

5. *Accept or reject research findings.* Decision-making is the manager's

responsibility, not the researcher's. It is the manager's responsibility to *avoid* a decision based on invalid research findings. Just as an evaluation should be made on a proposed research project before it is authorized, so also should an inquiry be made into the validity of the findings from completed research. Along with the researcher, the manager should review the research project to assure that it has been carefully carried out. Once assured, the manager will have confidence in the validity of the research findings and can then incorporate them into the decision-making process.

Concluding comments. A marketing research activity providing management with the maximum possible support will be one which reflects management's responsibility and involvement. Management's participation is most apparent in the early stages—when the project is being initiated and the problem and the information needs are being identified. However, management should also participate in the evaluation of the completed project, including the research findings.

Management preparation for marketing research participation

There are three ways managers can prepare themselves for participation in marketing research.

1. *Develop an understanding of the types of information which can be made available through marketing research.* Not all of the information a manager might want is obtainable through marketing research. For example, it is difficult for consumers to give valid answers to questions concerned with the distant future or the distant past. Similarly, while they can provide information about their current attitudes and behavior patterns, consumers may not be able to do so when asked about future intentions. Unimportant events—such as the brand of cinnamon purchased last—are less likely to be remembered than important events. People also have difficulty communicating their emotions and sensations. For example, consumers may be able to identify which of two coffees, two beers, or two soft drinks tastes better, but it is unlikely that they will be able to communicate to the interviewer the sensations they experienced in arriving at their choice. These considerations bear on the kinds of information which can be collected through marketing research. Manager-users of marketing research will serve themselves well if they spend some time reflecting on the kinds of valid information which can be obtained.

2. *Know what kinds of decisions marketing research can help resolve.* The above paragraph implies that not all marketing decisions can be resolved through the use of marketing research. The poor record of new product introductions indicates that consumers often are unable to report what they like and dislike about a proposed new product. Similarly, in tests of two advertising copy treatments, consumers can indicate which they recall or which they find most appealing, but they are unable to describe the long-run effect each will have on their attitudes and behavior. A recent study

went so far as to suggest that some managers believe research can identify a poor copy treatment, but not a good one.[10] Both of these examples involve future attitudes and behavior, which consumers cannot know with certainty. How, then, can marketing research predict future attitudes and behavior?

Although marketing research cannot predict the future, it can help reduce some of the uncertainty associated with decision-making. By gathering information on current and recent consumer attitudes and behavior, managers can gain a better understanding of the phenomenon with which they are dealing. They can then use their increased understanding to draw tentative conclusions about the outcome of the forthcoming decision. Thus, marketing research is most applicable to those situations where additional information about the present and recent past can help reduce a manager's uncertainty about the future.

3. *Understand the marketing research process, including the various causes of error and how each can be minimized or eliminated.* Errors can enter into a research project at every step in the research process—problem formulation, questionnaire design, sampling, fieldwork, tabulation, and analysis.[11] However, most causes of error can be minimized through the use of good research practices—questionnaires can be pretested, good sampling procedures can be used, fieldworkers can be carefully trained and supervised, and so on. With a good understanding of the marketing research process, managers will be able to judge whether proposed projects will be susceptible to too many sources of error. They can encourage the use of good marketing research practices by asking researchers the kinds of pertinent questions which will help them design research projects more in keeping with the manager's information and decision needs.

PLAN OF THE BOOK

The remainder of this book is divided into three parts. Although Parts II and III are strongly oriented toward the researcher, the materials presented there should be well understood by the manager who intends to utilize marketing research effectively. Part II (Chapters 2–6) is basic material needed for the understanding of almost any type of marketing research effort—basic research designs, data collection methods, secondary sources of data, and decision analysis. Part III (Chapters 7–18) presents the key aspects of the marketing research process—problem formulation, data collection forms, sampling, fieldwork, and analysis of data. In Part IV (Chapters 19–22) the emphasis returns to the manager's uses of marketing research. This part

---

[10] Victor P. Buell, *Changing Practices in Advertising Decision Making and Control* (New York: Association of National Advertisers, 1973), pp. 60–61.

[11] For an interesting checklist which suggests most of the sources of error which can enter into a marketing research project, see Charles S. Mayer, "Evaluating the Quality of Marketing Research Contractors," *Journal of Marketing Research* (May 1967): 135–38.

treats the research needs which fall within the administrative process framework suggested by Table 1–2 and which, therefore, can form the basis of a manager's marketing information system: defining and measuring markets; planning and developing the product; planning the advertising and marketing program; and measuring the effect of marketing expenditures on company sales, profits, and market share.

Case 1–1
MILLARD, INC.

The Millard Company was located in a large Southeastern city and had sales in excess of $20 million. The company was family-owned and had been in business under the same name for over 100 years. It consisted of three major divisions—printing, stationery, and office furniture. Each of the first two accounted for approximately 40 percent of sales. However, profits varied substantially between divisions, as did the amount of capital invested. Nor did all divisions necessarily sell to the same customers, although the company did use a common sales force. Overall company profits had declined substantially in recent years, and there was considerable disagreement among family members as to what corrective action to undertake. Recently, the board of directors requested the president and chief executive officer to hire a consultant to help management develop a strategic plan.

The consultant convinced the president that the development of a strategic plan required the participation of key company executives: the president, the accounting manager, the sales manager, and the three division heads. These six men plus the consultant constituted the strategic planning group. At the outset the consultant explained that the primary task facing the group was to define the company's various investment units in terms of product-market pairings, to determine for the foreseeable future the opportunities and threats for each, and finally, to determine whether on the basis of the trends in the external environment to change current allocations between investment units. Thus, he stated, "What we are going to do is largely directional in nature—that is, we have to set both financial and marketing objectives for each of our investment units. We also have to be sure we can attain these objectives and, thus, we have to specify the major actions we need to take to be successful and the costs involved."

The definition of the firm's major product-market pairings posed substantial problems at the outset. It was hard for the group to think in terms of market segments and not simply in products. The stationery and office supply division proved particularly different because of the number of items carried (over 5,000) and the number of product groups represented (e.g., writing instruments, typing supplies, files, paper products, and tapes). After much discussion the group decided to define the division's investment units as consisting of the following seven mutually exclusive units.

1. State contracts.
2. Local and city contracts.
3. Over-the-counter sales of stationery and other office supplies at the retail store the company maintained on its premises.
4. Computer supplies.
5. Sales to county banks and government offices through a separate sales force of six men who sold the products of all three divisions.
6. Commercial contracts, typically bid situations involving relatively few items.
7. Other commercial sales.

It was believed that they varied as to size, sales trends, costs, competition, and profitability. Similar difficulties were experienced regarding the definition of investment units for the other two divisions. This was particularly true with printing because of the number of different products which could be "manufactured" and the number of market sectors to which each could be sold.

Ultimately the group defined some 42 investment units—7 for stationery and supplies, 5 for furniture, and 30 for printing. The problem then became one of estimating costs and sales trends for each. The accounting department was assigned the task of estimating sales, costs, margins, and profitability for each unit. The department head planned to do this largely by sampling invoices from the past three years. The problem of estimating market sector sales over the next several years was another matter, since the company did not believe the needed data could be obtained from secondary sources. In addition to market data, the company wanted an analysis made of each of its major competitors with respect to the number of salesmen, amount spent on advertising, relative market shares, and profitability.

In discussing ways of obtaining the needed market sector data, the president suggested that perhaps the company should set up its own marketing research unit at this time. He said, "At least we can save the $5,000 or so it'll probably cost us to hire an outside research agency to get the data we need for the strategic plan. This idea about forming a company research unit is not really a new idea—at least as far as I'm concerned. The other managers have always said that we can't use such specialized personnel and that we've got all the data we can use anyhow. But now I think they probably have changed their minds since they have become involved in doing some strategic thinking. I'm not thinking big in the staffing of such a unit—a recent college graduate—a marketing major—and a clerk-typist who can do some tabulating. I'd probably have the unit report to the head of the accounting department since I'm too busy to look after it and the sales manager spends a lot of time in the field."

The consultant, whose major expertise outside of strategy was finance, asked the president if he could be more specific about what he wanted a marketing research unit to do. The president replied that while he had never put anything down in writing, he did have some specific ideas. "Generally," he said, "I want someone who is a self-starter—a person who will suggest ways we can better relate to our markets and will provide us with data to back up his suggestions. We need to do a lot of sales analysis work to better pinpoint our potential and to better control our salesmen. I'm constantly telling our sales manager this, but he's too busy handling our larger house accounts to do anything about it. He's also responsible—along with his assistant—for some 23 salesmen. Of course, they work mainly on commission, so they're pretty independent."

The president went on to say: "While we only spend about $200,000 a year in advertising, I'm not sure we're getting much in the way of results. Last year our advertising agency suggested we do some research work, but I couldn't understand what they wanted to do and turned down the request. I suppose I'm the guilty party as to the quality of our advertising, since I handle it. Another really important area is that concerned with financial analyses. We need to do this for our small accounts as well as in connection with our larger contracts. The unit would also keep our strategic plan updated. You told me this would have to be done annually. And finally, I'd like to have someone I could use for special projects. I really need help here. Only last week I had an idea that maybe, if we'd try handling our small stationery and office supplies accounts by phone, we might save a lot of money. I'd use a researcher to look into such an idea and report on his findings."

Should the Millard Company set up a market research unit?

How would you describe the job of the research director?

What would be his duties?

Who should he report to?

What research should be undertaken?

How else can the research need be satisfied by the company?

Case 1–2
MIDDLETON HOSPITAL

Alfred Robsen, superintendent of Middleton Hospital, became quite concerned after having read a consumer survey which indicated that public opinion toward hospitals, and the medical profession in general, was quite low. According to the survey, the public viewed the cost of health care to be as serious a problem as the high costs of food, clothing, fuel and other necessities. While three out of four survey respondents worried a great deal about product prices in general, almost 70 percent were equally concerned with the cost of medical care.

The public was also concerned with the quality of health services that they were receiving. One out of every four respondents felt that hospitals and the medical profession were doing a poor job in serving consumers, while only one out of five respondents felt that they were doing a good job. The only other major industries rated as significantly worse than hospitals and the medical profession were the oil industry and automobile manufacturers, which were judged to be doing a poor job by one out of every three respondents. Furthermore, when respondents with a favorable attitude toward consumer activism were asked to select industries which should receive the attention of the consumer movement in the near future, more than 40 percent of these respondents selected hospitals and the medical profession. This was second only to the food manufacturing industry, where the figure was 45 percent.

Robsen knew there was little he could do about the public's concern over the high cost of health care. Costs were rising for all hospitals and the most he could do would be to manage Middleton Hospital as efficiently as possible. However, he felt he could address the concerns patients had about the service they received. Middleton Hospital had always been regarded as the best of the city's four hospitals, and Robsen wanted to maintain that reputation.

Robsen described the findings of the study to his staff at its next meeting. He asked staff members to comment on particular areas of patient care that might be causes of patient dissatisfaction.

Ms. Bacon, who was responsible for admitting new patients, felt that waiting might be a real problem. In admitting and releasing patients, for instance, the delay could be considerable. Paperwork was heavy and getting heavier. There could also be delays, she knew, in other areas of the hospital; it was not uncommon to wait for physical therapy or for X-rays to be taken. Sometimes, in emergency situations, this was unavoidable. There were times, however, when patients were simply escorted to the special service area before personnel were available to take care of them.

The nursing supervisor, Ms. Hala, thought that patients would form their opinions of the hospital largely on the basis of whether their treatment was courteous and efficient. She felt that special care should be taken to see that patients were courteously escorted to their rooms, that their visiors were pleasantly received, and that their treatment and care were considerate throughout. Further, if calls for assistance were answered promptly, if food was served on time, if patients were bathed regularly, and rooms kept neat and clean, patients would most probably be pleased with the service.

Dr. Sentry, the hospital's chief of staff, thought that the attitude of the staff could be an important factor. A positive attitude on the part of doctors, nurses, and volunteers was a critical element of quality patient care. He said that the patient's care and treatment should be explained to him or her as fully as possible, and that he urged staff and other personnel to do so.

The supervisor of volunteer workers suggested that perhaps the volunteers were in a better position to hear certain complaints than any other of the hospital staff. Some of those complaints were minor, but they might be annoying to the patient. Such complaints might have to do with noise in the hallways, or not being able to get magazines and newspapers or books from the lending library. Another question that often came to the attention of volunteers concerned the availability of a chaplain or of religious services.

After having thought about what was said at the meeting, Robsen felt that it would be useful to conduct some research to find out which hospital characteristics and services were perceived as really important and how Middleton Hospital was rated on each of those characteristics. He thought that such information could reveal the hospital's reputation or image, and perhaps even tell him how the hospital was perceived in comparison with the city's other hospitals. It was unclear to Robsen, though, as to whether the research should involve only recent patients of Middleton Hospital, or recent patients of all the city's hospitals. There also appeared to be some merit in interviewing the general public, since most of the hospital's future patients would be drawn from that group.

How can Middleton Hospital use marketing research to advantage?

What actions will Mr. Robsen take as a result of the research?

Will the benefits be worth the cost?

What group or groups should be studied?

BASIC CONCEPTS

Part II has five chapters which are designed to acquaint the student with the basic concepts of the scientific method of studying problems and of research design, with basic methods of collecting data, with secondary sources of marketing information, and with decision analysis. Research designs are classified into two categories—those which are for the purpose of preliminary exploration of a problem area and those which are for the purpose of drawing definite conclusions relative to specific hypotheses. No matter what research design is used, one or both of two basic methods must be used to collect data in the field—questioning and observation. The strengths and weaknesses of each of these methods are discussed in detail. Before field research is attempted, secondary sources of information should be explored. Methods of doing this are covered in Chapter 5. Chapter 6 introduces the student to the use of decision trees and Bayesian analysis in evaluating the need for marketing research.

2

Scientific method and types of research

Marketing is more an art than a science. Successful decision-making in marketing depends on the skill and judgment of the individuals involved and cannot be reduced to an organized body of principles. Most decisions are made quickly and are based on experience, but sometimes information is collected to help.

When marketing managers make decisions, they normally use all available information to reduce their uncertainty as much as possible. If the available information is limited to that which they have accumulated as part of their general knowledge or which comes to them as part of the normal flow of day-to-day operating data, they have not used research. If, on the other hand, managers organize special projects to gather information pertinent to the decision, they are said to conduct research. It is the function of marketing research to reduce the degree of uncertainty in a decision. Whenever managers use research, they are applying the methods of science to the art of marketing.

SCIENTIFIC METHOD

No method known to man can entirely eliminate uncertainty. But scientific method, more than any other procedure, can minimize those elements of uncertainty which result from lack of information. By so doing, it reduces the danger of making a wrong choice between alternative courses of action.[1]

---

[1] Marie Jahoda, Morton Deutsch, and Stuart W. Cook, *Research Methods in Social Relations* (New York: Dryden Press, 1951) pt. I, p. 28.

The term *research* might be substituted for *scientific method* in this quotation without changing the general meaning, but no research is perfect and good research is better than bad research because it is done more "scientifically." Accordingly, it is worthwhile to consider what is the scientific method and what makes some research more scientific than other research.

The scientific method is characterized by two traits: validity and reliability. Validity is the characteristic used to describe research which measures what it claims to measure. For example, to measure television-viewing audiences, mechanical devices are put on sets to determine when they are turned on. This is used as a measure of audience but, in fact, it measures only sets turned on. On the surface, validity seems so obvious a factor as to be unimportant, but in practice subtle variations such as that in the above example make it necessary for researchers to consider validity carefully in each project.

Reliability is the characteristic of research methodology which allows it to be repeated again and again by the same and by different researchers, but always with the same results. Poor questionnaires or samples which are not representative of the population are two factors which make it unlikely that repetition of that same project will produce the same results.

Scientific method in the physical sciences and marketing

The scientific method, as a method of reducing uncertainty due to lack of information, has been developed primarily in the physical sciences. A centuries old tradition of careful problem definition combined with the use of measuring instruments which have been proven through many tests to measure specific characteristics provide validity for most physical science research. Much marketing research has equal validity, although the human factor in marketing may make differences in validity more subtle.

It is in the area of reliability, however, where the physical sciences appear to be significantly more "scientific" than marketing. In most physical sciences the reproducible experiment is accepted scientific method. In chemistry, for example, an experiment is conducted under controlled conditions. Such variables as temperature, atmospheric pressure, and quantities of chemicals are carefully measured and all but one held constant during the experiment. These conditions are reported in detail along with the results of the experiment so that others may reproduce the same conditions and verify the results.

In marketing it is difficult, if not impossible, to control all the conditions surrounding a research project so that the same researcher can see if his techniques produce the same results at different times and places or so that other researchers can attempt to reproduce the results. Even more important, most marketing research projects are done as one-time projects by private firms; no attempt is made to test the validity or reliability of the results and the methodology is not published so that others can check for these characteristics. Until recent years few marketing research projects could be called experiments, much less reproducible experiments, and even now only a small portion of all projects are real experiments.[2]

Distinction between the scientific and nonscientific methods

It is useful to think of the scientific method as a very general method which can be adapted to many widely varying situations according to the subject matter and specific problem involved. Since subject matter and problems vary across the whole range of human interest, it is obvious that the specifics of the methods applied will vary. Certain criteria, however, distinguish those methods that may be called scientific from other methods. Three major differences between the scientific and nonscientific methods which affect the reliability and validity of the results are in (1) the objectivity of the investigator, (2) the accuracy of measurement, and (3) the degree to which the investigation is continuing and exhaustive.

Objectivity of the investigator. Researchers must base their judgment on facts, not on preconceived notions or intuition, if their work is to be scientific. If an investigator is not completely objective in his thinking, if he is not just as anxious to find facts supporting one outcome of his study as another, it is unlikely his work will be scientific. Many marketing executives are strong-minded and put significant pressure on the researcher to obtain results supporting their positions.

How difficult it is to remain completely objective in any activity is brought out in a recent study of Sir Isaac Newton, the father of the modern scientific method and one of the great minds of all time. Newton challenged many of the basic concepts of science as they were known at the time and in so doing incurred strong attacks from scientists supporting accepted theories. Newton developed new mathematical theories of gravity and the velocity of sound. When he attempted to prove his theories by actual measurements of gravity and sound, he found significant differences. To strengthen his position vis-à vis his critics, he "fudged" his data to make the results match the theory.[3]

Accuracy of measurement. The scientific method attempts to obtain the most accurate measurements possible. Since the factors to be measured and the measuring devices available differ from one field of study to another, the accuracy of measurements differs widely. In the physical sciences, electronic measuring devices of great accuracy are available for some measurements. In marketing and in the social sciences, a relatively crude measuring device, the questionnaire, is often used. Both may be scientific if they are the best measuring devices which are available for the purpose at hand.

---

[2] Some indication of the growth of marketing as a science is the fact that the February 1979 issue of the *Journal of Marketing Research* was devoted to problems of validity and reliability in marketing research.

[3] R. S. Westfall, "Newton and the Fudge Factor," *Science* 179 (February 1973): 751–58.

Continuing and exhaustive nature of investigation. A scientific investigation considers all the facts that are pertinent to the problem at hand. No bit of evidence is passed over because it fails to fit a previously established pattern. But the mark of the scientific method is more than just refusal to overlook conflicting data; it is the aggressive searching for additional evidence to support, or confound, the existing conclusion. Scientists are never sure that they have found the ultimate truth. They know that many well-established conclusions have been found to be erroneous (for example, throughout the 19th century scientists accepted the "fact" that the atom was the smallest unit into which matter could be divided). It is this constantly challenging attitude which leads to continual progress in science.

In summary, the scientific method can be distinguished from other methods of investigation most easily by the degree to which it provides reliability. If researchers are completely objective, if their measurements are accurate, and if their studies are exhaustive, then their results will be reliable—they and other researchers will get the same results if they reproduce the investigation.

Difficulty of applying the scientific method in marketing

Three characteristics of the scientific method have been discussed above. General problems encountered in trying to achieve these characteristics in marketing research are worth noting along with their impact on the quality of the decisions managers can make using marketing research data. The main problems are identified in Table 2–1 and discussed thereafter.

TABLE 2–1. Problems in achieving scientific methodology in marketing research

Problems in achieving scientific method in marketing research	Characteristics of scientific method		
	Investigator objectivity	Accuracy in measurement	Exhaustive nature of investigation
Investigator involved in use of results	Lack of reliability		Lack of reliability
Nonprecise measuring devices		Lack of reliability	
Influence of measurement process on results		Lack of validity and reliability	
Time pressure for results			Lack of reliability
Difficulty in using experiments to test hypotheses			Lack of validity
Great complexity of subject	Lack of reliability	Lack of validity and reliability	Lack of validity and reliability

Investigator involved in use of results.   Marketing researchers are involved in the sales of their results, either directly as in the case of a commercial research firm or indirectly as in the case of the marketing research director of a manufacturing company. Marketing research data are usually sought for specific decisions which must be made promptly. Researchers are anxious to see the marketing organization prosper and for their careers to prosper as a result. They are, therefore, anxious for their results to be accepted. This may encourage some researchers to find data that support the views of their clients or superiors, either by consciously or unconsciously "fudging" the data obtained in the research (unreliable for lack of objectivity) or by drawing conclusions quickly from limited data (unreliable for lack of exhaustive study). All researchers may be subject to these pressures, as indicated by the Newton example, but the close association of the researcher with the decision action in marketing makes the problem greater there.

Nonprecise measuring devices.   One of the characteristics which distinguishes the scientific method from nonscientific activities is the emphasis put on accuracy of measurement. Since marketing is concerned with people, much of the information collected in marketing research is obtained by interview—a subjective procedure which rarely leads to accurate measurements. Furthermore, much of the information desired relates to opinions and attitudes which, at best, can be reduced to quantitative terms in only rough approximations. For example, the strength of an individual's liking for cigarettes can be measured, but only in a relatively crude way. The measuring devices available to the marketing researcher are, in general, not as accurate as those available to the natural scientist.

Contrast, for example, the accuracy obtained in measuring a teenager's attitude toward oatmeal with that obtained in experiments involving the measurement of time by atomic clocks. Such clocks keep time with an accuracy of one second within 31 trillion years. In the measurement of attitude toward oatmeal, data were obtained by questioning teenagers; there was no way of determining the accuracy of the measurement, but if the results were accurate within one part in ten they would be considered excellent. A number of interviewers were used; each differed from the rest in ability, experience, and training. Some interviews may have been conducted with one foot in the door or while the respondents were busy with their daily tasks. There are, however, examples of very accurate measurement in marketing research such as sales records, warehouse receipts, and recordings of when TV and radio sets are turned on and to what station they're tuned.

Influence of measurement process on results.   When chemists weigh the precipitate resulting from the combination of two chemicals or when physicists measure the speed of sound, neither are concerned with the effect their measurement process has on the results. They can repeat the measurement another day and get essentially the same answer. Such is not always the case in marketing research. When humans recognize that they are being measured, they frequently change. For example, the family which has an audimeter put on its television set may modify its viewing habits because it knows all the viewing is recorded. Similarly, individuals who are questioned about specific opinions may find their opinions changing as a result of the questioning. This is particularly important in studies which include interviews of the same people a second time at a later date to determine what changes have taken place in their opinions. People previously questioned frequently change their opinions in a different way than they would have done had they not been questioned. The interview may call their attention to the subject, say a brand of soap. Thereafter, they are more apt to note advertisements for this soap, the slogans used, and changes in the product than are other individuals whose attention has not been called to it.

The fact that measuring human attitudes and actions can change them makes for lack of both reliability and validity in research results. Measurements at other times and by other researchers may get other results, and it is not clear what is actually being measured. Decisions made with such data are precarious because of the interaction between attitudes and the measuring process.

Time pressure for results.   Marketing research is particularly subject to the pressures of time. Competition rewards the first entry into a new field · (for example, a new system for reducing car exhaust pollution) with a larger share of the market than the product would otherwise achieve. Consequently, decisions on new products, and other marketing variables, are made in a hurry. If research is to be used at all, it must be done quickly. As a result, most marketing research does not benefit from the continuing and exhaustive study that characterizes the scientific method. It should be noted, however, that while most marketing studies have an immediate short-range objective, similar types of studies are done over and over, for different products and at different times, so that a gradual improvement in methodology and understanding take place. The general result is the gradual development of something that approaches scientific method.

Difficulty in using experiments to test hypotheses.   Experimentation is particularly valuable as a research tool because it helps identify cause and effect relationships more clearly than any other research designs. Some consider experimentation the only type of scientific study. Unfortunately, the use of experimentation in marketing research is often impractical or even impossible. It is impossible to control all the factors affecting product sales, such factors as consumer attitudes, the weather, and competitive sales strategies. Therefore, it is impossible to reproduce the same experiment time after time. Thus, this powerful scientific tool is not completely available to marketing research. It is partially available, however, because methods of statistical control have been developed which permit many useful marketing experiments.

Great complexity of subject.   Marketing is concerned with the movement of goods from producers to consumers. The most important determinant of marketing activity is the reaction of people to given stimuli (for example, advertisements) or, more exactly, the anticipated reaction of people to stimuli. Thus, marketing research is concerned with individuals who in themselves and in their activities are more complex than the subjects of the physical scientist.

Perhaps this seems an overstatement to the physicist working on the project to land astronauts on Mars or to the pathologist trying to solve the mysteries of cancer. But individual people are different from these subjects; they have minds and the ability to reason and, therefore, they are able to alter their environment or their adjustment to it. A copper sulfate solution placed in a test tube by a chemist will be there tomorrow, but individuals placed in a given environment may change their location by their own will. The copper sulfate will be the same whether studied in Chicago or Bombay, whether studied today or next year. The same is not true of humans. Reactions of people to a given sales appeal would undoubtedly be different in Bombay than in Chicago. The style that is the fad this year may be discarded by next, and the advertising appeal that is most effective during the hot, humid days of July will likely have little influence next January. This complexity of the human race and their activities make the development of an exact science explaining these activities difficult.

Summary of the scientific method

Marketing research is sometimes defined as the application of the scientific method to marketing problems. In general, this means the application of valid and reliable research methods. Particular emphasis must be given to maintaining objectivity on the part of the investigator, emphasizing accuracy in measurement, and making exhaustive investigations.

There are several specific difficulties encountered in trying to apply the scientific method to marketing problems and these difficulties raise doubts as to the value of many marketing research results.

In approving proposed research projects or in using the results from completed projects, marketing managers should continually ask themselves: (1) Are the data in this project valid—do they measure what they should measure. (2) Are the data in this project reliable—would another study get the same results?

TYPES OF RESEARCH

Despite the difficulty of establishing an entirely satisfactory classification system, it is helpful to classify marketing research projects on the basis of the fundamental objective of the research. Consideration of these different types, their applicability, their strengths, and their weaknesses will help the student in selecting the type best suited to a specific problem. Two general types of research are (1) exploratory and (2) conclusive. Each of these is further subdivided as follows:

Exploratory research	*Conclusive research*
a. Search of secondary data.	*a.* Descriptive research.
b. Survey of knowledgeable persons.	1. Case study.
	2. Statistical study.
c. Case study.	*b.* Experimentation.

These terms are not generally used by marketing practitioners who tend to use the terms *qualitative* and *quantitative* instead of exploratory and conclusive. But the terms qualitative and quantitative suggest the character of the data gathering process rather than the fundamental objective of the research. The authors believe the terminology used here is more useful in guiding research planning. Exploratory research seeks to discover new relationships, while conclusive research is designed to help executives choose among various possible courses of action, that is, to make decisions.

Exploratory research

In well-established fields of study, hypotheses are usually drawn from ideas developed or glimpsed in previous research studies or are derived from theory.[4] Until recent years marketing has been seriously handicapped by a lack of significant theory and by a lack of thoroughly developed research programs to provide a background in depth for specific situations. By now, however, many companies have developed "data banks" on their standard products which include the results of studies made over a period of many years. Each study adds a little more to the total knowledge about the product and the marketing forces influencing it. General Electric reports that one study it made to identify community leaders in the adoption of new products led to a hypothesis for the next study that young people influenced their parents in this process. This led to further studies of the process of social learning in relation to age and family structure, each study providing hypotheses for the next.[5]

Marketing theory has developed rapidly in recent years and now provides the source for many research hypotheses. A large influx of behavioral scientists into marketing has spurred the development of theories of consumer attitude, motivation, and behavior. It now seems safe to say that in another few years a significant body of marketing theory will exist.[6]

---

[4] At this point, the student should become familiar with the term *hypothesis*. It is used frequently in research work and will be used frequently in this book. When researchers have a tentative answer to a question, they call it a hypothesis. For example, candy manufacturers on the basis of their experience, might establish the hypothesis that consumers will prefer crushed peanuts over whole peanuts in a particular candy bar. Once the hypothesis is stated, researchers attempt to design a research project to prove or disprove it.

[5] Nelson N. Foote, "Asking the Right Questions," *New Directions in Research Design* (*Proceedings: American Marketing Association, 2d National Conference on Research Design, 1965*), p. 9.

[6] For a series of examples of the use of theory to develop marketing hypotheses for testing see M. Venkatesan, ed., *Proceedings: 3d Annual Conference Association for Consumer Research* (College Park, Md.: Association for Consumer Research, 1972).

Too little is known, however, about consumer reaction to marketing stimuli to permit the drawing of sound hypotheses in many specific situations. As a result, much marketing research is of an exploratory nature; emphasis is placed on finding practices and policies that need changing and on developing possible alternatives.

Use of exploratory research.   Exploratory research usually results when a research firm is called in by a client who says, "We're not getting the sales volume we think we should. What's wrong?" The researcher might guess at a number of factors—the product might be inferior in quality or style, the wrong channels of distribution might be used, the number of sales representatives in the field might be too few, the advertising appeals might not be the best, and so on.

Since the number of possible difficulties is almost infinite, it is impractical to test them all. Exploratory research is required to find the most likely explanations. Such research may also be involved when the perceived problem is much less general; for example, the research department may be requested to find why one group of sales representatives is particularly unproductive or why certain market segments are buying less than others. Exploratory research is needed in each case to develop likely hypotheses.

The objective of the study determines whether or not it is exploratory and an appropriate research design is then developed. When definite hypotheses have been established, a study to test them is not exploratory.

The research design concepts applicable to exploratory studies are different from those applicable to conclusive studies so it is important to keep in mind the study objectives to assist in finding a good design. It should be noted, however, that the research process tends to become circular over a period of time. Exploratory research may define a problem which is then "solved" by conclusive research, but the conclusive research may have byproducts which are in effect new exploratory studies leading to new hypotheses.

Design of exploratory studies.   Since the object of an exploratory study is to find new ideas, flexibility and ingenuity characterize the investigation. As they go along, researchers must be on the alert to recognize new ideas. They then swing their search in the new direction until they have exhausted the possibilities in the idea or have found a better idea toward which to turn their investigation. Thus, they may be constantly changing their focus of investigation as new possibilities come to their attention.

Formal design is conspicuous by its absence in exploratory studies. The imagination of the researcher is the key factor. However, three lines of attack may aid in finding hypotheses of value: (1) study of secondary sources of information; (2) survey of individuals who are apt to have ideas on the general subject; and (3) analysis of selected cases.

Study of secondary data.   Probably the quickest and most economical way for researchers to find possible hypotheses is to take advantage of the work of others and of their own earlier efforts. Most large companies which have maintained marketing research programs over a number of years have accumulated significant libraries of research relating to their marketing activities. Reports from research organizations furnishing continuing data (for example, Nielsen reports on sales of branded products and American Research Bureau TV audience measures), trade association sales data, and company records such as those kept for accounting and sales analysis purposes are other fruitful sources. There is now a large volume of basic research reported in professional and trade journals and in government documents which may stimulate hypotheses. These sources are often maintained in company libraries, but are otherwise available in public libraries as are more general books, newspapers, and government documents. In a relatively short time, researchers can scan a large volume of published and unpublished ideas and data.

A large food manufacturer's experience furnishes an example of exploratory research based on study of secondary data. To get a particular network radio show that it wanted, this manufacturer had to "take" stations in markets in which it was already advertising as much as apparent potential warranted. In studying Nielsen data on sales in all markets, the marketing research director of this firm noted that sales had shown significant gains in those markets in which the new radio show caused an "overspending" on advertising. From this experience came the hypothesis that larger advertising expenditures generally would be profitable in all markets. Conclusive research of an experimental type substantiated the hypothesis, and advertising was increased from 5.6 percent to 9.3 percent of sales. Within three years, the firm's market share rose from 20 percent to 50 percent.[7]

A survey of previous work of this type can be expedited if it is organized. The fact that the exploratory study has no formal design and that investigators exercise their individual initiative in spotting and following leads does not mean that such a study is done in an aimless manner. Enough is known about marketing so that major areas which frequently are worth investigating can be identified. Also available are many guides and indexes which investigators can use to help locate published and some unpublished materials.[8]

Current developments are changing the traditional character of secondary data searches. Electronic data processing systems now make it possible to store large quantities of data and to retrieve such data rapidly with automated search techniques. At the same time the quantity of secondary data of the types both internal and external to the company is multiplying at a tremendous rate. The result is to make a much larger volume of secondary data operationally available to the researcher. The impact of this development is just beginning to be felt.

Survey of individuals with ideas.   Individuals with ideas on the general subject of interest may be found in widely diversified groups. All persons

---

[7] A. C. Nielsen, Jr., "Key Factors in Building and Maintaining a Strong Consumer Franchise" (undated monograph).

[8] Some of these are discussed in Chapter 5.

who have any association with the efforts to market the product in question are potential sources of information in a marketing research project. Such individuals may include the top executives and sales managers of the company in question and of companies making similar or related products; sales representatives, wholesalers, and retailers who handle the product or related products; and consumers who have used a product of the type in question or have had occasion to need such a product.

While people with ideas of this type may be found in the groups mentioned above, it does not follow that everybody in these groups will have such ideas. Unfortunately, because of limited experience with the problem at hand, lack of ability as observers, inability to express their ideas, or other reasons, most individuals are unable to give any new insights into a marketing problem. Therefore, if time and effort are to be used economically, it is necessary to single out those individuals who are the most imaginative. Among sales representatives and dealers this can partially be accomplished by getting suggestions from sales managers and sales representatives, respectively; among consumers it is difficult. In some instances, however, research departments have been able to locate consumers of special ability along these lines. General Motors, for example, at one time built up a list of consumers who had a special interest in automobile engineering and design and who were imaginative about future developments in these fields.

Despite the desire to find those individuals who have ideas, it is important not to concentrate the investigation only among the better educated, more articulate persons. Such individuals are apt to have similar ideas, whereas reactions to product characteristics or sales appeals may be quite different in other more important population groups. As a result of this desire to reach heterogeneous groups and because of the difficulty of finding those particular consumers with ideas, the typical exploratory survey is made by interviewing individuals known to be cooperative and to have ideas on the subject, plus some others selected somewhat haphazardly from among various population groups thought to be important. This is as good a practical solution as is available.

Since the objective of exploratory research is to find new ideas, it is important to give respondents the greatest possible freedom of response. Within the context of the problem at hand, respondents should be allowed to choose freely the ideas and topics they wish to discuss. At the same time, most respondents need stimuli to bring out their attitudes and ideas. Various techniques have been developed to aid in collecting exploratory data from individuals and they make up what is usually called qualitative research. When applied to consumers such research is generally aimed at finding the thoughts, feelings, and attitudes which influence consumer behavior. The techniques involve interviews with individuals and groups. Individual interviews involve depth interviews or a projective device by which the respondent is asked to project himself into a particular situation. Group interviews have come to be called *focus-group* interviews.

One type of projective device is that of role playing or role rehearsal. An example occurred in a study done for the U.S. Department of Agriculture to determine the maximum amount of poultry products consumers might consume.

> The interviewers asked respondents: "Suppose you were asked to serve chicken three times a week for a year to your family; in return for doing so you would be paid $15 a week; you could not tell anyone in your family that you were experimenting on them or that you were being paid. Will you do it?" The following responses were typical of those received:
> "I'd get out my cookbook again."
> "There are so many ways to make chicken. It doesn't have a lot of flavor itself."
> "I think that what would happen is that there would be more variety, and you'd be inventive and branch out."
> From the ideas obtained from these "role rehearsals," the researchers developed hypotheses that were later tested in a structured questionnaire.[9]

Focus-group interviews.   Focus group interviews have become by far the most widely used method of exploratory research. In 1979 a check among the largest consumer goods manufacturers in the United States showed that 93 percent used focus groups.[10] Focus groups usually consist of 6 to 12 consumers brought together at one place to discuss the topic of interest. Many research organizations now have elaborate facilities for such groups which permit the discussions to be tape-recorded or video-recorded and permit marketing and advertising executives to watch the proceedings through one-way glass or on closed-circuit TV. This latter aspect has become a major by-product of focus groups as it enables executives to get first-person feel of consumer attitudes and reactions to the product or advertisement in question.[11] Since the executives watching the process are higher ranking than the researchers, there is a growing tendency to run the focus group with their interests as the prime consideration. The obvious result of this "tail-wagging-dog" development is a loss in the quality of the research.

Research objectives of focus groups vary, but they are, or should be, consistent in *not* trying to measure quantitatively any of the topics of interest. Focus groups in exploratory research are intended to provide some of the complex, subtle aspects of the relationship between consumers on the one hand and products, advertising, and sales efforts on the other. They

---

[9] Herbert I. Abelson, "A 'Role Rehearsal' Technique for Exploratory Interviewing," *Public Opinion Quarterly* 30 (Summer 1966):302–5.

[10] *Consumer Market Research Usage Patterns and Attitudes* (Chicago: Market Facts, Inc., 1979).

[11] The following discussion draws heavily on Bobby J. Calder, "Focus Groups and the Nature of Qualitative Marketing Research," *Journal of Marketing Research* 14 (August 1977):353–64; R&D Sub-Committee on Qualitative Research, "Qualitative Research—A Summary of the Concepts Involved," *Journal of the Market Research Society* 21 (April 1979):107–24; and Myril Axelrod, "Two Part Series on Qualitative Research," *Marketing News* (February 28 and March 14, 1975):6–7, 10–11.

provide qualitative or subjective analyses of such things as consumer language used in talking about a product, emotional and behavioral reactions to advertising, lifestyle relationship to the product category and the specific brand, and unconscious consumer motivations relative to the product and its promotion.

Focus-group process. When a focus group is convened, the moderator (researcher) provides a brief general comment on the purpose of the meeting and suggests a specific topic to open the discussion. A typical approach is to have the group start talking about the general product category and the specific products within that category which they use. From this discussion the moderator may move the group to talk about how they feel about the products of interest and then to a discussion of their attitudes and behaviors towards the products, why they like some brands and not others.

The moderator attempts to let the group carry the conversation by itself. He intervenes only to introduce topics of importance that may not come up spontaneously, to move on when a topic has been exhausted, or to bring the discussion back to the area of interest when it has wandered into irrelevant areas. The interviews are usually taped so that the moderator can concentrate on keeping the discussion on track without fear of losing information, but can then analyze the results under conditions which permit careful attention to detail and thoughtful development of hypotheses.

The moderator must blend into the group so that she is accepted as one of them rather than as a director who will ask questions which the others must answer. This usually means female moderators for women's groups, young moderators for young groups, etc. Nevertheless, the moderator must enter the session with a detailed plan covering all areas which she wants to be discussed and the best way to introduce each area so as to encourage open discussion. At the same time the moderator must not dominate the discussion; each participant must feel free to bring up any topic she wishes.

Focus groups have become popular in marketing research because they give a direct "feel" of individual consumers. Other studies may result in averages, percentages, or more exotic calculations, but they seem impersonal as a result. Reports prepared on focus group interviews typically contain many direct quotations from the interview session. These can be highly useful and stimulating to marketing people, but it is important to remember that the value of focus groups is to provide such ideas, not to measure the size of market segments holding the ideas.

Problems with focus groups. To be successful, focus groups require a moderator who is well trained, typically in psychology and sociology, who has had experience with the product of interest, and has an intuitive skill for grasping the important points developed in the discussion. Since the moderator conducts the interview, analyzes the results, draws conclusions, and recommends action, it is clear that the results from this type of exploratory research depend on the skill and imagination of this individual. This is one of the weaknesses of this type of research, a weakness which leads to great scepticism on the part of many. The same results are not apt to be obtained by other researchers at other times. If focus groups are treated as exploratory research and the hypotheses developed are then tested with conclusive quantitative research, there is no problem. But much focus-group research is not followed by conclusive research, probably because of the cost. Critics of focus groups argue that the results obtained are little more than the creative ideas of the researcher and should not be considered research.

In early focus-group research the sessions were held in private homes which provided a relaxed atmosphere conducive to informal discussion of the bull session variety. As the value of these sessions for stimulating directly advertising and marketing creative people became recognized, it became necessary to hold the sessions in more formal settings with one-way mirrors and audio-video recording facilities. As a result there is a tendency to use formal conference rooms with the participants sitting around a large table. Most researchers would prefer a room made as casual and informal as possible.

Depth interviews were a predecessor of focus groups. They are used for many of the same purposes and are subject to the same criticisms. The difference is that depth interviews are made one at a time. Focus groups are a cheaper, less time consuming way of developing information on consumer views, habits and attitudes and also tend to clarify attitudes and feelings through the give-and-take of the group discussion. The good moderator enhances this advantage. But the groups have problems which even the best moderators can't entirely eliminate. Dominant personalities may take over groups and lead the discussion in their own way. This may result in the establishment of a group feeling which keeps less aggressive individuals with other views from expressing them. Other participants may tend to stray off the topic making it difficult to cover all the points of interest in the time available—usually a maximum of two hours per group.

Selecting samples for focus groups.   Sampling problems for focus groups are of two types—how many different groups to have and what the makeup of each group should be. A generally accepted rule of thumb is never to use only one focus group. The guiding concept is to keep running groups until the researcher is getting no more new ideas. In practice, three or four groups on a given topic are typical.

Makeup of each focus group is not determined by an objective process. Quotas are typically established for demographic factors such as age, sex, marital status and income level, but product and brand usage and frequency of purchase are also usually involved.

Quotas may be based on the proportion of a group in the general population or may be used to limit the focus group to a certain narrow category such as unmarried men between 18 and 30. Focus-group research is based on small samples and is designed to provide ideas rather than to measure the size of various attitudes in the population. Therefore, it is unrealistic and inefficient to try to get all segments of the population represented proportionately in focus groups. The one or few segments most useful for the project should dominate the sample. It is often useful to have different focus groups for different important segments rather than to have several segments in the same group. While the interaction among the different segments may be useful, it often leads to so much variation that no clear ideas develop. Some researchers, for example, don't have fulltime housewives with children at home in the same groups as working women without children because their lifestyles are completely different. Some practitioners never have men and women in the same focus group because they believe there is more "performing" when the two sexes are together. The market for the product and the purpose of the research are the determining factors in setting quotas. In almost all cases, however, it is desirable to have individuals who have had experience with the product in question and are articulate.

Organizations specialize in recruiting participants for focus groups. They usually have lists of volunteers such as PTAs or religious groups. Interviewers call names on these lists and screen them according to the quotas established. When difficulties are encountered in filling certain hard-to-find quotas, interviewers may resort to recruiting friends or pushing individuals into categories other than those in which they naturally fall. Many people enjoy focus group experiences and try to get into such groups frequently, but experience has shown that participants cease to react spontaneously if they are in more than one or two groups a year.

It must also be remembered that the individuals, usually women, who participate in focus groups are probably from a segment of the population that is more outspoken, more activist, more domineering than other women. Whether this means they are different in consumption attitudes and habits is not clear.

Analysis of selected cases.   In some instances, detailed case analysis of a few selected individuals or organizations may be particularly helpful in gaining ideas about possible relationships. Case studies are characterized by intensive study.[12] Emphasis is placed on understanding the subject of investigation as a whole. All aspects of the case are investigated. This intensive study of a case is apt to turn up relationships which might not otherwise be found. In one study to improve the productivity of the sales force of a particular company, the investigator studied intensively two or three of the best sales representatives and two or three of the worst. Data were collected on the background and experience of each representative and then several days were spent making sales calls with them. As a result, a hypothesis was developed. It was that checking the stock of retailers and suggesting items on which they were low were the most important differences between the successful and the poor sales representatives.

---

[12] Since case analyses are also used in the descriptive type of conclusive study, the case method is discussed further under that heading.

The reader will note that the concept of case studies differs from surveys of knowledgeable persons more in degree than in kind. Focus groups, for example, are almost case studies of a small group of consumers. If each consumer in a focus group were interviewed separately, but with the same plan, the process would be considered a series of case studies; when the consumers are interviewed as a group, the process is a focus group.

Conclusive research

When a marketing executive makes a decision, one course of action is being selected from among a number available. The alternatives may be as few as two, or virtually infinite; they may be well defined or only vaguely glimpsed. Conclusive research provides information which helps the executive make a rational decision. In some instances, particularly if an experiment is run, the research may come close to specifying the precise alternative to choose; in other cases, especially with descriptive studies, the research will only partially clarify the situation and much will be left to the executive's judgment.

Descriptive research.   Descriptive studies, as their name implies, are designed to describe something, for example, the characteristics of users of a given product; the degree to which product use varies with income, age, sex, or other characteristics; or the number who saw a specific television commercial. A majority of marketing research studies are of this type.

It should not be concluded because the emphasis is on description that such studies should be simply fact-gathering expeditions. Unfortunately, it is relatively easy to start a descriptive study with the vague thought that the data collected will be interesting. As a result many descriptive studies are made with only hazy objectives and with inadequate planning. Much of the data collected in such studies turn out to be useless. Descriptive studies of this type, in which there is no clear hypothesis, are actually more exploratory than they are conclusive. If such studies are conceived and conducted as exploratory projects, equal or better information can usually be obtained at smaller cost.

To be of value, a descriptive study must collect data for a definite purpose. Nevertheless, descriptive studies vary in the degree to which a specific hypothesis is the guide. In a market definition study, frequently no specific statement of a hypothesis is made. The idea that selling effort should be concentrated on the market most likely to buy is, however, implicit. The descriptive study is designed to find that market, with the assumption that selling effort will then be concentrated where it will do the most good. In other instances, descriptive studies may be guided by much more explicit hypotheses. A cereal company may find its sales slipping. On the basis of market contacts (or perhaps exploratory research), the company may hypothesize that teenage children do not eat its cereal for breakfast. A descriptive study can then be designed to test this hypothesis.

Importance of design in descriptive studies. Descriptive studies differ from exploratory studies in the formality with which they are designed. Exploratory studies are characterized by flexibility, while descriptive studies attempt to obtain a complete and accurate description of a situation. Formal design is required to insure that the description covers all phases desired. Precise statement of the problem indicates what information is required. The study must then be designed to provide for the collection of this information. Unless the study design provides specified methods for selecting sources of information (sample design) and for collecting data from those sources, the information obtained may be inaccurate or inappropriate.

Formal design is also required to forestall collection of unnecessary data. Since descriptive studies often cost many thousands of dollars, the unnecessary expenditures could be large.

Descriptive data are commonly used as direct bases for marketing decisions. After analyzing the data, the investigators attempt to predict the result of certain actions; for example, they may predict that concentration of advertising on upper-income people will increase sales volume. Descriptive data, however, do not show direct cause and effect relationships. Purchases of a product and income may vary together, but this does not prove high income is the cause of the purchases. Experimental data are needed to establish cause and effect. Frequently in marketing, however, investigators find that they have neither the funds nor the means of controlling a situation necessary to establish an experiment; thus, they must rely on descriptive data. If descriptive data are to be used as a basis for prediction, their collection must be designed so that the ambiguous nature of cause and effect relationships will be reduced as much as possible.

Careful design of descriptive studies is necessary, therefore, to insure complete description of the situation, to insure minimum bias in the collection of data, to hold costs to a minimum, and to reduce the errors to which the interpretation is subject.

Types of descriptive study designs. To facilitate the discussion on the design of descriptive studies, two types, or methods, of study are considered separately—the case method and the statistical method. The separation is required because analysis of result is approached differently in the two instances.

Case studies are not widely used in descriptive research; however, they are worth some discussion and perhaps more use than they have been given in the past. The term statistical method is unfortunate, since it suggests other studies are not statistical, which is not true. However, the term is used widely in social research, and no other term adequately describes the method involved.[13]

---

[13] The term *survey* is frequently used to describe the method covered by the term *statistical study*. However, survey is also used, and perhaps more frequently, to denote any study in which data are gathered by interviewing.

Case method.   The case method involves intensive study of a relatively small number of situations. For example, an investigator might make a detailed investigation of a few consumers, a few retail stores, a few sales control systems, or a few small town markets. In some instances, the number of cases studied is reduced to one. Whether one or a few units are examined, the process is called the case method and each unit is called a case. The emphasis is on obtaining a complete description and understanding of the relationships of factors in each instance, regardless of the number involved.

There is some question as to whether the case method should be considered a type of descriptive research or only a method of exploratory research or a step in the research process. One view considers the case method applicable only to exploratory studies and considers exploratory studies as the first step in the research process. Thus, the case method would be used to discover new ideas about relationships which could then be tested by conclusive research.

The case method is often used in the above manner—as a first step in the research process. Without doubt, this is the best application of the case method. In many instances, however, case studies are the end procedure as far as formal research is concerned. Testing of the conclusions reached occurs only as they are put into practice. The distinction between the case method in exploratory research and the case method in descriptive research, then, is largely a distinction based on the finality of the results. If further testing is planned, the work is exploratory. The procedure, in either instance, is much the same except that more flexibility is obtained in exploratory work. In descriptive research, the procedure may be more formalized, so that the points investigated are definitely known, and analysis can approach the quantitative analysis used with the statistical method.

Use of case method.   Case studies are of particular value when one is seeking help on a problem in which interrelationships of a number of factors are involved, and in which it is difficult to understand the individual factors without considering their relationships with each other. For example, independent wholesalers are constantly trying to improve their operations so as to enable their retail store customers to compete with chain stores. The case method might be applied to this problem. One researcher who has made such a study comments:

> [This] study is the first of a series of case studies designed to fill the gap on delivery cost data at the wholesale level. Subsequent discussions with other firms indicate that a number of the findings in [this] study have general application throughout the industry.[14]

Probably more than anything else, marketing executives would like to know why people buy or do not buy their products. The case method, using depth interviews, is one of the ways of studying this problem. A trained

---

[14] James R. Snitzler, "How Wholesalers Can Cut Delivery Costs," *Journal of Marketing* 23 (July 1958):25.

researcher interviews a small, selected group of consumers in a manner roughly similar to that used by the psychiatrist. The objective is to get at subsurface, even subconscious, motivations.

Case method design.   Analogy is the method of analysis most applicable in the case method.[15] Cases collected are typically studies to find three factors: (1) features which are common to all cases in the general group; (2) features which are not common to all cases, but are common to certain subgroups; and (3) features which are unique to a specific case.

Conclusions are formulated from comparisons of these similarities and differences. In some instances, the investigator is most interested in the first two groups of factors—those that are common to all in the class or those that are common to all in a subclass. For example, in a study of consumer motivations investigators would be interested in those motives which were common to all consumers or to all in certain subgroups such as those living on farms, those over 50 years of age, or those of German extraction. In other instances, the factors most important are those factors unique to the individual case. If grocery stores are being studied, the investigator may seek the characteristics which are common only to the profitable stores and the characteristics which are common to the unprofitable stores. In such a study good housekeeping was found common to virtually all stores, but good stock control procedures were found common only to the subclass of profitable stores.

Design of case studies, then, will be based on the specific objectives of the study, and is primarily a question of good judgment in selecting cases to be studied. If factors common to all items of a group are sought (for example, motivations of consumers buying sports cars), then a "representative group" of cases from the universe of sports car buyers might be selected. If it were desired to find what made some sales representatives more successful than others, the design might include cases from two abnormal subgroups—successful sales representatives and unsuccessful sales representatives.

Advantages and disadvantages of the case method.   This statement summarizes well the situation relative to case studies:

> To work it [the case method] well requires a rare combination of judgment in selecting cases, and of insight and sympathy in interpreting them. At its best, it is the best of all; but in ordinary hands it is likely to suggest more untrustworthy general conclusions than those obtained by the extensive method of collecting more rapidly very numerous observations, reducing them as far as possible to statistical form, and obtaining broad averages in which inaccuracies and idiosyncrasies may be twisted to counteract one another to some extent.[16]

---

[15] In fact, analogy is the only method of analysis which can be used in the real case method. If a number of cases are collected, there is a tendency to determine such measures as averages and frequency distributions. When these procedures are used, however, the method becomes "statistical" rather than "case."

[16] Alfred Marshall, *Principles of Economics,* 8th ed. (New York: Macmillan Co., 1930), p. 116.

The chief advantages of the case method are these: (1) inferences are obtained from study of an entire situation, an entity, rather than from study of one or several selected aspects alone; (2) a case study is a description of a real event or situation, whereas a statistical study involves abstraction from real situations (for example, an average may be typical of a large group, but not be descriptive of a single unit in the group); and (3) more accurate data are obtained, probably as a result of the longer, more intimate association of the researcher and respondent, the greater rapport that is normally developed between the two, and the reduced reliance on formalized questions and answers.

Disadvantages of the case method center around the lack of objectivity, which is inherent, and the sampling methods used. (1) Since case studies involve detailed description of complete situations, it is difficult to develop formal methods of observation and recording. Informal methods tend to become subjective rather than objective, and involve the danger that investigators will see what they hope or expect to see. (2) This lack of objectivity carries over into the analysis of case data. Since, by definition, formal statistical procedures are not used, the analysis is based on the intuition of investigators. As pointed out above, this may lead to unwarranted conclusions. (3) In analyzing cases, investigators are inclined to generalize, although the case method does not lend itself to generalization. Because the sample is usually very small, because cases are selected subjectively, and because a tendency exists to select unusual cases, any generalization is dangerous.

A good example of the problems encountered when the case method is inappropriately used occurred in a case study of promotion methods. A review of this project concluded:

> Instead of selecting cases from as widely varying backgrounds as possible to obtain as many ideas as possible, they studied only firms purposely selected to be as homogeneous as possible. Then instead of studying each case as an integrated unit, the cases were lumped into composites, thus losing the valuable interrelated aspects. At the same time, statistical analyses were attempted with a total sample of 12 and subsamples of 6 each. Conclusions as to the differences between consumer and industrial firms from samples of this sort can only be meaningless.[17]

In summary, the case method has its greatest value in exploratory research where the objective is to find hypotheses to be tested by more formal research methods. When data from a case study are classified and summarized, the study becomes statistical rather than case in nature. When this is so, statistical methods should be used.

Statistical method.   The statistical method differs from the case method in the number of cases studied and in the comprehensiveness of the study of each case. While the case method involves complete study of a few cases, the

---

[17] Ralph Westfall, book review, *Journal of Marketing Research* 2 (November 1965): 421.

statistical method involves the study of a few factors in a larger number of cases. Since more cases are involved, the statistical method must use different methods of analysis—methods designed for mass data. Instead of comparing individual cases by analogy, the statistical method ceases to identify individual cases and focuses instead on classes, averages, percentages, measures of dispersion, and more sophisticated statistical procedures. It is from the use of these statistical tools for analyzing quantities of data that the term *statistical method* is derived.

Use of statistical method.   Because it is difficult to apply the experimental method to many marketing situations, the statistical method has been substituted. The latter is the method most used in marketing research and in the collection and study of data of many types. Data which the accounting department compiles showing sales by type of customer, by geographical area, or by product are analyzed by the statistical method to find the most profitable allocation of selling effort. Standard surveys to find whether a product is used more by young or old people, whether a given advertisement was seen or not, the quantity of soft drinks consumed in the past week, or the attitude toward permanent-press clothes are also examples of the statistical method.

Concrete illustration will clarify the nature of these statistical studies. A milling company wishes to find out who eats its breakfast cereal and how much each consumer eats. Accordingly, the company makes a statistical study. A sample of approximately 1,000 consumers is chosen. From these consumers, the company obtains information as to whether or not they have ever eaten the company brand of cereal, and how many times, if any, they have eaten the cereal in the last week. In addition, information is obtained on the age, sex, income, occupation, and size of family of the consumer. The company can then compute such things as the percentage who have eaten the cereal in the last week; the average number of times that each consumer ate the cereal in a week; the percentage of "eaters" in each of several income, age, sex, occupation, and family-size groups; and the proportion of "heavy eaters" and "light eaters" of the cereal.

Statistical method design.   If a statistical study were to be purely descriptive, that is, if the objective were to present the situation exising at a particular time, the design of the study sample would tend to be a cross section of the universe under study. A cross section of the charge account customers of a department store might be obtained by selecting every hundredth such customer from the charge account files maintained by the store. The objective of such a design would be to select a relatively small group which would be similar to the entire group of the charge account customers. A description of this small group would then be obtained and used as if it were a description of the entire list of charge account customers.[18]

---

[18] The degree to which a description of a small group or sample coincides with a description of the total group or universe is discussed in the chapters on sampling.

Description for its own sake is rarely the objective of a marketing research study. From the descriptive statistics researchers hope to gain ideas about cause and effect relationships which will provide help in planning marketing programs. Since the statistical study does not lend itself to proof of cause and effect relationships, researchers must design their studies to give as much evidence as possible on such relationships. This is usually done by designing a system of classification and cross classification. The objective is to establish categories such that classification in one category implies classification in one or more other categories; for example, if older people consume product X heavily, classification in the older age group will imply classification in the heavy consumption group. Detailed analysis of an example may make this more clear. A study of 1,036 families found that 35 percent bought a household durable good (refrigerator, stove, and so on) during a given year.[19] If more could be learned about why those who bought did so, it would be helpful in planning selling effort for the next season. At an earlier date, these families had been questioned as to their plans for such a purchase. A cross classification of the two sets of data gave the result shown in Table 2–2.

TABLE 2–2. Durable goods purchase intentions of families and actual purchase behavior

	Planned to buy		Did not plan to buy		Total	
	Number	Percent	Number	Percent	Number	Percent
Did buy	128	54	236	30	364	35
Did not buy	108	46	564	70	672	65
Total	236	100	800	100	1,036	100

The table indicates that those who plan to purchase durables during a year do, in fact, purchase more than those who do not plan to purchase (54 percent to 30 percent). But "planning to purchase" is still not a very good predictor of actual purchase because 46 percent of those who planned to buy did not and 30 percent of those who did not plan to buy did. These findings suggest other factors are also related to the buying action. Researchers must use their judgment and general knowledge of the field to select the factors most likely to improve the prediction of actual purchase behavior. In the example at hand, researchers obtained information as to the consumers' expectations of an increase in prices (see Table 2–3).

Actual purchases differed little among those who thought prices would drop, stay the same, or rise. But the greatest value in cross classification does not come from analysis of one factor and then another; it comes from the

---

[19] The following example is drawn from Jean Namias, "Intentions to Purchase Related to Consumer Characteristics," *Journal of Marketing* 25 (July 1960):32–36.

TABLE 2-3. Effect of expected price changes on purchase of household durables

| | Expect price to | | | | | | | |
	Drop		Stay same		Rise		Total	
	Number	Percent	Number	Percent	Number	Percent	Number	Percent
Did buy	28	37	134	32	202	37	364	35
Did not buy	48	63	284	68	340	63	672	65
Total	76	100	418	100	542	100	1,036	100

TABLE 2-4. Fulfillment of plans to purchase durable goods classified by expected price changes

| | Planned to purchase, expect price to | | | | | | Did not plan to purchase, expect price to | | | | | |
	Drop		Stay same		Rise		Drop		Stay same		Rise	
	Number	Percent	Number	Percent	Number	Percent	Number	Percent	Number	Percent	Number	Percent
Did buy	6	46	52	50	70	59	22	35	82	26	132	31
Did not buy ..	7	54	52	50	49	41	41	65	232	74	291	69
Total	13	100	104	100	119	100	63	100	314	100	423	100

analysis of several variables at the same time. Table 2–4 shows the cross classification of actual purchases with plans to buy and with expectation of price changes.

When one considers only those who planned to buy, the percentage actually buying increases from 46 percent among those expecting a price drop, to 50 percent among those expecting stable prices, to 59 percent for those expecting price increases. Among those not planning purchases, the proportions actually buying are lower and do not follow the same pattern on the basis of price expectations. These data suggest that both price expectations and purchase plans influence actual purchases, but they do not prove it. Income, for example, may be closely related to buying plans and might explain more of the actual purchases. To separate this factor, different income classes could be established within each price expectation class within each purchase plan class.

Many more factors could be considered in the analysis, but it can readily be seen from Table 2–4 that more factors make the analysis complex and make presentation of results awkward. No matter how many factors are considered, one can never be sure there are not others that are more basic influences on the action under study. Cross classification is useful in indicating possible relationships, but it cannot prove cause and effect relationships.

Statistical study designs, then, must be such as to permit the cross classifications which are important to the analysis. The cross classifications which are desired must be determined in advance, and the study sample must provide enough respondents in each cell for proper analysis. In some cases a representative cross section may be satisfactory. In many instances, however, such a design would require an extremely large sample if each cross classification were to be represented adequately. In Table 2–4, for example, data from a fairly large cross-sectional sample of 1,036 are itemized, but this sample produced only 13 respondents who planned to purchase and also expected the price to drop. To increase this subsample to only 52 respondents would require a total sample of 4,144 if a cross section were used.

To overcome this problem, designs are frequently used in which unusual cross classifications are weighted more heavily than they actually occur in the universe under study. If it were possible to select separately respondents who planned to purchase and expected the price to drop, a subsample of 52 such respondents could be obtained by adding only 39 to the sample in Table 2–4 instead of 3,108 which a cross-sectional selection would require. Selection of such a subsample might be difficult in this case, but in others is simple. For example, the researcher may wish to contrast the purchase rate for dried milk among rural residents with the rate among city dwellers. Two samples, one of city residents and one of rural residents, could be selected easily to give the size needed in each category.

Advantages and disadvantages of statistical method.   Compared with case studies, statistical studies involve a relatively large number of observations. As a result the analysis uses techniques adapted to mass data. Each individual item tends to lose its identity. This is both an advantage and a disadvantage. The advantage lies in the objectivity with which the analysis can be made. Averages and percentages are computed. Two competent researchers, working with the same information, will get the same average or percentage. Such is not true with the case study. In the latter, the analysis is based largely on intuition and judgment and, hence, two researchers might easily differ in their analyses of the same data. A second advantage of the statistical method relative to the case method is that it permits the researcher to make more accurate generalizations. The tendency in case studies is to jump to general conclusions from a few sample cases which may or may not be typical of the universe under investigation. A properly selected sample for a statistical study, since it involves more cases, is apt to be typical of the universe. Furthermore, if the research is properly designed, the reliability of generalizations drawn from statistical data can be measured.[20]

Another disadvantage of the statistical method is its inability to prove cause and effect relationships. This is a disadvantage relative only to the experimental method, for the case method has the same inadequacy. No matter how many factors they have included in their cross classifications, researchers never know that they have all that are of importance. Thus, the statistical method may suggest cause and effect relationships, but it cannot be used to prove them in the way the experimental method can be used.

An additional problem is that the direction of the causal effect is not always clear in statistical studies. Where advertising and sales are found to vary together, for example, it is not clear whether advertising causes sales or sales cause the expenditure of more advertising effort because of greater apparent potential sales results.

SUMMARY

Marketing research projects are designed as either exploratory studies or conclusive studies, depending on the objectives. Exploratory studies are used when so little is known about a given area that useful hypotheses cannot be formulated. Their objective is to define relationships between two or more factors in a way that will permit statement of specific hypotheses. These can then be tested by conclusive research to select the best.

Exploratory studies are designed as searches of secondary data, surveys of selected individuals thought to have ideas (with focus groups being widely used), and analysis of selected cases.

Conclusive research requires more formal design than exploratory research. The most used type of conclusive research design is the descriptive design. Such designs provide a description of a specific situation in such a way as to help the researcher identify cause and effect relationships. The case method and the statistical method are two descriptive designs.

---

[20] Reliability of estimates made from samples can be measured where probability sampling methods are used. These are discussed in Chapters 10 and 11.

Case 2–1
J. M. THOMAS COMPANY

The J. M. Thomas Company was a large manufacturer of industrial vehicles with annual sales in excess of $200 million. These vehicles were gasoline-powered materials-handling tractors of various sizes and capabilities which were used in lifting and moving bulk materials such as soil, sand, snow and other heavy items such as crates and boxes. They were typically used by many different manufacturing, processing and service industries. Despite their high cost of several thousands of dollars, vehicles such as these were so efficient in materials handling and movement that they were found in almost every firm where heavy loads had to be moved.

The Thomas Company's line of industrial vehicles were marketed through 96 distributors who had exclusive territories and handled only the Thomas line. Each distributor had his own sales force which called on customers and prospects within the territory. The distributors also had the facilities and personnel to service the equipment they sold, and they carried a full inventory of replacement parts.

Richard Hersey, the sales manager of the Thomas Company, believed the company's vehicles held a good position in the industry, but this was based on his intuitive feeling and not on specific research or industry statistics. For example, he did not know whether the company was losing or gaining market share, or if they knew about all possible opportunities for increased sales. Since the distributors' salesmen didn't call on all users of industrial vehicles in their territories, Hersey knew they weren't aware of how many vehicles had been sold to those users by competitors. Because of this poor market information, Hersey asked the marketing research firm of Henry and Bell to propose research which could provide the needed information.

A few weeks later, Marty Holland, a project manager at Henry and Bell met with Hersey to discuss a four point research approach. First, he suggested they test the research on three Thomas distributors, one judged by Hersey as having achieved average sales performance, and one each judged to be above average and below average in their performance. By selecting three distributors of different performance, the reseach could help show if Thomas Company's market position actually was different in territories where their position was believed to be different.

Second, Hersey and other Thomas Company personnel would use their knowledge of their customer firms and the Standard Industrial Classification (SIC) system to identify the industries which they believed were users of industrial vehicles.[1] All industries which they judged to represent a significant level of sales potential would be included in the study.

---

[1] See Chapter 22 for a description of the Standard Industrial Classification (SIC) system.

Third, they would obtain information from the Dun and Bradstreet Company on all firms which were located in the three distributors' territories and which were listed in the SIC industry categories identified as industrial vehicle users in step two. The Dun and Bradstreet information would include the name, address, and telephone number of each firm, the name of the chief officer, the company's size in terms of number of employees, and the SIC industry affiliation of the company.

Fourth, Henry and Bell would use their long-distance telephone facilities to telephone these companies and interview the person responsible for purchasing industrial vehicles. Interviewers would try to obtain information regarding the company's current use of industrial vehicles, the number and brand names of their vehicles, whether they would need more vehicles in the near future, if they were aware of the Thomas Company's distributor in their area, and if they had recently been contacted by a salesman from the Thomas Company's distributor

In terms of project cost, Holland estimated that if 1,000 firms were contacted by telephone in each of the three territories, the research would cost approximately $10,000 per territory. Holland had considered and rejected using personal interviews rather than telephone, because he knew the cost would be considerably higher. If the Thomas Company decided to use this research approach, Hersey would have to select three distributors with different levels of sales performance who were willing to participate in the project.

Evaluate the proposed research. Should it be accepted, modified or rejected?

Should some other research approach be used?

If it is accepted as is or in modified form, how can the findings be used?

Case 2–2
PACKAGED PRODUCTS

Robert Yamani was marketing director of Packaged Products, a division of the General Milling Company, which specialized in cereals and ready-to-bake products. Packaged Products marketed a line of cake mixes, cookie mixes, pie crusts, and pastries, all of which were ready-to-bake with the addition of only one or two ingredients. Mr. Yamani felt that the division had been reasonably successful in developing a line of products which were generally well-received by homemakers and that the division should continue to be new-product oriented.

The division's continued growth, Mr. Yamani believed, could be assured only if there were a steady stream of new products being introduced on the market. Mr. Yamani's view on this matter was that the division's goal should be to introduce one new or improved product each year. Each new or improved product should increase the division's sales at a greater rate than could be expected as a result of increased population and economic growth.

One day Mr. Yamani noticed an interesting article in *Advertising Age,* a weekly trade newspaper in the advertising and marketing field. The article was basically a verbatim record of the comments of nine consumers on the subject of new products in supermarkets. The consumers had been brought together by the director of research of an advertising agency to serve as subjects in a focus group interview (see Exhibit 1). In reading the article, Mr. Yamani was struck by what appeared to be a very negative attitude toward new products by some of the consumers. This disturbed him quite a bit, because if a sizable portion of consumers had such a negative attitude, one implication could be that the division's new product objectives should be reconsidered.

Mr. Yamani sent the article and a memo to Nancy Schmidt, the division's marketing research manager. He asked her to read and study the article and then to meet with him for the purpose of discussing the article. He asked her to consider three points. First, did she notice anything in the recorded focus group interview which was of significance to Packaged Products? If so, what was it and in what way was it significant? Second, should Packaged Products undertake a series of focus group interviews in order to identify better consumer attitudes toward new products, reformulated products, packaging, and prices. Third, did the article contain any ideas or concepts the potential value of which to Packaged Products was so great that they could justify the undertaking of a large statistical study?

What answers should Nancy Schmidt prepare for each of the points raised by Mr. Yamani?

EXHIBIT 1. Too many new products? Dallas consumers think so*

Mr. Yob: Let's talk in general about new products in supermarkets. What is it that attracts you to new products?

Ann: Well, I like to buy things that will be useful to me and my family and that I think will appeal to them. I'm not going to buy a new product if I don't have a use for it, or if I feel that it is only going to benefit me.

Judith: I think the visual presentation of it would be the first thing.

Mr. Yob: What is it about the visual presentation?

Judith: The colors and the writing catch your eye so that you can pick it out from 100 million things on the shelf.

* An edited transcript of a focus group session conducted by Dick Yob, vice president/ director of research, Bloom Advertising, Dallas. Reprinted with permission from the September 8, 1975 issue of *Advertising Age.* Copyright 1975 by Crain Communications, Inc.

EXHIBIT 1 (*continued*)

Linda H.: I think the thing that attracts me to a product is the unhappiness I have with the present product. I mean you have to be attracted to a new product because of something that isn't the way you would like it to be with what you're presently using.

Looks for nutritional content

Elaine: If I see a product on the shelf that I know nothing about, I will stop and read the package. Then I'll read the contents to see if there is a possibility that my family would like it better than what we are presently using.

Mr. Yob: What do you look for on the package?

Elaine: Nutritional value. How many preservatives. If there is starch or sugar, I put it back, or if it starts with water, I put it back. Filler and stuff like that. I really got mad the other day when I looked for the nutritional content on a jar of Gerber's baby food and it wasn't there. I wrote them and I said I think for the general public's welfare they ought to say what the product contains. The first thing a mother is looking for is nutritional value, and they don't put that on baby food.

Mr. Yob: What recourse do you have?

Elaine: I still buy the product, but you can write them and give them the business about it. I think that if you don't write them you're neglecting your duty as a consumer.

Mr. Yob: Do you think it helps to write?

Mary Jane: Oh, yes, you get fantastically neat letters back from the presidents.

Mr. Yob: Are you satisfied with the response you get when you do that?

Mary Jane: Well, I think if enough people do it, yes. You know I haven't seen any instant change because I wrote, but I think eventually it will change.

Mary Elise: I wrote a letter to a toy manufacturer and got no response at all, and I was very angry.

Ann: I hate to admit it, but I don't really care. If a new product doesn't work, I usually say, all right, it didn't work and I won't buy it again. Even if I did complain they wouldn't change anything. Besides, I don't have time to sit down and write letters right now.

Elaine: I wrote to Spray 'N Wash, and they didn't change. They didn't change the labeling to indicate Spray 'N Wash cannot be used on certain kinds of acrylics. It leaves an oily stain and it doesn't say that on the label. I don't buy Spray 'N Wash anymore. I use Grease Relief.

Mr. Yob: Compared to a few years ago, are you more or less apt to take a new product back to the store that you're dissatisfied with?

Mickey: More now. Things cost more now and I want to get my money's worth.

Judith: The stores tend to be more receptive now than before, but I think a lot of people try to take advantage of them.

Linda F.: Supermarkets don't really care if you return things. The supermarket is the best place to take something back.

Mr. Yob: As opposed to what?

Linda F.: Well, writing a letter or telephoning. Have you ever tried to complain about an automobile?

EXHIBIT 1 (*continued*)

Elaine: The supermarkets aren't interested. I mean they didn't make the product and they're going to get reimbursed. So they don't care much one way or the other.

Mr. Yob: You mentioned your families before. Do you normally ask your family when considering a new product before you go to the store?

Ellen: I do because I'm only one person out of ten, and there's no way I'm going to be able to eat the amount I have to buy if they don't like it. My kids will tell me about a new product before I even know about it.

Kids pick Pringle's as "must try"

Mr. Yob: What kinds of products would kids usually suggest?

Ann: Well, Pringle's is one that comes to mind. My kids could hardly wait to try Pringle's. They wanted to dump the whole thing out and stack them up. I hadn't seen it, but my kids had been seeing it for weeks. I'm the first one to charge out and try every new thing before anybody else does.

Mr. Yob: You don't consult your family?

Ann: No. They may tell me once in a while, "Momma, let's try this," but as a rule, I don't consult them.

Mr. Yob: When you bring home a new product, do they know immediately it's a new product or do you tell them it is?

Mickey: Yes, they notice. All they [manufacturers] have to do is change the package and the kids are suspicious. Put a different person on the front [cereal box] and they ask if it's new.

Mary Jane: In our family we have always gone out of our way to try all kinds of new things, even when our children were very young. They developed very good eating habits because they've had to try everything that comes along.

Mr. Yob: What differences do you see in new products today compared to five years ago?

Ellen: They've come out with price per unit.

Mickey: There seem to be more added ingredients or even "gimmicks."

Mr. Yob: Give me an example.

Mickey: Well, like this new chewing gum. It's even got a breath freshener. Next they'll have one with a deodorant.

Linda H.: Packaging has changed. They're trying to make the packaging much more appealing, to strike your attention. I mean they're all doing it. They are playing up to your emotional and esthetic values. They hope you say, "That's a pretty package (or shape of a bottle). I think I'll buy that." Well, me, I'm more practical.

All you pay for are the boxes

Mr. Yob: Is new product packaging considerably different than five years ago?

Ellen: Yes. There are packages that come inside of another package—like a Pillsbury Bundt cake mix I bought. They put these three little boxes in a big box when a small box would have done the job. You get the impression that you're getting more than you really are. You feel very often that what

EXHIBIT 1 (*continued*)

you're really paying for is all of the boxes. I'm sure more money is going into the boxes than into the product.

Ann: One thing that really irritates me, and they're doing it more and more, is that all you can find is the smaller sizes—a lot of single-serving things instead of the giant sizes I want to buy. It costs me more per serving to buy the smaller sizes, but they don't seem to offer the bigger sizes. I don't know if it's the manufacturer or the store buyer.

Mr. Yob: Why do you think they are going to smaller sizes?

Ann: It's more convenient for single people who have been complaining for years that they have been overlooked.

Elaine: Another thing is, if it's a smaller can, they can put what looks like a smaller price on it. They reduce the size and leave the same price on it. This really burns me up. It's confusing and misleading.

Forget the new and improve the old

Mickey: I have something to say. It has been bothering me for a long time. I think there are too, too, too many new products on the market. If the manufacturers would concentrate on doing a good job with the few items that they make, or improve them instead of worrying about grabbing another hunk of a new market, the consumer would be better off. They should just stabilize the products they have.

Who needs to walk into a supermarket and find an entire long row of beans? I mean, how many kinds of bean can you eat? I don't need 16 different brands of baked beans. I don't need 25 different kinds of pinto beans. Who needs all of this? I think it's foolishness.

The American public has been swamped with an overabundance of gimmick items. Manufacturers are overextending themselves. I find this in the food items; I find this in the detergent items; and certainly it's true in the automobile industry. Every year they have to come out with a new model.

I think this has filtered down into other kinds of manufacturing so that they always have to come out with a new gimmick. Consumers are not so foolish. Housewives are more interested in quality, and they don't need 99 new products every year. They are not dissatisfied with some of the good stable ones.

Group. *Applause.*

Mr. Yob: Does this mean you won't try new products?

Mickey: No, it doesn't. But what most will end up doing is going back to the old products after trying the new ones—the ones we know are good standards. I've been with Mr. Campbell for years.

Ann: This reminds me of something I saw on television the other night. Kraft sponsored some show and, instead of showing new products, they showed a new way to use their old products. They showed what you can make on camping trips and you can write in and get the recipes. It really appealed to me. They used existing products to extend meals and make them more economical—like casseroles, which are much more reasonable for the housewife.

EXHIBIT 1 (*concluded*)

Mary Elise: The only reason I try anything is that I hear about it from a friend or I get a free sample on the door.

Mr. Yob: Any other differences between new products now and five years ago?

Mary Jane: Five years ago they were coming out with new things that would help you make things from scratch. Now it is all "convenience."

Linda H.: Convenience products tend to kill the taste. The taste is not there because of the necessity to use preservatives, which kill the natural flavors.

Mr. Yob: What about household convenience products?

Judith: Nobody loves housework, and anything that will make it easier and faster is usually a success. When you're thinking about food, however, you're thinking about something that affects the well being of your life.

Mr. Yob: Let's change tack. If you were an advisory council, meeting with a group of advertisers, what type of presentations would you recommend they consider in advertising their new products?

Ellen: They tend to use too many famous people. I really thought they did a better job when they put Miss Plain Jane on the television; people could associate with her more readily.

Elaine: What they should do is (1) tell us what it will do; (2) tell us the truth (we're not all dumb-dumbs); and (3) tell us how to use it.

Ellen: They're wasting their money the way they're advertising now. We don't believe it.

Ann: I agree with Elaine. I think I might be really interested in something if they told me the use of the product, the content, and the price.

Mr. Yob: Wouldn't that be rather boring, though?

Ann: No. That's what we want to know. It would save hours spent running around comparing prices.

Linda F.: Tell us how to vary our menus a little bit with the same product. We've been saying this for years. But the advertisers do not listen to us. They are manipulating us.

Convenience foods wave of future

Mr. Yob: Okay. What will new products be like in five years?

Ellen: More convenience foods all the time.

Mary Elise: Yes, that's right. The way the trend is going, foods will take less work and be more dehydrated or reconstituted with preservatives.

Judith: Well, I think it depends on how far the consumer is pushed as far as the economy is concerned. More convenience in household products is fine if they save me effort and time, but a convenience food product will really have to be good to get me interested.

Elaine: What bothers me is that they will continue to be working on the new and improved version even when the current version is on the shelf. They think that's the only way they will be able to sell us their products. They say, "Now it's improved," and you open it up and it tastes the same, or it doesn't do the job any better than the one it replaced.

The great big gimmick is "That's not Tide, that's NEW TIDE." Phooey!

3

Research types:
Experimentation

Conclusive research projects may be either descriptive or experimental in design. If the former design is used, cross classification is relied on to identify the effect of the causal factor. But as pointed out before, measurements of cause and effect by cross classification are never completely satisfactory. One is always able to think of other hypotheses that would explain the observed relationship, but which cannot be disproved by the available data.

Experiments are much more effective in measuring cause and effect relationships; the collection of data in an experiment is organized in such a way as to permit relatively unambiguous interpretation. One measure of the development of marketing science is the rapid growth of marketing experiments in recent years. Only by the use of experiments can one develop the understanding of cause and effect relationships that are the basis of a science.

Because of this importance of experimentation in the development of marketing science, experimentation is given more extensive treatment here than are the other basic types of research design. A second reason for this emphasis is that the design of experiments lends itself more readily to rational analysis and provides an "ideal" against which other research designs can be compared.

This chapter presents the general concept of experimentation and a number of the more common experimental designs.[1] In the process it points out the factors which obscure the conclusions which should be drawn from most

---

[1] For a more extended treatment of experimentation in marketing see Seymour Banks, *Experimentation in Marketing* (New York: McGraw-Hill, 1965); M. Venkatesan and R. J. Holloway, *An Introduction to Marketing Experimentation* (New York: Macmillan Co., 1970); and K. K. Cox and B. M. Enis, *Experimentation for Marketing Decisions* (Scranton, Pa.: International Textbook Co., 1969).

marketing research projects and shows how various experimental designs reduce or eliminate specific factors which contribute to this obscurity.

Definition of experiment

Experimentation is not easy to define. As used here, it will refer to that research process in which one or more variables are manipulated under conditions which permit the collection of data which show the effects, if any, of such variables in unconfused fashion. Such a definition indicates that the distinction between experimental and nonexperimental research may sometimes be a matter of degree rather than of kind.

Under most circumstances, experimenters must create "artificial" situations so that they can obtain the particular data needed and can measure the data accurately. Experiments are artificial in the sense that situations are usually created for testing purposes. This artificiality is the essence of the experimental method, since it gives researchers more control over the factors they are studying. If they can control the factors which are present in a given situation, they can obtain more conclusive evidence of cause and effect relationships between any two of them. Thus, the ability to set up a situation for the express purpose of observing and recording accurately the effect on one factor when another is deliberately changed permits researchers to prove or disprove hypotheses that they could otherwise only partially test. It is for this reason that experiments have been the basis for the advancement of knowledge in most scientific fields.

Laboratory versus field experiments

Marketing experiments can be conducted in a laboratory or in the field. In laboratory experiments, test subjects, usually consumers, are brought to a theater or conference room and exposed to an experimental variable such as a television commercial. In field experiments, the experimental variable is taken to the field—for example, a new package is tested in a store or a new product is taken to homemakers and they are asked to try it in their homes. In each case some measurement is made of test subject reaction.

A concrete example will illustrate field and laboratory experiments in comparison with a descriptive study. All three methods were used to measure the price elasticity of demand for four different products. In the field experiments the products were placed in 16 different stores and the prices varied according to a carefully controlled plan. Sales at each price level were recorded. In the laboratory experiment, an artificial "store" was set up and homemakers were asked to go through the "store" and select products as if on a regular shopping trip. Prices were varied in a manner similar to that used in the field experiment. Actual selections (comparable to sales in the field experiment) were recorded. In the descriptive study, homemakers were shown pictures of the different products at the different prices and asked what purchases they would make if they saw the same items while on an actual shopping trip. The findings from the three different studies are shown in Table 3–1.[2]

TABLE 3–1. Estimated percentage change in sales volume for a 1 percent increase in price for four products based on three methods of data generation

Product	Field experiment	Laboratory experiment	Descriptive study
A	−1.57	−1.25	−0.33
B	−1.27	−0.64	0.71
C	−1.58	−0.76	−1.86
D	−1.74	1.13	0.35

The researcher concluded that only the field experiment generated results that were significant and consistent. The laboratory experiment produced results more similar to those of the field experiment than did the descriptive study method. Other tests show similar results. The field experiment is clearly the preferred research design if it is feasible from a cost and operational standpoint.

In general, the student should be aware that all problems which can be studied by experiments can also be studied by nonexperimental statistical methods, but the results are not apt to be as clear or as useful. The percentage of people who say they prefer package A to package B does not tell the researcher as much as do the sales results from using each in the market. Researchers should always prefer experimental over nonexperimental studies except where cost and time are enough different to offset the advantages of the experiments. They should prefer field experiments over laboratory experiments except under similar variations in time and cost. In all research an experimental design should be the ideal concept that researchers approach as closely as possible.

SELECTED EXPERIMENTAL DESIGNS

To begin the discussion of specific experimental designs[3] it is useful to visualize an experiment in an oversimplified form. The researcher has a hypothesis that if an experimental variable (for example, advertising, shelf display, training) is applied to an experimental unit (for example, a group of consumers, a store, some sales representatives), it will have an effect which

---

[2] Roy G. Stout, "Developing Data to Estimate Price-Quantity Relationships," *Journal of Marketing* 33 (April 1969):34–36.

[3] The following discussion draws heavily on Donald T. Campbell and Julian C. Stanley, "Experimental and Quasi-Experimental Designs for Research on Teaching," in N. L. Gage, ed., *Handbook of Research on Teaching* (Chicago: Rand McNally, 1963), pp. 171–246.

can be measured (for example, the number remembering the brand name, units sold, calls made). A plan is developed for controlling conditions pertinent to the experiment so that some experimental units can be exposed to the experimental variable and the results measured. The following are some of the most common designs for marketing experiments.

"After only" design

This is the simplest of all experimental designs; in fact, it should not be called an experiment, but by starting with this design, it will be easier to see the need for the more complex designs. As the "after only" name suggests, this design consists of measuring the dependent variable after, and only after, the experimental subjects have been exposed to the experimental variable. In the notation that will be used hereafter, this can be shown as follows:

Experimental group

Experimental variable introduced . . . . Yes
"After" measurement . . . . Yes (x_1)

Effect of experimental variable $= x_1$

An example will illustrate. Roe herring was a traditional breakfast dish in Virginia, but it is no longer so widely eaten. In an attempt to widen the market, the firm owning the Tidewater brand ran an advertisement in the Sunday morning Richmond newspaper and in both the morning and evening newspapers during the following six days. This ad carried a coupon which could be exchanged at a grocery store for one free can of Tidewater roe herring. A total of 46,486 free cans were so claimed. The conclusion drawn from this study was that no other advertising medium could produce such immediate action at such low cost.

Presumably, the conclusion from the roe herring experiment is arrived at in the following manner. The 46,486 coupons redeemed is a large number— undoubtedly much larger than the number of cans that would have been consumed during the same period without the advertising. If the advertising had been run in other media, it is unlikely that the results obtained would have been so large as those obtained with newspaper advertising.

Problems of validity are so apparent in the above interpretation that one is inclined not to take the experiment seriously. Yet there is just enough logic on the surface to make the conclusion believable. This superficial believability leads to many studies of this type and to wide circulation of the results. Such studies are a dubious basis for current business decisions and no basis at all for long-run scientific development of marketing.

In the roe herring example, the conclusion that the number of cans of Tidewater roe herring obtained by consumers through coupon redemption was much larger than the number that would otherwise have been purchased is based on an implicit comparison of the 46,486 figure with some idea of the number of cans that consumers otherwise would have obtained. Executives of the company have, on the basis of experience, a general idea of what sales of Tidewater roe herring would normally be during a period similar to that in which the advertising ran. It would be more scientific, however, to make an explicit measurement of this "normal" sales volume rather than to rely on a vague implicit estimate. A further question is entirely ignored in the interpretation presented; namely, did the large number of free cans go to consumers who would otherwise have bought these cans, although perhaps over a much longer period of time? A comparison of actual sales following the advertising period with "normal" sales for the same period would help to answer this question.

The "after only" design is even weaker with respect to the conclusion that newspaper advertising brought larger results than a similar amount of advertising in other media would have achieved. This conclusion is based on a comparison of the results obtained from newspaper advertising with an implicit estimate of what would have been obtained from advertising in other media. The latter estimate is based on past experience with other media in other places and with other products and, perhaps, on general advertising philosophy. How much more scientific it would have been to divide the newspaper advertising money among several media in such a way as to permit measurement of the results actually achieved with each.

The "after only" experimental design is better considered an exploratory case study than a real experiment. If the results are looked at as suggestive and used to establish a hypothesis for testing with a properly designed experiment, they will serve a better purpose than if used as true experimental results.

"Before-after" design

In this design, the experimenters measure the dependent variable "before" exposing the subjects to the experimental variable and again "after" exposure to the experimental variable. The difference between the two is considered to be a measurement of the effect of the experimental variable. This is summarized in the following notation:

	Experimental group
"Before" measurement	Yes (x_1)
Experimental variable introduced	Yes
"After" measurement	Yes (x_2)
Effect of experimental variable $= x_2 - x_1$	

This design differs from the previous "after only" design in that an explicit measurement is made before the experimental variable is introduced, whereas in the "after only" design the before measurement is implicitly estimated on the basis of vague past experience. Therefore, the "before-after" design is definitely superior to the "after only" design, but it is still subject to many shortcomings.

A typical example of a "before-after" design is a laboratory experiment to test the effect of television commercials. A group of consumers in a theater is told that a drawing is to be held; the winner will receive, for example, $10 worth of shampoo. The consumers are asked to check on a card which of a list of major shampoo brands they would like if they should win. The drawing is held. Next, the consumers are shown a 30-minute movie in which three different commercials are interspersed. One commercial is for a given brand of shampoo. After the movie, another drawing is held. All consumers indicate the brand of shampoo they want if they should win this second drawing. The researcher counts the number requesting the brand promoted by the shampoo commercial. The difference between the percentage of consumers wanting the brand in the two drawings is used as a measure of the effectiveness of the commercial. The following data are reported from such a test:

	Experimental group (205 consumers)
"Before" measurement (percentage preferring Brand X in first drawing)	4.2% (x_1)
Experimental variable introduced (Brand X commercial)	Yes
"After" measurement (percentage preferring Brand X in second drawing)	12.4% (x_2)

$$\text{Effect of experimental variable (Brand X commercial)} = x_2 - x_1 = 12.4\% - 4.2\%$$
$$= 8.2\% \text{ increase in brand preference}$$

This design seems clear-cut: the dependent variable is measured, the experimental subjects (consumers) are exposed to the experimental variable (shampoo commercial) and the dependent variable is measured again. The difference between the two measures is the result of exposure to the advertising. More thorough study, however, will show that a number of other factors might have caused some, or all, of the variation found; at the least, they create doubt as to the validity of the measured effect of the experimental variable. The other factors are called uncontrolled variables. The most important of them are discussed here in some detail because they are common to all research projects and should be considered in designing all projects.

Uncontrolled variables. One factor that could cause the "after" measurement to differ from the "before" measurement is *history*. The amount of history in the example above, in which only 30 minutes separated the two measurements, is so small as to be an unlikely factor of importance. If, however, the two measurements were several days, or even months, apart, the effect of history might become a major factor. For example, if a period of several months were involved, advertising activities of other brands or changes in hair styles, such as a shift from curly to straight and sleek, could make major changes in the "after" measurement. Thus, the longer the time period between the two measurements, the greater the danger that history will confound the results. All happenings outside the sphere of the experiment may be considered a part of history.

In the television commercial example, it is possible that the entire situation would become boring to some of the subjects. By the time of the "after" measurement they would react differently than at the "before" measurement, regardless of what took place in the interim. Such biological or psychological changes which take place with the passage of time are called *maturation*. Experiments which require elaborate contrivances of an artificial nature and which require the willing cooperation of test subjects over a significant period of time are the most subject to maturation effect.

Pretest effect is a third factor which may endanger the validity of the "before-after" design. In the television example, when the consumers were asked at the start to indicate the brand of shampoo they would prefer, they immediately knew, even if they did not particularly think about it, that the researcher was interested in shampoo. This could easily influence their responses to the "after" measurement. For example, some consumers might be stimulated to think about shampoos, to notice the hair of other consumers or to discuss shampoos with other consumers. All of these might influence their response at the second request for brand preference. Simply remembering the brand preferred at the first drawing, a consumer might automatically report the same brand or, just to be different, report a different one to "change one's luck." Pretesting can influence later measures in many ways. It is difficult, if not impossible, to know what the net effect of these influences might be, or even their direction. The more artificial and the more obvious the measurement process, the more effect it may be expected to have on later results. On the other hand, if the measurement process is not apparent to the experimental subjects (for example, if the measurement is the adding up of sales at the end of a day), then it will probably not influence results.[4]

Measurement variation is another factor which may cause variations in the "before" and "after" measurements that may be confused with the effect of the experimental variable. It does not seem likely that this effect occurred in the shampoo commercial example, but in other experiments where interviewers are more active in determining the measurements, their techniques may vary between the two measurements. In testing two different formulations of breakfast cereals, for example, one cereal formula might be left with a sample of homemakers. At a later date, the interviewer would bring the second formula and interview the homemaker about the first. On a third call, the homemaker would report on the second formula. By the time of this

---

[4] *Pretesting* may have more complex interaction effects. These will be discussed with the "before-after with control group" design.

third call, it is likely that the interviewer would have become more experienced or blasé about the project, and would have become better acquainted with the test subject. Thus, the last interview would be apt to elicit somewhat different information than it would have if it had been made on the first call.

The four factors which raise doubt as to the validity of conclusions from a "before-after" design are *history, maturation, pretesting,* and *measurement variation.* These factors suggest the need of a control group against which to compare the results in the experimental group.

"Before-after with control group" design

This classical experimental design, developed to permit measurement of the effect of the experimental variable alone, may be depicted as follows:

	Experimental group	Control group
"Before" measurement	Yes (x_1)	Yes (y_1)
Experimental variable	Yes	No
"After" measurement	Yes (x_2)	Yes (y_2)

$$\text{Effect of experimental variable} = (x_2 - x_1) - (y_2 - y_1)$$

The experimental group and the control group are selected in such a way that they are similar, that is, they are interchangeable for test purposes. The control group is measured at the same times as the experimental group, but no experimental variable is introduced. Thus, the difference between the "after" and "before" measurements of the control group $(y_2 - y_1)$ is the result of uncontrolled variables. The difference between the "after" and "before" measurements in the experimental group $(x_2 - x_1)$ is the result of the experimental variable plus the same uncontrolled variables affecting the control group.[5] The effect of the experimental variable alone can be determined by subtracting the difference in the two measurements of the control group from the difference in the two measurements of the experimental group $(x_2 - x_1)$ $- (y_2 - y_1)$.

An experiment run by the National Broadcasting Company (NBC) illustrates this design. A carefully selected sample of 2,441 male and female household heads in a medium-sized midwestern market was interviewed at two different times three months apart. Purchases during the preceding four-week period of 22 different brands in 11 different household product categories varying from beer to toothpaste were determined in each of the two

---

[5] This assumes the effects of the various factors, experimental and uncontrolled variables, are additive. This is a common assumption which has not been proved. It is quite possible, for example, that the total effect is more nearly equal to the product of the factors than to the sum, or the relationship may be more complex. See Richard L. Solomon, "An Extension of Control Group Design," *Psychological Bulletin* 44 (March 1949):140.

interviews. In the first interview, the percentage buying one or more of the brands was determined for the entire sample and used as the "before" measure. In the second interview the sample was separated into two subsamples —those exposed to television and magazine advertising of the products and those not exposed to the advertising. The results were as follows:

	Experimental group (exposed to advertising)	Control group (not exposed to advertising)
"Before" measurement (percentage purchasing in past 4 weeks)	19.4% (x_1)	19.4% (y_1)
Experimental variable (exposed to advertising of products)	Yes	No
"After" measurement (percentage purchasing in past 4 weeks at time of second interview)	20.5% (x_2)	16.9% (y_2)

$$\text{Effect of experimental variable} = (20.5\% - 19.4\%) - (16.9\% - 19.4\%)$$
$$= (1.1\%) - (-2.5\%) = 3.6\%$$

Purchases by those exposed to advertising during the three-month period increased slightly, while purchases by those not exposed to the advertising decreased. The net effect of the experimental variable was an increase of 3.6 percent of the total sample, or an 18.6 percent increase over the rate of purchase in the starting period.

In this example, the control group is a group of consumers, presumably similar to the experimental group except for not being exposed to the experimental variable. Another type of control could have been purchases of similar, but unadvertised, products by the same consumers, or conceivably another market where the products were not advertised. When the experiment is limited to one medium-sized midwestern market, the degree to which the results can be generalized is limited to the one market studied, although strong suggestions may be drawn relative to other medium-sized midwestern cities and even beyond.

This design has definite advantages over the simple "before-after" design. The effects of the uncontrolled variables, *history, maturation, pretesting,* and *measurement variability,* should be the same for the control group as for the experimental group. In this case, these factors appear to have had a negative effect on purchases of 2.5 percent. If it had not been for the experimental variable, presumably the experimental group would have shown a similar drop in purchases during the period. The fact that the experimental group showed an increase in purchases indicates that the advertising overcame the negative effect of the four factors mentioned above and added a plus factor of 1.1 percent in addition.

Selection of test subjects is a further confounding factor that may occur in this design. The selection of people for the experimental and control groups was on the basis of whether or not they were exposed to advertising of the products in question. If the 2,441 subjects had been divided into two groups on a random basis and one group exposed to advertising while the other was not, no selection problem would exist. In the example given, however, the subjects were separated on the basis of their own verbal reports of whether or not they had been exposed to the advertising in question.[6] Thus, the respondents in each group were self-selected, almost automatically guaranteeing that those putting themselves in the experimental group would show a larger purchase rate for the products in question than those in the control group. Individuals who have purchased a product are more apt to be aware of the advertising than those who have not. The cause and effect relationship might be in reverse order to that inferred from the experiment. More generally, however, self-selection is almost sure not to give two groups that are comparable. The "after" measurement for two such groups is apt to differ even if neither is exposed to the experimental variable.

If the selection of test subjects for both the experimental and control groups is controlled by the experimenter and if the assignment to each group is on a random basis, the degree to which the two groups differ can be measured statistically. Such measurements will be discussed in the chapters on sampling. A tendency in early experiments was to "match" experimental and control groups by making them similar on various characteristics such as age, sex, income, nationality of origin, and so on. Since it is impossible ever to match two individuals—let alone two groups—on all possible characteristics, the "matching" of the two groups is only a little better than self-selection.

Even though *history* seems to be adequately controlled in the "before-after with control group" design, it is possible to have biases of this type if the two groups are handled differently, for example, are handled by different observers or at different times. Instructions by the experimenter or offhand comments by some of the participants may influence the result.

Mortality is a factor which becomes a particularly noticeable source of bias in the "before-after with control group" design. This is the loss of some test subjects between the "before" and "after" measurements. Such a loss can occur in the simple "before-after" design, but it is usually ignored for the sake of convenience. It is more serious to ignore losses when the mortality rate is different between the experimental and control groups. Even in the latter case, those who drop out are often disregarded, but the danger of bias as a result is more apt to be noted. If the rate of mortality is significantly different between the two groups or if the type of subject dropping out of one group is different from that dropping out of the other, the possibility that the results will be affected is clear. In experiments where the experimental group has to perform certain tasks during a period of time, mortality may become relatively heavy among the experimental group. For example, if the experi-

---

[6] Thomas E. Coffin, "Beyond Audience: The Measurement of Advertising Effectiveness," mimeographed.

mental group has to keep a diary of certain activities, many may become disinterested and fail to keep the diary or do so only in part.

While the "before-after with control group" experimental design is the classic for laboratory experiments, it has another serious weakness when applied to the study of opinions, attitudes, and ideas—these factors may change in the process of being studied. Since many marketing studies are of the type that can be influenced by the process of measurement, this design cannot be considered the ideal for marketing experiments.

When people are questioned about their attitudes, opinions, or ideas before the introduction of an experimental variable (for example, advertising), they may become more aware of the product or service and, thus, be more influenced by the advertisements than those individuals not questioned in advance. On the other hand, the "before" test may tend to crystallize the opinions of people interviewed and to reduce the influence of the advertisements on them. Or, of course, the pretesting may have no effect. All three of these types of effects have been found, but the results to date suggest that the interaction effect between pretesting and the experimental variable may not be an important factor in many cases. Nevertheless, *interaction* of this type must be considered a weakness of this design.

When considered in connection with the simple "before-after" design, the effects of the "before" measurement and the interaction between this measurement and the experimental variable reduce validity; that is, they bias the measurement of the effect of the experimental variable. When these effects are considered in connection with the "before-after with control group" design, the direct effect of the pretest is measured and can be accounted for. The *interaction* effect, however, occurs only within the experimental group. If the experiment is considered to be for the purpose of measuring the effect of the experimental variable on pretested subjects, validity is not damaged. It is inaccurate, however, to generalize from the effect of the experimental variable on a pretested population to the effect on an unpretested population, and it is the unpretested population, of course, which is almost always of interest.

A United Nations education campaign in Cincinnati provides an unusually dramatic example of the interaction between pretest and experimental variable.[7] Two equivalent samples of 1,000 individuals each were selected. The members of one of these samples were interviewed to determine their information and attitudes on the United Nations. After this a publicity campaign was conducted in the city for several months and the second sample was then interviewed to determine the effects of the campaign. Practically no results were discovered—the members of the second sample were not better informed and had no different attitudes than the members of the first sample

---

[7] S. A. Star and H. M. Hughes, "Report on an Educational Campaign: The Cincinnati Plan for the United Nations," *American Journal of Sociology* 55 (1949–50): 389.

had had prior to the publicity campaign. The second sample was generally not even aware that a publicity campaign had been going on. The first sample was then reinterviewed. It was found that the members of this group had undergone definite changes in attitude and information about the United Nations and were well aware of the publicity campaign. The "before" measurement had a definite effect on the influence of the publicity on the respondents.

"Four-group–six study" design

As shown above, when the investigator is obtaining information in an undisguised manner directly from persons, the "before-after with control group" design is inadequate. Both the experimental and control groups are apt to be influenced, and in different ways, by the "before" measurement. To overcome these difficulties, a "four-group–six study" design is established as the ideal where there is interaction between the respondent and the questioning process. It can be depicted as follows:

	Experimental		Control	
	Group 1	Group 2	Group 1	Group 2
"Before" measurement	Yes (x_1)	No	Yes (y_1)	No
Experimental variable	Yes	Yes	No	No
"After" measurement	Yes (x_2)	Yes (x_3)	Yes (y_2)	Yes (y_3)

Experimental group 1 and control group 1 form the "before-after with control group" design. An additional two groups, one experimental and one control, are added. Neither is measured before the experimental variable is introduced. The variable is introduced into the two experimental groups only, and all four groups are measured "after." All four groups are preselected in such a way that they are equivalent (that is, subjects are assigned to the four groups on a random basis). This means that the "before" measurement should be the same in all four groups except for random variations. It is presumed, therefore, that the two "before" measurements will be approximately equal ($x_1 = y_1$). It is then inferred that the other two groups would have shown similar measurements if they had been measured. The average of x_1 and y_1 is, therefore, taken to be the "before" measure of experimental group 2 and control group 2.[8] If the "before" measurements had no effect on the variable being studied (for example, purchases of dietetic colas), the two experimental groups should give the same "after" measurements and the two control groups should give the same "after" measure-

---

[8] It is necessary to have a control group for which no premeasurement is made because the "before" study may influence the "after" results for a control group as well as for an experimental group. In the instance of the control group, however, no interaction of the experimental variable with the "before" measurement occurs, because no experimental variable is introduced.

ments. If the experimental variable had any influence, the results in the two experimental groups will differ significantly from the results of the two control groups.

If the "before" measurement does influence the test subjects directly and also interacts with the experimental variable, as is probable, each of the four groups will give a different "after" measurement, and the differences between the "before" and "after" measurements in the four cases will be the result of various factors as shown in the following table.[9]

Group measured	Factors making up the difference between "before" and "after" measurements
Experimental group 1 ($x_2 - x_1$)	Experimental variable + "before" measurement + interaction of "before" measurement with experimental variable + uncontrolled variables
Experimental group 2 $[x_3 - \frac{1}{2}(x_1 + y_1)]$	Experimental variable + uncontrolled variables
Control group 1 ($y_2 - y_1$)	"Before" measurement + uncontrolled variables
Control group 2 $[y_3 - \frac{1}{2}(x_1 + y_1)]$	Uncontrolled variables

These results can be presented, as shown above, as four simultaneous equations with four unknowns. They can then be solved to obtain a value for each of the four unknown factors affecting the difference between the "before" and "after" measurements.

This "four-group–six study" design may be taken as a model for marketing experiments in which data are collected from individuals in such a way that they realize it is being done. The design, however, has little practical value. The expense of selecting four groups in such a way as to insure they are equivalent and the added expense of making six studies among these four groups make this design impractical for most marketing studies. The use of inferred "before" measurements also creates statistical difficulties in testing the significance of results.

Despite these practical and theoretical weaknesses, the "four-group–six study" design is a useful "ideal" against which to compare proposed designs. Such comparisons emphasize the assumptions on which the more simple designs are based and, thus, emphasize the limitations of the data collected in the more simple designs. Fortunately, marketing experiments often permit the collection of data without the knowledge of the consumers involved (for

---

[9] "Miscellaneous uncontrolled variables" includes all the confounding factors previously discussed (history, maturation, and so on) plus any other possible influences. No specific account is taken of possible interaction between these variables and the experimental variable or interaction among these variables themselves.

example, sales data) and, hence, the more simple "before-after with control group" design can be used. Even more fortunately, many marketing experiments lend themselves to the more simple "after only with control group" design.

"After only with control group" design

In the "four-group–six study" design, it is possible to determine the effect of the experimental variable from only two groups—experimental group 2 and control group 2. Referring to the summary table of the factors affecting the results in that design, one can see that the difference between the "before" and "after" measurements of experimental group 2 is made up of the effects of the experimental variable and uncontrolled variables; the difference between the "before" and "after" measurements of control group 2 is the result of uncontrolled variables. Since the "before" measurement in both these cases was inferred, it would be the same in both instances. Therefore, the effect of the experimental variable can be determined simply by computing the difference between the "after" measurements for the two groups $(x_3 - y_3)$.

This raises the question: Why include the other two groups in the experimental design? The answer for the scholar is that the four groups and six studies enable the experimental variable to be studied under different conditions, the individual cases to be studied concerning changes, and better methodology to be developed. To the average business executive, these may not be compelling enough reasons to sustain the added expense. Therefore, the "after only with control group" design becomes a logical modification. This would appear as shown:

	Experimental group	Control group
"Before" measurement	No	No
Experimental variable	Yes	No
"After" measurement	Yes (x_1)	Yes (y_1)

Effect of experimental variable $= x_1 - y_1$

The experimental and control groups are selected in such a way as to be equivalent. No "before" measurement is made in either group. The effect of the experimental variable is determined by computing the difference between the two "after" measurements $(x_1 - y_1)$. Notice that this design escapes the problems of pretest effect and interaction. Compared to the "four-group–six study" design, this "two-group–two study" design is much simpler to administer and much less expensive. It is not surprising that it is by far the most widely used design in marketing.

In a classic "after only with control group" study to determine the image of the homemaker who uses instant coffee, the following design was used.

Two comparable groups of consumers were shown similar shopping lists and asked to describe the homemaker who prepared the list. On the list shown the control group, one of the items was "Maxwell House Coffee (drip grind)." On the list shown the experimental group, this item was replaced by "Nescafe Instant Coffee." The results measured were the percentages of the respondents who described the shopping list author as having various characteristics. The effect of the experimental variable (Nescafe Instant Coffee user) was the difference in the percentage ascribing each characteristic to the "instant coffee user" from the percentage ascribing the same characteristics to the "drip grind user." The results are summarized below.[10]

	Experimental group	Control group
"Before" measurement	No	No
Experimental variable—(shopping list)	Instant coffee	Drip grind coffee
"After" measurement—(consumer description of shopper)	Lazy 18% Thrifty 36 Spendthrift 23 Bad wife 18	Lazy 10% Thrifty 55 Spendthrift 5 Bad wife 5

Effect of experimental variable = Lazy (18% − 10%) = 8%
= Thrifty (36% − 55%) = −19%
= Spendthrift (23% − 5%) = 18%
= Bad wife (18% − 5%) = 13%

No problems of "before" measurement effect were encountered because no premeasurements were made. Uncontrolled variables such as history and maturation influenced both the experimental and control groups to the same degree. On one basis, the "after only" design is at a disadvantage relative to the "before-after" design. The "before-after" design permits an analysis of the process of change, whereas the "after only" design does not. Thus, individual respondents can be identified and their reactions noted in a "before-after" study. For example, in an attitude and opinion study one can measure the effect of the experimental variable on those people who had favorable attitudes as contrasted with those who had unfavorable attitudes in the "before" measurement.

The "after only with control group" design fits many marketing problems and is easy to use. Many promotional devices can be tested this way. A dry milk company believed its biggest problem was to get consumers acquainted with its product. Therefore, it put most of its promotional money into sampling campaigns, but it had no real knowledge of their effect. An "after only" experiment was devised whereby the experimental group was given samples of dry milk. Then the experimental group and the control group were both

---

[10] F. E. Webster and F. von Pechmann, "A Replication of the 'Shopping List' Study," *Journal of Marketing* 34 (April 1970):61–63. Only part of the results are shown.

sent coupons for purchase of the dry milk at a discount at grocery stores. The coupons were coded to indicate whether they were sent to the experimental group or control group, and the number of coupons redeemed by each group was counted.

Frequently, product tests are also of the "after only with control group" design. General Motors ran such an experiment to determine the desirability of nylon cord tires as compared to the traditional rayon cord tires. Nylon cord tires were more expensive than rayon cord tires and were alleged to whine and thump, but there was little evidence as to the importance of these defects if, in fact, they existed at all. Accordingly, General Motors equipped 40,000 Chevrolets with nylon cord tires and kept track of the serial numbers of the cars. Later they interviewed owners of cars with both types of tires to get their appraisals of their tires.

Ex post facto design

One variation of the "after only" design is called the *ex post facto* design. This differs from the "after only" design because the experimental and control groups are selected *after* the experimental variable is introduced instead of *before*. One advantage is that the test subjects cannot be influenced, pro or con, toward the subject by knowing they are being tested, since they are exposed to the experimental variable before being selected for the sample.

Another advantage of this method is that it permits the experimenter to let the experimental variable be introduced at will and to control only observations. This is useful in advertising tests which use commercial media. A large grocery product manufacturer ran an advertising campaign in one midwestern city. Then, it selected an experimental group of consumers who reported they had seen the advertisements and a control group of consumers who said they had not seen the ads. The two groups were asked questions about the tendency of the manufacturer's product to cause people to gain weight. Since the advertising campaign had emphasized that the product was not fattening, it was hypothesized that those who had seen the advertisements would report the product as being nonfattening to a greater degree than would those who had not seen the campaign.

The results supported this hypothesis: the product was reported not fattening by 63 percent of those seeing the advertisements, but by only 56 percent of the control group. But members of the experimental and control groups were actually self-selected. Those who said they had seen the ads were very likely the ones on whom the ads made some impression. It is also quite likely that some of those who said they had not seen the ads actually had, but did not remember having seen them.

If the experimental variable is such that exposure to it can be determined objectively on an *ex post facto* basis, this bias of self-selection can be eliminated and the design becomes essentially the same as the "after only with control group" design. In this latter case, the *ex post facto* design may have a definite advantage over the other design, as the experimental variable will have exerted its influence in an entirely natural setting. An example would be a study to determine the effect of TV commercials in color as compared to black and white. The type of television set, if any, in the home can be determined objectively. It should be noted that the *ex post facto* design is the same as the statistical, cross-classification type of study discussed in the previous chapter. For example, families under study might be classified into two classes—those with color television sets and those without. The number of hours each group viewed each of the available television stations could then be recorded and comparisons made. Because the *ex post facto* design is essentially cross classification, some students prefer not to consider it an experimental design.

Continuous diary panel design

In most marketing research experiments, the subjects (individuals, dealers, and so on) from whom information is to be obtained are selected by some sampling procedure. After the information required by the project is obtained, these subjects are not "used" again. In some instances, however, a sample is recruited, and information is obtained from the members continuously or at intervals over a period of time. A permanent or fixed sample of this type is called a panel. Panels are used for both exploratory and conclusive studies. The procedure in using them is basically the same in each case; however, when used in an experiment the panel must be viewed as having a design which can be depicted in the manner shown in the accompanying table.

	Experimental group
First measurement	Yes (x_1)
Second measurement	Yes (x_2)
First experimental variable	Yes
Third measurement	Yes (x_3)
Second experimental variable	Yes
Fourth measurement	Yes (x_4)
Fifth measurement	Yes (x_5)
Third experimental variable	Yes
etc.	

Measurements are taken at intervals (for example, weekly reports by consumers on food products purchased), and experimental variables (for example, a new package size) are introduced when desired. The result is a design similar to a series of "before-after" experiments.

Any of the measurements can be considered "before" measurements for the introduction of experimental variables thereafter. Similarly, any measurement can be used as an "after" measurement for preceding variables. When used in this simple manner (for example, using the second and third measurements in the above table as the "before" and "after" measurements around the first experimental variable), panel data become essentially the same as the "before-after" design. As such, panel data are subject to criticism with respect to the lack of control of *history*. Such use of panel data is weak at best.

Better experimental design is achieved with panel data if the data are looked at as a time series—numerous measurements are made both before and after the introduction of the experimental variable. Trends can then be established as a base from which to measure the effect of the experimental variable. From the following hypothetical examples, however, it can be seen how difficult this may be.

FIGURE 3–1. Hypothetical sales of selected products at various times before and after experimental variable

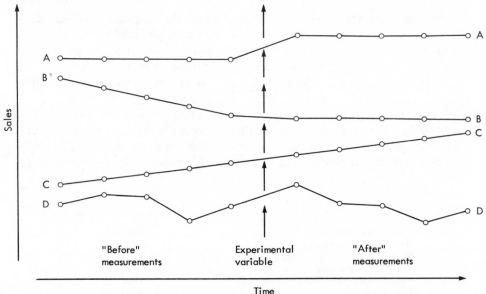

In the graph, the small circles to the left of the vertical arrows labeled "experimental variable" are meant to indicate on a vertical scale the relative size of a series of measurements of some particular factor under study, for example, consumer purchases of a product; the circles to the right of the "experimental variable" arrows are a series of measurements after the introduction of the experimental variable. Assume that the experimental variable is a shift in channel of distribution. In example A and B in the graph, one would be inclined to infer that the experimental variable (change in channels) had a favorable effect on sales. In C and D, it seems unlikely that the change in channels had any effect.

To use panel data as an effective experiment, it is important that experimenters predict in advance the trend that they would expect if the experimental variable were not introduced. This prediction becomes, in effect, a control group measurement against which the measurement obtained after the introduction of the experimental variable is compared. Even so, it is clear that any of innumerable factors of *history* could influence the subject under study (consumer purchases in the example) and, thus, confuse the interpretation of the effect of the change in channels. Intimate knowledge and observation of the subject under study will enable the experimenter and executives using the study results to make judgments as to the probability of uncontrolled variables affecting the outcome.

The practice of hunting through past panel data to find a time when sales (or another factor) changed and then attempting to find some causal factor that changed at the same time cannot be considered experimentation. Such practice may be good exploratory research, but hypotheses drawn in this manner must be subjected to more controlled study.

Use of panels.   Effective use has been made of panels in developing early forecasts of long-run sales for new products. A consumer panel is established in one or more test markets and the new product then introduced to those test markets. The percentage of consumers buying the product and the percentage making repeat purchases are obtained from continuing reports furnished by the panel. For example, the hypothetical results shown in Figures 3–2 and 3–3 might be obtained for a new cold breakfast cereal.

FIGURE 3–2. Cumulative percentage of all cold cereal buyers buying brand A the first time

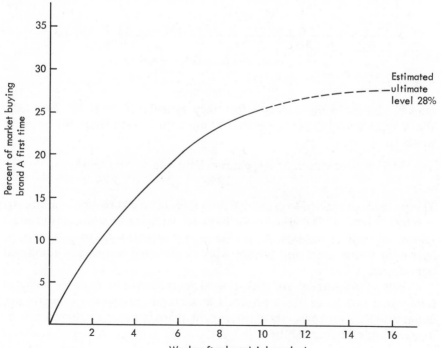

The data in Figures 3–2 and 3–3 suggest that 28 percent of all cold cereal buyers could ultimately be persuaded to buy brand A at least once (market penetration), and that these buyers would continue to buy brand A at a rate that would stabilize at about 12 percent of their cold cereal purchases (repeat purchase rate). The dotted lines at the outer ends of the curves are intended to suggest that the leveling-off points can be predicted from the

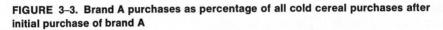

FIGURE 3–3. Brand A purchases as percentage of all cold cereal purchases after initial purchase of brand A

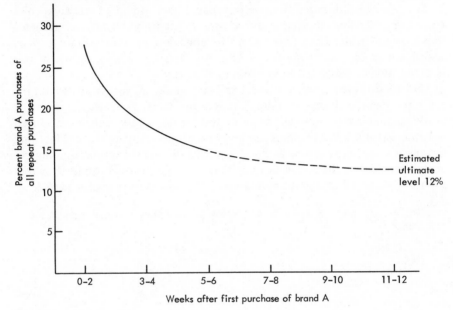

rates of change in the curves before they actually do level off. From the above hypothetical data the predicted long-term market share for brand A would be

Market penetration $\times$ Repeat purchase rate = Market share
28% $\times$ 12% = 3.36% of market

This percentage applied to estimated total sales of cold cereal gives a forecast of sales of brand A. The above is the basic model for forecasting new product sales from early panel data. A number of refinements have been developed by various researchers and further work is expected to provide additional improvements.

Panels of consumers are widely used to study the type of person and family that purchases given products and brands, frequency of purchase, quantity at each purchase, retail prices paid, place of purchase, brand switching, and other buying habits.

Advantages in using panels. The various methods used in collecting data from panel members have both advantages and disadvantages; however, these apply to any type of sample and will be discussed in the chapter on data collection. Other advantages and disadvantages, however, are unique to the panel design.

More detailed analyses available. Probably the most important single advantage of the panel design is analytical. Since data are collected from the same individuals over time, the specific individuals who change or who do not change (for example, those who switch to different brands and those who are loyal to a specific brand) can be studied. This enables the researcher to study the kind of person who changes brands and who does not change, thus suggesting the segment of the population on which promotional effort can most successfully be concentrated.

When panels are maintained over a period of time, a succession of tactics, such as advertisements or new products, may be introduced as experimental variables. Interpretation of the results may be made as described above. In some instances, the panel members may be divided into experimental and control groups (for example, those who have television sets and those who do not.) When an advertising campaign over television is begun, purchases of the product by the two groups can be compared. In this case, the panel would take on the characteristics of the "before-after with control group" design.

More data can be obtained. People who belong to a panel have agreed to cooperate with the researcher over a period of time. The person who joins panels is probably the type who is willing to give time to research and to complete longer and more exacting interviews than are other people.

Data collected are more accurate. A growing body of evidence indicates that well-run consumer panels using continuous reporting diaries yield fairly accurate projections of total retail sales of a variety of consumer products. Comparison of such data with data obtained from surveys in which consumers are asked to recall purchases of various products during a previous period and checking both against known total sales indicates that the panel-with-diary method gives considerably more accurate results than does the recall method. The direction, however, of the error in recall methods is not consistent. One study has shown recall methods tend to overstate the sales of well-known national brands, and to understate sales of private brands by as much as 50 percent.[11]

Changes in the workload imposed on panels seem to have little effect on the accuracy of reporting, but it is necessary to pay panel households to keep them reporting accurately. Small payments are as effective as larger ones.[12]

---

[11] Yoram Wind and David Lerner, "On the Measurement of Purchase Data: Surveys versus Purchase Diaries," *Journal of Marketing Research* 16 (February 1979): 39–47.

[12] Seymour Sudman, "On the Accuracy of Recording of Consumer Panels: II," *Journal of Marketing Research* 1 (August 1964): 69–83.

Panel costs may be lower.   Much of the cost of panels is fixed or sunk cost. Recruiting, training, and maintaining a proper assortment of panel members is a major share of a panel's cost and must be incurred before any information is obtained. The cost of the data for any particular study based on the panel depends on how much the panel is used, that is, over how many projects can the costs be averaged.

Disadvantages of using panels.   Basic panel disadvantages can be grouped into two categories: (1) those relating to the nonrepresentativeness of the members of a panel; and (2) those relating to bias in responses from panel members.

Panels may not be representative samples.   Since participating in a continuous diary panel involves some effort on the part of panel members, many individuals will decline to serve on panels. This raises the question of whether the sample can be truly representative of the universe being studied, regardless of the fact that the sample may correspond with the universe on certain selected characteristics. To hold refusals of this type to a minimum, many panels pay the members in money or merchandise; but this raises the further question of whether or not premiums attract a special type of panel member. It is often assumed that both the highest and the lowest social classes are underrepresented in panels. The former are not interested in the small payments and the latter lack the ability to perform the reporting tasks. No direct evidence is available that higher income groups will not cooperate, but it is established that inner-city families will cooperate more if the method of communication is by telephone rather than by mail.

The best continuing panels use an objective sample design to designate the individuals or homes to be included in the original panel. Refusal to participate immediately eliminates a significant percentage of those so designated, usually 50% or more. These losses are replaced by substitutes with similar characteristics, such as geographical area and city size in which they live, income level, and age of homemaker.

It is usually assumed that a panel is made up of the same individuals each time information is collected. To keep the same individuals active in the panel, most researchers offer inducements such as payments that increase as continued cooperation is obtained. Nevertheless, every panel has a certain mortality—often as much as 20 percent per year for those operating over that long a period. Some people die, others move away, and others just quit. These losses are replaced by new members with similar characteristics as far as these characteristics are known, but the probability that the replacements differ from the original group in some significant, but unknown, ways is always present.

Despite these alarming rates of original noncooperation and mortality thereafter, the few studies that have attempted to measure the effect of such losses on the makeup of the panel have tended to conclude that those remaining have similar purchasing, television, and radio habits.

Panel members may report inaccurate data.   The accuracy of data from panels was reported as one of the advantages of the use of panels. The evidence supports this for well-run panels. There is enough danger of response bias, however, that it is wise to note the likely sources.

Response errors by panel members are generally thought to result from change of habits, from self-consciousness, development of "expertise," attempts by the panel members to "look good," the bias of boredom or annoyance from continuous reporting, failure to keep diaries on a current basis, and fatigue from completing overly long diaries. The latter is no different from that which occurs with single surveys, except that panel diaries tend to be made longer than questionnaires because of the established rapport with the panel members. Some consumer purchase diaries are, in fact, quite lengthy.

Most operators of commercial "continuous" panels concede that the actions of new members of their panels are not typical, but they provide little data as to the extent of this bias or the length of time that it persists. The tendency appears to be for new panel members to increase the activity that is being recorded, for example, television viewing or food purchasing. To eliminate the effects of this bias, panel operators exclude the data from new members from final results. When members have belonged to the panel for a period of four to six weeks, they are included in the tabulation of the entire panel.

As the novelty of panel membership wears off, interest may decline and cooperation may tend to become mechanical. Diaries may be filled out just before they are sent in rather than as the events recorded take place. Panel operators try to overcome such tendencies by encouragement, emphasis on the importance of the data, remuneration, and "inspirational" communications. An experiment with a special shopping trip record that was designed to get the homemaker to open the diary after each shopping trip proved to increase measurably the purchases recorded.

Factorial designs

In the experimental designs that have been discussed, a single experimental variable, with usually only one "level," was considered. In the "after only with control group" design, the possibility of testing several versions of the variable was pointed out; for example, several different ads could be tested, each with a separate group. All but one group alternately could be considered as control groups against which to compare the experimental group, or an additional control group not exposed to any advertising could be used to protect against possible negative effects of all ads.

Factorial designs permit the experimenter to test two or more variables at the same time and to determine not only the main effects of each of the variables, but also to measure the interaction effects of the variables. Consider the problem of determining the proper concentration of sugar and flavor in a soft drink. A simple approach would be to make up a batch of the optimum mixture as judged by the producer and to have a sample of consumers taste it and competing products and indicate an order of preference. The consumers might even be asked to comment on the degree of sugar and flavor in a soft drink. Another approach would be to make up several batches with differing levels of sugar content, but with the flavor held constant. Consumers could then taste a sample of each and indicate a preference. Sugar could then be held constant and flavor varied.

The latter approach might indicate that heavy sugar and heavy flavor were both preferred, but a product with such a mixture might turn out to be unpalatable. When the flavor is strong, sugar may become less desirable. Such considerations make it important to test various levels of sugar content combined with various levels of flavor. Suppose four different degrees of sugar content and four of flavor were selected as possible characteristics of the final product. Sixteen different combinations can be made from these variations, as shown in the following table.

Flavor intensity	Sugar content			
	1	*2*	*3*	*4*
1	a	b	c	d
2	e	f	g	h
3	i	j	k	l
4	m	n	o	p

Each of the 16 formula variations (*a* to *p*) can be given to a sample of consumers and their reactions measured on various bases—for example, a preference scale from one to ten. The following hypothetical data illustrate results that might be obtained.

Flavor intensity	Sugar content			
	1	*2*	*3*	*4*
1	4.9	6.0	5.0	3.6
2	6.1	7.3	5.1	3.8
3	8.1	9.2	8.3	4.6
4	6.2	6.4	6.2	3.2

The second degree of sugar content and third degree of flavor intensity are each preferred over all levels of their own variable, no matter what the level of the other variable. The combination of these two is the preferred product formula, that is, it has the highest preference rating of 9.2. The combination of the fourth level of each of the variables is the least preferred product formula; its preference rating is 3.2.

In the above example, each of the two variables was tested at four different levels. Actually, the number of levels for each variable is determined by the thoroughness with which the experimenter wishes to study the problem, the range over which it is considered useful to study the variable, the degree of change necessary to make a discernible difference to the consumer, and the cost.

While two variables were considered in the factorial design given above, it is possible to test three or more variables. Assume that color was a third factor that might influence consumer preference for a drink. Four different colors could be tested, but to include each color variation with each possible combination of sugar and flavor would require 64 different cells and would make the experiment an expensive one. To economize in situations of this sort a variation of the factorial design has been developed—the Latin Square.

The Latin Square.   Suppose a researcher wishes to evaluate the effects of three alternative shelf arrangements (A, B, and C). He plans to do this by observing the sales generated by each variation in each of three stores in each of three time periods. He designs an experiment so that each shelf arrangement is used once, and only once, in each store and once, but only once, in each time period. The following arrangement meets these specifications:

Time period	Store		
	1	*2*	*3*
1	A	C	B
2	C	B	A
3	B	A	C

Such a geometric pattern, in which each letter is represented once and only once in each row and each column of a square, is called a *Latin Square*. Its utility in experimentation arises from this balanced property, from the fact that comparisons among treatments will be free from differences between "rows" (here, time periods) and between "columns" (here, stores). Thus, the Latin Square removes from experimental error *two* sources of extraneous variation in the experiment, one associated with different time periods (the rows) and one associated with different stores (the columns). This results in a greater precision in the evaluation of experimental results than is possible in the experimental designs described previously.

The Latin Square above for three treatments is said to be of size 3×3, referring to the number of rows and columns in the square. Latin Squares of any size exist; in marketing research, 2×2 to 6×6 squares are the most useful, since experiments generally do not attempt to evaluate more than half a dozen different variations at once. Because the number of variations must equal the number of rows (and columns) in a Latin Square, this range determines the most useful square sizes. With small Latin Squares (say, 4×4 or less) a single square will usually not provide adequate precision of results. A solution is to use more than one square.

As with the other experimental designs discussed, it is essential that randomization be used to decide which variable in a Latin Square is to be assigned to which experimental unit. In marketing research experiments using the Latin Square principle, the following structure is relatively common:

1.   There are *several repetitions* of the Latin Square arrangement, that is, several squares of the same size used to provide adequate total sample size.
2.   In each square, the *columns* represent different marketing units (for example, geographic areas or individual stores).
3.   In each square, the *rows* represent time periods, these being common to all the squares in the experiment if more than one is used.

Table 3–2 shows results of a Latin Square store test in which five squares were used to test three alternative shelf arrangements (A, B, and C) during three months, the same months being used in each of the five squares. The data shown are unit sales volumes for a breakfast cereal under the specified circumstances. Shelf arrangement C was used in store 1, in square 1, during month 1, and sales for that period were 202; the other tabular entries are similarly identified.

TABLE 3–2. Sales volumes in units from a test of three shelf arrangements (A, B, and C) obtained from five 3 × 3 Latin Squares with common rows (months) and different columns (stores)

Month	Square 1			Square 2			Square 3		
	1	2	3	4	5	6	7	8	9
1	C–202	B–246	A–1047	B–603	C–428	A–283	C–511	B–899	A–940
2	B–218	A–185	C–186	C–556	A–518	B–210	A–328	C–321	B–678
3	A–203	C–183	B–343	A–647	B–457	C–271	B–390	A–639	C–393

Month	Square 4			Square 5		
	10	11	12	13	14	15
1	A–119	B–346	C–203	B–291	C–319	A–600
2	C–143	A–390	B–269	C–267	A–363	B–614
3	B–245	C–397	A–190	A–164	B–243	C–716

PROBLEMS IN MARKETING EXPERIMENTATION

Experimental studies were rare in marketing before 1950. Since then the number of experiments has grown steadily and at an increasing rate. While the number of experiments is still small as a percentage of all marketing research projects, the advantages of experiments in determining cause and effect are so strong that one is safe in predicting continued expansion in their use. Some of the factors which limit the use of experiments have been brought out in the above discussion; however, there are additional practical problems which deserve comment.

Lack of theoretical base

True experimentation cannot take place without hypotheses to test. Such hypotheses are usually developed from underlying theory which in turn develops from extensive observation and description. Marketing research of the past has been primarily descriptive; as a result, extensive information on markets and marketing methods is now available. Little theory is yet available, but conditions are ripe for more extensive development in the future. This situation suggests that the researcher in the future will be able to develop more useful hypotheses and, thus, will be able to conduct more experiments.

Time factors

Individual markets vary from one time to another, and the same is true, of course, with people. Preferences and motivations change from year to year or even day to day. This dynamic nature of the consumer is particularly important because of the time factor involved in many marketing experiments. Sales tests must be given a considerable period of time if complete results are to be obtained. How long after an advertisement is run is its impact on sales felt? No one knows for sure, but it is likely that some effect may carry over a period of several weeks or even months. If various tests are to be rotated among the same markets as in Latin Square designs, the time required for the entire experiment may run into many months, or even years. By the time such a test is finished, consumer opinions may have changed. As experiments are continued over longer periods, mortality becomes a greater threat to validity.

Brief experiments measure only short-term effects. Most experiments assume that the immediate results (for example, sales) measure the effect of the experimental variable. But what are the cumulative effects of advertising which may build goodwill and consumer acceptance over a long period of time? Innovations in product design may be immediate successes, but they lose popularity in the long run. Other products may meet initial resistance only to go on at a later date to become successes. Experiments should cover long enough periods to enable the "after" measurement to include most, or all, of the effect of the variable. This is simply not feasible with many business problems, since decisions are usually made at an early date.

Cost of experimentation

Experimental research is often expensive. In most cases, at least one control group will be required in addition to the experimental group. In some instances, these groups will have to be measured twice or data will have to be collected continuously over a period. Thus, the cost of an experiment tends to be greater than the cost of a descriptive study.

In some experiments, control of the experimental variable is relatively simple (for example, the number of shelf "facings" in display of the product in the store), but in other instances control of the variable can be extremely expensive. Preliminary investigation of a possible experiment involving the substitution of local variables in a nationally televised commercial indicated that the cost of controlling the experimental variable in this manner would be $180,000.

Test marketing of a new product is another form of experimentation that may become very expensive. Since the costs of introducing a new product into even a relatively small market may be quite high, the tendency is to test new products in only one or a few markets. This may keep cost within feasible limits, but it raises serious questions. Variation among markets is probably greater in many cases than variation in preference among different test products. In general, the effect of the experimental variable is often relatively small as compared to the effects of miscellaneous variables. While the latter can be prevented from biasing the results through randomization, very large samples (which mean very large costs) are necessary if the experimental effects are to be measured accurately.

Administrative problems of experimentation

Many administrative problems are encountered in conducting experiments. Frequently, cooperation must be obtained and maintained from individuals who find this interferes with their normal work, or who are at least aware that "something different" is going on. In order to see that the experiment conditions are properly controlled the experimenter may have to maintain very close (and expensive) supervision. An experiment to determine the effect of a sampling campaign, for example, may measure the number of consumers redeeming a coupon for a second package. Grocers, however, are more concerned with maintaining friendly relations with their customers than they are with conducting research for a manufacturer. When consumers seek to redeem coupons for cash or for brands other than the one specified, the grocer, frequently, is inclined to cooperate, thus destroying the value of the coupon as a measure of consumer willingness to repurchase the brand. Only careful supervision can prevent such developments.

Competitive circumstances may create difficult experimental conditions. Experiments are more open to observation by competitors than are "one shot" surveys. If a new product is tested in the market, competitors are apt to become aware of the test and are thus alerted to new developments. If the results of the test are measured in sales, the competitor may be able to learn as much from the test as the experimenter, and at considerably less expense. Some firms maintain an emergency special promotion plan which they can throw into any competitor's test market and confuse the results. The longer the term of an experiment, the more possible these competitive reactions become.

CONCLUSIONS ON EXPERIMENTAL RESEARCH

Experiments have a basic advantage over descriptive studies—they are less apt to be useless. By their very nature, experiments are conducted to determine cause and effect. Before an experiment can be made, the researcher must develop a hypothesis. This forces researchers to state specifically what cause and effect they expect to find. They are, thus, likely to face in advance the question of "What will I do with the results." Experimental results, therefore, are more likely to relate to a specific decision that must be made than are descriptive data.

As marketing becomes more scientific, it seems inevitable that experimental research will be more widely used. When new products are developed, they are tested and retested in many technical experiments before the final models are determined. Months, or even years, are spent in experimental work of this type. Marketing programs, however, are designed in more limited time periods. The marketing department has no equivalent to a "tooling-up" time. Yet the cost of an erroneous marketing decision may be as staggering as a mistake in technical development. In many marketing situations, the alternatives from which a choice must be made can be tested at a relatively small cost. Experiments are particularly useful for this purpose.

Both laboratory and field experiments are useful in marketing, although the latter are preferred whenever possible. Many different experimental designs are available and ingenious researchers are finding more and more ways to adapt them to marketing problems.

Case 3–1
INTERNATIONAL HARVESTER COMPANY (A)

In addition to being a world leader in the manufacture of agricultural and construction equipment, International Harvester produces a line of trucks, which until recently included a full line of pickups and all-purpose vehicles. Among these were a line of light trucks (one-half ton and three-quarter ton pickups), heavy-duty station wagons (the Travelall), and all-purpose vehicles (the Scout II travel top and pickup) which were on-and-off highway vehicles with part-time four-wheel drive. Mr. Panelli, the marketing manager for light trucks and utility vehicles, was concerned with the number of products in the line of light-duty vehicles and their relatively low volume and market penetration.

Following an analysis of these products and the markets they served, Mr. Panelli and other company officials made the decision to simplify the line of light-duty vehicles. The two series of pickup trucks, the heavy duty Travelall wagon, and the Scout II pickup, were to be eliminated. Of the original line, the only vehicle to remain was the Scout II travel top, an all-purpose vehicle of 100″ wheel base with on-off highway capability, including four-wheel drive. It was also decided that two new vehicles would be added to the Scout line, both of which would have a wheel base of 118″. One of the new vehicles was a Scout pickup truck with cargo space inside the cab behind the seat, and the other was an extended all-metal station wagon with four-wheel drive as an option. Table 1 summarizes all of the product line changes.

TABLE 1. Product line changes

Products to be dropped
½ ton pickup
¾ ton pickup
Scout II pickup
Travelall heavy-duty station wagon

Products to be retained

Scout II travel top:	100″ wheelbase all-purpose vehicle with 4-wheel drive and on–off highway capability

Products to be added

Scout II pickup:	118″ wheelbase light-duty truck with 4-wheel drive, on–off highway capability, and in-cab cargo space behind seat
Scout II station wagon:	118″ wheelbase heavy duty, extended all-metal station wagon with optional 4-wheel drive

---

Most of the International Harvester management, Mr. Panelli included, believed that this product line extension was "dramatically different from the present line," that the benefits it offered to the consumer were "substantial," and that the line would "expand the market" for this type of vehicle. No other manufacturer offered anything exactly like this new line. The strong family resemblance of the new line items would allow them to be marketed through the same dealers handling the Scout II.

From his previous experience, Mr. Panelli felt that the new line could appeal to owners of all-purpose vehicles, including current owners of a Scout II pickup, and that the two new vehicles would appeal to current owners of heavy-duty station wagons such as the Travelall. Past research indicated that some owners of regular station wagons moved up to an all-purpose vehicle on their next purchase; such people could be attracted to the new line. In all, the company was able to identify six types of vehicle owners who would find some appeal in the two new vehicles: Scout II owners, owners of other brands of all-purpose vehicles, owners of heavy-duty station wagons, owners of large station wagons, owners of pickups, and owners of small- and medium-sized station wagons. These were established as the six market segments toward which the company's marketing efforts would be directed.

Mr. Panelli next had to address the question of "How to position the products creatively so that we attract the largest number of purchasers while minimizing the cannibalization of our Scout II travel top?" That is, what main ideas and themes should be used in the company's advertising and promotion for the new line in order to attract purchases from people not currently driving an International Harvester vehicle. He decided to use research to help resolve this issue. The research would be designed to achieve two objectives: (1) identify a creative strategy which would position the new line optimally, relative to both the company's Scout II travel top and competitors' existing lines; (2) identify those segments of the market with the highest probability of purchasing the new line. Marketing Analysts, Inc., a well-known marketing research firm, was asked to submit a complete written proposal for a research project which would address these two objectives. Their proposal is described below.

Description of proposal

Because of the marketing characteristics of the new line extension, Marketing Analysts, Inc. recommended research which would use a consumer panel and would employ both telephone interviews and mail questionnaires. Their proposal explained the reasoning behind their recommendation to use this type of research design.

> You have unique products which give rise to a unique research problem. The positioning of these products will not be easy and can only be accomplished by talking to that very small proportion of the population who either profess an interest in purchasing this type of product or who can be considered somewhat representative of those who will buy the product—that is, those who have recently purchased a product similar to your product.
>
> The best way to approach your problem of creative positioning is to establish a multiquota sample and to find out how each possible segment of your market will position your products in the current competitive milieu. While doing this, you can also find out the likelihood of purchase and thereby determine the proper weighting which should be applied to each segment in contributing to the overall positioning. By following this approach, you will be allowing only those individuals who fall into your market to position the vehicle and you will be asking them to position it competitively—that is, in direct comparison to other products which will constitute the major competition once your new product is offered for sale in the new marketplace. And, by utilizing the purchase probabilities as weights, you will arrive at a selection procedure that accurately reflects the total potential of the market.

The proposed research design consisted of three phases: (1) the members of a large panel were to be screened to locate qualified prospects for the new product; (2) a medium-size sample of qualified prospects would be interviewed "in-depth" to identify possible creative strategies; (3) a large sample of qualified respondents would be surveyed by mail to test their response to alternative creative strategies.

Phase 1. Marketing Analysts, Inc. maintained a file of almost 100,000 households which had agreed to cooperate in research projects undertaken by the firm. The first phase of the proposed research would be to screen this panel to locate some 5–10,000 households which were qualified prospects for the new line. A qualified prospect would be an owner of one of the six types of vehicles identified above who also indicated being "very likely" or "fairly likely" to buy an all-purpose vehicle or pickup within the next few years. Each such owner would be identified according to the type of vehicle currently owned; these households would then be used in phase 2 and phase 3 of the proposed research project.

Phase 2. In this phase approximately 300 qualified households would be interviewed using a combination of mail and telephone. These households would be mailed pictures, specifications, and line drawings of the new International Harvester products, although they would not be identified by the International Harvester name. The line drawings would include side and top views showing the seating arrangement, space usage, leg room, cargo space, and other features. The specifications would include such things as carrying capacity, dimensions, horsepower, available options, transmission and power train information, driving range, and similar information. Similar materials of International Harvester's present line and of competing products, all identified by brand, would also be included.

After reviewing these materials, respondents' reactions and impressions would be obtained through telephone interviews using open-ended questions. Interviewers would be told that the objective was to obtain qualitative data useful for ascertaining how potential buyers perceived the new vehicles, both in an overall sense, and with respect to power, acceleration, handling ease, riding comfort, ruggedness, interior styling, and other features. Interviewers would be instructed to record verbatim responses and told that it was very important to do so because none of the responses would be tabulated or analyzed statistically.

Responses to the open-ended questions would be studied to identify four or five ideas or themes which might be considered for use as creative strategies in advertising for the new line. Illustrative creative strategies which might emerge from this phase of the research could be "a really rugged vehicle for outdoors people," "an in-town, off-road wagon for the entire family," or some other statements reflecting who would be likely to use the vehicle, when, and under what circumstances.

Phase 3. This phase would be undertaken after four or five creative strategy statements had been identified. In this phase, some 3,600 households would be selected on the basis of their being potential purchasers of the new line; that is, owners of one of the six types of vehicles described above who indicated being "very likely" or "fairly likely" to buy an all-purpose vehicle or pickup within the next few years. Because these six types of owners would represent the six market segments likely to be interested in the new line, the total sample would consist of six samples of approximately 600 each, that is, one sample of current owners of pickups, one sample of current owners of heavy-duty station wagons, and so on. All of the house-holds in each market segment would be sent pictures, line drawings, and specifications of the International Harvester line extension, the present Inter-national Harvester line, and competing lines, all identified by brand. Each of the six segments would be randomly divided into four subsamples, each of which would receive only one of the creative strategy statements being tested for the new line. In addition, each of the four subsamples would be further subdivided into two groups, one of which would receive information that the price of the new vehicles would be on a par with competitive ve-hicles. The other group would receive information that the new vehicles would be priced slightly higher than competitive vehicles.

This study design is illustrated in Exhibit 1. The total study would consist of six samples of approximately 600 households in each market segment.

EXHIBIT 1. Proposed study design for phase 3

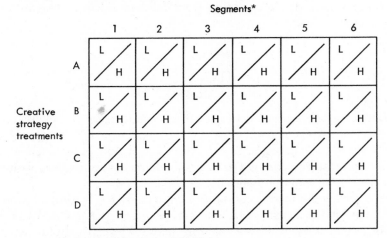

* Owners of different types of vehicles.
Key: L = competitive price and H = slightly higher price.

Each sample of 600 would be broken into four subsamples of approximately 150 households receiving the same creative treatment. Each of these sub-samples would be broken into two groups, one of which would respond to a competitive price and one to a slightly higher price.

Analysis. The evaluation of each creative strategy-price combination would be based upon three measures: the degree to which it (1) resulted in the new International Harvester line being rated as most appealing, (2) led respondents to indicate that they might visit a dealer to look at the new line, and (3) led respondents to indicate that they would be most likely to select a vehicle in the new International Harvester line when they made their next purchase. For each creative strategy-price combination, the research would yield three percentages: for example, for creative strategy A and the "popu-lar price," the research might show that 38 percent of the respondents found a vehicle in the new International Harvester line "most appealing" among all the vehicles reviewed; that 26 percent indicated that they "might visit a dealer showroom" to look at the line; and that 17 percent indicated that they "most likely would purchase" a vehicle in the new International Harvester line. By comparing these three percentages for each creative strategy-price combination, it would be possible to identify the most effective combinations. These could be weighted by the relative size of each market segment to decide which combinations were likely to be most effective in generating sales interest in the new line.

Should Mr. Panelli accept the proposal from Marketing Analysts, Inc.?

If the proposal is accepted, how should the data from phase 3 of the research be used?

If the proposal is not accepted, what alternate research design do you propose be used?

Case 3–2
GAM, INC.

GAM, Inc. was a long established regional manufacturer of jackets, skirts, and other sportswear apparel designed for women in the 18–25-year age group. Over the years, their advertising had been mainly of the image building type, and was concentrated in regional editions of appropriate women's magazines during January, February, and March.

The company monitored consumer attitudes toward its product line by conducting a comprehensive telephone survey each March in GAM's market area. In these surveys, 1,000 women in the 18–25-year age bracket were asked a number of questions concerning themselves and their clothing preferences. They were also asked questions regarding their awareness of, and attitude toward, the GAM product line and the product lines of their major competitors. The company used the responses to certain of these questions to develop an index called "the propensity to buy GAM." This index was an estimate of the percentage of 18–25-year-old women who seemed to show a propensity to buy the GAM brand when shopping for an apparel item of the type sold by GAM. The trend of the index was causing much concern, because in the period of 1975–79 it fell from 15 percent to 11–12 percent. The trend of the index was confirmed by a gradual decline in sales over the same time period.

During the 1980 Plans Review, the Merchandising Manager proposed that a major change be made in the company's advertising strategy. She suggested a doubling of the advertising media budget, with the additional funds to be spent on spot television commercials during April, May, and June. She argued that such a change would reach women who were not readers of the magazines GAM regularly used in their advertising campaign. Also, the television commercials would increase the frequency of exposure to GAM advertisements among women who were both magazine readers and television viewers. Finally, the change would have an overall beneficial effect because it would extend the company's advertising campaign from three months to six months, which was the typical length of their competitors' advertising campaigns.

Because of their concern, management agreed to test the proposed change in a handful of markets. Six markets reflecting good, average and poor sales results for GAM products were judgmentally selected using the company's Brand Development Index (BDI). A market's BDI was defined as GAM's per capita sales (among 18–25-year-old women) in that market divided by GAM's per capita sales (among 18–25-year-old women) in the company's entire marketing area. Markets A and E with BDIs of 1.62 and 1.95, respectively, were the markets with "good" GAM sales. Markets with "average." GAM sales, and their BDI's, were C (BDI = 0.91) and D (BDI = 1.02). "Poor" markets were B (BDI = 0.43) and F (BDI = 0.66).

These markets were divided into two groups, with A, B, and C assigned to one group, and D, E, and F assigned to the other. In the following year, markets A, B, and C were given the regular magazine advertising campaign in January, February, and March, and then given the proposed spot television campaign in April, May and June. Markets D, E, and F were given only the regular magazine advertising campaign in January, February and March. A telephone survey of 200 women (18–25 years old) was carried out in the usual manner in each of the markets in late March. In late June the surveys were repeated in all markets, but with different respondents. Table 1 shows how "the propensity to buy GAM" index changed in the six markets.

TABLE 1. Propensity to buy GAM at two selected dates

	Selected dates	
Market	March	June
A	15%	19%
B	3	9
C	10	18
D	10	6
E	12	2
F	5	1

Evaluate the GAM advertising experiment. In what ways could the experimental design have been improved?

Do you need any additional information in order to draw conclusions and make recommendations? If so, specify.

What do you recommend regarding change in advertising strategy?

4

Basic methods
of collecting data

No matter what the basic design of the research, it is necessary to collect accurate data to achieve useful results. For this reason, it is helpful to consider methods of collecting data and the quality of information they may be expected to produce. Questioning and observation are the two basic methods of collecting data in marketing research. Questioning, as the name suggests, is distinguished by the fact that data are collected by asking questions of people who are thought to have the desired information. Questions may be asked in person or in writing. A formal list of such questions is called a questionnaire.

When data are collected by observation, researchers ask no questions. Instead they keep track of the objects or actions in which they are interested. Sometimes individuals make the observations; on other occasions, mechanical devices note and record the desired information. Observations may be made of information such as census reports, of objects such as the number of signs for a given company, or of people and their activities. No matter what research design is used, the necessary data are collected by one or both of these two methods.

General accuracy of data collected

Surveys have become so commonplace in today's world that the average person seldom questions the idea that useful information can be obtained in this manner. The fact that findings of one type or another are developed and usually seem plausible furthers this acceptance. When formal efforts are made to check the accuracy of survey data, however, the results are often disquieting.

Accuracy of survey data. Perhaps the best study of the accuracy of responses to questionnaires was one in which a carefully selected sample of 920 individuals was asked a variety of questions for which correct answers were available from official records. Table 4–1 shows some of the results of this survey. Ninety-eight percent of the respondents reported accurately on telephone ownership, but as few as 56 percent reported correctly on whether or not they contributed to the Community Chest.

TABLE 4–1. Accuracy of data obtained by survey when compared to official records

	Percentage of respondent reports			
	Correct	Exagger- ated	Under- stated	Other*
Telephone in house	98	1	1	0
Home ownership	96	3	1	0
Automobile ownership	94	3	0	3
Age	92	4	4	0
Possession of driver's license	88	10	2	0
Valid library card	87	9	2	2
Registered to vote	82	16	2	0
Voting in congressional election	69	19	2	10
Contributed to Community Chest	56	34	0	10

* Such as "no answer."
Source: Don Cahalan, "Correlates of Respondent Accuracy in the Denver Validity Study," *Public Opinion Quarterly* 32 (Winter 1968–69): 610.

Errors of the above size on factual data are upsetting enough, but of even more concern to the marketing researcher are data obtained by questionnaire, presumably accurately, but which report incorrectly what the situation actually is. For example, a food manufacturer, who was testing three possible designs (three colors, five colors, and six colors) of a new package, asked consumers to pick the one they preferred. Sixty-two percent reported they liked the six-color package best. When three packages were put on the shelf and sales observed, only 11 percent bought the six-color package; 16 percent bought the five-color package; and 72 percent bought the three-color package.[1]

Accuracy of observation data. Such results as the above have led to the substitution of observation for questioning where at all feasible. In general, observation data are more accurate than questionnaire data, especially when observation of an action can be obtained in place of a verbal report of what action the respondent would take (as in the above example).

On the other hand, observation does not automatically produce accurate data. Physical difficulties in the observation situation or on the part of the observer may result in errors. Even more important, however, is the influence

[1] Louis Cheskin, *Why Is She Buying Package 2?* (undated brochure).

on observations of the observer's training, philosophy, opinions, and expectations. Significant variations in observation of the same phenomena have been reported for such diverse projects as the state of repair for telephone poles, the transit of stars in a telescope, and the reading of chest X-ray films.[2] Perhaps Bertrand Russell's comment on the study of animal behavior summarizes the situation as well as any:

> One may say broadly that all the animals that have been carefully observed have behaved so as to confirm the philosophy in which the observer believed before his observation began. Nay, more, they have all displayed the national characteristics of the observer. Animals studied by Americans rush about frantically, with an incredible display of hustle and pep, and at last achieve the desired result by chance. Animals observed by the Germans sit still and think, and at last evolve the solution out of their inner consciousness.[3]

From the above it is obvious that data collected by any method are subject to considerable error and can be used only with caution. Questionnaire and observation are the only methods available, however, for collecting data. More detailed discussion of the two methods will help in understanding how each can be used most effectively.

QUESTIONNAIRE METHOD

If one wants to know what type of dentifrice people use, what they think of television commercials, or why they buy particular brands of cars, the natural procedure is to ask them. Thus, the questionnaire method has come to be the more widely used of the two data collection methods. Many homemakers are now familiar with the telephone caller who greets them with, "We are making a survey," and then proceeds to ask a series of questions. Half of the U.S. public has participated in one or more such studies.[4] Business executives also frequently receive written or oral requests for information. The common factor in all varieties of the questionnaire method is this reliance on verbal responses to questions, written or oral.

Some interviews are conducted in person, others by telephone, and still others by mail. Each of these procedures has its special advantages and limitations. Each will be discussed later in this chapter. The questionnaire method in general, however, has a number of pervasive advantages and disadvantages. Discussion of particular variations will be more meaningful if these characteristics of the general method are brought out first.

---

[2] Herbert Hyman, *Interviewing in Social Research* (Chicago: University of Chicago Press, 1951), p. 13.

[3] Bertrand Russell, *Philosophy* (New York: Norton, 1927), p. 30.

[4] Frank D. Walker, "Surveys' Image Better," *Marketing News* (January 12, 1979):1.

Advantages of questionnaire method

Versatility. Probably the greatest advantage of the questionnaire method is its versatility. Almost every problem of marketing research can be approached from the questionnaire standpoint. Every marketing problem involves people. Therefore, ideas relative to the problem and its solution can be obtained by asking these people about the problem. Many problems can be studied only by questioning. Knowledge, opinions, motivations, and intentions are usually not open to observation. Except where records have been maintained, past events can be studied only through the questionnaire method. Similarly, it is not normally feasible to observe personal activities such as brushing teeth. All this does not mean that the questionnaire method can be used satisfactorily to solve all marketing problems. It can be used, however, to get some data relative to most problems.

Speed and cost. Questioning is usually faster and cheaper than observing. Interviewers have more control over their data-gathering activities than do observers. As a result, less time is typically wasted in a questionnaire study. For example, in a research study to find whether consumers prefer beer in bottles or cans, one could either ask people their preference or wait in package liquor stores to observe which containers customers ask for when they come in to buy beer. The latter method would require observers to wait until customers came into the store to buy beer. Interviewers, however, could proceed from one interview to another with no wait in between. Thus, the lost time would be less with the questionnaire method. Some events that take place over a period of time, such as the number of trips to the supermarket in a week, would require lengthy observation, but a question on this behavior can be answered in a few seconds. In many cases, however, this advantage of the questionnaire may be negligible.

Disadvantages of questionnaire method

Despite the fact that the questionnaire method is widely used in marketing research, it has several important limitations.

Unwillingness of respondent to provide information. Most interviews are obtained at the sufferance of the respondent. The respondent answers the telephone to be greeted by an interviewer with a list of questions. The interviewer is unknown to the respondent, and the subject of the proposed interview may be of little or no interest. The interviewer counts on the natural politeness and good nature of most people to gain their cooperation. But in some cases potential respondents will refuse to take the time to be interviewed or will refuse to answer some specific questions. Questions about income or about very personal subjects frequently meet refusals. The number of such refusals varies with individual interviewers and with the subject of the interview, but in some cases refusals run as high as 55 percent of the attempted calls. A more typical refusal rate for a household survey is probably 5 to 10 percent. When questionnaires are sent through the mails, the percentage which is not returned may exceed 90 percent, although a non-response rate of 50 percent is more typical, and among skilled researchers 25 percent or less is common.

Various methods of reducing unwillingness on the part of respondents have been developed. The most important of these is salesmanship on the part of the interviewer or a covering letter with mail questionnaires. Rewards in the form of premiums or cash often help to gain cooperation. Assurance that the information will be held in confidence and in no way will be related to the individual may reduce refusals when data are particularly personal or of value to competitors.

Inability of respondent to provide information.   Despite a willingness to cooperate, many persons are unable to give accurate information on questions which the marketing interviewer would like to ask. Many motivations, for example, are largely subconscious. How many consumers analyze their reasons for buying a particular bar of soap or suit of clothes and then formulate those reasons so that they can be expressed quickly and clearly when an interviewer unexpectedly asks about them? Most products are bought without any conscious array of reasons for and against. Questions on such motivations are, therefore, apt to be useless. Current work on motivation is attempting to obtain the information indirectly by asking questions which can be answered and which, by their pattern, indicate motivation.[5]

In other cases, respondents cannot furnish information because they are unable to remember the facts desired or because they have never known the facts. One can ask: How many times did you eat corn flakes for breakfast last month? Few could answer such a question accurately because most people do not attempt to note or remember such information.

Many times the only way to overcome this problem is to make the survey at a time when the events of interest are fresh in the respondent's mind. Memory, however, is related to other factors besides recency. One experiment found that respondents could report correctly only 31 percent of the programs to which their radios were tuned the previous day. When a consumer panel that reported purchases of convenience items changed the reporting period from monthly to weekly, the volume of purchases reported increased 20 percent. Most people, however, could probably remember for many days, or even years, the place at which they bought their present car.

In some situations, it is possible to help the respondent's memory. Aided-recall techniques are used for this purpose. If a consumer is asked what ads she has seen recently, she may be able to mention a few; if she is asked about ads for Sanka coffee, she is more apt to recall; and if she is shown pictures of the ads, she is even more apt to remember. In one study, respondents who were known to have seen a TV newscast, were asked if they could recall any

---

[5] This is discussed more extensively in Chapter 9 on attitude measurement.

stories from the newscast. The average respondent could remember only 1.2 stories. But when the interviewer read the "headlines" to the respondents they remembered an average of 8.7 stories.[6]

Using aids to recall involves dangers which must be considered when the technique is used. Such aids may cause respondents to think they have seen or heard the item in question even when they have not. One experiment to measure the extent of such erroneous reporting found that just as many individuals reported having seen certain elements of an advertisement they were shown when the elements had not been in the advertisement as when they had been.[7]

If consumers are asked any question which they cannot answer correctly because they do not know and have never known the information requested, they may still answer. Such answers are sometimes honest mistakes and at other times are made to impress the interviewer. In any case, these answers appear as valid responses and so give erroneous results.

It is important, then, to ask people *only* those questions they are qualified to answer. Where alternate respondents are available, the one most apt to have the information should be used. Because homemakers are at home more than other members of the family, they are frequently asked questions about activities and opinions of the other members. In many cases this may be satisfactory, but in some cases this undoubtedly leads to incorrect responses. One study of family expenses over the previous six months found homemakers failed to report 28 percent of the cars and 21 percent of the major appliances purchased.[8]

Influence of questioning process.   A third major limitation of the questionnaire method is the effect of the questioning process on the results obtained. The situation in which a person is questioned about routine actions is an artificial one at best. As a result, respondents may furnish reports quite different from the facts.

If the true answer to a question would be embarrassing or damaging to the ego, some respondents will manufacture an answer. Whereas respondents may answer accurately questions such as whether or not they attend professional football games or what brand of washing machine they have, they may tend to modify answers to questions on their income or the magazines to which they subscribe. One study found that beer consumption as reported by consumers was considerably less than sales by brewers. When the approach to the problem was changed to obtain beer purchases, such purchases reported by consumers exceeded reported beer drinking

---

[6] W. Russell Neuman, "Patterns of Recall among Television News Viewers," *Public Opinion Quarterly* 40 (Spring 1976):118.

[7] Eric Mander and Mort David, "Recognition of Ad Elements: Recall or Projection," *Journal of Advertising Research* 1 (December 1961):23–25.

[8] John Neter, "Measurement Errors in Reports of Consumer Expenditures," *Journal of Marketing Research* 7 (February 1970):21.

by 37.6 percent.[9] Consumers reporting purchases of food and drug items by brand reported 45 percent more purchases of the best known national brands than was known to be the case, but 62 percent less purchasing of leading chain store brands.[10]

Often respondents attempt to give answers that they think will please the interviewer. For example, if respondents know the product for which a particular survey is being made, the percentage reporting use of that product tends to be higher than otherwise. Some respondents use the interview as an occasion to amuse or astonish the interviewer or reader of the questionnaire.

QUESTIONNAIRE STUDIES CLASSIFIED BY STRUCTURE AND DISGUISE

As noted previously, it is possible to classify questionnaire studies on a variety of bases. Three such bases which are of importance are (1) the degree to which the questionnaire is formalized or structured; (2) the disguise or lack of disguise of the objectives of the questionnaire; and (3) the communication method used. The first two of these bases are considered together.

Questionnaire studies can be conducted either with or without formal lists of questions. When no formal questionnaire is used, interviewers adapt their questioning to each interview as it progresses or perhaps elicit responses by indirect methods such as showing pictures on which the respondent

TABLE 4–2. Types of questionnaire studies

	Structured	Nonstructured
Nondisguised	Most questionnaires	Some focus groups Some depth interviews
	Example: Does your family own a piano?	Example: Ask respondent(s) to discuss what they think when canned soup is mentioned.
Disguised	Some attitude measurements	Projective techniques
	Example: Which of the following eat a lot, and which a little, oatmeal: Farmers Movie actors etc.	Example: Nescafé example discussed below.

---

[9] Elmo Roper organization house organ (September 1960).

[10] Seymour Sudman, "On the Accuracy of Recording of Consumer Panels: II," *Journal of Marketing Research* 1 (August 1964):77.

comments. Following a prescribed sequence of questions is referred to as structured study while the other is nonstructured. Questionnaires can be constructed so that the objective is clear to the respondent (nondisguised), or they can be constructed so as to disguise the objective. Using these two bases of classification, four types of studies can be distinguished.[11]

Structured, nondisguised questioning.   Most questionnaire studies made in marketing research are of the first type—they are structured and are not disguised. If the sales manager for a musical instrument company wants to find out how many and what type of people play various types of instruments, a formal list of questions may be set up which ask directly about the ownership and playing of various instruments. Each of a selected group of persons is then asked this set of questions in the given sequence. Answers are frequently limited to a list of alternatives which is stated or implied. Several questions taken from an actual survey of this type are given below:

> Does your family own a piano?
>   Yes _____   No _____
> (If yes, ask):
> What type of piano do you have?
>   Upright _____ Spinet _____ Grand _____ Other _____
> Did you buy it or was it a gift?
> Which members of your family, if any, can now play the piano?

Collection of data in a structured interview of this type has definite advantages in marketing research. By reducing the chance for interviewers to influence results through different phrasings of questions and even different questions, and through different judgments of answers and what to record, the structured questionnaire produces more reliable results—that is, if the research project is repeated in the same manner, similar results will be obtained. Perhaps the ultimate in structuring was accomplished in one study in which respondents were seated in a chair which was fastened to the floor a given distance from the chair in which the interviewer sat. The interviewer asked questions by handing the respondent cards on which the questions were printed.

The greater reliability which comes with structuring may be obtained at the loss of some validity. An established procedure prevents the interviewers from trying to obtain more information when it appears the respondent has more to give, or to explore points when the respondent's answer appears misleading, evasive, or otherwise inaccurate. However, to do this effectively, interviewers must be skilled in the art and well trained for the specific project. In most marketing research projects interviewers are neither.

Data obtained in structured, nondisguised studies are easier to tabulate and interpret than data gathered in other ways. This does not necessarily

---

[11] This cross classification was first suggested by Donald T. Campbell, "The Indirect Assessment of Social Attitudes," *Psychological Bulletin* 47 (January 1950):15.

mean that they are more useful or valid in solving the questions at hand, as will be shown later. But answers to formal questions of clear purpose can be counted and their apparent meaning determined in a more objective fashion than is true for data obtained by other methods.

Structured, nondisguised studies can be handled by telephone, mail, or personal interview. Unfortunately, such studies tend to be limited to the collection of factual information or opinions. They are subject to the three limitations of the questionnaire method—respondents may be unable to furnish the information desired, they may be unwilling to furnish it, or the questioning process may tend to stimulate incorrect or misleading answers.

Nonstructured, nondisguised questioning.   More than anything else, marketers want to know why people buy or do not buy their products. Direct questions dealing with motives rarely elicit useful answers. As pointed out above, most people do not have a clear idea as to why they make specific marketing decisions. Direct questions do not measure the relative importance of the various types of reasons, and many individuals will not report motives which might be considered base or socially unacceptable. The family which bought a new Cadillac to make the neighbors envious, would be unlikely to report such a motivation. Instead, the statement that Cadillacs are really economical in the long run might be made.

To overcome these difficulties, researchers have developed depth interviews and focus group interviews. Instead of approaching respondents with a fixed list of questions, the interviewer attempts to get respondents to talk freely about the subject of interest. By so doing, the interviewer hopes to put respondents at ease and to encourage them to express any ideas which they have on the subject. If some idea of interest is passed over too quickly, the interviewer may seek more information by "probing." For example, the interviewer may comment, "That's interesting. Why do you feel that way?" This encourages further discussion of the point. The objective of these interviews is to get below the surface reasons for particular marketing decisions and to find the underlying or basic motives. Such interviews do not involve the use of formal questionnaires, yet the discussion is directed to the specific problem at hand. They are nonstructured, nondisguised questioning.

The advantages of focus groups and depth interviews were discussed in Chapter 2. They tend to obtain more information from respondents because the latter are encouraged to express any ideas they have and points of particular interest can be explored at length. The interviewer is free to adjust to each situation as it develops. This flexibility on the part of the interviewer is a major advantage, but it is also a major weakness. Since each interviewer handles each interview differently, it is difficult to compare results. Averages and percentages cannot be computed with validity. Thus, focus groups and depth interviews are best used in exploratory research where the objective is to find ideas for specific hypotheses which may be tested with other methods.

This reliance on the judgment of the individual interviewer also creates other problems. An interviewer who has a strong preference for one brand of car will be apt to find different attitudes toward that car than one who dislikes the car. In some cases, such interviews are taken verbatim by recording machines. This reduces interviewer bias, but may put respondents ill at ease.

Depth interviews take longer than the typical structured interviews. Many of them last an hour or more and so are costly. As a result, group interviews have become the prevalent method of conducting this type of research. In both cases the time involved creates difficulties in securing respondent cooperation and, hence, may lead to biased samples.

A final disadvantage of the nonstructured, nondisguised type of questionnaire lies in the difficulty and cost of interpretation. Trained psychologists are usually used. Even then it is subjective and will probably vary from one analyst to another.

Nonstructured, disguised questioning.   Many people are either unwilling or unable to give accurate reports as to their own attitudes and motivations. Thus, even focus groups (nonstructured, nondisguised questioning) probably give biased results. To overcome this difficulty, clinical psychologists have developed disguised methods of gathering such data. Disguised methods are designed so that the respondents do not know what the objective of the study is. Such disguised methods may also be nonstructured. Projective techniques are an example of this type.

The theory of projective techniques is that all individuals, in describing a situation, interpret that situation to a degree. The description given reflects a certain amount of the individual giving it. Then, when individuals describe a situation, they are actually describing their interpretations of the situation.

Various projective techniques are used, but the most common are word association, sentence completion, and story telling. In word association, a series of words is read one at a time to respondents. After each word respondents say the first thing that comes into their minds. Sentence completion requires respondents to complete partial sentences. In story telling, respondents are shown pictures or given descriptions and asked to tell a story about them.

A classic study of instant coffee illustrates the general approach.[12] When asked why they did not like instant coffee, most consumers said they did not like the flavor. Since this seemed to be a stereotyped answer, one researcher decided to use a disguised method to test it. Two grocery shopping lists were constructed which were identical except for the coffee; on one it was Nescafé Instant Coffee and on the other it was one pound Maxwell House Coffee (drip grind). Two matched samples of homemakers were then selected. One

---

[12] Mason Haire, "Projective Techniques in Marketing Research," *Journal of Marketing* 14 (April 1950):649–52, and F. E. Webster, Jr. and F. von Pechmann, "A Replication of the 'Shopping List' Study," *Journal of Marketing* 34 (April 1970):61–63.

grocery list was shown to one sample and the other list was shown to the other sample. Each homemaker was asked to describe the consumer who made up the shopping list.

Some of the differences in the consumers described as making up the lists are revealing of attitudes toward instant coffee.

Nescafé consumer	*Maxwell House consumer*
48% said lazy	4% said lazy
48% said failed to plan household purchases	12% said failed to plan household purchases
4% said thrifty	16% said thrifty
12% said spendthrift	0% said spendthrift
4% said good wife	16% said good wife

Since projective techniques are unstructured, they have much the same limitations as focus groups. Interpretation is very subjective; hence it is subject to the criticism that it reflects the interpreter as much as the respondent. Cost, time, and difficulty in securing competent fieldworkers are problems which plague projective techniques in a manner similar to focus groups.

The big advantage of projective techniques lies in their ability to uncover subconscious and socially unacceptable attitudes and motives. When consumers were asked why they did not use instant coffee, they said they did not like the taste. When they were asked to describe the consumer who had instant coffee on the shopping list, they described a lazy, unskilled housekeeper.

A further advantage of projective techniques over focus groups lies in the greater standardization of the stimulus given to the respondent. Stimuli are not standardized in depth interviews; hence, comparisons of results are not valid. But all respondents can be given exactly the same stimulus in projective tests, for example, word associations. Results are, therefore, more comparable and less subject to bias. Direct comparison of projective results, however, is still not as easy as with most structured studies, because each answer is given in the respondent's own words rather than in terms of one of several established answers.

Despite the obvious merits of projective techniques for obtaining data on motives and attitudes, some evidence indicates that imaginative use of structured questionnaires can obtain similar results with the accompanying advantages of economy. One study with the express purpose of testing this hypothesis found close correlation between the results.[13]

Structured, disguised questioning. Questioning of the structured, disguised type has the advantages of disguise which were pointed out above—

---

[13] B. A. Maher, Norman Watt, and Donald T. Campbell, "Comparative Validity of Two Projective and Two Structured Attitude Tests in a Prison Population," *Journal of Applied Psychology* 44 (August 1960):284–88.

primarily that respondents do not know what is being measured and, hence, are not biased in their answers. The advantages of structure lie in the reduction of interviewer and interpreter bias, in quicker and less costly interviewing, and in easier tabulation of results.

Some structured, disguised tests of attitudes are based on the theory that individuals' knowledge, perception, and memory are conditioned by their attitudes. For example, Democrats listen to more speeches by other Democrats than by Republicans; therefore, Democrats have more information about Democratic candidates than about Republican candidates. A simple test of information about candidates would then serve to separate Democrats from Republicans. A straightforward question—Are you a Democrat or a Republican?—might get a biased answer.

Similarly, it is theorized that if respondents are asked questions to which they do not know the answers, they will tend to guess in the direction of their own attitudes. For example, when asked whether various types of people ate hot cereal for breakfast, most respondents reported doctors ate a lot of it, but movie actors ate very little hot cereal. This suggests that those respondents thought hot cereal was healthful but "unglamorous."

Data collected by structured, disguised techniques on attitudes toward instant coffee were compared with the similar data collected by nonstructured, disguised techniques as described above. Although the samples in the two studies were not directly comparable, the results obtained with the simple structured, disguised questionnaire were similar in nature to those obtained by the nonstructured approach. The structured study, however, benefited from having the prior data as a guide to the study design.[14]

These studies suggest that it is possible to obtain the advantages of disguise and structure in the same study with the attendant ease of handling in doorstep interviews, ease of comprehension by respondent, ease of administration and tabulating, objectively measurable reliability, and economy.

QUESTIONNAIRE STUDIES CLASSIFIED BY METHODS OF COMMUNICATION

In the preceding discussion, questionnaires were classified on the basis of a combination of structure and disguise. Another classification, which overlaps the preceding one but which is useful for illustrating other types of opportunities and problems, is classification on the basis of the method of communication used. Three different methods of communication with questionnaires are available: (1) personal interview, (2) telephone, and (3) mail. Personal interviews are those in which an interviewer obtains information from respondents in face-to-face meetings. Telephone interviews are similar except that communication between interviewer and respondent is

---

[14] Ralph Westfall, Harper Boyd, Jr., and Donald T. Campbell, "The Use of Structured Techniques in Motivation Research," *Journal of Marketing* 22 (October 1957): 134–39.

via telephone instead of direct personal contact. In most mail surveys, questionnaires are mailed to respondents who also return them by mail. Sometimes, however, mail questionnaires are placed in respondent hands by other means, such as by attaching them to consumer products, putting them in magazines or newspapers, or having fieldworkers leave them with respondents. Respondents complete the questionnaires by themselves and return the completed forms though the mail. Occasionally, a survey mails questionnaires to respondents and fieldworkers go to pick them up.

For years the bulk of all marketing research studies was conducted by personal interview at the respondent's home. This is no longer the case. A study in 1978 of individuals who had been interviewed in the past year showed the following methods of communication:[15]

Telephone	40%
Mail	26
Personal interview at shopping center	20
Personal interview at home	14
	100%

When personal interviews are used, they now occur more often in shopping centers than at home. Telephone and shopping center interviews are the most rapidly growing of the above types, primarily because they tend to be cheaper than the other methods of communication, yet give satisfactory results. Personal interviews at home are declining in use.

Since any of the communication methods can be used to collect data on a wide variety of topics, cost frequently is a deciding factor in the method to be used. Costs for each of the methods range widely so that the characteristics of a given study determine which method of communication will be the cheapest, but, in general, mail tends to be the cheapest per completed interview followed by telephone, personal interviews in shopping centers, personal interviews at home, and focus group interviews as shown in Table 4–3.

TABLE 4–3. Cost per completed interview for selected methods of communication

Method of communication	Cost range		
	High	Low	Typical
Mail	$ 15	$ 4	$ 8
Telephone	25	6	12
Personal—shopping center	40	8	15
Personal—home	100	25	40
Per group (5–12 people)	$3,000	$1,000	$1,800

---

[15] "1978 Industry Image Survey Results," *The Researcher* (November 1978).

The high costs in the table are for 20–30 minute complex interviews with respondents who are difficult to find (for example, last year's stereo purchasers) while the low costs are for 5–10 minute, simple interviews with respondents who don't have to be screened from the general population.

Cost per completed interview is not always a sound basis for comparison of communication methods. If a particular communication method will not reach a particular population group or will not secure accurate information from a group on the subject of interest, there is no point in considering its use no matter what the cost. Cost per unit of accurate information would be a more desirable basis for comparing communication methods, but "accurate information" can only be quantified arbitrarily. Factors which influence the accuracy of the data which can be obtained by a given method are the character of the population to be studied, the subject of interest, the questionnaire length, the questionnaire complexity, the geographic area to be covered, the time available for the study, and budgetary limitations.

Questionnaires which are of the structured type, disguised or nondisguised, can generally be handled by any of the three communication methods, but nonstructured interviews cannot be handled by mail and only with some limitations by telephone. Every type of study, however, can be handled by personal interview, in shopping centers or at home.

Each of the three methods of communication is discussed in more detail in the following pages.

Telephone interviews

As stated earlier, telephone interviews[16] have become the most widely used of the three methods of collecting data. They are not as versatile as personal interviews as it is difficult to handle over-the-telephone interviews which need props; interviews which are relatively unstructured or have questions which require long, descriptive answers; or interviews which call for observation of the respondents or their environment. Imaginative researchers, however, continue to find methods of overcoming these problems. If product samples are needed, they may be mailed or delivered in advance. Audio aids may be found to replace video aids.

Modern technology and organization have changed the nature of telephone surveys in a major way. Wide Area Telephone Service (WATS) offered by the Bell System makes it economically feasible to handle nationwide surveys from one location. Random Digit Dialing (RDD) makes it feasible to select probability samples of all telephone homes, including those homes with unlisted numbers. Cathode Ray Tubes (CRT) and computer systems make it possible to have questionnaires programmed to appear on

---

[16] For an extensive discussion of telephone interviews see Robert M. Groves and Robert L. Kahn, *Surveys by Telephone* (New York: Academic Press, 1979). The following discussion also draws heavily on Tyzoon T. Tyebee, "Telephone Survey Methods: The State of the Art," *Journal of Marketing* 43 (Summer 1979):68–78.

the tube (similar to a TV picture) in front of the interviewer in the sequence in which the questions are to be asked. Answers to the questions, except for discussion type responses, can be recorded by the interviewer directly into the computer system thus simplifying the tabulation problem. Each of these major developments will be considered at greater length in the following discussion of the factors which determine which method of data collection should be used in a given situation.

Information obtained.   Several studies have collected data by different methods (telephone, mail, personal interview) and have generally concluded that the information obtained by the various methods tends to be comparable. Nevertheless, there are some variations that should be noted.

Most people tend to respond more briefly to open questions over the telephone and it is difficult to hold their interest while the phone is "dead" when the interviewer is recording answers. It is desirable, therefore, to limit the number of questions which may require lengthy answers and to eliminate gaps in the conversation, perhaps by interviewers repeating answers, while they are writing them down.

Compared with personal interviews, telephone interviews produce more noncommittal answers than definite choices. People are reluctant to report over the telephone personal items such as family incomes, plans to buy a car, and use of installment credit, yet some studies have obtained such data successfully by telephone. When the nature of the survey requires probing on particular issues, for example, probing on problems encountered by the respondent in using a given product, respondents tend to give fewer responses over the telephone than when interviewed in person. For many years it was assumed that telephone surveys had to be limited to short questionnaires made up of questions which could be answered briefly. It is still true that telephone interviews tend to be shorter than those conducted face to face. Interviews taking up to 30 minutes, however, are frequently conducted by telephone.

Quality of information.   The quality of the information obtained in telephone interviews tends to be better than that from personal interviews because the interviewing process can be controlled and supervised better. The number of interviewers needed is fewer for telephone and they can be concentrated in a few locations, perhaps just one, even for national surveys. This makes it feasible for research organizations to employ full-time interviewing staffs, to train them well, and to supervise their work closely. This advantage of the telephone method is magnified by the WATS telephone service which makes it economically feasible to centralize telephone surveys even for national studies.

WATS provides unlimited telephone calls for 240 hours a month to a given zone of the United States for a fixed charge. Monthly charges from Chicago range from $1,150 for a five-state zone around the city to $1,660 for the entire country.[17] Using WATS, a small number of interviewers can make

---

[17] Illinois Bell Telephone Company.

a sizable survey quickly from one central location. The fixed line rental charge makes this feasible. The major benefits from using WATS are (1) accurate control of persons interviewed (the sample); (2) control over what the interviewers ask and how they ask it; and (3) control of the quality of the interviewing as measured in such things as number of refusals, interviews per hour, number of incomplete interviews, and amount of editing required on completed interviews. When planning is done so that WATS lines are used to capacity, the cost of surveys using WATS is about the same as for local telephone procedures.

Centralization of telephone interviewing also makes it feasible for research organizations to provide interviewers with CRT displays and computer control of questionnaires. The computer brings the questions on the CRT display in the proper sequence, even skipping questions when called for by the answer to a previous question. This reduces variation and error in presentation by the interviewers. The latter can enter the respondent's answers directly into the computer via a typewriter-like terminal. This greatly reduces the time and error involved in collecting, editing, coding, and tabulating results as compared to mail and personal interviews. The computerization process permits customizing and personalizing each interview which improves respondent rapport and quality of response. For example, at one point in the interview the respondent may report that she usually shops at the Jewel Food Store. Later the questionnaire may return to ask about the store and the computer will put the name Jewel Food in the question as it appears on the CRT display.

Telephone and personal interviews have another important advantage—they can be used to collect information on events at the time they are happening, thus reducing the errors resulting from failure of memory. Radio and television listening are often checked in this manner. Telephone interviews are particularly good in this respect as the speed with which they can be conducted permits a relatively large number of interviews during a short period, for example, the period during which a particular television program is on.

Control of sample.　On the surface it appears that telephone interviewing is ideally adapted to the selection of random samples. Lists of the population are available in telephone books and a routine procedure can be established for selecting names from these lists. This advantage of the telephone method does tend to be available, but the problem is more complex. About 4.5 million households do not have telephones. The proportion with telephones is steadily expanding, however, and now 95 percent of all homes have telephones. Ownership varies among income groups. Virtually all families with incomes over $25,000 have phones, but only 80 percent of those with family incomes below $4,000, in the South and in rural areas, have phones. For most marketing research studies the loss of those without telephones is probably not important, but for some special studies the homes without telephones could be significant.

A greater problem than nontelephone homes is the growing number of homes with unlisted telephone numbers. Nationally, about 20 percent of all households with telephones have unlisted numbers, but this figure becomes 30 percent in major metropolitan areas. In Chicago it is estimated that 33 percent of the residential telephones are unlisted and another 13 percent are "directory assistance only."[18] Thus, 46 percent of the residential phones in Chicago are not in the phone book. In addition to being high in large cities, the incidence of unlisted phone numbers is twice as high among non-whites as whites and higher in households with three or more persons and in households with one or more children.[19]

This large number of unlisted telephones would probably have limited the growth in collection of data by telephone were it not for the development of a method of selecting phone numbers randomly whether they are listed or not. This procedure, called Random Digit Dialing (RDD), is based on the fact that all telephone numbers are a subset of all possible ten-digit numbers (area code—three digits; exchange—three digits; number—four digits). A computer can be used to generate a series of random ten-digit numbers, a process that will give every phone number, listed or unlisted, an equal chance of being selected.

RDD is not as simple, however, as the above suggests. Only about 1 out of every 200 numbers generated in the above way will be a residential number. If the area codes are restricted to just the 103 such areas in the continental United States, the production of "good" numbers rises to about 1 in 20. This can be improved to a 1 in 5 probability with knowledge of the working exchange numbers and further improved with knowledge of the blocks of numbers currently in use by the various exchanges. Multiple listings and business and professional numbers further complicate the sampling problem and require special procedures.

A different approach to the unlisted number problem is to select listed numbers from directories at random and then add a standard number, say 3, to get the number actually dialed.

These methods, while somewhat cumbersome, provide good control of the sample selection process and provide a probability sample of telephone households.

Response rates.   Once a sample of telephone homes has been selected, it is still necessary to secure the desired information from those homes. Some homes will not be reached even if repeated calls are made and others will refuse to cooperate when contact is made. On the average, 40 percent of the telephone households selected to be in the sample are never reached in telephone surveys. Of the 60 percent that are reached, over 25 percent refuse to cooperate. The net result is that the average telephone survey col-

---

[18] Donald Zochert, "Unlisted Phones: It's Privacy by Numbers," *Chicago Daily News* (October 3, 1977):13.

[19] "A Better, More Cost-Efficient Telephone Sample," *The Nielsen Researcher* 2 (1978):10.

lects data from only about 45 percent of the households selected for the sample.[20]

If those not reached by phone and those who refused to cooperate were no different from the other households in the sample, this nonresponse rate would not be of major concern. If repeated efforts are not made to reach the households designated in the sample, the following groups will be overrepresented:

Over-64 age group.

Low-education group.

Low-income group.

Respondents with home related
    occupations.

Those outside large cities.

To reduce the not-at-home bias most organizations call back several times —three or four callbacks are common, but as many as eight may be made for specific studies. Four callbacks typically reduces the number not reached to about 20 percent. One researcher reports reaching 98.4 pecent of a selected sample of over 10,000 after making seven callbacks, but this is a higher percentage of success than is usual.[21] The rate of successful contact can be increased by calling at night.

Not-at-homes are somewhat lower in telephone surveys than in personal interviews at home because some people who will not answer the door to a stranger will answer the telephone. Of course, interviews made in shopping centers do not have this problem. Most investigators report lower refusal rates in telephone surveys than in personal interviews, but this can vary. Surveys on intimate and controversial topics tend to get larger refusal rates when done by telephone. A letter in advance significantly lowers refusal rates.

Time factor.   Telephone interviews are by far the fastest of the three methods of data collection. With short questionnaires as many as 20 calls per hour can be made. Interviewers calling at homes cannot approach that figure even if working in a small geographical area. Personal interviews in shopping centers can approach the speed of telephone in the data collection process, but the editing, coding, and tabulating process typically takes several weeks whereas computer-controlled telephone studies have the data entered into the computer during the interview and preliminary reports can be available within a day or two after completion of the interviews.

---

[20] Frederick Wiseman and Philip McDonald, *The Nonresponse Problem in Consumer Telephone Surveys* (Cambridge, Mass.: Marketing Science Institute, 1978), p. 3 ff.

[21] Glen H. Mitchell, *Telephone Interviewing* (Wooster, Ohio: Ohio Agricultural Experiment Station, undated), p. 7.

Cost. The number of man-hours involved tends to determine the cost of most surveys—especially for personal and telephone interviews. The administrative problems of quality control are another factor. Since both man-hours and administrative problems tend to be less for telephone than for personal interviews, the former tends to be cheaper.

Table 4–3 shows typical field costs for the various data collection methods. While the telephone tends to be relatively cheap, this is a tendency only. In a study of food purchases where each homemaker completed a long questionnaire, the telephone was found to be no cheaper generally than a system of delivering the questionnaire and picking it up. Telephone interviews were conducted everyday whereas the self-administered diaries were delivered and picked up once a week.[22]

Personal interviews

As already indicated, the personal interview is the most versatile and flexible of the three communication methods. Projects which involve the use of props such as product samples or copies of advertisements or which require the interviewer to make observations at the time of the interview are almost limited to the use of personal interviews. Unstructured questioning and long difficult questionnaires are more effective when handled by personal interviews. Shopping center interviewing, particularly when the research organization has a "store" in which to conduct the interviews, is particularly advantageous when the interviewer needs to show things such as in package evaluations, taste tests, and advertising pretests.

During the interview itself, the presence of the interviewer permits flexibility in procedure. The questioning can be adapted to the situation, further explanations or clarifications can be requested if desired, mechanical aids or displays can be used, also sets of cards can be given to the respondent for sorting. The respondent can be questioned on the brands in the pantry.

Unfortunately, these advantages of the personal interview tend to be more than offset by the high cost of door-to-door interviewing and by sampling problems in shopping center interviewing. At one time personal interviewing in the home was the dominant method of collecting data, but cost differentials are leading to more use of telephone interviews. Interviewing respondents in shopping centers reduces the costs as compared to home interviews, but makes it impossible to control the sample in a way required for many studies. Even the flexibility inherent in personal interviews is not as advantageous as it seems. Relatively little advantage is taken of the possibilities because variations by interviewers may bias the results.

A further advantage to projects using personal and telephone interviews is that such projects can be stopped or altered at any point during the study.

---

[22] Seymour Sudman and Robert Ferber, "A Comparison of Alternative Procedures for Collecting Consumer Expenditure Data for Frequently Purchased Products," *Journal of Marketing Research* 11 (May 1974):134.

Such is not possible with a mail study. Once the questionnaires are mailed, such a study is committed, and the sample or the questionnaire cannot be changed.

Information obtained.   Both quantity and quality of information obtained are important. Most commercial research organizations operate on the assumption that long questionnaires (that is, large quantities of data) can best be handled by personal interview, next best by mail, and least well by telephone. Although this is a sound principle, there is increasing evidence that the latter two are less limited in length than has been assumed. The University of Michigan Survey Research Center, however, limits its telephone interviews to 11 minutes in length; personal interviews may run to 75 minutes.[23] The time that an interview can run, however, is determined at least as much by the clarity of each question, the perceived relevance to the topic, and the lack of redundancy as by the method of communication.

In some cases, it is desirable to combine questioning and observation in collecting the basic data. To find out whether or not homemakers know the brand of coffee they use, a combination of methods might be used. First interviewers could inquire as to what brand was being used. Then they could seek permission to observe the brand in the pantry. Interviewer observations of the quality of the interview, that is, the respondents' apparent knowledge of the subject and their willingness to cooperate, are sometimes helpful in interpretation of results.

Accuracy of information.   It is generally assumed that the personal interview obtains the most accurate information of any of the three methods, but there is little empirical evidence that proves this. Well-conducted studies have been found to obtain similar data from the same respondents whatever method of communication was used. One national study found the data obtained on demographic variables and on public policy opinions to be essentially the same whether it was collected by telephone or personal interview at home.[24] Another experiment compared the reporting of hospitalization experiences by personal interview and by mail with actual hospital records. Little difference was found, but if anything, the mail results were more accurate.[25]

Respondents report they enjoy personal interviews more than mail questionnaires and the latter more than telephone interviews. Respondents over the telephone show more suspicion, ask more frequently how much longer the interview will take, and give much shorter answers to open questions than do respondents in personal interviews. People are usually found to be reluctant to report over the telephone personal items such as family income,

---

[23] Jay W. Schmiedeskamp, "Reinterviews by Telephone," *Journal of Marketing* 26 (January 1962):30.

[24] See, for example, Groves and Kahn, *Surveys.*

[25] Charles Cannell and Floyd Fowler, "Comparison of a Self-Enumerative Procedure and a Personal Interview," *Public Opinion Quarterly* 27 (Summer 1963):250–64.

use of installment credit, or plans to buy a car, but some studies find more accurate reporting of such sensitive issues over the phone.

Influence of interviewer.   The presence of the interviewer undoubtedly has some effect on the accuracy of data obtained; the effect may be in both directions. It is more tense when interviewers are present in person than when they are on the telephone. When an interviewer is present, it is hard for respondents to report incorrectly if the environment does not support their statements (for example, do they live in a house or an apartment). Interviewers can probe and explain when they think it is useful and they can do this better in person than on the telephone.

On the other hand, much effort is often put to limiting the interviewer in adapting to individual interviews. The interaction between interviewer and respondent may bias the respondent's replies, and the personal interests and attitudes of interviewers will cause them to interpret responses differently.

Personal interviews at home can have a positive effect on the accuracy of information obtained by asking respondents to check the specific brands they may have on hand rather than relying on memory. Mail permits more flexibility on the part of the respondent in this regard, but does not provide the same degree of motivation. Telephone interviews presumably have the same advantage as home interviews in this regard, but most researchers do not want to send respondents away from the telephone because some won't come back.

A final consideration on the quality of information obtained is that of cheating on the part of interviewers. Personal interviewers, whether working door-to-door or in shopping centers, work alone and under little supervision in most cases. Some are tempted to fill in questionnaires in full or in part without completing the interviews. Procedures for checkbacks with respondents and for testing patterns of responses enable most well-planned studies to minimize cheating, but telephone interviewing which is done at centralized locations and under direct supervision provides the best control.

Control of sample.   The largest difference among the three methods of communication is in the amount of control they permit over the sample from which information is collected. A method is weak if it does not permit objective designation of the individuals from whom data are obtained. There are two elements involved: the original designation of individuals or organizations from whom it is proposed to obtain information and the determination of the individuals, if any, from whom information is actually obtained. The first element will be considered here while the second element will be considered in the following section on response rates.

Theoretically it is easy to designate a precise probability sample of consumers for a study using personal interviews at home since all members of the population can be reached with this method. In practice, however, it is usually necessary to have a list of all members of the universe, if a representative sample is to be obtained. For most large universes such as all consumers in the United States or even all homemakers in St. Louis, such lists are not available. It is possible to substitute lists of areas, for example, city blocks and so to obtain adequate samples, but to do so for a national project is difficult, time consuming, and expensive.[26] Few marketing research studies now use personal interviews with such elaborate area samples. Where lists of the universe to be studied are available (for example, the charge account customers of a department store), strict sample control is feasible.

When personal interviews are made at shopping center locations, no good control of the sample is possible. Usually respondents are selected at different locations within the shopping center, at different hours of the day, and on different days of the week. Nevertheless, samples selected at shopping malls are composed of respondents who are much younger than the average, are more likely to have children under 18, and have higher than average incomes.

Response rate. Obtaining data from all the individuals designated for a sample is impossible for all practical purposes. In fact, information is seldom obtained by personal interview from more than 90 percent of the designated sample and completion rates between 65 percent and 85 percent are typical for studies which use an original call and two callbacks.[27]

Problems of collecting data from the designated sample are of two types: finding the individuals and inducing them to provide the information. Door-to-door interviewers are finding increasing problems in obtaining interviews in high-rise apartments, many of which control entry to the building. Further problems arise from not-at-homes. The growing number of families with two working parents increases the not-at-home problem. Personal interviews are limited to the period between 8:00 A.M. and 9:00 P.M. During much of that time only about 57 percent of all households have any person over 14 years of age at home.[28]

By timing calls to fit the times when respondents are most apt to be home, the not-at-home problem can be minimized, but is still sizable. Callbacks at other times and other days will find more of the designated individuals, but callbacks are expensive.

Refusals tend to average about 10 percent in personal interviews whether made at home or in shopping centers. Interviewers rely primarily in their sales ability to convince individuals to cooperate with a study. Most projects provide a specified introductory statement that is designed to help secure cooperation, but the interviewer's presence is the important factor.

Since individuals who are not at home or who refuse to cooperate may well be different from those who are cooperative, the problem of nonresponse can cause significant error in results. Personal interviews are considered the strongest of the three methods in coping with the problem.

Obtaining data from the specific individuals selected for the sample is so

---

[26] This, and other, sampling procedures are discussed in more detail in Chapters 10 and 11.

[27] Charles S. Mayer, "Data Collection Methods: Personal Interviews" in Robert Ferber, *Handbook of Marketing Research*, pp. 2–82 to 2–89.

[28] Bureau of the Census, U.S. Department of Commerce, *Who's Home When*, working paper 37 (Washington, D.C.: U.S. Government Printing Office, 1973).

important in obtaining accurate results that various measures of success in this regard are often considered measures of the quality of the data collection process. Several measures used in this way are:[29]

1. Percentage of refusals.
2. Percentage of completed interviews.
3. Number of callbacks required to locate respondent.
4. Average number of interviews per hour.
5. Percentage of questionnaires that have to be returned for editing.
6. Supervisor rating of interview process.

All these factors are primarily related to telephone and personal interviews. The first five can be measured in both types of studies. Fieldwork assignments vary in personal interviews (high-rise apartments, slums, or rural areas, for example), so that comparison of interviewers is questionable and time lags between field locations and the central office make it difficult to correct weaknesses. Supervision of the actual interview process is almost impossible with personal interviews. When telephone interviewers all work at a central location, each can be given an assignment comparable with the others, and supervisors can listen to the actual interviews. Corrections can be made quickly.

Time factor.   The administrative problems of planning and controlling fieldwork are large for personal interviews made at home. The elapsed time from the beginning of fieldwork to the completion of the project is lengthy. Once the sampling locations have been selected, researchers must select interviewers convenient to those locations. Often new interviewers must be recruited and trained. Materials must be distributed to the interviewers, schedules set, and supervision maintained to insure that the work is being done properly and on schedule. Except for small studies done in one or a few locations, personal interview studies are almost always longer in elapsed time than mail or telephone studies. This is not true of shopping center interviews for which the field work can be done almost as rapidly as by telephone for some studies.

Cost.   Personal interviews require the most interviewers and take the longest time. As a result, they are expensive. Typical costs per interview for the various methods of communication are shown in Table 4–3.

Mail surveys[30]

There is no interviewer in mail surveys to explain the purpose and to induce cooperation, to ask the questions, to record the answers, and in gen-

---

[29] J. O. Eastlack, Jr. and Henry Assael, "Better Telephone Surveys through Centralized Interviewing," *Journal of Advertising Research* 6 (March 1966):4.

[30] The following discussion draws heavily on Paul L. Erdos, "Data Collection Methods: Mail Surveys," in Robert Ferber, *Handbook of Marketing Research,* pp. 2–90 to 2–104; Arnold S. Linsky, "Stimulating Responses to Mailed Questionnaires: A Review," *Public Opinion Quarterly* 39 (1975):82–101; and Thomas Danbury, "Large-Scale Mail Surveys of the General Population," paper presented to the Advertising Research Foundation (New York: October 19, 1976).

eral to cope with any problems. This is the main difference between mail and the other two methods. It puts a great deal of importance on the construction of the questionnaire and any transmittal letters which may accompany it.

Mail cannot be used to conduct an unstructured study where an interviewer is relied on to improvise the questioning as each interview progresses. Personal and telephone interviews are also more flexible in that they can be stopped or altered at any point, whereas once a mail survey is put in the mail the researcher can only let it run its course.

Mail surveys are particularly versatile in reaching all types of people, in all geographic areas, in rural or urban areas at the same cost. On the other hand, while mail may make it easy to reach a particular group, and only that group, this is true only where a mailing list is available. Members of specific organizations or all licensed automobile owners are examples where such lists are available. The purchasers of a particular product can be reached by attaching questionnaires to the product package and subscribers to particular magazines or newspapers can be reached by including questionnaires in the publications.

Information obtained.   Many commercial research organizations operate on the rule that questionnaires longer than six pages should not be used to collect data by mail. This seems to fit with common sense, but a number of experiments suggest that longer questionnaires can be used effectively by mail. Questionnaires as long as 32 pages or containing 1,100 questions have been used successfully. Evidence suggests that the manner in which the proposition is presented and the appearance of the first page may have more to do with completing the questionnaire than does length.

From a specific respondent, a mail questionnaire probably produces as good or better information than personal or telephone interviews where an interviewer can bias the results. The Bureau of the Census has shifted from the use of personal interviews to mail surveys because it believes they provide ". . . more reliable answers supplied directly by respondents instead of through a more or less inhibiting intermediary, the enumerator."[31]

Mail questionnaires have been shown to be generally superior to either telephone or personal interviews in collecting data on topics that might be embarrassing. Data from one of the best studies of this problem are shown in Table 4–4. Even though the questions asked appear to be only mildly embarrassing at most, the differences in answers obtained by mail and by personal interview are large.

Sequence bias is also a threat in mail surveys—respondents can change their answers after seeing later questions. This bias may not be as great as it is usually thought to be. In an experiment to determine the extent of sequence bias, a questionnaire was loaded with references to a particular brand of gasoline before a question as to the brand of gasoline used. Only a

---

[31] Bureau of the Census, U.S. Department of Commerce, *Planning Notes for 1970 Decennial Census,* (Washington, D.C.: U.S. Government Printing Office, 1966), p. 2.

TABLE 4–4. Responses to the same questions by mail and personal interview

Subject	Personal interview	Mail
Have used hair rinse	37%	51%
Have used eye shadow	46	59
Have purchaser margarine	75	82
Have borrowed money at regular bank	17	42
Have borrowed money at credit union	16	22
Have borrowed money at small loan company	11	13
Sample size	200	100

Source: William F. O'Dell, "Personal Interviews or Mail Panels," *Journal of Marketing* 26 (October 1962):34–39.

6 percent increase in the proportion reporting use of the specified brand occurred with the mail questionnaire.[32]

In answering open-ended questions, that is, questions which respondents must answer in their own words, respondents tend to be more brief and more general in mail surveys than in personal or telephone interviews. Complex questions with rating scales or other procedures that can be confusing tend to draw more "no answers" in mail surveys.

Control of sample. To conduct a mail survey it is necessary to have a mailing list. Since it is almost always prohibitively expensive to create one for a specific project, established lists are used. Typical lists are city directories, telephone directories, real estate tax lists, car registration lists, business directories, subscription lists, and organization membership lists. A list approximating the general U.S. household population is maintained by Reuben H. Donnelley Corporation. It consists of 64 million households (almost 90 percent of all 72 million households) and was developed by merging a list of the 53 million households shown in the 4,700 telephone directories and the 47 million households having autos registered (only 40 states release such registration lists). Each household is classified on the basis of about 60 different variables (actual or estimated). A number of firms now provide established mail panels—lists of families that have agreed to answer mail questionnaires on almost any topic. These panels are set up to be representative of the population on various characteristics, but there is always the fact that only about one family in five will join such a panel, which suggests that those that would not join may differ in some respects from the others.

For some universes, such as charge card customers, complete lists of the universe are available, but for many studies the universe of interest has to be approximated from more general groups such as those described above. The households to which questionnaires are sent are known and controlled

---

[32] William F. O'Dell, "Personal Interviews or Mail Panels," *Journal of Marketing* 26 (October 1962): 34–39.

at a central location, but 8 to 12 percent of general mailings are not delivered for a variety of reasons.

Response rate. For many years mail surveys were suspect because of low response rates, often below 25 percent, which made users suspect that those who returned the questionnaires were different from the rest of the universe. Most well-run general population surveys now get 50 percent or greater return and surveys of special groups, such as recent purchasers of recreational vehicles, often get over 90 percent return. The established mail panels maintained by commercial research firms are made up of individuals who have agreed to participate in surveys; returns from mailings to them, therefore, routinely produce very high rates of return, but one is uncertain as to how representative the returns are. These rates of return make mail surveys very competitive with the other methods of communication in this regard. Table 4–5 shows response rates by the various communication methods from selected population groups as reported by one research organization. The response rate on mail surveys was larger than on the other methods for almost everyone of the 52 population groups reported. The exceptions were for households in which the head had only a grade school education, in which the annual income was under $5,000, which were located in black neighborhoods, or which consisted of a widowed woman.

TABLE 4–5. Survey response rates according to various methods of communication by selected population groups

Population group	Mail	Tele- phone	Personal interviews Door- to-door	Shopping centers
Single family home	65.8%	52.1%	50.9%	58.5%
Mobile homes	48.5	39.2	29.5	44.9
Male	65.1	54.7	53.6	59.4
Female	61.8	45.3	59.6	56.6
Grade school education	50.7	45.3	58.0	57.6
College graduate	68.0	54.6	53.2	57.9
Income under $5,000	60.8	46.8	65.0	63.0
Income over $25,000	68.9	54.6	52.7	55.0
Married	64.8	53.5	54.6	58.8
Widowed	55.8	51.3	57.8	63.4
In black neighborhood	52.9	72.6	75.9	81.4

Source: Thomas Danbury, "Surveys in America," paper presented to the Advertising Research Foundation (New York: October 18, 1977).

Another portion, probably small, of the returns received from mail questionnaires have been filled out by some member of the family other than the one for whom it was intended, by a secretary, or some other unknown person.

There is evidence that the results from a mail survey with a 40 percent return are, in most cases, the same as the results after 60 or 80 percent return. It is increasingly expensive to increase the return by sending a second, third, fourth or more additional mailings to those who haven't responded. Table 4–6 shows a typical result of three waves of mailings. The percentage of return drops with each mailing and the cost per return doubles. For this reason some researchers question the desirability of pressing for returns beyond 50 pecent.

TABLE 4–6. Cost per return for repeated mailings

	Wave 1	Wave 2	Wave 3
Number mailed out	1,000	605	486
Returned questionnaires	395	119	44
Percent returned	40%	20%	9%
Cost of mail-out	$1,400	$847	$680
Cost per return	$3.54	$7.12	$15.45

Source: Danbury, "Large-Scale Mail Surveys," p. 15.

If it is possible to increase the response rate on the first mailing, the cost will tend to be less per return. There is a large and steadily growing literature on methods of doing this. Some results are conflicting, but the methods can generally be classified in three categories: general motivation, direct incentive, and mechanical and perceptual means.

General motivation.   The best motivation respondents can have to complete a mail questionnaire is their interest in it. Table 4–7 illustrates how widely returns will vary among segments of the survey population when their interest in the subject varies. Obviously, if some of the segments differed significantly in their opinions on the subject under investigation, such large differences in rate of response would bias the general results.

Since the subject of a given survey cannot be changed to fit each respondent's interest, it is important to make the questionnaire as interesting as possible. An interesting title and first questions are generally believed to be important, but there is no clear evidence of the effect these have. All researchers try to make the questionnaire attractive by printing on good quality paper and leaving plenty of white space. Some use paper of various colors.

TABLE 4–7. Returns of mail questionnaires on value of audit committees by various population segments

Population group	Questionnaires mailed	Questionnaires returned	Percentage returned
Chief executive officers	1,732	420	24%
Nonofficer directors	1,950	245	13
Independent CPAs	186	140	75
Internal auditors	51	37	65
Total	3,919	842	21%

Source: R. F. Mautz and F. L. Neumann, "The Effective Corporate Audit Committee," *Harvard Business Review* 48 (November-December 1970):58.

Experiments indicate that none of these make much difference within reasonable alternatives.

Most researchers believe it is important to develop a "personalization" of the survey, that is, to make respondents feel there is some personal connection between themselves and the researcher or research organization. At the same time most researchers feel that one advantage of the mail questionnaire is that it can be made relatively anonymous. Obviously, these two efforts are at cross purposes. Some studies show distinctly larger returns for questionnaires identified only by number as compared to those identified by name, but some show little such effect. Personalization, the opposite of anonymity, is achieved through cover letters sent with questionnaires and by having questionnaires signed or otherwise identified with the specific respondent. Cover letters can be personalized by addressing the respondent by name and hand signing them. This adds significantly to the cost, but cannot be counted on to increase returns by much; some tests have shown personalization actually reduced returns. If respondents are being assured their replies will be anonymous, a personalized letter may reduce the researchers credibility.

Direct incentives.   Cash enclosed with the questionnaire, a promise of cash if a completed questionnaire is returned, or a premium enclosed are the direct incentives used to obtain completion of mail questionnaires. Cash awards always seem to increase returns; numerous studies show the number of respondents not replying is reduced an average of one third. Table 4–8 shows some typical results.

Table 4–8 indicates that the larger the incentive, the larger the return. It is not clear what the optimum amount is. Some believe 50 cents to $1 may be the most productive. Promises of cash payments for returned questionnaires have almost no impact on returns. Almost any type of premium included with the questionnaire tends to increase returns. Trading stamps, ballpoint pens, pencils, flat packages of coffee, and lottery tickets suggest the variety of premiums that can be used.

Cash payments or premiums obviously increase the costs of a survey, but the important cost measure is the cost per completed questionnaire. It appears that cash payments probably produce a given proportion of returns

TABLE 4–8. Percentage of sample responding to mail questionnaires with different prepaid cash incentives

Study		Incentive				
	None	$0.01	$0.05	$0.10	$0.25	$1.00
A	22%					70%
B	40			54%	63%	
C	23				40	54
D	52	55%	54%	57	70	

Source: J. S. Armstrong, "Monetary Incentives in Mail Surveys," *Public Opinion Quarterly* 39 (Spring 1975):112.

somewhat more cheaply than follow-up letters and other efforts to get nonrespondents to cooperate.

Mechanical and perceptual devices. There are many mechanical and perceptual devices that can be used to increase returns on mail surveys. Contact with the respondents before they receive the questionnaire telling them of the research and its purpose and requesting cooperation tends to increase returns. Telephone contact is the most effective, but letters and postcards are also effective.

The method of mailing affects the return. First class mail gets better results than third class; special delivery and registered mail bring even better results. In case of the latter two, it is desirable to include some explanation for the special handling. One study obtained a 66 percent return on special delivery, 60 percent on airmail, and 52 percent on first class.

Return envelopes result in larger returns; one study obtained only 26 percent return with no return envelope, but got 90 percent return when a stamped return envelope was enclosed. Another study obtained 26 percent return with a stamped envelope as compared to 17 percent with an unstamped return envelope. In general, hand-stamped return envelopes bring greater returns than metered envelopes.

To obtain a good return it is usually necessary to have a follow-up campaign to those who do not reply to the first mailing. This is expensive as pointed out above; some question whether it would not be wiser to expand the size of the original mailing. When follow-ups are used, the first is usually done by mail and includes another questionnaire with another request that it be completed and returned. This is sent as soon as returns begin to dwindle. If a choice must be made between a precontact letter and a follow-up letter, the latter is preferred. When a high return is particularly desired, additional follow-ups may be made by telephone, telegram, or special delivery. These bring results, but several additional waves of follow-up letters could be sent for the same cost and probably would bring results as good. Three studies that have reported essentially 100 percent returns, however, used intensive follow-ups by telephone, telegram, and special delivery.

Time factor. If research results must be obtained in hours or even days, mail is not the data collection method to use. Once questionnaires are put in the mail, the researcher can do nothing to change the character of the response process and little to speed it up. A period of two weeks is usually necessary to receive the bulk of the returns from one mailing. If a follow-up letter is sent, another two weeks is required. Some researchers are now finding they can speed this up by sending the follow-up after only one week. Very large samples can be covered by mail in the same period required for small samples.

Cost. Improved methods which now provide returns of 70 percent on many surveys have changed the relative cost of collecting data by mail as compared to telephone and personal interview. On the average, mail surveys are probably the cheapest per completed interview of the various methods although on many specific studies telephone will be cheaper. Mail is almost always cheaper than personal, door-to-door interviews. Typical relative costs are shown in Table 4–2.

Selection of method to use

The use of either telephone, mail, or personal interviews involves advantages and disadvantages. Fundamentally, however, the decision to use one or the other method is based on thinking as to the accuracy of the information which will be obtained. If the same results will be achieved by each method of collecting data, the decision can be made on the basis of cost or speed.

OBSERVATIONAL METHOD

Observation is the second method of collecting data. It is the process of recognizing and noting people, objects, and occurrences rather than asking for information. For example, instead of asking consumers what brands they buy or what television programs they view, the researcher arranges to observe what products are bought and what programs are watched. Very few of the "one-shot" research projects done in marketing are of this type— perhaps no more than 1 percent. Some of the major continuing services, however, such as the Nielsen Television Index of television viewing do use observation methods. The coming development of the Universal Product Code and scanning at supermarket checkout counters, moreover, may make observation a much more important method of collecting data than it has been.

Advantages and disadvantages of observation

Some of the advantages of this method of collecting data as compared to the questionnaire method are obvious. If the researcher observes and records events, it is not necessary to rely on the willingness and ability of respondents to report accurately. Furthermore, the biasing effect of interviewers or their phrasing of questions is either eliminated or reduced. Data collected by observation are, therefore, more objective and generally more accurate. Several comparisons of observation and questionnaire data were presented in the early part of this chapter showing the relative accuracy of the observation method.

Unfortunately, the observational method also has a number of weaknesses which keep it from being more widely used. Researchers have long recognized the merits of observation as opposed to questioning, yet the vast majority of marketing research projects continue to rely on the questionnaire. Probably the most limiting factor in the use of observation is the inability to observe such things as attitudes, motivations, and plans. Only as these factors are reflected in actions can they be observed, and then they are confounded with so many other factors as to make their identification difficult, if not impossible.

Events of more than short-term duration also pose observational problems. For example, a family's use of leisure time, frequency of visits to the drugstore, or the use of hotels or motels on the last trip are items which do not lend themselves to observation. Personal and intimate activities such as brushing teeth and watching television late at night are more easily discussed with questionnaires than they are observed.

On the other hand, there are some things which can be observed, but which cannot be reported with any accuracy by respondents. Tone of voice, nervous habits, and spatial relationships in interpersonal encounters are examples of things of which most people are too unaware to report accurately, but which can be observed.

Observation eliminates much of the subjective element encountered with questionnaires, but it is not entirely objective. Observers are still necessary in most cases and, being human, they are subject to error. Many times these observers are well trained and are required to record only facts in which they have no personal interest. Results under these circumstances should be objective and accurate. In other studies, however, observers may be active participants and, therefore, may not be objective reporters. For example, observers may go into a store acting as customers. They are to observe the activities of the salesclerk. This involves interaction between the two. Different observers might interact differently with the salesclerk; the results obtained will have subjective elements.

In some observational studies, it is impractical to keep respondents from knowing that they are being observed. This results in a biasing effect similar to the one found in questionnaire studies. If respondents know their actions are being observed, they are apt to act differently than they otherwise would.

Cost is a final disadvantage of observation. Under most circumstances, observational data are more expensive to obtain than survey data. It is necessary to station observers where they can see the pertinent phenomena. Frequently, this requires the observer to wait, doing nothing, between events to be observed. For example, to observe the consumers who ask for a specific brand of canned milk, an observer would have to wait in a store until customers came in for canned milk. This unproductive time is an increased cost.

Modern technology, however, is providing more and more methods for observing by machine with both increased accuracy and decreased labor costs. The mechanical scanning of Universal Product Codes at checkout stations and the "observation" by audimeters of TV shows turned on are examples.

Methods of observation

Observational studies[33] can be classified usefully on five bases: (1) whether the situation in which the observation is made is natural or con-

---

[33] The following discussion draws heavily on E. J. Webb, D. T. Campbell, K. D. Schwartz, and Lee Sechrest, *Unobstrusive Measures: Nonreactive Research in the Social Sciences* (Chicago: Rand McNally, 1966).

trived, (2) whether the observation is obtrusive or unobtrusive, (3) whether the observation is structured or unstructured, (4) whether the factor of interest is observed directly or indirectly, and (5) whether observations are made by observers or by mechanical means. Various combinations of these bases are used to establish the following classes.

Natural, direct, unobtrusive observation. When an observer is stationed in a grocery store to note how many different brands of canned soup each shopper picks up before selecting one, there is unobtrusive, direct observation in a natural situation. If the observer looks and acts like another shopper, the regular shoppers do not realize they are being observed. If a camera is positioned to record shopping actions, the observation is by mechanical means. If the observer counts the specific cans picked up, the observation is structured; but if the observer has a less clear assignment, such as to observe how shoppers go about selecting a brand of soup, the situation is unstructured.

Structured direct observation is used when the problem at hand has been formulated precisely enough to enable researchers to define specifically the observations to be made. Observers in a supermarket, for example, might note the number of different cans of soup picked up by each customer buying soup. Such observations are not as apt to have a subjective bias by observers as are unstructured observations. A form can be easily printed for simple recording of such observations. Even if the observers must wait for an unnoticed moment to record each observation, they are not apt to have as much bias in their memory as with unstructured observations. Not all structured observations are as simple as this example, but experiments have shown that even observers with different points of view on a given question will tend to make similar observations under structured conditions.

Unstructured, direct observation is similar to unstructured questioning; observers are placed in situations and observe whatever they deem pertinent. For example, in an effort to find ways of improving the service in a retail store, observers may mingle with customers in the store and look for activities that suggest service problems. Such observation is subject to subjective errors in both the actual observation and recording. No one can observe everything that is going on; hence, the observer must select certain things to note. The actual observation also has subjective elements because of the difficulty of separating observation from inference; customers standing at a counter with annoyed looks on their faces may be observed as irritated because of lack of service. The latter inference follows so easily from the observation that it may not be separated from it.

The following is the report of one out of a large number of observations of shopping behavior in supermarkets:[34]

---

[34] W. D. Wells and L. A. LoScuito, "Direct Observation of Purchasing Behavior," *Journal of Marketing Research* (August 1966):227.

A school-age boy and his parents enter the aisle.

The parents hurry down the aisle, looking straight ahead and not even glancing at the cereals.

"Can't I have some cereal?" asks the boy very winningly.

"No," answers the father very sternly, and quickly continues up the aisle.

"You dirty crumb," is the boy's reply as he walks up the aisle with his head lowered.

This is a somewhat dramatic observation. Did the drama cause the observer to overlook more mundane aspects of the family's behavior? Would similar adjectives have been used by other observers to describe the behavior? The example suggests the possibilities for observer bias. In this particular study, the researchers found two major problems: (1) to get observers to record their observations in detail and (2) to prepare permanent records of observations at the earliest opportunity. Extensive training was necessary to overcome these problems. The second problem above is common to observations where an effort is made to keep the observer unnoticed. In such cases, the observer cannot easily record the data except from memory—another invitation to error.

Sampling is another problem common to natural observation studies. Because it is necessary to let events happen as they do naturally, it is often difficult to get a cross-sectional sample. Efforts are usually made to sample at different geographical locations (for example, different stores) and to make a representative sampling of time periods.

Contrived observation. When researchers rely on natural direct observation, they frequently find observers have a great deal of waste time while they wait for the desired event to happen. To reduce this problem, it may be desirable to contrive situations so that observations may be made more efficiently. To study the bargaining that goes on between automobile sales people and customers, for example, researchers may have their observers pose as customers and take various bargaining attitudes from the most-eager-to-buy to the toughest price-seeking. In each case, the observer would note the sales person's response. As long as the sales person believes the researcher to be a *bona fide* customer, there is no bias in the observation. It is often much easier for the observer-customer to maintain a natural situation than for an intruder-observer to do so. As a result, contrived observations often have a validity advantage as well as an economic one.

Mechanical observation. In the discussion of both natural direct observation and contrived observation, it was assumed that humans were used as observers. A number of imaginative methods of mechanical observation and devices for making such observations have been developed. The most widely known device of this type is the audimeter, a device used by the A. C. Nielsen Company to record when radio and television sets are turned on and the stations to which they are tuned. The tape on which this information is recorded is mailed at regular intervals to the Nielsen Company, where it is analyzed. The newest generation of this system uses the Storage Instantaneous Audimeter. This device automatically stores in electronic memory data on television stations tuned in. Nielsen has a central computer which dials these memories on the telephone twice a day and collects the information from them.

Another device for making observations is the psychogalvanometer. This machine measures minute emotional reactions through changes in the rate of perspiration, much like a lie detector. Advertisements can be tested for relative impact by showing them to respondents and measuring the emotional response of the respondent on the galvanometer. More recently a computer-based technique for analyzing changes in voice pitch has been found effective in measuring changes in emotional reaction. This has been used to test reactions to advertisements and to new products.

The eye-camera is a device to record the movements of the eye. A respondent can be given an advertisement and the eye-camera can then be used to record the movements of the eye in looking at the ad—what parts are noted first, in what sequence the various copy blocks are read, and what parts attract the longest attention. Similar analyses can be made of consumer reactions to packages or to pictures of many brands displayed on store shelves.

The eye camera, voice pitch, and psychogalvanometer tend to be limited to laboratory settings; therefore, questions are raised as to the bias of observation in unnatural circumstances and when respondents know they are being observed. The audimeter raises more subtle questions. This device is placed on the radio or television set in a manner that has no effect on the way these appliances are used. Even though the subjects can use their radios and television sets in a normal manner, there is some question whether or not they will be "natural" if they know they are being observed. Will the family that knows its television set has an audimeter on it watch the same programs, no more or no less, as it otherwise would? Research on this question indicates that whatever bias occurs when the audimeter is placed on the television set soon wears off. On the other hand, a small bias does occur because some families, ones who view television relatively little on the average, will not permit audimeters to be placed on their sets.

There is general belief that the greatest development in marketing research in the next decade will be the development of automated scanning of Universal Product Codes in supermarkets and perhaps later in other types of retail outlets. Manufacturers mark each package with a code that identifies the brand, package size, color, flavor, etc. At the checkout counter the clerk passes this code over a scanner which puts all the data into a computer where price is also stored. Theoretically every purchase is thus identified in some detail and summaries can be easily made.

By 1980 something over 1,000 supermarkets representing about 5 percent of total grocery store sales had scanning and the number was growing rapidly. One industry source estimates that scanning may be economically viable in stores with sales of $80,000 a week or more. Such stores do about half of all grocery sales and are the leading stores.[35] This means, of course, that insofar as sales in smaller stores are different, manufacturers will not have a complete picture of their sales. There are also many technical and organizational problems still to be worked on to make scanning data accurate. Every product must be coded, clerks must "scan" each item purchased, methods must be found for scanning cumbersome items such as 25-pound packages of dog food, and codes must be printed so that the equipment can read them correctly.

Further extensions of the opportunities brought by scanning are suggested by the service offered under the name BehaviorScan.[36] In two cities that receive all their TV by cable, 3,000 households have identification cards which are scanned along with their grocery purchases. Commercials on TV are controlled by a split cable so that half the households, for example, may see a Wheaties commercial and half a Cheerios commercial. This setup will permit close analysis of the effect of advertising on sales.

Indirect observation.   Methods discussed above are all direct observations of the factors of interest. One type of observation, however, focuses on the physical traces left by the factor of interest. These traces are of two types—accretions left or erosion that has resulted—similar in character to the delta built up at the mouth of a river as compared to a canyon carved by the same river. To define the trading area of cities, researchers have found it useful to observe the formations where farm roads enter the main highways leading to a city. Where the corners of these intersections have been rounded off the most on the side toward a given city, it is safe to assume that the majority of the time farmers entering the main highway are turning toward that city and are, in fact, a part of the city's trading area. At the point where the "round-off" begins to be more in the opposite direction, the farmers belong to the trading area of another city. When flying over an area, this breaking point between two trading areas can often be seen clearly.

Other accretion studies have involved the observation of liquor bottles in trash to estimate the liquor consumption in cities without package stores, and the determination of the best radio stations on which to advertise to car-listeners by observing the stations at which radios were set in the cars brought to a car dealer for repair. Brand preference studies are often based on observation of brands on consumer pantry shelves, and relative store emphasis on different brands is noted by observing the size of the inventory displayed.

Erosion observations are less frequent in marketing research, but examples are a study of the relative popularity of different museum displays done by observing the relative wear on floor tiles around the exhibits, and a study of the relative readership of different sections of an encyclopedia by measuring the wear and tear on the pages.

---

[35] "Turning Scanning Data into Information," *The Nielsen Researcher* (1979):2–7.

[36] "New 'BehaviorScan' System Ties Grocery Sales to TV Ads," *Marketing News* (September 21, 1979):7.

Observation of the results of past actions will not bias the data if done on a one-time basis. Pantry audits can determine what products have been bought previously. If such audits are made regularly, however, as with some store audits, biased data may result. It is rumored, for example, that manufacturers' sales representatives attempt to find the stores which are audited and put special sales effort on these stores. In this way they hope to make it appear that they are building large stocks with their retail store customers.

Observation of records.   Whenever researchers use data collected for another purpose, they are employing the observation method in a manner very similar in character to the observation of physical traces.[37] In one sense, the records of previous activities (for example, sales, inventories, newspaper accounts, population census, highway usage) are physical traces of previous periods. In recent years computerized warehouse inventory and movement data have become a major source of information on brand shares.

SUMMARY

If one wishes to find what people think or know, the logical procedure is to ask them. This has led marketing researchers to use the questionnaire technique for collecting data more than any other method.

It is not as easy as it might appear, however, to collect facts or opinions from people. Unless the point of interest has been impressed on respondents' minds very recently, they are apt to have trouble remembering it exactly. Another problem is the unwillingness of some people to answer questions from strangers. Different wordings of questions will often obtain different results; yet there is no way of knowing what is the correct way to ask the question. When the survey method is properly used, these disadvantages can be minimized. The versatility of the questionnaire method, its speed, and its relatively low cost are important advantages relative to the observation method.

Interviews can be handled in various ways. The general purpose of the survey can be disclosed to respondents or it can be disguised. Interviews can follow a formal list of questions which are asked as written, or interviews can be nonstructured and proceed as the interviewer's judgment dictates. The cross classification of these two characteristics establishes four classes of interview, each of which fits certain situations.

Three methods of communication are used with the questionnaire method —telephone, personal interview, and mail. Each has advantages and limitations. Personal interviews are the most flexible, but also the most costly, so telephone and mail are the most widely used. When well done, each provides data of similar accuracy.

Theoretically the observational method is superior to the questionnaire method. Observations are made at the time events occur. The collection of

---

[37] The particular problems associated with the use of secondary data are discussed at length in Chapter 5.

data by observation involves less chance for bias, with the possible exception of cases where the observer is an active participant in the event.

On the practical side, the advantages are in favor of the questionnaire method and have led to its widespread use. Almost any marketing problem can be approached with the questionnaire, whereas the observational method cannot get data of many types. The observational method also tends to be more expensive than the survey. Mechanical methods of observation are becoming increasingly important. Many studies combine the use of questionnaires and observation.

Case 4–1
THE MIDWEST BANK

The Midwest Bank was the oldest and second-largest bank in a major midwestern city. Its current assets were about $800 million, and earnings for the most recent year exceeded $30 million.

Down through the years the Midwest Bank had tried to maintain an image of a pleasant, convenient, and comfortable place to do one's banking. Of late, officials at the bank were concerned because they had learned that certain services were causing some dissatisfactions among customers. Specifically, complaints seemed to fall into four categories: (1) slow-moving lines, (2) a "pressured" feeling of doing business with other customers crowded against one's back, (3) withdrawals and check cashing transactions being easily observed by other customers, and (4) having to wait a long time to make a relatively minor transaction.

In light of these complaints, bank officials were currently considering two proposals which might help improve customer service. The first of these was a Fast Teller service. Under the present system, the bank used teller units with 12 windows each, and a customer seeking service would enter any one of the 12 lines of people which had formed in front of the windows. In the proposed Fast Teller arrangement, all customers would enter the same single line and, as a teller became available, the first person in that line would move up to the available teller.

Management felt that this set-up might eliminate at least three of the major complaints. First, a customer would no longer have to wait in a particularly slow-moving line while the line next to him or her moved more rapidly. Second, since only one person at a time would be standing at a teller window, that person's transactions would be less easily observed by others. Also, that person would feel less pressured to finish his or her business in a hurry, since no one would be standing behind them.

The second proposal being considered was Express Service. Currently, a wide range of transactions could take place at any teller window, including savings deposits and withdrawals, check cashing and checking deposits, purchase of money orders and cashiers checks, charges on a national credit card, and still others. The Express service would utilize specialized teller windows where a customer would be limited to one, or possibly two, specific transactions. Although management believed that this arrangement would expedite service, they were uncertain as to which particular transactions were used in combination by enough customers to warrant Express Service.

Bank officials gave George Riley the assignment of studying and making recommendations concerning the addition of the two proposed services. Riley had been with the bank for two years, ever since his graduation from the state university. He had only recently been transferred to his present position in the bank services department. As Riley reviewed the assignment given to him, he felt that the bank's information regarding the complaints was inadequate for making a recommendation, and that more research would have to be done.

Riley felt that either of two approaches could be used to obtain the information needed to evaluate the Fast Teller service. He could conduct an attitude or image survey, getting at complaints in an indirect or disguised manner. Or, he could conduct a survey asking directly for the bank's good and bad points. Regardless of which approach was used, he would have to determine how to select respondents, and whether to interview in person, or by mail or telephone.

Riley believed that the evaluation of the Express Service proposal might be somewhat more complicated. This was due to the fact that management wanted to know what specific transactions would qualify for Express Service, and which transactions could be most feasibly combined at any given window. Riley wondered whether, through observing and keeping a record of the transactions made by a sample of customers, he would be able to gather sufficient data to answer these questions. If he could get the needed information by this method, he would have to decide on how to select the customers to be observed. Also, he would have to decide if he should combine observations with interviews, or if observations alone would suffice. Furthermore, Riley wondered if this research on Express Service should be carried out jointly with, or independently of, the research on the Fast Teller service.

What information should Riley collect in order to evaluate each of the proposed services?

What research project(s) should be used in the evaluation of each of the proposed services?

Design each of those projects. What method of collecting data should be used in each?

CASE 4–2
RAINBOW STORES

Rainbow stores was a chain of 26 supermarkets located primarily in large west coast metropolitan areas. Reputedly one of the best-run chains in the country, Rainbow owed its success in large part to the creativity and resourcefulness of its president, Clark Samuels, a leader in progressive food retailing practices and, most recently, a pioneer in the use of electronic scanning equipment at check-out counters. Samuels had already fully equipped 7 of his stores with the scanner devices, and in the other 19 stores had installed electronic cash register (ECR) systems which could be readily upgraded to full scanning status. At the time, less than 1 percent of the food stores in the country were using scanning equipment. Samuels had been impressed with the "hard savings" resulting from the use of the equipment (mostly in the form of labor savings and reduced inventory shrinkage), and customers had generally seemed pleased with the faster check-out process and the reduced incidents of error on their bills. Samuels felt, however, that the benefits of the system had just begun to surface; he was intrigued with the research possibilities presented by the scanners.

Scanners such as those used in Rainbow Stores were developed by the computer industry to accommodate the Universal Product Code (UPC), a band of parallel lines, approximately one-inch square, which appeared on grocery products, drug products, records and magazines. The UPC was jointly conceived by food processors, supermarket retailers and equipment manufacturers, and when decoded by an electronic scanner, the UPC would identify the manufacturer, size, flavor, color and other features of a product. At the time, the UPC appeared on more than 170 billion packages sold in the United States.

In a scanner-equipped store, the UPC of each item purchased by a shopper would be read electronically as it passed over a laser slot in the check-out counter. The product information disclosed by the UPC was then matched to price information stored in the scanner's computer, and the ECR printed out a customer receipt which identified each item purchased by the individual product name and price. As a by-product of this system, the store management was given a detailed item-by-item record of product movement and price; it was this latter feature which led Samuels to believe the scanner could be a valuable research tool.

Samuels realized that before the scanner system could be used in any kind of conclusive research the seven fully equipped stores would have to be matched in some way according to the characteristics of the customers who shopped there. With that thought in mind, he retained the research firm of Robert Chapman and Associates to study age, income, family size and other demographic characteristics of each store's clientele. Although the study revealed some minor store-to-store differences, Samuels felt they were not so great as to preclude the use of the seven scanner-equipped stores as research sites. In fact, three or four of the stores were so well-matched on some of the variables studied that Samuels felt, through careful selection, it would be possible to use combinations of stores which would not cause a bias due to different types of customers. Furthermore, since the study had shown the seven scanner-equipped stores to be somewhat representative of the Rainbow chain as a whole, Samuels felt that some of the research findings might be applied to nonscanner-equipped stores as well.

Encouraged by the findings of the demographic study, Samuels next turned to consider the particular areas which might possibly be researched with the scanner-computer equipment. Three areas seemed to be especially promising.

1. Determination of the best price to charge for store brands relative to national brands in a given product category.
2. Measurement of the true effectiveness of end-of-aisle displays (EAD) on both current and future purchases.
3. Evaluation of the effect of different advertising practices.

In regard to the first area of research, Mr. Samuels was confident that the profitability of the Rainbow Stores' house brand could be considerably improved. He focused on one product in particular which he felt was underpriced compared to national brands. This item, frozen orange juice, was currently priced at 83 cents per package, approximately 10 cents lower than competing national brands. Historical data had shown that the store brand accounted for 30 percent of total sales volume in this product category—a figure which represented over 600,000 packages per year. Samuels figured if he could raise the price to 85 cents a package without significant loss in sales volume, he could increase profits by $12,000 per year (600,000 × $.02); at a price of 87 cents a package, profits would increase by $24,000 per year if volume remained steady. Such figures could be significant to Rainbow Stores, which operated in an industry whose earnings were less than one percent of sales. Samuels felt the scanner could help him determine the most profitable price for this and many other store-branded items.

End-of-aisle displays (EAD) represented another potential research area of interest to Samuels. Like other food retailers, he knew that EAD increased the sales of the displayed item during the display period. Intuitively, however, Samuels felt that perhaps these display-induced sales increases might only borrow from future sales when the item was returned to its normal position on the shelf. The situation could be aggravated if the EAD featured a reduced price; such a practice might even result in a loss in terms of overall profits. Samuels felt the scanner might help him quantify the true effectiveness of this display technique by measuring: (1) the sales increase while the product was in EAD, (2) the sales increase or decrease for a certain number of weeks following EAD, and (3) the total profitability of the EAD effort.

A third area of interest to Samuels was the effectiveness of various forms of advertising. Advertising was essential to the food retailer, but with so many alternatives available, the retailer had only his hunches to tell him which were most effective. Samuels knew, for instance, that major items featured in bold print in Rainbow's weekly newspaper advertisements were effective in drawing customers. But what was the most effective way to advertise minor sales items? Was a small advertisement for the item in the regular weekly full-page advertisement preferable to merely flagging the item with a small cardboard sign at its display space in the store? Or was the one-sheet flier, which was picked up by customers as they entered the store, more effective than these other techniques? Samuels was also interested in the true effectiveness of various loss leaders—specials on meat, dairy, coffee, etc. that were priced significantly below their normal retail price to draw people to the store. If customers bought only the loss leader, profitability would suffer during the course of the sale. If, however, the use of different loss leaders could be shown to be related to increases or decreases in the average amount purchased on the shopping trip, Samuels would know which loss leaders to use more frequently. He also felt that appropriate research could help him determine the most effective loss leader price and the length of time which should elapse before any given loss leader was featured again.

How can Samuels use the scanning system as a research tool?

Which of the areas of interest to Samuels can be researched with the use of the scanning system? How?

Design a specific research project for each area in which you believe the scanning system can make a contribution. Could questionnaire studies be used to obtain the needed information?

5
Secondary data

When marketing information is needed, a decision is frequently made to undertake a field survey when, in fact, this should be done only if the information cannot be obtained in any other way. A search will sometimes find the data have already been collected by a field study or may even be free.

Broadly speaking, the data available to the marketing researcher are either primary or secondary data. Secondary data can be defined as data collected by someone else for purposes other than solving the problem being investigated. Such data can be obtained *internally* (for example, accounting records) or *externally* (for example, government reports, trade association reports, commercial services). *Primary data,* on the other hand, are generated in a study specifically designed to accommodate the data needs of the problem at hand. If, for example, a machine tool manufacturer gathered data from its prospective customers about what features were wanted in a given machine tool, the resulting statistics would be primary data.

Since the majority of marketing research is concerned with either individual brands or a change in company marketing activities, much primary data must be gathered. The needed information is specific to a particular company and, hence, is not available from secondary sources. Nevertheless, the researcher should not assume that primary data are the only "answer." When sufficient secondary data are available, considerable time and money may be saved. The researcher, however, needs to know how to evaluate such data. This chapter will deal with the problems and opportunities associated with the use of secondary data and the chief sources of secondary information which are important to marketing.

USING SECONDARY DATA

The overwhelming flow of information which engulfs the world shows no sign of abating. On the contrary, its magnitude justifies the mixed metaphor that "it can drown us—or cause us to die of thirst." One scientist predicted that by the year 2010, in the United States alone, about 1.3 million scientists will be publishing annually 3 million articles in 60,000 journals.[1] Indeed, by 1974, 49,440 scientific and technical journals were being published in the world, including 8,460 in the United States.[2] Even confining the count to the "scholarly" category of such journals still leaves the international total at 1,945; and, within that select group, some 150,572 articles were published.[3] In 1975, the ISSN-Index (International Standard Serial Number) listed about 70,000 serials of all types as being in current publication.[4] The number of articles carried by this full complement of serials exceeded 1 million. Moreover, it has been predicted that the number of journals published will double every 15 years.[5]

The publication of books has been equally overwhelming. Fifty million books have been published since Gutenberg printed the Bible in the middle of the 15th century.[6] In 1976, over 425,000 books were in print. Currently, about 30,000 new titles and 10,000 new editions are introduced each year, while only about 15,000 titles go out of print.[7] In 1977, for example, the final listing of the American book title output was 42,780, which comprised 33,292 new books and 9,488 new editions.[8] The United States economy is based upon information; by 1967, 25 percent of GNP ". . . originated in the production, processing, and distribution of goods and services."[9] By 1970, close to half the work force were "information workers," who earned over 53 percent of all labor income. What is more, the trend persists and, the importance of mastering the major sources of secondary data is clear. Competent researchers not only must become thoroughly acquainted with these major sources—especially those pertinent to the researchers' organizations—but must also know how to locate valuable data in out-of-the-way places.

---

[1] In Morton F. Meltzer, *The Information Imperative* (New York: American Management Association, 1971), p. 4.

[2] David E. Allen, Jr., unpublished paper, SRI International, Menlo Park, California, 1976.

[3] Ibid.

[4] Fritz Machlup, "Stocks and Flows of Knowledge," *Kyklos,* XXXII (1979), fasc. 1/2, 402.

[5] Derek de Solla Price, as cited by Machlup, "Stocks and Flows," p. 402.

[6] Ibid., p. 403.

[7] Allen, *paper.*

[8] *Publishers Weekly* (February 19, 1979):53.

[9] Marc Uri Porat, "Global Implications of the Information Society," *Journal of Communication* 28 (Winter 1978):70.

Advantages of secondary data

Economy is clearly the greatest advantage of secondary data. Instead of printing data collection forms, hiring fieldworkers, transporting them throughout the field area, and editing and tabulating the results, researchers, alone or with some clerical assistance, may go to the library and take information from a published record compiled by somebody else. Secondary data are cheaper than primary data and can also be more quickly obtained. While a field project often takes 60 to 90 days or more, secondary data can be collected in a library within a few days.

Another advantage of some secondary data sources is that they provide information which could not be obtained by the typical organization. The Bureau of Census, for example, can require individual retailers to divulge sales, expenses, and profit information which would normally be inaccessible to the typical researcher. Moreover, data of this category, collected in the ordinary course of events, are less subject to the biases that might occur if the researcher were to gather the information for a specific purpose.

Drawbacks of secondary data

In utilizing secondary data, two major difficulties must be overcome: finding information which exactly fits the needs of the project at hand and being sure that the data are sufficiently accurate.

Finding data to suit the project. Quite often, secondary data do not satisfy immediate needs because they have been compiled for other purposes. Even when directly pertinent to the subject under study, secondary data may be just enough off the point to make them of little or no use. Three variations of this type which frequently impair the value of secondary data are: (1) units of measurement, (2) definitions of classes, and (3) recency.

Variation in the units of measurement is a common deficiency of secondary data. Consumer income, for instance, may be measured by individual, family, household, spending units, or tax return, depending on the source. In view of the differences in the units of measurement, the various data can be used together only for rough approximations.

Another common variation in secondary data is the different construction given to classes in different projects. A chain of stores, for example, may be defined as more than one store, four or more stores, ten or more stores, and so on. Similarly, age groupings may be under 20, 20 to 30, and over 30, or they may be under 25, 25 to 40, and over 40. Continued efforts are being made to establish uniform classifications, so as to avoid this sort of variation. The definitions employed by the U.S. Bureau of Census are often adopted by others, because it probably produces more statistics than any other single body. Unfortunately, however, neither these nor other standards, such as the breakdowns of population data suggested by the American Marketing Association as far back as 1951, have been generally accepted.[10]

Yet another common variation in secondary data is the date on which they are collected. Marketing is seldom concerned with historical statistics. Data which are invaluable one year may have become useless by the next. The census, for example, contains some of the most indispensable marketing data, yet six to eight years after a census is taken, much of that information will have largely lost its value.

Finding data of known accuracy. Once having discovered appropriate secondary data, the researcher must determine whether or not the information is accurate enough for the purposes at hand. Before using secondary data, the researcher must subject them *and* the circumstances under which they were gathered to a critical and pressing evaluation.

Of critical importance in this evaluation is the identification of the data's source. Secondary data may be derived from a secondary source or from an original source. If the researcher obtains secondary data from the party who gathered them, the original or primary source is being utilized. But if the data are derived from a source which, in turn, procured them elsewhere, then a secondary source is being used. Whenever feasible, secondary data ought to be collected from original sources.

One of the main advantages of *original* sources is that they usually explain how the data were collected. This facilitates an appraisal of their reliability. One of the main disadvantages of using secondary sources is that they not only frequently omit this explanation, but they may also make errors in copying data.[11] Unwary researchers are likely to perpetuate such errors in their own work. Still another failing of secondary sources is their frequent tendency to abbreviate the information given in the original sources; explanatory or cautionary footnotes, for example, may be omitted.

Secondary sources must be used with caution because they frequently report preliminary data as final and fail to incorporate revised data when they become available. The federal government often releases preliminary data which are later adjusted into "final" data. Moreover, the "final" data are sometimes revised as a result of additional information or a change in procedure. These alterations are more likely to be picked up if the original source, rather than a secondary source, is monitored.

Evaluating secondary data

On many occasions, researchers will be obliged to choose from among two or more sources of data. Clearly the choice will be guided by the determination of which data scores highest on the following four considerations.

---

[10] "Standard Breakdowns for Population Data," *Journal of Marketing* (April 1951): 476–478.

[11] See Oskar Morgenster, *On the Accuracy of Economic Observations,* 2d ed. (Princeton, N.J.: Princeton University Press, 1963), p. 305 and elsewhere.

Pertinency to the data.   To be usable, the data must use the same units of measurement specified in the project, must be applicable to the period of time in question, and must be derived from the universe of interest. Classes of data must be constructed in the same way as in the project.

Who collects and publishes the data—and why.   In evaluating secondary data, the researcher must necessarily examine the organization which collected the data and the purposes for which they were published. An organization which makes the collection and publication of data its chief function is apt to furnish accurate data. Obviously, the success of any firm of this sort depends on the long-run satisfaction of its clients that the information supplied is accurate.

The ability of an organization to procure the wanted information is naturally a pivotal consideration. This often reduces itself to a matter of authority and prestige. The U.S. Bureau of Internal Revenue, for instance, can obtain accurate information about income more easily than any private firm simply because it has legal authority to do so.

When feasible, the capabilities and motivation of the individuals responsible for the data collection should also be appraised. Reputation, experience, and degree of independence on the particular project are all germane considerations in assessing the reliability of an "expert." An individual working for an independent research agency would be more likely to turn out an accurate report than the same individual working for an organization which is committed to one side of a question.

Discovering the purpose for which data are published is mandatory for an adequate evaluation of secondary data. Data published to promote the interests of a particular group, whether it is political, commercial, or social, are suspect. At the same time, not all data credited to sources with an "axe to grind" should be dismissed out of hand. Nevertheless, information so procured should always be handled with care.

Method of collecting data.   If a source fails to give a detailed description of its method of data collection, researchers should be hesitant about using the information that it provides. Only too often, shyness about procedures in the collection of data suggests the employment of sloppy methods. Most primary sources, however, describe their methods.

When the methodology is described, researchers should subject it to a painstaking examination. Even if the procedures appear to be sound, caution must be exercised, because weaknesses tend to be camouflaged. Searching questions must be answered positively before the data can be put to work.

If a sample was used, was it selected objectively? Was it large enough, particularly in the subsamples? Was it chosen from the universe of interest? Was it the most objective possible? Data gathered by observation tend to be more objective (and, therefore, more accurate) than data collected through questioning. Was the questionnaire employed adequate for getting the desired information? Accumulating data in the field requires administration. What kind of supervision was exercised over the people who actually collected the data? Were any checks made on the accuracy of the fieldworkers' results?

General evidences of careful work. An indispensable point of evaluation is the general evidence that the data have been collected and processed carefully. Is the information presented in a well-organized manner? Are the tables constructed properly, and are they consistent within and among themselves? Are the conclusions supported by the data?

Conflicting data. If several sources of data relating to a researcher's problem are available, the data can be submitted to a quality control analysis of the sort applied in production. After dividing the data into "good" and "poor" on the basis of criteria like those mentioned in the foregoing section, correlations on points of interest can be run between the two groups, and statistical tests can be made with the results. In projects which rely heavily on secondary data, this technique is particularly valuable.[12]

TYPES OF SECONDARY DATA

Secondary data are either internal or external to the company considering their use. Internal data are typified by summaries of sales representatives' reports, invoices, shipment records, and operating statements. A research manager must necessarily become thoroughly familiar with all of the material of this type that is available within the company. Company records must be constantly explored so as not to overlook information needed for current marketing research projects.

The collection of internal data is largely a matter of knowing the company's operating procedures and establishing systematic methods for recording the desired information. Collection of external data is more difficult because the data have much greater variety and the sources are far more numerous.

External data may be divided into four classes: (1) census and registration data; (2) individual project reports publicly circulated in encyclopedias, books, monographs, bulletins, and periodicals; (3) data collected for sale on a commercial basis; and (4) miscellaneous data.

Census and registration data

The U.S. Bureau of Census continually produces many studies which are indispensable sources for the market researcher. Originally limited to a population count for purposes of taxation, the "census" has long since come to mean enumerations of far wider variety, and the broadening of its significance promises to persist.

The major uses of census data are in sales forecasting, development of market potentials, construction of sales territories and quotas, store location,

---

[12] See Charles S. Mayer, "Quality Control in Research," *Journal of Advertising Research* (June 1971):9–14, and Charles S. Mayer, "Evaluating the Quality of Marketing Research Contractors," *Journal of Marketing Research* (May 1967):135–38.

and plant location. These by no means exhaust the possibilities of exploitation. Enterprising marketing researchers can probably employ the data-rich census for their firms in many ways.

None of the censuses is without interest to the marketing researcher. Together with other reports issued by the Bureau, they constitute the most fruitful single source of data useful in marketing research.[13] The experience, resources, and authority of the Bureau combine to give the data a high reputation for validity.[14] In 1963 Congress authorized that all censuses—with the exception of the Census of Population and Housing—be conducted every five years. The following censuses are of particular interest.

Census of Population.   The 1980 Census of Population is the 20th since 1790. It will report the population count by state, county, city, metropolitan area, and, in large cities, by census tract. *Census tracts* are fixed areas of around 4,000 in population—very convenient for marketing surveys as constant bases from one census to another. The Census will cover many characteristics of the population such as age, sex, race, mother tongue, citizenship, education, families and their composition, employment, place of work, veteran status, occupation, and income. Planning for the 1980 census began in July 1973; release of all totals is due by April 1, 1981. Greater accuracy and other improvements in the data collection were developed for the 1980 Census. The Bureau issues the *Current Population Survey* every month; this publication comprises a scientific sampling of data on personal and family characteristics of the population, mobility of the population, income, consumer buying indicators, school enrollment, and other subjects.

Census of Housing.   Made in conjunction with the Census of Population, this census enumerates types of structures, year built, equipment (including some appliances), water source, sewage disposal, fuel used, rent paid, value, number of persons per room, occupancy and tenure, ethnic category of occupants, condition and size of dwelling, and mortgage status. For cities of over 50,000 data are reported by blocks. *Current Housing Reports,* a quarterly publication, provides data on housing vacancies by rate, condition, and other characteristics.

Census of Manufactures.   This census, last taken in 1977, provides detailed data covering all establishments in some 450 industries, a geographic area series (all states and the District of Columbia), and a subject series (17 special reports). Data are provided on the number and size of establishments, the legal form of ownership, payrolls, man-hours, sales by customer class, inventories, selected costs, book value of fixed assets, capital

---

[13] In addition to the censuses described below, the Bureau also collects data on import and export trade. See "The Census Bureau and Trade Statistics—Part of a Long Tradition," *Commerce America* (May 27, 1978), inside front cover.

[14] Even the Bureau of the Census, however, is reproachable. For an example of the Bureau's imperfection, see William E. Cox, Jr., "The Census of Business: Some Contrary Evidence," *Journal of Marketing* (July 1967):47–51.

expenditures, industrial water use, selected metalworking operations, fuels and electric energy consumed, value added by manufacture, quantity and value of materials consumed, and products shipped. The Bureau also publishes the *Annual Survey of Manufactures* which furnishes intercensal statistics for many pivotal aspects of U.S. manufacturing. In addition, constant updating is provided by the Bureau's *Current Industrial Reports.*

Census of Retail Trade.   The 1977 enumeration of retail establishments was published in final report form in April 1980. It includes data on total sales, number of employees, payrolls, and merchandise lines. The enumerations are broken down by state, county, and city.

Census of Wholesale Trade.   Final reports for this 1977 census were published in March 1980. They are organized by geographic area and wholesale commodity line sales and include data similar to that in the retail census.

Census of Mineral Industries.   Publication of this 1977 census was made in 1980. It shows the number of companies, mines, and preparation plants in various mineral industries or groups of related industries, as well as the number of employees, principal expenses, capital expenditures, power equipment, value of shipments, and water use.

Census of Agriculture.   The latest census, covering 1977, tabulated data on counties with ten or more farms within some 50 geographical divisions. Information in the report includes number of farms, size, acreage value, farm expenditures, crops and livestock, value of products, facilities and equipment, number and characteristics of persons living in farm households, farm labor, irrigation, and the use of fertilizers.

Census of Transportation.   The 1977 census was comprised of four separate studies—national travel, truck inventory and use, survey of motor carriers and public warehousing, and commodity transportation.

Census of Governments.   In a series of publications, the 1977 Census of Governments presented data concerning numbers and characteristics of governments in the United States, the value of taxable property, public employees and payrolls, as well as governmental revenues, expenditures, debt, and financial assets.

Registration data.   These data are collected routinely by legal requirement or as a part of administrative procedure. Most of this information is compiled by governmental agencies and is sometimes difficult to locate. Its wide variety is illustrated by the following list, which is far from exhaustive: births, deaths, marriages, school enrollment, income-tax returns, social security tax payments, unemployment, sales-tax payments, sales and prices at public markets, export declarations, trade association (and other organizational) membership lists, customers lists (particularly credit customers), automobile registrations, and license requirements for various business activities.

Finding census and registration data.   Perhaps the most helpful guide to census data is the quarterly *Catalog of U.S. Census Publications* which contains tentative publication dates of preliminary and all other census reports.[15] A number of helpful guides to the publications of the Bureau of the Census are readily available from the U.S. Department of Commerce, Social and Economic Statistics Administration and the Bureau of the Census.

Knowing the field. Nothing can replace familiarity with the field of study. A marketing researcher who works with a manufacturer for a substantial length of time inevitably becomes acquainted with the important census and registration data pertinent to the relevant field. Whenever involved in problems connected with a relatively strange field, it is profitable to seek out sources by "picking the brains" of experienced professionals.

Special problems in using census and registration data. Census and registration data suffer from the defects common to secondary data. Above all other failings, they were naturally not collected to meet the exact needs of the researcher's immediate project. In general, however, the data gathered by the U.S. Bureau of the Census serve as standards for other data. Even so, care must be taken in their use. Definitions are sometimes changed from one census to another. Different definitions may be applied to different areas within the same census. New England metropolitan areas, for example, are defined differently in the census than are other metropolitan areas.

Publicly circulated reports of individual projects

This category of references includes a broad sweep of sources and items of extremely differing value. Among the materials incorporated in this group are books, monographs, bulletins, journal articles, commercial reports, and encyclopedia sections. Items are taken to be "publicly circulated" when the originators clearly sought to expose their work to a significant slice of the public.

Some of these items describe the results of extensive original research, some summarize the research of others, and some are statements of opinion. They tend to include more discussion and less statistics than do census and registration data, although statistical information is included in many items of this type.

---

[15] For a more extended discussion of how to locate data, see Allan Rawnsley (ed.), *Manual of Industrial Marketing Research* (New York: Wiley, 1978); Christine Hall, *Principal Sources of Marketing Information* (in the U.K.) (London: The Times Information and Marketing Intelligence Unit, October 1976); Robert Ferber et al., *A Basic Bibliography on Marketing Research,* 3d ed. (Chicago: American Marketing Association, 1974); Theodore A. Nelson and Toledo W. Chumley, *Measuring Markets: A Guide to the Use of Federal and State Statistical Data* (Washington, D.C.: U.S. Department of Commerce, 1974); B. A. Greenberg, et al., "What Techniques Are Used by Marketing Researchers in Business?" *Journal of Marketing* (April 1977):62–68; and W. E. Cox, Jr. and L. V. Dominguez, "Key Issues and Procedures of Industrial Marketing Research," *Industrial Marketing Management* (January 1979):81–93.

A useful annotated list of 52 journals directly pertinent to marketing research is available in Christopher H. Lovelock (ed.), "Periodicals of Interest to Researchers in Marketing," working paper (Boston: Division of Research, Harvard Business School, May 1979), pp. 79–131.

Sources of publicly circulated reports of individual projects. Materials of this sort originate with almost every conceivable source such as the federal government, state and local governments, colleges and universities, foundations, professional associations, trade associations, chambers of commerce, publishing companies, and commercial organizations.

Finding publicly circulated reports of individual projects. A number of guides are available for locating materials of this type:

General guides

Brownstone, David M., and Carruth, Gorton, comps., *Where to Find Business Information: A Worldwide Guide for Everyone Who Needs the Answers to Business Questions* (New York: John Wiley & Sons, 1979). Lists over 5,000 publications of current interest. Books, periodicals, and data bases. International scope, but English-language sources only. Subject, title, and publisher indexes.

Daniells, Lorna M., comp., *Business Information Sources* (Berkeley: University of California Press, 1976). A modernizing of Edwin T. Coman, Jr.'s classic *Sources of Business Information,* 2d ed. (Berkeley: University of California Press, 1964). Selections intended to meet the information needs of business in "this . . . computerized age."

White, Carl M., et al., *Sources of Information in the Social Sciences: A Guide to the Literature,* 2d ed. (Chicago: American Library Association, 1973). Bibliographical essays and annotated lists in all major fields, including "economics and business."

Guides to books, monographs, bulletins, and reports

Bibliographic Index: A Cumulative Bibliography of Bibliographies (New York: H. W. Wilson and Co., since 1937). Subject list of bibliographies with 50 or more citations. Mostly titles in Germanic (including English) and Romance languages. Semiannual with annual cumulation. Books, pamphlets, and periodicals. About 2,400 journals are monitored.

Dissertation Abstracts (Ann Arbor: University Microfilms, since 1952). Monthly. Since 1962, cumulated subject and author indexes.

Bibliography of Publications of University Bureaus of Business and Economic Research. Annual. Indexed by institution, author, and subject. (Published before 1963 under the title *Index of Publications of Bureaus of Business and Economic Research.*)

Monthly Catalog of U.S. Government Publications. Published monthly since July, 1945 (annually from 1895 to 1945). Lists publications of all branches of the government. Includes subject index.

Degan, Diana, and Miller, Thomas E. (eds.), *Findex: The Directory of Market Research Reports, Studies and Surveys* (New York: FIND/SVP, 1979). Includes reports by investment research firms on companies and industries. Over 2,500 commercially available reports. Published annually with a mid-year supplement. Indexed by subject and company name.

Guides to periodicals

Business Periodicals Index. Published since 1958 (part of *Industrial Arts Index, 1913–58*). Monthly (except for July), with cumulations quarterly, semi-annually, and annually. Subject index. Covers 272 periodicals published in the United States, Canada, and the U.K. (or by selected international organizations).

Social Sciences Index. Started in April, 1974. Covers over 265 periodicals, mostly professional journals in law, psychology, economics, and other social sciences. English language.

Journal of Advertising Research. Published by the Advertising Research Foundation. Includes reviews, resumes, and listings of the current literature.

Journal of Marketing. Published quarterly by the American Marketing Association. "Marketing Abstracts," a special section, classifies selected articles from numerous business, economic, and social science periodicals under 26 headings; the articles are briefly summarized.

Readers' Guide to Periodical Literature. Since 1900. Semimonthly and annually. Subject and author arrangement. Indexes over 180 U.S. periodicals of the popular type.

New York Times Index. Since 1913. Semimonthly, with annual cumulation. Subject index.

Wall Street Journal Index. Since December, 1957. Monthly, with annual cumulations. Corporation and subject indexes.

Commercial information

The growing demand for marketing data in recent years has given rise to a number of companies which make a business of collecting and selling marketing information. Such companies typically fall into one of two categories. Many restrict themselves to research on specific problems faced by their clients. Another group of companies are those which collect certain marketing data on a continuing basis. This information is sold on subscription to all buyers. Some of the kinds of data provided and selected companies in each area are described below.

Consumer purchase data. Such data are relevant to almost all marketing problems, but are especially critical in defining market segments, identifying competitors and evaluating their activities, scheduling production and controlling inventories, targeting advertising, and assessing the results of merchandising efforts. A number of commercial services provide continuous data on consumer purchases. National Purchase Diary, Inc. (NPD) is the largest supplier of diary panel data in the United States. This organization maintains a panel of some 13,000 families which are selected so as to be representative of the entire U.S. population. This size is sufficiently large to enable regional "breakouts" in areas representing as little as 5 to 8 percent of the total continental U.S. population. Further, the company can provide local market data in 35 separate areas. These panels are of particular importance in the testing of new products.

Panel members keep diaries in which they record all of their purchases of 50 different product classes. Products which are purchased frequently, such as packaged food and personal care products, make up the list. Members submit diaries monthly and are compensated annually or biannually. NPD data are reported by selected demographics, regions (tailored to client needs), product ownership and media habits. Panel data permit analysis of sales and share trends by brand, package size, product type, and retail outlet. Special analyses can provide insights into heavy versus light users of a product class, dealing strategy, price ranges, and brand loyalty.

In general, continuous consumer panels cannot adequately represent the total universe buying any product. Foreign speaking and illiterates do not participate, and black families are typically underrepresented (about half the rate they should be in the NPD). And some people simply do not want to be bothered with keeping a continuous record of their purchases.

Continuous consumer purchase data are also provided by NPD on a number of specialized "products." Thus, panel data are available on consumer buying habits with respect to chain restaurants through the *Crest Report*. Also provided are similar consumption data on gasoline and allied products, toys and games, records and prerecorded tapes, textiles, and wine.

National Family Opinion, Inc., has a sample universe of over 200,000 families and household panelists which enable it to set up ad hoc panels (both as to size and composition) tailored to the needs of the client. Data are collected by mail and by telephone via WATS lines. In addition, continuous panel data are provided on all beverage consumption (except water), textiles and clothing, and automotive products including petroleum products, parts, and service.

Another service involving the use of a continuous panel is the national menu census provided every year by Market Research Corporation of America. Information is provided on each menu served at each meal, snack items, and carry out food items; whether the item was used as a basic dish, an ingredient, or an additive; how the item was prepared; who was present at the meal; what was done with leftovers; and so on. The panel consists of 4,000 families who report continuously for a whole year.

Retail sales data.   The best known service of this type is the Nielsen Retail Index which provides continuous sales data on food, proprietary drugs, cosmetics including perfumes, photographic products, jewelry, traffic appliances, tobacco, and some alcoholic beverages. These data are obtained every 60 days by auditing inventories and sales of a carefully selected sample of stores. In the food area Nielsen audits some 1,600 stores distributed nationwide.

Clients of the audit program typically receive regular reports of total sales of the applicable product class, sales of own and competing brands, retailer inventory and stock turn, retail and wholesale prices, retail gross margin, percentage of stores stocking, special manufacturer deals, and local advertising. These data are made available for the total United States and by regions, store ownership groups, and sales volume groups. Nielsen's subsidiaries do store audits in over 20 foreign countries. The company also provides custom research based on a sample of UPC scanner equipped stores located in an Eastern market. The growing use of such scanners is expected to change the nature of this type of marketing research.

IMS is a large international company specializing in research pertaining to the pharmaceutical and medical fields. The company's major service consists of providing continuous retail sales data on ethical drugs through an audit of prescriptions at sample stores. It also operates panels of doctors regarding their patient treatment. These data as well as those from a variety of special research projects can be accessed by clients using an on-line CRT.

Wholesale data.   Selling Areas-Marketing, Inc., (SAMI) provides product movement data to retail food stores from more than 400 chain and wholesaler warehouses as well as rack jobbers. Dollar volume and share-of-market data are issued every four weeks involving some 28,000 individual items. These data are reported for 39 marketing areas covering about 77 percent of national food sales. Because most large warehouses track product movement by the computer, large amounts of data of this type can be collected at a relatively low cost.

SAMI also offers a service called SARDI which measures product availability at the retail level. Not unlike Nielsen, the company is experimenting with data obtained by UPC scanner. SAMI operates a service in the Kansas City/Topeka area which reports weekly product movement from a sample of scanner equipped stores. It has linked a panel of 1,300 households to this store sample by recording their retail purchases using the UPC scanners. Each household has an identification number which is included in the data recorded by the scanners.

Advertising data.   Because of the many billions of dollars spent on advertising each year, it is not surprising that there is a large amount of advertising research data available from a variety of sources. While a substantial sum of money is spent on copy research, the majority is spent on media research. Copy research, by its very nature, is a situational activity, but there are a number of firms which make available a testing environment.

ASI Marketing Research, Inc., provides an example of one such service. While this firm has a number of different research services, its major activity utilizes in-theater testing of TV commercials. Recruitment of respondents is done by personal interview in an effort to obtain representative audiences. A predetermined number of respondents are seated in the theater at locations equipped with electronic interest recorders and finger sensors (to measure emotional responses). All respondents complete a classification questionnaire and provide a preexposure brand preference measure presented in the form of a prize list before the viewing starts.

The program consists of a cartoon and a TV pilot film followed by five commercials. Respondents report their reactions to each, using a self-administered questionnaire. After the commercials are shown, the audience is broken down into small groups which discuss their reactions to the commercials. At the very end a new brand preference prize list is completed as well as an open-ended questionnaire which asks respondents to write down all the brands and commercials they can remember. ASI provides three kinds of measures for a test commercial: (1) interest and involvement (derived from the electronic interest recorders and finger sensors); (2) ability to communicate (based on the data obtained from the interviews and discussions); and (3) effectiveness (from the pre/post brand-preference measure).

ASI also provides on-air testing using some 40 cooperating CATV systems located throughout the United States. By showing a special first-class movie on an unused channel and inviting (by phone) a selected audience to view it, a sufficient and representative sample is obtained. The test commercial is mixed with others during the movie. Phone interviewing on an aided and unaided basis provides the evaluation data.

There are a number of services similar in one way or another to the above in theater design and the use of before and after measures. All are, in reality, laboratory tests in which the commercial to be tested is the experimental variable. Thus, some companies use trailers as their laboratories, while others use 23-inch TV monitors. And, many companies provide an after only recall measure to an on-air exposure in one or more markets. Tests of radio copy can be undertaken in ways similar to those discussed above.

Pretesting of print advertising is typically done by the research department of advertising agencies, although some is done on a custom basis using independent research agencies. One of the few print advertising services is provided by ASI. The technique consists of imbedding both test and control ads in unreleased copies of appropriate general distribution magazines and placing these in the homes of a representative sample. At the time of placement respondent demographics and brand preferences are obtained. A later interview, on an aided and unaided basis, measures recognition/recall, quality of communication, and persuasive appeal of the test ad.

The Starch Readership Service is a post-measurement service that reports on the reading of ads in more than 90 consumer, business, trade and professional magazines, and newspapers. Each year over 75,000 ads are studied. The purpose of the research is to show the extent to which respondents have seen and read the advertisements in each study vehicle. Measures are provided on "noting" (percent remembering having seen the ad), "associate" (percent who saw or read some part of the ad which clearly indicated the brand or advertiser), and "read most" (percent reading half or more of text material). Each Starch report utilizes a minimum sample size of 100 men and/or women readers. Starch also provides services which are based on in-depth interviews regarding the impressions and perceptions of respondents to a given print ad. These latter services are used for both pretesting and posttesting of ads.

Media audience data are made available from a number of companies on a continuous basis. The Nielsen Television Index is one of the most widely used. Data are collected electronically via a device which is installed in the home of a respondent family. This device records when the set is on, what channel it is tuned to, and when it is switched to another channel or off. At frequent intervals, the program data recorded by this device are transferred electronically to a central computer. A separate panel of households provides data on who in the household is watching at 15-minute intervals via a diary.

Clients are provided with an impressive array of data, including audience size and characteristics for any TV program and type of program (e.g., comedy and mystery), flow of audiences from and to alternative programs, and audience duplication between various program combinations. The sample size for the electronic device based service is over 1,200 households. Findings are augmented by reports from a 2,000 consumer panel.

Arbitron also provides a continuous service which measures both television viewing and radio listening. Most of these data are obtained using the diary method. Over 2 million households are contacted yearly in an effort to provide detailed audience data by local markets. Metered TV set panels are operated in several of the larger metropolitan areas. Other companies also provide similar information with respect to radio listening by local markets.

Other commercial research services

Many other research agencies provide either continuous marketing data or have a specialized service which is designed to help solve a particular marketing problem. Examples of the former include the Audit Bureau of Circulations which supplies data on the paid circulations of newspapers and magazines, Media Records which gives newspaper linage purchased by advertisers, Publishers Information Bureau which reports monthly expenditures by advertisers in major media vehicles, Dun and Bradstreet which furnishes credit information on individual firms, J. W. Dodge Corporation which compiles construction statistics, and SMRB which measures magazine readership. Yankelovich, Skelly, and White provide a service which tracks social trends, public policy issues for business, and consumerism pressures.

A number of firms provide laboratory type facilities and procedures for pretesting new products. These services typically attempt to replicate the real world by exposing respondents to advertising and the purchase of the new product. Most base their market share and sales forecasts on measures pertaining to awareness, trial, and repeat buying. An example of such a service is the Elrick and Lavidge COMP system which is designed to evaluate consumer reactions to new and old products, packages, positionings, and prices.

Market Facts' Marketest Store Auditing Service is concerned with controlled store testing for new products. Marketest is able to obtain distribution of new food and drug products through cooperative agreements with leading chains and independents in eight metropolitan areas. Warehouse facilities and a fleet of trucks are maintained to support such tests.

ADTEL is probably the most elaborate service dealing with the sales effect of advertising and promotion on new and established products. Through the use of controlled cable television and diary panels to measure sales results, a variety of experiments can be conducted in the three test markets which ADTEL provides.

Data banks

Perhaps the most dramatic emergence in the world of information has been the application of computer systems to data of all types. At a constantly increasing rate, all sorts of information is being put into forms readable by a machine and made commercially available to users. While the transaction is commercial, many of the data banks have been developed through the financial encouragement of the U.S. Office of Science Information Service and are therefore accessible on a nonprofit basis. Other institutions, such as universities and libraries, have also developed information banks that are publicly accessible. The private data banks are accessible upon payment of scheduled fees. All data banks fall within one of three categories: (1) bibliographic (excerpts from published literature, commonly searchable by means of key words); (2) statistical (usually brought up to date at periodic intervals); and (3) computational (the raw data of the other two types of data banks are enhanced computationally). While data banks are not without their disadvantages, their use by market researchers is becoming indispensable.[16]

Guides to information banks

Kruzas, Anthony T., and Sullivan, Linda Varekamp (eds.), *Encyclopedia of Information Systems and Services,* 3d ed. (Detroit: Gale Research Co., 1978). A guide to information storage and retrieval services, data base producers and publishers, online vendors, computer service companies, computerized retrieval systems, micrographic firms, libraries, information centers, data banks, and research centers. Over 2,500 organizations are described in some detail. Eighteen indexes present varied access to the material.

Auerbach Computer Technology Reports. Vol. M–1 includes directories of distributors and suppliers as well as indexes of data banks, distributors, and subjects. The directories contain explicit details about who maintains the bank, how to obtain access to it, how often the bank is updated, span of time covered, the class of users, fees, and clear descriptions of the data in the banks. The service is looseleaf and continuingly updated.

Pratt, Gordon (ed.), *Data Bases in Europe: A Directory to Machine-Readable Data Bases and Data Banks in Europe* (London: Aslib, 1976).

---

[16] Marshall B. Romney, "Should Management Jump on the Data Base Wagon?" *Financial Executive* 47 (May 1979):24–30.

Sanders, Eusidic and James B. (eds.), *Information Market Place 1978–1979: An International Directory of Information Products and Services* (New York: R. R. Bowker Company, 1978). This directory has seven divisions: information products (including data bases); information distribution; information retailing; support services and suppliers; associations and governmental agencies; conferences and courses; and sources of information. The data bases are categorized (for example, banking; business, economics, and management).

Problems in using commercial data.   Although commercial agencies do not have the user's specific problem in mind when they collect data, they do collect information oriented toward a specific purpose—measuring industry or product sales, measuring the intensity of advertising activity by brand, measuring recall of an advertisement, and so on. When a researcher has need for such information, the data from commercial agencies may be very helpful.

In buying commercial data, the researcher must be sure that the data are accurate enough for the purposes of the research. Such a judgment is easier to make with these data than it is with most other secondary data, because detailed descriptions of the methods of data collection can be easily obtained. In some cases, essentially similar data can be bought from two or more sources which differ in their collection methods. The buyer must decide which of the methods most adequately meets the project's needs. The measurement of radio and television audiences, for example, is accomplished by organizations which use such differing techniques as audimeters, spot telephone calls, diaries, recall interviews, and combinations of these. Whoever buys such audience data must make an evaluation of these alternative techniques in the context of the problems which the data are expected to help in solving.

Fortunately, most continuing services are operated by competent technicians who employ sound procedures. However, even the best of these organizations are limited by financial considerations, and all are hampered by the difficulties inherent in collecting valid and reliable data from consumers and other respondents. For these reasons, researchers considering the use of a commercial service should carefully evaluate that service before subscribing to it.

Miscellaneous secondary data

Probably the most rewarding single source of secondary data is a competent reference librarian. Another major source is the field offices that the U.S. Department of Commerce maintains in major cities throughout the land. These offices are equipped to aid the researcher in the search for data on any given business topic.

Trade associations.   Companies in similar businesses often form associations which can refer the researcher to the more relevant major sources of information related to their lines of business. Most associations compile data on members of the trade, and some gather additional data which are directly germane to a particular industry.

Most of the trade associations of the United States and Canada are listed in the following sources:

Gale Research Co., *Encyclopedia of Associations,* 13th ed., 1979. Vol. 1, *National Associations of the United States,* gives detailed descriptions of 13,589 organizations; vol. 2, *Geographic and Executive Index;* vol. 3, *New Associations and Projects,* which by October 1979, had listed 846 new associations.

Klein, Barry T. (ed.), *Guide to American Scientific and Technical Directories,* 2d ed. (Rye, N.Y.: Todd Publications, 1975). Covers more than 2,500 publications, including many concerned with special trades and industries.

Colgate, Craig, Jr., and Boida, Patricia (eds.), *National Trade and Professional Associations of the United States and Canada and Labor Unions* (Washington, D.C.: Columbia Books, Inc., 1979). This annual lists about 6,000 associations. It is alphabetically arranged, and offers key-word, geographic, executive, and budgetary indexes.

Other guides to marketing data.   In addition to trade association directories, there are many guides for helping the researcher locate data. Among the major ones are the following:

Harvey, Joan M., *Sources of Statistics,* 2d ed. (Hamden, Conn.: Linnet Books, 1971). This inventory is arranged by category of activity, for example, prices, or tourism, and is mainly confined to the United States and the United Kingdom. The author has also published: *Statistics Africa: Sources for Social, Economic and Market Research,* 2d ed. (Beckenham, Eng.: CBD Research, 1978); *Statistics Europe: Sources for Market Research* (1976); *Statistics Asia & Australia: Sources for Market Research* (1974); and *Statistics America: Sources for Market Research* (North, South, and Central America) (1973).

Andriot, John L. (ed.), *Guide to U.S. Government Statistics,* 4th ed. (McLean, Va.: Documents Index, 1973). Annotated guide to over 1,700 recurring publications. Lists over 3,200 titles in the main statistical series. Includes a reprint of Parts 1 and 2 of the Bureau of the Budget's *Statistical Services of the United States Government* (1968).

Wasserman, Paul, and Berners, Jacqueline (eds.), *Statistics Sources: A Subject Guide to Data on Industrial, Business, Social, Educational, Financial, and Other Topics for the United States and Internationally,* 5th ed. (Detroit: Gale Research Co., 1977). Alphabetical subject listing.

F(unck) and S(cott) Index of Corporations and Industries Annual. Covers company, product and industry information from over 750 financial publications, business-oriented newspapers, trade magazines, and special reports. Since 1968. Now quarterly. Index is arranged by SIC classification and by organizational title.

Sources of summary statistics.   The publications listed below summarize statistics from many sources. While valuable as sources of information in themselves, they also indicate original sources in which more detailed data can be found.

Axel, Helen (ed.), *A Guide to Consumer Markets: 1977/1978* (New York: The Conference Board, 1977). An array of statistics is included which ranges from population to prices. It has been published since 1970.

Board of Governors, Federal Reserve System, *Federal Reserve Bulletin* (Washington, D.C.: U.S. Government Printing Office). Monthly. It includes statistics on retailing, prices, consumer credit, and national income. Current and trend data are also included.

Commodity Research Bureau, Inc., *Commodity Year Book* (New York). Annual. Data on production, prices, consumption, and import and export flow are provided for a great many commodities. The commodities and their areas of production are also briefly described.

Editor and Publisher Market Guide: 1979 (New York: Editor and Publisher Co., Inc., 1979). Published annually since 1924. Gives market data relevant to over 1,500 daily newspaper markets in the United States and Canada. It estimates disposable personal income, disposable income per household, and retail sales.

Bureau of Labor Statistics, U.S. Department of Labor, *Monthly Labor Review* (Washington, D.C.: U.S. Government Printing Office). This title presents statistics on employment, wages, consumer price indexes, wholesale price indexes, labor turnover, economic sectors, and so on.

Social and Economic Statistics Administration, U.S. Bureau of the Census, *Guide to Foreign Trade Statistics*. The latest edition, issued in 1975, fully describes the program and where specific statistics can be located.

U.S. Department of Agriculture, *Agricultural Statistics* (Washington, D.C.: U.S. Government Printing Office). Annual. Agricultural production, prices, consumption, costs, and facilities are among the subjects reported.

U.S. Bureau of the Census. *County and City Data Book: 1977* (Washington, D.C.: U.S. Government Printing Office, 1978). This publication presents 195 statistical items for each census region, division, state and county; 161 items for SMSA's (standard metropolitan statistical areas); and 190 items for each city that had 25,000 inhabitants or more in 1975.

U.S. Bureau of the Census, *Statistical Abstract of the United States* (Washington, D.C.: U.S. Government Printing Office). In the 1978 edition of this annual, over 1,500 tables and charts are covered in more than 1,000 pages. The data are derived from private and governmental publications and from unpublished records. Valuable guidance to other statistical sources, both federal and state, is also provided.

The American Statistics Index (ASI), initiated in 1972, is designed to be a master guide and index to all statistical publications of the U.S. government. It is published annually in two volumes, one of which contains multiple indexes (subject and name, category—such as geographical, title, and agency report number). The other volume is devoted to abstracts. Monthly supplements are issued throughout each year.

SUMMARY

Before deciding to collect expensive primary data, the researcher should always explore the possibilities of using secondary data. Such data are cheaper and more quickly obtainable than primary data and may also be available where primary data could not be obtained at all. It is difficult, however, to find secondary data that exactly fit the needs of a specific project and to determine the accuracy of such data. In evaluating secondary data, the researcher must consider the following items: (1) pertinency to the problem, (2) the organization collecting the data, (3) the reasons for publishing the data, (4) methods used in collecting the data, and (5) general evidence of careful work.

Secondary data are either internal or external. Internal data must be found through knowledge of the recordkeeping procedures of a particular company. External data are more varied, more dispersed, and more difficult to locate. External data can be classified into four groups: (1) census and registration data, (2) publicly circulated individual project reports, (3) data collected by a commercial marketing research service, and (4) miscellaneous data. Although knowing all of the sources of such information is impossible, the researcher should be acquainted with most of the basic sources and be familiar with the guides to other secondary sources.

Case 5–1
COMMONWEALTH FOODS

Commonwealth Foods was one of the nation's largest processors of all types of fruits and vegetables. Their products were packaged in all sizes of jars and cans, whose contents might be whole fruits and vegetables (for example, tomatoes, plums), fruit and vegetable pieces (for example, sliced peaches, green beans), or creamed and sauced fruits and vegetables (for example, creamed corn, pickle relish). Users generally considered Commonwealth to be one of the better brands, and it could be found in most supermarkets in the country.

Commonwealth Foods had a large salaried sales force which sold every item in the line. These sales representatives called on chain store buyers, managers of large independent supermarkets, and food wholesalers. They were responsible for seeing to it that as much of the Commonwealth line as possible was sold in as many stores as possible. They were also expected to visit a number of stores each day and to report to their superiors the competitive conditions found in those stores.

The annual promotional budget for the entire Commonwealth line was well in excess of $20 million, most of which was spent on advertising in various women's magazines, in newspapers in major markets, and on television programs whose audiences included a high proportion of homemakers. In recent years a growing proportion of the promotional budget was being spent on coupons, promotions, trade dealing, and cooperative advertising (that is, Commonwealth Foods would pay for part of a retailer's large newspaper advertisement if it included a small advertisement for a Commonwealth Foods product). This trend caused some concern among the management of Commonwealth Foods, because the company had made very few attempts to measure the effectiveness of the promotions which were now being used more heavily.

The vice president of marketing asked the corporate marketing research manager, Arthur Barnsdale, to review the kinds of information the company would need in order to evaluate the effectiveness of promotions. In discussing the matter with Mr. Barnsdale, the vice president indicated that the purpose of consumer promotions (for example, cents-off coupons, refunds with proof of purchase, recipe booklets with proof of purchase, specially priced packages, and so on) was to get current users of the Commonwealth brand to buy even more, to get users of other brands to switch to the Commonwealth brand, and to get nonusers of the product to try it. The purpose of trade-oriented promotions (primarily discounts and cooperative advertising) was to get retailers to give better displays to the Commonwealth line, to get them to carry items or sizes not previously carried, and to obtain distribution in stores which had not previously carried any of the Commonwealth line.

In considering his assignment, Mr. Barnsdale listed the data sources he would probably have to study very carefully.

1. *Company shipments to chains, wholesalers, and large independent stores.* These data were not easily related to specific promotions, because the company had no information as to when the items were actually sold.
2. *Warehouse withdrawal data, such as those offered by SAMI.* These data could be loosely related to certain kinds of promotions, but one had to keep in mind the fact that the data reflected warehouse withdrawals and not consumer purchases. (A description of the SAMI service appears as Appendix A of this case.)
3. *Retail sales, such as data available from the Nielsen Retail Index.* These data represent final sales, but they do not isolate the effects of certain kinds of consumer promotions. (A description of the Nielsen Retail Index appears as Appendix B of this case.)
4. *Purchase diary data, such as those available from MRCA.* These data show consecutive purchases by the same families and identify whether a coupon was used, as well as the price paid for the item. (A description of the MRCA panel diary service appears as Appendix C of this case.)

5.   *Field surveys.* The company can design special field studies to obtain data which might be used to evaluate the effectiveness of promotions.

> *What data sources should Mr. Barnsdale use to evaluate each of the different kinds of consumer promotions?*
>
> *Show how you would use those data sources to measure promotional effectiveness.*
>
> *What data sources should be used to evaluate each of the different kinds of trade promotions?*
>
> *Show how you would use those data sources.*

APPENDIX A
Selling Areas—Marketing, Inc. (SAMI)*

Selling Areas—Marketing, Inc. is an organization which reports the amount of product shipped from warehouses during a four-week period to food stores in the market area served by the warehouses. This information is available for 68 product groups (for example, baking mixes, canned fruit, paper products, snacks), which are further broken down into more than 400 categories (for example, pie crust mix and pancake mix, pretzels, and salted nuts). SAMI's reporting service is available for 39 market areas which account for more than 77 percent of total food sales in the United States (see Exhibit A–1).

In each market area, data are obtained from chain warehouses, wholesalers, health and beauty-aid rack operators, and frozen food warehouses. In Chicago, for example, food operators participating with SAMI include A&P, Certified, Dominick's, Hillman's, Jewel, National Tea and others. On the average, the product shipment information gathered in a market by SAMI represents about 85 percent of the market's commodity food volume.

SAMI divides the year into 13 equal periods. At the end of each four weeks, product movement data from individual warehouses, are placed on computer tapes and sent to SAMI headquarters. There the tapes from all warehouses in a market are processed together to arrive at total commodity food volume movement in that market for the most recent four-week reporting period. Firms which subscribe to this service receive case movement and dollar volume data in a report usually received about three weeks after the end of the reporting period. Subscribers receive this information for their own brand, competing brands, and private label.

---

* All charts are presented through the courtesy of Selling Areas—Marketing, Inc.

EXHIBIT A–1. SAMI market areas

Albany/Schenectady	Miami
Atlanta	Milwaukee
Baltimore/Washington, D.C.	Minneapolis/St. Paul
Birmingham/Montgomery	Nashville/Knoxville
Boston/Providence	New Orleans
Buffalo	New York
Charlotte	Norfolk/Richmond
Chicago	Oklahoma City/Tulsa
Cincinnati/Columbus/Dayton	Philadelphia
Cleveland	Phoenix/Tucson
Dallas/Ft. Worth	Pittsburgh
Denver	Portland, Oregon
Des Moines/Omaha	Raleigh/Winston-Salem
Detroit	Salt Lake City/Boise
Houston	San Antonio/Corpus Christi
Indianapolis	San Francisco
Jacksonville/Tampa	Seattle/Tacoma
Kansas City	St. Louis
Los Angeles/San Diego	Syracuse
Memphis/Little Rock	

Each food operator also reports the price at which it sells an item. Since different food operators may not set the same price on an item, each operator is likely to sell different quantities during the four-week period. Because of this, an average price is calculated for the sales of a brand by all food operators in a market. This price is a weighted average of the price and quantity reported by each food operator during the four-week period.

Every four weeks, participating food operators receive reports showing total movement in their markets of each of the more than 400 categories reported by SAMI. Each food operator is also given the share of total movement of each item which it accounted for, but this information is kept confidential from other food operators.

A manufacturer who subscribes to the SAMI service will receive a report every four weeks showing product description, package size, case movement (for the last 4 weeks and the last 52 weeks), the item's dollar share of total category sales (for the last 4 weeks and the last 52 weeks), and the number of food operators carrying the product. These data can be broken out for each of the 39 SAMI markets or summarized for the total United States. These same data can also be presented as trends by showing the results from the most recent 13 reporting periods. Other report forms are also possible.

Exhibit A–2 illustrates how SAMI data can be used to monitor the competitive environment. The exhibit shows what happened to four established brands (A, B, C, D) when two new brands (E, F) were introduced. The trend data show that one established brand (A) was unaffected by the new introductions, that established brands C and D appear to be losing out to new brand E, and that new brand F is in serious trouble.

EXHIBIT A–2. Brand share trend data

Percent share of market

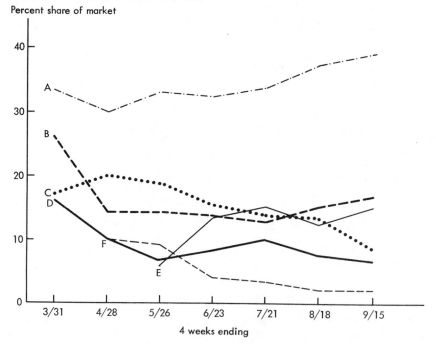

4 weeks ending

Exhibit A–3 illustrates how a manufacturer can use SAMI data to measure the effectiveness of two different promotions—a 20-cent price reduction and a bonus package containing extra volume at no extra price. By comparing average case movement before the promotions with average case movement during the promotions, the effectiveness of the two promotions can be measured. Thus, Exhibit A–3 shows that the bonus package promotion resulted

EXHIBIT A–3. Case movement data in different markets

	Case movement	
	Market A 20 cents off	Market B bonus pack
4-week period ending		
6/9	5,937	8,620
7/7	3,301	6,407
8/4	2,820	4,710
9/1	3,314	4,830
Total 16-week period ending 9/1	15,372	24,567
Average per 4-week period during test	3,843	6,142
Average per 4-week period during previous 28 weeks	3,122	4,710
Average increase per 4-week period	721	1,432
Percent of increase	23%	30%

in a 30 percent sales increase, while the price-off promotion resulted in a 23 percent sales increase.

A manufacturer can purchase the SAMI service for all 39 markets, for only one market, or for any combination of markets. The cost of the service varies according to the product category, the sales volume of the category and the time needed to process data in the category. When purchasing the service on an individual market basis, larger markets are more costly than smaller markets.

APPENDIX B
A. C. Nielsen Company*

The A. C. Nielsen Company provides a variety of fact-finding services. One of these is the Nielsen Retail Index. This index measures consumer sales continuously (every 60 days) by personally conducting audits of invoices and inventories in 1,600 typical chain and independent food stores. The consumer sales figures obtained from the sample are expanded to a total for the United States. These stores are selected in such a manner that their sales furnish a representative cross section of the sales of all stores. The sample stores are located in 600 counties selected on a probability basis. Contracts are signed with each store and with chain headquarters under which Nielsen auditors have the privilege of taking inventories, and auditing the invoices for all goods coming into the store. Cooperating stores are compensated with cash and general marketing information.

The Nielsen Company uses a highly trained, permanent full-time auditing staff. Most of the auditors are college graduates and their average length of service with the firm is approximately eight years. A field supervisor is employed for every eight auditors to insure accuracy in the fieldwork. Essentially the same stores are included in the bimonthly audits, and thus trend data show the long-term direction of the total market and of each important brand. The basic data obtained as a result of these audits are shown in Exhibit B–1. These data are charted every two months and a presentation made to the client. The company maintains a trained group of client service personnel who analyze and interpret the data regularly. The annual cost of this basic service could range from $25–100,000 per year, depending upon the client brand's sales volume, the number of items the client has in the product category of interest, and the number of different analyses and reports the client desires. The cost could run much higher for clients with large sales in many product categories.

The Nielsen service determines the consumer sales of competitors and provides an index of a client's competitive progress which is expressed as a percentage of the total market. These are illustrated in Exhibit B–2.

---

* All charts are presented through the courtesy of the A. C. Nielsen Co.

EXHIBIT B–1. Complete list of data secured every 60 days in food stores

1. Sales to consumers.
2. Purchases by retailers.
3. Retail inventories.
4. Average monthly sales.
5. Store count distribution.
6. All commodity distribution.
7. Out-of-stock stores.
8. Prices (wholesale and retail).
9. Special factory packs.
10. Dealer support (displays, local advertising, coupon redemption).
11. Total food store sales (all commodities).
12. Major media advertising (from other sources).

Data breakdowns available

Brand, type, and size	Territory	Client areas		County sizes	Store types	
	New England	1	10	Metro New York	Drug	Grocery
All other brands	Metro New York	2	11	Metro Chicago	Chain (4 or more)	Chain (4 or more)
Private label	Mid–Atlantic	3	12			
	East Central	4	13	Metro Los Angeles	Independents	Independents
D	Metro Chicago	5	14	A Counties	Large ($200M and over)	Large (over $500M)
C	West Central	6	15		Medium ($100 to $200M)	Chain and large combined
B	South East	7	16	B Counties		
A	South West	8	17	C Counties	Small (under $100M)	Medium ($100 to 500M)
	Metro Los Angeles	9	18			Small (under $100M)
Client brand	Rem. Pacific			D Counties		

(Competitors)

The service is valuable in noting the difference between factory and consumer sales. Since manufacturers may be spending large sums of money for various advertising and merchandising efforts to increase the flow of their goods at the point of consumption, they need to know promptly the volume of their consumer sales. They cannot use factory sales as a measure of the success or failure of their efforts since the trend of such sales is generally slow in reflecting the ups and downs of consumer sales trends. Exhibit B–3 illustrates this point.

A client can use the service to detect profitable and unprofitable promotional methods. Since the Index measures consumer sales of a product (and its share of total consumer sales) both before and after any change in promotional effort, it is felt that much can be learned about the company's promotional activities. Exhibit B–4 illustrates the situation in which, if factory sales had been used to judge the success of an advertising switch, a serious mistake would have been made.

EXHIBIT B–2. Consumer sales—all brands ($000)

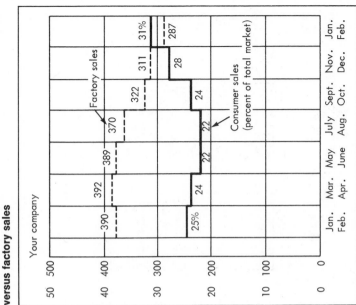

EXHIBIT B–3. Consumer sales in percent of total market versus factory sales

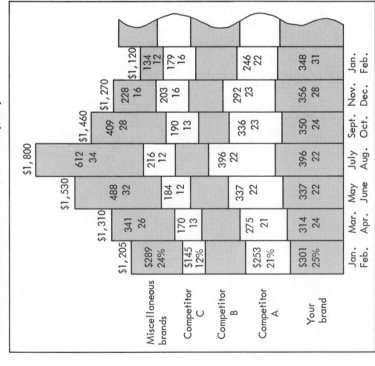

EXHIBIT B–4. A change in advertising (quantity, type, copy, media)

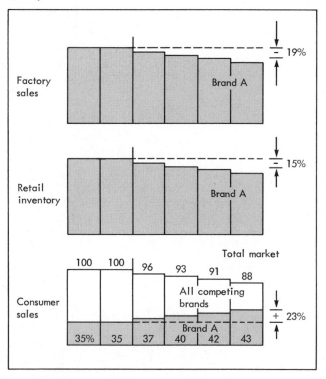

The Nielsen Index can separate the consumer take-away of regular merchandise from that purchased during the various promotions, such as one-cent sales and two-for-one. Some clients make frequent use of such promotions. Use of the Nielsen Index can identify whether a promotion is successful or unsuccessful. Exhibits B–5 and B–6 illustrate how the Index can be used in this manner.

EXHIBIT B–5. A successful promotion—case 328—brand H metropolitan Chicago

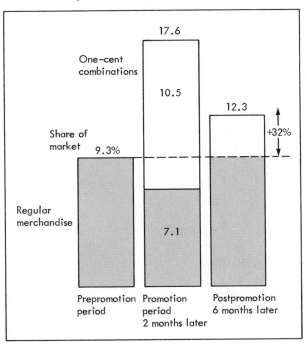

EXHIBIT B–6. An unsuccessful promotion—case 508—brand T metropolitan Chicago

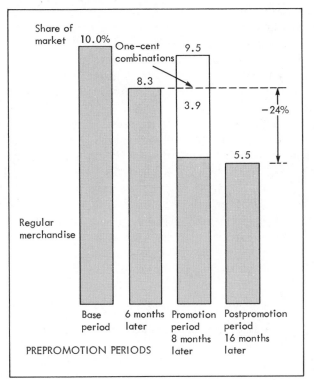

APPENDIX C
Market Research Corporation of America*

The Market Research Corporation of America (MRCA) offers clients monthly reports of consumer purchases of items sold in food and drugstores. The MRCA data are obtained from a consumer panel of approximately 7,500 families throughout the United States. These families keep "diaries" which they send in each week. Each family records the requested food and drug purchases as they are brought home. Thus, any "memory error" is reduced or eliminated. For each purchase the following information is recorded:

Date and day of week.
Brand name.
Number of items purchased.
Type of container (glass, tin, and so on).
Exact weight or quantity.
Where purchased (including store name).
Normal transaction or deal (one-cent sale, coupon, and so on).
Price paid.

The 7,500 families used in the sample are carefully selected on a probability basis and are representative of the total population on major characteristics such as geographic region, city size, income, presence of children, education, size of family, and age of homemaker.

When a family is selected for the panel, a member of the MRCA staff calls on it, enlists its cooperation, and trains it in the procedures. Each family receives compensation in the form of points which are exchangeable for merchandise.

Each month MRCA will deliver to clients a report for the preceding month showing total consumer purchases in the United States of the product category of interest to the client, along with purchases of each important brand individually. A study of this information over a period of months would enable clients to tell whether they were gaining or losing in market position. Exhibit C–1 shows the type of analysis that might be made.

In addition to this basic consumer purchasing information, the monthly report would include analyses of such things as deal versus nondeal purchases and average prices paid by consumers. This monthly report would be delivered within 10 to 15 days after the end of the month.

---

* All charts are presented through the courtesy of Market Research Corporation of America.

EXHIBIT C–1. Food product—volume and brand shares U.S. total

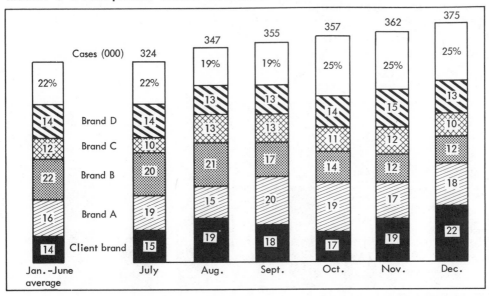

EXHIBIT C–2. Food product—volume and brand shares client company's sales regions (April–December)

Every three months a separate quarterly report would be submitted. This would include analyses of purchases by regions and by type of retail outlet as shown in Exhibits C–2 and C–3 and, on occasion, it would include other

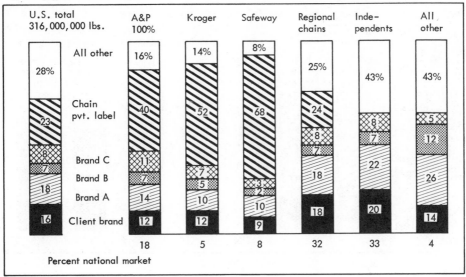

EXHIBIT C–3. Food product—market and brand performance major chains and other outlets (October–December)

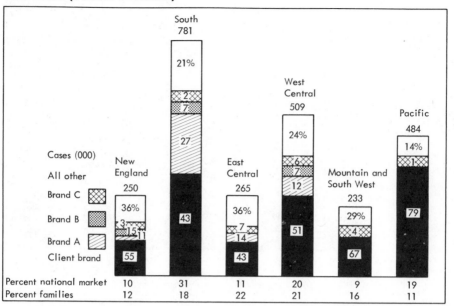

special analyses such as concentration of purchases among families as shown in Exhibit C–4.

Other special studies would be made on an annual basis, such as a study of the trend in product types (fresh, canned, and frozen) as shown in Exhibit C–5.

EXHIBIT C–4. Drug product—market concentration (six months' period)

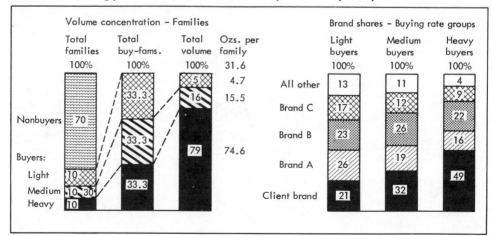

EXHIBIT C–5. Food product—consumer purchases by type (October through March each year)

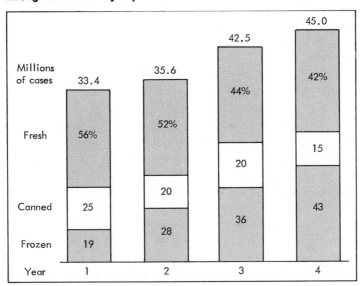

The cost of the service described above could range from $20–50,000 per year, depending upon the clients' particular product category of interest, the number of items they have in the category, and the number and type of special analyses and reports clients would want. The cost could run much higher for clients who wanted a number of special analyses for many different brands in different product categories. MRCA offers a wide variety of such services and report formats, many of which can be especially tailored to fit the needs of clients.

Case 5–2

BENNETT FROZEN FOODS

Floyd Menaugh, president of the Bennett Frozen Food Company, was concerned with the fact that his company was lacking good sales and marketing information. The company had monthly shipment figures, broken down by product and the market areas serviced by the company's food brokers. However, the company did not have up-to-date sales figures, and it did not know how well its competitors were doing. As a result, Mr. Menaugh was thinking of subscribing to a commercial marketing research service which could supply the kind of competitive information the company did not have.

Mr. Menaugh was considering the services offered by Selling Areas—Marketing, Inc. (SAMI) and the A. C. Nielsen Company. The two services were similar in some ways, but they were quite different in others. Mr. Menaugh was wondering which of the two services would most satisfy the

company's needs. He judged that the SAMI service would cost about
$100,000 per year, and the Nielsen service would cost much more, perhaps,
as much as $175–225,000 per year.

The Bennett Frozen Food Company was a national supplier of frozen
desserts, pies, cakes, rolls, biscuits, and other bakery items. All products
were prepared in the company's only plant, a large, modern baking and
freezing facility located in an East Coast city. Its product line was the largest
in the frozen bakery goods field, of high quality, and typically priced slightly
higher than the average competitor's product. The company's products were
sold in the frozen food sections of supermarkets and were generally viewed
by the consuming public as belonging to one of the industry leaders.

The sales of Bennett products occurred mostly in the larger cities. The ten
most important cities accounted for almost 50 percent of total sales and the
next twelve most important cities accounted for an additional 22 percent of
sales. Because local market conditions varied so tremendously due to local
and regional competitive brands—of both the fresh and frozen variety—
marketing efforts for the Bennett line tended to be tailored to reflect the
intensity of competition present in each market. Promotional support usually
consisted of trade allowances, trade promotions, and spot television commercials, all of which could be adjusted to local market conditions.

Sales of the company's products were under the direction of the company's
24 sales representatives. These sales representatives called on and assisted
some 72 frozen food brokers located throughout the country. These food
brokers had exclusive responsibility for selling the company's products in
their own market areas, which typically consisted of a central city with two or
three surrounding counties or two or three neighboring cities with their surrounding counties. In some southern and western regions, a broker's market
area might consist of all or parts of two or three states. The food brokers
called on the major chains and larger independent stores in their respective
market areas. Orders from large customers, such as retail chains, were
shipped directly from the Bennett plant. Smaller orders were supplied to
customers from a number of regional frozen food warehouses.

The Marketing Department of the Bennett Frozen Food Company was
responsible for developing new products, preparing advertising campaigns
and budgets, pricing, packaging, promotions, and marketing research. In
general, the Marketing Department was responsible for all aspects of the
company's marketing planning and programs except those associated with
the Bennett sales force, the food brokers handling the Bennett line, and the
retail trade which displayed and sold the line to final consumers.

Mr. Menaugh met with Walter Malinson, the sales manager, and with
John Gerlinger, the marketing manager, to discuss the matter of which com-
mercial marketing research service would best serve the company's needs.
Mr. Menaugh felt that the company should buy the retail service offered by
the A. C. Nielsen Company or the warehouse withdrawal service offered by
SAMI, but not both. Prior to the meeting, Mr. Menaugh had sent each

EXHIBIT 1

To: Floyd Menaugh, President

From: Walter Malinson, Sales Manager

   With respect to the issue of which marketing research service the company should purchase, the Sales Department feels that its needs would best be served by the warehouse withdrawal data available from Selling Areas—Marketing, Inc. The reasons for this preference are as follows:

1. Every 28 days (13 times a year) SAMI provides complete sales volume data for each of the 39 markets it serves. For each product category, they make available total sales by all competitors and total sales by brand, in both units and dollars. These data are actual shipments from warehouses, not estimates based on sampling.
2. The data would be useful to our district offices, because frequently the sales of a district accrue primarily from the one or two metropolitan areas in the district. In many cases, the district's metropolitan area is among those included in the SAMI reporting system. (Nielsen data are on a regional basis and, therefore, cannot serve this purpose.)
3. Since many of our important retail customers operate primarily in one market, they are only interested in sales figures from their markets. They obtain this information from SAMI. Our sales force and our brokers need the same information when talking with retailers, especially when the retailers use SAMI data as a basis for taking an action unfavorable to one or more Bennett products. It is important to remember that bakery goods are essentially a "local" industry, and that data from SAMI are "local" in nature. (Again, Nielsen data are too regional to be of much use to our sales representatives in this regard.)
4. Since we normally test new products in two or three test markets, SAMI sales figures of successful new product tests could be used to convince the retail trade in other markets that the new product will be a profitable addition to their lines.
5. In most markets, many items in the Bennett line are either the industry leader or a close second or third. Because of the breadth of our line and the high volume and high markups associated with most of our items, SAMI sales data will demonstrate to wary and uncertain retailers how much more profitable the entire Bennett line is, compared with competitors' lines. Such demonstrated profitability can be used by our brokers and our sales representatives to gain greater retail availability in general and additional shelf space in stores where only a portion of our line is already merchandised.

of the men descriptive materials of the two companies' services. (Descriptions of the services offered by the two companies appear as appendixes to Case 5–1.) After a discussion of a number of relevant points, Mr. Menaugh asked Walter and John to consider the matter and to recommend the service their respective departments would prefer to have available and to list the reasons for their preference. He then adjourned the meeting. A week later he received the memos shown in Exhibits 1 and 2 from the two managers.

EXHIBIT 2

To: Floyd Menaugh, President

From: John Gerlinger, Marketing Manager

After carefully considering the advantages and disadvantages of both the Nielsen and SAMI commercial research services relative to the needs of the Marketing Department, I have concluded that the Nielsen data would be of greater value. The following points are offered in support of this conclusion.

1. Nielsen data represent retail sales to the final consumer, while SAMI data represent product withdrawals from warehouses. The latter data can appear as "sales," when in fact they include inventory on the store's shelves and in the store's storage area. On the other hand, Nielsen data are "final sales" and, as such, are a much better measure of "what has been happening lately to sales." Because of the sampling procedures used by Nielsen and their gathering of data from broader market areas, the data can be used to project sales and brand share at the national level. This capability is especially important when attempting to measure the effectiveness of advertising and promotion over time. In addition, because Nielsen is based on sample data of sales made by specific stores at specific locations, the data can be customized (that is, specially analyzed) to reflect the sales in specific food broker areas.

2. Nielsen will present sales of our brand and all competing brands broken down by chain stores and independents, by four different store size categories, and by county size. Such data would tell us more about where our distribution is strong and where it is in need of improvement. It could tell us the percentages of stores in different type and size categories which stock all or some of our products. These data could identify if a successful product was not being carried by certain types of stores (that is, chains versus independents, or large stores versus small stores). This would be especially helpful for giving guidance to our sales force and our brokers. Programs could then be undertaken to gain distribution for that product in those stores. (Because they are from warehouse withdrawals rather than from retail store sales, the SAMI data cannot be broken down into sales by type or size of retail store.)

3. Because the source of Nielsen data is the retail store, included among the reported data are price on our brand and competitors' brands for different package sizes, out-of-stock conditions, the availability of special packages, the amount of space allotted to the product, the number of brand facings, and the availability of special displays, coupons, or other point-of-purchase promotions. Such data allow better tracking of competitive activity and of the competitive environment. They are available from Nielsen, but not from SAMI.

Which of the two commercial services should Mr. Menaugh purchase? Why?

What are the most important factors to consider when making the decision?

6

Decision trees and Bayesian analysis

When a problem or opportunity occurs, managers must choose between doing A, or B, or C, . . . and so on. To make a choice, managers must *both* evaluate the results of doing A or B *and* estimate the certainty that A or B will actually lead to the expected results. For example, if a manager is 100 percent certain that doing A will result in profits of $125,000 and 100 percent certain that doing B will result in profits of $55,000, a decision is easy and no research is required. But, if the manager does not know for sure what the results of doing A (or B or C) will be, the manager may authorize research which will clarify the situation. In general, *the more uncertain managers are about the consequences of a major decision, the more likely they are to ask for information or research which will help reduce that uncertainty.*

Whenever marketing managers face a major decision, they must decide whether to make the decision on the basis of what is known or to delay the decision until additional information is gathered. This chapter presents two methods which can be used to analyze situations where managers may have to decide on whether or not to do research.

DECISION TREES

The risk and uncertainty associated with decisions can be analyzed with the aid of decision trees. The latter are tree-like diagrams (for example, Figure 6–1) consisting of four major components: (1) decision forks, (2) outcome forks, (3) probabilities associated with each outcome, and (4) rewards or penalties associated with each outcome.

To illustrate, assume that the Acme Bakery is planning a new promotion program in the city in which it is located. The program will consist of either newspaper advertisements or direct mail coupons. Newspaper advertisements are less costly and will reach a larger audience than direct mail coupons, but also are more easily observed by the competing bakery. Consequently, the use of newspaper advertisements is more likely to trigger a counterpromotion by the competing bakery. After careful consideration, the marketing manager constructs a decision tree of this situation (see Figure 6–1).

The left side of Figure 6–1 shows the decision fork, which represents *all* of the alternative courses of action being considered—using either newspaper advertisements or direct mail coupons. Moving to the right along one of the branches of the decision fork, one encounters an outcome fork, which represents *all* of the possible outcomes that might occur if that decision is made. For example, if the decision is made to use newspapers, Figure 6–1 shows the possible occurrence of two outcomes—the competing bakery reacts to the Acme Bakery promotion or it does not. Associated with each possible outcome is the marketing manager's estimate of the probability that the outcome will occur. In the case of the Acme Bakery using newspaper advertisements, the marketing manager estimates there is a 0.8 probability

FIGURE 6–1. Decision tree for the Acme Bakery promotion decision

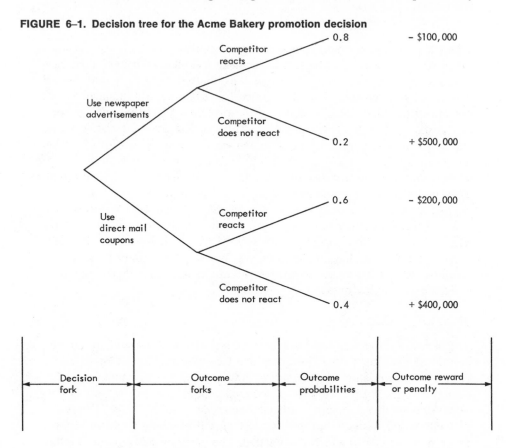

that the competing baker will offer a counterpromotion and a 0.2 probability that it will not. Finally, using the best information available, the Acme Bakery marketing manager estimates that Acme will either realize a profit of $500,000 or a loss of $100,000 if it uses newspaper advertisements, depending upon whether the competing bakery reacts to the promotion.

The same reasoning applies to the branch associated with the decision alternative of using direct mail coupons. The latter are more costly to use, but they are less likely to be noticed by the competitor. These facts are reflected in Figure 6–1, which shows a larger probability of no competitive response and a smaller profit for the direct mail coupon branch. Thus, Figure 6–1 is a tree diagram for the Acme Bakery promotion decision, and it contains a decision fork, outcome forks, outcome probabilities, and outcome rewards or penalties.

When the decision tree is completed, the Acme Bakery marketing manager can use it to evaluate the two alternatives being considered. This is done by calculating an "expected value" for each alternative. An expected value consists of two components—the reward or penalty associated with an event and the probability that the event will occur. Thus, if one buys a ticket in a $500 lottery in which 100 tickets are sold, the expected value of buying the ticket is equal to the probability of winning the lottery (1 in 100, or 0.01), multiplied by the reward associated with winning ($500). This expected value of $5 (= $500 × 0.01) is a measure of the value of one lottery ticket.

In the Acme Bakery example, expected values can be calculated by starting at the end of one of the decision alternative branches (the right side in Figure 6–1) and then multiplying the outcome probability by the outcome reward or penalty. By doing this *for each outcome and summing,* one can calculate the expected value of each decision alternative. In the Acme example, the expected value of using newspaper advertisements is

$$(0.8) \, (- \$100,000) + (0.2) \, (\$500,000) = + \$20,000.$$

Similarly, the expected value of using direct mail coupons is

$$(0.6) \, (- \$200,000) + (0.4) \, (\$400,000) = + \$40,000.$$

These expected values are based on *the best information currently available* to the marketing manager—that is, information relative to possible outcomes, outcome probabilities, and outcome rewards or penalties. As such, they are measures of how good each alternative is relative to the other. The marketing manager can compare the two expected values and use them when making a decision on which alternative to use.

It should be noted that both alternatives involve uncertainty (will the competitor react to the promotion?) and risk (losses of $100,000 and $200,000 if the competitor does react). By using a decision tree analysis, including expected value calculations, a manager's evaluation of decision alternatives can take risk and uncertainty into formal consideration.

Evaluating the need for research

A decision tree analysis can help management evaluate their needs for marketing research. For example, consider the case of a firm which has successfully tested a new product within a laboratory setting. The three major decision alternatives being considered by the firm are (1) to introduce the product nationally, (2) to test market the product in one market only, or (3) not to introduce the product at this time. These are shown on the left side of Figure 6–2.

FIGURE 6–2. A decision tree diagram for evaluating the need for research

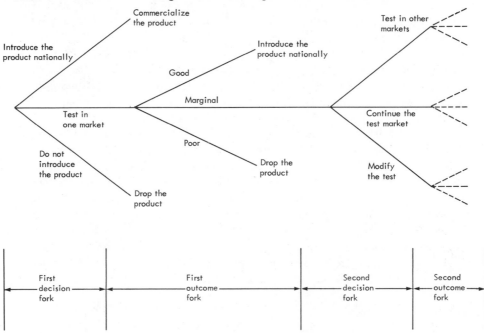

If the firm's management is confident that the product will be a success, they may choose the first alternative. If they are confident that the product will not be a success, they may choose the third alternative. Presumably either decision will reflect the case where management has relatively little uncertainty about the consequences of these decisions. On the other hand, if management is uncertain about the profitability of introducing the product nationally or the opportunity loss associated with dropping it, they may choose to undertake a test market.

If the second alternative is chosen, there are three possible test market outcomes—good, marginal, and poor. If the outcome is "good," management may then make the decision to introduce the product nationally. A "poor" outcome may result in a decision to drop the new product. In either case, the research (the test market) will have provided management with the additional information needed in order to make a decision.

On the other hand, if the outcome of the test market is "marginal," the research may not lead to enough reduction of uncertainty to permit management to decide either to introduce the product or to drop it. That is, the level of uncertainty will still be greater than management will accept. In such a case, a second decision fork will be attached to the "marginal" outcome, and such a decision fork may involve such alternatives as testing in other markets, continuing the present test market, or modifying the test marketing program. This fork indicates that additional research can be undertaken—and can continue to be undertaken—until the new information adequately reduces management's uncertainty and allows them to make the decision to introduce the product or to drop it.

Uncertainty and the need for research

The issue of whether or not research is needed can be better understood by graphing management's expectations of the consequences of a decision. For example, assume in the new product illustration above that the product will be profitable if it gains more than a 10 percent market share. If management were to decide on introducing the product nationally, what do they think the consequences of such a decision will be? Their choice of this alternative would be based on their estimate of the market share the product will attain if it is introduced.

In order to develop this information, individual managers will have to estimate the probability that the product will achieve a 10 percent market share, the probability that it will achieve an 11 percent market share, the probability that it will achieve a 12 percent market share, and so on. The right side of Figure 6–3a shows such information from one manager. This manager estimates that there is a 0.10 probability that the new product will attain a 16 percent market share, a 0.20 probability that it will attain a 17 percent market share, a 0.40 probability that it will attain an 18 percent market share, and so on. This probability distribution reflects some uncertainty—the manager is uncertain as to where in the 16–20 percent range the actual market share will be. However, it also reflects certainty, in the sense that this manager feels the product will achieve a market share at least as large as 16 percent—which is much larger than the break-even market share of 10 percent. If other managers also "feel certain" that the product will attain a market share of at least 16 percent and possibly as high as 20 percent, the decision can be made to introduce the product without doing further research.

The left side of Figure 6–3a shows similar information from a different manager. This manager estimates that there is a 0.05 probability that the new product will attain a 4 percent market share, a 0.30 probability that it will attain a 5 percent market share, a 0.30 probability that it will attain a 6 per-

FIGURE 6–3. Uncertainty and research

A. Adequate certainty, no research needed prior to decision

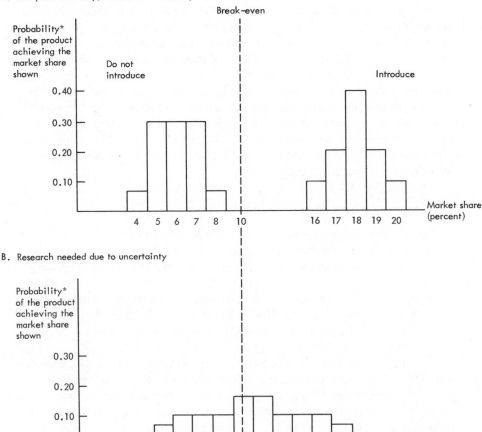

* Management's best estimates.

cent market share, and so on. This probability distribution reflects some uncertainty—in the 4–8 percent range—but it also indicates that this manager feels certain that the product will not attain the 10 percent break-even market share. If other managers also "feel certain" that the product will attain no more than a 4–8 percent market share, they need not do any research prior to deciding not to introduce the product.

Figure 6–3b illustrates a different type of uncertainty. This probability distribution shows that a manager has estimated that the product may attain a market share as low as 6 percent, as high as 15 percent, or some other market share in between. Furthermore, the manager is not very sure of any of these market shares—all have approximately the same probability. This case differs from the two above in that this manager *is uncertain as to whether the product will be profitable, only break even, or incur a loss.* This manager may choose to do research—that is, select the second alternative (see Figure 6–2)—before making a decision to introduce or drop the product.

By doing research, the managers would obtain additional information which might lead them to alter the probability distribution shown in Figure 6–3b. In fact, if their altered probability distribution looked like either of those in Figure 6–3a, the research will have reduced the managers' uncertainty to a level which will allow them to choose between introducing and dropping the product. Thus the question of whether or not research should be done is typified by Figure 6–3; a large degree of uncertainty fosters the decision to do research, with the hope that it will lead to a sufficient reduction in uncertainty to permit either a final decision (drop the new product idea or introduce it nationally), or an interim decision (continue testing).

The foregoing discussion has been mainly qualitative. This issue can also be analyzed with a more sophisticated quantitative approach which utilizes the concepts presented so far in this chapter—decision trees, decision forks, outcome forks, outcome rewards or penalties, outcome probabilities, and expected values. The application of more quantitative methods to the issue of whether or not research should be done is illustrated below.

Decision tree analysis to determine the need for research

A coffee company was considering the adoption of a new container which could have a major impact on the company's market share.[1] Six alternative courses of action were being considered.

1. Adopt the new container nationally as soon as possible.
2. Stay with the present container until a major competitor converts and then decide what action to take.
3. Convert one of the company's plants to the new container, test market, and then decide.
4. Same as 3 above, except order all needed conversion equipment now.
5. Undertake two months of consumer research and then decide.
6. Same as 5 above, but order all conversion equipment now.

The decision tree for this situation involves six alternatives at the first decision fork, followed by six *different* outcome forks, one for each alternative. Figure 6–4 shows only the outcome fork associated with alternative one (A_1). The figure shows that the company's management thought there were three possible responses by their major competitor if their decision was an immediate introduction of the new container nationally. These were (1) major competition does not convert—branch B_1; (2) major competitor follows conversion to the new container—branch B_2; and (3) independent con-

---

[1] Adapted from Joseph W. Newman, "An Application of Decision Theory under the Operating Pressures of Marketing Management," working paper no. 69 (Stanford, Calif.: Stanford University Graduate School of Business, 1965).

FIGURE 6–4. Expected value of decision to convert to new container as soon as possible ($000)

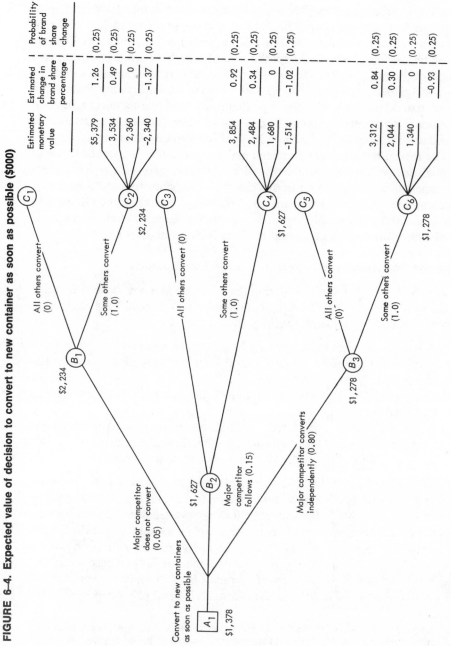

Dollar values assigned to A_1, B_1, B_2, B_3, C_2, C_4, and C_6 are expected values.
Source: Adapted from Joseph W. Newman, "An Application of Decision Theory under the Operating Pressures of Marketing Management," working paper no. 69 (Stanford, Calif.: Stanford University Graduate School of Business, 1965).

version by major competitor—branch B_3. The managers of the coffee company then estimated the probabilities associated with the occurrence of each possible type of reaction by the major competitor. These were 0.05 that the competitor would not convert, 0.15 that the competitor would follow the company's action, and 0.80 that the competitor would convert independent of the coffee company's action.

It was also believed that the major competitor's response would be followed by decisions from the rest of the industry—branches C_1 to C_6. It was considered a certainty (1.0) that some others in the industry would convert —C_2, C_4, and C_6—and a certainty (0.0) that all others would not convert— C_1, C_3, and C_5. Finally, for each "branch" (C) of the tree, changes in the company's market share were estimated. Each of four possible market share changes was given a 0.25 probability of occurring, that is, each of the four was believed to have an equal chance of occurring.

With this portion of the decision tree completed, it is possible to calculate the expected value associated with alternative A_1—the immediate nationwide introduction of the new container. To do so, one begins at the right side and calculates the expected value associated with each C branch. For example, the C_6 expected value of $1,278 thousand is obtained by multiplying each of the four monetary value figures ($3,312, $2,044, $1,340, and −$1,586) by the appropriate probability (0.25). This total is then weighted by 1.0 and combined with zero from C_5 to get the expected value of B_3— $1,278. This procedure is used to calculate expected values for C_4 (and B_2), and for C_2 (and B_1). The expected values (in thousands) of the B outcomes are weighted by their probabilities and summed

$$(\$1,278) (0.80) + (\$1,627) (0.15) + (\$2,234) (0.05) = \$1,378$$

to obtain the expected value of the first alternative (A_1). The expected values of each of the alternatives similarly computed are

Alternative	Expected value ($000)
1	$1,378
2	212
3	769
4	823
5	1,246
6	1,554

Alternatives 6 and 1 appear to be the most promising, and both favor the new container. Should management use the findings of this analysis and choose either alternative 6 or 1? Management should recognize that the entire analysis is based on the estimates *they* provided—the monetary values associated with different market shares and the probabilities assigned to the various outcomes such as competitors' reactions and resulting market shares.

If the estimates are based on the best information available, they represent management's best judgment without the benefit of further research. Thus, if management is confident that the identified outcomes and the probabilities assigned to them are correct, alternative 6 would be the best choice, and the firm would begin two months of consumer research and order all conversion equipment at once.

The above analysis illustrates a case in which management may not need research to make a decision. The results of the analysis, however, are determined by management's estimates of the monetary value of the various outcomes and of the probability that each will occur. If management feels secure in these estimates, no further study is necessary. If there is considerable uncertainty about the accuracy of the estimates, however, management may wish to do some research.

BAYESIAN ANALYSIS

Bayesian analysis is another method which can be used to help management decide whether or not to do research. The diagram in Figure 6–5 introduces this method.

FIGURE 6–5. Framework of a typical Bayesian analysis

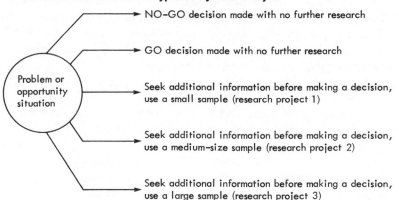

The figure suggests that a management facing a problem situation will consider a number of possibilities, of which the first two have already been discussed—making either a GO or NO-GO decision without further research. In most cases, it is reasonable to assume that some other possibilities exist, namely, doing various amounts of research before making a decision. Figure 6–5 shows the case where management is considering undertaking one of three research projects prior to making a decision. Here management can ask, "Are we better off making a decision without doing further research, or will we be better off delaying the decision until after we have obtained the findings from research project 1 (or 2, or 3)?" To answer this question, management will have to make judgments about what additional information the research will produce and how valuable that information will be. An alternative question to the one above would be: "How much should we be willing to pay for that information?"

Value of perfect information. A soft drink company is faced with the decision of whether to introduce a new brand. The company assigns a 0.80 probability to a favorable sales reaction and a 0.20 probability to a "failure." If the new brand is successful, the company expects to make $500,000 additional profit, but if it is unsuccessful, the company expects to lose $300,000. As a result, the expected value of introducing the new brand is

$$\$340,000 = (\$500,000)(0.8) + (-\$300,000)(0.2).$$

Suppose now that the decision-maker could undertake marketing research which would yield *perfect* information, that is, the research would tell with certainty whether or not the new brand would be successful. How much would such information be worth? At present, the expected payoff is $340,000 if the new brand is introduced. If the decision-maker knew *for certain* that the new brand would succeed, it would be introduced and realize $500,000 additional profits. If the decision-maker knew *for certain* that the new brand would not be successful, it would not be introduced and the payoff would be zero. The decision-maker believes probabilities are 0.8 for success and 0.2 for failure. That is, if perfect information could be obtained, there is a 4 out of 5 chance that it would indicate the new brand would be successful and a 1 out of 5 chance that it would indicate the new brand would fail. Therefore, if the decision-maker had perfect information, the expected value of decision making would be

$$\$400,000 = (0.8)(\$500,000) + (0.2)(\$0),$$

because the potential loss of $300,000 would be avoided. How much should the decision-maker be willing to pay for such perfect information? The *value of perfect information* is the difference between $400,000, the expected value with certainty, and $340,000, the expected value with uncertainty, or $60,000. If the proposed research would cost more than $60,000 to conduct, it should definitely not be undertaken.

This calculated value of perfect information is useful because it gives the manager an estimate of the upper limit that should be spent on research. However, it does not tell the manager *how much should be spent on a specific research project.* To arrive at such an estimate, one must use a more complete Bayesian analysis.

A Bayesian analysis. Assume that the soft drink company manager feels the introduction of the new brand will lead to one of three possible results, each called a state of nature. If the market is highly receptive to the new brand, it will achieve a market share larger than 5 percent and profits will amount to $500,000. If the new brand's reception is only average, its market share will be 1–5 percent and the company's profits will be $300,000.

A poor market reception (less than 1 percent market share) will result in a loss of $500,000.[2] Thus, the manager knows that one of these three states of nature (that is, market shares) does exist but the manager is not certain which. Using best judgment, the manager estimates a 0.30 probability that the "highly receptive" market condition will be the true state of nature. Probabilities of 0.50 and 0.20 are also estimated for the "average" and "poor" market receptions being the true states of nature. Table 6–1 shows a payoff table containing this information with the three different states of nature identified as S_1, S_2, and S_3.

TABLE 6–1. Payoffs from introduction of new brand

	States of nature					
	$S_1 > 5\%$		$S_2 = 1{-}5\%$		$S_3 < 1\%$	
Alternative decisions	*Probability S_1 exists*	*Profit if decision taken*	*Probability S_2 exists*	*Profit if decision taken*	*Probability S_3 exists*	*Profit (loss) if decision taken*
Introduce new brand ...	0.30	$500,000	0.50	$300,000	0.20	(−$500,000)
Do not introduce	0.30	0	0.50	0	0.20	0

The expected value of introducing the new brand is $200,000:

$$(0.3 \times \$500,000) + (0.5 \times \$300,000) + (0.2 \times -\$500,000)$$

If the executive had perfect information, that is, if all uncertainty could be eliminated, the correct decision could be made depending upon which state of nature existed. If S_1 or S_2 existed, the new brand would be introduced making a profit of $500,000 or of $300,000, respectively. If S_3 were the state of nature, the new brand would not be introduced and there would be a profit of zero. Since the probability of the three states of nature existing are 0.3, 0.5 and 0.2, respectively, the expected value of the decision under certainty, that is, with perfect information, is

$$\$300,000 = (0.3 \times \$500,000) + (0.5 \times \$300,000) + (0.2 \times \$0).$$

The value of perfect information would be the difference between the expected value of the decision under uncertainty and the expected value of the decision under certainty, or $100,000 ($300,000 − $200,000). Therefore, no research should be undertaken in this situation if it would cost more than $100,000.

At this point in the analysis, the manager knows the expected value of introducing the new brand without doing further research ($200,000), the expected value of not introducing the new brand ($0), and the value of per-

---

[2] The Bayesian analysis requires that *all possible states of nature be listed.* In this case, the three states of nature are collectively exhaustive, that is, no other states of nature are possible.

fect information ($100,000). Assume now that the manager is considering a marketing research test using one of three possible sample sizes—small (project 1), medium (project 2), and large (project 3). The manager faces the issue illustrated in Figure 6–5; namely, should a decision be made with no further research, or should research project 1, research project 2, or research project 3 be used? This can be evaluated by applying a Bayesian analysis, first, to research project 1, and then to research projects 2 and 3. That analysis consists of seven steps, which are illustrated using the small sample test (project 1) as an example.

Step 1.   Establishing prior probabilities.   Prior probabilities are the probabilities which a manager assigns to the possible existence of each state of nature. The probabilities of 0.3, 0.5, and 0.2 shown in Table 6–1 are called prior probabilities because they exist prior to obtaining additional information. They are subjectively determined by the manager using experience, past research, and any other pertinent input. They are the manager's best estimates of the likelihood that a state of nature is the one which actually exists in the real world.

In considering whether or not to use the small sample research project, the manager will want to consider how the new information *will change the prior probabilities*. For example, if the research project shows the new brand attaining a 3 percent market share, should the manager change the prior probabilities to 0.0, 1.0, and 0.0, or should they only be changed to 0.2, 0.7, and 0.1? At issue here is the recognition that research findings will approximate the true state of nature (i.e., the market share that would be obtained), but will not identify it perfectly. The Bayesian analysis takes this into consideration. In the explanation which follows S_i (where i can be set equal to 1, 2, 3, . . .) will be used to identify the states of nature, and E_j (where j can be set equal to 1, 2, 3, . . .) will be used to identify research outcomes. Four different types of probability will be discussed: conditional probability, joint probability, marginal probability, and posterior probability.

Step 2.   Determining conditional probabilities for different test outcomes.
If the small sample research project is undertaken, the results can show a market share of less than 1 percent (E_3), a market share between 1–5 percent (E_2), or a market share greater than 5 percent (E_1).[3] These three outcomes *include all possible research outcomes*—a condition which must be satisfied for the Bayesian analysis.

If the true state of nature is that the brand will attain a market share greater than 5 percent (that is, S_1 exists), what is the probability that the research outcome will show a market share less than 1 percent (that is, what is the probability that research outcome E_3 will result)? If S_1 exists, what is the probability that research outcome E_2 will result or that research outcome E_1 will result? These are conditional probabilities, and they are

---

[3] For simplicity three possible research outcomes are stated to cover all possibilities. Obviously, the possibilities could have been divided into a larger number.

shown in the first row of Table 6–2 for state of nature S_1.[4] Similar conditional probabilities are shown in the second and third rows of Table 6–2 for states of nature S_2 and S_3. (Note that for each state of nature the sum of the probabilities is 1.00, that is, one of the three outcomes must occur. Note also that the column probabilities do not necessarily sum to 1.00).

TABLE 6–2. Conditional probabilities that research outcome E_j will occur if S_i is the true state of nature.

	Possible research outcomes			
If state of nature is:	E_1 (Over 5 percent market share)	E_2 (1–5 percent market share)	E_3 (Below 1 percent market share)	Total
S_1 (over 5 percent share)	0.60	0.30	0.10	1.00
S_2 (1–5 percent share	0.20	0.50	0.30	1.00
S_3 (below 1 percent share)	0.10	0.20	0.70	1.00

Table 6–2 indicates that, if S_1 is the true state of nature, there is a 0.60 probability that the research will show outcome E_1, a 0.30 probability that the research will show outcome E_2 and a 0.10 probability that the research will show E_3. Similarly, if S_3 is the true state of nature, there is a 0.70 probability that the research will show outcome E_3, a 0.20 probability that it will show outcome E_2, and so on.

This second step in the Bayesian analysis requires that the manager and the researcher estimate the conditional probability that research outcome E_j ($j = 1, 2, 3$) will occur if the true state of nature is S_i ($i = 1, 2, 3$). These probabilities must be estimated for all combinations of E_j and S_i. They are then used in the calculation of joint probabilities.

Step 3.   Calculating joint probabilities.   If the manager knew which of the three states of nature actually existed, research would not be needed. However, research is being considered because the manager is uncertain as to what market share the new brand might achieve.

If additional information were obtained from new research, managers could ask how likely it is that state of nature S_1 (or S_2, or S_3) actually exists. If there is confidence in the research, managers will usually judge that the actual state of nature is close to that shown by the research. However, managers know that research results can easily differ slightly from the actual state of nature, and occasionally can differ quite a bit. Managers must also have confidence in their own estimates of the market. If the research results are

---

[4] Estimating conditional probabilities is similar to asking the classical sampling question: If a universe of 1,000 people contains 10 percent with red heads, what is the probability that a sample drawn from the universe will have 8–12 percent red heads; will have more than 12 percent red heads; will have less than 8 percent red heads? These issues are discussed at length in Chapters 10 and 14.

similar to the managers' estimates of the market, they are more confident that they are right. If the research conflicts with their estimates, they must decide how the new research findings can be used to modify their estimates. The next steps show a way of combining the new research information with prior estimates.

The probability that a given research outcome will be obtained if a given state of nature exists (conditional probability) is combined with the probability that the specified state of nature does in fact exist (prior probability). This is the joint probability that a given state of nature exists and that research, if conducted, will provide a given result (E_1, E_2, or E_3). The reader will recall that the manager estimated the probabilities of the existence of each of the three states of nature (S_1, S_2, S_3) at 0.30, 0.50, and 0.20, respectively. These are shown in column (a) of Table 6–3. The conditional probabilities that outcome E_j will occur, given that S_i is the true state of nature, are taken from Table 6–2. These appear in columns (b), (d), and (f) in Table 6–3. The joint probability that state of nature S_1 is the true state of nature *and* that test outcome E_1 will occur is equal to $0.30 \times 0.60 = 0.18$. See columns (a), (b), and (c) in row 1 of Table 6–3. This probability indicates that, according to the manager's best judgment, there is a probability of 0.18 that state of nature S_1 exists *and* that outcome E_1 will result if the research is undertaken. Similarly, the 0.03 which appears in row 1, column (g) indicates that there is a joint probability of 0.03 (0.30×0.10) that state of nature S_1 exists *and* that outcome E_3 will result if the research is undertaken.

Step 4. Estimating the occurrence of research outcomes (marginal probabilities).   The joint probabilities calculated in the step previous are used to estimate the probability that research outcome E_1 will occur, the probability that research outcome E_2 will occur, and so on. Each of these new probabilities is called a marginal probability.

A marginal probability can be calculated by summing the joint probabilities associated with *one research outcome.* For example, column (c) of Table 6–3 shows the joint probability of the following occurring together:

$$\text{State of nature } S_1 \text{ and research outcome } E_1 = 0.18$$
$$\text{State of nature } S_2 \text{ and research outcome } E_1 = 0.10$$
$$\underline{\text{State of nature } S_3 \text{ and research outcome } E_1 = 0.02}$$
$$0.30$$

These are *the only* conditions under which research outcome E_1 can occur because S_1, S_2, and S_3 represent all the states of nature that can exist. It follows that the best estimate of the probability of research outcome E_1 occurring is 0.30. Similarly, the best estimates that research outcomes E_2 and E_3 will occur are the marginal probabilities of 0.38 and 0.32, respectively, shown at the bottom of columns (e) and (g) in Table 6–3. Thus, the manager's best judgment (that is, the manager's prior probabilities and the esti-

TABLE 6-3. Joint probabilities for combinations of given states of nature and given research outcomes

		Possible research outcomes					
		E_1		E_2		E_3	
States of nature	(a) Probability of S_i being true state*	(b) Probability of E_1 research outcome if given S exists†	(c) Joint probability of E_1 and S_i [(a) × (b)]	(d) Probability of E_2 research outcome if given S exists†	(e) Joint probability of E_2 and S_i [(a) × (d)]	(f) Probability of E_3 research outcome if given S exists†	(g) Joint probability of E_3 and S_i [(a) × (f)]
S_1	0.30	0.60	0.18	0.30	0.09	0.10	0.03
S_2	0.50	0.20	0.10	0.50	0.25	0.30	0.15
S_3	0.20	0.10	0.02	0.20	0.04	0.70	0.14
	1.00		0.30		0.38		0.32

* Probabilities of S_1, S_2, or S_3 being the true state of nature are taken from Table 6-1.
† Probabilities of E_1, E_2, and E_3 outcomes occurring with given states of nature are taken from Table 6-2.

mated conditional probabilities) indicates that, if the small sample research project is undertaken, the probabilities of research outcomes E_1, E_2, and E_3 occurring are 0.30, 0.38, and 0.32, respectively.

Step 5.   Calculating posterior probabilities.   This step in the analysis involves calculating the posterior probabilities, *which are really "revised" prior probabilities.* They are called "posterior" because they are the manager's probabilities that various states of nature exist *after* the new information has been obtained from the research.

At the outset of the analysis (step 1), the manager estimated prior probabilities of 0.3, 0.5, and 0.2 for the existence of states of nature S_1, S_2, and S_3, respectively. After research findings are obtained, the manager will use the new information to revise those prior probabilities. To illustrate, assume that the small sample research project is undertaken and results obtained are E_2 —the research indicates the brand's market share will be 1–5 percent. The manager can now ask, "What is the probability that S_1 is the true state of nature? What is the probability that S_2 or S_3 is the true state of nature?" These posterior probabilities can be calculated using the data in Table 6–3.

Table 6–3 shows that research outcomes E_1, E_2, E_3 have probabilities of occurring of 0.30, 0.38, and 0.32, respectively [totals in columns (c), (e), and (g)]. Considering column (c), one can see that, if E_1 is the research result (a probability of 0.30), any one of the three states of nature (S_1, S_2, S_3) could exist, but the probability of S_1 actually being the true state of nature is larger than the probability of either S_2 or S_3 being the true state of nature (0.18 is larger than either 0.10 or 0.02). The specific probability that S_1 is the true state of nature, if E_1 is the research result obtained, is 0.18 ÷ 0.30 = 0.60. Similarly, if E_1 is the research result, the probability that S_2 is the true state of nature is 0.33 (0.10 ÷ 0.30) and the probability that S_3 is the true state of nature is 0.07 (0.02 ÷ 0.30).

These posterior probabilities are shown in Table 6–4, along with posterior probabilities for all other possible states of nature and test outcomes. In general, Table 6–4 reads as follows: If E_3 is the research outcome, the probability that S_2 is the true state of nature is 0.47, if E_2 is the research outcome, the probability that S_3 is the true state of nature is 0.10, and so on.

Step 6.   Developing a decision tree for research project 1.   Steps 1 through 5 are carried out primarily to obtain the marginal probabilities and

---

TABLE 6–4. Probability of a given state of nature being the true state if a given research outcome is obtained (posterior probabilities)

States of nature	Possible research outcomes		
	E_1	E_2	E_3
S_1	0.18/0.30 = 0.60	0.90/0.38 = 0.24	0.03/0.32 = 0.09
S_2	0.10/0.30 = 0.33	0.25/0.38 = 0.66	0.15/0.32 = 0.47
S_3	0.02/0.30 = 0.07	0.04/0.38 = 0.10	0.14/0.32 = 0.44
	1.00	1.00	1.00

posterior probabilities presented in Tables 6–3 and 6–4. Those probabilities are needed for the analysis made at this step.

Assume, for example, that outcome E_3 has been observed in the test market. The expected value of the decision to introduce the new brand, given that outcome E_3 has been observed, is a loss of $34,000. This calculation is made in the upper right corner of Table 6–5 and is based on (1) the posterior probability of each state of nature being the true state of nature *given that E_3 has been observed* and (2) the reward—that is, the profit or loss—expected from the introduction of the new brand if S_1 or S_2 or S_3 is the true state of nature. If the product is introduced and S_1 is the state of nature, a profit of $500,000 will be made; if S_2 is the state of nature, profits will be $300,000; if S_3 is the state of nature, a loss of $500,000 will be incurred. The probabilities that S_1, S_2, and S_3 are the real states of nature if E_3 is found in the research are 0.09, 0.47, and 0.44 respectively (see column labeled "Posterior probability that state of nature is S_i" in Table 6–5). Thus, if outcome E_3 oc-

TABLE 6–5. Decision tree analysis for research project 1

Expected value of decision making after research project 1	Possible research outcomes	Marginal probability of occurrence of outcome E_j	Expected value of introducing the new brand given the occurrence of outcome E_j	Posterior probability that state of nature is S_i	Rewards ($000)	States of nature
				0.09	$500	S_1
			–$34,000	0.47	300	S_2
			Introduce	0.44	–500	S_3
	E_3	0.32	Do not introduce			
				0.09	0	S_1
			$0	0.47	0	S_2
				0.44	0	S_3
				0.24	500	S_1
			$268,000	0.66	300	S_2
			Introduce	0.10	–500	S_3
$211,040	E_2	0.38	Do not introduce			
				0.24	0	S_1
			$0	0.66	0	S_2
				0.10	0	S_3
				0.60		S_1
			$364,000	0.33	300	S_2
			Introduce	0.07	–500	S_3
	E_1	0.30	Do not introduce			
				0.60	0	S_1
			$0	0.33	0	S_2
				0.07		S_3

curs, the expected value of introducing the new brand is a loss of $34,000:

$$(0.09) (\$500,000) + (0.47) (\$300,000) + (0.44) (-\$500,000).$$

The expected value of not introducing the brand is $0:

$$(0.09)(\$0) + (0.47)(\$0) + (0.44)(\$0).$$

These same calculations are made for the occurrence of test outcomes E_2 and E_1. Those results are shown in the center right and lower right portions of Table 6–5. The expected values of introducing the new brand if outcomes E_2 or E_1 occur are $268,000 and $364,000 respectively. (Since the decision not to introduce the new brand results in neither a profit nor a loss, the expected value of this decision is always $0, regardless of research outcome.)

Step 7. Calculating the expected value of decision making after research project 1. The final step in the analysis answers the important question asked at the outset: "What is the value of the information which will be generated by the research project?" The left half of Table 6–5 attempts to answer that question by using the marginal probabilities calculated at the bottom of Table 6–3—the probabilities that each of the research outcomes would occur.

This analysis indicates the manager would introduce the new brand of soft drink if test outcome E_2 or E_1 resulted; because that action would have an expected value of $268,000 if research outcome E_2 occurred, or an expected value of $364,000 if outcome E_1 occurred (see Table 6–5). If test outcome E_3 occurred, the manager would not introduce the new brand because the expected value of doing so would be $-$34,000. (The fact that this alternative is *not selected* is shown in Table 6–5 by the double bar across the line after the E_3 marginal probability.) The expected value of decision-making *using the information from the small sample research project* is, therefore, $211,040:

$$(0.32) (\$0) + (0.38) (\$268,000) + (0.30) (\$364,000).$$

The data for this calculation are shown in columns 2–4 of Table 6–5, and summarized in Table 6–6.

TABLE 6–6. Expected value of decision making after research project 1

(a)	*(b)*	*(c)*	*(d)*	*(c) ×(d)*
Research outcome	Decision if outcome E_j occurs	Expected value of decision	Marginal probability of occurrence of outcome E_j	Expected value of decision after research
E_1	Introduce	$364,000	0.30	$109,200
E_2	Introduce	268,000	0.38	101,840
E_3	Do not introduce	0	0.32	0
				$211,040

Calculating the expected value of decision making after research projects 2 and 3. The foregoing analysis was concerned solely with the contribution a small sample research project could make to a manager's decision making. That analysis can be summarized as follows: the expected value of introducing the new soft drink brand without doing further research is $200,000, while the expected value of introducing the new brand after research project 1 is $211,040. Thus, the maximum value derived from research project 1 is $11,040, and the manager would be well advised not to undertake the research if it will cost more than that amount.

But at the beginning of this discussion, three possible research projects were considered. The above analysis should now be repeated for research project 2 and for research project 3. The only changes will be in the assigned conditional probabilities discussed in step 2 (see Table 6–2); these are the probabilities that various research results will occur if given states of nature exist. These changes in conditional probabilities will occur because project 2 was to have a medium-sized sample and project 3 a large sample. The manager will expect the medium sample to be more likely to produce results indicating the true state of nature than the small sample (project 1). Similarly, the manager will expect even more accuracy from the large sample (project 3). For example, in the large-sample research project, the manager would assign a higher probability to the occurrence of research outcome E_1 if the true state of nature were S_1 than the 0.60 probability in the small-sample project (see Table 6–2). Similarly, the manager would assign a higher figure than 0.50 (see Table 6–2) to the probability of research outcome E_2 in the large-sample study if the true state of nature were S_2.

After the manager and the researcher develop sets of conditional probabilities for the medium- and large-sample projects, the analysis for each would follow the seven steps discussed above. Such analyses (not shown here) indicate that the expected value of decisions on introducing the new soft drink brand after research projects 2 and 3 would be $239,600 and $260,100 respectively.[5]

If the costs of doing research projects 1, 2, and 3 are $10,000, $20,000, and $30,000, respectively, the manager can use the information shown in Table 6–7 to decide whether to do research and, if so, which project to undertake. Table 6–7 indicates that project 1 is of little worth (its net value is only $1,040), but that both projects 2 and 3 are worth doing because they have a positive net value. However, project 3 has a higher net value and, therefore, should be preferred over project 2.

---

[5] These results are based upon the seven-step analysis discussed earlier, with the exception that the two sets of conditional probabilities shown below were used for research projects 2 and 3. Compare to Table 6–2.

Project 2			Project 3		
0.70	0.25	0.05	0.80	0.20	0.00
0.15	0.60	0.25	0.10	0.70	0.20
0.05	0.15	0.80	0.00	0.10	0.90

TABLE 6–7. Summary of Bayesian analysis of value of proposed research

(1) Research project to be undertaken	(2) Expected value of new brand introduction	(3) Value of research*	(4) Cost of research	(5) Net value of research†
None	$200,000	—	—	—
1	211,040	$11,040	$10,000	$ 1,040
2	239,600	39,600	20,000	19,600
3	260,100	60,100	30,000	30,100

* Column (2) minus $200,000, the expected value of new brand introduction without research.
† Column (3) minus column (4).

The above procedure illustrates how a Bayesian analysis can be used to determine whether anything is gained by doing research, and which research project appears to offer the greatest value. It should be noted in Table 6–7 that, if research projects 1, 2, and 3 cost $5,000, $10,000, and $15,000, respectively, all would show a positive net value. If the projects cost $25,000, $50,000, and $100,000, respectively, none would show a positive net value, and, therefore, none would be worth doing.

The reader will note that the above illustration is simplified. In practice there would be complicating factors such as more possible states of nature, and more possible research outcomes. Nevertheless, this type of analysis provides an explicit basis for appraising the value of marketing research.

SUMMARY

With the emergence of a problem or opportunity situation, the decision makers must determine what courses of action will be considered and must estimate the consequences of each. If managers are faced with uncertainty— either with respect to a clear understanding of the problem or opportunity, or with respect to the consequences of possible decisions—they may use research to reduce that uncertainty.

Managers and researchers can use a decision tree analysis in such situations to help them determine if a decision can be made without doing further research, or to identify information areas in which additional data should be gathered through research. If some research is to be undertaken, a Bayesian analysis can help managers and researchers identify the research project which appears to offer the greatest information value relative to its cost.

Case 6–1
PRENTICE DISTRIBUTING COMPANY

The Prentice Distributing Company sold a line of home and commercial garden and lawn power equipment, electric golf carts, power maintenance items for golf courses, and spare parts for these items. It served one entire state and part of another located in the southwestern part of the United States. Prentice operated both as a wholesaler and a distributor. In the former capacity, it purchased in quantity its lawn and garden items from a variety of sources and sold them to retailers who, in turn, sold to the ultimate users—mainly households. As a distributor, it sold items direct to industrial buyers—primarily golf courses. Its sales force of 16 men and women sold to both retailers and industrial users.

Prentice competed with a variety of wholesalers and distributors, but in the home and garden area competed mainly against one other distributor whose sales of these items were estimated to be about the same as Prentice for the equivalent geographical area. The two collectively were estimated to have about a 60 percent share of the market. Both carried different brands of lawn and garden equipment although both emphasized their higher priced lines.

In late February Prentice executives became aware of a substantial amount of price competition at the retail level on home lawn mowers. While a certain amount of price competition was inevitably present on the lower priced, less well-known brands, the extent of price-cutting on the higher priced brands was considered highly unusual. Some retailers, especially those in the larger metropolitan areas, were selling one or more leading brands at prices 15 percent to 18 percent below "usual" or "suggested" prices. In the case of Prentice retailers, this was not due to excessive inventories nor was this thought to be the case with the other retailers involved.

Further investigation revealed that brand A, the high-priced, top-of-the-line brand which was distributed by Prentice, was being sold by many retailers at $310 which represented a reduction of $50 off its list price of $360. Its primary competitor, brand B, which was distributed by Prentice's major competitor, was priced in a similar fashion—at $305, down from a list price of $352.

An examination of Prentice's price schedule to retailers for brand A versus that of the competitor for brand B revealed that while approximately the same, there was a difference in unit prices in larger order sizes which favored brand B (Exhibit 1). Prentice operated at a 16 percent margin on the under 20-unit lots.

EXHIBIT 1. Prentice retail quantity discount schedule for brand A versus competitor's schedule for brand B (as of April 1)

	Per unit	
	Brand A	*Brand B*
Retail unit suggested price	$360.00	$352.00
Wholesale unit delivered price in lots of		
Under 20 units	$288.00	$278.00
20–29 units	280.80	271.04
30–49 units	273.60	264.00
50 and over	266.40	256.96

In early March brand B's distributor announced a $40 trade-in sale; that is, for an indefinite period retailers were to allow $40 off the list price to customers who had a machine to turn in, regardless of its make or condition. This offer was promoted with heavy newspaper advertising and store signs and displays. Retailers could dispose of the trade-ins any way they wished but had to absorb the entire price reduction: that is, the price paid by retailers for brand B remained exactly the same as before.

Within a week Prentice noticed a substantial decline in its sales of brand A (Exhibit 2 shows the monthly sales of this brand for last year and the current year). Total unit sales were forecast at 10,000 units for the current year. If

EXHIBIT 2. Prentice monthly unit sales of brand A last year and projected sales current year

Month	Last year	Current year*
January–February	600	652
March	1,656	1,792
April	2,576	2,740
May	2,024	2,134
June	736	750
July	368	412
August–December	1,240	1,520
Total	9,200	10,000

* January–February current year sales are actual; all others are estimates.

the situation continued, it was thought that sales for April, May, June, and July would be "down" by 40 percent, 45 percent, 50 percent, respectively.

With these "facts" in mind, Prentice considered its options, which were thought to be as follows:

1. To match the competitor's trade-in offer of $40 and advertise this offer in strength at a cost of $15,000. The retailer would absorb the cost of the trade-in while Prentice would pay for all advertising. Prentice estimated that the results of this option would be a $+6$ percent increase over estimated current year sales (with 0.6 probability), a $+3$ percent increase over estimated current year sales (with 0.3 probability), $+0$ percent increase over estimated current year sales (with 0.1 probability).

2. To offer an outright price reduction of $40 to counteract the trade-in. Again, this would be absorbed by the retailer. This was thought to be a questionable option, since competition had already been making such an offer for some time. Prentice estimated the results of this option to be a $+1$ percent sales increase (with 0.1 probability), a $+0$ percent increase (with 0.2 probability), a -1 percent decrease (with 0.3 probability), a -2 percent decrease (with 0.4 probability).

3. To increase cooperative advertising allowances given to retailers on brand A from 2 percent of sales to 4 percent. Because of brand A's reputation, Prentice felt that this might be an effective course of action. Prentice

estimated the results of this option to be a $+2$ percent sales increase (with 0.4 probability), a $+1$ percent increase (with 0.2 probability), a $+0$ percent increase (with 0.2 probability), a -1 percent decrease (with 0.2 probability).

4.   To provide a special retail sales incentive of $15 per unit, paid for by Prentice. Retailers would find this an attractive option because it represented $55 more gross profit per unit than was available from brand B. Prentice estimated the results of this option to be a $+4$ percent sales increase (with 0.5 probability), a $+2$ percent increase (with 0.5 probability), a $+0$ percent increase (with 0.0 probability).

Since many of the retailers of brand A also sold brand B, Prentice felt that action of some kind must be forthcoming in the immediate future. It was not thought that similar action was necessary, or desirable, on other lawn mowers although these also were experiencing price erosions.

What market research should be undertaken in order to help Prentice decide which options to undertake?

Before making your recommendations, set up a decision tree analysis which will enable you to determine better what options are most feasible.

Case 6–2
LERNER PAINT COMPANY

The Lerner Paint Company was a medium-sized firm producing a high quality paint which was sold nationally through stores franchised to handle the Lerner brand. Lerner sold a complete line of paints with the various bases—oil, alkyd, water, and latex. The line included all of the ordinary colors and some special colors developed by Lerner. The firm was intrigued by a new type of roller for applying paint which had been brought to it by a hitherto unknown individual, Mr. Swenton.

The new roller had a chamber above the actual roller which was as wide as the roller itself—ten inches in the standard size—one inch thick, and extended about eight inches up the handle. A plastic bag of paint could be placed in this chamber. The bag was perforated at one end; when it was inserted in the chamber, a tape covering the perforation was removed to permit the paint to ooze out onto the roller. The chamber could be made smaller by squeezing the lid down tighter and tighter. A series of catches in the lid made this easy to do. As the bag was squeezed, more paint was forced out through the perforations. This made it possible to keep a constant flow of paint on the roller and, hence, made it unnecessary for the painter to stop and dip the roller in a pan of paint. The roller model which Mr. Swenton had developed held a plastic bag holding ⅘ quart of paint. All of the different base paints could be used in this manner.

The Lerner management tried the new product in the company laboratories. It seemed to perform adequately and with a few minor adjustments was ready for the market. In appraising the possible sales of this product, management felt that it had appeal primarily for the household do-it-yourself market. Professional painters had resisted the use of paint rollers, inasmuch as such rollers speeded up painting and, thereby, presumably reduced the need for painters. This suggested to the Lerner management that this new device, which would speed painting more, would be further resisted by professional painters. The device would have a great deal of convenience for the typical consumer, however, and might be received very well by the household market.

Looking over statistics of the household paint market, the Lerner management found that there were varying estimates. One mail survey made by a trade association among 6,000 consumer panel members showed that, on the average, families in the United States painted two and a fraction rooms in their homes each year. This included bathrooms, kitchens, and game rooms, as well as living rooms and bedrooms. On the average, these families had five such rooms which were painted, as opposed to being papered, in their homes. Among these families, 70 percent painted their rooms themselves, that is, some member of the family actually put the paint on the walls.

Another survey, which had been made by mail by one of the major home magazines among its subscribers, found that 60 percent of the subscribers answering the questionnaire had painted one complete wall or ceiling or more during the past 12 months. Among this 60 percent of the families, 70 percent had done the painting themselves. Painting of interior rooms in homes was a seasonal activity. During each of the months from April to September, 10 to 14 percent of the families did some interior painting. In March and October about 8 percent of the families did such painting, while in the other four months 5 percent or less did interior painting. Both men and women did a considerable volume of interior painting. The proportion was about equal, according to replies received in the survey. The percentage of women doing the painting, however, was larger among lower income groups and among families living on farms and in smaller towns. As income rose and as the size of the city in which families were located increased, the percentage of women doing painting declined; however, there was a significant proportion of families, about 20 percent, in which women did painting even in the population groups where women were less inclined to do this work.

The most recent survey of household interior painting indicated that about 60 percent of those families doing their own painting had used rollers the last time they had done such painting. This survey, however, was several years old. Data on household painting by the members of the family showed that there were fairly common practices in this regard throughout the various sections of the United States.

The cost of producing the new type of roller which Mr. Swenton had developed was relatively small. Lerner executives believed that they could produce a medium-quality roller of this type so that it would sell for about $1 at retail level.

In estimating the possible profit opportunities in the new product, Lerner executives made the following estimates:

1. There were 50 million families in the United States that might be considered possible customers for the product.
2. One percent of those families which painted 200 square feet or more in a year might be induced to try the product.
3. No profit would be made on the sale of the new type of roller, but one bag of paint would be sold with each roller.
4. Paint sold with rollers would be paint that would not otherwise be sold.
5. Lerner's margin on the added paint sales would be 60 cents per bag regardless of volume.
6. To complete the engineering and marketing of the product would require an investment of $100,000.
7. From the data available the best estimates Lerner executives could make of the proportion of the 50 million families who were potential customers that painted 200 square feet or more in a year were as follows:

Percent of families painting 200 square feet or more in a year	Probability of being fact
60 percent or more	0.05
40–59 percent	0.40
20–39 percent	0.50
Under 20 percent	0.05
Total	1.00

Research to test the product in actual consumer use and to determine the percentage of families who painted 200 square feet or more a year would cost an estimated $5,000.

Do the secondary data available indicate a large enough market to warrant further investment in marketing research?

How much confidence should Lerner executives have in these data? Are they all of equal reliability?

Should the additional research expenditure of $5,000 be made?

PART III

THE MARKETING RESEARCH PROCESS

The basic concepts of research design, methods of obtaining data from respondents, and sources of secondary data have been discussed in the preceding chapters. The discussion has been general in nature, and the matters of identifying a specific research situation and of organizing and executing the resulting research project have been avoided. The next 12 chapters trace a research situation from its inception to the analysis of the collected data and preparation of the report. Each major step faced by the researcher on a typical project is discussed.

7

The marketing research process: Planning the research project

In planning and designing a specific research project, it is necessary to anticipate all of the steps which must be undertaken if the project is to be completed successfully. These steps—often referred to collectively as the research process—are not a mechanically contrived sequence of independent steps. They consist of a number of interrelated, frequently overlapping, activities. Each step is dependent to some extent on each of the others, and the first step must be planned with the second, third, and so on, in mind. For example, one must have a good understanding of the problem in order to identify the information needed for "solving" the problem. The form and content of the "needed information" strongly affects the questionnaire, which in turn affects how the collected data will be analyzed.

This chapter and all of the other chapters in Part III are concerned with the individual steps in the marketing research process. If it were broken down into very small parts or activities, the marketing research process would consist of a great number of steps.[1] On the other hand, if the various parts are clustered according to major activities, the marketing research process can be viewed as consisting of the following seven steps.

1. Formulating the study.
2. Preparing a list of the needed information.
3. Designing the data collection project.
4. Selecting a sample type.
5. Determining sample size.

---

[1] For example, see the breakdown found in Charles S. Mayer, "Evaluating the Quality of Marketing Research Contractors," *Journal of Marketing Research* (May 1976): 131–41.

6. Organizing the fieldwork.
7. Analyzing the collected data and reporting the findings.

Sources of error

If not properly designed, each step in the research process can be a potential source of error. Table 7–1 is a list of some of the errors and difficulties associated with the major steps in the research process. The desired result of any research project is the information needed by management to resolve the problem which gave rise to the project. Such information must be relatively error free. Consequently, a research project should be designed in such a way that the magnitude of the overall error is small enough to allow the findings to be used by management. To do so, the research design should anticipate the sources of error which can affect a research project and the precautions which can be taken to minimize those errors.

TABLE 7–1. Research process steps and potential sources of error

Step	Sources of error or other difficulties
1. Problem formulation	Management identifies the "wrong" problem or defines the problem poorly.
2. Determining information needs	Management is unable to identify the specific information needed for decision making.
3. Research design, including questionnaire	Ambiguous questions or poor experimental designs result in responses which are not reliable or valid.
4. Sample type	Sample procedures result in the selection of a biased sample.
5. Sample size	Some error arises from the random fluctuations normally associated with sampling.
6. Fieldwork	Errors are caused by nonrespondents, by poor selection of respondents, by the interviewer, or by the nature of interviewer-respondent interaction.
7. Tabulation and analysis	Errors occur during the process of transforming raw data from questionnaires into "research findings."

The seven steps shown in Table 7–1 are described in more detail in this chapter and the other chapters in Part III. The discussions attempt to point out the major errors which can occur at each research process step, and what can be done at each step to minimize or eliminate such errors.

INITIAL STEPS IN DESIGNING A RESEARCH PROJECT

The first three steps in the marketing research process tend to be highly interrelated. "Formulating the study" cannot take place without a tentative "list of needed information." Similarly, these two steps cannot be completed without some preliminary ideas about the design to be used in collecting data. These first three steps are discussed in greater detail now.

Formulating the study

In this step of the research design process, the researchers must first attempt to answer the questions, "What is the purpose of this study?" and "Why is the study being undertaken?" If these questions are not properly answered at the outset, the project may very well be directed at vague goals, with the probable result that the collected data will be inadequate for the manager's purposes. Perhaps the best way to identify specific research objectives is to put them in written form. The manager and the researcher can then discuss the written statement, modifying it where necessary. Once it has been approved both by the manager and the researcher, it can serve as the researcher's guide to what it is that the manager expects from the research.

Clearly, this step in the research process must involve both the manager and the researcher. One source of research error is a poorly formulated study. Much of the responsibility for study formulation necessarily lies with the manager. Researchers cannot be expected to answer such questions as "What is the purpose of this study?" without a great deal of assistance. Hence, if this step in the research process is not to be a major source of error, the manager and the researcher must collaborate in a clear and precise identification of the study objectives. Only then can the researcher begin to formulate the study, that is, to consider whether to use exploratory or conclusive research, whether to collect case study or statistical data, and whether to use a descriptive or experimental design. Before making these decisions, the researcher should gain a good understanding of the situation which led to the request for research. Was it the recognition of an urgent problem, was it a need for information which can identify the existence of a problem, or was it for a more precise identification of a potential opportunity?

If a *potential opportunity* stimulated the request, the researcher may be asked for information of the sort to be obtained by an exploratory study involving such things as a search of secondary information sources, discussions with knowledgeable individuals, or unstructured interviews with potential customers. In general, this type of study is likely to involve explorations in a number of directions, each of which will make some contribution to the manager's understanding of the potential opportunity. As the opportunity becomes more clearly identified, the manager may either discontinue the research activities, or request research which is more conclusive, that is, more decision oriented.

A *poorly defined problem* has research implications similar to those described in the above paragraph. No one can envision all of the many factors that may have a bearing on a problem. Consider the company faced with a decline in its sales. What researcher can list all of the possible causes of this decline and can then array these possible causes in order of their probable importance? Before attempting to do this, researchers should get ideas from as many useful sources as possible. When they have collected as many tentative explanations as they can, they are better able to set up hypotheses that are likely to support further research.

Probably the first investigation that should be done in such a situation is research among secondary sources, including all applicable company records. An example of the value of this type of effort occurred when a producer of commercial laundry equipment experienced declining sales. The management was worried that the product had declined in quality or price appeal relative to competitors. A research firm charted the company's sales and the industry's sales over the past ten-year period. Company sales had gone down, but the industry's sales had declined more rapidly. This changed the whole line of thinking as to the problem. Instead of suffering from competition within its industry, the firm was losing business to a change in the environment. The investigation then turned in the direction of finding new products which had growth potential.

Frequently, a manager requests information which will help *identify the existence of problem situations*. Information useful for this purpose may include data on company sales and costs and either the company's market share or total industry sales. Much of this information is available from internal sources, but field studies or secondary data sources such as commercial services, trade associations, and government agencies are also useful. Sales, costs, and market share are analyzed by products, sales districts or markets, sales representatives, and types of accounts. This information is compared with some standard, such as last year's sales or this year's quota, to see how the firm is progressing. If standards are not being met, management will be alerted that a problem may exist.

Other studies may be directed toward understanding and *solving specific problems*. Some typical examples are

1. Of three proposed advertising copy approaches, which will lead to the largest increase in brand awareness?
2. Which will most effectively counter a competitor's new product introduction—a 50 percent increase in mass media advertising, a 15-cent coupon in consumer magazines, or a 10 percent discount to the trade?
3. How important is a reduction in delivery time to the firm's largest accounts?

Studies of this sort are likely to utilize conclusive research designs, probably experimentation, and will be much more structured and statistically oriented than exploratory studies. Unlike the research described in the previous paragraph, these studies will not rely heavily on internal information or other secondary sources.

Preparing a list of needed information

When satisfied with the statement of research objectives, the researcher will prepare a list of the information which is needed to attain the objectives. In setting down what information is needed, the researcher must anticipate limitations of the data-gathering process. For example, it does no good to list desired information which cannot be obtained because consumers cannot, or will not, answer questions on such a subject or because dealers consider such information a competitive secret. The researcher has to know what information can realistically be obtained.

In a study to determine the reasons why consumers used, or did not use, instant rice, the following information was sought.

1. How many homemakers have heard of instant rice, and of these, how many are current users and how many nonusers of the product?
2. Why has the product not been tried by those who have heard of it but have never used it?
3. Why did some homemakers try the product, but not continue to use it?
4. How is the product used for each major use, and why is the product used instead of substitute items?
5. In each of the above questions, how do the results compare among classes by age of homemaker, family income, family size, education of homemaker, and race?

The above listing is presented as an example of the listing of information desired in an actual research project. The reader should note improvements that could have, and should have, been made. For example, in point one, what is a "current user," and in point four, what foods will be considered substitute items?

The researcher should evaluate the usefulness of the listed information by anticipating the possible findings of the study and then trying to answer the question, "What will management do if these are the findings?" It is possible that some findings may suggest courses of action which cannot be undertaken, for example, because of limited financial resources. If the firm can take no action regardless of what the findings are, then there is no reason to undertake a research study. Or, if it appears that only one course of action is open to the firm *regardless of the findings,* there is no decision to be made; hence, there is no need for research to be undertaken.

A research proposal for an agricultural chemical company provides a good illustration of this point. The study objectives were to obtain a profile of the company's image versus the images of competing companies with regard to such attributes as research skills, aggressiveness in introducing new products, maintaining an effective dealer organization, and competency of technical field staff. A number of possible findings could have been obtained, but the most likely one was that, because it was a new company, the firm's profile would not be as good as its competitors'. Given such a finding, what would management do? In this case, the management decided it would do nothing different from what it was already doing, since current actions were based on this assumption. The research director then set up a number of other alternative profiles, including one which was superior to the competitors on all counts. Only in the latter case did management indicate it would change what it was then doing (by reducing its corporate advertising budget); since the probability of such a "superior" profile was assessed at less than 0.01, the image study was abandoned.

Thus, it will sometimes be found that a research study is not necessary. Too frequently the assumption is made that research is always desirable, when, in fact, research expenditures should only be made when a firm will be able to act on the findings.

Yet many situations requiring a research input do arise and, when they do, the reader should recognize the importance of research process steps 1 and 2. The "formulation of the study" and the "list of needed information" reflect to a very great extent the managers' understanding of the competitive evironment in which they operate and the possible ways they can respond to problems and opportunities which they see in the environment. In effect, managers have some kind of model—either explicit or implicit—of the world within which they operate. If researchers do not have a good understanding of how a manager sees the real world, any research project they design is likely to gather some information which is *not useful* to the manager and, perhaps, *not gather* some information which the manager needs. This is a type of data-collection error which should be avoided. To do so, the researcher and the manager must work closely during steps 1 and 2. Together they should identify the decision model which the manager will use in making a decision. For example, after discussions with a researcher, a manager may state the decision model as follows: If research findings show X, then my decision will be A; if research findings show Y, then my decision will be B; if research findings show Z, then my decision will be C; and so on.

Although researchers have little chance of identifying such a decision model without the manager's cooperation and participation, they can contribute substantially to its formulation, and thus greatly enhance the utility of the research. The problem will become precisely defined, and information which is needed will become clearly identified. Since researchers will then know which data are needed, they can proceed into step 3 of the research process.

Designing the data collection project

This activity usually consists of two parts—the overall data collection design and the design of the data collection form. Since the latter is treated in detail in the next two chapters, only the former is discussed here.

After the list of needed information has been prepared in step 2, the researcher should determine whether such information is already available, either in company records or in outside sources. Certainly, the researcher should not collect data from the field until the appropriate secondary sources of information have been reviewed.[2] However, information obtained from secondary sources must be examined carefully to make sure that it fits the particular needs of the researcher. Since it was obtained for another purpose, it may not be adequate. Outside data may have been gathered and tabulated using different definitions—or the information may be outdated. While it is often difficult to determine the reliability of such data, a careful check should be made for internal consistency to determine whether data have been collected and reported with care and precision. The reputation and experience of the organization collecting the data are often the best guide to their accuracy.

If the needed information is not available from secondary sources, the researcher will have to collect data in the field. The next task is to identify who has the needed information and how it can be obtained. For example, in a study of attitudes toward hot cereals, the researcher must decide if only current users of hot cereal are to be studied or if potential users are also to be included. The researcher must decide if the data are to be collected through observations or interviews and, if the latter, whether the interview is to be a personal one in stores near the cereal display, or a telephone interview to the home where the cereal is consumed.

An important research design issue is whether to gather the data through a few case studies or through a large statistical sample. If the study is a conclusive one (that is, if the findings are to be "representative" of the universe), the researcher may want to use a large sample statistical study. However, if the project is concerned with finding a "best" way rather than a typical way of doing something—such as organizing a voluntary chain or laying out the main floor of a store—the research may well consist of the analysis of a few selected cases. The cases will be selected on the basis of the researcher's judgment as to what are the most successful cases available and, possibly, the least successful for comparison. A few cases only would be chosen—perhaps eight to ten, maybe only three or four.

If an experiment is part of the research design, the researcher must decide such things as where the "before" and "after" measurements will take place. The form of the experimental variable and how it will be applied must be determined. In the testing of advertising copy, for example, a before-after study could employ pilot versions of the proposed copy, or the study could be integrated with the initial appearance of the new copy in the mass media. Similarly, if a before-after-with-control-group experiment is to be part of the research design, the researcher must determine how the experimental and control groups are to be selected.

At this point in the research design process, the researcher will have deter-

---

[2] See Chapter 5.

mined (1) whether the research should be exploratory or conclusive, (2) who to interview, and how, (3) whether to study a few cases only, or sample a large group, and (4) whether or not to use experiments. These issues are concerned with the overall research design.

OTHER STEPS IN DESIGNING A RESEARCH PROJECT

What the researchers do in the last four steps of the research process will be greatly dependent upon what was decided in the first three steps. The last four steps of the marketing research process are described briefly here, and then are treated in detail in Chapters 10–18.

Selecting a sample type

The first task in sampling is to define carefully just what groups of people, stores, and so on are to be sampled. For example, if the study calls for collecting data from appliance dealers, then it is necessary to define what is meant by an appliance dealer (are discount stores selling appliances to be included?), and to define the precise geographical area which is of interest (e.g., the metropolitan Chicago area).

The researchers must also decide on the type of sample which is to be selected. There are two general methods which can be used to select respondents—probability and nonprobability. Probability methods use a procedure which insures that each member in the group from which the sample is to be drawn has a known probability of being chosen. There are various probability techniques such as simple random sampling, sampling systematically from a list of all items in the group, stratifying the group by certain characteristics and then randomly selecting within each stratum, and so on.

Determining sample size

The researchers must also decide on how large a sample to select. Marketing research samples vary from 10 or 15 to several thousand. The researcher must consider the problem at hand, the budget, and the accuracy needed in the data before the question of sample size can be answered. The sample size will have an effect on the level of confidence managers will have in the study's findings. For example, if 18 percent of Chicago's households report that they regularly view a certain television program, a manager can ask: "How close is this estimate to the real or true percentage existing among *all* Chicago households?" The manager is likely to have more confidence in the accuracy of the estimate if a large sample is taken rather than a small one.

Organizing the fieldwork

The fieldwork will include selecting, training, controlling, and evaluating the members of the field force. The methods used in the field are very important since they usually involve a substantial part of the research budget and are an important potential source of bias. Fieldwork methods are dictated largely by the method of collecting data, the sampling requirements and the kinds of information which must be obtained.

In studies involving personal interviews in the home, the fieldwork is widely dispersed and the fieldworkers themselves have varying skills. In such studies, it is difficult, expensive, and time-consuming just to determine whether the interviews or observations were actually made, let alone to determine whether each worker followed the field instructions to the letter. On the other hand, the fieldwork associated with some telephone studies is easier to monitor and control if the interviewers are all operating from a central location. In such situations the fieldworkers can be more closely supervised.

Analyzing the collected data and reporting the findings

After the fieldwork has been completed, there remains the difficult task of processing the completed data forms in a way which will yield the information which the project was designed to obtain. First, the forms need to be edited to make sure that instructions were followed, that all questions were asked or observations made, and that the resulting data are consistent and logical within each form. Next, the data must be prepared for tabulation. This means the data must be assigned to various categories, and then coded so the responses can be put on computer cards or tapes and then tabulated and analyzed by a computer.

The tabulation and analysis function is guided by the needed information which was identified in the second step of the marketing research process. This means that the researchers must establish procedures which transform the raw data in the computer into the information needed. Tables of data must be compiled, percentages and averages must be computed, and comparisons must be made between different classes, categories, and groups. In some projects researchers will use more advanced statistical or multivariate methods of analysis. Whatever the actual procedures used to process the raw data, the end result should be a set of information which coincides well with the list of needed information established in step 2 of the marketing research process.

The reporting of research findings represents the end product of the research process. No matter what the proficiency with which all previous steps have been dispatched, the project will not be successful if the findings are poorly reported.

The type of report will vary greatly depending on the nature of the project and the audience for which it is prepared. Some reports should include considerable descriptive material covering the details of the research methodology used to obtain the data. Other reports are concerned primarily with a presentation of the conclusions reached.

INTERRELATING THE STEPS: AN ILLUSTRATION

The first paragraph of this chapter points out that the marketing research process consists of interrelated steps. Now that the steps of the marketing research process have been introduced, readers will find it helpful to see a simple example which illustrates how the steps are interrelated.

The mayor of Millfort was thinking of asking the city council to vote funds for the development of a system of bicycle paths throughout the community.[3] Before doing so, he felt he should determine the percentage of bicycle owners and nonowners in favor of developing a system of bicycle paths. He discussed the matter with a local marketing research firm, which was asked to submit a proposal for research. Some of the highlights of that proposal are described below.

1.   The *purpose of the study* is to determine if enough bicycle owners and nonowners are in favor of the development of bicycle paths throughout the community. (The mayor, along with the city council, will specify the percentage that constitutes "enough".)
2.   The *information needed* is: How many people own bicycles, and are they in favor of, or opposed to, the development of a system of bicycle paths? How many people don't own bicycles, and are they in favor of, or opposed to, the development of a system of bicycle paths?
3.   The *data collection form* will include the two questions illustrated on the left side of Table 7–2.

TABLE 7–2. Questions and tabulations for the Millfort bicycle path study

Questions	Tabulations		
Do you own a bicycle? _____Yes _____No	Bicycle owners who	Number	Percent
	Strongly agree	_____	_____
	Somewhat agree	_____	_____
Will you please indicate the	Undecided	_____	_____
degree to which you agree or	Somewhat disagree	_____	_____
disagree with the following	Strongly disagree	_____	_____
statement: A system of bicycle			
paths should be developed in	Subtotal	_____	_____
our community.	Nonowners who		
_____Strongly agree	Strongly agree	_____	_____
_____Somewhat agree	Somewhat agree	_____	_____
_____Undecided	Undecided	_____	_____
_____Somewhat disagree	Somewhat disagree	_____	_____
_____Strongly disagree	Strongly disagree	_____	_____
	Subtotal	_____	_____
	Total	600	100%

---

[3] This illustration is adapted from William R. Wynd, "Six-Step Basic Program Can Help Volunteers Solve Research Problems," *Marketing News* (September 9, 1977):12.

4. After a representative sample of 600 community residents are inter-
    viewed, their responses will be *tabulated* in the manner shown on the
    right side of Table 7–2.

A close inspection of the above will reveal that the four steps of *purpose
of the study, information needed, data collection form,* and *tabulation* are
highly interrelated. The information needed follows directly from the purpose of the study, and the data collection form is strongly related to information needed. Not only does the tabulation follow logically from the data
collection form, the tabulation also coincides strongly with the information
needed.

SUMMARY

Chapter 7 is concerned with a transition from the basic research concepts
discussed in Part II to the identification of a specific research situation and
the research project which can help management handle the situation. In
order to design a specific project, it is necessary to anticipate all the steps
in the research process. These steps represent seven interrelated activities
which frequently overlap one another. They are (1) formulating the study;
(2) listing the needed information; (3) designing the data collection project;
(4) selecting a sample type; (5) determining sample size; (6) organizing the
fieldwork; and (7) analyzing the collected data and reported findings.

Case 7–1
BOLAN TRUCKS, INC.

Bolan Trucks, Inc. was a distributor of the complete line of International
Harvester Trucks, including a four-wheel-drive sports utility vehicle called
the Scout. Bolan Trucks was located in a large midwestern city, which was a
commercial and industrial center. In addition, five college campuses were
located within a short drive of the city's center.

Tom Bolan, the owner of Bolan Trucks, knew that there had been significant growth in the sales of four-wheel-drive vehicles over the last five to
six years. That growth, which had also occurred in Bolan's market area, was
due to at least two factors: increased interest in hunting, fishing, camping,
and other summertime and wintertime outdoor activities; and a shifting of
the population out of big cities into suburban areas and small cities and
towns. Four-wheel-drive vehicles had grown in popularity because of their
ability to maneuver on unpaved roads and trails not suitable for travel with
a standard automobile. This was possible because, in a typical car, power
from the motor was transmitted to only two of the wheels, but in a four-
wheel-drive vehicle the motor could drive all four wheels. Since four-wheel-
drive vehicles could take sportsmen way off the beaten track where a regular automobile could not go, those vehicles were becoming more popular

with outdoorsmen. Because of the International Harvester Scout, Bolan was interested in this growing market segment.

Bolan knew that his sales of the Scout had not kept pace with the sales growth of four-wheel-drive vehicles in general, and that most of those sales were being made by Jeep and the Chevrolet Blazer. He felt that the poor sales performance of the Scout was not due to an inferior product, because the Scout was a high-quality vehicle with attractive exterior styling and with interior appointments much like those in medium-priced station wagons. Unlike the Chevrolet Blazer, which was built on a pickup truck chassis, and the Jeep, which was designed as a World War II combat utility vehicle, the Scout had been specially designed as a four-wheel-drive passenger vehicle.

Research findings from a variety of studies had shown that the bulk of four-wheel-drive vehicle owners had been to college, were under 35 years of age, and were employed as professionals and managers. Because four-wheel-drive vehicle owners tended to be young and college educated, Bolan wondered if advertising in college newspapers and radio stations would help the International Harvester Scout capture a greater share of the four-wheel-drive market in his area. He believed that one factor contributing to the Scout's lower sales growth was that college students were probably more aware of Jeep and the Chevrolet Blazer than the Scout. If that were true, and if recent college graduates didn't even consider the Scout when contemplating the purchase of a four-wheel-drive vehicle, advertising to college students might prove to be a good long run strategy.

Bolan discussed the idea with Dr. Hall, a professor in the Business College at Allen University, which was located in the city. Hall suggested that the idea might be an interesting subject for a marketing research project in one of his classes. It would expose students to a real situation in which marketing research could be applied, and it might help Bolan determine whether his idea was a good one. Bolan agreed, and together they worked out a list of five items of information that should be obtained from current college students.

1. Were students aware that some vehicles had four-wheel-drive capability, and were they aware of the different brands offering that capability?
2. Based on their interest in outdoor activities and the expected location of their place of residence after graduation from college, did students have a potential need for a four-wheel-drive vehicle?
3. Were they dissatisfied with their present vehicles, especially in regard to performance capabilities when the owner was engaged in outdoor activities?
4. Did the students intend to purchase a motor vehicle within a few years after graduation from college?
5. Did they read their college newspapers and listen to their college radio stations?

Dr. Hall and his students then carried out a small pilot study designed to obtain the information Bolan needed to evaluate his idea of advertising to college students. Exhibit 1 shows the questionnaire used by the class when it completed 122 personal interviews of college students on the Allen University Campus and on two other nearby college campuses. Respondents were selected on a convenience basis in or near the student center. Interviewing was varied by time of day and day of week in an attempt to avoid bias. After the students had tabulated and analyzed the findings from their pilot study, Doctor Hall selected what he thought were the five most important ones.

1. Sixty-five respondents knew what it meant to have four-wheel-drive and 58 could name two or more brands which offered such a capability. Of these 58 respondents, 14 were aware of the Scout, but only 3 respondents said it was the best four-wheel-drive vehicle on the market. Jeep and Blazer were judged the best four-wheel-drive vehicles by 21 and 17 respondents, respectively.
2. Thirty-three respondents thought that they would have a need for a four-wheel-drive vehicle, while 89 did not. These findings were broken down by future place of residence (see Table 1) and by the degree of respondent participation in favored outdoor activities (see Table 2).
3. Only 32 of the respondents were dissatisfied with their present vehicles, but no one reported being dissatisfied because of the lack of four-wheel-drive.

TABLE 1. Need for four-wheel-drive, broken down by future place of residence

Need four-wheel-drive?	Future place of residence				
	Large urban	Small or medium city	Small town	Don't know	Totals
Yes	18	7	6	2	33
No	62	21	5	1	89
	80	28	11	3	122

TABLE 2. Need for four-wheel-drive, broken down by time spent on favorite activities

Need four-wheel drive?	Time spent on favorite activities						
	Great deal	Often	Occa-sionally	Sel-dom	Never	Don't know	Totals
Yes	8	15	8	1	1	0	33
No	12	42	24	8	2	1	89
	20	57	32	9	3	1	122

4. Seventy of the respondents reported that they intended to buy a motor vehicle within two years of their graduation from college, but only three respondents were thinking of purchasing a four-wheel-drive vehicle.

5. All of the schools at which respondents were interviewed had their own newspapers. Two thirds of the respondents reported that they read their college newspapers regularly.

Hall cautioned Bolan to recognize that these findings were from a pilot study and not from a full-scale marketing research project. If Bolan thought this type of research could help him make a decision regarding advertising the Scout on college campuses, Hall suggested that Bolan should first undertake a larger study involving professional interviewers and a more scientifically selected sample.

Evaluate the pilot study described in the case. Were the findings of any use to Bolan?

How could the study have been improved?

Should Bolan undertake a full-scale project and, if so, what should it be?

EXHIBIT 1

Good morning/afternoon/evening, my name is _____. I'm a student at Allen University, and one of my classes is doing a survey. Would you be so kind as to take a few minutes to answer some questions? Thank you!

1. Are you a student here at _____ (name of college) _____?
   _____Yes   _____No (STOP INTERVIEW)

2. Are you a senior, a junior, a sophomore, or a freshman?
   _____Sen. _____Jun. _____Soph. _____Fresh.
   _____Other (specify)_____

3. What kind of work do you expect to do after you've completed your education, that is, after you are no longer a full-time student?
   _____Professional   _____Military service
   _____Business   _____Other (specify)_____

4. If you were to estimate what your annual income will be three years after completing your full-time education, which of the following would you estimate, A, B or C? (show card)
   _____A. Less than $15,000
   _____B. $15,000 or more, but less than $20,000
   _____C. $20,000 or more

5. After completing your full-time education do you think you will live in a large urban area, in a medium-sized or small city, or in a small town?
   _____Large urban   _____Small town
   _____Medium/small city   _____Don't know

EXHIBIT 1 (continued)

6. What are your two most favorite outdoor activities?

_____Hunting   _____Hiking   _____Other (specify)
_____Fishing   _____Boating
_____Camping   _____Skiing

7. When you are on vacation, or when you have free time, how much do you participate in your favorite outdoor activities? (show card)

_____Great deal   _____Seldom
_____Often   _____Never
_____Occasionally

8. Do you own a motor vehicle?

_____Yes   _____No (SKIP TO Q13)

9. What brand and type of vehicle do you own?

Brand_____   Type_____

10. Are you in any way dissatisfied with your motor vehicle?

_____Yes   _____No (SKIP TO Q12)

11. Why are you dissatisfied with it?

_____Not big enough   _____Doesn't have four-wheel drive
_____Not powerful enough   _____Other (specify)

12. Will you buy essentially the same type of vehicle when you make your next automobile or vehicle purchase?

_____Yes. Why?_____
_____No. Why not?_____

(GO TO Q15)

13. Do you expect to buy a motor vehicle within two years of your graduation from college?

_____Yes   _____No (GO TO Q15)

14. What type or types of vehicles will you consider buying?

_____Station wagon   _____4-wheel-drive vehicle
_____Van   _____Other (specify)
_____Truck

15. What does it mean if a motor vehicle has four-wheel-drive capability?

_____Correct response   _____Incorrect response
_____Don't know

(Explain four-wheel-drive to respondent)

16. Do you think you would have need for a motor vehicle which had four-wheel-drive capability?

_____Yes. Why?_____
_____No. Why not?_____

17. Do you know the brand names of any motor vehicles which have four-wheel-drive capability? Do you know the name of the company that manufactures the vehicle?

Brand   *Manufacturer is*

_____Bronco ⎫ If only   _____Ford
_____Blazer ⎬ one brand   _____Chevrolet
_____Jeep   ⎬ mentioned,   _____Jeep (American Motors)
_____Scout   ⎭ GO TO Q20   _____International Harvester
_____Other   _____
_____Don't know any (GO TO Q20)

EXHIBIT 1 (concluded)

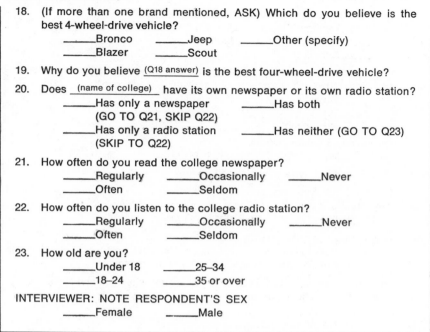

18. (If more than one brand mentioned, ASK) Which do you believe is the best 4-wheel-drive vehicle?

_____Bronco _____Jeep _____Other (specify)

_____Blazer _____Scout

19. Why do you believe (Q18 answer) is the best four-wheel-drive vehicle?

20. Does (name of college) have its own newspaper or its own radio station?

_____Has only a newspaper _____Has both
(GO TO Q21, SKIP Q22)

_____Has only a radio station _____Has neither (GO TO Q23)
(SKIP TO Q22)

21. How often do you read the college newspaper?

_____Regularly _____Occasionally _____Never

_____Often _____Seldom

22. How often do you listen to the college radio station?

_____Regularly _____Occasionally _____Never

_____Often _____Seldom

23. How old are you?

_____Under 18 _____25–34

_____18–24 _____35 or over

INTERVIEWER: NOTE RESPONDENT'S SEX

_____Female _____Male

Case 7–2
THE GRAYSON COMPANY

The Grayson Company was a relatively small detergent manufacturer which had prospered by producing specialty washing and cleaning products. Over the years a substantial portion of its marketing expenditures had been allocated to in-store merchandising activities. The company considered itself to be one of the more effective merchandisers in the industry and attributed much of its continued success to its expertise in this area. When a new marketing manager, Thomas Kirkland, was appointed, one of his first acts was to question the amount spent for in-store promotions. He found little evidence to indicate how effective the company's merchandising activities had been.

In discussing this problem with his marketing research director, Dr. James Mayer, Kirkland learned that before any major merchandising effort was undertaken a financial report using marginal contribution analysis was prepared, but that no evaluation was made of the actual results obtained. After further discussion the research director was asked to prepare a proposal for measuring the results derived from the company's major promotion "deals." In doing so, he was advised that his proposal should be sufficiently flexible to evaluate any specific promotional activity including price-off, contest, premium, coupon, and tie-in offers (that is, joint product offerings). Dr. Mayer's proposal is presented in the appendix.

> *Critically evaluate the proposal. What information is needed to evaluate the effectiveness of various promotions?*
>
> *Will the proposed research obtain that information?*
>
> *Can you suggest ways to improve the research?*

APPENDIX

TO: Thomas Kirkland, vice-president of marketing

FROM: Dr. James Mayer, research director

SUBJECT: A proposed research process for evaluating promotions

This proposed process can, as per your instructions, be used for any promotional activity or merchandise "deal" regardless of its incentive. It provides an objective "profitability" measure by which results can be determined and compared to targets, break-evens, and other promotions. While there are costs associated with the implementation of this process, the cost savings which will result from overall company increased promotional efficiency should more than offset them. The steps involved are set forth below.

1. A sample should be drawn from the large stores which are contacted at regular intervals by our direct sales force. The sample should be comprised of 50 stores which are located in five metro areas which, in turn, are located in our Eastern, Southern, Midwestern, Rocky Mountain and Southwestern, and Far Western sales regions. Thus, each metropolitan area will be represented by 10 stores.

    At periodic points in time and depending on the number of promotions involved, the sample should be "turned over." After every promotion 10 stores should be "dropped" and 10 new stores added—two per metro area. This means that each such test can be compared against several previous studies using identical stores. This should enhance the reliability of the comparisons. The exact manner of selecting the stores and the incentives offered can be determined at a later date.

2. Since these stores are contacted at regular intervals, the number of cases sold to each should be easily determined as it is a matter of record. Although our sales force calls on chain units to place merchandising pieces, they do not ordinarily call on such units to solicit orders. Thus, organizations which engage in central buying will not be included in our sample.

The number of cases sold to each sampling unit will be totaled for the 13-week period prior to the deal period. Weekly sales will be estimated by dividing this total by 13. This assumes that store weekly inventory remains pretty much the same over the time period.

3. The sales representatives involved will note for each sampling unit each time they call, the size and type of competitive displays for each of our products and the exact nature of any competitive deals.

4. When a promotion is scheduled the sales representatives will inventory each store before the promotion starts as to the number of our units in stock (for only the promotion item). They will do this at the end of the promotion period. This may cause them to shift the timing of their scheduled calls, but since a number of different sales representatives are involved the disruption overall to the sales force should be slight.

5. Step 4 should enable us to compute the sales during the deal period since we will know shipments from our records.

6. From the previous 13-week data we can calculate what sales during the deal period would have been under "normal" conditions. By subtracting normal case sales from the sales occurring during the deal period we can obtain an estimate of the number sold because of the deal. We can do the same for the after-deal period. Given the nature of our deals, I suggest using a two-week period.

7. The cost per deal-case sold will be calculated by taking into account the incentive (coupon plus handling cost, cents off, cost of any "free goods," and so on) and the cost of the merchandise display. Any media costs will not be included at this stage. The merchandise display cost will be estimated by costing out set-up time and travel to which will be added the cost of the display. The total here will be divided by the total number of cases sold. By subtracting these costs per case from the standard per case marginal contribution, we will be able to get a net marginal contribution per case sold as well as a total net contribution for the 50 stores.

8. The advertising department in cooperation with the application product manager will indicate the amount of media money involved and estimate *in advance* of the promotion the amount which should be charged against the specific promotion. This amount should be subtracted from the "net" obtained from the step above by estimating media costs per case sold and, then, multiplying this figure by the cases sold in the 50-store sample.

9. The results from step 8 can be compared with targets, break-even, or the results from other promotions.

8

Data collection I: Basic forms

When researchers have specified the information they need to solve the problem at hand, they must proceed to find that information. It is cheaper and simpler to use secondary data, data which someone else has collected previously, if such data are available. If secondary data cannot be found, researchers are faced with the necessity of collecting original information themselves. This collection and analysis of primary data occupy most of the time of marketing researchers. Accordingly, the next several chapters are devoted to consideration of primary data problems.

Questioning and observing are the two basic methods of collecting primary data.[1] Regardless of which of these data collection methods is used, some procedure must be developed to standardize the process and, thereby, standardize the data accumulated. If researchers go out to ask people questions and ask each person somewhat different questions, they will get answers that are not directly comparable. If 50 different fieldworkers in cities and rural areas throughout the country are sent out to observe sales representatives in retail appliance stores, they will be extremely unlikely to observe the same things unless they are given a guide to follow. Thus, some standardized procedure must be developed if the data collected in the field are to be comparable.

A second reason for needing a standardized procedure is to achieve speed and accuracy in recording data. If the fieldworkers have an established pattern to follow in their work and a standardized form on which to record the

---

[1] The general advantages and weaknesses of each of these methods were discussed in Chapter 4.

data collected, they can proceed more rapidly and more accurately. A third reason for standardized data collection procedures is to achieve speed and accuracy in handling the data in the office. If all the information coming into the central office from the fieldworkers comes in on a common form, it can be summarized more quickly and with less error than if fieldworkers report data in whatever form they choose.

To collect good primary data, then, it is necessary to develop standardized forms to guide the procedure. These forms are one of the main sources of error in the typical marketing research project. This is particularly true in the case of questionnaire studies where verbal communication is involved. Since questionnaire studies are also more prevalent than observation studies, the major part of this chapter will be devoted to the problems encountered in constructing good questionnaires. Some of this will also be pertinent to observation forms; however, a section at the end of the chapter will take up the latter specifically.[2]

IMPORTANCE OF QUESTIONNAIRE

When information is to be collected by asking questions of people who may have the desired data, a standardized form called a questionnaire is prepared. The questionnaire is a list of questions to be asked respondents and spaces in which to record the answers. Each question is worded exactly as it is to be asked, and the questions are listed in an established sequence. Figure 8–1 shows a page from a typical questionnaire.

At first, one is inclined to think that the construction of a questionnaire is simple. All that is necessary is to write down the questions that are to be asked and have them printed on sheets of paper. Unfortunately, the problem is deceptive. It is easy to write down questions, but are they the right questions? Will a question mean the same thing to Mrs. Longstreet in Fort Collins, Colorado as it does to Mrs. Vanderbilt in New York City? Will it mean the same to either of them as it means to the researcher? Slight variations in question wording may make a considerable change in the answers obtained. Which is the "correct" alternative? If one question is asked before another, it may get a different answer than if it is asked after the other. If some questions are asked, respondents may refuse to answer them at all. On the other hand, respondents may knowingly answer other questions incorrectly.

Questionnaires are *the* measuring instruments used in marketing research. If they are to produce useful measurements, they must be both valid and reliable. In one public opinion survey, the following question was asked with the results shown:

---

[2] Questionnaires are used with telephone, mail, and personal interviews. Since the most demanding from a questionnaire construction standpoint is the personal interview, the discussion here will be from the standpoint of a personal interview in structured form. Where the means of communication will have an impact, that will be pointed out.

FIGURE 8–1. Page from steam iron questionnaire

16.   Some steam irons also have a spray device on them which sprays water from the
       front of the iron. This is in <u>addition</u> to the steam which comes out through the
       holes in the soleplate or bottom of the iron. Does your steam iron have a spray
       device like this on it?

| 71– |
| 72– |
| 73– |
| 74– |
| 80– |

Yes – *1*   No – *2*   Don't know/not sure – *3* | 4 |

                    SKIP TO Q. 18a

17a.   Do you use the spray device on your iron always, sometimes, or never when you
       iron?

Always – *1*   Sometimes – *2*   Never – *3* | 5 |

IF "SOMETIMES" OR "NEVER," ASK:

   17b.   Why don't you use the spray device on your steam iron (more often)?
           . . . Why else don't you use it? (PROBE)

                                                                    | 6– |
                                                                    | 7– |

18a.   Aside from using a spray device on your iron, do you <u>ever</u> sprinkle or pre–dampen
       your clothes before ironing them with your steam iron?

Yes – *1*   No – *2*

                    SKIP TO Q. 19a

IF "YES," ASK:

   18b.   Do you <u>always</u> sprinkle or pre–dampen your clothes in that way before you | 8 |
           iron them with your steam iron, or do you sometimes do it and sometimes
           not?

           Always – *4*   Sometimes – *5*

19a.   In addition to the electric cord attached to the iron, do you <u>usually</u> use an extension
       cord with your steam iron?

Yes – *1*   No – *2* | 9 |

  b.   Would you prefer that the cord that comes attached to your iron be longer, or
       shorter, or is it about the right length as it is?

Would prefer longer – *1*   Would prefer shorter – *2*   About right as is – *3* | 10 |

*Which of the following statements most closely coincides with your opinion
of the Metallic Metals Act?*

Thirty percent of the respondents had no opinion; the other 70 percent
distributed their answers as follows:

  It would be a good move on the part of the United States (21.4 percent).
  It would be a good thing but should be left to the individual states (58.6
      percent).

It is all right for foreign countries but should not be required here (15.7 percent).

It is of no value at all (4.3 percent).

If these data were included with other information and presented in a leather-bound report, they would be impressive evidence in favor of the second alternative. Of course, the point is that there is no such thing as a Metallic Metals Act. Questions will get answers, but do the answers mean anything? In this case the question was not valid; it did not measure what it was presumed to measure.

Political differences over American involvement in Vietnam in the late 1960s and early 1970s led many politicians to conduct polls among their constituents to determine the latter's attitudes on the question. Two such polls, both conducted in New York City at about the same time, asked the following questions with the results shown:[3]

Do you approve of the recent decision to extend bombing raids in North Vietnam aimed at oil reserves and other strategic supply depots around Hanoi and Haiphong?

Yes 66%
No or don't know 34

Do you believe the United States should bomb Hanoi and Haiphong?

Yes 14%
No or don't know 86

While the wording of these questions differs slightly, they seem to be getting at the same issue. They leave one less than sure what the "true" sentiments of the public are on this question. The questioning is not reliable as it produces different results when the same thing is asked in different ways.

In May 1975 the British government was faced with a decision to remain in the European Common Market or to withdraw. The prime minister decided to have a public referendum on the issue. He stated that he wanted a single straightforward question that the public could answer "yes" or "no." One can hardly imagine a more crucial question-wording problem. Many different versions were proposed, but the one finally selected was the following:[4]

Do you think that the United Kingdom should stay in the European Community (the Common Market)?

The authors of this text do not believe this was the best possible wording. After studying this chapter, students may want to try their hands at improving the question.

---

[3] Leo Bogart, "No Opinion, Don't Know, and Maybe No Answer," *Public Opinion Quarterly* 31 (Fall 1967):332.

[4] *Keesing's Contemporary Archives* (May 26–June 1, 1975), pp. 27141–2.

The preceding examples are extreme cases, but they illustrate factors which the researcher must consider in preparing a questionnaire. Other problems are so many and so varied as to lead one outstanding researcher to conclude after a major project

> . . . that error or bias attributable to sampling and to methods of questionnaire administration were relatively small as compared with other types of variation—especially variation attributable to different ways of wording questions.[5]

QUESTIONNAIRE CONSTRUCTION PROCEDURE

Questionnaire construction is still much more of an art than a science. No procedures have been established which will automatically lead to a good questionnaire. Most of what is known about making questionnaires is the result of general experience. Neither a basic theory nor even a fully systematized approach to the problem has been developed. Nevertheless, the extensive experience of many researchers and a limited number of organized experiments have led to a considerable understanding of the problem and to a long list of "dos and don'ts" and rules of thumb. These can help a beginning researcher avoid many pitfalls, but they cannot be substituted for creative imagination in designing a questioning procedure. In the following discussion, the generally accepted "rules" are organized so as to provide a step-by-step approach to the development of a questionnaire.

Determine what information is wanted

Basically a questionnaire must serve two functions: it must translate research objectives into specific questions the respondent can answer, and it must motivate the respondent to cooperate with the survey and to furnish the information correctly. Therefore, before a questionnaire can be formulated a specific statement of the information which is needed must be made. The complete analysis must be anticipated. For example, it is not enough to know that the objective is to find what type of person forms the market for the product. The specific characteristics that are thought to be important must be stated. Thus, a deodorant soap company wishing to define its market might specify that the survey determine the proportion of individuals using the soap within the groups shown in Table 8–1. With such a listing, the questionnaire framer could develop a series of questions that would elicit the information needed for the proposed analysis. This statement of objectives is part of the problem definition step. It is repeated here to emphasize that a questionnaire cannot be started until the precise information sought is known.

---

[5] Samuel A. Stouffer et al., *Measurement and Prediction, Studies in Social Psychology in World War II,* vol. 4 (Princeton, N.J.: Princeton University Press, 1950), p. 709.

TABLE 8–1

Age	Sex	Income	Geographical area	City size
Under 20	Male	Under $10,000	Northeast	Over 1 million
20–29	Female	$10,000–14,999	North Central	50,000–1 million
30–45		15,000–24,999	South	2,500–49,999
Over 45		25,000 and over	West	Rural

Determine the type of questionnaire to be used

Questionnaires can be used by personal interview, mail, or telephone. The choice among these alternatives is largely determined by the type of information to be obtained and by the type of respondents from whom it is to be obtained. It is necessary to decide on the type of questionnaire at this point since the questions asked, the way in which they are asked, and the sequence in which they are asked will all be influenced by this decision. The influence of the type of questionnaire on these factors will be brought out in the following discussion.

Determine the content of individual questions

Once the needed information is specified and the method of communication is decided, researchers are ready to begin formulating their questionnaire. A first problem is to decide what to include in individual questions. The following points are in the nature of standards against which to check possible questions; obviously, they leave much to the originality of the researchers.

Is the question necessary? It seems an obvious point that no question should be included in a questionnaire unless it is necessary;[6] however, there is a strong tendency to include interesting questions which have no particular value for the study objectives. This has become a particularly important point in recent years as the average questionnaire has become longer.

Extra questions add to the expense of the survey and increase the demands made on respondents, thus decreasing the likelihood of their cooperation. It is reported that the addition of one question to a U.S. Census questionnaire adds approximately $1 million to the total cost of the census. While the typical marketing research project is extremely small compared to the census, this example indicates the problem.

To determine whether a question is necessary or not, the researcher must turn back to the objectives of the study. Is the information definitely called for? Will something actually be done as a result of the information obtained? If the answer to either of these is "no," the question should be eliminated.

---

[6] There is one exception to this statement. Occasionally a "useless" question is asked to gain respondent interest or to provide transition from one subject to another.

Does the respondent have the information requested? The trick question quoted previously on the Metallic Metals Act shows that people will answer questions that they do not understand. Similar tests, in which dummy advertisements are inserted in magazines, find people who report having seen the ads before. Such answers do not necessarily stem from dishonesty. Many result from confusion. Results of this type emphasize the importance of asking only questions for which the respondents have the necessary information to answer. Several aspects of this point, which researchers should consider in planning their questions, are discussed in the following paragraphs.

Is the point within the respondent's experience? Even questions which seem quite ordinary may not fall within a given respondent's experience.

How do you think All compares with other packaged soaps and detergents? This question seems straightforward. Unless respondents have used All, however, their answers are not apt to mean much. It would be better to determine in advance whether or not the respondent has ever used All. Even then some respondents will be comparing All with Tide and Era, while others will be comparing it with Ivory and Lux. It is important, then, to determine whether or not the question is meaningful in the respondent's experience. When there is doubt, "filter" questions should be used. In this example, the researcher might ask: *What packaged soaps and detergents have you used during the last year?* If All is reported among others, the next question might be: *How do you rank these in order of your preference?* The filter question shown here is indirect. It is probably preferable to a direct question in this case, since the latter might introduce some bias. If an indirect question is not feasible, however, a direct filter question should be used. For example: *Have you used All during the last year?* More people will say "no" to such a question than will volunteer that they have not used All if asked a question which assumes they have used it, such as, *"How do you think All compares with other detergents?"*

Can the respondent remember the information? How many can name the brand of shirt they are wearing, the license number of their car, or the amount of the deductions from their paycheck? Most people have known all these points at one time or another, but they are not apt to remember them when questioned specifically. Many things that one might expect everyone to know are not remembered. In fact, where memory is involved at all, researchers must be cautious not to over-estimate the accuracy with which respondents will remember the information they want.

A great many questions asked in marketing research involve memory in varying degrees. What brand of soap do you use? Have you seen this advertisement before? What stories did you read in this magazine? What television programs did you watch yesterday? Memory of such events is influenced by four factors: (1) the event itself, (2) the individual remembering, (3) the length of time since the event, and (4) the stimulus given to the individual's memory. The first two of these factors are beyond the researchers' control, but they must consider them in deciding what questions to include in their survey. The last two factors they can affect.

When the prosecuting attorneys ask the classic question, "Where were you on the night of January 3, 1972?" the witness always seems to know. This may be the result of prior coaching, but, if the witness saw a murder on that night, it is quite likely that it would be remembered for the rest of the witness' life. Thus, the importance of the event has much to do with its recollection. Few consumers will recall the brand of canned peas purchased three weeks ago, but most can remember the brand of car bought years ago. Unusual events are remembered well. Most people have trouble remembering all of the television shows they watched the night before, but everyone who saw the first game of the World Series probably remembered it for at least several days. Events which are part of an established pattern or which interrupt an established pattern are remembered better than unrelated events. Consumers who always buy Colgate toothpaste will remember what brand they bought last time better than the person who has no established favorite. This is true even if the Colgate consumer bought Crest the last time.

Any woman remembers her wedding date, but most of the bridesmaids would be unable to recall it a few years later. The difference is in the importance of the event to the individual. Researchers cannot change the ability of a person to remember things, but they can try to ask the person most apt to remember. Thus, the homemaker is usually sought as the respondent on questions about household purchases. Homemakers make most of them and, since they often establish habits, they are more apt to remember purchases than are other members of the family.

Researchers can control the length of time between an event and the date of their questioning only by limiting their questions to events that have happened recently. This means that questions on purchases are usually limited to the most recent purchase; questions on television programs watched are limited to the previous day, the immediately preceding hours, or even to the current moment; and questions on the readership of magazines are asked on the latest issue.

Ability to remember is influenced by the stimulus which calls for the remembering. Thus, it is easier for respondents to recognize a past event if it is presented to them than it is for them to recall the same event without any clues. The latter is referred to as *unaided recall*. Suppose a respondent is asked, "What radio programs did you listen to last night?" Experiments have shown that such a question may locate as little as 10 percent of those who actually listened to a program. Many more can recall the same programs if they are given a list of the programs from the previous evening and asked which ones they heard. This is called *aided recall*.

The considerable advantage of aided recall which comes with these stimuli to the respondent's memory is, at least partially, offset by the bias resulting from the suggestions offered by each such stimulus. Every multiple choice question is subject to suggestion bias of this type. The extent of this bias and methods of reducing it are discussed in the section on multiple choice questions.

An extreme of the aided-recall approach is the recognition method of stimulating recall. Instead of describing possible answers, researchers show the respondent the actual items in which they are interested. For example, researchers trying to determine purchases of Jell-O might show respondents actual boxes of Jell-O. To determine the readership of advertisements, researchers often go through magazines with respondents, showing them each advertisement and asking if they remember having seen it before. This recognition method furnishes an excellent stimulus to memory, but it is also subject to suggestion bias as is all aided recall.

Will the respondent have to do a lot of work to get the information? In a survey for a trucking firm, traffic managers of manufacturing plants and department stores were shown a map of the United States with a section equivalent to about eight states outlined in red. The traffic managers were then asked: *What annual volume in tons do you ship to or from the area outlined in red on the map?* It is likely that most of the traffic managers had this information, but it is also likely that most of them would have had to compile the data from written records to give a very accurate report. Few respondents will take a lot of time to collect the information needed to answer a questionnaire. They may make the best guess they can. If it is a mail questionnaire, they are apt to drop the questionnaire in the waste-basket. Such questions, even if answered, tend to irritate respondents and, hence, to damage cooperation with the rest of the survey. In most instances, such questions should be avoided.

Will respondents give the information? Even though they know the answer, respondents will sometimes not answer questions. There are two reasons for this: (1) they are unable to phrase their answers, or (2) they do not want to answer. It goes without saying that such questions hurt coop-eration for the rest of an interview and, therefore, should be eliminated. It is often possible, however, to change such questions so as to secure the desired information.

General Motors developed a classic questionnaire to get consumer opin-ions on car styling. Few consumers could describe the type of car grill work that they liked best, but if they were shown pictures of ten cars they could point out the grill they liked best. The pictures made it possible for respon-dents to report their answers.

Even though they could answer accurately, respondents may hesitate to do so if the question is seen as embarrassing or as relating to their social status. A questionnaire on magazine readership, for example, showed relatively little readership of pulp magazines in the upper-income groups.

On the theory that these people might feel it was degrading to admit reading such "trash," the study was revised. People were asked to contribute their old magazines to charity. A count of these magazines showed that the number of people contributing certain magazines exceeded the number who reported reading them by 50 percent.

When asked on what matters they were least willing to be interviewed, one group of respondents reported money matters, family life, political beliefs, and religious beliefs in that order. Some income classification, however, is desirable on many research projects. Other embarrassing or status-damaging questions may be necessary for particular surveys. Numerous techniques, of which the following are examples, have been developed for the purpose.

1. The question may be included in a group of others that are more innocuous and the whole list asked quickly.
2. The interviewer may make a statement indicating that the behavior in question is not unusual and then ask the specific question of the respondents. The statement tends to make respondents feel that their own behavior is not out of place.
3. The question may be phrased to refer to "other people." For example, the respondent may be asked if most people report errors on their bills that are favorable to themselves. They will presumably answer in terms of their own practice.
4. A special ballot may be provided which respondents can complete personally and drop in a sealed box. This can be used only in personal interviews.
5. Another approach that can be used in personal interviews is that of handing respondents cards with alternatives listed and identified by letters or numbers. They can then respond in terms of the letter or number. For example, the interviewer may hand out cards on which the following information is entered and ask respondents in which class their annual income falls:

   Class L .... Under $10,000
   Class M .... $10,000–$20,000
   Class N .... Over $20,000

   It may be desirable to have enough classes so that both extremes are so extreme that few will be in those groups.
6. For income data an effective approach is to start at a midpoint and go up or down as in the following:[7]

---

[7] William B. Locander and John P. Burton, "The Effect of Question Form on Gathering Income Data by Telephone," *Journal of Marketing Research* 13 (May 1976): 189–92.

What was the approximate annual income of all members of your family before taxes in 1980—was it $25,000 or more or was it less than that?

If $25,000 or more, ask:	*If under $25,000, ask:*
Was it under $35,000?	Was it over $20,000?
If over $35,000, ask:	*If under $20,000, ask:*
Was it under $40,000	Was it under $15,000?
or over $40,000?	*If under $15,000, ask:*
	Was it under $10,000?

Are several questions needed instead of one?   Some questions may have two or more elements. If these are left in one question, interpretation of the answers becomes impossible. In a survey on laundry detergents one might ask: *Do you think Tide gets clothes clean without injuring the fabric?* A "yes" answer would presumably be clear, but suppose the answer is "no." Would this mean that Tide doesn't get clothes clean, or that it injures fabrics? Or suppose the homemaker thinks Tide damages silks and rayons but does not hurt other fabrics. A series of two or more questions could clarify these points.

A more subtle example of the multielement question is the "why" question. *Why do you use Era detergent?* One can imagine answers such as "to get the clothes clean," "it's easier on my hands than others," and "my neighbor recommended it." Actually, each of these answers is a reply to a different element in the question. The first answer tells why the homemaker uses a detergent; the second answer tells what the homemaker likes about Era as compared to other detergents; and the third answer tells how the homemaker happened to get acquainted with Era. Thus, the three answers cannot be compared. Useful comparisons might be obtained if the question were changed into separate questions:

1. *What do you like about Era as compared to other detergents?*
2. *How did you first happen to use Era?*

Almost any "why" question about the use of a product involves these two elements: (1) attributes of the product and (2) influences leading to knowledge of it.

Determine the type of question to use

Once the content of individual questions is decided, researchers are ready to begin forming the actual questions. Before they can work on the wording of each question, they must decide on the type of question to use. Part of this decision is whether to use disguised or nondisguised, structured or unstructured questioning. These tend to be issues of general research strategy. But individual questions may have different degrees of structure. The three main types of questions from least structured to most structured are (1) open, (2) multiple choice, and (3) dichotomous.

Open questions.   *What industries are your best potential markets for hydraulic equipment? How many families occupy this home? How long have you had this piano? Why do you smoke Marlboro cigarettes?* Each of these is an example of an open, or free-answer, question. Respondents are free to answer in their own words and to express any ideas that they think pertinent. No alternatives are suggested. Three of the four examples would probably result in short answers. The question on cigarettes might draw a lengthy discussion which interviewers would have to record verbatim or attempt to summarize.

Open questions are good as first questions. They introduce the subject and obtain general reactions which are relatively uninfluenced by the question itself. If the question is left especially wide open, almost every respondent will be able to give some answer and will thus begin to warm up to the questioning process. In a survey on cable television the following was the first question: *In general, how do you feel about cable television?* This question acquaints the respondent with the subject of the survey, gets general attitudes which may be helpful in later interpretation of results, and opens the way for more specific questioning on cable television.

Open questions influence the answers obtained less than multiple choice or dichotomous questions. A survey on shaving habits among men might ask: *With what type of instrument do you shave?* Or a multiple choice question might be used: *Do you shave with a safety razor, straightedge razor, or electric shaver?* The latter suggests alternatives and may, as a result, influence the answers obtained. The open question does not suffer from this weakness.

Since the open question suggests no answers, the variety of answers obtained is often extreme. Take the question: *What are the things you look for in buying a suit?* The researcher could list a number of the answers that would be forthcoming—color, style, price, and so on. But some respondents will mention items that are not likely to occur to the researcher. Long open questions also have a decided advantage in obtaining accurate information of the "how much" or "how many" type on threatening items such as quantity of drinking or use of drugs.[8] Thus, the open question is particularly useful in exploratory research where new ideas and relationships are sought. On the basis of the replies received in the exploratory study, the researcher may be able to establish the alternative answers that appear and use them in a multiple choice question in further research.

Despite these advantages of open questions, certain disadvantages limit their usefulness. A principal weakness is the large degree of interviewer bias which they permit. Interviewers may be instructed to record answers to open

---

[8] Ed Blair, Seymour Sudman, Norman Bradburn, and Carol Stocking, "How to Ask Questions about Drinking and Sex," *Journal of Marketing Research* 14 (April 1977):316–21.

questions verbatim or to set down the main points mentioned by respondents. In either instance, the interviewers' reports will vary. Interviewers skilled in shorthand will get down every word; other interviewers will have to ask respondents to give their answers phrase by phrase if they are to get each word. Obviously, in the latter case the interview will drag and respondents will lose interest. Answers given a few words at a time will differ from answers which are given in more or less normal conversation. If interviewers are told to digest replies, bias is even more likely. Interviewers interpret the replies they receive in terms of their own ideas. The result is a mixture of interviewer and respondent, rather than respondent alone. Where verbatim reporting is important, tape recorders may be used.

A second main disadvantage of open questions lies in the difficult and time-consuming tabulation problems which they pose. Since respondents answer in their own words, each answer is unique. For some questions, answers may run several sentences or more in length. If generalizations are to be drawn from such answers, some way must be found for summarizing them. This is usually done by having an editor read some or all of the answers and establish classifications. Then each answer must be read and marked to indicate into which class or classes it falls. A tabulator can then go over the answers and count the number in each classification. The process is time consuming and open to subjective errors on the part of the editor. Since answers differ in wording and degree of explanation, it is difficult to classify all answers in any given categories. In a survey on packaged soaps for automatic washing machines the question, *What do you like about "X" soap for washing clothes?* brought the frequent answer, "suds." Usually homemakers like lots of suds from a soap, but in automatic washers too much suds flow over and are a nuisance. Some soaps make a point of a fact that they make little suds. The answer "suds" could mean the respondent thought the soap produced either a lot or a little suds. Classification is almost impossible.[9]

This expensive job of editing can be eliminated or reduced without losing the advantages of the open question when the subject is well formulated and the possible answers are limited in variety. The probable answers can be set down so the interviewer can check the one given. This speeds up the field-work and eliminates the editor's job of classification. The following question illustrates the method:

For how many months or years have you been buying gasoline at this station?

Less than 6 months _____	1 to 5 years _____
6 months to 1 year _____	5 years or more _____

The alternatives listed are not mentioned aloud to the respondent; if they were, the question would become a multiple choice one. Whenever possible,

---

[9] The question used in this example is also a leading question unless it has been preceded by a series of questions that established that the homemaker liked "X" soap for washing clothes.

lists of answers, as shown above, should be used with open questions because of the time-savings both in fieldwork and tabulating.

Answers to open questions can be limited to fairly specific areas in some cases by phrasing the question properly. In one study, a bottle of orange drink was shown to respondents who were asked:

How much orange juice do you think it contains?

Among the answers obtained were the following:[10]

One orange and a little water and sugar	Small amount
	One-fourth
25 percent orange and 75 percent carbonated water	Very little, if any
	Doubt it
Juice of 6 oranges	Don't know
Three ounces	Not very much
Full strength	Part orange juice
A quarter cup	A pint
None	Most of it
Not much	About a glass and a half

The answers in this case reflect so many different frames of reference that they are relatively useless. They would have been more comparable if the question had been worded: *What percentage of this drink do you think is orange juice?*

Another disadvantage of the open question is the implicit weighting which it may give to the upper-income, better-educated segment of the population. Individuals in these groups are more articulate than others and, hence, tend to mention more points in answering open questions. For example, this group might mention three reasons for liking "X" soap on the average, while the average for others might be one. Then, if 100 from the articulate group and 100 others are interviewed, 400 reasons for using "X" soap will be recorded. Three out of every four, however, will be reasons given by the articulate group. If the two groups differ in attitude, the resulting summaries will be biased.

Compared with more structured questions, open questions are three to five times more costly because of the added time required to record answers; to edit, classify, and code answers; and to tabulate the results.[11]

Researchers are coming more and more to the conclusion that open questions are useful in exploratory research and as a means for opening up topics, but that otherwise their disadvantages outweigh their advantages in large surveys. An excellent study of the open question has concluded:

---

[10] *U.S. v. 88 Cases (Bireley's Orange Beverage)*, 5 FRD 503 (U.S. D.C.N.J., 1945).

[11] Jeffrey L. Pope, "12 Ways to Cut Marketing Research Costs," *Marketing News* (June 6, 1975), p. 6.

1.   Average response to open questions is three times as long as to closed questions.
2.   The meaningful, relevant, nonrepetitive response is no more in open than in closed questions.
3.   Pertinence of responses is the same in both types of questions.
4.   Factual reporting is less accurate in open questions.
5.   Open questions get less valid responses on subjective topics.
6.   Self-revelation is greater on factual topics but less on attitudinal topics when open questions are used.[12]

Multiple choice questions.   Questions of this type offer respondents a number of specific alternatives from which they are to choose one or more, as the case may be. The following are examples:

Do you buy this brand of motor oil exclusively, more than any other brand, or just occasionally?

Exclusively _____   Just occasionally _____
More than any other _____   Don't know _____

Which of the following reasons do you think explain your patronage of this service station?

It's closest to my home _____
It's clean and attractive _____
It sells the gasoline brand I prefer _____
Its prices are lower _____
It gives complete service _____
The personnel are courteous _____
They are good mechanics _____
They are personal friends _____
Other reasons _____
Don't know _____

Notice in each case the alternatives are actually repeated to the respondent. If the second question were asked without actually mentioning the alternatives, it would be an open question rather than a multiple choice.

The two questions above illustrate some of the difficulties in using multiple choice questions. In the first question, the three alternatives are mentioned in the question proper. In the second question, there are too many alternatives to mention in the question proper; instead, they are listed at the end. But the list is so long that respondents would not be able to remember it when it was read to them.

Whenever a list of alternatives is as long as this in a personal interview, the choices should be put on a card and handed to the respondent. In telephone interviews lists this long should be avoided.

---

[12] B. S. Dohrenwend, "Some Effects of Open and Closed Questions on Respondents' Answers," *Human Organization* 24 (Summer 1965):175–84, as repeated in Stanley L. Payne, "Are Open-ended Questions Worth the Effort?" *Journal of Marketing Research* 2 (November 1965):417–18.

In the first illustration above, it is clear that the respondent is to select one alternative only. In the second question, this is not so clear. If uniformity of response is to be obtained, it is necessary to make clear to the respondent how many choices may be selected.

In the second illustration above, the last alternative is "other." It is common practice to give this choice, since some alternative may have been omitted. Respondents who had an answer not listed might be confused or feel forced to select another choice if they did not have this escape. Actually, any alternative that is not listed will usually be mentioned so seldom as to amount to little. Therefore, it is imperative to list all alternatives that may be of any importance at all. For example:

Approximately which of the following percentages of the total gasoline purchases for your car are made at this station?

25 to 50% _____	75 to 100% _____
50 to 75% _____	100% _____

Consumers who bought less than 25 percent of their gasoline at the designated station would be unable to select one of the alternatives. This question also illustrates another problem. Suppose respondents estimated they bought 50 percent of their gasoline at the designated station. Would they select the first or second alternative? This is particularly troublesome in cases where the overlap is in the round numbers in which answers will probably be formulated. Thus, care should be taken to avoid overlap among alternatives.

It is also desirable in questions with quantitative answers to select alternatives so that the most probable answers will fall in the middle of a class. In the above example 25, 50, and 75 percent would be frequent answers and so should be near the middle of classes instead of at extremes. As it is, most of the answers in the second class would probably be at one extreme or the other—50 percent or 75 percent. The class average of 62.5 percent, however, would be used to represent the class. But this would be an answer few would give.

Multiple choice questions overcome some of the disadvantages of open questions, but incur some new ones. Open questions are subject to interviewer bias in the recording of answers. This is not nearly as important with multiple choice questions where answers are in one or more of the stated alternatives. All the interviewer has to do is check the applicable reply. Thus, the multiple choice question is faster and less subject to bias in the interview.

Similarly, the multiple choice question simplifies the tabulating process. The difficult and time-consuming editing process is reduced to a rapid check for mechanical accuracy.

Multiple choice questions tend to bias results by the order in which the alternative answers are given. When ideas are involved, the first item in the list of alternatives has a favorable bias. More respondents pick a given idea when it is first than will pick it when it is in another position. In an experiment to test this, four ideas were presented as alternatives to a multiple choice question. Each of the four was shown alternately in each of the four positions. Each was selected more times when it was in the first position than in any other. In total, the percentage of respondents selecting a choice when it was first on the list was 6 percent larger than the percentage selecting the idea when it was in one of the two central positions and 4 percent above the percentage picking it when it was last.

This bias of position can be overcome by alternating the order in which alternatives are listed. If six choices are offered, six different groups of cards are printed. The order of listing is different on each card. Each item appears first on one of the six different cards, second on one, and so on. Thus, in one sixth of the interviews, item A is first, in one sixth it is second, and so on. This, of course, does not eliminate the bias, but it averages the upward and downward bias of the various positions.

When the alternatives in a multiple choice question are numbers, this bias of position changes. Central positions are chosen more than either extreme. Respondents guess that the answer expected is apt to be near the middle. They are usually correct. It is common in constructing questionnaires to put down the likely answer and to add one or two alternatives on either side of it. Unfortunately, it is not easy to rotate positions when numbers are used. If a series of numbers is involved, it is logical to put them in order from small to large or vice versa. Even if they are out of this order, the respondent will tend to sort them into a sequence. An effort should be made to have a class at each end that is more extreme than any respondent is apt to be. This will enable all respondents to report accurately without being in an extreme category.

Dichotomous questions.   The dichotomous, or two-way question, is an extreme of the multiple choice question. The idea is to offer only two choices —yes or no, did or did not, cash or credit, railroad or airline, and so on. Such questions are the most widely used of the three basic types. The following are examples of dichotomous questions:

Would the service proposed by "X" Lines make motor freight service more useful to you? Is any of this discount normally passed on to others? Did you buy it or was it a gift? Was it new or used when you got it?

In the last two questions the two alternatives are both stated; in the first two, one alternative is stated, while the other is implied. In the second question it seems obvious that the other alternative is that none of the discount was passed on or, putting it another way, that all of the discount was kept by the firms reporting. Probably there would be no confusion as to what the two alternatives were in this case. It is also likely, however, that different results would have been obtained had both alternatives been stated explicitly. For example: *Is any of this discount normally passed on to others or is all of it kept by your firm?*

An experiment to test the effect of stating only one alternative used the following two questions.[13] *Do you think the United States should allow public speeches against democracy? Do you think the United States should forbid public speeches against democracy?*

The following results were obtained:

First question		Second question	
Should allow	21%	Should not forbid	39%
Should not allow	62	Should forbid	46
No opinion	17	No opinion	15

Since the two questions ask exactly the same thing—one in a positive way and one in a negative way—the answers should be directly comparable. Those who say the U.S. should allow such speeches should also report that these speeches should not be forbidden. The results show that this did not occur. Only 21 percent wanted to allow speeches against democracy, but 39 percent were against forbidding them. A closer estimate of the true feeling on the subject would probably have been obtained if the question had stated both alternatives: *Do you think the United States should allow or forbid public speeches against democracy?*

Dichotomous questions have about the same advantages as multiple choice questions. They are quick and easy for an interviewer to handle. Editing and tabulation are relatively simple. They offer less opportunity for interviewer bias to creep into the results. The straight yes-no type of answer makes it easy for the respondent to reply. But dischotomous questions may be deceptive in their seeming simplicity. Few dichotomous questions, for example, are actually only two-way. Take the following question: *Do you expect to buy another piano some day?* Undoubtedly some people definitely plan to buy another piano and others definitely plan not to, but a large middle group may have no definite plans either way. Some of these might properly report, "don't know." Others might be in a "maybe" class. Even the "maybes" might fall into distinct groups—those who probably would but were not sure and those who probably would not but were not sure. This would mean that instead of two possible answers there would be five: yes, no, probably, probably not, and don't know. If the piano question were reworded to include explicit statement of both of the original alternatives and to take into account the five alternatives actually existing, it might appear as follows:

Do you expect to buy another piano some day, or not?

Yes _____	No _____
Probably _____	Don't know _____
Probably not _____	

The five alternatives would not be suggested to the respondents, but if one of them qualified an answer, the interviewer could then check the appropri-

[13] Donald Rugg, "Experiments in Wording Questions: II," *Public Opinion Quarterly* 5 (March 1941):91–92.

ate space. At the very least, the "don't know" category should be provided. Then the "probablys" would be classified in the "yes" category and the "probably nots" in the "no" category. As was pointed out in the discussion of multiple choice questions, however, if the alternatives are not actually stated to the respondent, fewer persons will report them than would otherwise. Therefore, if the "probably" answers are not actually indicated to the respondent, the number reporting them will have a downward bias and the number saying "yes" and "no" will have an upward bias.

Dichotomous questions may be more than two-way questions for another reason—instead of one or the other of the two alternatives, the correct answer may be both. In a survey on shaving habits among college men, the question was asked: *Do you shave with an electric razor or a safety razor?* As it turned out, many college men use both. They use an electric razor for everyday shaving, but when they have a date and want an especially close shave, they use a safety razor. It would be better in this case to have the "both" category available for the interviewer to check, or to make the question multiple choice by including the "both" possibility in the actual question.

Summary.   Researchers must consider the advantages and disadvantages of each of the three basic types before deciding which type to use for each question in their survey. In general, the expense of editing open questions militates against their use if it is at all possible to avoid them. If preliminary work has pretty well established the answers which will be forthcoming, the open question may well be changed to a multiple choice question. Even if the question is left open, it may be possible to set down the various answers which will be given and, thus, to permit the interviewer to check one or more of the alternatives rather than to record the answer verbatim. If the open question is used, the question should direct answers to a particular framework so that they will be comparable. Otherwise results as useless as those in the orange drink questionnaire may be obtained.

If a multiple choice question is used, all alternatives should be stated and should be mutually exclusive. A "don't know" category should be left on the questionnaire even though it may not be suggested to the respondents.

If dichotomous questions are used, they must actually be two-way questions. If qualified answers or combination answers are possible, space should be left for recording them and also for a "don't know" answer.

Decide on wording of questions

In the preceding discussion of question content and types of questions, much has been said on question wording. A number of other important ideas, however, should be considered. Unfortunately, these ideas are more rules of thumb which have been developed from experience than they are underlying concepts.

Define the issue.   Beginning newspaper reporters are admonished to include in their lead paragraphs the six points: who, where, when, what, why, and how. This can also serve as a guide to the researcher preparing a questionnaire. Each question should be checked against these points to be sure that the issue is clear. *Who, what, where,* and *when* are particularly important. The *why* and *how* may be applicable in some questions.

Take the question: *What brand of cigarettes do you smoke? Who?* In this case the "you" seems clear, but in some cases this word may leave confusion as to whether it applies to the respondents, their families, their companies, or some other plural application. *What?* "Brand of cigarettes" and "smoke" are stated. The word "brand" may be slightly confusing, but otherwise the "what" in this question is clear. *When?* This is not clear. Does the question mean usually, always, last time, ever, or what? The question makes the fundamental error of assuming something. It assumes that all respondents smoke one brand of cigarettes to the exclusion of all others. Of course this is not true. A better way to get at the same information might then be to ask: *What brand of cigarettes did you buy the last time you bought cigarettes?* This makes the "when" specific. In this question the where, how, and why are not applicable.

Should question be subjective or objective?   Many questions can be stated in either subjective or objective form. *Do you think the Ford is a better car than the Chevrolet? Is the Ford a better car than the Chevrolet?* The first phrasing is subjective; it puts the question in terms of the individual and is apt to elicit a response in terms of the individual's feelings. The second phrasing tends to cause the respondent to think more in terms of what people in general think. One study of the effect of subjective-objective statements used questions of the following type:[14] *Did you see a demonstration of Foley Kitchen Utensils in the housewares department? Was there a demonstration of Foley Kitchen Utensils in the housewares department?* The results of this study indicated that subjective, rather than objective, questions tended to give more reliable results. Researchers have no available rules to follow in deciding whether to make their questions subjective or objective. They must be aware, however, of the fact that the choice will influence their results.

Positive or negative statement.   In a survey to determine the attitudes of executives towards advertising, every question was stated in both a positive and a negative way. Two different questionnaires were prepared, one using half of the positive and half of the negative wordings in an interspersed way, and the second using the other half of the questions. Several issues were presented in either positive or negative statements and respondents were to indicate one of five alternative reactions to other statement: agree generally, agree partially, can't say, disagree partially, and disagree generally. Presumably one who agreed with a favorable statement of one issue would disagree

---

[14] Alfred W. Hubbard, "Phrasing Questions," *Journal of Marketing* 15 (July 1950): 48–56.

with an unfavorable statement of the same issue. While this was generally true, considerable variation obtained, as shown in Table 8–2.

TABLE 8–2. Effect of positive and negative wording of questions on attitude toward advertising

Nature of question	Agree		Can't say	Disagree	
	Generally	Partially		Generally	Partially
Effect on standard of living:					
Raises it	51%	34%	6%	6%	3%
Lowers it	2	1	5	14	78
Effect on products for the public:					
Better ones	47	30	6	9	8
Poorer ones	2	6	6	20	66
Most efficient way to stimulate mass buying:					
Advertising	66	23	4	4	3
Other methods	3	10	16	16	55
To hasten recovery in a recession:					
Substantially increase advertising	18	36	14	13	19
Substantially decrease advertising	2	3	7	9	79
Advertising effect on prices:					
Lower prices	30	24	13	14	19
Higher prices	14	14	10	17	45

Source: S. A. Greyser, "Businessmen re Advertising: 'Yes, but . . .'," *Harvard Business Review* 40 (May–June 1962): 28.

This study used positive and negative statements alternately to average out the effect of each wording. Another approach would have been to state both alternatives, the positive and the negative in each question, as follows: *Do you think advertising should be increased or decreased to hasten recovery in a recession?*

Use simple words. Words used in questionnaires should be words which have only one meaning, and that meaning known by everyone. Unfortunately, it is not easy to find such words. Many ordinary words have different meanings listed in the dictionary, and even other meanings among certain groups of the population or in certain sections of the country. What is "soda pop" in some sections is "tonic" in others, and "root beer" and "sarsaparilla" are the same thing.

Do you require all prospective sales representatives to go through training? In this question, "prospective" can readily be picked out as an unusual word which might not be understood by everyone. But what about "require"? It is a common enough word. The dictionary, however, shows eight different meanings. Does it mean that all new sales representatives must, or do, go through a training program? If so, why not ask: *Do all new sales representatives go through training?*

It is best to err on the side of simplicity if doubt exists. There are many examples of misunderstandings of what seem to be everyday words.

Avoid ambiguous questions.   Ambiguous questions mean different things to different people. Naturally, comparable replies cannot be received from respondents who take a question to mean different things. The question *How often do you serve soup at home?* obtained answers that showed soup was served less frequently than was believed to be the case. Further study showed that to many homemakers "served" meant a special occasion such as when entertaining. Soup may have been eaten when the family was alone, but it was not *served.* A better wording turned out to be: How often do you use soup at home?[15]

Questions which use such terms as usually, normally, frequently, and regularly are ambiguous: *What brand of cigarettes do you smoke regularly?* What does "regularly" mean—always, almost always, more than any other, or what? Some respondents will interpret it one way and some another. When the researcher wants to find out typical behavior, it is probably best to inquire about a specific time, such as the last time: *What brand was the last cigarette you smoked?* The last brand smoked by some respondents will be different from the one they usually smoke, but, if the sample is adequate, this will average out. This study concluded that for repetitive studies of this type it would be useful to determine the meaning of words such as the above in terms of probabilities and then to use questions involving such words.

Avoid leading questions.   In a study to evaluate the service of automobile insurance companies, a series of questions on claim service was preceded by a statement which began as follows: "It has been alleged that some low-rate companies are much tougher in adjusting claims than standard rate companies, and that you are more likely to have to go to court to collect the sum due you."[16] It is obvious that this statement would influence the answers to the questions on claim service which followed. Most marketing research studies do not have the obvious bias of the above, but it is easy to lead respondents toward one answer unless care is taken not to do so.

Do you have a General Electric refrigerator? This question will result in more reports of GE refrigerators than will a question: *What brand of refrigerator do you have?* When respondents get an idea that a survey is being made for a particular company or product, they have a tendency to respond favorably toward the sponsor. In a mail survey among FM radio owners in

---

15 J. M. Bowen, "Questionnaire Design for the Personal Interview," in *Fieldwork, Sampling and Questionnaire Design* (Amsterdam: European Society for Opinion Surveys and Market Research, 1973), pt. 1, p. 79.

16 J. Stevens Stock and Barbara K. Auerbach, "How Not to Do Consumer Research," *Journal of Marketing* 27 (July 1963):21.

the area covered by a small FM radio station, respondents were asked to list the four FM stations to which they listened most. The sponsoring station came out on top by far. A study of the individual questionnaires, however, showed that many of the respondents had associated the survey with that station, apparently through the address to which the questionnaire was mailed. Many of the returned questionnaires had additional comments such as, "We think you're wonderful," and "We like your station but not quite as well as X."

Do not ask questions in a way that will involve generalization. Questions should always be stated in specific terms. If generalizations are desired, the researcher should make them from the specific data obtained. Consider the following question: *How many machine tool sales representatives have called on you in the last year?* The only way the respondent could answer this questions would be to estimate about how many sales representatives came in during a typical week or possibly a month and then to multiply. The results would be more accurate if the question asked: *How many machine tool sales representatives called on you last week?* The researcher could then multiply by 52.

"Cushion" questions which may seem unreasonable to the respondent. In many marketing research projects it is desirable to know the income of the respondent so that comparisons can be made among income groups. A sudden question: *What is your income?* may impress the respondent as being too personal. A brief explanation as to the reason for asking such a question is often used to ease the respondent's reaction. Interviewers may explain, for example, that they would like to get some personal information to help classify respondents. Then the request for income data may seem more reasonable to the respondent.

Consumer surveys have become commonplace enough in recent years that difficulties of the above type may be less important than in the past. To test this point, a survey that inquired about insomnia alternated three different introductory remarks: *"I would like to ask you about*

1. . . . *certain ailments."*
2. . . . *certain common ailments."*
3. . . . *certain common ailments which most people have."*

No difference was found in the response to the question which followed as to whether the respondent had insomnia. On the other hand, when "buffer items" (questions as to the incidence of colds and allergies) were introduced between the above introduction and the question on insomnia, 23.2 percent of the respondents reported insomnia as compared to only 12.5 percent when no "buffer items" were used.[17]

---

[17] Frederick J. Thumin, "Watch for Those Unseen Variables," *Journal of Marketing* 26 (July 1962):59.

Use split ballot wherever possible.   No one wording is the correct one for a question. Different wordings may get different answers, yet no one can say one wording is right and the others wrong. It is important for the researcher to realize this situation exists and to understand what effect a particular phrasing may have on the results. To do this the split ballot technique can be used. Whenever there are two wordings from which to choose but no basis on which to pick one over the other, one can be run on half the questionnaires and the other on the other half. Comparison of the two halves of the questionnaires will permit a better interpretation of the results than would be possible were only one wording used.

Decide on question sequence

Once the wording of the individual questions has been determined, it is necessary to set them up in some order. The sequence can influence the results obtained.

A questionnaire has three major sections: (1) basic information, (2) classification information, and (3) identification information. Since questions pertaining to these sections tend to be of declining interest to the respondent, the sections are usually put in the order shown. Questions relating to the basic information sought form the body of the questionnaire. To help in analyzing this information, it is usually necessary to be able to classify respondents on such bases as age, sex, income, education, and nationality. Questions on these points form the classification section. The identification section identifies all parties involved. This includes the name and address of the respondent, and the names of such individuals as the interviewer, editor, and card puncher. These are used to verify that the actual respondents shown were interviewed and to assign responsibility for and to evaluate the quality of the tasks done.

Opening questions must win respondent's interest.   When respondents agree to be interviewed, they have made a concession—often partly out of curiosity. The questionnaire must capture their interest at once or they may break off the interview. Therefore, the first question should be an interesting one, even if it is necessary to insert a question which is not strictly necessary for the survey. Questions asking the respondents' opinions are good starters as everyone likes to think their opinions are important. In contrast, consider the opening question in a shopping habits survey which was *Who lives here?* This could hardly be expected to excite the respondent. Undoubtedly the next few questions were received rather coldly. A study among apartment dwellers started with *Do you own a horse?* The latter seems sure to create curiosity among most people.

It is also important to make the first few questions particularly simple—questions that everyone will be able to answer easily. This builds the confidence of respondents so they feel they can handle the project. If the opening questions "stump" respondents, they are apt to say something like, "I don't know. I'm not the type of person you should be talking to anyway,'' and the interview may be lost.

Place questions which are apt to cause difficulty in the body of the questionnaire. Questions which might embarrass respondents and those which may have little interest for respondents should be well down in the questionnaire so that the questioning process is well established before they are reached. After respondents have answered a number of questions, they are more at ease with the interview and are less apt to balk at personal questions such as those relating to income, knowledge, ability, and status.

Consider influence of questions on succeeding questions. In discussing leading questions, it was pointed out how mention of the product sponsoring the survey would bias answers. Thus, if it is necessary to mention the project specifically in some questions, those questions should be left to the end of the questionnaire.

In another study to test the effect of question sequence, a researcher set up five different question sequences before asking respondents how interested they would be in buying a new product described as a combination pen and pencil selling for 29 cents. One set of respondents was asked their buying interest immediately after the product was described to them; a second set was first asked what advantages they saw in the product; a third set was asked the disadvantages; a fourth was asked both advantages and disadvantages in that order; and a fifth, disadvantages and then advantages. The results are shown in Table 8–3.

It is clear that mention of the advantages of the product increased the expressed buying interest, whereas mention of the disadvantages decreased the interest. Other types of question sequence bias may be more subtle.

TABLE 8–3. Effect of question sequence on reported buying interest

Degree of buying interest	Interest in buying questions asked				
	Immedi-ately	After asking advantages	After asking dis-advantages	After asking advantages and dis-advantages	After asking disadvantages and advantages
Very much interested	2.8%	16.7%	0.0%	5.7%	8.3%
Somewhat interested	33.3	19.4	15.6	28.6	16.7
A little interested	8.3	11.1	15.6	14.3	16.7
Not very interested	25.0	13.9	12.5	22.9	30.6
Not at all interested	30.6	38.9	56.3	28.5	27.7
Total	100.0%	100.0%	100.0%	100.0%	100.0%

Source: Edwin J. Gross, ''The Effect of Question Sequence on Measures of Buying Interest,'' *Journal of Advertising Research* 4 (September 1964):41.

Arrange questions in logical order.   Questions should follow one another in some logical order, that is, logical to respondents. Sudden changes in subject confuse respondents and cause indecision on their part. In an experiment to test the effect of sudden shifts in thought, one interviewer asked a given group of questions in a series of related questions and another interviewer included these questions in a series of unrelated questions. In the second case, the number of indecisive answers such as "don't know" ran 7 to 13 percent higher than in the first case.[18]

A useful way to develop the best question sequence is to put each question on a card so that they can be sorted easily until a desirable sequence is found.

Mail questionnaire a special problem.   Mail questionnaires raise unique problems in question sequence. Since the mail questionnaire must sell itself, it is particularly important that the opening questions capture the respondent's interest. Questions should then proceed in logical order. It is not possible, however, to take advantage of sequence position in the same way as in personal interviews. Questions that are at the end to avoid biasing the answers to other questions will still bias the others because respondents can go back and change their responses to earlier questions.

Precode questionnaire.   Virtually all surveys are now tabulated by computer. As pointed out earlier, some telephone interviews are conducted using equipment which permits the interviewer to record the answers directly onto computer tape. After most interviews, however, the information must be transferred from the questionnaire to punch cards or computer tape. To speed this process questionnaires are precoded, that is, the codes which will be entered in the computer (the specific punch on a punchcard) are printed on the questionnaire so that, when a respondent checks an answer, it identifies the code to be transferred to the computer. A typical code identifies the column and position in the column which is to be punched in the card. For example, a question and possible answers might be shown as follows:

Do you use the spray device when you iron?

	Col. 12
Always	1
Sometimes	2
Never	3

The answer given would be marked with an X in the appropriate box and the card puncher would know to punch that position in column 12.

While precoding is designed to speed the tabulation process, it also has a desirable effect in forcing the researcher to think through each question and the possible answers. If the answers that will be obtained won't provide the information needed for action, a new or reworded question is called for. At

---

[18] Albert B. Blankenship, *Consumer and Opinion Research* (New York: Harper & Brothers, 1943), pp. 77–78.

this point it is clear why open questions that lead to longer answers are shunned by researchers whenever possible.

Figure 8–2 shows a page from a questionnaire on rice usage which illustrates precoding.

FIGURE 8–2. Page from questionnaire showing precoding

8. About how often do you use rice in your home? (SPECIFY BELOW)

More than once a week	-1	# times/week	27	
Once a week	-2	
Once every two weeks	-3	
Once every three weeks	-4		28	
Once a month	-5	
Less often than once a month	-6	

REFER TO Q. 2c ANSWER ON FLAP. RECORD BRAND USED MOST OFTEN BELOW UNDER "USE MOST" COLUMN AND USE IN ASKING Q. 9a.

9a. You mentioned earlier that you use (BRAND FROM Q. 2c) most often. What other brands of white rice, if any, do you use occasionally? . . . Any others? (RECORD BELOW)

ASK Q. 9b FOR EVERY BRAND USED — INCLUDING BRAND USED MOST:

9b. How often do you use (BRAND)   ? Would you say . . . more than once a week . . . once a week . . . once every 2 weeks . . . once every 3 weeks . . . once a month, or less than once a month?

	2c. Brand use most	Q.9a Use occas.	Q.9b Frequency of use						
			More than once a week	Once a week	Once every 2 wks.	Every 3 wks.	Once a mo.	Less than once a mo.	
Minute Rice	1	2	3	4	5	6	7	8	29
Uncle Ben's	1	2	3	4	5	6	7	8	30
Adolphus	1	2	3	4	5	6	7	8	31
Carolina	1	2	3	4	5	6	7	8	32
MJB	1	2	3	4	5	6	7	8	33
Mahatma	1	2	3	4	5	6	7	8	34
Riceland	1	2	3	4	5	6	7	8	35
Other (specify):	1	2	3	4	5	6	7	8	36
		2	3	4	5	6	7	8	37
									38
None	1	2							

FOR EACH BRAND LISTED BELOW NOT USED:

39
40

9c. Have you ever used (BRAND)   ?

	Yes	No	OK	
Minute Rice	1	2	X	41
Uncle Ben's	1	2	X	42
Adolphus	1	2	X	43

ASK ABOUT EACH BRAND TO WHICH RESPONDENT ANSWERED "YES" TO Q. 9c:

9d. When did you last use (BRAND)   ?

	Minute Rice	Uncle Ben's	Adolphus
Six months ago (or less)	1	1	1
Over 6 mos. to 1 yr. ago	2	2	2
Over 1 yr. to 2 yrs. ago	3	3	3
Over 2 years ago	4	4	4
Don't remember	X	X	X
	44	45	46

Decide on layout and reproduction

The physical layout and reproduction of a questionnaire can influence its success with respondents and can affect the problems encountered in handling it in the researcher's office. Three major points should be considered in planning the layout and reproduction of the questionnaire: (1) securing acceptance of the questionnaire by respondents, (2) making it easy to control the questionnaires, and (3) making it easy to handle the questionnaires.

Securing acceptance of the questionnaire. The physical appearance of a questionnaire influences the attitude of the respondent towards a mail or personal interview survey. If the questionnaire is mimeographed on a poor grade of paper, the respondent is apt to think the project does not amount to much. Printing on a good quality of paper, however, makes the questionnaire appear to be of some value.

The name of the firm sponsoring the project and the name of the project should appear at the top of the first page or on the cover if the questionnaire is in book form. Most companies use fictitious names on their questionnaires in order to prevent biased answers from respondents, and also to forestall phone calls from respondents asking information about the survey.

Experiments made in preparing the mail questionnaire for the 1980 Census showed that the general format, spacing, and positioning of questions had significant effect on the results, especially on the reaction to the questionnaire and, hence, full completion of it. Questions at the top of the page got more attention than when placed at the bottom. Instructions printed in red made little difference except they made respondents think that the questionnaire was more complicated than otherwise.[19]

Ease of control. To make it possible to control the questionnaires in the field operation and in the editing and tabulating procedures, the questionnaires should be numbered serially. This enables the research director to verify that all questionnaires are accounted for or to determine which ones are lost. Mail questionnaires are an exception. If these are numbered, respondents will assume that the number identifies a given questionnaire with them personally. It is generally believed that some respondents will refuse to reply or will answer differently under this condition. Recent research, however, suggests that the loss of anonymity influences results very little, if any.

Similarly, the questions on the questionnaire should be numbered serially. This makes reference to individual questions more simple and speeds up editing and tabulating.

Ease of handling. Proper reproduction of a questionnaire can facilitate the fieldwork and the office work on surveys. The size of the questionnaire is

---

[19] Naomi D. Rothwell and Anita M. Rustemeyer, "Studies of Census Mail Questionnaires," *Journal of Marketing Research* 16 (August 1979):401–9.

important. Small forms the size of a post card are easy to carry in the field and easy to sort, count, and file in the office. It is not wise, however, to crowd material into a small space. If the questionnaire is crowded, it makes a bad appearance and leads to errors in data collection. If small spaces only are available for answers to open questions, interviewers will digest the answers received to make them fit the space available. When interviewers have to crowd answers into small spaces, it is frequently hard to read the answers and tabulation errors appear.

Questionnaires that are too large become awkward for the interviewer to handle. Something near letter size, 8½ × 11 inches, is probably about the right size.

When a questionnaire runs to several pages, it should be made into a booklet form rather than a number of sheets of paper clipped or stapled together. A booklet is easier for the interviewer to handle and does not come apart with use as do clipped and stapled papers.

Questions should be laid out so as to make it easy for the fieldworker or respondent to follow the sequence. Numbering the questions in sequence helps, but confusion is particularly apt to come on filter-type questions. If question 4 is to be asked only of those respondents who answered "yes" to question 3 it is helpful if the layout of the questionnaire guides this procedure.

By showing the proper question sequence as a flow diagram on the questionnaire, the designer can help the interviewer move through the questionnaire quickly and accurately. Figure 8–3 is an example. Some researchers have found color coding useful—the color of the space in which the answer is recorded is the color under the number of the next question to be asked.

Many opportunities exist for improving the average questionnaire in layout in such a way as both to improve the quality of data collected and to reduce costs. One of the few reported efforts along these lines resulted in a reduction in printing costs for the questionnaires in a study from $1,150 to $214.20.[20]

New equipment is making possible a more mechanized system of tabulating data with accompanying improvements in both accuracy and cost. One of these, the optical scanner, requires that responses be recorded by code, which requires special questionnaire layout and may introduce errors in the recording. Answers are recorded with a heavy pencil similar to that used by many students in standardized tests and usually must be recorded on a sheet separate from the questionnaire proper. While this system has been used successfully, it is still experimental in nature.

---

[20] David F. Wolfe, "A New Questionnaire Design," *Journal of Marketing* 21 (October 1956):186–90.

FIGURE 8–3. Example of a flow diagram on a questionnaire

5. What brand of coffee did you buy last time you bought coffee?

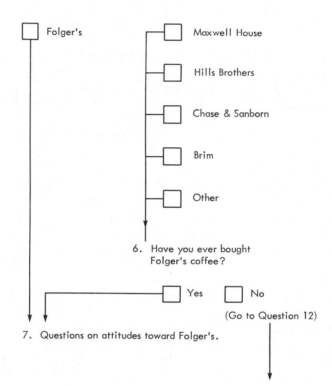

6. Have you ever bought Folger's coffee?

7. Questions on attitudes toward Folger's.

Pretest

Before a questionnaire is ready for the field, it needs to be presented under field conditions. No researcher can prepare a questionnaire so good that improvements cannot be discovered in field tests. Researchers have reported pretesting, changing, and pretesting again for as many as 25 times before they were satisfied with some questionnaires. One pretest is as much, however, as most questionnaires get.

Pretests are best done by personal interview even if the survey is to be handled by mail or telephone. Interviewers can note respondent reactions and attitudes which cannot otherwise be obtained. After any pertinent changes in the questionnaire have been made, another pretest can be run by mail or telephone if those methods are to be used in the survey. This latter pretest should uncover any weakness peculiar to the method of communication.

The people interviewed in a pretest should be roughly similar to those who will be covered in the final study. Ordinarily, the number of interviews in a pretest is small—perhaps 20, but, if major changes are made as a result, the new questionnaire should be pretested again. Only the best interviewers should be used in pretest work, since they must be able to perceive uneasiness, confusion, and resistance among respondents. Poor interviewers may not be aware of these difficulties.

Interviewers in pretests should watch particularly to see if the issue in each question is clear to respondents. Any requests for explanation, comments, or other reactions by the respondents should be noted. After an interview is over, interviewers may discuss it with respondents to get explanations of what meaning they got from individual questions and why they answered "don't know" where they did.

Wording of some questions should be improved as a result of the pretest. Interviewers should note words which are not understood by all respondents. If there is any doubt as to the wording of a question, interviewers can try alternate wordings and compare reactions of respondents to the different phrasings.

As a result of the pretest, some questions may be eliminated from the questionnaire and others may be added. Interviewers will observe questions which cause embarrassment or resistance, the point at which respondents begin to get bored and impatient, and the places where relaxed cooperation seems to break down.

Pretests should also test question sequence. Do the first questions catch the respondent's interest? Are some answers influenced by the questions which preceded them? Interviewers should report mechanical difficulties encountered, such as confusion in following question sequence and difficulty in squeezing answers into the spaces allotted.

Revision and final draft

After each significant revision of the questionnaire, another pretest should be run. When the last pretest suggests no new revisions, the researcher is ready to print the actual questionnaires to be used in the survey.

Summary

Questionnaire construction has been discussed in nine steps. These steps may vary in importance in individual projects, but each step must receive attention in each case. The nine steps are: (1) decide what information is wanted; (2) decide what type of questionnaire (personal interview, mail, telephone) to use; (3) decide on the content of individual questions; (4) decide on the type of question (open, multiple choice, dichotomous) to use; (5) decide on the wording of the questions; (6) decide on question sequence; (7) determine form, layout, and method of questionnaire reproduction; (8) make a preliminary draft and pretest it; and (9) revise and prepare the final questionnaire.

FORMS FOR OBSERVATIONAL STUDIES

Forms for the recording of observational data are much more simple to construct than are questionnaires. The psychological impact of the form on the source of the information does not need to be considered. All that is necessary is to develop a form which makes it simple for the fieldworker to record the desired information accurately, which identifies the information properly, and which makes tabulation of the results easy. Figure 8–4 is an

FIGURE 8–4. Example of form for recording observational data

	2 lb.	5 lb.	10 lb.	25 lb.		
Item No. (11–14)	0 3 0 1	0 3 0 2	0 3 0 3	0 3 0 4		
Item Description Page 4	Purina Dry Dog Food 2 lb.	Purina Dry Dog Food 5 lb.	Purina Dry Dog Food 10 lb.	Purina Dry Dog Food 25 lb.		
Shelf Loc. (15–16)	1 of 3	1 of 3	3 of 3	3 of 3	of	of
Inches Fac. (17–18)	2	3	2	2		
Quantity (19–20)	1	1	1	1		
For Price (21–23)	3 7	6 9	1 2 9	2 7 9		
Other Inv. (24–27)	1 2					
Display Inv. (28–31)						
Shelf Inv. (32–35)	2 1	4 9	2 2	1 7		
Total Inv.	3 3	4 9	2 2	1 7		
Prev. Inv. (76–80)	1 3	3 4	1 0	1 4		
Difference + –	– 2 0	– 1 5	– 1 2	– 3		
Deliveries: Date – Amount	4/15-12 4/22-12 7/6-12	4/15-20 6/22-20	4/15-5 6/22-10 6/27-10	4/15-4 6/22-10 6/29-10		
Product Credits						
Net Purch. (36–39)	3 6	4 0	2 5	2 4		
Current Sales	S/Days 1 6	S/Days 2 5	S/Days 1 3	S/Days 2 1	S/Days	S/Days
Sales Last Period (Date)	21	46	20	15		
Sales 2 Periods Ago (Date)						

Courtesy: Market Facts, Inc.

example of a page from a form used in collecting data on retail store displays, prices, inventories, purchases, and sales of Purina Dog Food during a market test.

This page is one actually used by a fieldworker in collecting data in a store. The figures entered by hand were put there by the fieldworker. Note that a separate column is provided for each package size. Spaces are provided for each observation to be entered separately, for example, shelf location, width of the face of the display, price, inventory, and each delivery. Calculation of net purchases, current sales, and sales last period is made in the office where the environment and equipment are available for doing an accurate job.

A good observation form permits researchers to record individual observations, but it does not force them to make a summary of their observations, which would be subject to error.

Physical layout and reproduction of observation forms should follow the same rules discussed for questionnaires.

Recording of disguised and unstructured observations is more difficult. Usually in such situations it is not feasible for observers to record observations at the moment they are made for fear of influencing the event of interest. In a shopping observation, for example, where observers are posing as prospective customers in an appliance store, they can hardly stop after each exchange with the salesperson to note what took place. The salesperson would begin to wonder what was going on. Under such circumstances, the observation must be written up as soon after the event as possible—in the example, as soon as the customer-observer leaves the store. To help in remembering what has taken place, it is useful to have an outline of the desired observations in mind before undertaking the actual observations. The observer might have in mind to note the following events: (1) the salesperson's opening; (2) the number of sales points made; (3) if certain major sales appeals were brought up; (4) the method of handling selected objections; (5) the salesperson's understanding of the product mechanics; (6) how the question of price was handled; and (7) how the salesperson attempted to close the sale. With these as a framework for observation, observers would be able to recall what occurred if they recorded it immediately. In some cases, it may be possible to record some of the observations by checking items on a list; for example, did salesperson demonstrate the automatic ice cube maker; did salesperson volunteer price?

Mechanical recording of observations is accomplished in some cases by such devices as the Nielsen audimeter or the eye camera. Moving pictures are used to record consumer action in such shopping activities as picking products from supermarket shelves. These mechanical methods give accurate records of the factors recorded, but the factors may be limited to only part of the total activity.

Case 8–1
ARKANSAS MOTORISTS*

The Arkansas Department of Public Safety was planning to undertake a study to obtain data on the attitudes, beliefs, and behavior patterns of Arkansas drivers regarding a number of safety-related issues. More specifically, the study's purpose was to investigate (1) the perceptions, attitudes, and behavioral patterns of motorists with respect to the 55mph maximum

---

* Adapted with permission from a case prepared by Conway Rucks, Associate Professor of Marketing, University of Arkansas at Little Rock, and Carol Crain, Director of Research, Area Market Research Associates, Little Rock, Arkansas.

speed limit, and (2) motorists' attitudes toward and usage of safety devices such as seat belts and child restraint systems. The study called for a sample of 400 Arkansas motorists to be selected at random throughout the state, and to be interviewed by telephone. The interviews would be conducted over a two week period from 5:00 PM to 8:30 PM. Callbacks would be made to minimize any bias which would result from the nonrespondent group.

Exhibit 1 shows the questionnaire which was developed after a detailed review of similar studies conducted by other states and numerous interviews with personnel of the Arkansas Department of Public Safety. The questionnaire also included questions (not shown in Exhibit 1) concerning sex, age, location of residence, occupation, annual total family income, education, and marital status.

Critically evaluate the questionnaire. How well will it satisfy the information specified in the study?

What changes would you make in the questionnaire? In the research design?

EXHIBIT 1

Arkansas Motorist Questionnaire

Hello, I'm _____ with Area Market Research Associates, an opinion research firm in Little Rock. We have been commissioned to make a survey of Arkansas motorists. We would appreciate it if you would give us a few minutes of your time and help us in this survey. (Circle the number(s) of the answer(s) given.)

1. *a.* What type of driver's license do you carry? (*you may read list*)

    (1) Operator   (4) Endorsed
    (2) Chauffeur   (5) Other
    (3) Motorcycle

  b. How many vehicles are in your household?

    (1) One   (4) Four
    (2) Two   (5) Other
    (3) Three

  c. Which one do *you* drive most often?

Passenger cars	*Trucks*	*Cycles*
(1) Regular	(4) Pickup	(7) Motorcycle
(2) Compact	(5) Van/Camper/RV	(8) Motor scooter/
(3) Sports car	(6) Commercial truck	Moped

  d. Please give me your best estimate of how many miles *you* drove in 1978.

    (1) Under 4,999   (4) 15,000–19,999
    (2) 5,000–9,999   (5) 20,000–49,999
    (3) 10,000–14,999   (6) 50,000 or more

  e. How many years have you been driving a vehicle? _____

EXHIBIT 1 (*continued*)

f. How likely do you think it is that *you* will be involved in an automobile accident of any kind this year, either one caused by you or someone else? Are your chances

(1) 1 in 10
(2) 1 in 100
(3) 1 in 1,000
(4) 1 in 10,000
(5) 1 in 100,000

g. How much control do you feel *you* have in preventing *your own* involvement in automobile accidents?

(1) Almost total control
(2) A lot of control
(3) Some control
(4) Very little control/none

2. a. The maximum legal speed limit on Arkansas highways today is 55 mph (miles per hour). What proportion of drivers on Arkansas highways, in your opinion, are usually observing the speed limit? (Pause for an answer & if the person does not understand, read the list at that time.)

(1) Almost all/75%–100%
(2) Over half/51%–74%
(3) Half/50%
(4) Fewer than half/25%–49%
(5) Very few or none/0–24%

b. Of the people who are driving over 55 mph, about how fast would you say they are driving?

(1) 56–60
(2) 61–65
(3) 66–70
(4) Over 70

c. There may be times you find yourself driving over 55 mph on the freeways & highways. What percentage of the time do you find yourself doing this?

(1) Almost all the time/75%–100%
(2) Over half the time/51%–74%
(3) About half the time/50%
(4) Less than half the time/ 25%–49%
(5) Only very rarely/1%–24%
(6) Never/0%

d. At what speed do you usually feel the most comfortable driving on the highway? (*Use highest mph given in answer*)

(1) 55 or less   (4) 66–70
(2) 56–60   (5) Over 70
(3) 61–65

e. At the times when you're driving 55 mph *or less*, what are your reasons for driving at that speed?

(1) Afraid of getting a ticket
(2) Feel safer
(3) Feel more relaxed
(4) To conserve gas
(5) To save money
(6) Other _____

f. At those times when you're driving *more than* 55 mph, why do you feel that you're going at that speed?

(1) Want to get where I'm going
(2) Get bored
(3) Feel less safe driving slower
(4) Engine performs better at higher speed
(5) Get better gas mileage
(6) Fear of getting run over by faster-moving traffic

EXHIBIT 1 (*continued*)

(7) Interstate designed for higher speeds

(8) Other _____

3. *a.* In your opinion, *why* was the 55 mph speed limit law passed?

(1) To save lives
(2) To cut down on accidents
(3) To save gas
(4) To get people to relax
(5) Government intervention
(6) Don't know
(7) Other _____

b. Are you in favor of keeping 55 mph as the *maximum* speed limit on Arkansas highways?

(1) Yes, in favor
(2) No, not in favor

c. What are your reasons for feeling this way? _____
_____
_____

d. (*If "no" on question 3b*) In your opinion, what should be the speed limit on Arkansas highways?

(1) 60
(2) 65
(3) 70
(4) 75
(5) Other _____

e. Do you think the 55 mph maximum highway speed limit is here to stay or will be changed?

(1) Here to stay
(2) Will be changed

	Yes	No
f. Do you feel that the 55 mph speed limit saves lives?	1	2
g. Do you feel that the 55 mph speed limit saves gas?	1	2
h. Do you feel that the 55 mph speed limit increases your travel time on a trip so that it's a problem for you?	1	2
i. Do you feel that 55 mph reduces your maintenance & repair costs on your vehicle?	1	2

j. What could be done to get you to drive 55 mph more frequently than you do now?

(1) More State Police
(2) Stricter enforcement/ no speed tolerance
(3) Never drive over 55 mph
(4) Other _____

k. Do you believe that the 55 mph speed limit has helped, hurt, or hasn't affected the transportation industry, such as trucks and buses?

(1) Hurt it
(2) Helped it
(3) Hasn't affected it

EXHIBIT 1 (continued)

4. *a.* Do you think the Highway Patrol/State Police allow a few miles over the 55 mph limit before writing a ticket?

(1) Yes
(2) No (*skip to Q.4c*)

b. (If yes on Q.4a) How much do you think they allow?

(1) 5 mph
(2) 10 mph
(3) 15 mph
(4) 20 mph
(5) Varies with officer
(6) Other _____

c. How does the Ark. State Police enforcement of 55 mph compare with other states?

(1) Not as good
(2) As good
(3) Better
(4) Other _____

d. In your opinion, do you think that 55 mph is being enforced enough in Arkansas?

(1) Yes
(2) No

e. In your opinion, if the State Police use surveillance planes for speed control enforcement, do you think this is fair or unfair?

(1) Fair
(2) Unfair

f. Do you own a CB radio or CB monitor?

(1) Yes
(2) No

g. Do you own a "fuzzbuster"?

(1) Yes
(2) No

5. *a.* How many vehicles in your household are equipped with safety belts in working order?

(1) None
(2) One
(3) Two
(4) Three
(5) Four
(6) Other _____

We are interested in finding out how and when people use safety belts.

	Always	Most of the time	Seldom	Never
5. *b.* When you're driving, how often do you normally wear a safety belt?	1	2	3	4
c. When you're riding in someone else's car, how often do you normally wear a safety belt?	1	2	3	4

d. Please tell me why you wear your safety belt _____ _____. (*Insert answer from Q.5b in blank; don't read following answers; three answers possible*)

(01) Safety reasons/prevent injury
(02) Because of the warning system in the car
(03) Habit
(04) Feel more secure/comfortable
(05) Don't want to be bothered
(06) Forgetful/lazy
(07) Uncomfortable
(08) Inconvenient
(09) Feel trapped

EXHIBIT 1 (*concluded*)

	(10) Afraid of being trapped In vehicle in accident involving water or fire
	(11) Doubt value of belt
	(12) Belts give false sense of confidence
	(13) Wrinkles clothing
	(14) In and out of vehicle all the time
	(15) Other _____

e. How many children in your family are living at home?
   (1) None (*skip to Q.5j*)
   (2) One–two
   (3) Three or more

f. Please tell us how many children you have in each age category. (*read categories.*)
   (1) Age 1 to 5 _____
   (2) Age 6 to 10 _____
   (3) Age 11 to 15 _____
   (4) Age 16 to 18 _____
   (5) Other _____

(If all children over ten years, skip to 5j)

g. Do you have any special safety belt or carriers for your children?
   (1) Yes
   (2) No (*Skip to Q.5i*)

h. (If yes to Q5g) How often do you put your children in these safety belts or carriers?
   (1) All the time (*skip to Q.5j*)
   (2) Most of the time
   (3) Seldom
   (4) Never

i. Please give me your reasons for _____ putting your children in the safety carrier/seat belt. (*In the blank, substitute usually, seldom, or never, depending on how they answered Q.5g or 5h; 3 answers possible)*
   (01) Too big a bother
   (02) Uncomfortable
   (03) Forgetful
   (04) Lazy
   (05) Children can't see out
   (06) Won't stay put/fusses
   (07) Fear of children being hurt
   (08) Don't think belts work
   (09) In and out of vehicle all time
   (10) Use them on long trips only
   (11) Other _____

j. In your opinion, how safe is a child riding on an adult's lap?
   (1) Safer than when belted
   (2) As safe as if in safety belt
   (3) Not as safe as in safety belt

k. If a law were passed in Arkansas that required people to wear safety belts, would you favor or oppose such a law?
   (1) Favor it
   (2) Oppose it

Case 8–2
PETERSEN'S DEPARTMENT STORES

Petersen's was a leading department store located in one of the most fashionable shopping areas of a major metropolitan city. It was the newest of a rapidly growing chain of stores specializing in a full line of high quality merchandise for customers with distinctive tastes. Because of the store's prime location and access to a large, upper-income clientele, Mr. Cameron, the company's president, felt that the new store would soon out-perform all others in the chain. The new store's only disadvantage was the presence just down the street of a major competitor which specialized in the same quality of merchandise handled by Petersen's. Mr. Cameron felt, however, that Petersen's could offset this competition by promoting a fashion image and unparalleled customer services. Charles Bernardi, recently hired as vice president for Customer Services, was given the responsibility for seeing that the store's services attained the high level expected by Mr. Cameron.

Mr. Bernardi, who had been part of the management team of a competing department store in another city, was generally pleased by what he saw when he arrived at the new Petersen's store. Merchandise was well chosen and attractively displayed, sales people were courteous and well-groomed, and a wide array of customer services was already being offered.

A few weeks after taking over his new responsibilities, Bernardi learned of a potential problem from his wife, who had just met one of their new neighbors, Mrs. Curtis. On hearing of Bernardi's new position, Mrs. Curtis remarked that she had been shopping at Petersen's recently and was very impressed by the new store. She complained, however, that it had taken an extraordinary amount of time to make her purchase. First, she had had trouble finding a salesperson to take her payment. Then, when she paid by check, there was another long delay when the saleslady had to leave the counter to find someone authorized to approve it. While she was gone, three or four customers were waiting anxiously to be served.

When Bernardi returned to work the next morning, he decided to investigate Mrs. Curtis' complaint. He sought out a salesman in the menswear department and asked him to describe the transaction procedures that were involved when a customer made a purchase. The sales ticket, Bernardi found, was designed so that the date, department code and the salesperson's identification number had to be repeated in three places. With each purchase, the salesperson was also required to prepare a manual inventory record, indicating the size, color, style, vendor and price of the item sold. For payments made by personal check, the customer had to present a driver's license and a national credit card, and the information on these had to be transferred to the reverse side of the check. A telephone call was then made to verify the person's good credit standing and, this done, a supervisor had to be located to approve the payment by check.

Still other problems could arise, Bernardi found, if the customer decided to pay with a gift certificate. If the value of the gift certificate exceeded the customer's purchases, the salesperson would have to leave the floor to go to the business office to obtain change in the form of "script" (that is, Petersen's paper money). Also, since each salesperson started the day with only $25 in change, often they would have to borrow change from each other if purchases were made with large bills.

Although there may have been good reason for instituting such procedures, Bernardi felt that they caused a great deal of customer inconvenience and, if so, should be changed. The credit and inventory control departments might be opposed to such a change, however, since new systems would have to be set up, new forms printed, and personnel retrained. Because of the potential opposition to such a change, Bernardi knew that he would have to prove to his superiors that the transaction procedures were causing at least some customers to be greatly inconvenienced. What he needed to know was the extent of the disatisfaction among customers, the particular reasons the procedures represented an annoyance to the customers, in which departments slow service was most prevalent, and whether it occurred at all times or only sporadically. Bernardi also wanted to know what types of customers were most inconvenienced by the slow service—males or females, regular customers or only occasional ones, customers in a hurry (for example, those on their lunch hours) or those casually browsing through the store. After thinking through the situation, Bernardi knew that some research would have to be undertaken to provide him with more definitive answers.

Bernardi wondered about the kinds of research that might be used for this problem. On the one hand, he could arrange to have some customers interviewed; on the other hand, he felt that much could be learned by first observing a customer's transaction and then asking certain questions if the transaction was long and drawn out. If he decided that the best way to find out if customers were dissatisfied with the store's service was to ask them, should the interviewing be done in the store, by a personal interview in the customer's home, by a telephone interview, or perhaps with a mail questionnaire? There was also the matter of selecting the customers to be interviewed. If in-store interviewing were to be utilized, should customers be selected randomly as they enter or leave the store, or should customers be randomly selected in different departments at different times of the day? If a telephone interview or a mail questionnaire were to be used, should respondents be selected from a list of the store's credit card holders, from names on sales slips, from the telephone book, or by some other means? Furthermore, Bernardi wondered, just how could one go about measuring customer dissatisfaction?

What information does Bernardi need?

What research project(s) can gather the information?

Design the research project(s) and questionnaire or observation forms needed.

9

Data collection II:
Attitude measurement

Interest in consumer attitude measurement now seems to be at an all-time peak. Attempts to "position" products in certain market niches are often based on estimates of the attitudes of different market segments toward similar products. Most of the strategy of market segmentation is based on attitudinal segmentation. Attitude measurement is also a key factor in the increased efforts to measure the effectiveness of advertising. To measure the effectiveness of advertising, it is necessary to measure changes in attitudes which may be caused by the advertising. A knowledge of attitudes helps the marketer predict consumer reactions to products and to advertising messages about products. This importance of attitudes, combined with the difficulty of measuring them, warrants separate attention to attitude measurement. What has been said in the previous chapter on constructing questionnaires applies to the construction of forms for collecting information on attitudes. But special problems are encountered in attempts to measure attitudes.

Attitudes and scaling

Attitude has been defined as a predisposition to respond to an idea or object.[1] In marketing this relates to the consumer's predisposition to respond to a product or service. If the predisposition is favorable, it is assumed that this means the consumer is more likely to purchase the item. The process, however, is more complicated than this suggests. Attitudes have a number

---

[1] This section draws on Gene F. Summers, *Attitude Measurement* (Chicago: Rand McNally, 1970), pp. 1–6.

of elements to them—three according to one generally accepted concept. This concept holds that attitudes are composed of *beliefs* about the object of concern such as its strength or economy; *emotional feelings* about the object such as "like" and "dislike"; and a readiness of the individual to *respond behaviorally* to the object, that is, to buy it. There is a tendency in marketing to bring these three elements into something called *image*. When the car manufacturer, the movie producer, or the insurance company refer to the consumer images of their products, they are referring to some general averages of many individual attitudes toward the products and each individual attitude is made up of various elements such as those suggested above.

It is clear that attitudes are complex and not fully understood. It is believed that attitudes can be changed, but that they tend to be persistent. Strongly held attitudes can be changed only with great pressure. Attitude measurement in marketing tends to focus on measurement of beliefs about a product's qualities and the emotional feelings about those qualities. Until now the devices developed for measuring attitudes have been crude at best. They apparently measure some general attitude, but they are just beginning to separate the various elements of an attitude. None of the existing devices is able to measure with any high degree of accuracy.

Scaling is the term commonly used to refer to the process of measuring attitudes. Measurement, or scaling, suggests some form of quantification which can be expressed in numbers such as we use to scale distances (feet, miles, and so on) or weights (pounds, kilograms, and so on). But this is difficult to do for attitudes. No one is entirely sure what an attitude is and there is no clear point from which to start measuring. In the latter respect, attitudes are something like temperature. Zero has been arbitrarily assigned on the thermometer (at different places for Fahrenheit and Centigrade), but this leads to difficulties such as the one identified in the conundrum: How cold is twice as cold as zero? There is no agreed upon "zero" at which to start measuring attitudes. The most common procedure is to measure in two directions from some neutral point such as measuring degrees of liking or disliking a product from some point between the two, a point of indifference.

GENERAL METHODS OF COLLECTING ATTITUDE DATA

Attitude measuring techniques[2] can be classified in general into two groups—those that are based on questioning and those that are based on observation. Each of these can be subdivided in the following ways:

Questionnaire methods

1. Self-reports—individuals are asked to report on their own attitudes.
2. Verbal reaction to partially structured situations—individuals are shown

---

[2] This section draws on Stuart W. Cook and Claire Selltiz, "A Multiple-Indicator Approach to Attitude Measurement," in Summers, *Attitude Measurement,* pp. 23 ff.

pictures of the product in use or in some setting and are asked to comment.

3. Performance on objective tasks—individuals are asked to report on factual matters and their attitudes are inferred from their knowledge about products.

Observation methods

1. Overt actions—individuals are given opportunities to select items they prefer.
2. Physiological reactions—when individuals are exposed to the item in question, sweating in the hand, dilatation of the eye, or change of voice pitch is measured.

These methods of collecting attitude data have the advantages and disadvantages associated with the questionnaire and observation methods generally. The self-reporting method is by far the most widely used. It has definite weaknesses in being open to respondent bias, but its advantages are still enough to make it preferred in most cases over other methods. The remainder of this chapter will focus on specific methods of scaling, that is, measuring attitudes by direct self-reporting methods and by methods using reactions to partially structured stimuli. These methods tend to emphasize either measurement of beliefs about a product or measurement of emotional feelings about it, but some attempt to do both. Some combination of beliefs and emotional feelings generally is assumed to determine readiness to buy.

SPECIFIC METHODS OF MEASURING ATTITUDES

If attitude measurement data are to be collected by self-reporting methods, questionnaires must be developed for the purpose. But there are further problems involved in designing attitude measurement instruments and a number of specialized techniques have been developed for such measurements. Some of the more fundamental and widely used of these methods are discussed here.

Suppose a coffee company wants to know the attitude of consumers toward the color of coffee in the cup (preference for light, dark, or in between), and toward bitterness, aroma, and flavor. No standard yardstick exists for measuring these factors; researchers must create their own devices. Or suppose the company wants to know how consumers "see" coffee in their lives—is it important, does it play a major social role, is it harmful to children, is it a masculine drink, is it consumed primarily within the family or at more social occasions, do people like it or is it a habit, what product attributes are particularly important in selecting one brand of coffee over another, how ready to buy are individual consumers for particular kinds of coffee (percolator, drip, instant) or for particular brands?

The above points suggest some of the kinds of attitudes which the marketer may want to measure. Methods of getting at them vary widely and will be discussed according to whether they are structured or nonstructured and disguised or nondisguised.

Nondisguised, nonstructured techniques

The reader will recall from the discussion in Chapter 4 that the terms *disguise* and *structure* refer to whether the respondent knows the purpose of the interview and whether there is a formal structure or procedure for the questioning.

Depth interviews. Depth interviews are the most commonly used technique that makes no attempt to disguise the subject of interest and uses no structured framework for eliciting information. To be effective, depth interviews must be conducted by highly trained interviewers, often individuals with training in psychology. Such interviewers get respondents talking about the subject of interest, for example, coffee, and attempt to explore the respondents' attitudes in depth by probing extensively into any areas which come up. Interviewers will have a general series of topics which they will introduce, perhaps topics such as those suggested about coffee, and will introduce these from time to time if the respondent does not bring them up. But the tone of the interview is one of permissiveness and the respondent is encouraged to talk as freely as possible.

Obviously, the interviewers' skill is the key factor in depth interviewing. They must be imaginative and thorough in probing the leads provided by respondents, yet they must be careful not to let their questioning influence the answers. Interpretation of interview results is equally subjective. There is no basis for counting answers. Researchers must use their knowledge of human behavior to analyze the responses and to discover the attitudes they suggest. There are numerous opportunities for bias in the results. Depth interviews are also costly, both in the data collection and the analysis stages. This leads to the use of small samples which can be another source of error.

Focus group interviews. In principle, focus group interviewing[3] is the same as depth interviewing except that groups are interviewed at one time. This tends to reduce the cost of obtaining information from a given number of respondents and has the added advantage of stimulation that each respondent receives from the others in the group. The disadvantages are the same as described for depth interviewing plus the added problem of possible group domination by one or a few individuals.

Conclusions. Nondisguised, nonstructured interview techniques were widely used in the 1950's. Then, for almost two decades they declined in popularity, but they have now become popular again. The focus group interview, particularly, has been found to provide leads to consumer thinking and attitudes that are difficult to obtain with other methods. For exploratory studies, nondisguised, nonstructured methods are hard to replace.

---

[3] This technique was discussed at length in Chapter 2.

Disguised, nonstructured techniques

Many people are unwilling or unable to provide investigators with insight into their conscious or unconscious attitudes. Disguised methods, usually referred to as projective techniques, have been developed to overcome this problem. Projective techniques are vague or incomplete stimuli to which the respondent is asked to respond. In doing so, it is believed that respondents reveal elements of their attitudes that they would not reveal in response to direct questions. Unconscious attitudes which a respondent cannot verbalize or conscious attitudes which a respondent will not report because they are socially unacceptable may be explored by the projective method.

Projective techniques suffer from the same kinds of weaknesses as do depth interviews. Some psychologists question their validity, but studies have shown that such techniques can provide more valid data than do direct questions.

There are a variety of projective techniques, including word association, sentence completion, story completion, and pictorial tests. Each of these will be discussed briefly.

Word association. Word association is one of the oldest and simplest projective techniques. Respondents are presented with a number of different words, one at a time. After each word they are asked to give the first word that comes to mind. If the list of words presented is related to the subject of interest, respondents may indicate some of their attitudes toward the subject with their responses. The underlying assumption is that by "free associating" with certain words, respondents will reveal their inner feelings about the subject being studied. Responses are timed so that those answers which respondents "reason out" are identified and taken into account in the analysis.

Word association tests are not difficult to administer, since to most respondents, taking the test is like playing a game. Nor is it difficult to construct a word list. It does require, however, some skill and experience to interpret the results. The usual way of constructing such a test is for researchers to prepare a list composed of a combination of stimulating and neutral words. What stimulating words to include depends on the study purpose. For example, if the purpose is to find responses to alternative advertising appeals, then the key words in these appeals will certainly be included in the list. On the other hand, if one is undertaking an exploratory study on, say, consumers' feelings about a particular food, then a great variety of words that might relate to food in general as well as that specific type of food would be used.

The words are usually read to the respondent one at a time and the interviewer records the first word "associated." Respondents should not be asked to write their answers because an additional variable is thereby added, namely the delay required for the respondent to put the association into written form.

There are several variations to the simple test situation described above. For example, respondents may be asked to give not only the first word that comes to mind, but the first three or four. Variations of this technique may be run as controlled tests, as contrasted to free association. For example, respondents may be asked, *What brand of cake mix comes to your mind first when I mention a moist cake?* or *What brand of detergent comes to your mind first when I mention soft and fluffy clothes?*

In analyzing the results of word association tests, the usual practice is to arrange responses along such lines as favorable-unfavorable and pleasant-unpleasant. Individual questionnaires should be checked for consistency and for evidence of "blocks." The latter are usually indicated by a person's inability to associate within a time limit such as five seconds. This is why interviewers time respondents and proceed to the next word if no answer is forthcoming.

Sentence completion.   This technique is quite similar to word association. Respondents are presented with a number of incomplete sentences and asked to complete them. As with the word association test, respondents are asked to complete the sentence with the first thought that comes to mind. To insure that this is done, respondents are timed. Sentence completion tests may provide more information about the subject's feelings than word association; but they are not as disguised, and many respondents are able to diagnose the investigator's purpose.

Sentence completion can be used in a number of different ways in marketing research. Some examples taken from a magazine study are:

"A man who reads *Time* magazine is . . . ."
"A man who receives a gift certificate good for *Newsweek* magazine would be . . . ."
"*Business Week* magazine appeals to . . . ."
"*Fortune* magazine is most liked by . . . ."

Sentence completion questions can be worded in either the first or third person. No evidence exists to indicate one approach is better than the other.

Story completion.   This technique provides respondents with part of a story—enough to center attention upon a particular issue, but not enough to indicate the ending. Respondents are then asked to give the conclusion in their own words.

An example of the use of the story completion technique is as follows:

A man purchased gasoline at his regular service station which sold a nationally advertised brand of gas. The station attendant, who knew the man, said, "Mr. Harris, your battery is now nearly two years old. We have a new product which when added to the water in your battery will prolong its life by about a year. It's a real good buy at $1.75."
What is the customer's response?
Why?

The story completion technique is quite versatile and has numerous applications to marketing problems, the most important of which is probably to provide the seller with data on the images and feelings that people have about a particular product. Obviously such findings are highly useful in determining advertising and promotional themes as well as desirable product characteristics.

Pictorial techniques.   The pictorial techniques are similar to story telling except that pictures are used as the stimuli. The two main pictorial techniques are (1) Thematic Apperception Tests, and (2) cartoons.

Thematic Apperception Tests.   Thematic Apperception Tests, commonly referred to as TAT, have long been used by clinical psychologists. They have been described as consisting of:

> . . . a series of ambiguous pictures, about each of which the subject is asked to tell a story ("What's happening in the picture? How did it come about? What will happen next?"). It is assumed that in describing the characters depicted, in setting forth their actions and the influences which affect them, the subject indirectly tells something about himself. Any person in the story with whose actions the subject concerns himself, with whom the subject may be conceived as identifying, represents a medium through which the subject expresses his own inner tendencies. The thoughts, the feelings, the attitudes, the inhibitions, etc., expressed by the characters with whom he identifies provide clues to his own tendencies. This does not mean that basic tendencies are always directly revealed; unconscious defense mechanisms may transform their expression even in the TAT, but the TAT will often provide indications of the operations of these mechanisms.[4]

An example of the pictorial technique is contained in Figure 9–1. The researcher found that the answers elicited through the use of this projective drawing were substantially different from those obtained through the use of direct questions and seemed to be better predictors of milk consumption. In commenting on the use of this technique, and projective techniques in general, the researcher states that "it can be particularly helpful in checking the veracity of responses to more direct questions, in obtaining information from consumers not easily obtained by more direct methods (i.e., where inhibitions are raised for one of several reasons), and in providing supplementary information."[5]

Some projective materials elicit more and better responses than others. This depends upon the ambiguity of the material, the extent to which the respondent is able to guess the conclusions, and the vagueness of the probe questions.

Cartoon tests.   Cartoon tests are a version or modification of the TAT, but they are simpler to administer and analyze. Cartoon characters are shown in a specific situation pertinent to the problem. One or more of

---

[4] Marie Jahoda, Morton Deutsch, and Stuart W. Cook, *Research Methods in Social Relations* (New York: Dryden Press, 1951), pt. 1, p. 215.

[5] Howard L. Steck, "On the Validity of Projective Questions," *Journal of Marketing Research* 1 (August 1964):49.

FIGURE 9–1. Example of Thematic Apperception Test

Would you think that Mrs. A or Mrs. B drank more milk, or possibly both about the same amount? (Reason given?)

Mrs. A.   Mrs. B.

Source: Howard L. Steck, "On the Validity of Projective Questions," *Journal of Marketing Research* 1 (August 1964):46.

the "balloons" indicating the conversation of the characters is left open and the respondent is asked to fill it in. In comparing the cartoon technique with the direct question in a study of the loyalty of buyers to industrial suppliers, one researcher concluded that the indirect approach provided a better insight and measure of resistance to change than did the direct method. This researcher used a cartoon which showed a conference in progress. One of the participants (Pete) was saying:[6]

"Now this is our present supplier list. We've been with them for quite a

---

[6] George M. Robertson, "Motives in Industrial Buying," in Robert S. Hancock ed., *Dynamic Marketing for a Changing World* (Chicago: American Marketing Association, 1960), p. 394.

while and they've been doing a good job. I see no reason for making any changes. The next subject is . . . ."

Tom, another man at the conference, interrupts to say: "Hold on Pete . . . loyalty is fine, but there are a lot of other considerations. I think we're due for a change."

The interviewer asked the respondent, "In this case, with which man would you be in most agreement? Why is that?"

In preparing cartoon tests, the researcher must be careful to use situations into which respondents can project themselves easily. That is, the picture must present a situation which is familiar to the respondent—one with which the respondent can identify.

Conclusions. Disguised, nonstructured techniques have one advantage over nondisguised, nonstructured techniques—they may get responses in some cases which respondent would not, or could not, give if they were clear as to the issues at hand. Otherwise, the two groups of techniques have similar advantages and disadvantages. Both groups have their advocates, but the nondisguised methods are more used at present.

Disguised, structured techniques

Nonstructured techniques described earlier have two major disadvantages: (1) they are slow, and hence, costly to administer in the field and to tabulate, and (2) the data collection process and the interpretation of results are subjective and, hence, open to bias. Structured techniques overcome these problems, but they are difficult to use in situations where respondents may hesitate to report their attitudes. Where the direct purpose of the study can be disguised, this problem can be overcome. Ingenious researchers have found ways to gain the advantage of structure and disguise by trading on the fact that people tend to know more about things that they favor or, if forced to guess factual information, will guess in a direction that is favorable to items or ideas that they favor.

The basic premise underlying such tests is that respondents will reveal their attitudes by the extent to which their answers to objective questions vary from the correct answers. Respondents are provided with questions which they are not likely to be able to answer correctly. Thus, they are forced to guess at the answers. The direction and extent of these guessing errors is assumed to reveal their attitudes on the subject. For example, individuals tend to gather information which supports their attitudes and, therefore, the extent and kind of information individuals possess on a given subject indicates something of their attitude.

In a hot cereal study, the disguised, structured technique was used by asking such questions as the following:[7] *How much do you think it costs for the hot cereal alone in an average bowl of cereal such as you'd serve at breakfast?*

---

[7] Ralph L. Westfall, Harper W. Boyd, Jr., and Donald T. Campbell, "The Use of Structured Techniques in Motivation Research," *Journal of Marketing* (October 1957): 138.

(¼ cent or less, ½ cent, ¾ cent, 1 cent, 2 cents, 3 cents, 4 cents, 5 cents, 6 cents, plus, don't know?) *Which of the following cereals do you think costs more per serving than a hot cereal, and which costs less? Do corn flakes cost more or less than hot cereal? Do Cheerios cost more or less than hot cereal?*

Questions similar to these were asked regarding vitamins, protein content, and the fattening qualities of hot cereals as contrasted to selected brands of cold cereal. Data from these questions revealed, for example, that dry cereal users exaggerated the cost of hot cereal. Considerable differences were evident between regions and city-size groups as to perceived vitamin content; the larger the city size, the better the vitamin rating for dry cereals.

Conclusions. Disguised, structured techniques have many of the advantages of nonstructured methods while eliminating much of the subjective element with which such methods are plagued. The authors have expected the disguised, structured methods to replace gradually the nonstructured methods as researchers become more imaginative in their use. This has not happened, but the potential advantages are large enough to warrant further efforts.

Structured, nondisguised techniques

The nonstructured techniques for attitude measurement are primarily of value in exploratory studies, where the researcher is looking for the salient attributes of given products and the important factors surrounding purchase decisions as seen by the consumer. Structured, disguised techniques provide a more objective measurement system, but the disguise factor makes the measurement indirect and, hence, difficult to compare accurately with measurements of competing items. This weakness has provided major incentive for the development of a standard attitude measuring instrument comparable to a scale or a yardstick. The term *scaling* has been applied to the efforts to measure attitudes objectively and a number of scales have been developed which are useful.

Ordinal scales are the simplest attitude measuring scales used in marketing research. They serve to rank respondents according to some characteristic such as favorability toward a certain brand or to rank items such as brands in order of consumer preference. Such scales make no attempt to measure the degree of favorability of the different rankings, that is, the distances between the different rank positions may vary widely. All the scale tells is that the individual or item has more, less, or the same amount of the characteristic being measured as some other item. This is the most widely used type of scale in marketing research.

Interval scales not only separate individuals or items by rank order, but measure the distance between rank positions in equal units. Such a scale permits the researcher to say that position 4 on the scale is above position 5, and also that the distance from 5 to 4 is the same as the distance from 4 to 3. Such a scale, however, does not permit conclusions that position 6 is twice as strong as position 3 because no zero position has been established. If one measures the distance between two points as four feet and between two other points as two feet, it is possible to say that the one distance is twice that of the other because each distance is measured from an absolute zero. A scale which permits such measurements is called a *ratio* scale. While ratio scales are common in physical science, the measurement of attitudes is still so crude that they are of no significance in marketing research.

Ordinal scales are the most widely used in marketing research, although interval scales have had some minor use. The more common variations of these two basic types are discussed in the following paragraphs.

Self-rating scales.   The simplest ordinal scale is the rating scale in which respondents rate themselves in one of two categories. This may result from a dichotomous question such as: *Do you like or dislike television commercials?* In answering this question, respondents classify themselves in one of two categories—those who like television commercials and those who do not. A possible third category would include those who refuse to take a position saying they neither like nor dislike commercials.

To simplify the process for the respondents, these alternatives may be specified so that they can check the ones that described themselves. A further refinement is to provide additional alternatives in the form of degrees of liking or disliking and listing them in sequence so that the alternatives form a type of scale. Two variations of such self-rating scales, the graphic rating scale and the ranking process, are discussed here.

Graphic rating scales.   The most widely used scale in marketing research is that in which respondents are asked to rate themselves by checking the point at which they would fall on a scale running from one extreme of the attitude in question to the other. In a study to determine attitudes toward private brands as compared with national brands, respondents were given the following task:[8]

Suppose that a large, new A&P store has recently opened up in your neighborhood and you have decided to shop there. Listed below are several brands of products that the store carries. Check in one of the spaces beside each brand how you think you might feel about using the brand.

	Use regularly	Use occasionally	Might use	Probably never use	Would never use
	1	2	3	4	5
Libby's canned peas					
Camel cigarettes					
Breck shampoo					
A&P aspirin					

---

[8] John G. Myers, "An Investigation of Socio-Psychological Variables as Determinants of Brand Imagery and Brand Choice" (manuscript, Northwestern University, 1964).

Many variations of the above scaling device have been developed; a number of these are shown in Figure 9–2.[9]

As can be seen from Figure 9–2, scales can have a few points (e.g., 3) or many points (e.g., 11); the number of points can be odd or even; the scale can be measured numerically, verbally, or a combination of both; the scale can be balanced or the majority of the points (even all) can be on the positive or negative side; scales can be numbered positively or positively and negatively around a zero point; and people can be scaled by their responses to a question such as in 13 in Figure 9–2. All of these variations seem to have some effect on the result. In the study from which the above 13 variations were taken the authors tested each variation in a number of ways:

1. All the scales seemed to discriminate among various brands in several different product areas such as coffee, toothpaste, detergents, and analgesics.
2. Number 13, an awareness measure, was clearly the best in discriminating among different brands followed by number 4, the paired comparison test. But there was variation in different product categories.
3. The scales that tended to discriminate the best all tended to limit in some way the number of strongly favorable responses (e.g., in number 13 only one brand could be the first mentioned).
4. Five-point scales seemed to discriminate better than 11-point scales. More than seven points in a scale seemed to lessen its ability to discriminate.
5. In the test, respondents were asked which brand of each product they had purchased last. There was a strong relationship between this brand purchased and a high rating on each of the 13 scale variations.
6. Respondents were found to choose the verbal labels rather than the numerical when both were used in the same scale. This resulted in a tendency to ignore the numerical points where a verbal label was not attached.
7. In general three scales were definitely preferable over the others:

> #13—awareness of brands
> #8—verbal purchase intent
> #4—paired comparison.

8. Paired comparison had a disadvantage of being more cumbersome to administer and is limited in that it measures only relative to other brands which may change over time.

A number of the scales shown in Figure 9–2 were graphic scales (1, 2, 6, 8) in which respondents could mark a position on a line or in a series of

---

[9] The examples shown and the related discussion are adapted from Russell I. Haley and Peter B. Case, "Testing Thirteen Attitude Scales for Agreement and Brand Discrimination," *Journal of Marketing* 43 (Fall 1979):20–32. Reprinted by permission of the American Marketing Association.

FIGURE 9–2. Variations of basic attitude scales

Description	*Format*
1. 7–point verbal balanced scale	For each of the following brands, check the degree it is acceptable to you.

☐ Extremely acceptable
☐ Quite acceptable
☐ Slightly acceptable
☐ Neither one nor the other
☐ Slightly unacceptable
☐ Quite unacceptable
☐ Extremely unacceptable

2. 11–point numbered and verbal scale

What is the chance of your buying (*brand*) the next time you purchase this product?

☐ 100 absolutely certain
☐ 90
☐ 80 strong possibility
☐ 70
☐ 60
☐ 50
☐ 40
☐ 30
☐ 20 slight possibility
☐ 10
☐ 0 absolutely no chance

3. 6–point verbal unbalanced scale

What is your opinion of (*brand*)?

☐ Excellent
☐ Very good
☐ Good
☐ Fair
☐ Not so good
☐ Poor
☐ Don't know

4. Score by brand, but constant sum

The number of brands to be considered are presented two at a time so that each brand is presented once with each other. In each pair, respondents are asked to divide 10 points between the two brands on the basis of how they like one compared to the other. A score is then totaled for each brand.

5. 3–point, small number of favorable ratings

If you were to purchase this product tomorrow, which brand would be your first choice? Which would be your second choice?

_____ First choice
_____ Second choice
_____ No mention

FIGURE 9–2 (continued)

	Description	*Format*

6. 10–point numerical scale

Check your opinion of (_brand_) on the following scale.

Poor | | | | | | | | | | | Excellent

 1 2 3 4 5 6 7 8 9 10

7. 11–point numerical and verbal scale

Mark on the following scale how you like (_brand_).

_____ 100
_____ 90 excellent
_____ 80 like very much
_____ 70 like quite well
_____ 60 like fairly well
_____ 50 indifferent
_____ 40 not like very well
_____ 30 not so good
_____ 20 not like at all
_____ 10 terrible
_____ 0

8. 5–point verbal

What is the chance of your buying (_brand_) the next time you purchase this product?

Definitely will buy	Very likely will buy	Probably will buy	Might or might not buy	Definitely will not buy

9. 5–point verbal

Check your agreement with the following statement: (_brand_) is considered one of the best.

Agree completely	Agree somewhat	Don't know	Disagree somewhat	Disagree completely
☐	☐	☐	☐	☐

10. 11 value positions, but constant sum

Respondent is given 10 pennies and a number of brands and asked to allocate the pennies over the brands on the basis of how she likes them.

11. 7–point verbal balanced

How do you rate the quality of (_brand_)?

_____ Extremely high quality
_____ Quite high quality
_____ Slightly high quality
_____ Neither one nor the other
_____ Slightly low quality
_____ Quite low quality
_____ Extremely low quality

FIGURE 9–2 *(concluded)*

Description	*Format*

12. 11–point numerical scale

What is your opinion of (__brand__)?

Poor | | | | | | | | | | | | Excellent

$-5 \ -4 \ -3 \ -2 \ -1 \quad 0 \ +1 \ +2 \ +3 \ +4 \ +5$

13. 5–point scale

When I mention micro-wave ovens, what brand do you think of? Any others? Have you heard of *(mention other brands of interest not reported)*?

_____ First unaided mention
_____ Second unaided mention
_____ Other unaided mention
_____ Aided recall
_____ Never heard of

(Each brand to receive a score based on the category into which it falls.)

Source: Adapted from Russell I. Haley and Peter B. Case, "Testing Thirteen Attitude Scales for Agreement and Brand Discrimination," *Journal of Marketing* 43 (Fall 1979):20–32. Reprinted by permission of the American Marketing Association.

boxes that indicated their position. Graphic scales generally are relatively simple to construct, use, and interpret, and they permit the use of various degrees of gradation as the researcher may choose. It is doubtful that consumers can distinguish between points if more than six or eight are used. If this is true, additional information is not obtained by putting more points on the scale. In practice, scales of five or six points are generally accepted.

When descriptive terms are used to define the points on the scale, each term should be as closely related to the numerical points as possible. It is impossible to do this exactly; who's to say if "very good" is twice as far from neutral as "fairly good." One effort to measure the relative size of "very" and "fairly" found that, while they were usually equated with $+2$ and $+1$, respectively, by researchers, the weight in respondents' minds was more nearly $+3.74$ and $+1.22$, respectively.[10]

This problem of the relative weights of various points on a scale emphasizes again the point made earlier: ordinal scales rank points, but say nothing about the relative distance between points. Unfortunately, it is very common to compare brands or individuals by computing averages, for example, the average "likingness" for different brands. The median rather than the mean should be the measure used when the scale is ordinal. If researchers want to combine ratings from several different scales into one overall score, they

_____

[10] Cliff Holmes, "A Statistical Evaluation of Rating Scales," *Journal of the Market Research Society* 16 (1974):91. See also James H. Myers and W. G. Warner, "Semantic Properties of Selected Evaluation Adjectives," *Journal of Marketing Research* 5 (November 1968):409–12.

have to assume the scale is an interval one even though they know it is ordinal. When this is done, the questionable value of the result should be emphasized.

Ranking.   In the graphic rating scales discussed above, respondents rated brands on a scale without reference to other brands. From the results it would be possible to rank brands with respect to the particular attitudes being measured. Another way to approach the problem, if rankings are desired, is to ask respondents to rank the brands or other subjects of interest according to the attitude being studied. In the previously mentioned study of attitudes toward private and national brands, the following technique was used:[11]

Beside each of the products listed below are four brand names. Mark 1, 2, 3, or 4 alongside each brand according to how often you use the brands—1 for most used, 2 for next, and so on. If the brands you use are not shown, choose those that you would be most likely to use.

1. Canned peas	_____Del Monte	_____Green Giant	_____Libby's	_____Jewel
2. Cigarettes	_____Kent	_____Camel	_____Benson & Hedges	_____Salem
3. Liquid shampoo	_____Prell	_____Breck	_____Halo	_____Pamper
4. Headache remedy	_____Bayer aspirin	_____Bufferin	_____Walgreen	_____Excedrin

Rankings of this sort separate the items in the group studied, but of course give no absolute rating—all the items could be considered good or bad. This technique is also limited by the number of items that a respondent can consider meaningfully at one time.

Rating scales of the graphic and ranking variety are simple in concept and use, yet seem to give results, in most cases, comparable with those obtained with more complex techniques. The most significant problem in using such scales has to do with their *validity,* that is, do they measure what they are presumed to measure? It is difficult to find standards against which to measure validity. The most common effort has been to compare opinions of products with their market shares or with purchases following the opinion measurement. These tests tend to support the validity of various attitude measures, but the correlation is far from perfect. Price is a confusing factor in these validity tests, as the most expensive brand is often considered the best even though many consumers may not choose to pay the high price.

Indirect scales.   Attitudes are complex and difficult to measure, as the above discussion has indicated. Few people spend much time analyzing their own attitudes. This means that when individuals are asked to mark the point on an attitude scale that accurately indicates their attitude on the subject in

---

[11] Myers, "Investigation of Socio-Psychological Variables."

question, they must make a judgment under difficult circumstances. It would be strange if such judgments were uniformly accurate. In an effort to improve the measurement of attitudes, indirect approaches to the problem have been developed. Rather than ask individuals for self-assessments, a series of statements related to the attitude is developed and individuals are asked to indicate agreement or disagreement with them. On the basis of the responses, a score is determined which is a measure of individual attitudes. Some of the several different types of indirect scales will be discussed in the following paragraphs.

Thurstone scale.   Thurstone developed his method of equal-appearing intervals on the concept that, even though people could not assign quantitative measurements to their own attitudes, they could tell the difference between the attitude represented by two different statements and could identify items that were approximately halfway between the two.[12] The procedure is as follows:

1. Collect a large number of statements (perhaps as many as several hundred) related to the attitude in question.
2. Have a number of judges (perhaps 20 or more) sort the statements independently into 11 piles which vary from the most unfavorable statements in pile one, to neutral statements in pile 6, to the most favorable statements in pile 11.[13]
3. Study the frequency distribution of ratings for each statement and eliminate those statements that different judges have given widely scattered ratings, that is, that are in a number of different piles.
4. Determine the scale value of each of the remaining statements, that is, the number of the pile in which the median of the distribution falls.
5. Select one or two statements from each of the 11 piles for the final scale. Those statements with the narrowest range of ratings are preferred as being the most reliable. They are listed in random order to form the final scale.

The following statements are taken in order, one from each of the 11 positions, from a scale to measure attitude toward television commercials. They give an idea of the range covered by such a scale.

1. All TV commercials should be prohibited by law.
2. Watching TV commercials is a complete waste of time.
3. Most TV commercials are pretty bad.
4. TV commercials are monotonous.

---

[12] L. L. Thurstone and E. J. Chave, *The Measurement of Attitude* (Chicago: University of Chicago Press, 1929).

[13] Thurstone recommended a large number of judges, 100 or more, but current work indicates such a large number is not necessary for reliability. See Allen L. Edwards, *Techniques of Attitude Scale Construction* (New York: Appleton-Century-Croft, 1957), pp. 168–69.

5. TV commercials do not interfere too much with enjoying TV.
6. I have no feeling one way or the other about most TV commercials.
7. I like TV commercials at times.
8. Most TV commercials are fairly interesting.
9. I like to buy products advertised on TV whenever possible.
10. Most TV commercials help people select the best products available.
11. TV commercials are more fun to watch than the regular programs.

Respondents whose attitudes are to be scaled are given the list of statements and asked to indicate agreement or disagreement with each statement. Presumably each respondent will agree with only one statement or with a few statements that are from immediately adjacent scale positions. For example, a respondent might agree with statements the scale values of which were 8, 9, and 10. Such an agreement in the above list on television commercials would be interpreted as representing a favorable attitude toward commercials. Respondents' scores are computed as the median of the item numbers with which they agree. If respondents agreed with statements 1, 4, 7, and 11, it would be interpreted to indicate they did not have organized attitudes on the topic. If the scale has been properly prepared, few respondents should show such a varied group of attitudes.

The scale as originally developed by Thurstone had 11 positions, this number is still commonly used. Actually, there is no particular reason for this number and either more or less could be used. An odd number is preferred by most so that a central, neutral position can be identified.

Thurstone scales are not widely used in marketing research, probably because of the time-consuming task of preparing them. The preparation of long lists of statements and the rating of these statements by a number of judges is more easily adapted to the classroom than to commercial field operations. Some interesting examples are available, however, such as the readiness-to-buy scale used to indicate the degree to which consumers are ready to purchase various brands of convenience goods.[14]

A number of questions have been raised as to the value of the Thurstone scaling technique. The scale position of each item is determined by a group of judges; their ratings may be influenced by their own attitudes. Many experiments have shown these ratings to be independent of the judges' opinions, but more recent studies indicate that, at least on some subjects, a definite correlation exists between the judges' attitudes and their ratings.[15] Even where this correlation is clearly shown, however, judges with different attitudes themselves still arranged the statements in the same rank order. This

---

[14] William D. Wells, *Readiness to Buy* (paper delivered to American Association for Public Opinion Research–World Association for Public Opinion Research Conference, May 6, 1960).

[15] R. T. Granneberg, "The Influence of Individual Attitude and Attitude-Intelligence Interaction upon Scale Values of Attitude Items," *American Psychologist* 10 (August 1955):330–31.

suggests that Thurstone scales should not be used as interval scales as originally intended, but as ordinal scales.

Another problem with the Thurstone scale comes from the fact that different individuals can obtain exactly the same scores from agreeing with quite
different items. A respondent who agreed only with item 7 would have a
score of 7, but so would a respondent who agreed with items 3, 7, and 11.
Some would argue that an individual who could agree with an item as extreme as number 11 could not possibly have the same attitude as one who
could agree with no item above number 7. The contrary argument would be
that attitudes are a composite of reactions to a large number of factors; no
two people have been exposed to the same factors or have reacted exactly
the same way to all of them. Each person's attitude, therefore, is an average
of a number of factors and the same average (attitude) can result from many
different combinations of factors.

A final criticism of Thurstone scaling is that it does not obtain information
as to the degree or intensity of agreement with the various statements. It is
this criticism that leads to the next type of scale to be considered, the Likert
scale.

Likert scales.   As with Thurstone scales, Likert scales involve a list of
statements related to the attitude in question. Instead of checking only those
statements with which they agree, however, respondents are asked to indicate
the degree of agreement or disagreement with each of the statements. Each
degree of agreement is given a numerical score and the respondent's total
score is computed by summing these scores from all the statements. The
following example on attitudes towards hot cereal will illustrate. Respondents were given a card on which the following was shown:

1. Agree very strongly.
2. Agree fairly strongly.
3. Agree.
4. Undecided.
5. Disagree.
6. Disagree fairly strongly.
7. Disagree very strongly.
X. Don't know

The respondents were then given a list of statements about hot cereal and
asked to select one of the above answers for each statement. Some of the
statements were as follows:

1. Hot cereal has a taste I like.
2. Hot cereal is a mess to make.
3. Hot cereal sticks to your ribs.
4. Hot cereal is expensive.
5. Hot cereal is high in vitamins.

The responses were scored from one to seven, as indicated above, except that the values were reversed for statements unfavorable to hot cereals, for example, statements 2 and 4. The sum of scores from all the statements made the total score for the respondent. In this example, a person with a very favorable attitude toward hot cereal could receive a score of five (one on each of the five statements) while someone with a very unfavorable attitude could receive a score as high as 35 (seven on each statement times five statements).

Likert scales are developed in a manner similar to that used for Thurstone scales.

1. Collect a large number of statements relevant to the attitude in question which can be clearly identified as either favorable or unfavorable.
2. Select a series of responses that represent various degrees of agreement or disagreement. Five variations such as agree strongly, agree, undecided, disagree, and disagree strongly are often used, but various other numbers can be used. It is doubtful that respondents can make meaningful distinctions among more than seven or nine variations. An odd number is usually used in order to have a middle, or zero point, but this is not necessary. If respondents are forced to choose between a favorable or unfavorable response when they in fact have no opinion, they should pick the mildest degree of agreement and disagreement about an equal number of times.
3. Administer the collected statements to a group reasonably representative of the universe to be studied and have them check one of the classes of agreement or disagreement for each statement.
4. Compute each individual's score by summing the scores of the responses to each question. The responses must be scored so that the most favorable response has the same rating for each statement. Since some statements will be favorable and some unfavorable, this will mean reversing the ratings of the responses for one of the groups of statements.
5. Eliminate those statements that do not discriminate between the high and low scorers on the total test. This can be done by selecting the high and low quartiles of respondents according to total score. Determine the average score on each statement among those in the high quartile and similarly among those in the low quartile. Those statements on which these averages differ by the largest amount are the most discriminating.

Likert scales are of the ordinal type; they enable one to rank attitudes, but not to measure the difference between attitudes. They take about the same amount of effort to create as Thurstone scales and are considered more discriminating and reliable because of the larger range of responses typically given in Likert scales. They have the same disadvantage as the Thurstone scales—similar scores can be achieved through varying combinations of responses. In this connection, the same argument as was presented in the discussion of Thurstone scales is pertinent to Likert scales.

Comparison of Thurstone and Likert scaling methods.   It is obvious that the Thurstone and Likert scaling methods have much in common. They have been two of the most widely used methods, yet there have been relatively few tests of the comparative validity, reliability, and efficiency of the two. The evidence to date indicates that the Likert scale is probably more reliable and faster than the Thurstone method, but there is no sound evidence on the comparative validity.

Semantic differential.   The Semantic differential has come to be used widely in marketing research. Perhaps its main use has been in connection with brand and company image studies; it permits the development of descriptive profiles that facilitate comparison of competitive items. For example, the following profiles of three beer companies were developed with this technique:[16]

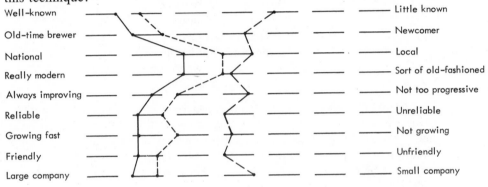

The unique characteristic of the semantic differential is the use of a number of bipolar scales, such as those shown above, to rate any product, company, or concept of interest. Respondents are given a group of these scales and asked to check on each one the point that indicates their opinion of the subject in question. As originally developed, each scale consisted of two opposing adjectives, such as good/bad and clean/dirty, which were separated by a continuum divided into seven segments. Each segment is assumed to represent one step in moving from the meaning of the adjective at one end to that at the other. Respondents check the segment which represents the degree of the characteristic involved which most closely coincides with their opinion of the product or other item being rated. There is no reason why the space between the opposing adjectives must be divided into seven segments; any number will work if it does not get so large as to represent distinctions too small to be meaningful to respondents. In one project, the entire scale

---

[16] W. A. Mindak, "Fitting the Semantic Differential to the Marketing Problem," *Journal of Marketing* 25 (April 1961):28–33.

was omitted and respondents were asked to pick one or the other of the polar adjectives, which most nearly coincided with their opinion of the subject.[17] Many researchers now use an even number of segments to force respondents to take a position. The neutral midpoint in a semantic differential seems to attract many respondents, thus resulting in nondiscriminating scores.

Although the original semantic differential scales could presumably be used for rating any item, most researchers develop their own scales for specific projects. For example, in a study to determine how people viewed a picture which was to be used in an advertisement, the following pairs of adjectives were used:

Rich—Poor

Intelligent—Unintelligent

Worried—Unworried

Honest—Dishonest

Healthy—Unhealthy

Likable—Unlikable

Wholesome—Unwholesome

Cheerful—Sad

The basis for selection of opposing adjectives to use is the purpose of the project at hand. In the above example, the advertisement was for an insurance company which was particularly concerned that the man pictured should not be thought to be worried or sad. Opposing adjectives must be such as to be readily understood as opposites by respondents.

The basic concept of the semantic differential has been modified in various ways. Figure 9–3 shows three variations, all of which are reported to have produced highly reliable data.

Semantic differential scales can be used to obtain total attitude scores similar to those obtained by the Likert method. Pairs of adjectives must be selected that are relevant to the attitude to be measured. In a study to determine the relative favorability of consumer attitudes toward two brands of the same product, pairs such as fair tasting/excellent tasting, average value for money/excellent value, and very healthful/not very healthful were used.[18] The adjectives were separated by a six-segment scale; the least favorable location on each scale was given a value of 1, the next least favorable a value of 2, and so on. After all the scales had been completed for each brand, these values were summed to obtain an attitude score for each brand. It should be noted that the paired adjectives in this project did not represent opposing extremes in each case. It was apparently reasoned that few people would consider any food product on the market as less than fair tasting.

---

[17] Louis Cheskin Associates as quoted in *Advertising Image* (Richmond, Va.: *Richmond News Leader,* 1963).

[18] William D. Barclay, "The Semantic Differential as an Index of Brand Attitude," *Journal of Advertising Research* 4 (March 1964):30–33.

FIGURE 9–3. Three alternative versions of the semantic differential

Form A (The upgraded semantic differential)
Rate the 10 residences in terms of how much you would like to live in each.

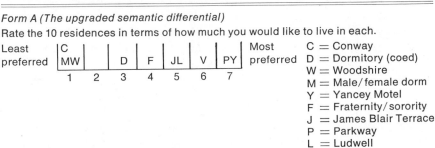

	C = Conway
	D = Dormitory (coed)
	W = Woodshire
	M = Male/female dorm
	Y = Yancey Motel
	F = Fraternity/sorority
	J = James Blair Terrace
	P = Parkway
	L = Ludwell
	V = Village

Form B
Rate the 10 residences in terms of how much you would like to live in each.
Merely circle the number that reflects your preference for each residence.

	Extremely low preference						Extremely high preference
Conway Apartments	1	2	3	4	5	6	7
Dormitory (coed)	1	2	3	4	5	6	7
Woodshire Apartments	1	2	3	4	5	6	7
Male/female dormitory	1	2	3	4	5	6	7
Yancey Motel	1	2	3	4	5	6	7
Fraternity/sorority house	1	2	3	4	5	6	7
James Blair Terrace	1	2	3	4	5	6	7
Parkway Apartments	1	2	3	4	5	6	7
Ludwell	1	2	3	4	5	6	7
Village Apartments	1	2	3	4	5	6	7

Form C
Rate Conway Apartments along the four residence attributes listed below. Merely place an X at the position on the scale that reflects your opinion.

Expensive	: X : : : : : :	Inexpensive
Not luxurious	: : : : X : : :	Luxurious
Far from Jones Hall	X : : : : : : :	Close to Jones Hall
Provides little social opportunity	: : : : X : : :	Provides an abundance of social opportunities

Source: Philip E. Downs, "Testing the Upgraded Semantic Differential," *Journal of the Market Research Society* 20 (April 1978):100.

The use of a total score obtained in this manner as an indication of the overall attitude toward a brand assumes that all the important factors that determine consumer attitude toward a brand have been included and that they are all of relatively equal weight. In the study cited earlier, a positive correlation was found between attitude scores so determined and brand purchases.

When the semantic differential is used to develop an image profile, it provides a good basis for comparing images of two or more items. When it is used as in the last example above, it is presumably serving as a scale on which some underlying attitude is measured. If it is to be used in this manner, some procedure must be inserted to sort out the nondiscriminating adjectival pairs in a manner similar to that suggested in step 5 of the Likert scale procedure. The question of validity is so serious here that the semantic differential is not recommended for overall attitude measurement; it is best when used for image-descriptive purposes. The one big advantage of the semantic differential is its simplicity, while producing results comparable with those of the more complex scaling methods. The method is easy and fast to administer, but is also sensitive to small differences in attitude, highly versatile, reliable, and generally valid.

MULTIDIMENSIONAL SCALING

The scaling methods discussed above all enable the researcher to measure to some degree consumer attitudes toward products and brands. In general, they permit one to determine such things as which brand is perceived by consumers to be more economical than another, less glamorous, more old fashioned, and so on. Two or more brands can thus be compared on as many different characteristics as the researcher considers significant or is imaginative enough to bring into consideration. But the various brands are measured against each characteristic one at a time. The measurement process tells little about the relative importance of the different characteristics or how the characteristics relate to each other in reference to the various brands.

Multidimensional scaling[19] is a term used to describe a group of analytical techniques used to study consumer attitudes, particularly attitudes relating to perceptions and preferences. These techniques attempt to identify the product attributes that are important to consumers and to measure their relative importance. They are useful in studying questions of the following types:

1. What are the major attributes of a given class of product (for example, soft drinks, fabric softeners, modes of transportation) that consumers perceive in considering the product and by which they compare different brands of the product?
2. Which brands compete most directly with each other? Which the least?
3. Would consumers like a new brand with a combination of characteristics not found in the market?

---

[19] This discussion is based primarily on Paul E. Green and Frank J. Carmone, *Multidimensional Scaling* (Boston: Allyn & Bacon, 1970); Paul E. Green, "Marketing Applications of MDS: Assessment and Outlook," *Journal of Marketing* 39 (January 1975):24–31; and James R. Taylor, "Management Experience with Applications of Multidimensional Scaling Methods" (Cambridge, Mass.: Marketing Science Institute working paper, not dated).

4. What would be the consumer's ideal combination of product attributes?
5. What sales and advertising messages are compatible with consumer brand perceptions?

An example may clarify the idea. Suppose consumers are asked to compare each of a group of cars with each of the others and to specify the two they perceive as being the most similar, the pair that is next most similar, and so on. Respondents are to use any criteria they choose. For the following 11 cars this would mean ranking on similarity all 55 possible pairs:[20]

1. Ford Mustang.
2. Mercury Cougar.
3. Lincoln Continental.
4. Ford Thunderbird.
5. Ford Pinto.
6. Chrysler Imperial.
7. Jaguar Sedan.
8. AMC Matador.
9. Dodge Dart.
10. Buick LaSabre.
11. Chevrolet Vega.

This could be done by putting each of the pairs on one of 55 cards. The respondent could separate these into two groups—those that have pairs that tend to be similar and those with pairs that tend to be different. He could then take the "similar" pile and separate it into those that are very similar and those not so similar. Within one of these groups, the respondent would then choose the most similar, the next most, and so on. In this step-by-step procedure a complete ranking on similarity would eventually be obtained.

One consumer might come up with results such as those shown in Table 9–1. The number 8 in the upper left corner shows that cars 1 and 2 were the eighth most similar; cars 3 and 6 were the most similar in the consumer's judgment (see figure 1 at intersection); and cars 3 and 5 were least similar.

TABLE 9–1. Pairs of cars ranked by similarity*

Car no.	1	2	3	4	5	6	7	8	9	10	11
1	—	8	50	31	12	48	36	2	5	39	10
2		—	39	9	33	37	22	6	4	14	32
3			—	11	55	1	23	46	41	17	52
4				—	44	13	16	19	25	18	42
5					—	54	53	30	28	45	7
6						—	26	47	40	24	51
7							—	29	35	34	49
8								—	3	27	15
9									—	20	21
10										—	43
11											—

* Read as follows: Pair 3 and 6 are most similar, 3 and 5 least similar.
   Source: Paul E. Green and Frank J. Carmone, *Multidimensional Scaling* (Boston: Allyn & Bacon, 1970), p. 33.

---

[20] This example is developed from data provided by Green and Carmone, *Multidimensional Scaling*, pp. 23–33, but some of the car names have been altered and the presentation is changed.

Analysis of these results by multidimensional methods is at a level of sophistication beyond this book. In general, the procedure requires the power of a computer to be practical. A number of computer programs are available for the purpose. Three basic questions are typically considered:

1. How many dimensions (product attributes) underlie the consumer's perceptions of the cars?
2. What is the actual configuration of the consumer's perceptions of the brands—which cars are the most alike and which the least?
3. What are the actual attributes underlying the configuration?

The general analysis can be seen by following the car example in an overly simplified form.

The computer program proceeds with the analysis of the first question by testing the data to see if there is a configuration of points on one dimension that fits the rank order data satisfactorily. Dimensions as referred to here relate to product attributes such as price, full economy, and performance, but it is important to note that what attributes are actually involved is not known. If one dimension does not provide a fit, two dimensions are tried; if these do not give a satisfactory configuration, three dimensions are tried, and so on. Since the fitting of a configuration to the data is a matter of degree, the researcher must trade off goodness of fit against a large number of dimensions. A lack-of-fit index called "stress" is calculated by the computer program. Rule-of-thumb policies for acceptable levels of this index have been established, but the general goal is to find a reasonably small number of dimensions which will eliminate most of the stress. In Figure 9–4 three di-

FIGURE 9–4. Example of stress index and number of dimensions

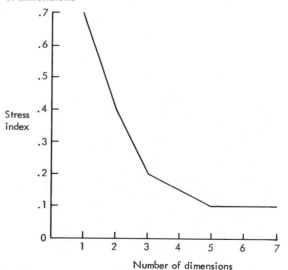

mensions appear to eliminate most of the stress; the addition of more dimensions reduces stress very little.

Assume that the program in the above example actually found one dimension eliminated almost all the stress, that is, that one attribute apparently was the basis for the comparison of the different cars. A configuration such as the one in Figure 9–5 might be the result.

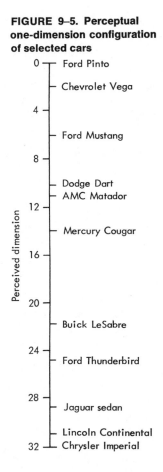

FIGURE 9–5. Perceptual one-dimension configuration of selected cars

The Ford Pinto and Chevrolet Vega are perceived as quite similar to each other, but quite different from the Lincoln and Chrysler. There is a significant gap between the Cougar and the Buick even though they are next to each other in the rank ordering.

While the computer program will develop the type of configuration shown in Figure 9–5, it tells nothing about the name of the attribute on which consumers were making their comparisons of cars. Marketing managers or researchers must guess what the attribute is on the basis of their knowledge of consumer attitudes toward cars, or they may collect additional data to help make the judgment. Additional information might be obtained by asking consumers to rank the same cars on several specified characteristics; if one of these gave a similar pattern to that already obtained, that characteristic might be concluded to be the attribute used in the original comparisons. Or researchers might test some objective factors; if they placed the cars on a scale according to price, for example (see right hand side of Table 9–2), they might find a configuration much like that obtained from the computer configuration. This might lead them to conclude that price was the basic attribute on which the consumers compared cars. This subjective way of naming the attribute (dimension) or attributes on which consumers based their comparisons is one of the weaknesses of multidimensional scaling.

Consumer preferences. After the consumer's perception configuration has been developed as suggested above, a next step may be to determine the preferences with regard to the product under study. Suppose consumer A is asked to rank the 11 cars in the example according to preference. The results might be as shown in the hypothetical data in the left-hand column in Table 9–2. Researchers, on the basis of their knowledge of the market, might then rank the cars on the basis of price as in the right-hand column in Table 9–2.

From the results in Table 9–2 the researcher would tend to conclude that price is the factor that underlies this consumer's preference choices and that the "ideal" car is also the lowest priced. The term "ideal point" is used to

---

TABLE 9–2. Ranking of cars by one consumer's preferences and by price*

Consumer's preference		Price	
Most preferred:	Ford Pinto	Lowest price:	Ford Pinto
	Chevrolet Vega		Chevrolet Vega
	Ford Mustang		Ford Mustang
	Dodge Dart		Dodge Dart
	AMC Matador		AMC Matador
	Mercury Cougar		Mercury Cougar
	Buick LeSabre		Buick LeSabre
	Ford Thunderbird		Ford Thunderbird
	Jaguar Sedan		Jaguar Sedan
	Lincoln Continental		Lincoln Continental
Least preferred:	Chrysler Imperial	Highest price:	Chrysler Imperial

* Data are hypothetical.

---

refer to the "point" which describes the consumer's preference, in this case the lowest price.

Suppose that other consumers, B, C, and D also provide data on their perceptions of product similarity and product preferences. Assume (an unlikely event) that all have the same similarity rankings as that given for consumer A, but their "ideal" points are at different locations on the configu-

**FIGURE 9–6. Ideal point
location on prime dimension**

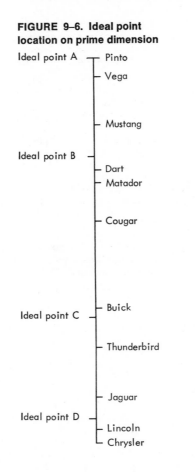

ration as shown in Figure 9–6. "Ideal" points A, B, C, and D correspond to consumers so designated.

Table 9–3 shows the order of preference of the 11 cars for each of these consumers.

Note the preference rankings are based on the distance of the brand from the consumer's ideal point as shown in Figure 9–6. All four consumers are assumed to have compared the cars on the basis of one attribute only, that is, price. But while consumer A preferred cheap cars and so had preferences ranking in order of price, consumers B, C, and D each had different "ideal" points and so preferred cars of increasing price.

If a larger sample of consumers, say 100, provided data on the same basis as above and all based their comparisons of cars on the one attribute of price (unlikely event), their ideal points could be plotted and might give a distribution like that in Figure 9–7. Such a distribution would suggest that there were three main market segments—one for low-priced cars, one for low- to middle-priced cars, and one for high-priced cars.

TABLE 9–3. Ranking of cars by preference of four consumers

	Consumer A	*Consumer B*	*Consumer C*	*Consumer D*
Most preferred:	Ford Pinto Chevrolet Vega	Dodge Dart AMC Matador	Buick LeSabre Ford Thunderbird	Lincoln Continental Chrysler Imperial
	Ford Mustang	Ford Mustang	Jaguar Sedan	Jaguar Sedan
	Dodge Dart	Mercury Cougar	Mercury Cougar	Ford Thunderbird
	AMC Matador	Chevrolet Vega	AMC Matador	Buick LeSabre
	Mercury Cougar	Ford Pinto	Lincoln Continental	Mercury Cougar
	Buick LeSabre	Buick LeSabre	Chrysler Imperial	AMC Matador
	Ford Thunderbird	Ford Thunderbird	Dodge Dart	Dodge Dart
	Jaguar Sedan	Jaguar Sedan	Ford Mustang	Ford Mustang
Least preferred:	Lincoln Continental Chrysler Imperial	Lincoln Continental Chrysler Imperial	Chevrolet Vega Ford Pinto	Chevrolet Vega Ford Pinto

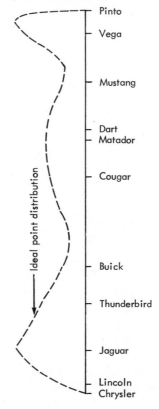

FIGURE 9–7. Distribution of consumer ideal points on price dimension

Multidimensional considerations. All of the above example is based on the unrealistic assumption that a consumer comparing different car brands would perceive the differences on the basis of only one attribute (dimension). In fact, the perceptions of cars by different consumers undoubtedly involve different attributes and any one consumer undoubtedly perceives each car as a composite of a number of different attributes. The term multidimensional scaling applies to those techniques which enable the researcher to study the combination of these various attributes. Since it is difficult to comprehend the complex interaction of a number of attributes and the technical analysis used, the overly simplified example above has been used. It is impractical to diagram the relationship of a number of variables at once, but Figure 9–8 shows one consumer's two dimensional comparison of 11 cars.

FIGURE 9–8. Illustration of consumer perception of similarities of selected cars on two dimensions

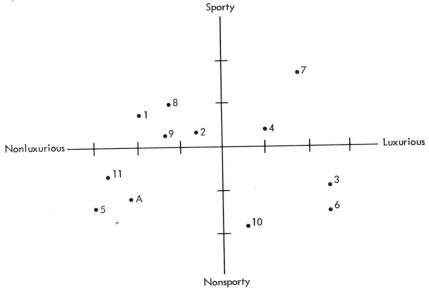

Source: Paul E. Green and Frank J. Carmone, *Multidimensional Scaling* (Boston: Allyn & Bacon, 1970), p. 23. Names of the cars have been modified.

The individuals who carried out this analysis named the two variables sportiness and luxuriousness. The consumer's ideal point is identified as A. Note that the preference ranking (distance from each car's location) will be different from that which would exist if only one of the dimensions were used. Cars 5 and 11, Ford Pinto and Chevrolet Vega, are still seen as quite similar (near each other on diagram), but 7 and 3, Jaguar Sedan and Lincoln Continental, which were seen as relatively similar on one dimension, are seen as quite different on two dimensions. This consumer's ideal point is nearest

Ford Pinto and Chevrolet Vega (5 and 11) and farthest from Jaguar Sedan (7).

The above discussion has been presented largely in terms of data from one consumer. Similar sets of data will be collected from a sample of consumers in an actual study. They will tend to have different configurations and efforts will be made to find groupings. Specific market segments, for example, income or age groups, may tend to give similar configurations. Such similarities will suggest market segments that may warrant separate marketing attention.

Uses of multidimensional scaling.   There are many possible uses for this method of scaling which have already been glimpsed; undoubtedly other applications will be developed as the technique becomes more widely used. Some of the uses which have already been identified are the following:

Market segmentation.   If brands are located as points in preference-space, as in the example, and consumers' ideal points are similarly located, market segments might then be viewed as subspaces in which consumers had similar ideal positions and perceived the brands similarly.

Product life cycle.   By analyzing respondent perceptions at different times, researchers might be able to relate movement along various dimensions (characteristics) to some measure such as market share and, thus, develop a new concept of product life cycle.

Vendor evaluations.   Industrial purchasing agents must choose among vendors who differ, for example, in price, delivery, reliability, technical service, and credit. How purchasing agents summarize the various characteristics to determine a specific vendor from whom to purchase would be information that would help vendors design sales strategies.

Advertising media selection.   What magazines should be used for an advertising campaign to reach a given audience? Different possible media could be identified as points in similarity-space (as were cars in the example) and members of their audiences located as ideal points. This would be similar to the market segmentation process. A similar approach might be taken to locate the best media for specific ads.

Limitations of multidimensional scaling.   In the above discussion, it has been suggested that many problems remain to be solved before the apparent full potential of multidimensional scaling is achieved. Some of these problems are significant limitations in current use of the technique. These limitations can be classified in the following three categories:

Conceptual problems.   Definitions of "similarity" and "preference" that are conceptually clear and that can be communicated accurately to respondents have not been developed and may not be achievable. Criteria on which similarities are gauged may vary during an interview with respondents; they may vary by the context in which respondents think, such as a purchase for themselves or as a gift; and small variations in one criterion may be more important than large variations in another. None of these factors is fully understood or amenable to control at present.

Current studies assume that each stimulus (brand in the example) is a first choice. If the preferred brand were not available, it is assumed the consumer would take the second choice. But what if the consumer purchases two items; for example, two cars. After the first choice has been bought, will the order of preference change for the second car?

How do preferences change over time? Do they change frequently, or are they relatively stable? The answers to these questions would have much to do with the operational use which a firm would make of a multidimensional analysis.

Empirical problems. In the discussion of the multidimensional scaling process, it was pointed out that the "labeling" of the various dimensions (criteria) of importance to respondents is subjective and, hence, open to question.

The data collection process is as open to bias in multidimensional scaling projects as in any other, but the relative impact of such biases is less well known. Procedures for collecting data and the general background conditions or "scenarios" in which a project is presented have yet to be standardized.

The example presented here was for one respondent. The problem of aggregating responses over a large group of people has not been worked out.

Computational problems. All analyses of the type discussed here require computer programs. Several different ones are used, but it is not known how, if at all, they vary in results according to variation in such inputs as number of points and experimental error.

Most computer programs assume the measurements between points, that is, the distances between items that are seen as different, are straight line or linear distances. Computer programs are available which use different distance functions, but researchers do not know what functions are appropriate. As a result, the linear assumption is made.

Summary on multidimensional scaling. This technique has become highly popular with academic students of marketing and is being increasingly used by practitioners. As it is applied by more researchers, the limitations are being better understood and, to some extent, solved. Further refinement is certain to come and the technique will continue to contribute to marketers' understanding of consumer behavior.

SUMMARY

Attitudes are complex and not completely understood. They are a composite of such things as beliefs, preferences, and readiness to respond behaviorally. Efforts to measure attitudes are not entirely successful in separating these elements and in many cases confuse them.

Measurement of consumer attitudes is a major concern of marketing researchers. The techniques used vary from completely unstructured to highly structured, from disguised to completely open, and from simple and direct to highly complex. All provide some contribution to understanding consumers, but none of the methods has been completely validated. Ranking of individuals along a given attitude or group of attitudes is about the best that can be done. Reliable interval and ratio scaling methods are not yet available. The semantic differential is simple in concept and gives results comparable with more complex, one-dimensional methods. As a result, it is widely used. Multidimensional methods are currently the fad and appear to add significantly to the analysis of attitudes.

Case 9–1
GOVERNOR'S COMMISSION

Over the past ten years the general public has become increasingly aware of business practices that lead to some form of environmental pollution. Recently more and more attention has been focused on the problem of litter. Citizens in many states have become alarmed and upset by the sight of growing amounts of paper trash and nondisposable glass bottles and cans on their highways, beaches, and public parks. In the states of Oregon, Maine, and Vermont, the outcry against litter was so strong that the use of throwaway bottles and cans has been banned by law. Several other states were studying the litter issue with the idea of creating legislation to control the problem.

The litter problem was becoming a major concern of many citizens in a midwestern state where tourism was an important industry. This state, which for many years was recognized for its beautiful parks and beaches, was finding that these areas were being despoiled by trash, cans, bottles and other litter. Many people felt that the litter problem, if left unresolved, would have a negative effect on the state's reputation as a recreational area, and cause a decline in the state's tourist trade. After consulting with several of his aides, the governor of the state determined that the litter issue was a major concern to many people in the state, and that it would be to his advantage to take a leadership position in this matter. The governor felt that the best way to approach the problem would be to establish a committee to study the litter situation in the state.

The Governor's Commission, as it came to be called, was comprised of nine distinguished citizens from all walks of life—law, medicine, education, labor, and business. The various backgrounds of the committee members allowed the problem to be viewed in a number of different perspectives, which was deemed essential to gaining a good overall insight to the litter situation. The chairperson of the commission, Ms. Mendenhall, was the president of the state's chapter of a well-known nature society, and had been actively involved in many other environmental issues. The charge of the commission was to advise, consult and make recommendations to the governor on what should be done concerning the litter problem, that is, the commission could recommend legislation and executive directives, but they had no power to execute orders of their own.

After meeting for several months the commission felt that the governor could consider six possible alternative courses of action. One alternative was for the state to undertake a major advertising campaign to persuade people not to litter. The second alternative was to tax each nonreturnable bottle and can and use the resulting revenues to pay for cleaning up the environment. Another was to put a complete ban on nonreturnable cans and bottles, as some other states had done. A variation of the third alternative was to institute a complete ban on nonreturnable bottles and cans, but not until some three to five years in the future. The thinking behind this alternative was to give bottlers time to writeoff presently used capital equipment and to retool for future operations. There was also a recommendation to pass a tax to be effective at some time in the future on all nonreturnable bottles and cans, and, in the meantime, give bottlers a chance to convert to making and using returnable containers. The commission also recognized that one alternative would be to do nothing and just ignore the problem, although feelings among the commission members were such that this seemed an unlikely recommendation.

As the commission proceeded it became clear that there was no single best course of action to recommend, due to the convincing arguments posed by the various interested parties, including both environmentalists and bottlers. Environmentalists argued that a ban or curb on nonreturnable cans and bottles would save much of the expense of litter cleanup, would help retain the beauty of the state's parks and beaches, and thus help keep the state's tourism revenues at a high level. In addition to the beautification effects, such laws would lead to an increase in jobs because of increased handling and transportation of returnable bottles at both the wholesale and retail levels. Environmentalists also argued that returnable bottles would be cheaper to use because they could be refilled.

On the other hand, bottlers believed that thousands of jobs would be lost at glass and can factories if legislation banned the use of nonreturnable bottles and cans. Bottlers also believed that millions of dollars would have to be spent on converting old plants to the production of reusable bottles and to provide warehouses for storing the bottles. Many bottlers felt that they might have to cease operation if they had to bear this expense.

The issue was further clouded by the fact that both the bottlers and the environmentalists used the results of Oregon's ban on nonreturnable containers to support their views. Environmentalists frequently quoted a study that found an 82 percent decline in beverage container litter, and a 47 percent decline in overall litter. Bottlers and other commercial people argued instead that the decline occurred because the state started spending more money to clean up the litter. Another industry argument was that beer, soft drinks, and packaging companies had to spend $6.4 million dollars for the conversion in Oregon while profits fell and jobs were lost.

As a result of the conflicting points of view, Ms. Mendenhall and the other members of the commission concluded that the littering issue was a political one as well as an economical and social one. After much delibera-tion, the commission concluded that it did not have enough information con-cerning either the facts about the effects of the Oregon law, or the reaction of the state's citizens to some of the alternatives then being considered by the commission. The commission decided to recommend that three of their members be charged with gathering all of the facts about the effects of the Oregon law, and that a research firm be hired to study the views of the state's citizens as to how the litter problem should be handled.

After the governor had given his approval, Ms. Mendenhall made ar-rangements to hire the research firm of Fischer and Associates, which had a good reputation as a research supplier on such projects as retailers' ad-vertising effectiveness, usage of consumer products and services, and public attitudes on political and community issues. The governor and Ms. Menden-hall met with Mr. Fischer to discuss the work of the commission, the data they had accumulated concerning the issue, and the alternative recommen-dations being considered. The governor indicated that he needed to know how the people of his state felt about the can and bottle litter problem, and what they thought should be done. He felt he wouldn't be able to come up with good legislation without such information. Because he considered the issue an important one, the governor indicated that a generous budget could be made available if Mr. Fischer could come up with a good research proposal.

After Fischer assigned the project to Lynn Benning, one of the firm's project directors, the two of them met to sketch out some general approaches which might be considered for use. With regard to the type of interview, they believed that a telephone or personal interview most likely would be used, but a mail questionnaire might work out if it were well designed. If a personal interview were used, they noted that it could take place in homes, in stores or shopping centers, or even at some parks and beaches. If the latter locations were used, they felt that it might be possible to do some observing as part of the study. When talking about the questionnaire, Ms. Benning wondered whether a structured, nondisguised questionnaire would be able to get at respondents' real attitudes and opinions. Mr. Fischer mentioned that it might be necessary to use a partially disguised questionnaire, and to ask such ques-tions as, *How important to you are the state's parks and beaches?* and *What are the major problems facing the state's parks and beaches today?* in order to find out how people really felt and how important the can and bottle litter problem was to them. The two also spent some time discussing how to phrase the questions which would measure a respondent's attitude toward, and preference for, the five or six alternatives being considered by the Governor's Commission.

Design the research project that Lynn Benning should recommend. What information should be obtained?

What should be included in the questionnaire?

Design the questionnaire you would recommend.

Case 9–2
PAUL'S PREMIUM BEER

Paul's Brewery, which was located on the west coast, introduced a premium beer to the three-state market in which it distributed its line of beers. Since its founding in the 1880s, this family-owned business had enjoyed almost continuous success. Since the early 1960s, the company had added a number of new malt beverage products including a price brand, a malt liquor, a light beer, and most recently a premium beer. The latter was designed to take advantage of the trend favoring premium beers. The new premium product had been extensively researched as to taste and package, including label and brand name. The new product, to be sold under the name of one of the founders of the company, featured a recipe he had used in Germany before immigrating to the United States.

In an attempt to create a unique identity for the new product, the company requested its advertising agency to develop several alternative advertising campaigns which would communicate the unique taste of this premium brand, as well as create a strong identity which differentiated it from other premium brands on the market.

The advertising agency developed three alternative campaigns, each of which centered on the use of 30-second television commercials. All three were designed to accomplish the same objective. In an effort to determine which approach was best and why, the company authorized the agency to undertake a research project. The three commercials would be shown in finished form despite the high cost of doing so.

The agency recommended that a central location study be conducted in one of Paul's largest metropolitan markets to evaluate the three new commercials. A total of 150 interviews were to be conducted—50 for each alternative. Each sample would be matched with respect to the following:

1. Employed males, 25 years of age or older, with incomes over $20,000 per year.
2. Beer consumption—all had to be medium or heavy beer drinkers (1 or more six-packs per week).
3. Have consumed a premium beer in the past four weeks.

Respondents were to be preselected by phone in accordance with quotas reflecting the above characteristics. If qualified, they were invited to participate in "an interesting research study" for which they would receive $3 and have a chance to win a $50 or $25 prize.

Upon arrival at the test site, respondents would be administered the preliminary questionnaire which obtained brand preference, beer usage data, and demographic information.

Respondents, in groups of ten, were then to be taken to the viewing room where they would be shown one of the commercials to be evaluated. Following this each respondent would fill out a self-administered questionnaire which consisted of the following open-ended questions:

1. What thoughts or feelings did you have while watching this commercial?
2. Other than trying to get you to buy the product, what was the *main* idea the commercial was trying to get across?
3. What *other* ideas about the product was the commercial getting across to you?
4. What was the name of the product advertised in the commercial?
5. What else (if anything) would you like to know about the product that was not mentioned in the commercial?
6. Please respond to how you feel about the product's taste as a result of having seen the advertising just shown you. (*Circle one answer.*)

Definitely would like taste	1
Probably would like taste	2
Neither would nor would not like taste	3
Probably would not like taste	4
Definitely would not like taste	5

Part two of the self-administered questionnaire contained over 40 pairs of opposite phrases which could be used to describe the respondent's reaction to the recently viewed commercial. Each was scaled to a 7-point basis. Respondents were instructed to:

... place an X on the line that best describes how strongly you feel *based only on the commercial you just saw*. Remember, if you place an X on the line to the far left, that means that you feel strongly that the statement on the left is very descriptive of this commercial. If you place an X on the line to the far right, you feel strongly that the statement on the right is very descriptive of the commercial. The lines in between represent various degrees of your reaction to the commercial.

An example of this type of scaling was:

A beer with an __ __ __ __ __ __ __ A beer with
excellent taste   a poor taste

The opposite phrases covered a variety of subject areas including taste (excellent/poor), price (low/high priced), kind of people drinking the brand advertised (younger/older, active/passive, sophisticated/unsophisticated, and followers/leaders), occasions (everyday/special occasions), quality (high/low), purchase intentions (would/would not buy), recommend to others (would/would not), evaluation of commercial (different/same as other premium beer commercials), and situation shown (enjoyable situation shown/not an enjoyable situation shown).

Part three of the questionnaire sought to obtain an overall evaluation of the commercial through a series of rating scales. First, respondents were asked to provide a summary rating using a 7-point scale (extremely good/extremely poor). Next, the commercial was scaled as to how it compared to other premium beer commercials (extremely similar/extremely different). The next two questions were concerned with believability and relevance. Questions 5 and 6 dealt with how Paul's compared with other premium beers.

Evaluate the proposed research design. What changes would you make to improve it?

Carefully show how your proposed research design would provide the company with the information it wants.

10

Introduction to sampling

Sampling is a commonplace idea. Everyone is accustomed to drawing conclusions about a large group on the basis of a small sample. Almost every day newspapers report the results of studies in which public opinion on some question is estimated by collecting opinions from a few selected individuals. Much marketing information is obtained through the use of samples. It is important, therefore, that the student of marketing research understand the advantages and limitations of collecting data through samples. This discussion of sampling will be limited to an examination of basic concepts. The reader is assumed to have only a limited knowledge of mathematics.[1]

Lower cost is the major reason why data are collected by sampling in place of complete enumerations. However, samples possess other advantages. For example, to make a census of all women homemakers in the United States it would be necessary to recruit, train, and supervise a very large number of field enumerators if the work were to be completed within a reasonable period of time. This would be a difficult administrative task. A sample would require fewer fieldworkers. Therefore, better personnel could be selected and trained, and their work could be more closely supervised.

These considerations are nonstatistical in character. They are important, however, because in practice researchers are *not* concerned exclusively with

---

[1] The reader who is interested in more technical discussions of sampling is referred to the following: W. G. Cochran, *Sampling Techniques* (New York: John Wiley & Sons, 1977); W. E. Deming, *Sample Design in Business Research* (New York: John Wiley & Sons, 1960); M. H. Hansen et al., *Sample Survey Methods and Theory,* vols. I and II (New York: John Wiley & Sons, 1953); N. L. Johnson and H. Smith, Jr., eds., *New Developments in Survey Sampling* (New York: Wiley-Interscience, 1969); R. K. Som, *A Manual of Sampling Techniques* (London: Heinemann, 1973).

the problem of sampling per se. They are concerned with the total research process instead of any particular aspect. They may find, for example, that the lesser administrative problems encountered in collecting data from a sample lead to more accurate data than could be obtained by collecting data from all units. The procedure which leads to the greatest accuracy in the final data is the procedure desired.

Confusion between sampling errors and data collection errors

Any data collected from a sample are a function of two factors, the "underlying reality" and the method used to collect the data. Researchers are interested in estimating this "underlying reality"; therefore, they must be aware of the possible errors in their data collection method. When data are collected from a sample, an additional source of error is introduced—that of sampling. In sampling studies these factors are often confused. If the results of a sampling study are found to be incorrect, the tendency is to assume that the sample was in error. Actually, the method of collecting data from the sample might have been inaccurate, or both factors may have been involved. For example, assume the problem of finding the percentage of households in Denver, Colorado owning a microwave oven. If a count of all households were made, an incorrect answer might still be obtained because the method of determining whether the household owned a microwave might be inaccurate. If only a sample of households was studied, the inaccurate method of measuring ownership would still be present, but, in addition, there would be error because the sample would not be exactly representative of the universe. Both types of error—the sampling error and the data collection error—must be considered in designing a research project. The following discussion of sampling deals primarily with sampling error. The reader must keep in mind that the final choice of sampling method will involve consideration of the nonsampling factor as well.

BASIC SAMPLING PROBLEMS

Definition of the universe being studied

The first problem in any sampling operation is to define the universe, or population, being studied.[2] The universe is the entire group of items which the researchers wish to study and about which they plan to generalize. For a given project, the universe might consist of all women homemakers over 40 years of age residing in the United States, all families within the corporate limits of the city of Chicago, or all grocery stores in the New York metropolitan area. Thus, the definition of the universe, in any particular case, is determined solely by the research objectives of the particular study.

---

[2] Some statisticians make a distinction between the terms *universe* and *population*. In this book the terms are used synonymously.

Many decisions usually must be made if the universe (or population) is to be sharply defined. For example, to define the universe of grocery stores located in the New York metropolitan area, such questions as the following must be answered: *What is a grocery store? Are both chains and independents to be considered? Are stores which sell primarily cooked foods (delicatessens) to be considered? What point or period of time is involved? Exactly what geographical area is to be considered?*

Definition of the variables being studied

The second problem to consider is the definition of the variables to be studied. For example, assume a bottler wishes to determine whether New York metropolitan area grocery stores stock a particular brand of soft drink. In this case, only one variable is being studied and it may be given a strict definition—a store either has the drink in stock or it does not.

In practice one often studies universe characteristics which are less sharply defined and, therefore, are difficult to measure accurately. For example, it is difficult to define precisely the attitude of homemakers toward frozen foods. Since this attitude is difficult to define, it is difficult to measure, because it is not exactly clear what one is trying to measure. This problem of "variable definition" is also present when a complete census is planned.

Sample design

Sample design is the third question raised in any sampling operation. This subject may be divided into (1) determining sampling units, (2) selecting the sample items and determining sample size, and (3) estimating universe characteristics from sample data.

The sampling section of this book will be devoted to an examination of these topics, with particular emphasis on methods of sample selection.

Choice of sampling units. Consider the problem of finding the proportion of grocery stores in the New York metropolitan area which stock Pepsi-Cola. Here grocery stores would be the units observed and, therefore, it would be reasonable to consider a *direct* sampling procedure. Given a list of all New York metropolitan area grocery stores, it would be relatively easy to choose a sample. If no such list were available, however, it would be necessary to resort to some *indirect* method of sampling stores. One might, for example, choose a sample of areas (such as city blocks) and observe all, or a specific fraction, of the grocery stores located in the chosen blocks. Thus, where a list of the units to be studied is not available, sampling units (such as blocks) which contain the particular units being studied (such as stores), and for which a list does exist, can be used. This method will be discussed in some detail in the section on area sampling.

Selecting the sample. Another part of the sample design problem is the method of choosing the sample items. Two general classes of methods exist for selecting samples: probability methods and nonprobability methods.

Probability sampling methods are those in which every item in the universe (for example, every grocery store in the New York metropolitan area) has a known chance, or probability, of being chosen for the sample. This implies that the selection of sample items is *independent* of the person making the study, that is, the sampling operation is controlled objectively so that the items will be chosen strictly at random. *Nonprobability sampling methods* are those which *do not* provide every item in the universe with a known chance of being included in the sample. The selection process is, at least partially, subjective.

The Pepsi-Cola distribution example provides an illustration of each of these two general classes of sampling methods.

1. A probability sampling method. From a list of all New York metropolitan area grocery stores, select a sample of 50 stores at random, that is, in such a way as to give each store an equal chance of being selected.[3] Fieldworkers visit all 50 stores and observe whether Pepsi-Cola is in stock.

2. A nonprobability sampling method. Ten New York metropolitan area fieldworkers visit five "average" grocery stores near their homes and observe whether Pepsi-Cola is in stock.

Each method will provide a sample of 50 stores. The first method will cost more because the sample stores will likely to distributed throughout the New York area. The use of such a method, however, would guarantee that every store had an equal chance of being included in the sample. The second method of sample selection would cost less, since the store would be near the observers' homes and the observers would not spend as much time traveling among them. But there is no rigorous way of determining whether the sample is representative of all the stores in the New York area.

In this book, the major emphasis will be placed on methods of probability sampling. One cannot think intelligently about nonprobability samples without using probability sampling theory as a reference point. However, several nonprobability sampling techniques are widely used in marketing research. They will be discussed in a later section.

Estimating universe characteristics from sample data. Marketing researchers are usually interested in summary numbers which describe particular properties of a given universe, for example, the arithmetic mean or the percentage of observations which show a given characteristic. In practice researchers do not usually know these summary values for the universe. They estimate them by measuring the given characteristics in a sample. Thus, researchers are forced to rely on *estimates* of the universe values, which will generally be different from the true universe values. It is important to note that any universe value (for example, mean or percentage) is a fixed number—even though generally it is not known. In contrast, the estimate of

---

[3] This makes the selection of a random sample sound deceptively easy. Actually, it is necessary to establish a formal procedure to insure that the selection is really random. This will be discussed in some detail later in this section.

the universe value obtained from a sample will vary from one sample to the next. Thus, if researchers were to take 100 independently selected samples of X items, each from the same universe, they would expect to obtain a different sample mean or percentage each time—even though there was only one real universe mean or percentage.

As an example consider the universe that exists when all face cards are removed from an ordinary deck of 52 playing cards. Such a universe contains 40 items. Each element of such a universe can be classified in three ways: numerical value, suit, and color. Some characteristics of this universe are:

1. The arithmetic mean (5.5).
2. The proportion of cards represented by any suit (0.25).
3. The proportion of red cards (0.50).

It must be emphasized that in the usual marketing study researchers do not know the value of the characteristics of the universe with which they are dealing. It will help develop the reader's understanding of the behavior of sample values, however, to consider samples drawn from a universe for which they know the true values.

From the universe of 40 cards described above, 50 independent random samples of 5 cards each were drawn. After each sample was selected, those 5 cards were replaced in the universe of 40 before the next sample was selected.

For each of these 50 samples, the proportion of red cards was determined. This proportion was taken to be an estimate of the proportion of red cards in the universe (which was known to be 0.50). In each sample this proportion could take any one of six values: 0.00, 0.20, 0.40, 0.60, 0.80, or 1.00. The results of this experimental sampling from a known universe are given in Table 10–1.

A first observation that can be made about these data is an obvious one: *all samples do not lead to the same estimate of the universe value.* In this case, sample estimates of the proportion of red cards varied from 0.00 to 1.00, when in fact the universe proportion was 0.50. Unless all items in a

TABLE 10–1. Distribution of 50 sample proportions taken from samples of 5 cards each (universe proportion of red cards = 0.50)

Sample proportion of red cards	Number of times proportion occurred
0.00 (all black)	2
0.20 (1 red, 4 black)	3
0.40 (2 red, 3 black)	14
0.60 (3 red, 2 black)	21
0.80 (4 red, 1 black)	8
1.00 (all red)	2
Total	50

universe are identical, different samples may lead to different estimates. That some sample estimates differ in extreme fashion from the universe value being estimated (in the above illustration the 0.00 and 1.00 values are examples) is an inevitable consequence of sampling. It is the price which must be paid for generalizing about a universe characteristic on the basis of a sample.

A second observation from the example is that *most of the estimates tend to cluster around the true universe proportion of red cards*. It is this property which gives faith in probability sampling. Unless there were some reason for believing that a sample estimate would ordinarily be close to the true value, there would be little point in using samples. Actually, there is no objective basis for supposing that this will happen unless probability sampling methods are used in selecting the items for the sample. In the above example, of course, it is possible to verify the existence of this tendency for the sample estimates to cluster around the universe value. But, in general, the universe value is unknown and, therefore, it is impossible to verify directly that a sampling process gives estimates which are close to the true value.

The sampling illustration presented above is artificial in other respects besides the fact that the universe value being estimated is known. Under practical research conditions, the universe would ordinarily consist of more than 40 items; usually only one sample is chosen; and the sample generally consists of more than 5 items. Nevertheless, the experiment demonstrates some features of the sampling process.

SIMPLE RANDOM SAMPLING—SAMPLE SELECTION

Probability sampling is the only sampling technique available which will provide an objective measure of the reliability of sample estimate. The simplest possible probability sampling method is called *simple random sampling*. In probability sampling, every possible sample of a given size drawn from a specified universe has a known chance of being selected. In simple random sampling, every possible sample has a *known and equal* chance of selection.

Simple random sampling is discussed in detail for two reasons:

1. It is the easiest probability sampling method to understand. It will serve as a vehicle for introducing some of the more complicated ideas involved in drawing inferences from samples.
2. It may serve as a good approximation to some of the more complex methods used in practice.

What is a simple random sample?

Assume a universe for which there is an *accurate list* of all items in the universe. How can one select a "simple random sample" from this universe, that is, how can one choose a sample in such a way that every possible sample of a given size has the same known and equal chance of being chosen?

It is easy to grasp the concept from a simple illustration. How does one choose a simple random sample of two homemakers from a universe list of six: A, B, C, D, E, and F? There are 15 possible samples: AB, AC, AD, and so on, if the sample AB is considered the same as BA. To give each possible sample an equal and known chance of selection, first number 15 poker chips from 1 to 15, and then set up a correspondence between chip numbers and each of the possible samples of two homemakers:

Chip number	Sample homemakers
1	AB
2	AC
3	AD
.	.
.	.
15	EF

Next, place the 15 chips in a bowl, mix thoroughly, and choose 1 chip "blindly." The number on that chip identifies a random sample of two homemakers.

Note the consequences of repeating this process a large number of times, each time returning to the bowl the chip previously obtained and mixing again before the next selection. In the long run every chip and, therefore, every possible sample will be obtained with equal frequency and with a known probability of 1 in 15. Although the term "a simple random sample" is used to describe such a sample, what is actually meant is a sample chosen by a *process* that guarantees, in the long run, that every possible sample will be represented with equal and known frequency.

The process of selecting a simple random sample guarantees that every universe item has an equal chance of being selected. In the above illustration, homemaker A will be found in one third of all possible samples (AB, AC, AD, AE, AF of the 15), and so will each of the other homemakers.

This fact makes it possible to choose a simple random sample by selecting universe items one at a time "at random," rather than by picking the entire sample (two homemakers in the illustration) at one time. This procedure—selecting universe items individually—generates a simple random sample equivalent to that achieved by the selection of the entire sample at one time.

The use of tables of random numbers

In the practical selection of a simple random sample, tables of random numbers are used rather than choosing chips from a bowl. Table 10–2 is a short table of random numbers.

The table consists of 400 digits arranged in ten columns of four digits each in ten rows. There is no pattern to the occurrence of any particular digit. If, for example, the pattern of occurrence of the digit 7 in the first row is studied, it is found that this digit occurs in the columns 14, 28, 30, 31, and 37. If the

TABLE 10–2. Short table of random numbers

Row number	Column number									
	1–4	5–8	9–12	13–16	17–20	21–24	25–28	29–32	33–36	37–40
1	3125	8144	5454	6703	2444	1518	3387	8772	6538	7532
2	1496	9980	1454	3074	3889	9230	2398	1598	3947	6917
3	4905	4956	3551	6836	6512	8312	9283	6663	8606	9580
4	9967	5765	1446	9288	0555	2591	8307	5280	5948	7869
5	5414	9534	9318	7827	5558	8651	7679	9983	5528	8922
6	5750	3489	9914	5737	6677	8288	7957	0899	1918	7684
7	9867	7825	0690	3990	2075	5402	8168	1601	0830	7544
8	4099	0087	9042	8818	0716	0373	6561	0855	3654	5997
9	2082	0918	8491	6480	8460	9663	2426	2816	1263	8430
10	7884	3991	1608	1489	7127	0563	1140	8816	9437	0495

Source: M. G. Kendall and B. Babington Smith, Tables of Random Sampling Numbers in *Tracts for Computers No. 24* (Cambridge, England: Cambridge University Press, 1946), p. 33. The fact that the digits are shown in groups of four has no significance. This grouping is to make it easier to read the numbers.

7s are traced throughout the remaining columns of the table, one finds no systematic pattern of their occurrence. The 7s occur "at random" in the table, and make up approximately 10 percent of the digits in the table.

To illustrate the use of a table of random numbers in sample selection, suppose it were desired to choose a simple random sample of 15 furniture stores from a universe of 83 furniture stores. The first step would be to assign the numbers 1 to 83 to the universe items. Then, beginning at a preselected place in a table of random numbers, select two-digit random numbers between 1 and 83 until 15 furniture stores are identified. Suppose, for example, the digits in columns 10 and 11, row 1, are selected as a starting point. The sample of furniture stores would then consist of the stores numbered as follows: 45, 46, 70, 32, 44, 41, 51, 83, 38, 78, 77, 26, 53, 21, and 49. The reader will observe that: (1) two-digit random numbers were chosen since the universe had more than 10 but not more than 100 members; (2) once a particular random number had been chosen it was ignored thereafter; (3) random numbers exceeding the last element on the list (83) were ignored.

Generalizing, the procedure for choosing a simple random sample with a table of random numbers is:

1.   Number each item in the universe serially from 1 to N (the total number in the universe). The arrangement of the list itself is immaterial.

2.   Beginning at any preselected place in a table of random numbers, proceed systematically through the table utilizing as many rows as are needed. If the universe has between 1 and 10 items, take one digit at a time; if the universe has between 11 and 100 items, take two digits at a time; and so on.[4]

---

[4] The random number table given is too small for most uses. See The Rand Corporation, *A Million Random Digits with 100,000 Normal Deviates* (Glencoe, Ill.: The Free Press, 1955).

3.   The sample will be comprised of those universe items whose numbers are chosen.

ESTIMATION AND THE CONSTRUCTION OF CONFIDENCE LIMITS

After selecting a simple random sample, how does one estimate universe values from the sample data? Many such values might be of interest, but the treatment here will emphasize the estimation of the two most commonly used—the *arithmetic mean* and a *percentage*.

Sample values as estimates of universe values

Assume one is interested in the total sales of Colgate toothpaste in Detroit grocery stores during a given week. For each of the grocery stores the value of this characteristic (sales of Colgate toothpaste) could be measured. The sum of these values would be the total sales of Colgate in Detroit grocery stores during the given period. The *arithmetic mean* would be the average sales of Colgate toothpaste per store for the given week, that is, the total sales divided by the number of stores.

Another parameter of common interest is the *percentage,* or proportion, of items in the universe possessing a particular characteristic. For example, in the toothpaste study one might be interested in the percentage of grocery stores stocking Colgate toothpaste.

How does one estimate a universe mean from sample data? Intuition suggests that the mean of the sample might be a good estimate of the universe mean. In this, intuition tends to be correct. If all possible simple random samples of a given size are drawn from a universe and the mean computed for each sample, the average of these sample means will be the same as the universe mean. The sample mean is an *unbiased estimate* of the universe mean, that is, sample means do not tend, on the average, to be higher or lower than the universe mean. This does *not* mean that each sample mean will be exactly equal to the universe mean. Only rarely will this happen; in general, the two will differ.

It may be helpful to illustrate this lack of bias in sample means as estimates of a universe mean. Consider a universe of four items with the values of $A = 1$, $B = 3$, $C = 4$, and $D = 8$. Assume all possible samples of size three are selected from this universe. The possible sample means would be:

Sample	Sample mean	Sample	Sample mean
A,B,C	2⅔	A,C,D	4⅓
A,B,D	4	B,C,D	5

In this case only one of all the possible sample means is equal to the universe mean, but the average of all possible means

$$\frac{2\frac{2}{3} + 4 + 4\frac{1}{3} + 5}{4}$$

is equal to the universe mean of 4. The sample mean, then, affords an un-biased estimate of the universe mean, but any one sample mean is unlikely to be exactly the same as the universe mean.

The proportion (or percentage) of the universe items having a particular attribute is simply a special case of the arithmetic mean.[5] Hence, a sample proportion (or percentage) provides an unbiased estimate of the correspond-ing universe proportion (or percentage). For example, from a simple random sample of 200 drugstore owners, it was found that 150 preferred to buy directly from the manufacturer, that is, a sample percentage of 75 per-cent. This percentage is an unbiased estimate of the universe percentage which prefers to buy directly. If a large number of simple random samples were drawn from this universe and the sample percentage computed each time, then the average value of these sample percentages would tend to equal the universe percentage.

Although both the sample mean and proportion are unbiased when based on simple random sampling, not all sample values provide unbiased esti-mates of the corresponding universe values. A conspicuous example is a group of estimates called *ratio estimates* which, as often used, are biased estimates of their population counterparts. Structurally, estimates of this type involve a ratio of quantities, *both* of which vary from sample to sample.

An example is provided by brand share. Suppose we have a universe of five stores, with sales of Brand X and the product class of which it is a part, as follows:

		Sales of	
Store		*Brand X*	*Total product class*
A		1	10
B		5	10
C		16	20
D		14	30
E		14	30
Total		50	100

---

[5] By this we mean that the *proportion* of items having a particular characteristic is equal to the *arithmetic mean* of the items, when items having the characteristic are given the value of 1, and those without it are given the value of 0. As an illustration, suppose there are five items, of which four have a specified characteristic. The pro-portion with this characteristic is 0.8. This is identical with the arithmetic mean when the four items with the characteristic are scored 1, and the item without it is scored 0:

$$\frac{4(1) + 1(0)}{5} = 0.8.$$

The fact that this so-called scoring system (0,1) enables us to regard a proportion as a special kind of mean simplifies the theory, since it permits immediate attribution of properties of the mean to a proportion.

Using samples of size two, it will be shown that the average brand share for all possible samples is not equal to the brand share for the universe as a whole. The ratio estimate of brand share is a biased estimate of universe brand share. The possible samples, and the brand share for each, are as follows:

Possible sample	X	Sample total of Product class	Sample brand share
A B	6	20	6/20
A C	17	30	17/30
A D	15	40	15/40
A E	15	40	15/40
B C	21	30	21/30
B D	19	40	19/40
B E	19	40	19/40
C D	30	50	30/50
C E	30	50	30/50
D E	28	60	28/60

The average of all ten possible sample brand shares is 0.493, compared to 0.500 for the universe. Hence, the sample value in this case is a biased estimate.

This example has been used mainly to illustrate the fact that not all estimates derived from simple random samples provide unbiased estimates of the analogous universe values. The sample mean and proportion are unusual in this regard.

Despite the bias in sample ratio estimates, such estimates find frequent application in sample surveys, particularly in more complex forms of probability sampling. Although they will often be biased estimates, in many situations the bias will be small (as in the above example) and other considerations will recommend their use.

Interval estimation

Different samples from the same universe will give different estimates of the universe value. The estimate from a particular sample will generally differ from the universe value because of *sampling error,* that is, because the sample chosen will not be a precise replica of the universe. If researchers took another random sample from the same universe, the resulting estimate could differ a little, somewhat, or a great deal from the estimate obtained from the first sample. They are then faced with determining how precise, or reliable, their sample estimates are.

Investigators would like to determine a range of values within which they could be quite sure that the true value lies. That is, they would like to construct an *interval estimate* of a parameter such as the universe mean. They would like, also, to be able to specify quantitatively how *confident* they are that the indicated interval estimate will in fact include the true universe mean.

What is wanted here is called a *confidence interval estimate* of the universe parameter. The researcher wishes to say, with a particular degree of confidence, that the universe parameter lies between two specified numerical values (confidence limits).

The theory of random sampling (and of probability sampling generally) provides methods for establishing such interval estimates. This permits the researcher to evaluate the reliability of sample estimates. Thus, with simple random sample data, one can measure the sampling error associated with an estimated mean or percentage, thereby setting bounds within which the universe value being estimated will likely lie. This is a great advantage of probability sampling over other methods.

The first concept needed in developing the idea of confidence intervals is that of sampling distribution.

The sampling distribution concept.   It has been emphasized that different samples from the same universe will lead to different estimates of the universe mean or universe percentage. For example, assume one chooses all possible simple random samples of two from a universe of six persons in a department store. Each person is carrying the following amount of cash: A—$20, B—$80, C—$100, D—$100, E—$100, and F—$200. The universe mean is $100. Seven different sample means ranging from $50 (sample AB) to $150 (samples CF, DF, and EF) would be obtained, with the following relative number of occurrences:

Sample mean	Relative number of occurrences	Sample mean	Relative number of occurrences
$ 50	1 out of 15	$110	1 out of 15
60	3 out of 15	140	1 out of 15
90	3 out of 15	150	3 out of 15
100	3 out of 15		

Such a listing of the possible random sample means together with their relative frequencies of occurrence is called the *random sampling distribution of the mean* for samples of two each from the given universe. Any such distribution of sample values under random sampling is called a *sampling distribution*.

Given a sampling distribution, one can predict the average behavior of the sample estimate under study. In this case, for example, if repeated simple random samples of two each were drawn from the universe of six persons and a sample mean computed each time, on the average 60 percent (9 out of 15) of these sample means would lie between $60 and $100, inclusive. Again on the average, about 73 percent (11 out of 15) of the sample means would be within $40 of the universe mean ($100), and so on.

The fact that knowledge of the sampling distribution makes it possible to predict the sampling behavior of the mean or a percentage is of fundamental importance in statistical inference. If one knew only that a particular sample estimate would vary under repeated sampling and had no information as to *how* it would vary, then it would be impossible to devise a measure of the sampling error associated with that estimate. Since the sampling distribution of an estimate describes how that estimate will vary with repeated sampling, it provides a basis for determining the reliability of the sample estimate.

Sampling distribution of the mean in large samples. In practical sampling work, the composition of the universe from which the sample is drawn is seldom known. Therefore, the sampling distribution of an estimate based on observations from the universe will also be unknown. On the face of it this would seem to rule out the possibility of constructing interval estimates of the type discussed above.

However, mathematicians have derived a theorem called the Central Limit Theorem, which makes it possible to construct interval estimates whose properties are known sufficiently well for most practical purposes. In rather crude terms, the Central Limit Theorem states: The sampling distribution of the mean, for a large sample, will be approximately a *normal distribution.*[6]

This large sample distribution of sample means will be distributed symmetrically around the true universe mean as shown in Figure 10–1. The

FIGURE 10–1. Distribution of large sample means around universe mean

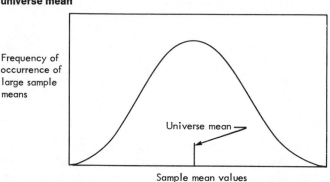

Frequency of occurrence of large sample means

Universe mean →

Sample mean values

sample means tend to cluster around the universe mean. Small deviations from the universe mean are more frequent than large ones. Sample means that deviate very widely from the universe mean are rare. Positive and negative deviations of equal magnitude occur with equal frequency.

If a number of samples of a large size is drawn at random from the same

---

[6] Cochran, *Sampling Techniques,* gives a discussion of the validity of the normal approximation in sampling from a finite universe.

universe, the means of the samples will tend to form a normal curve around the universe mean. The larger the individual samples, the more closely will the sample means cluster around the universe mean. That is, the larger the the sample, the greater the reliability of the sample mean. This accords with common sense since it would be expected that a large sample would be more similar to the universe than would a small sample.

Figure 10–2 illustrates the closer clustering of sample means around the

FIGURE 10–2. Distribution of sample means around universe mean for very large samples

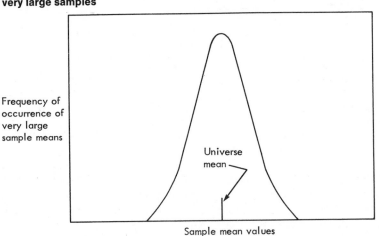

Frequency of occurrence of very large sample means

Universe mean

Sample mean values

universe mean when very large samples are used. Compare this distribution with that shown in Figure 10–1. Note that both are distributed symmetrically, but the distribution of sample means for large samples has fewer values that deviate widely from the universe mean. The larger the samples, the more closely the sample means will cluster around the universe mean. However, no matter how large the sample, unless it approaches the size of the universe, some sample means will be different from the universe mean.

If a universe is normally distributed, the proportion of the universe items located between any two limits is determined by the distance of those limits from the universe mean, measured in terms of standard deviation (SD).[7]

---

[7] The standard deviation of a universe is a measure of the dispersion of the items in the universe around their mean. The standard deviation of a finite universe may be defined by the formula

$$\sigma = \sqrt{\frac{\Sigma x^2}{N-1}}$$

where

σ = Standard deviation.
x = Deviation of an item from the universe mean.
N = Number of items in the universe.

In a normally distributed universe, about 68 percent of the items will be within one standard deviation of the mean, about 95 percent within two standard deviations of the mean, and virtually all (99.7 percent) within three standard deviations of the mean. These facts are exhibited in Figure 10–3.

FIGURE 10–3. Area under the normal curve

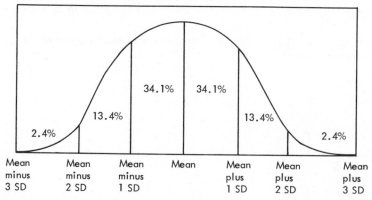

Because sample means will be approximately normally distributed about the universe mean, it is possible to make analogous statements about the deviation of sample means from the universe mean. When applied to the sampling distribution of the mean, however, the term *standard error of the mean* is used instead of standard deviation. The following statements apply.

1. About 68 percent of sample means will fall within 1 standard error on either side of the universe mean.
2. About 95 percent of sample means will fall within 2 standard errors on either side of the universe mean.[8]
3. Practically all sample means will be located within 3 standard errors on either side of the universe mean.

It is often convenient to refer to the number of standard errors under consideration by a common term; Z is used here. In statements 1, 2, and 3, above, Z is 1, 2, and 3, respectively.[9]

Nothing has been said as to how large the sample must be before the Central Limit Theorem may be applied. For fairly symmetrical universes, the sample can be as small as ten and the approximation will hold very well. On the other hand, for very skewed universes, the approximation may

---

[8] Technically, 95 percent of the sample means will fall within 1.96 standard errors on either side of the universe mean. The 1.96 is rounded to 2 to simplify the illustrations used in this section and to conform to common usage.

[9] The table in Appendix A uses this notation. Various values of Z are shown in column (1) there. Column (2), Appendix A shows the percentage of sample means falling within 1, 2, and 3 standard errors of the population mean (Z values of 1, 2, and 3) as 0.6826, 0.9544, and 0.9972, respectively.

be a relatively poor one, even for a sample of 200. For most applications it is satisfactory to assume that means based on samples of 30 will be approximately normally distributed.

Standard error of the mean and universe standard deviation. In constructing a confidence interval, one must also know how the standard error of the mean is related to the standard deviation of the universe. In a simple random sample, that relationship is

$$\sigma_{\bar{x}} = \frac{\sigma}{\sqrt{n}}$$

where

$\sigma_{\bar{x}}$ = Standard error of the mean.
σ = Standard deviation of the universe.
n = Number of observations in the sample.

This formula applies if less than 5 percent of the universe is included in the sample.[10]

Construction and interpretation of a confidence interval estimate for the universe mean

How does the researcher construct a confidence interval estimate of the universe mean? The first step is for the researcher to decide on the *level of confidence* he or she wishes to have in the results. Roughly, a "level of confidence" is the probability that one's confidence interval statement about the universe mean is correct, that is, that the obtained interval will in fact encompass the universe mean.

---

[10] If more than 5 percent of the universe is included in the sample, then the standard error may be computed as:

$$\sqrt{\frac{(N-n)}{N}} \cdot \frac{\sigma}{\sqrt{n}}$$

where N is the universe size and n is the sample size. The factor

$$\sqrt{\frac{N-n}{N}}$$

is called the "finite population correction." It takes account of the fact that a sample from a finite population partially exhausts that population. That some such correction is necessary becomes clear when one considers the limiting case $n = N$, that is, when a complete census is done. If no finite population correction were made, this would make the standard error of the mean equal to $\sigma/\sqrt{N}$, an obviously erroneous result. With the correction factor, the standard error of the mean based on a complete enumeration of the population becomes

$$\sqrt{\frac{N-N}{N}} \frac{\sigma}{\sqrt{n}} = 0,$$

as it should, since the estimate contains no sampling error when a census is conducted.
There is nothing magical about the use of 5 percent as the division point for the use of the finite correction factor. Some writers recommend 10 percent. Ignoring the correction factor is conservative, since it results in an overestimate of the standard error.

The higher the confidence level, the more likely that the confidence interval will in fact be correct. It is commonly chosen to be 80, 90, 95 or some higher percent, depending on how confident the analyst wishes to be about the location of the universe mean. For illustration, it is assumed that a *95 percent confidence interval estimate* of the mean is wanted. In terms of the foregoing discussion of the sampling distribution of the mean, 95 percent confidence implies that the researcher wishes to work with $Z = 2$.

Once the confidence level is decided, the analyst performs certain calculations (illustrated below) based on the available information. This will consist of the size of the simple random sample used (n), the mean of the sample (always symbolized by $\bar{x}$), and information about the universe standard deviation (denoted by σ). The course of the calculations depends on whether the universe standard deviation, σ, is *known* (possibly from previous work), or whether it is *not known* and must be estimated from the sample. The simplest case is when σ is known.

If the universe standard deviation (σ) is known.   Assume σ is known, and, to make matters as concrete as possible, that there are data from a simple random sample of size $n = 64$. A 95 percent confidence interval estimate of the universe mean is to be constructed, using this information and $\bar{x}$, the mean of the sample.

The applicable theory to be used is that the sample mean, based on $n = 64$, has a normally shaped sampling distribution which has a mean, M (universe mean), and a standard error of:

$$\sigma_{\bar{x}} = \frac{\sigma}{\sqrt{n}} = \frac{\sigma}{\sqrt{64}} = \frac{\sigma}{8}$$

This implies that about 95 percent of all possible random sample means, based on $n = 64$, from the sample universe, will fall within $Z = 2$ standard errors $\left(2\sigma_{\bar{x}} = 2\left(\frac{\sigma}{8}\right) \text{ units} \right)$ of M, the universe mean. That is, *before* the sample was selected, the chances were about 95 out of 100 that the interval:

$$M - (2)\left(\frac{\sigma}{8}\right) \quad \text{to} \quad M + (2)\left(\frac{\sigma}{8}\right)$$

or,

$$M \pm (2)\left(\frac{\sigma}{8}\right)$$

would include the mean of a sample of n = 64.

After the sample is drawn and its mean, $\bar{x}$, is calculated, one asserts—with 95 percent confidence—that the *obtained* sample mean, $\bar{x}$, is one of those sample means that is within $Z = 2$ standard errors of the universe mean, *M*. If, in fact, the obtained sample mean is one of those sample means within 2 standard errors of *M*, then the *95 percent confidence interval*

$$\bar{x} \pm (2)\left(\frac{\sigma}{8}\right)$$

will include (or cover) the universe mean, *M*.

More generally, because of the theory outlined earlier, we can always calculate a 95 percent confidence interval on the universe mean, M, using this formula:

$$\bar{x} \pm 2\frac{\sigma}{\sqrt{n}}$$

where $\bar{x}$ is the obtained sample mean based on a simple random sample of size n, and σ is the universe standard deviation. There is a 95 percent probability that the statement

$$\bar{x} \pm 2\frac{\sigma}{\sqrt{n}} \text{ includes } M$$

is correct, in the sense that 95 percent of the intervals calculated in this manner, using a large number of different samples, will in fact cover the universe mean. This is the meaning of 95 percent confidence.

Numerical example of calculating 95 percent confidence interval, when σ is known. Suppose that, in a simple random sample of $n = 49$ stores, average sales of a given brand are $72 per store in a particular week. It is known from past experience that, while average sales per week vary, the standard deviation of sales per store is constant and equal to $10. One can develop a 95 percent confidence interval estimate of M, the universe mean sales per store during the week considered.

The procedure is to solve numerically the two equations

$$\text{Lower confidence limit} = \bar{x} - 2\frac{\sigma}{\sqrt{n}}$$

$$\text{Upper confidence limit} = \bar{x} + 2\frac{\sigma}{\sqrt{n}}$$

because the 95 percent confidence interval is

$$\bar{x} \pm 2\frac{\sigma}{\sqrt{n}}$$

The lower confidence limit is

$$72 - (2)\left(\frac{10}{\sqrt{49}}\right) = 72 - 2.9 = 69.1$$

and the upper confidence limit is

$$72 + (2)\left(\frac{10}{\sqrt{49}}\right) = 72 + 2.9 = 74.9$$

Therefore, a 95 percent confidence interval for M is 69.1 to 74.9 dollars per store. The analyst is 95 percent confident that the true sales mean per store is between 69 and 75 dollars per week. This is a 95 percent confidence interval, because if repeated samples of $n = 49$ were drawn from this universe, and each time the analyst calculated the confidence limits

$$\bar{x} - (2)\left(\frac{10}{\sqrt{49}}\right)$$

and

$$\bar{x} + (2)\left(\frac{10}{\sqrt{49}}\right)$$

then 95 percent of the intervals so defined ($x \pm 2.9$) would in fact include the unknown universe mean, M.

By the same reasoning, a confidence interval almost certain to cover the universe mean is computed using the limits:

$$\text{Lower confidence limit} = \bar{x} - (3)\left(\frac{\sigma}{\sqrt{n}}\right)$$

$$\text{Upper confidence limit} = \bar{x} + (3)\left(\frac{\sigma}{\sqrt{n}}\right)$$

This interval is calculated using $Z = 3$ standard errors because almost all (99.7 percent) of the observations in a normal distribution are within three standard deviations of the universe mean (see Appendix A, column 2, Z value $= 3$). It should be noted that confidence levels other than 95 percent ($Z = 2$) and 99.7 percent ($Z = 3$) may be developed by using other values of Z.

It bears emphasis that the notion of "confidence" used here is defined in terms of what would occur if a very large number of samples were drawn. Any particular confidence interval either will or will not cover the universe mean. What is guaranteed is that, for example, over the long run, 95 percent of confidence interval assertions about the location of the universe mean will be correct, if a 95 percent confidence interval is used.

If standard deviation of universe is not known.   Up to this point it has been assumed that the standard deviation of the universe is a known quantity. In practical marketing research problems this value will almost never be known. Therefore, an estimate of the standard error ($\sigma_{\bar{x}}$) must be substituted in the confidence interval formula. The standard deviation of the sample is used for this purpose, that is, to calculate an estimated standard error,

$$s_{\bar{x}} = \frac{s}{\sqrt{n}}$$

where

$s_{\bar{x}} =$ Estimated standard error of the mean.
$s =$ Standard deviation of the sample.
$n =$ Number of observations in the sample.

This estimate tends to distort the accuracy of the estimation of confidence limits, but for practical purposes it will be satisfactory if the sample is large.[11]

Illustration. A random sample of 100 consumers provided the following information about the amount of money spent during a two-month period on certain food items:

$$\text{Sample mean } (\bar{x}) = \$400.$$
$$\text{Sample standard deviation } (s) = \$\ 80.$$

The problem is to estimate the mean of the universe with a 95 percent confidence interval and to interpret the result. The algebraic expression for this confidence interval is

$$\bar{x} \pm 2 \left(\frac{\$80}{\sqrt{100}} \right) = \$400 \pm 2 \left(\frac{\$80}{10} \right) = \$400 \pm \$16.$$

Therefore, one is 95 percent confident that the universe mean will be between $384 and $416. This finding is interpreted in the following way: If a very large number of samples of 100 consumers each were selected at random from this universe and for each such sample the confidence interval

$$\bar{x} \pm 2 \frac{s}{\sqrt{n}}$$

were computed, then about 95 percent of the intervals so computed would include the universe mean.

It is to be emphasized that the interpretation did not say the particular interval, $384–$416 (as calculated from a single sample), will bracket the universe mean. Rather, the interpretation said that, if a large number of random samples were selected and the interval computed each time, then about 95 percent of the intervals would cover the universe mean.

It should be noted in the above example that if the sample size were 256 rather than 100, the confidence interval would be $400 ± $10, or $390–$410. This demonstrates the effect of larger sample sizes on the confidence interval, and gives an indication of how researchers can control the width of the confidence interval through the use of different sample sizes.

Confidence limits for percentages. As in the case of the universe mean, the researcher may also wish to construct confidence limits for universe percentages. Fortunately, the theory is identical to that used to construct confidence limits for the universe mean since a percentage is but a special case of the mean. It follows that the sampling distribution of a percentage is, for large samples, approximately normally distributed. The standard error of a percentage from a simple random sample is estimated by the formula

$$s_p = \sqrt{\frac{pq}{n}}$$

---

[11] If the sample represents 5 percent or more of the universe, this expression may be revised downward, as described in footnote 10.

where

p = Percentage of items in the sample possessing a given characteristic,
q = Percentage of items not possessing the characteristic,
n = Sample size.

Suppose that a simple random sample of 100 families shows 40 own a dog and 60 do not. The estimated standard error, s_p, would be computed as follows:

$$s_p = \sqrt{\frac{(p)(q)}{n}} = \sqrt{\frac{(40)(60)}{100}} \%$$
$$= 4.9\%$$

The 95 percent confidence interval would be

$$p \pm 2s_p = 40\% \pm 2(4.9\%) = 40\% \pm 9.8\%$$

Thus, one would be 95 percent confident that the true percentage of dog ownership was between 30.2 and 49.8 percent.

In the above example, if the sample size were 600 instead of 100, the confidence interval would be $40\% \pm 2$ (2%), or 36–44 percent. This again demonstrates how researchers can control the width of the confidence interval through the use of different sample sizes.

One caution is in order with regard to this method of constructing a confidence interval for percentages. For values of p less than 30 percent or more than 70 percent, a sample of more than 100 is needed if the normal approximation to the sampling distribution of a percentage is to be a good one. If, for example, one were sampling an infrequent attribute, one which only 2 percent of the universe had, it could not be realistically assumed that the sample percentage would be distributed normally under repeated random sampling unless very large samples were used.

ESTIMATION OF SAMPLE NECESSARY FOR SPECIFIED RELIABILITY

The sample size needed to estimate the mean of a population, with a specified level of reliability, can be calculated using the principles presented on the preceding pages. An example will help. Two marketing executives wish to estimate the average monthly sales of a particular brand of cat food in chain grocery stores. After some discussion, it is decided that an estimate is needed which is correct within 10 percent of the actual sales. If simple random sampling is used, how big a sample of chain stores is needed?

On the basis of their previous experience, perhaps assisted by a pilot test, the executives estimate that the average monthly sales per store are 30 cans. Therefore, they estimate that to be within 10 percent of the actual mean will require a sample result within ±3 cans of the actual average; this means that they will want a confidence interval of ±3 cans. Recall the earlier theory that indicated that a sample mean is virtually certain (99.7 percent) to be within three standard errors of the universe mean. If they wish to be virtually certain of this result, this fact can be applied to the above confidence interval (±3 cans), and the sample size (n) needed must then be such that

$$3s_{\bar{x}} = 3 \text{ cans}$$
$$s_{\bar{x}} = 1 \text{ can}$$

They must also use their knowledge of actual sales conditions to estimate the standard deviation (s) of monthly sales per store. For commonly encountered distributions (i.e., positively skewed ones), the marketing executives can arrive at a reasonable estimate of s by dividing the range of the assumed distribution of monthly sales per store by four (4).[12] For example, if the executives felt that 60 cans per month and 12 cans per month would approximate the range of monthly sales per store, the estimated standard deviation (s) would be $(60 - 12)/4 = 12$ cans per month.

The formula

$$s_{\bar{x}} = \frac{s}{\sqrt{n}}$$

can then be used to determine the required sample size.

$$s_{\bar{x}} = \frac{s}{\sqrt{n}}$$
$$1 \text{ can} = \frac{12 \text{ cans}}{\sqrt{n}}$$
$$\sqrt{n} = 12$$
$$n = 144$$

The average sales from a sample of 144 chain stores should be within 3 cans of the actual universe average; that is, if $\bar{x}$ is the average monthly sales of the stores in the sample, the executives will be almost certain that average sales of all stores in the universe are within the range of $\bar{x} \pm 3$ cans.

Before measuring the sales in the sample of 144 stores, the executives will estimate the cost of doing so. If the cost will be more than they believe the information is worth, they will reconsider the certainty requirements which had previously been specified. A decision might be made not to conduct the study at all or the executives might decide that they were willing to accept the chance of 95 percent, rather than almost 100 percent, that the sample average sales will be within 3 cans of the universe average. The sample size needed must then be such that

$$2s_{\bar{x}} = 3 \text{ cans}$$
$$s_{\bar{x}} = 1.5 \text{ cans}$$

and by using the formula shown above, one can determine that the necessary sample size would be $n = 64$ chain stores.

---

[12] See Deming, *Sample Decisions in Business Research*, p. 260.

Or the executives might decide that they would be satisfied if they could be virtually certain (99.7 percent) that the sample mean was within 15 percent of the population mean: 15 percent of 30 cans = 4.5 cans; that is, the confidence interval would be ± 4.5 cans. Then

$$3s_{\bar{x}} = 4.5 \text{ cans}$$
$$s_{\bar{x}} = 1.5 \text{ cans}$$

and the necessary sample size would be $n = 64$ chain stores.

Note that the example of a change in the confidence required (from 99.7 percent to 95 percent) and the example of a change in degree of precision sought (from an estimate within 10 percent of the mean to within 15 percent) both result in the same new size of sample, that is, 64. It is the combination of these two factors, the confidence requirement and the degree of precision sought, which determines the sample size needed in a given situation. Individual judgment as to the risk involved, based on the type of decision to be made with the results, and the individual variations in willingness to take risks, determine the choice made in a given situation. The reader will recognize that all samples do not have to be based on virtual certainty ($3s_{\bar{x}}$) or 95 chances out of 100 ($2s_{\bar{x}}$), but that any probability can be chosen, for example, 90/100, 75/100, and so on. Most marketing samples tend to be based on the probability of at least 80 chances out of 100 that the sample will give results within the selected confidence interval.[13]

The above formula and the example given are based on the assumption that the universe size (N) is large relative to the projected sample size (n). If the indicated sample size is an appreciable proportion of the universe (more than 5 percent), this formula overestimates the sample size required. If the ratio n/N exceeds 0.05, the indicated sample size should be revised downward using the formula

$$n' = \frac{n}{1 + \dfrac{n}{N}}$$

As an example of this refinement, suppose that in the first cat food example, the relevant universe size is $N = 500$ chain stores. Then, since $n/N = 0.29$, the required sample should be reduced to

$$n' = \left(\frac{144}{1 + 144/500}\right) = 112$$

Determining sample size when estimating a percentage

To determine the necessary sample size when estimating a percentage, the researcher will use the basic formula shown earlier for calculating confidence limits for percentages:

---

[13] See Appendix A, column 2, for the number of standard errors of the mean which will include various probability ranges.

$$s_p = \sqrt{\frac{pq}{n}}$$

or

$$n = \frac{pq}{(s_p)^2}$$

As an example of application of this formula, suppose one wishes to estimate the percentage of families which serve a specific hot cereal during a particular week. The researcher believes that 40 percent of families do so—that is, $p = 40$ percent. He wants to be 95 percent confident ($Z = 2$) that the sample percentage will be within 4 percentage points of the actual universe percentage. Then

$$2\, s_p = \quad 4\%$$
$$s_p = \quad 2\%$$
$$p = 40\%$$
$$q = 60\%$$

Using the formula above

$$n = \frac{40 \times 60}{(2)^2} = \frac{2,400}{4} = 600.$$

As was the case when determining sample size for a mean, the size indicated by the basic formula for a percentage should be revised downward if the indicated sample comprises over 5 percent of the universe.

Additional remarks on the determination of sample size

The actual application of the sample size formulas given in this section requires consideration of a number of related issues. These include the following:

1.   The formulas given are applicable strictly to only *simple random sampling*. Sampling systems which are more efficient statistically (such as stratified random sampling, to be discussed later) will require fewer observations for equally satisfactory results. Similarly, there are other sampling systems, commonly used in practice, for which the simple formulas provided will underestimate the actual number of observation units which must be contacted.

2.   These formulas relate to the sample size needed for one particular characteristic of interest. Hardly ever is a survey done to answer only one question. Typically, several values are of interest and each may require a different sample size. One consequence is the necessity for compromise on this question, some estimates being provided with less precision than is really wanted and others having greater reliability than is necessary.

3.   In addition to varying reliability requirements for different universe characteristics of interest, various universe segments may have different pre-

cision needs. For instance, in chain stores, it might be necessary to have results that are correct within 10 percent; in independent stores, this require-ment might be relaxed to 15 percent. In general, simple random sampling would not be the best approach to this problem, but, regardless of sampling method, the broad problem of differential reliability needs must be con-sidered.

4.   In order to be useful, the sample size formulas must be based on ade-quate information about the universe, and the more that is known of a uni-verse, the more efficiently it can be sampled.

5.   Management's concern for the precision of the results must be real-istic. Executives sometimes overestimate the reliability with which estimates must be provided. Because of the importance of this factor on the sample size needed, it is critical that a realistic appraisal be made.

The student of marketing research should also be aware that the sample size determination method described here is not the only approach to the problem. If a given research project is designed to answer a highly specific decision problem, and certain information is available, then it may be pos-sible to arrive at a formally optimal (or near-optimal) solution to the sample size problem. The methodology used is generally described as the Bayesian approach to the question.[14]

PRACTICAL PROBLEMS IN USING SIMPLE RANDOM SAMPLING

Although simple random sampling serves well to introduce the basic ideas of sampling, it is not suitable for most sampling problems in marketing re-search. Its use is severely limited by the four factors discussed below.

Cost

One of the most important factors limiting the use of simple random sampling is the cost. Since the method guarantees that every possible item in the universe has the same chance of being chosen, the actual sample selected often consists of universe items which are widely dispersed geographically. If personal interviews are then used, interviewers may have to travel con-siderable distances, thereby increasing the costs of the field operation.

Availability of a current listing of population elements

A second very serious limitation to practical use of simple random sam-pling is the need for an accurate list of universe elements. It is usually diffi-cult to obtain such a list for even a relatively fixed universe such as all grocery stores in the state of Illinois. For human universes it may be impos-sible to obtain an accurate list. This is partly the result of the large numbers

---

[14] The basic reference is R. Schlaiffer, *Probability and Statistics for Business De-cisions* (New York: McGraw-Hill), especially chap. 35. See also Seymour Sudman, *Applied Sampling* (New York: Academic Press, 1976), especially chap. 5.

and high mobility of humans, but it is also true because many universes are a small percentage of the total and are not easy to identify, for example, people who have purchased a stereo in the last month.

Statistical efficiency

A third difficulty associated with simple random sampling is that it is often *statistically inefficient.* One sample design is said to be statistically more efficient than another when, for the same size sample, a smaller standard error is obtained. Given some knowledge, or perhaps just "educated guesses," about a universe, one may ordinarily improve the reliability of the sample mean or percentage by imposing certain restrictions on the sampling procedure. Methods for doing this are described in the next chapter.

Administrative difficulties

A number of difficulties are associated with the administration of simple random samples. One is the conceptually simple, but sometimes troublesome, problem of selecting the sample. The random selection of, say, 5,000 names from a list of 2 million is a difficult job if errors are to be avoided.

Another administrative problem in simple random sampling is the difficulty of maintaining supervisory control in personal interview studies. The geographic dispersion of sample units to be contacted makes interviewer supervision difficult and expensive.

Simple random sampling occasionally a feasible method

In spite of the difficulties enumerated above, some use is made of simple random samples in practical marketing research. Sometimes one wishes to sample a universe with the following properties:

1. It is small.
2. A satisfactory list of universe items exists.
3. The cost per interview is practically independent of the location of the sample items.
4. Other than a list of items, no other universe information is available.

In such a case, simple random sampling might be a practical procedure. An example of such a situation would be a telephone survey of dentists in Chicago. Another would be a mail survey of company salesmen.

In general, however, the practical limitations of simple random sampling are severe enough to limit seriously its application in marketing research. Accordingly, various alternative probability and nonprobability sampling methods have been devised. In subsequent sections a few of these alternate methods will be considered. Particular attention will be paid to their relationship to simple random sampling. It will be found that a knowledge of simple random sampling helps one understand more complex sampling methods.

SUMMARY

The first two steps in sampling are to define the universe and to specify the variables to be studied. Next, the sample must be designed. This involves a determination of sampling units, planning the selection of sample items, and preparing to estimate universe characteristics from sample data.

The two basic methods of selecting sample items are probability and non-probability methods. Probability sampling methods are the only ones which enable the researcher to measure objectively the precision of sample estimates. Simple random sampling is the simplest type of probability sampling. In simple random sampling, the sample mean provides an unbiased estimate of the universe mean. This does not mean, however, that any particular sample mean will be the same as the universe mean.

The sampling distribution of a mean or percentage describes how that value will vary under repeated sampling. While in practical sampling work the sampling distribution is not known, it is still possible to make use of an approximate sampling distribution and so to construct confidence limits.

If a large number of samples is drawn from a given universe, the means of these samples will tend to form a normal distribution around the universe mean. The larger the samples, the more tightly are the sample means clustered around the universe mean. Therefore, the larger the sample, the greater the reliability of the sample mean.

In simple random sampling, the distribution of sample means is approximately normal. Thus, if a great many samples of the same size are selected at random from the same universe, about 68 percent of the sample means will fall within one standard error of the universe mean, 95 percent within two standard errors, and practically all within three standard errors. From this information one may construct a confidence interval estimate of a mean or a percentage which will, with a given confidence, include the universe value of the mean or percentage.

By substituting a desired value of the standard error into the standard error formula, it is possible to determine the sample size required for a specified reliability.

Simple random sampling is infrequently employed in marketing research because of the problems associated with its cost, the necessity of having a list of the universe items, the fact that it is not always statistically efficient, and the difficulties of administering data collection by personal interview in simple random samples.

Case 10–1
PAINTCO, INC.

Paintco was a regional paint manufacturer with a strong reputation for making a premium-priced, exceptionally high quality paint in its own limited marketing area. Currently, the company's management was considering a program for gradual regional expansion. It was recognized, however, that expansion could be very expensive because paint was largely a commodity business, with only a few brands enjoying a reputation of being above average in quality. Because of this, Paintco might have to advertise extensively during the expansion program in order to create an awareness of the brand's exceptionally high quality.

Bill Clayborn, the company's sales manager, proposed that expansion be tested in three medium-sized cities adjacent to the region in which Paintco already marketed. Each of the three cities would receive introductory newspaper advertising during the first month, to announce the availability of the Paintco brand in local outlets. Dealers would receive significant incentive to stock the brand and give it some display support. In addition, as part of the expansion test, the three cities would receive different levels of television advertising support in the second, third, and fourth months after introduction. One of the cities would receive television advertising expenditures equivalent to about $4 million if the same advertising program were done on a national basis. A second city would receive only half the advertising expenditures allocated to the first city, and the third city would receive no television advertising. The effectiveness of the three different advertising levels would be monitored, to help the company's management establish a basis for deciding on how to advertise in future expansions.

The effectiveness of the three advertising programs would be monitored in two ways. The company would keep track of the sales of Paintco products to the dealers in the three cities. Because much of the initial sales would be to provide dealers with inventory to display, Clayborn knew that company sales figures would not accurately represent dealer sales to final consumers. Nevertheless, he felt that the sales figures would give an indication of how well the dealers were receiving the Paintco introduction in each of the cities.

Clayborn also wanted to use consumer research to measure aided and unaided brand awareness, and advertising awareness, among male homeowners 30 years of age and older. (Exhibit 1 shows a rough outline of the questionnaire being considered for the research.) This information would be collected just before and just after the television advertising period. Clayborn's best guess was that awareness levels would reach as high as 30 to 40 percent in the city receiving the heavy television advertising support, and approximately 20 to 25 percent in the city receiving only moderate television advertising. It seemed unlikely that awareness would exceed 10 percent in the city in which no television advertising was to be used.

Because men were not likely to be home except in the evenings and on weekends, Paintco's marketing research firm recommended that the research be carried out over the telephone. In addition, the desired information was not lengthy, personal, or confidential. These conditions seemed to favor telephone interviewing over all other approaches, especially since Clayborn wanted to obtain a representative sample in each city.

EXHIBIT 1. Questionnaire Draft Outline

1. When you think of paint, what brand do you think of first?
2. What other paint brands can you think of?
3. Have you seen or heard any paint advertising in the past three months?
4. (*If yes*) What brands were advertised?
5. (*If any recalled*) What did the advertising say about (*each brand recalled*)?
6. Which of the following brands of paint have you ever heard of:
   - _____ DuPont
   - _____ Glidden
   - _____ Pittsburgh
   - _____ Paintco
   - _____ Sears
   - _____ Sherwin Williams?
7. (*For each brand heard of*) Have you ever seen or heard any advertising for (*each brand*)?

Also in favor of doing the research by telephone was the fact that the marketing research firm had experienced telephone interviewers in each of the cities involved in the expansion. Paintco's marketing research firm believed that essentially all households in the test cities had telephones. They also estimated that over 90 percent of the telephones in the three cities were listed in the telephone directories, which could be used to select the sample in each city. The marketing research firm also estimated that approximately 75 percent of telephone calls made in the evenings or on weekends would be completed calls, that approximately 50 percent of the completed calls would reach a qualified respondent, and that fewer than 10 percent of the qualified respondents would refuse to cooperate.

> *Develop specific procedures and instructions to be used in selecting the samples in each of the three cities.*
>
> *Assuming that each city's telephone directory contains approximately 38,000 lines, and that Clayborn wants to be 80 to 90 percent confident and have results that are accurate within 5 to 10 percent, how many households should be called in each test city?*
>
> *What callback or substitution policy should be used for not-at-homes, unqualified respondents, and refusals?*

Case 10–2
THE NORWELL COMPANY

The Norwell Company produced a men's hair spray which was sold through drugstores, supermarkets, and variety and department stores. Sales totaled

$14.8 million and 30 percent of this revenue was spent on advertising. For some time the company and its advertising agency had felt the need to undertake a study to obtain more data on the characteristics of their users as contrasted to those of other leading brands. Both the company and the agency believed that such information would help them find better ways to promote and sell the Norwell product.

Preliminary discussions between the advertising department of the Norwell Company and the research department of the advertising agency resulted in the following study objectives:

1. To determine the characteristics of Norwell users versus competitors by such factors as age, income, occupation, marital status, family size, education, social class, leisure time activities, types of hair (fine, coarse), and so on.
2. To determine the image of the Norwell brand versus competitors on such attributes as masculinity, expensiveness, oiliness, stickiness, and user stereotypes (such as for young men, factory workers, young executives, and men living in small towns).
3. The meaning to consumers of certain words which were used to describe men's hair spray in general.
4. The media habits of users by television programs, magazines, and newspapers.

In discussing the sampling universe, the advertising manager stated that he thought the study results should be broken down by heavy versus light users of the Norwell product. In his opinion as few as 15 to 20 percent of the users might account for 60 percent of the total purchases of the Norwell product. He had no idea how many containers a user would have to buy during a specified time period in order to qualify as a heavy or a light user. The research director and the advertising manager disagreed on a definition of user: the research director thought that anyone who had used the Norwell product within the past year should qualify as a user, and therefore, be included in the study, while the advertising manager thought that a user should be defined as one who had purchased the product within the past three months. In fact, the advertising manager went on to say, "I am really interested only in those people who say that the Norwell brand is their favorite brand or the brand that they purchase more than any other."

After much discussion about what constituted or should constitute a user, the research director pointed out that, in his opinion, the advertising manager was not being realistic about the whole sampling problem. He had conducted a pilot study to determine how many qualified users he could obtain out of every 100 persons interviewed in Columbus, Ohio. While he did not feel that the findings were completely representative, he did think that they provided a crude estimate of the sampling problem and the costs which would result from using any kind of a probability sample. The research director said:

In the Columbus study we were interested only in finding out how many males 18 years of age or older used hair spray, what brands they had purchased during the past year and the past three months, and what brand they bought most frequently. All interviewing took place during the evening hours and over the weekend. The findings revealed that only about 70 percent of the male respondents were at home when the interviewer made the call. Of those who were home and who agreed to cooperate, only 65 percent were users of men's hair spray: that is, affirmatively answered the question: "Do you ever use hair spray?" Of those who used hair spray, only 7 percent had purchased the Norwell brand within the past three months, while 15 percent reported having purchased it within the past year. The costs of the Columbus job figured out to about $2.90 per contact including the not-at-homes, refusals, and completed interviews, all as contacts. The sample size for the Columbus pilot study was 212 male respondents and the field costs were $615. These costs will be increased substantially if the sample includes smaller towns and farm interviews.

The research director believed that the best sample size they could hope for would be one which provided about 100 interviews with Norwell users plus 100 interviews with users of other brands in each of 10 to 15 metropolitan areas. This would provide a total sample size of two to three thousand and would require contacts with between forty and fifty thousand respondents. The research director indicated that this size sample would permit breakdown of the results for the United States by heavy versus light Norwell users.

The advertising manager did not think this would be an adequate national sample. He said:

I can't present these results to my management and tell them that they are representative of the whole country, and I doubt if the sample in each of the 10 to 15 metropolitan areas is big enough to enable us to draw reliable conclusions about our customers and noncustomers in that particular area. I don't see how you can sample each metropolitan area on an equal basis. I would think that the bigger areas such as New York and Chicago should have bigger samples than some of the smaller metropolitan areas.

The research director explained that this way of allocating the sample between areas was not correct since the size of the universe had no effect on the size of the sample. He said:

If we do it the way you are suggesting, it will mean that in some of the big metropolitan areas we'll end up with 150 to 200 interviews while, in some of the smaller ones we'll have only 50 or 75 interviews. Under such conditions it would be impossible to break out the findings of each metropolitan area separately. If we sample each area equally, we can weight the results obtained from the different metropolitan areas so as to get accurate U.S. totals.

When the discussion turned to costs, the advertising manager complained:

I can't possibly tell my management that we have to make 40–50,000 calls in order to get 2,000 to 3,000 interviews. They're going to tell me that we're wasting an awful lot of money just to find Norwell users. Why can't we find Norwell users by selecting a sample of drugstores and offering druggists some money for getting names and addresses of those men who buy hair spray. We could probably locate Norwell users for maybe 35 to 50 cents each.

The research director admitted that this would be a much cheaper way, but pointed out that he would not have any idea what kind of sample would result, and therefore it would be impossible to tell anything at all about the reliability of the survey. The advertising manager thought the Norwell management would provide no more than $20,000 for the study. The research director estimated that the results could be tabulated, analyzed, a report written, and the results presented to management for about $5,000, thus leaving around $15,000 for fieldwork.

How should the sampling universe be defined?

How large should the sample be?

Should a probability sample design be employed?

How should the sample be distributed geographically?

11

Application of sampling methods to marketing problems

Although simple random sampling has the important advantage of simplicity, it is not appropriate for many problems in marketing research. Some alternative sampling designs which, while more complex, have more general applicability are considered in this chapter. The first to be examined is *stratified random sampling*.

STRATIFIED RANDOM SAMPLING

This procedure may be summarized as follows:

1. The universe to be sampled is subdivided (or *stratified*) into groups which are mutually exclusive, and include all items in the universe.
2. A simple random sample is then chosen independently from each group —or stratum.

This sampling procedure differs from simple random sampling in that with the latter the sample items are chosen at random from the *entire* universe. In stratified random sampling the sample is designed so that a designated number of items is chosen from *each* stratum. In simple random sampling the distribution of the sample among strata is left entirely to chance.

Reasons for stratification

Greater reliability. Stratification is often used in marketing research. Although there are several reasons for the widespread use of this procedure, the leading one is that it usually will lead to sample estimates which have a greater reliability than would otherwise be obtained. This basic idea involved may be grasped by reference to Figures 11–1 and 11–2. Suppose the curve

FIGURE 11–1. Graphical representation of the universe

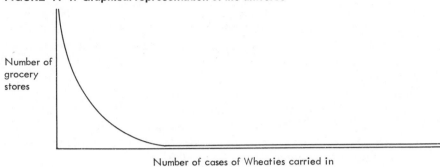

Number of grocery stores

Number of cases of Wheaties carried in stock by individual grocery stores

depicted in Figure 11–1 represents the distribution of the number of cases of Wheaties stocked in United States grocery stores. The objective is to estimate the average number of cases of Wheaties in stock per store.

The universe represented by this curve is typical of many encountered in marketing research. A very small proportion of the universe "contributes" heavily to the mean. A relatively few large stores account for a high percent of the total inventory. The presence or absence in a simple random sample

FIGURE 11–2. Partitioning of universe into subuniverses (strata)

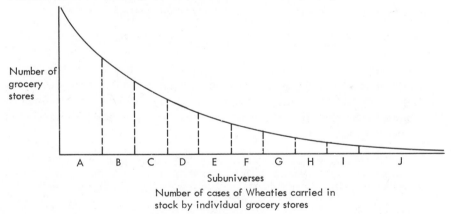

Number of grocery stores

| A | B | C | D | E | F | G | H | I | J |

Subuniverses

Number of cases of Wheaties carried in stock by individual grocery stores

of a few extreme stores would determine whether or not the sample mean would be reasonably close to that of the universe. Unless a very large simple random sample were used, there would be reason to expect that the extreme members of this universe would be represented somewhat more or less than their actual proportion in the universe.

Now, suppose information were available which made it possible to partition this universe into strata: A, B, C, and so on, as indicated in Figure 11–2.

A relatively small sample taken within each stratum would provide a good estimate of the mean of that stratum because of the similarity of the items included in that partition. If the proportion of the universe included within each stratum were known, the estimated means of these strata could be weighted together so as to provide an estimate of the mean of the entire universe.

If the variable being studied varies little among items in the same stratum, but a great deal among strata, this stratifying procedure will ordinarily provide a better estimate of the mean than could be obtained by using simple random sampling. In practice, the researcher usually does not know enough about the universe to subdivide it in quite this way. However, information will often be available about a variable which is highly correlated with the variable of interest. This may be used to make up the strata.

Obtaining information about parts of the universe. A second reason for stratification is that information may be desired about the component parts of a universe. For example, in a national study of coffee consumption, information might be wanted as to how the rate of consumption per family varies among geographic regions. Similarly, in a study of pancake mix sales in grocery stores, data might be wanted separately for chains and independents, and by store sizes. If individual estimates are desired for each of the component subuniverses, these subuniverses may be regarded as strata and an independent random sample drawn from each.

Estimation of the universe mean, with a stratified random sample

Since a stratified random sample is just a group of simple random samples, the sample mean of each stratum is unbiased. The means of the individual strata can be combined (weighted) into an unbiased estimate of the overall universe mean. Thus, the estimate of the universe mean is simply a weighted average of the strata means. For example, assume a two-stratum universe. From each stratum, the following observations are made using simple random sampling:

Stratum number	Number of observations	Value of each observation	Total value of all observations
1	2	10, 30	40
2	4	50, 100, 150, 200	500

In stratum 1 the arithmetic mean is 20 (40 ÷ 2), while in stratum 2 it is 125 (500 ÷ 4). The weight assigned to each stratum is the proportion of universe items included in that stratum. Assuming each stratum was sampled proportionate to its weight in the universe, the mean of stratum 1 would receive a weight of 2 and the mean of stratum 2 a weight of 4. The universe mean would be estimated by multiplying each stratum mean by its assigned weight, adding the results, and dividing by the sum of the weights. In the case at hand, the estimate for the universe mean would be

$$\frac{(20 \times 2) + (125 \times 4)}{2 + 4} = 90.$$

In the general case, one wishes to estimate the universe mean when there are k strata, where k can be any number greater than one. For each of the k strata, the following data must be obtained:

1. The mean of the sample for that stratum.
2. The ratio of the total number of items in that stratum to the total number in the universe. This is the relative "weight" of the stratum, denoted by W.

The data can be summarized as follows:

Stratum	Sample mean in stratum	Relative weight of stratum
1	$\overline{X}_1$	W_1
2	$\overline{X}_2$	W_2
3	$\overline{X}_3$	W_3
•	•	•
•	•	•
•	•	•
k	$\overline{X}_k$	W_k

With the information in the above table, the universe mean is estimated by the formula

$\overline{X}_{sr}$ (estimated mean based on stratified random sampling)

$$= W_1\overline{X}_1 + W_2\overline{X}_2 + - - - - - + W_k\overline{X}_k.$$

Note that this formula provides a weighted sample mean, each stratum mean being weighted in proportion to its share of the total number of elements in the universe. For the two-stratum example on page 332, the calculation is

$$\overline{X}_{sr} = W_1\overline{X}_1 + W_2\overline{X}_2$$
$$= \tfrac{1}{3} (20) + \tfrac{2}{3} (125) = 90$$

the same answer obtained before.

As another example, suppose the researcher has these data:

Store stratum	Sample mean unit sales per store	Number of stores in stratum
Large stores	200	20,000
Medium stores	100	30,000
Small stores	50	50,000

Then the estimated universe mean sales per store would be

$$X_{sr} = W_1 X_1 + W_2 X_2 + W_3 X_3$$
$$= (.2)\,(200) + (.3)\,(100) + (.5)\,(50) = 95 \text{ units.}$$

Interval estimation with stratified random samples

Little new theory is required to develop confidence limits for a universe mean estimated from a stratified random sample. As in the case of simple random sampling, an estimated standard error of the mean is first secured. Then the appropriate multiple of this figure (two for 95 percent confidence, three for virtual certainty) is added to and subtracted from the estimated mean. The resultant two numbers are the confidence limits.

To estimate the standard error of the mean of a stratified random sample, the data required are these:

Stratum	Sample variance in stratum	Sample size in stratum	Weight of stratum
1	s_1^2	n_1	W_1
2	s_2^2	n_2	W_2
3	s_3^2	n_3	W_3
•	•	•	•
•	•	•	•
•	•	•	•
k	s_k^2	n_k	W_k

The quantity s_1^2 is the variance (standard deviation squared) of the sample in stratum 1, and n_1 is the number of observations in that stratum. For stratum 2, the sample variance is s_2^2 and the sample size is n_2 and so on.

To estimate the standard error, first calculate the quantity,[1]

$$s_{\bar{x}_{sr}}^2 = \frac{W_1^2 s_1^2}{n_1} + \frac{W_2^2 s_2^2}{n_2} + - - - - + \frac{W_k^2 s_k^2}{n_k}.$$

The estimated standard error sought is $s_{\bar{x}_{sr}}$, the square root of $s_{\bar{x}_{sr}}^2$

As an illustration of the calculations, suppose that in the store sales example (page 333), the stratum sample variances and sample size are these:

---

[1] For each stratum in which the sample size exceeds 5 percent of the number of universe elements, a finite population correction factor needs to be applied to the appropriate term in the expression given for $s_{\bar{x}_{sr}}^2$. Although this situation is fully analogous to the corresponding correction for simple random sampling, this refinement will be ignored here for simplicity.

Store stratum	Sample variance in stratum $= s^2$	Sample size in stratum $= n$	Weight of stratum $= W$
Large stores	4,000	100	0.2
Medium stores	1,400	70	0.3
Small stores	400	80	0.5

The square of the estimated standard error is

$$ s^2_{\bar{x}_{sr}} = (.2)^2 \left(\frac{4000}{100} \right) + (.3)^2 \left(\frac{1400}{70} \right) + (.5)^2 \left(\frac{400}{80} \right) = 4.65. $$

So the estimated standard error of the mean is

$$ s_{\bar{x}_{sr}} = \sqrt{4.65} = 2.2 \text{ units, approximately.} $$

Multiplying this standard error by 2, and adding and subtracting the resulting quantity to the estimated mean of 95 units, gives a 95 percent confidence interval for the population mean of 90.6 to 99.4 units. An interval which is virtually certain to cover the population mean is 95 units $\pm$ 3 (2.2) units, or, 88.4 to 101.6 units.

Note that the method for calculating the standard error here is different from that used for simple random sampling. In general, different methods of probability sampling require different methods of evaluating means and associated standard errors. The more complex the design, the more complex will be the analysis.

Issues in the selection of stratified random samples

The preceding part of this chapter has dealt with how to make certain simple estimates from the data secured by a stratified random sample. It is now necessary to consider some of the issues involved in setting up a stratified random sample:

1. *Bases of stratification*—What characteristics should be used?
2. *Number of strata*—How many strata should be constructed?
3. *Sample sizes within strata*—How many observations should be taken in each stratum?

In a practical situation, these questions must be answered before data can be gathered and the estimates prepared. They are considered at this point, rather than earlier, because it is easier to discuss them after the general procedure of stratified random sampling and estimation has been sketched out.

Bases of stratification

An early decision in the development of a stratified random sample is the selection of bases of stratification. How should the total universe of interest be subdivided into component strata?

Intuitively, it seems clear that the best basis would be the frequency distribution of the principal variable being studied. For example, in the earlier Wheaties inventory illustration it is plausible that creation of strata on the basis of inventory would provide an optimal stratification. However, two difficulties arise in attempting to proceed this way. First, there is usually interest in many variables, not just one, and stratification on the basis of one may not provide the best stratification for the others. Second, even if one survey variable is of primary importance, current data on its frequency distribution will not be available. If they were, the study would not be needed.

Under these circumstances, a reasonable approach is to create strata on the basis of variables, for which information is available, that are believed to be highly correlated with the principal survey characteristics of interest. The stratification may be on the basis of a single, simple variable (for example, store dollar volume), or a compound variable (for example, store dollar volume *within* geographic region), depending on such matters as availability of detailed information and number of strata to be used.

In general, it is desirable to make up strata in such a way that the sampling units within strata are as similar as possible. The effect of this is that a relatively limited sample within each stratum will provide a generally precise estimate of the mean of that stratum. Similarly, it is desirable to use a stratification system which will maximize differences among stratum means for the key survey variables of interest.

In practical marketing research, one or more of a few stratification bases will often be found useful. For example, such stratification variables as geography and population density will typically be of value if either human or institutional populations are being sampled. In the case of institutional samples, it will virtually always be desirable to stratify on some measure of size (dollar volume, number of employees, and so on), since stores, wholesalers, and so on may exhibit enormous variability in such important characteristics as sales, inventories, and the like.

Number of strata

Common sense suggests as many strata as possible be used so that each stratum will be relatively homogenous. Each stratum mean can then be estimated with high reliability, and the overall population mean will be estimated with high precision.

However, practical problems limit the number of strata used. Past a certain number, little is gained by creating more strata. The costs of adding more strata (for example, sample selection and tabulation) may soon outrun benefits. More than six strata may be unprofitable when a single overall estimate is to be made.[2] If estimates are required for universe subgroups (for example, regions), then more strata may be desirable.

---

[2] W. C. Cochran, *Sampling Techniques* (New York: John Wiley & Sons, 1977), pp. 132–134.

Sample sizes within strata

Once strata have been established, the question of how big a sample should be drawn from each must be decided. To illustrate the problem, and some ways of approaching it, consider one particular situation which is of fairly common occurrence in marketing research. Suppose a budget has been fixed and that the cost per observation is known and equal for all strata. This amounts to saying that the total sample size (for all strata combined) is fixed. How should this total sample size be allocated among strata—how many observations should be taken from the first stratum, how many from the second, and so on?

As a concrete example, suppose the researcher wishes to estimate the mean value of some characteristic in this two-stratum universe:

Stratum	Number of items in stratum
A	10,000
B	90,000

Suppose further that the budget for the job is $3,000 and that the cost per observation is $6 in each stratum, so the available total sample size is 500. With this total sample size, there are 499 possible sample allocations between the two strata:

	Sample size in stratum	
Allocation	A	B
1	1	499
2	2	498
•	•	•
•	•	•
499	499	1

The problem is to decide which of these allocations is to be used.

Proportional allocation. One intuitively plausible approach would be to sample the same proportion of items in each stratum, that is, to sample all strata at the same rate. In the example being considered, the overall sampling fraction is

$$\frac{\text{Sample size}}{\text{Universe size}} = \frac{500}{100,000} = 0.5\%$$

so that this method of sample allocation would provide a sample of 50 in stratum A (10,000 $\times$ 0.5%) and a sample of 450 in stratum B (90,000 $\times$ 0.5%).

This method of allocation, sampling each stratum at the same rate, is called *proportional sampling*. It is probably the most widely used method.

As a general rule, it is also the preferred procedure when the objective is to estimate the overall universe mean and the only statistical data available on the strata are their sizes (number of items in each).

The major practical advantage of proportional allocation is that it leads to estimates which are computationally simple. In general, as noted earlier, it is necessary to weight the estimated stratum means in order to provide an estimate of the overall universe mean:

$$\overline{X}_{\mathrm{sr}} = W_1\overline{X}_1 + - - + W_k\overline{X}_k$$

With proportional allocation, this formula reduces to just

$$\frac{\text{sum of sample observations}}{\text{total sample size}}$$

That is, no special weighting is needed; all one has to do is add up the sample observations for all strata and divide by their number. Proportional allocation automatically weights the stratum means in their correct proportions. The reader may verify that this process works in the simple example considered on page 332. For that case, the sum of the sample values is $40 + 500 = 540$, and it is based on $2 + 4 = 6$ observations. Since this was a proportionally allocated sample, the above formula leads to $540/6 = 90$, which is the same estimated mean obtained by using the general formula involving weights.

Optimal allocation. As a rule, proportional allocation is recommended when all one knows of the strata is their sizes. If, in addition, the standard deviation of the observations in each stratum is known, then a *disproportionate allocation* may be desirable.[3]

To illustrate a situation where a disproportionate allocation would be clearly indicated, suppose all the observations in stratum B of the above example had the same value. In this instance, a sample of one from stratum B would be sufficient and the remaining 499 observations would be taken from stratum A. This allocation would be optimal, in the sense of giving the most information possible about the overall universe mean for a total available sample size of 500. It would obviously be wasteful, in this situation, to take a proportional sample (450) from stratum B.

In general, an allocation of a total sample size among strata is said to be the *optimal allocation* if, for that sample size, it provides the smallest possible standard error of the estimated mean. In any specific situation where the stratum standard deviations are known, it would be possible to identify the optimal allocation by going through the following process:

1. First enumerate the possible allocations, as in the illustration on page 337.
2. Then, for each allocation, calculate the standard error of the mean, us-

---

[3] If the unit *costs* of sampling vary among strata, a disproportionate sampling may similarly be desirable. Although account may be taken of these variations in arriving at optimal sample sizes, this facet is ignored here for simplicity.

ing the formula given on page 334, with the known standard deviations substituted for the estimated values in that formula.

3. Finally, select the allocation which leads to the smallest standard error. This is the optimal allocation.

Fortunately, it is not necessary to go through the steps indicated above to identify the optimal distribution of the sample. Mathematical analysis provides formulas which give the answer at once. For the two-stratum case, the optimal sample size (n_A) in stratum A, is

$$n_A = \frac{nN_A\sigma_A}{(N_A\sigma_A + N_B\sigma_B)}$$

where

$n =$ Total available sample size.
$N_A =$ Number of items in stratum A.
$N_B =$ Number of items in stratum B.
$\sigma_A =$ Standard deviation of the observations in stratum A.
$\sigma_B =$ Standard deviation of the observations in stratum B.

The optimal sample size in stratum B will be $n_B = n - n_A$.
Note in the above formula that the optimal allocation depends on two factors:

1. *The sizes of the strata, N_A and N_B.* In general, the larger the stratum, the larger the sample from that stratum.
2. *The variabilities within strata.* As a rule, the stratum with the larger standard deviation is sampled more heavily.

Observe also that, if the strata standard deviations are equal ($\sigma_A = \sigma_B$), then the formula says to take a proportional sample from each stratum. That is, proportional allocation is optimal when the strata are equally variable.
Consider the problem originally posed:

$$n = \quad 500$$
$$N_A = 10,000$$
$$N_B = 90,000$$

if

$$\sigma_A = 50$$
$$\sigma_B = 10$$

then in stratum A

$$n_A = 500\left(\frac{(10,000)(50)}{(10,000)(50) + (90,000)(10)}\right)$$
$$= 179 \text{ observations.}$$

In stratum B, $500 - 179 = 321$ observations would be taken. With this allocation, the standard error of the estimated universe mean would be 0.63.

This is about one-fourth less than the standard error that a proportionally allocated sample would provide (0.83), as may be verified. This represents a substantial increase in statistical efficiency, considering that just the allocation of the sample among strata was involved.

Application of optimal allocation. Few readers of this book will have occasion to use the formula for optimal allocation that has been given. Nevertheless, the reader should be broadly familiar with the idea of optimal allocation and have some understanding of its basis. The principle is applied fairly often in practical marketing research, especially where institutions (for example, stores) rather than families or individuals are being sampled. It is also of greater importance when measurement data (sales, inventories, and so on) are being gathered rather than attribute data (simple presence or absence of a characteristic).

A good illustration of the use of this general principle in practical application is provided by the Nielsen Retail Index (see page 148). Although the Nielsen sample comprises about 0.5 percent of the food stores in the continental United States, its stores account for more than 1.5 percent of the grocery store business. Because large food stores have more variable sales of almost any product, Nielsen samples them at a disproportionately heavy rate. This results in a much more efficient sample than would be obtained with a proportionally allocated sample.

Concluding remarks on stratified random sampling. Stratified random sampling is generally (and sometimes dramatically) more statistically efficient than simple random sampling. This is paid for at the price of greater complexity, both in sample design and analysis.

Stratified random sampling shares some of the limitations of simple random sampling. A complete universe list of individual elements is again necessary, and, in addition, one must be able to classify these elements into meaningful strata. Costs of data collection may be quite high, if on-site interviewer presence is required, because of the likelihood that the sample will be widely dispersed geographically.

These difficulties aside, the idea of stratification is widely used in marketing research studies. Its use in specific problems is often more complex than the particular application to stratified random sampling described here. However, the rationale for its use and principles of application remain the same.

Stratification, and the associated idea of optimal allocation, are most useful when sampling highly skewed universes (where elements vary greatly in size) and some measurement parameter (such as average sales, inventory, etc.) is to be estimated.

CLUSTER SAMPLING

In the sampling methods discussed so far, each item is chosen individually. In some probability sampling methods, however, groups or clusters of items are chosen at random. A simple example will illustrate the idea. Consider the following universe of 16 items arranged arbitrarily into four groups:

Group	Elements
1	X_1, X_2, X_3, X_4
2	X_5, X_6, X_7, X_8
3	$X_9, X_{10}, X_{11}, X_{12}$
4	$X_{13}, X_{14}, X_{15}, X_{16}$

Suppose it is desired to choose a probability sample of 8 elements from this universe.

One way of proceeding would be to choose a simple random sample of 8 items. But suppose that for some reason it is not feasible to carry out such a sampling method. An alternative way would be to select two of the four groups at random and enumerate their items *completely*. Clearly such a sampling technique would be a probability sampling scheme, since every element would have a known chance of being chosen—namely, a chance of one in two. Every possible combination of universe items, however, would *not* have the same chance of being chosen. This is true since the selection of one item in a cluster automatically means the inclusion of the other items in the cluster. Thus, with this sampling procedure (called *simple, one-stage cluster sampling*), it is impossible for some random samples to be chosen. For example, in the cluster sample described above the following combination, among others, could not occur: $X_1, X_2, X_5, X_6, X_9, X_{10}, X_{13},$ and X_{14}.

This procedure amounts to sampling from a universe of groups or clusters of items rather than sampling from a universe of individual items. The original universe of 16 items had been redefined as a universe of four clusters and a random sampling of two clusters has been made. Probability sampling techniques of this kind in which clusters of items are chosen with known chances are called *cluster sampling methods* and are widely used in the sampling of human populations. In this chapter, some of the basic ideas involved in cluster sampling will be explored, although the complexity of the subject will not permit a detailed discussion.

Relative efficiency of simple one-stage cluster sampling and simple random sampling

How does the sampling behavior of an estimate obtained by simple one-stage cluster sampling compare with that obtained by simple random sampling? A comparison of the two methods will indicate the circumstances under which cluster sampling will be more precise than simple random sampling, and vice versa.

Relative statistical efficiency. Consider the statistical efficiency of the mean of a simple, one-stage cluster sample relative to that of a simple random sample. One method will be regarded as superior to the other if it has a smaller standard error for the same total number of items sampled. The relative efficiency of the two sampling systems depends on the degree of similarity among items in each cluster. The greater the similarity of the observations in a cluster, the *less* efficient will be cluster sampling. The greater the dissimilarity among the observations in a cluster, the *more* efficient will be cluster sampling.

Suppose that two clusters of four elements each are to be selected from a universe with the following numerical values: four items with a value of 1, four with a value of 2, four with a value of 3, and four with a value of 4. Next, consider the two extreme ways of grouping the 16 elements into four clusters. The first clustering method gives a maximum of similarity within each cluster. The second method gives a minimum of similarity within each cluster.

Degree of similarity within cluster	Cluster number	Values of the observations in cluster
Maximum	1	1111
	2	2222
	3	3333
	4	4444
Minimum	1	1234
	2	1234
	3	1234
	4	1234

With the first of these clustering methods, the standard error of the mean of the cluster sample will be *more* than that of a simple random sample because, regardless of which two clusters are chosen, information will be obtained on only two of the four different values. One observation in each cluster in the sample gives information. The other six observations in the sample do little more than repeat this information. Thus, simple random sampling would be more efficient. With the minimum similarity clusters the standard error of the means of the cluster samples is zero, that is, each cluster has the same mean. Cluster sampling will be more efficient than simple random sampling in this case.

This example illustrates the basic principle that the statistical efficiency of cluster sampling depends on how the clusters are constructed—that is, on the degree to which each cluster can be made to include all the values in the universe. If the observations within a cluster represent only a few of the values in the universe, a simple cluster sample will be less efficient statistically than a simple random sample having the same total number of items. Clusters are often constructed in such a way that the items within a cluster are relatively homogeneous. This implies that in practice cluster sampling is often less efficient statistically than simple random sampling.

Relative net efficiency

The preceding discussion has been in terms of statistical efficiency only, that is, in terms of the relative magnitude of the standard errors under the two sampling systems. When *economic efficiency,* the relative cost per observation, of the two systems is considered, it will often be found that simple cluster sampling is the superior method. In a practical situation one will generally be interested in *net efficiency,* which consists of maximizing the information obtained per dollar of cost. A consideration of this latter criterion will often lead to the adoption of cluster sampling, since the gain in economic efficiency will usually offset the decline in statistical efficiency which may result from cluster sampling.

At this point in the discussion some of these ideas may seem rather abstract. For the moment, the essential conclusions are these:

1. Simple cluster sampling may be either more or less efficient statistically than simple random sampling. This depends on the degree of intra-cluster heterogeneity which is obtained.
2. In practice, clusters are often constructed in such a way that the observations within a cluster are relatively homogeneous. When this is the case, simple cluster sampling will be less efficient statistically than simple random sampling.
3. The lower relative cost of obtaining observations in cluster sampling often offsets the loss in statistical efficiency. The net efficiency is often greater for cluster sampling.

The reasoning behind the second and third conclusions will become more clear when a special type of cluster sampling, called *area sampling,* is discussed. Some idea of the interplay between statistical efficiency and economic efficiency in a practical situation will also become clear at that time.

Systematic sampling

One type of cluster sampling is called systematic sampling. An illustration will show how such a sample is drawn. From a list of 100 food stores, it is desired to choose a probability sample of 20 stores. One way of doing this is as follows:

1. Draw a random number between 1 and 5. Suppose the number chosen is 2.
2. Include in the sample the stores numbered 2, 7, 12, 17, 22 . . . 97; that is, starting with the number 2, take every fifth number.

The above is an illustration of *systematic sampling.* That this is a particular kind of cluster sampling is readily seen if the possible samples produced by this procedure are considered. This particular example has only five possible samples:

Sample	Identification of stores in sample	
1	1, 6, 11, 16, 21	96
2	2, 7, 12, 17, 22	97
3	3, 8, 13, 18, 23	98
4	4, 9, 14, 19, 24	99
5	5, 10, 15, 20, 25	100

Each of these samples amounts to a *cluster* of stores and each has a chance of 1 out of 5 of being included in the sample. In effect, the original universe of 100 stores has been redefined as a universe of five clusters of stores and each cluster is given an equal chance of being chosen by the sampling process. A *single* random number determines all 20 sample stores. As a consequence, the 20 sample stores are not independently chosen. Once random number 2 is chosen, the whole sequence of stores 2, 7, 12, 17, 22, and so on is *automatically* included in the sample.

To choose a systematic sample, the first step is to determine the total number of items in the universe. Divide this figure by the desired sample size. The result is called the sampling interval. Next select a random number between 1 and the sampling interval figure. This identifies the first element on the list to be included in the sample. Add to this random number the sampling interval. The result identifies the second item to be included in the sample. Continue adding the interval and taking the items so identified until the sample is drawn.

Advantages of systematic sampling. In one form or another, wide use is made of systematic sampling. The principal advantage of this technique is its simplicity. When sampling from a list, it is easier to choose a random start and select every *n*th item thereafter than to make a simple random selection. The technique is faster and less subject to error than simple random selection. Hence, systematic sampling is often used in place of simple random sampling. For example, it might be used instead of random sampling for selecting items within strata in a stratified design.

In common with simple random sampling, the mean of a systematic sample is an unbiased estimate of the universe mean.[4] This property is clear in the example used to introduce systematic sampling on page 343. Since each of the five possible samples shown has the same chance of being chosen and the average of the five sample means is equal to the universe mean, the sample mean provides an unbiased estimate.

It is often found that systematic sampling is somewhat more efficient statistically than is simple random sampling. This will be the case when adjacent universe items on the listing are similar and items widely removed

---

[4] Technically, for this to be true, it is necessary that the ratio of the number of universe elements to the sample size (that is, the sampling interval) be a whole number. The small variations from this that are usually encountered will not bias the estimate to an appreciable extent.

from one another are dissimilar. For example, if a list were made up by listing grocery stores in order according to dollar sales volume and the variable being sampled was correlated with sales, then it would be expected that systematic sampling would be more precise than simple random sampling. The ordering of stores by dollar volume in this case would set up an implicit stratification, and the systematic sampling would operate much like a stratified random sampling, with a single store chosen out of each stratum.

To illustrate the basic ideas of systematic sampling, it has been assumed that a listing of all universe items was available. It is not necessary that a complete listing be available at the time the sampling is begun. For example, one might sample systematically through time by collecting the carbon copy of every fifteenth sales slip in a store, or one could sample systematically through space by interviewing at every ninth dwelling unit on a block, even though a list of the dwelling units was not available beforehand.

Difficulty in estimating sampling error of a systematic sample.   One difficulty arising from systematic sampling is that an unbiased estimate of the sampling error attached to the estimated mean cannot be obtained without making some assumptions, because the selection process only identifies *one* cluster (even though this may contain several items for observation). At least two independently chosen sampling units (here, clusters) are needed to evaluate sampling error.

One might, for example, assume that the universe items were listed in random order. If this were the case, a systematic sample would be equivalent to a simple random sample and the usual formulas would apply. In some situations it may be quite reasonable to make this assumption—for example, when the list is in alphabetical order.

It may be possible to obtain an unbiased estimate of the sampling error by drawing a number of systematic samples instead of just one. For instance, instead of drawing one systematic sample of 500, it might be feasible to draw 10 independent systematic samples of 50 each. The variation among sample estimates yields a measurement of sampling error.

Danger of periodicities in universe listing.   Another basic difficulty may arise in systematic sampling when the universe listing contains "hidden periodicities." An example will again clarify the point. Suppose the problem is to sample from a list of 100 grocery stores consisting of 20 chains and 80 independents. The list of stores is made up as follows:

$$I,I,I,I,C,I,I,I,I,C, \ldots \ldots \ldots \ldots I,I,I,I,C.$$

I denotes an independent store and *C* denotes a chain store. A systematic sampling of 1 out of 5 stores on this list is to be made.

With a systematic sampling scheme, one would obtain either all independent stores in the sample (4 times out of 5) or all chain stores (1 time out of 5). Because the list contains a periodicity equal to a multiple of the sampling interval (1 in 5), such a sampling procedure would yield an estimate with a greater standard error than would simple random sampling. If the sampling interval were 1 in 10, 1 in 20, or any other multiple of 5, the difficulty would still persist.

In the illustration cited, if the characteristic being surveyed were independent of the type of store ownership, no difficulty would arise. Where periodicities do exist, however, it will often be found that the characteristic studied will *not* be independent of the periodically recurring phenomenon. For example, in sampling daily department store sales one would not choose to study sales every seventh day because of the weekly sales cycle.

Area sampling

Up to this point the discussion has been concerned with sampling from a list which identifies every individual item in the universe. In many marketing problems, either no such list is available or what is available is badly out of date or otherwise inadequate. To meet problems of this kind a very ingenious method of cluster sampling known as *area sampling* has been devised. Although the basic principles of area sampling are easy to understand, their application to particular problems requires considerable experience and ingenuity. Only the more important basic principles will be considered here.

Suppose it is desired to estimate the number of packages of Jell-O in households located within the corporate area limits of Philadelphia. No accurate listing of these households is available. How might one deal with this problem? One approach might be the following:

1. Choose a simple random sample of (n) city blocks from all those (N) which make up the city of Philadelphia.
2. Determine the number of Jell-O packages in all households located on the sample blocks. Add up these data to obtain the total inventory for all households located on sample blocks.
3. Multiply the total sample inventory by N/n, which is the reciprocal of the sampling ratio. The resulting figure will be an unbiased estimate of the total inventory of Jell-O in Philadelphia households.

Such a sampling procedure is a probability sampling method, since each Philadelphia household has a known chance (n/N) of being included in the sample. However, in this illustration the universe (Philadelphia households) was not sampled directly. A universe of *areas* (city blocks) was first defined and a sample of those selected. Then, the households located on the sample blocks were audited, and the total inventory of these households was used to estimate the inventory for all Philadelphia households.

Reasoning back of area sampling.   Consider in detail the reasoning behind this particular procedure. Philadelphia may be defined precisely in terms of a particular area. Further, it is possible to subdivide this area into a number of blocks such that (1) each block is clearly defined in terms of location and extent, and (2) the total number of blocks, N, is known. Since this operation is possible, Philadelphia may be considered a universe of areas (in this case, blocks). Because all of these blocks are identified and their total number is known, it is possible to draw a probability sample from this block universe.

Thus, the original universe (for which no list was available) is transformed into a universe of areas for which a listing (in the form of maps) does exist. The existence of a list for this block universe permits the selection of a probability sample of blocks. Since a rule of association between households and blocks has been established, the investigator may regard the households located on the sample blocks as a sample of households. This sample of households will be a probability sample because the cluster of households associated with each block has a known chance of being selected. This chance is equal to the chance that the block with which it is associated will be selected.

Simple, one-stage, area sampling. The above example of area sampling is an illustration of simple, one-stage, area sampling. The distinguishing feature of this process is that the areas chosen for the sample are completely enumerated; for example, every household on each block selected was included. A one-stage area sample of, say, 1,000 households (stores, and so on) may not be as efficient as a simple random sample of the same size. The principal reason for this is that the elements in the same area cluster may tend to be alike. For example, the families living on a particular city block will in general be relatively similar with regard to such characteristics as income, race, occupation, family size, and social class. Similarity in these socioeconomic characteristics makes it likely that the families on a block will give relatively similar responses on attitude surveys, will buy the same general types of merchandise, and will respond similarly in other ways of interest to the marketing researcher. Because of this intracluster similarity, the statistical efficiency of a one-stage area sample will ordinarily be less than that of a simple random sample having the same number of units.

Simple, two-stage, area sampling. In the previous section, a method of area sampling was discussed in which all households (stores, and so on) associated with the areas selected in a sample were enumerated. Actually, it is not necessary to enumerate all the items associated with a selected area; the elements associated with a sample area may be subsampled. This method of sampling, in which the sample units are themselves sampled, is called two-stage sampling. For example, in sampling households in a city, one might first choose a sample of blocks and then choose a sample of households on the selected blocks. Such a technique would be a two-stage sampling scheme since there would be two stages of sampling, first blocks and then households on the chosen blocks.

An illustration of two-stage area sampling. The basic idea involved in two-stage sampling may be illustrated as follows. Consider a universe of 40 blocks. Suppose that each block contains 8 households. Assume further that a sample of 20 households is to be chosen by sampling blocks and then subsampling households on the selected blocks. Since there are 320 (40 × 8) households in the universe, this amounts to saying that the overall sampling ratio for households is to be 20/320, or 1 out of 16.

One way of selecting this sample would be to sample blocks at the rate of 1 in 8 and then to subsample the households on the selected blocks at a rate of 1 in 2. This procedure would identify 20 households since 5 blocks would be selected ($\frac{1}{8}$ × 40) and 4 households would be chosen on each block ($\frac{1}{2}$ × 8).

This particular scheme is not the only way of choosing 20 households within the two-stage framework. Some other possibilities are:

1. Choose blocks at a rate of 1 in 2 and households on selected blocks at a rate of 1 in 8.
2. Choose blocks at a rate of 1 in 4 and households on selected blocks at a rate of 1 in 4.

In all of these cases, it will be observed that the product of the block sampling fraction and the intrablock subsampling fraction is equal to $\frac{1}{16}$. This is an essential requirement in this example because the overall sampling ratio is established at $\frac{1}{16}$.

The general two-stage sampling scheme exemplified above is called *simple two-stage area sampling*. Its distinguishing features are these:

1. Each first-stage unit has the same probability of being selected for the sample.
2. All second-stage units in the selected first-stage units have the same chance of being selected for the sample.

Concluding comments on area sampling

Area sampling is a powerful technique for applying the ideas of probability sampling to a universe for which (1) there is no satisfactory list of universe elements, (2) it is possible to associate each universe element uniquely with a specific geographic area, and (3) suitable maps exist. The basic idea has been widely used in marketing research, most often in connection with in-home personal interviews.

In practice, the design (and subsequent analysis) of area samples is a very complex undertaking, ordinarily requiring expert statistical counsel. This discussion has been confined to only two stages of sampling, at each of which the units were selected with equal probabilities. Many area sample designs use more than two stages, and vary the probabilities of sample selection from unit to unit at each stage.

Selection of a suitable area sample design necessitates detailed consideration of study purposes and of available information in the form of statistical data, map materials, interviewing resources, and cost parameters.

NONPROBABILITY SAMPLING

The methods of sampling previously discussed have all been probability sampling methods. In each case discussed, the basic requirement for probability sampling has been fulfilled; namely, every element in the universe sampled has a known chance of being chosen for the sample. Some methods of sampling in which this condition is not met will now be discussed. These are called *nonprobability sampling methods* and include any sampling method in which the chance of choosing a particular universe element is unknown.

As so defined, nonprobability sampling includes a great variety of techniques ranging in complexity from a sample chosen purely on the basis of convenience to an elaborate "quota sample" in which respondents are chosen on the basis of several socioeconomic characteristics. Any sampling procedure which does not specify the chance of selecting any universe element is a nonprobability sampling method, no matter what else is included in the specifications.

Convenience sampling

As the name implies, a "convenience sample" is chosen purely on the basis of convenience. The items of such a sample are chosen simply because they are accessible or articulate or otherwise easy to measure. "Speak-out" interviewing is an illustration of this general approach.

For obvious reasons, this method of sampling should only be used in special cases in marketing research. The items of the universe to be sampled may occasionally be sufficiently homogeneous so that any kind of sample will suffice. A convenience sample may be of value during the pretest phase of a study to improve the questionnaire, but it should rarely be used in any serious effort to estimate values of a universe.

In general, it will be found that the "convenient" items of a universe differ substantially from the less convenient items, thereby introducing a bias of unknown magnitude and direction into any estimate based on a convenience sample.

Judgment sampling

A second method of nonprobability sampling which is sometimes advocated is the selection of universe items by means of "expert judgment." Using this approach, specialists in the subject matter of the survey choose what they believe to be the best sample for that particular study. For example, a group of sales managers might select a sample of grocery stores in a city that they regarded as "representative" in some sense. This approach has been found empirically to produce unsatisfactory results. And, of course, there is no objective way of evaluating the reliability of sample results. Despite these limitations, this method may be useful when the total sample size is extremely small. Such uses should be rare.

Quota sampling

Perhaps the most commonly used sampling technique is a nonprobability technique called *quota sampling*. Although the elaborateness of quota samples varies considerably, they all embody three basic steps:

1. *Selection of the "control characteristics" and determination of the proportion of the universe having each set of characteristics.* This step involves the subdivision of the universe into component subuniverses and is similar to the stratification described earlier. The resultant subuniverses are usually called "cells" and the bases for the stratification are called "controls." These controls are usually chosen on two bases : (1) they are believed to be correlated with the characteristic to be studied, and (2) reasonably up-to-date information is available on their distribution within the universe.

Suppose that two control characterstics, age and family income, have been decided on for a survey of consumers in a particular city. The resulting cells for the universe would then appear as in Table 11–1.

TABLE 11–1. Cells in two-control quota sample

Family income	Age of consumer		
	Under 35 years	35 years and over	Total
Under $15,000	21%	27%	48%
$15,000 and over	12	40	52
Total	33%	67%	100%

In the universe to be sampled, 21 percent of the consumers are under 35 years of age and have family incomes under $15,000, 12 percent are under 35 years and have incomes of $15,000 and over, and so on.

2. *Allocation of the sample among cells.* Once the strata or cells have been established, the next step is to decide how large a sample should be taken from each cell. Usually, but not necessarily, a proportional sample is taken. In the two-control example given, if a total sample of 200 were wanted, a proportional distribution of interviews by cell would be as follows:

Description of consumer	Number in sample
Under 35 years, family income under $15,000	42 (21%)
Under 35 years, family income $15,000 and over	24 (12)
35 years and over, family income under $15,000	54 (27)
35 years and over, family income $15,000 and over	80 (40)
	200 (100%)

3.   *Selection of the sample items*. When the total number of respondents in each cell has been decided on, the next step in the sampling procedure is to assign a "quota" to each fieldworker. That is, each fieldworker is told to secure X observations with items having one set of characteristics, Y observations with items having another set of characteristics, and so on until the total sample has been allocated. In the consumer illustration, one interviewer might be told to secure a quota of 8 interviews with consumers under 35 having a family income under $15,000 and 14 interviews with consumers under 35 having a family income of $15,000 or over. This is the origin of the adjective "quota" in the name quota sampling.

The field representatives then seek out and interview or observe items (for example, consumers) who appear to have the characteristics specified by their quotas. Usually, the interviews are obtained in the most expeditious way possible.

Some difficulties with quota sampling.   Quota sampling and stratified random sampling are similar. In both methods, the universe to be studied is partitioned into subuniverses, and the total sample is allocated among the subuniverses. At this point, however, the two procedures diverge radically. In stratified random sampling, the sample within each stratum is chosen at random. In quota sampling, the sampling within each cell is not done at random; the field representatives are given wide latitude in the selection of respondents to meet their quotas.

This distinction between quota sampling and stratified random sampling is important. The two sampling systems are sometimes mistakenly thought to be equivalent, and the data from a quota sample are sometimes treated as if they were derived from a stratified random sample. The two systems would in fact be equivalent *if* it could be assumed that the within-cell samples of a quota sampling represented simple random samples. However, experience indicates that this assumption is not warranted. In using a quota sample, the implicit assumption is almost always made that the selection within cells is random or that the differences between items within cells is so small that even if a sample is drawn from extremes, it will not seriously affect the estimates. Thus, some researchers incorrectly apply the same principles to determine sample size and sampling error of a quota sample as they use with probability sampling.

Because the choice of respondents within a cell is left to the field representatives and is not governed by a random selection, the more accessible and articulate people within a cell will usually be the ones who are interviewed.

It will often be found, in addition, that quota samples differ from stratified random samples in ways other than the nature of the within-stratum sampling. For example, the "quotas" may be based on out-of-date or otherwise inaccurate information.

Another problem occurring in the execution of quota samples arises in connection with the fieldworkers' identification of the eligible respondents.

Even though the field representatives may be conscientious and alert, it is often difficult to determine such control characteristics as age in interviews. As a result, the interviews conducted to meet a particular quota may not in fact have the characteristics specified by the quota. For example, a group of interviews ostensibly conducted with consumers under 35 years of age may actually include consumers who are over 35 years old.

An additional fundamental methodological difficulty with quota sampling pertains to the nonstandardized, essentially idiosyncratic character of each quota sample: "Quota sampling is not one defined scientific method. Rather, each one seems to be an artistic production, hard to define or describe. Hence, a general critique cannot be detailed, and a specific critique of one procedure may not fit another."[5]

Special forms of nonprobability sampling

Group interview sample.   In recent years, several specialized forms of nonprobability sampling have achieved wide usage. One is the *group interview sample* which is used in focus group studies. A "group" is usually a quota sample of 5–10 consumers (possibly all product users, nonusers, etc.) assembled for a one to two hour *joint* interview by a person specially trained in group dynamics. Usually several such "groups" are conducted, one at a time.

The number of "groups" used is often small for two reasons: they are expensive and the information obtained from each group is highly unstructured because it is based on a simultaneous, free-form interview with a number of people. The difficulty of aggregating information over groups means that one can often learn as much as this method will usefully provide from just a few group interviews. The number of respondents per group is restricted to about ten, because of the practical difficulties experienced in maintaining control over a larger group.

One study involved three groups of male tequila drinkers under 30, with six respondents per group. The groups were geographically widely dispersed to elicit a broad range of reactions. The interviews, which included tasting a new brand, lasted about two hours. Discussion subjects included brand usage and perceptions, frequency and circumstances of purchase and use, and reactions toward advertising. The respondents for this study were recruited via telephone screening and offered $25 each for their participation.

This kind of sampling is typically done in exploratory research to learn something about the range of consumer beliefs and practices with respect to the subject at issue. Each group is a "fishing expedition," rather than a rigorous attempt to estimate the parameters of some universe. Used in this way, group samples can contribute importantly to the development of hypotheses. They should *never,* however, be regarded as providing evidence

---

[5] Leslie Kish, *Survey Sampling* (New York: John Wiley & Sons, 1965), p. 563.

on the size of some parameter. One reason is the difficulty of defining what universe is sampled by this technique. A second is that each group interview is essentially a sample of one, consisting usually of a vaguely defined cluster of responses. In practice, it is common to vary the form and content of the questioning from group to group. The respondents within a group are interviewed at the same time and each person's responses, therefore, are conditioned by those of the other respondents. Because groups are quota cluster samples, the data from four groups of five respondents each, for example, cannot be regarded as the equivalent of 20 independent, randomly chosen observations.

Shopping mall intercept samples.   Another widely used nonprobability sampling technique is the shopping mall intercept sample. Respondents are recruited for individual interviews (using assigned "quotas") at fixed locations in shopping malls. It is common in a given study to use several malls, each serving different socioeconomic populations, in each of several cities.

Such samples are frequently used in moderate size studies (100–200) that are *experimental* in character, for example, to compare responses to two or more TV commercials, two or more product concepts, and so forth, rather than to estimate the parameters of a single existent universe. Mall samples can be informative for such purposes, assuming that the *differences* in experimental results do not depend importantly on the characteristics of the sample. If, for example, the difference in effectiveness of two commercials varies with frequency of mall shopping, demographic characteristics of mall shoppers versus nonshoppers, or any characteristic related to availability for mall interview, then mall samples should not be used.

Mall sample advantages are speed and economy relative to a probability sample of personal interviews. Their limitations derive from the expediency of selecting the sample and the atypical character of the population sampled (that is, mall customers).

Controlled panel samples.   A third nonprobability sampling device often used is the controlled panel sample. This technique, pioneered by National Family Opinion, Inc. (NFO) of Toledo, Ohio is an elaborate and highly controlled form of quota sampling. NFO and similar organizations have developed huge files of names, addresses, telephone numbers and a wide array of demographic characteristics for households willing to be interviewed by mail or telephone. Using computers, they have constructed "panels" (often of 1,000 households each) that approximately replicate the U.S. household universe in demographic characteristics such as age, income, etc. known to be related to consumer attitudes and behavior. In a given project one or more panels are interviewed via mail or telephone to obtain the requisite information.

A major advantage of this approach is that large national samples can be provided relatively cheaply and easily. Such samples are particularly valuable when sampling rare populations, those that make up less than 5 percent of the population. What one does is to sample in two phases. In the first, a large sample is used to identify members of the rare population, using an inexpensive screening questionnaire. Then a more detailed questionnaire (usually by mail) is used with the sample so identified.

The disadvantages of controlled panel samples are those attendant on any quota sample plus the obvious bias that such samples are comprised of people who are willing to be included in controlled panels and to participate in surveys from time to time. Such bias may be particularly acute when the panel is a continuing one that demands extensive cooperation over an extended interval.

The three specialized nonprobability sampling techniques described are all variants of convenience and quota sampling, as discussed earlier. All are widely used and can, under appropriate circumstances, be informative. As with any nonprobability sampling method, it is essential that the researcher recognize their limitations compared with probability sampling and actively consider the trade-offs involved in their use for the particular problem at hand.

CHOICE OF SAMPLE DESIGN IN PRACTICE

This book has emphasized probability sampling. The widespread use of nonprobability sampling in marketing research has also been noted, and a number of commonly used techniques of this type have been described. In this section, some of the issues which influence the choice of one design over another in a given case are discussed, and certain compromise solutions to the design problem are described.

The major consideration in design choice is *quality of sample design required,* a vague and intuitive, but nevertheless useful, concept. As is shown by the common use of nonprobability designs, probability sampling—despite its many advantages—is not always essential. The "quality" of sample design required varies from one problem situation to another. It is convenient to think of a continuum of "quality of sample design required," as schematized below:

Quality of Sample Design Required

<--->

Extremely low   *Extremely high*

(Convenience sampling,   (Probability sampling,
from an accessible   from most relevant
universe)   universe)

In some situations, a low quality sample design, as represented by convenience sampling from an accessible universe, may be adequate. An example would be an exploratory study to help define issues, rather than to estimate parameters, when virtually nothing is known of the subject.

At the other extreme, high quality data will sometimes be necessary. If the analyst requires parameter estimates with calculable precision from a universe that corresponds closely to the universe of interest, then probability sampling is essential. These extremes can be regarded as the endpoints on a continuum of "sample design quality required."

Both researchers and managers usually want high quality data, and the advantages of probability sampling are widely recognized. There is a continuing conflict between this perceived need and the limitations of time, money and complexity. The result is that many studies utilize a sample design that falls somewhere between naive convenience sampling and probability sampling from the precise universe of interest.

The decision as to sample design in a particular case can be very difficult. While it is clear that "quality of sample design required" is the key consideration, there are no wholly objective methods of determining this quality. Judgment and experience necessarily play a crucial role in assessing how much "quality" is required and how best to proceed. For small scale studies, preliminary in character and limited in resources, the decision will frequently be between some form of nonprobability sampling or no primary research at all.

For large scale studies, supported by major resources, some form of probability sampling will be the tentative initial choice. From that beginning, other factors will influence the final decision.

For example, it is seldom, if ever, possible to obtain *complete* information on all units of a designated probability sample from human populations. Less than 100 percent response (sometimes as low as 30 percent) should be expected, owing to refusals, not-availables even after repeated callbacks, and the like. The potential negative impact of nonresponse—and resources needed to minimize the problem—will require consideration. The nominal advantages of probability sampling are lost if there is high nonresponse. One also must consider appropriate allocation of resources between sample design and collection of accurate information from designated sample units. On certain studies such as store sales audits and continuous consumer panels, it is expensive and operationally complex to obtain the needed data from designated sample units. As a result, it may be wiser to devote a large portion of resources to accurate data collection, recognizing that, as a consequence, fewer resources will be available for sample design.

The adoption of a probability sample design from the precise universe of interest is not automatic, even when resources are substantial for a large scale study. Individual features of the problem, combined with researcher experience and judgment, will determine the choice of design—an ultimately subjective decision.

Probability sampling theory, however, will always provide a rational basis for thinking about a sampling problem. Minimally, it will help identify possible pitfalls if some type of nonprobability sampling is used. Moreover, it is sometimes possible to adopt some features of probability sampling, even though its use in "pure" form may not be practical.

Compromise solutions: Probability sampling adaptations

Cognizant of the advantages of probability sampling, yet confronted with limited resources, many researchers have used compromise solutions to the sampling problems posed. These are intended to achieve some of the benefits of probability sampling from the precise universe of interest, without incurring the typically associated high costs.

Area sampling modifications. One such compromise involves the selection of *interview areas,* using probability sampling, but identifying respondents for interview in the selected areas by nonprobability methods. For example, a several stage area probability sample might be used to identify areas (e.g. blocks) as places of interview. Then, sample respondents could be identified for interview using a systematic pattern (e.g. every fifth house) from an arbitrarily designated point within each sample area (e.g. the southeast corner). Methods akin to this are widely used.

Probability sampling with quotas. One application assigns quotas, within probability-selected areas, based on estimated numbers of four groups within each area: Men under and over 30, and unemployed versus employed women.[6] Such a system retains some of the features of probability sampling, in that objective selection of where to interview is maintained rather than leaving it to interviewer choice. The imposition of quota controls ensures that certain hard-to-find people are represented, with appropriate frequency, in the sample. The procedure is substantially faster and cheaper than standard probability sampling for individual, in-home field interviews. These virtues are bought at the expense of the assurance provided by "pure" probability sampling.

Approximating the relevant universe with a listed one. Another acceptable compromise solution is to use probability sampling from a universe that only *approximates* the precise universe of interest. In effect, the precise universe of interest is assumed to be little different from the approximated universe for which a satisfactory list of universe elements exists. A common example is the use of probability sampling from a universe of telephone-accessible households, rather than a universe of all households.

Tracking studies, designed to trace trends in brand awareness, attitudes and product use are often conducted at periodic intervals using probability samples from telephone-accessible universes. Because some 90 percent of U.S. households have telephones, the researcher can often use probability sampling from this universe which approximates the universe of all households. An important advantage with such samples is that high response rates

---

[6] Sudman, *Applied Sampling,* pp. 191–200.

can often be obtained because the costs of repeated callbacks to reach not-at-homes are relatively inexpensive. Of course, for this use to be of value, it must be possible to obtain the requisite information via a telephone interview.

Many commercial research agencies execute telephone probability samples using various forms of such sampling. One company uses what amounts to two stage stratified cluster sampling.[7] At the first stage, clusters of "central telephone offices" were systematically selected from a universe of eight strata (groups of "central offices," stratified by metro versus nonmetro areas within four U.S. regions). At the second stage, household telephone numbers are randomly selected within the sample "central offices" chosen at the first stage. The result is a probability sample of telephone households of the U.S. telephone universe.

This general method—redefining the universe of interest to correspond with a listed universe—can be helpful in securing probability samples, where, as in the case of telephone-household universes, the approximation is a close one. Many easily accessible universe lists, however, are seriously defective, and caution is required in their use.

SUMMARY

This book has emphasized probability sampling and has given comparatively little discussion of nonprobability sampling, even though nonprobability sampling enjoys wider usage. To gain added insight into the issues impinging on the choice between these two general methods, the advantages and disadvantages of probability sampling are summarized briefly.

Advantages and disadvantages of probability sampling

Probability sampling is the *only* sampling method that provides essentially unbiased estimates having measurable precision. If the investigator requires this level of objectivity, then some variant of probability sampling is essential.

A second advantage is that probability sampling permits the researcher to evaluate, in quantitative terms, the relative efficiency of alternate sampling techniques in a given situation. Without added assumptions, this is not possible in nonprobability sampling.

A third major advantage is that probability sampling requires relatively little universe knowledge. Essentially, only two things need to be known: (1) a way of identifying each universe element uniquely and (2) the total number of universe elements. If, as in area sampling, a correspondence can be established between area units and universe terms and area maps are

---

[7] For description, see "A National Probability Sample of Telephone Households Using Computerized Sampling Techniques," *Chilton Research Services,* Radnor, PA, undated.

available, then probability sampling can be used. In contrast, nonprobability sampling methods may require substantial information about the character of the universe.

The principal disadvantages of probability sampling are its relative complexity, cost, and time requirements. Except in very simple situations, more resources are needed to design and execute a probability design than a nonprobability design. In many marketing research situations, the limitations of budget and time will require that nonprobability sampling be considered.

Choice between probability and nonprobability designs in marketing research practice

In practice, many forms of nonprobability sampling are in use, ranging in complexity from simple convenience sampling to elaborate variations of quota sampling. Some special forms enjoying wide application are: group interview samples, shopping mall intercept samples, and controlled panel samples.

The major consideration in choosing between some kind of probability design, or one of the nonprobability designs, is the *quality of sample design required,* a vague but useful concept. Because there are typically many factors involved in design choice, experience and judgment play key roles in the actual selection of a design in practice. The result is often a design that is intermediate in "quality" between naive convenience sampling and a perfectly executed probability sample from the precise universe of interest.

It is sometimes possible to adopt some of the features of probability sampling to improve results. One approach is to identify areas by probability sampling, but to identify respondents within areas by nonprobability methods. Another is to sample, by probability methods, an accessible universe for which a list of elements exists, assuming this universe does not differ importantly from the actual universe of interest. The latter method is widely used for probability samples in telephone surveys.

Case 11–1
MILWAUKEE MACHINE COMPANY (A)*

Milwaukee Machine Company was one of the major U.S. producers of turning and boring machines. It sold these products through 34 distributors, each of which had an exclusive territory. Sales averaged about $125 million annually.

To appraise the quality of the work done by its various distributors, the firm decided to develop estimates of the sales potential in each distributor's territory by measuring the installed inventory of turning and boring machines and by obtaining estimates of brand preferences among purchasing firms.

---

* Data provided by Management Research and Planning, Inc.

From study of trade association data and their own sales records, executives identified 13 industries (defined by 3-digit Standard Industrial Classification [SIC] codes) that bought turning or boring machines or both. Government information was available on the number of plants by number of employees in each of these industries in each county in the United States. From these data it was possible to calculate the number of plants of each of the 13 industries in each distributor's territory.

The research director decided to survey a sample of plants in each of these industries. For each plant the interviewer would ascertain the number of turning and boring machines installed and the brand preference for the next purchase of each type. From this information it would be possible to estimate the average number of machines per plant by plant size classification in each industry, and to estimate the inventory of machines in each distributor's territory by multiplying the average per plant by the number of plants in the territory in each size classification. Since plants varied widely in size and the number of machines per plant was related to size, it would be important to have the sample properly distributed by size of plant.

Three different categories of plants were represented in the 13 industries —manufacturing, construction, and metal wholesaling. The director believed manufacturing firms of a given size would have more machines than would either of the other types. Equipment more than five years old would be more apt to need replacement than newer machines; therefore, it would be desirable to find the inventory of machines in each of two age categories—less than five years old and five or more years old.

Trade and government sources reported the number of plants in various categories to be as shown in Tables 1 and 2.

Executives of the firm estimated that machines in use were about evenly divided between those over five and those under five years of age. They also

---

TABLE 1. Number of plants by industry

Industry	Number of plants in United States
Metal construction contractors	11,176
Furniture and fixture manufacturers	3,668
Smelters, refiners, rolling mills	2,501
Structural metal fabricators	9,673
Metal product fabricators	5,887
Manufacturers of farm and construction equipment	6,804
Manufacturers of metal working machinery	8,121
General industrial equipment manufacturers	3,415
Service machinery manufacturers	12,227
Electrical transmission equipment manufacturers	1,974
Communication equipment manufacturers	3,057
Manufacturers of automobile, airplane and railroad equipment	5,707
Metal wholesalers	17,497
Total	91,702

TABLE 2. Number of plants by number of employees (13 industries under study)

Number of employees	Number of plants in United States
1– 19	66,313
20– 49	10,256
50– 99	5,839
100–249	5,332
250 and over	2,195
Total	91,702

TABLE 3. Executive estimates of number of turning and number of boring machines per 100 employees by industry

Industry	Number of machines per 100 employees	
	Turning	Boring
Metal construction contractors	5.1	2.6
Furniture and fixture manufacturers	1.1	2.0
Smelters, refiners, rolling mills	7.8	4.5
Structural metal fabricators	5.6	7.1
Metal product fabricators	7.5	10.0
Manufacturers of farm and construction equipment	3.2	4.0
Manufacturers of metal working machinery	2.5	0.2
General industrial equipment manufacturers	2.2	1.8
Service machinery manufacturers	1.2	1.2
Electrical transmission equipment manufacturers	6.7	9.3
Communication equipment manufacturers	5.3	8.7
Manufacturers of automobile, airplane, and railroad equipment	3.6	8.8
Metal wholesalers	3.2	1.8

estimated the number of machines per employee for the 13 different industries as shown in Table 3.

Many of the smaller plants, they knew, had no machines and even some of the larger plants had none. Dividing firms into those with under 20 employees and those with 20 and over, the research director asked the sales representatives to estimate what proportion of firms in each size class of the 13 SIC industries had at least one machine of each type. An average of the answers is shown in Table 4.

A small pilot study showed brand preferences for the next purchases as shown in Table 5. The same study indicated that about 90 percent of the firms approached would supply the information requested.

Milwaukee executives decided they wanted estimates of the installed inventories in each distributor's area to be accurate within 10 percent and the national inventory of machines by each of the 13 SIC industries to be accurate within 15 percent.

TABLE 4. Percentage of plants by industry estimated to have at least one machine

Industry	Percent of plants with under 20 employees having				Percent of plants with 20 or more employees having			
	Turning machines	Boring machines	Both	Neither	Turning machines	Boring machines	Both	Neither
Metal construction contractors	40%	12%	12%	60%	67%	67%	60%	27%
Furniture and fixture manufacturers	12	12	12	88	51	53	46	41
Smelters, refiners, rolling mills	13	4	4	87	21	13	10	77
Structural metal fabricators	32	29	16	55	57	44	39	39
Metal products fabricators	32	27	18	59	44	38	34	52
Manufacturers of farm and construction equipment	8	4	—	89	34	31	24	59
Manufacturers of metal working machinery	7	4	—	89	25	14	14	75
General industrial equipment manufacturers	5	10	5	91	28	20	18	71
Service machinery manufacturers	7	—	—	93	30	24	24	70
Electrical transmission equipment manufacturers	11	5	5	90	29	23	20	68
Communication equipment manufacturers	9	9	4	87	27	38	31	56
Manufacturers of automobile, airplane, and railroad equipment	5	10	5	90	27	24	18	67
Metal wholesalers	23	15	8	69	61	20	20	39

TABLE 5. Brand preference of next purchase of turning and boring machines

	Turning machines	Boring machines
Milwaukee Machine Co.	36%	25%
Victoria	26	29
Smith, Oberdig, & Crenshaw	5	15
Harrison, Inc.	15	7
All others	18	24
Total	100%	100%

An alphabetical listing of companies in each industry showing the number of employees, the location, and the telephone number was available from Dun and Bradstreet. The research director planned to interview the production manager in each plant by WATS telephone through a local field-service firm.

How should the sample of firms be selected?

How large a sample should be used?

Case 11–2
BERRY SUPERMARKETS, INC.

The Berry Supermarket chain was headquartered in a medium-sized southern city and had eight stores serving the local area. Founded in the late 1930s, it had succeeded to a point where it was the volume leader within the metro area. It faced severe competition from other local groups as well as from several national and regional chains. Berry's basic strategy for building in-store traffic was to stock and display attractively fresh fruits and vegetables, meats, and bakery goods. In addition, it advertised that it had the lowest prices in town.

In the spring of 1976, Berry came under increasing price competition as did the rest of the industry. The situation at times bordered on a full-fledged price war. Part of the price declines could be traced to a drop in commodity prices, especially those for beef, poultry, pork, dairy products, and fresh fruits and vegetables. But it was also thought that the situation reflected an overpopulation of food stores and a leveling off of the area's population growth.

During the first quarter of 1976, Berry's profit margin on sales dropped to 0.2 percent, down from 1.2 percent for the same period in 1975. Worse yet, there was some evidence of a loss in market share. Increasingly, the management questioned whether the firm was, in reality, featuring the lowest prices in the area on comparable merchandise. At one of the weekly management meetings, W. F. Berry, president and chief executive officer, suggested that the group consider seriously commissioning a local marketing research firm to undertake periodic surveys to determine Berry's competitive position.

In brief, what was being suggested was a monthly study to determine to what extent area residents were satisfied with Berry versus leading competitors on the basis of price, service, assortment, and quality. Respondents would be asked to rate Berry versus individual competitors on these "dimensions" by department (for example, fresh meats, fruits and vegetables, bakery, canned goods, and laundry supplies). Store loyalty and demographic data would also be obtained.

The task of determining how such an idea could be made operational was assigned to the advertising manager who, in turn, consulted with a local marketing research firm. From the outset, the problem of sample design dominated the discussions. Both recognized the desirability of a probability sample, but they also knew the expense involved in setting up such a sample. Further, there was the problem of interviewing minority groups which comprised over 40 percent of the population of the city proper. Despite the use of trained and experienced minority interviewers, it had become increasingly difficult to interview successfully such respondents. Not-at-homes and refusals typically exceeded 50–60 percent in minority areas, and those who did cooperate often gave "conflicting" answers. The difficulties were confounded when the interview dealt with food purchases since respondents, many of whom were on welfare, frequently believed that the government was undertaking a check on them.

Because of the above, a plan was worked out whereby all interviewing would be done outside of a selected sample of supermarkets, including Berry stores. Interviewing would be done on Thursday, Friday, and Saturday during the first week of each month. One interviewer would be assigned to each sample store for all three days. The "interviewing" hours would be staggered in order to interview as many different kinds of shoppers as possible. Thus, on Thursday the hours would be 9–12 and 2–6; on Friday, from 2–6 and 7–10 in the evening; and on Saturday, the hours assigned would cover mornings, afternoons, and evenings. No interviewing was to take place on any of the other days although the stores were typically open from 8:00 A.M. until 10:00 P.M. on Monday through Saturday and 9:00 A.M. until 7:00 P.M. on Sunday.

Interviewers were to approach potential respondents with a request for an interview and at the same time offer, where applicable, to help put the groceries in the respondent's car. (Store personnel often carried the bags.) In addition, interviewers were to indicate they had a gift gasoline certificate worth $1 to award in return for cooperating. The certificate could be redeemed at any of several local gasoline service stations. Berry's sponsorship could not be detected in any way from the gift certificate. The number of

interviews which could be obtained daily under such conditions was estimated to be 30–35 per store or approximately 100 per store over a three-day
period.

Another matter of some importance had to do with whether the same
stores should be interviewed each month. After considerable discussion, it
was agreed that a new sample of stores should be drawn monthly. These
could include stores already sampled since the plan was to list the target
stores (approximately 120 in number) and select 8 each month at random
with the constraint that no more than one store from each chain group would
be included.

*Evaluate the proposed interviewing and sampling plans. What changes
do you recommend?*

12

Data collection and the field force

Methods of designing data-collection forms, particularly questionnaires, and methods of selecting samples from which to collect data have been discussed in the previous chapters. Ways of coping with the most common problems which endanger accurate results have been described. But no matter how carefully a sample is drawn or a questionnaire designed, the data collected will not be accurate unless the field force executes its job properly. As it is usually performed, fieldwork is one of the major sources of error in the typical research project—especially in questionnaire studies. There seems to be considerable agreement among social scientists that interviews are likely to produce unreliable data. Some go so far as to say that ". . . it is indefensible to assume the validity of purportedly factual data obtained by interview."[1]

There are many reasons why the interview is suspect as a way of obtaining data, but one of the most important is the complex nature of the memory process. Despite good intentions on the part of respondents they may not be able to recall past behavior accurately. Events which intervene between the interview and the time of the past behavior may cause respondents subconsciously to "juggle" the facts. Respondents also experience selective recall. Memory for all events does not decay at the same rate, since those elements which were most pleasant or most unpleasant tend to be remembered longest. Memory is further complicated by the fact that most people begin with selective perception in which they note only certain parts of an event—typically those parts which they expected to note.

---

[1] David J. Weiss and Rene V. Davis, "An Objective Validation of Factual Interview Data," *Journal of Applied Psychology* 44 (1960):384.

In addition to encountering memory difficulties, interviewing ". . . contains many unknowns or only partially understood sources of bias. It is necessary to know what occurs in the interviewing process in order to appraise the validity and reliability of the information."[2] This chapter is devoted to an examination of these biasing factors and to a discussion of how to aid the interviewers in overcoming these problems.

FIELDWORK PROCEDURE

Research directors have two major alternatives for getting their fieldwork done—they can develop their own organizations or they can contract with a fieldwork agency to do the job. In either case it is a difficult and costly step in the research process. Fieldwork involves the selection, training, supervision, and evaluation of individuals who collect data in the field. Data collection may be by either interview or observation, but since the problems are greater in the interview process, the following discussion is primarily in terms of interviewing—by the telephone and in person. Mail surveys do not have these problems.

Most fieldwork organizations now have a central location from which they can do telephone interviews nationwide and they can maintain a full-time staff of interviewers who are well trained and experienced. This set-up may be combined with "store" space in a shopping center where personal interviews are conducted and where full-time staff is available for that purpose. These interviewers are able to handle most fieldwork assignments and, with such centralization, training, supervision, and control of the data collection process can be detailed and close.

When data are collected personally at more dispersed locations, the fieldwork problem becomes more difficult. The research director must develop job specifications for the specific project, decide what characteristics the fieldworkers should have, and try to find interviewers with those characteristics. Since the sample design often calls for data to be collected at many different places, one or more fieldworkers with the desired characteristics must be found at each of these places. Most fieldwork organizations keep a file of such workers by geographical location. The sampling sites are matched against these files and qualified workers selected. Letters are sent to the selected interviewers telling them about the pending work and asking them to indicate by return mail their availability. Usually it is necessary to recruit some new workers for each job, since qualified interviewers may not be available at all locations and some may not be available for the specific job. This recruiting is often done with the help of such local sources as newspapers and educational institutions.

After fieldworkers are selected they have to be trained. Since most field-

---

2 J. Allen Williams, Jr., "Interviewer-Respondent Interaction: A Study of Bias in the Information Interview," *Sociometry* 27 (1964):338.

work must be done within a limited time period and interviewers are widely dispersed, training is usually done by mail. Under such conditions the training program consists of written instructions which the interviewer is asked to study carefully to learn the purpose of the study, how to locate and approach respondents, to establish rapport, to ask questions, and to obtain and record accurate answers. On some projects their training is given by supervisors in person at one or a few central locations.

Following the training program, the interviewers commence the fieldwork. During this time interviewers need to be supervised, at least to the extent of making certain that they are proceeding on schedule and that their work is satisfactory. Since factors such as sickness or bad weather may prevent some interviewers from completing their assignments on time, the director needs to keep tight control on the day-to-day field operations and must be ready to replace individual interviewers quickly, if necessary.

After the fieldwork is completed and the completed forms are returned to the home office, a verification check is made to make certain that the interviews were actually made, that is, to insure that interviewers did not cheat. The work of each interviewer is then evaluated. The questionnaires or other data forms turned in are checked for completeness, compliance with instructions, and apparent ability of the worker to obtain useful data. Such information helps the research director to select the best fieldworkers for future projects.

ERRORS IN FIELDWORK

While marketing researchers are aware of the need for good fieldwork and the professional journals have many discussions of the problems involved, little improvement was made until the telephone made it possible and economic pressures made it desirable to centralize the process. With a small full-time field force concentrated in one location it is feasible to develop experienced individuals, to provide special training as needed for each project, and to control the process by listening to samples of all interviewers' work to be sure they are following the prescribed procedures.

Compare this situation to that of the dispersed personal interview project where part-time interviewers with unknown capabilities are used. The only home office contact with them is likely to be through a written set of instructions which may be studied with varying degrees of care. Completed interviews are "edited" for mechanical procedure, and routine checks for cheating are made. The collected data are then tabulated and assumed to be correct.

But all types of interviews continue to suffer from common problems—the proportion of interviews that cannot be completed due to difficulties in finding respondents or their unwillingness to cooperate, variations in the way questions are presented, and the influence of the interviewer on the respondents and their responses. Knowledge of methods for coping with these problems has grown over the years, but it has not led to principles which insure the collection of accurate data. Despite these difficulties survey leaders must make every effort to be aware of and understand the kinds of errors which occur in the field. They may be able to take preventive action.

The remainder of this chapter discusses the field operation as it applies to telephone and personal interview situations. Most of what is discussed, however, applies also to the collection of data by the observational method.

Respondent selection errors

Selection errors with quota samples. In quota samples, interviewers select the individuals to be included in the survey, subject only to quotas for various population groups. This interviewer control of the selection of respondents is unlikely to result in the equivalent of a random sample. Interviewers tend to follow the paths of least resistance and of greatest convenience. One study showed that even when interviewers were given economic level quotas, they tended to underselect in both the high- and low-income classes. Errors or falsification also occur in classification; interviewers who classify the same respondents on an income basis may differ in as much as 30 percent of the cases; and interviewers tend to select households they "like" and which they think have higher incomes, even when controls are used to discourage this.

An effort is often made to overcome this respondent selection bias by setting up more elaborate controls or quotas. This can create biases of another type. When the number of controls gets beyond three or four, the fieldworker finds difficulty in locating respondents who meet all the characteristics prescribed. As a result interviewers tend to "push" a 35-year-old into the 40-and-over age group or to "force" their quotas in some other way.

In the case of shopping center interviews, respondents are selected almost by convenience. It cannot be said that errors are made in respondent selection, but it is highly probable that respondents tend to be those who appear easiest to interview.

Selection errors with probability samples. One of the common reasons given for the use of probability samples is that they eliminate the bias that comes from interviewer selection of respondents as described above. For telephone interviews this is largely true except as noted below, but for door-to-door interviews the use of a probability sample provides no guarantee *per se* that respondent selection bias will be eliminated. The use of such a design may cause different biases such as errors in listing dwelling units, in selecting dwelling units, and in selecting individuals within dwelling units.

Evidence indicates that in listing dwelling units interviewers tend to underlist in low-income blocks. One study found a 13 percent underlisting in such blocks. Once dwelling units have been listed, the specific dwelling units to be included in the sample must be selected. When fieldworkers make their selections in the field from listings, they find ways to avoid lower-income households as contrasted to when random selections are made in the office.

Interviewers also tend to select the more accessible individuals in the household in both telephone and personal interviews. Despite instructions which indicate the random procedures to follow in selecting respondents within the household, interviewers will "rig" the selection system to prevent making callbacks for the not-at-homes.[3]

The difficulty of listing and locating households for personal interviews is severe in the lower-income neighborhoods, as indicated in the following comment:

> The Central Harlem Adult Survey conducted in 1964, which encountered problems in the listing and location of housing units, as well as in contact, had an interview completion rate of only 63 percent. Comparison with the 1960 census figures revealed that the uninterviewed were heavily concentrated in the lowest income category (under $3,000 a year). The National Opinion Research Center interviewers reported the persistent feeling that people were reluctant to answer the doorbell.[4]

Nonresponse errors.   In almost every study, no response is obtained from a certain part of the sample, that is, from those who refuse cooperation, those who cannot be located, and those who are unsuitable to interview, such as the ill, deaf, and senile. In most studies, it is assumed that the replies from those who are interviewed are also representative of the nonresponse group. In some cases this may be so, but in many instances the nonresponse group differs markedly from the group which cooperates. If this nonresponse group is large, it may easily bias the results of the study.

Nonresponse problems are increasing; in the 1960s many research firms obtained 80 to 85 percent completion of surveys with 3 or 4 callbacks, but completion rates dropped to 55 to 65 percent in the 1970s. The nonresponse group usually includes a significant number of both not-at-homes and refusals. Table 12–1 shows the results from two large, very carefully done surveys—one done by telephone and one by personal interview with a probability sample.[5] Seventeen or more calls were made in the telephone study to try to reach each respondent in the sample and eight or more calls were made at households to try to complete the personal interviews. This is a much larger number of callbacks than is usually attempted, but significant portions of both samples were nonrespondents. The components of the nonresponse group were roughly similar in the two surveys except for the no-answer or not-at-home group which included 20.7 percent of the telephone sample and only 3.3 percent of the personal interview sample.

---

[3] Dean Manheimer and Herbert Hyman, "Interviewer Performance in Area Sampling," *Public Opinion Quarterly* 13 (Spring 1949):84–85.

[4] Carol H. Weiss, "Interviewing Low-Income Respondents," *Welfare in Review* (October 1966):3.

[5] Robert M. Groves and Robert L. Kahn, *Surveys by Telephone* (New York: Academic Press, 1979).

TABLE 12–1. Nonresponse components for telephone and personal interview surveys

	Telephone	Personal interviews
Completed interviews	55.9%	74.3%
Partial interviews	3.4	—
Refusal by respondent	7.5	10.9
Refusal by other member of household	4.3	1.9
Noninterview for other reasons (senile, deaf, foreign language, proper person not home, etc.)	8.0	9.6
No answer or not at home	20.7	3.3
Total	99.8%	100.0%

Source: Robert M. Groves and Robert L. Kahn, *Surveys by Telephone* (New York: Academic Press, 1979), pp. 66–67.

Not-at-homes.   The percentage of not-at-homes varies by city size, day of the week, time of day, season of the year, age, and the sex of the respondent, as well as with the provisions made to control not-at-homes in individual studies. It is, however, almost always surprisingly large. Table 12–2 shows the percentage of sample homes reached on each call for both the telephone and personal interview surveys mentioned above.

Only one fourth of the calls by either telephone or door-to-door were completed on the first attempt as shown in Table 12–2. Over 75 percent of the households which were ultimately reached for the sample had been

TABLE 12–2. Percentage of sample homes reached with each call in telephone and personal interview surveys

	Telephone		Personal interview	
Call	Percent	Cumulative percent	Percent	Cumulative percent
1	24	24	25	25
2	18	42	25	50
3	14	56	18	68
4	11	67	11	79
5	8	75	7	86
6	6	81	5	91
7	5	86	3	94
8	3	89	6	100
9	3	92		
10	2	94		
11	1	95		
12	1	96		
13	1	97		
14	1	98		
15	0	98		
16	1	99		
17	2	101		

Source: Groves and Kahn, *Surveys,* pp. 56 and 58.

reached by the fourth personal call and the fifth telephone call. This suggests why researchers have now concluded that three or four callbacks are about the optimum number in most surveys.

Failure to include not-at-homes may bias survey results because population groups vary in this probability of being at home. Young males particularly are not likely to be home, but other groups that are also more likely than the average to be not-at-home include families with no children, employed women, high income families, young people of both sexes and those who live in large cities.

With quota samples on door-to-door surveys, the survey directors seldom have any knowledge of the not-at-home problem. In quota samples for shopping center interviews, of course, there are no not-at-home problems. When probability samples are used, the director is aware of the not-at-homes and must decide how much effort is desirable to get more of them into the sample. Because of the differences between the at-homes and not-at-homes, it is usually wise to make at least three callbacks to interview the original not-at-homes.

Refusals. Refusal rates vary from project to project and may range up to 25 percent. Since refusals are often the result of personality and mood, it can be argued that they will occur randomly and will not bias results. Moreover, refusals are a matter of degree and of circumstances such as convenience at time of call. Repeated efforts to obtain compliance can reduce the refusal rate to a low level, five percent or less in general population surveys. Tendency to refuse is related to age, social class, and size of city.[6] The older the respondent, the lower the social class, and the larger the city, the more probable is a refusal.

In addition to general refusals, refusals may occur on specific questions, particularly those relating to income. In one study, those who refused to answer an income question were compared to those who did. The group not reporting income had a larger percentage of upper-income households (as inferred from rental data), highly educated persons, small families, older family heads, managerial and professional people, American born, Protestants, and Jews.[7]

Measurement of nonresponse. A first step in coping with nonresponse is to develop accurate information on the problem. Surprisingly, standard measures of nonresponse (or response) have not been established in the field. A study of 40 different firms to find how response was measured turned up 29 different methods. Applying these methods to a single survey resulted in response rates varying from 10 percent to 88 percent.[8] The researchers

---

[6] E. M. C. van Westerhoven, "Covering Non-Response: Does it Pay?" *Journal of Market Research Society* 20 (October 1978):246.

[7] Mildred B. Parten, *Surveys, Polls and Samples* (New York: Harper & Brothers, 1950), pp. 412–14.

[8] Frederick Wiseman and Philip McDonald, "Management Begins toward Much Needed Response Rate Standards," *Marketing News* 14 (January 11, 1980):1.

presented data from a hypothetical survey and asked a group of research companies how they would calculate the response rate. The hypothetical survey was described as a telephone survey among a sample taken from telephone directories with the following results:

Category	Frequency
Total numbers dialed	4,175
Disconnected, nonworking numbers	426
No answer, busy, not at home	1,757
Interviewer reject (language barrier, deaf, etc.)	187
Household refusal	153
Respondent refusal	711
Ineligible respondent	366
Termination by respondent	74
Completed interviews	501

The three most frequently reported methods of calculating response (each given by 7.5 percent of the firms) were the following:

(1)
$$= \frac{\text{Household refusals} + \text{Rejects} + \text{Ineligibles} + \text{Terminations} + \text{Refusals} + \text{Completed interviews}}{\text{Total numbers dialed}}$$

$$= \frac{153 + 187 + 366 + 74 + 711 + 501}{4,175} = 48\% \text{ response}$$

(2)
$$\frac{\text{Rejects} + \text{Ineligibles} + \text{Terminations} + \text{Refusals} + \text{Completed interviews}}{\text{Total numbers dialed}}$$

$$= \frac{187 + 366 + 74 + 711 + 501}{4,175} = 44\% \text{ response}$$

(3)
$$\frac{\text{Completed interviews}}{\text{Total numbers dialed}} = \frac{501}{4,175} = 12\% \text{ response}$$

In the first reported calculation the researchers are apparently defining responses as any contact made with the sample telephone numbers. The second calculation apparently considers response as a contact with the appropriate individual in the house and the third calculation defines response as a completed interview. The only way that methods one and two can be said to reflect a true rate of response is to assume that those who were reached by phone, but with whom interviews were not completed, were the same as those with whom interviews were completed. As has been shown earlier, such an assumption is dangerous; one might as well assume the no answers, busy signals and not at homes are similar to those with whom an interview was completed.

In door-to-door interviewing the response rate is calculated in a similar manner, but the factors are somewhat different. There are hardly any personal interviews that are terminated-by-respondent and the ring-no-answer is much more definite. As a result the proper calculation for a door-to-door probability sample will tend to be:

$$\frac{\text{Completed interviews}}{\substack{\text{Completed interviews} + \text{Not-at-homes} + \\ \text{Respondent refusals} + \text{Household refusals} \\ + \text{Rejects} + \text{Ineligibles}}} = \text{Response rate}$$

If the sample is a quota sample or if neighboring households are substituted for not-at-homes or refusals, a calculation of response rate is not meaningful.

Treatment of nonresponse. Proper field methods can reduce substantially the nonresponse rate—both refusals and not-at-homes—but they cannot eliminate the problem completely. Since most researchers are agreed that the bias of nonresponse is usually considerable, definite provisions to reduce it are almost always warranted.

In door-to-door interviews with probability samples, neighboring dwelling units are often substituted for not-at-homes or refusals. It is clear that this procedure does not solve the problem if the universe is thought of as consisting of two strata—one from which information will be obtained if its members are included in the sample and one from which no response will be obtained. Substituting new households just adds to the sample from which information is obtained; it does nothing to obtain information from the other stratum.

Callbacks are the only useful method of obtaining information from the non-response stratum. This applies to both telephone and door-to-door personal interview studies. For most surveys it is wise to select a smaller sample with four or more callbacks than to spend the same budget on a larger sample with no callbacks.

In door-to-door surveys the cost of callbacks can be reduced by leaving the questionnaire at the sample home with a request that the resident complete it and return it in the envelope provided. This has some of the problems of mail surveys, but does reduce the size of the non-response group. Costs may also be reduced by using the telephone to schedule callbacks. The telephone is particularly useful in locating, screening, and interviewing relatively unique populations such as individuals who have exercycles in their homes.

Care in the construction of the questionnaire, particularly in pretesting, can reduce the number of refusals as can training of interviewers with that objective in mind.

Errors in stimulating responses

Stating the question. In asking questions, interviewers are usually expected to follow certain rules. A typical set of such rules runs as follows:

1. Each question must be asked exactly as worded.
2. The interviewer must not comment on the question meaning or indicate in anyway what kinds of answers might be acceptable.
3. Every question must be asked unless the interviewer is instructed to do otherwise.
4. Questions must be asked in the same sequence as given on the questionnaire.

There is considerable evidence that even with a relatively simple, straightforward, structured questionnaire, interviewers do not follow the above rules. Concealed tape recorders in a personal interview study provide evidence that

> ... one third of the ... interviewers deviated frequently and markedly from their instructions, sometimes failing to explain the key terms or to repeat them as required, sometimes leaving them out altogether, shortening questions, or failing to follow up certain ambiguous answers in the manner required.[9]

Standardized interviewer performance is particularly difficult to obtain when using open-ended questions.

If a question is not easily understood by respondents, interviewers will rephrase it in ways which will cause less confusion. Since no two interviewers are apt to rephrase a question in the same way, different respondents get different stimuli which produce variations in replies. A variation of this problem occurs when interviewers are instructed to probe with additional questions to secure more complete answers. In either case, the addition of a comment by the interviewer raises the possibility that the respondent will be influenced in a different way than other respondents. Failure to probe adequately, when probing is necessary to obtain a meaningful answer, is one of the most serious sources of interviewer error. Table 12–3 shows the average

TABLE 12–3. Average number of errors in stating questions by error type in personal interview survey

Type of error	Number of errors per question
Reading error	0.293
Speech variations	0.116
Probes	0.140
Feedback to respondents	0.161

Source: Norman M. Bradburn and Seymour Sudman, *Improving Interview Method and Questionnaire Design* (San Francisco: Jossey-Bass Publishers, 1979), p. 29.

[9] W. A. Belson, "Increasing the Power of Research to Guide Advertising Decisions," *Journal of Marketing* (April 1965):38.

number of errors of various types made by interviewers per question asked in one carefully controlled personal interview survey.[10]

Questions which state the alternative answers, such as multiple choice questions, are particularly subject to interviewer bias. This bias occurs because the interviewer puts too much emphasis on one alternative in stating the question. The interviewer's method of asking questions will also influence results in other, more subtle, ways. For example, slight variations in tone of voice will change the entire meaning of some questions.

Some field-interviewing organizations require the interviewer to indicate on the questionnaire what additional comments were made in order to elicit satisfactory answers. Presumably, these are evaluated later to determine whether they biased the respondent sufficiently to warrant elimination of that questionnaire from tabulation.

In some interviewing situations, such as in group interviews, a tape recorder may prove helpful in reducing bias by recording both questions and answers verbatim. Experiments have shown that, contrary to general expectations, respondents will accept the use of tape recorders. The most critical element in gaining acceptance of the recorder is the interviewers' own attitudes toward it and their resulting behavior. The recorder, however, may introduce bias. One study found that tape-recording increased the accuracy of reported responses of lower-class respondents, but reduced the reported accuracy of middle- and upper-class respondents.

Bias from the interviewer's method of stating the question is lower in telephone surveys than in personal interview surveys, but there are more subtle factors involved than just the method of communication. Fewer interviewers are needed in telephone studies, but this means that "averaging out" of such interviewer bias is less apt to take place in telephone surveys. On the other hand, the smaller number of interviewers and their concentration at one location makes more training feasible and permits supervisors to listen in to a sample of each interviewer's work and, thus, to identify interviewers who are deviating from established procedures and to take corrective action. Computerized telephone surveys appear to have the potential for reducing this type of interview bias even further, but more experience is needed before definite conclusions can be drawn.

Respondent's perception of the interviewer.   Interviews involve a social relationship between two persons. Respondents adjust their conduct to what they consider to be appropriate to the situation. Interviewers, whether they like it or not, will be cast into some role by respondents. They must be conscious of the alternative roles at their disposal and attempt to establish the role which will best further the purposes of their study. "Interviewers, as the primary link between the researcher and the respondent, are instrumental in setting the level of a respondent's desire to cooperate. Interviewers

---

[10] Norman M. Bradburn and Seymour Sudman, *Improving Interview Method and Questionnaire Design* (San Francisco: Jossey–Bass Publishers, 1979), p. 26 ff.

who obtain the most complete personal interviews do so because they are able to induce respondents to work hard. . . ."[11]

When interviewing takes place on a subject about which there is some expectation regarding social approval or disapproval, or in which there is a strong ego involvement, respondents err by idealizing their behavior. Low-income respondents, in particular, tend to give the kinds of answers they think that society, through the interviewer, wants to hear. In interviews among blacks, white interviewers obtain significantly higher proportions of what may be called "proper" or "acceptable" answers than do black inter- viewers. Middle-class interviewers find more conservative attitudes among lower-income groups than do working class interviewers. The greater the social distance between the interviewers and the respondents, the greater the likelihood of bias. Respondents are used to talking about personal experi- ences only to listeners who share a great deal of experience and symbolism with them and with whom they can safely assume that words and gestures are assigned similar meanings. But in the interview, these assumptions break down.

Age, race, and income of the interviewer all tend to influence the re- sponses obtained from personal interviews. Age and race are not so appar- ent in telephone interviews and can be expected to have less influence in that method of communication. Older interviewers are perceived as authority figures and responses are modified accordingly. Black interviewers with white respondents or the opposite cause some tension. In each combination the respondent tends to answer in a way that will be least apt to have racial implications.[12] Interviewers who have higher incomes themselves tend to find higher incomes among respondents.[13]

In view of the evidence showing the influence of age, race, and income of the interviewer on information obtained, extensive efforts to control these effects would be expected. Unfortunately, the composition of the field staff can usually be modified only slightly for individual studies. Typically, the same interviewers are used to do many different kinds of projects; they work by assignment and interview all types of respondents. Most interviewers are middle-aged, middle-class women, while respondents are drawn from all classes. There is no relatively simple and economical way of matching inter- viewer and respondent nor of correcting for the biasing effect of given inter- viewer characteristics.

A basic condition for optimum communication is that respondents per- ceive interviewers as people who are likely to understand and accept them and what they have to say. Interviewers must be perceived as "within range"

---

[11] Charles F. Cannell and Floyd J. Fowler, Jr., "A Note on Interviewer Effect in Self Enumeration Procedures," *American Sociological Review* (April 1964):270.

[12] Shirley Hatchett and Howard Schuman, "White Respondents and Race-of-Inter- viewer Effects," *Public Opinion Quarterly* 39 (Winter 1975–76):523 ff.

[13] Barbara Bailar, Leroy Bailey, and Joyce Stevens, "Measures of Interviewer Bias and Variance," *Journal of Marketing Research* 14 (August 1977):337–43.

—that is, they must be seen as people to whom the respondents' statements and experience will not be foreign or offensive. This does not mean that respondents need to see interviewers as similar to themselves, but they must view interviewers as capable of understanding their points of view, and of doing so without rejecting them.

In general, the more characteristics interviewers and respondents have in common, the greater the probability of a successful interview. An economically feasible method of achieving this pairing has not been developed.

Errors in interpreting and recording answers

Not only can interviewers bias survey results by their impact on the respondents, but they may influence results by the way they react to respondents. Differences in the characteristics of interviewers such as experience, attitudes, and opinions also affect the recorded answers. Door-to-door interviewers are commonly faced with the problem of recording answers by writing on clipboards while trying to keep the respondents interested. The result is frequently a number of clerical errors. One research worker has found serious mistakes being made by interviewers in recording things not said, as well as not recording things which were said. These errors, however, were not as serious as errors resulting from failure to press for further comment on incomplete or "don't know" answers.

Interviewers also vary in the answers they record according to the amount of space available on the questionnaire. If a large amount of space is left for an answer, more will be recorded than if a small space is provided.

Recording of information is more accurate in telephone surveys because interviewers can have all appropriate materials and tables on which to write. This advantage should become greater as direct recording into the computer becomes more widely used.

It should not be inferred that interviewers do not usually interpret and record data accurately. It has been common practice in classifying respondents by ocupation to have interviewers record factual data from which office "experts" would determine the proper occupational class. Results of an experiment in which interviewers made the occupational classifications showed these classifications to be as accurate as those made by the office staff.[14]

Cheating

It is difficult to know to what extent cheating is a serious problem—partly because cheating is hard to define. The most glaring example of cheating is the interviewer who fills out questionnaires without making interviews. More frequently, cheating is confined to falsification of certain data within the

---

[14] K. E. Bauman and C. L. Chase, "Interviewers as Coders of Occupation," *Public Opinion Quarterly* 38 (Spring 1974):107–12.

questionnaire. Because of the difficulty of supervising door-to-door interviewers, cheating is a particular problem in such studies. It may be present at
any point in the interviewing process, including enumeration of dwelling
units, selection of dwelling units, and selection of respondents within dwelling units.

Although the field force used on a typical marketing research project
probably is not selected with great discretion and is given a minimum of
training, very little follow-through is made to detect cheating of any but the
crudest type. Under such conditions it seems likely that cheating is an important source of interviewer bias. There are many causes for cheating other
than those personality characteristics inherent in the interviewers themselves.
Study design and implementation influence the predisposition to cheat. If
respondents are difficult to locate and interview, cheating increases. Other
"causes" are unreasonable deadlines and difficult-to-complete questionnaires.

Many investigators are coming to the conclusion that cheating is as much
a problem of morale as of morals. The more the interviewer knows about
what is expected of her, the less likely she is to cheat. When situations develop which are confusing, embarrassing, difficult, unexplained, or impractical, the interviewer is tempted to find a way around them. To the extent that
factors of this type cause cheating, research directors can reduce or eliminate
the problem.

MINIMIZING FIELDWORK ERRORS

There are many points at which errors can creep into marketing research
studies during the fieldwork phase as described above. To reduce such errors
to a minimum and to hold costs to acceptable levels, research organizations
pay particular attention to five factors:

1. Selection and training of fieldworkers—interviewers or observers.
2. Administrative procedures for handling projects in the field.
3. Supervision of fieldworkers and the data collection process.
4. Quality and cost control procedures.
5. Validation of fieldwork.[15]

Administrative control of projects in the field

Most fieldwork, whether done by telephone or personal interviewing is
done by individuals recruited and organized to do fieldwork for a wide variety of research studies. Some research organizations maintain a staff of
fieldworkers on a national basis; others contract out the fieldwork to organizations specializing in that phase only. Some fieldwork organizations maintain a national organization while others have lists of independent supervisors who have groups of interviewers in their local areas. This discussion

---

[15] The following draws particularly on Groves and Kahn, *Surveys,* pp. 40–45.

will not deal with the problems of recruiting these interviewers and maintaining the organizations. When a project is approaching the fieldwork stage, the organization to be used is alerted. If it is believed that certain types of interviewers are required (e.g., men or women under 30), that will be stated, but to a significant degree it is necessary to use those fieldworkers who are available.

Personal interview surveys on a national basis may require hundreds of interviewers at dispersed areas around the country, supervisors who oversee their work directly, and field coordinators who control the whole process. A national telephone survey could be organized in a similar manner using the same or similar interviewers with local telephone service. The WATS service, however, makes it feasible to handle the telephone survey from one central location.

For the centralized telephone project a much smaller number of interviewers (e.g., 10–40) are sufficient. If any are new interviewers, they must be given general instructions on interviewing techniques. All interviewers are then assembled for training on the specific features of the project at hand. Sometimes these are brief sessions, but for major projects of particular importance, the training session may take as much as two days. Each interviewer does a practice interview which is then discussed with a supervisor.

For personal interview projects such centralized training is not practical. The usual procedure is to send written instructions and questionnaires to the local supervisors who are expected to conduct the training. This means that there is considerable variation in the amount and quality of training the various interviewers receive.

To insure that fieldwork is started and proceeds on schedule, researchers establish starting and completion dates and quotas for completion by certain intervals. When materials are mailed to the fieldwork supervisors, a list of all materials is included along with a postcard to be returned, acknowledging receipt. Interviewers turn in their completed questionnaires daily to local supervisors. These are tabulated to provide a running total of completed interviews by interviewer and for the project. If the project falls behind schedule, the director can identify those who must be speeded up. Additional interviewers may be added if necessary.

In centralized telephone surveys the same activities must take place, but they are much simpler because the people and materials are all at one place. Delays and losses of materials in the extra handlings and in the mails are eliminated.

As completed questionnaires come in they are edited to be sure the interviewers are proceeding properly. Any mistakes can be corrected before further interviews are made. Since most projects are on a tight schedule in the field, it is important that problems be identified as early as possible and proper action taken. In addition to the checks suggested above, interviewers must know what to do in case of difficulty. In personal interviews these things must be done by the local supervisors, with the resulting delays and variations among them, whereas centralized telephone studies provide quick and uniform controls.

Quality and cost control

If good fieldwork is to be achieved, it is necessary to provide supervision. For personal interview studies which are geographically larger than one metropolitan area, this requires local supervisors. In most instances they work for more than one research organization. It is important that they have close contact with the central research office, that they be trained for work with the organization, that they receive periodic visits from representatives of the central organization to review their work, and that they have written instructions and forms for each specific job.

Control.   Local supervisors have personal contact with the field force under their supervision. It is they who, typically, receive the completed questionnaires daily and check them to insure that instructions are being followed and that the quality is good. Supervisors should keep daily records on the number of calls, number of not-at-homes, number of refusals, and number of completed interviews for each interviewer and the total for all interviewers under their control. In addition, they record hours worked and expenses. These permit them to determine the cost per completed interview, whether the job is moving on schedule, and which interviewers, if any, are having trouble. Supervisors report similarly to the central office and a total progress report can be maintained.

Quality control by the supervisor usually is based on verification that the sampling procedure is being followed insofar as addresses, names, and demographic characteristics can show this. Questionnaires are examined to see if all questions have been completed, if directions have been followed in terms of questions to be asked, if particular answers are received to previous questions, if unsatisfactory or incomplete answers have been accepted without sufficient probing, and if writing is legible.

All of the above is much simpler in telephone surveys. Monitoring equipment permits a small number of specialized supervisors, perhaps only one, to listen to ongoing interviews and to provide any needed corrective action as soon as the interview is over. The sample is identified by telephone numbers. Every day the status of each number is put into the computer which generates a daily report showing interviews completed, the number left to do, response rates, and work completed by each interviewer.

Detection of cheating.   A special aspect of quality control is that of validation or detection of cheating. Since interviewers work independently it is not always easy to detect cheating or to distinguish cheating from honest misunderstandings as to procedure. All well-run field surveys check a sample of each interviewer's work to see if it represents actual interviews with the individuals shown. The close supervision provided in centralized telephone studies makes cheating a very small problem, but checks are typically made anyway. In personal interview surveys local supervisors do this by phoning a sample of respondents and asking if they were interviewed. When interviewers are spread over too wide an area for this to be feasible, postcards are mailed asking acknowledgment of the interview. This is usually done by saying the interview has been reported and asking if the interviewer was polite and efficient. An opportunity to report that no interview took place is provided. The number of such postcards returned is usually so low that reports of no interview can only be taken as suggestions for further investigation.

Central office control.   The quality and cost controls begun by the field supervisors are summarized at the central office. Other controls are often added. For example, answers to key questions may be tabulated by interviewer. One such study asked: "Certain new brands of instant coffee have recently appeared in the shops. Can you tell me what brands these are?" One brand was Fine Blend. The results for some selected interviewers were as follows:[16]

Interviewer	Number of interviews	Percent reporting Fine Blend
A	15	13%
B	16	25
C	15	0
D	15	20
E	16	88
F	14	14
G	16	19

In total, 51 interviewers completed 1,168 interviews and the average percentage reporting Fine Blend was 18 percent and the standard deviation was 15.4 percent. Casual inspection finds that interviewer E is quite different from the rest. The 88 percent of her interviews which reported Fine Blend is almost 5 standard deviations from the mean—an extremely unlikely event. One is inclined to suspect that the interviewer filled in the questionnaires without interviewing the respondents—that is, cheated. But perhaps this sample was unusual. A check showed that those interviewed by E were similar in age, social class, and household composition to those interviewed by others. A supervisor then visited E and discussed the situation. It developed that the instructions had been misunderstood, and E was prompting respondents. As a result, this interviewer was given closer supervision in subsequent surveys and greater care was given to the preparation of instructions.

Probably the major advantage of telephone interview surveys over personal interview surveys is in the fieldwork area. Great reductions in travel time and expense are an advantage to the telephone, but the major advan-

---

[16] Based on data in R. C. King and P. M. Trotman, "Experience of a Computer System for the Quality Control of Interviewers," in ESOMAR Seminar, *Fieldwork, Sampling and Questionnaire Design,* pp. 262–65.

tage lies in the smaller number of people involved and the easier communication among them. In one study done both by telephone and personal interview, the following comparison was found:[17]

	Personal interview	Telephone interview
Completed interviews	1,550	1,700
Field coordinator	1	0
Field supervisors	11	1
Field "contacts"	Several	0
Interviewers	144	37
Cost per interview	$54.82	$23.45

Evaluation of interviewers

Interviews are checked for quality as the completed questionnaires are turned in. Costs are monitored while the survey is progressing. These activities are necessary to insure successful completion of the project. On a long-term basis, it is important to evaluate interviewers in a way that will enable the organization to identify the better ones and so to build, gradually, a better field force.

The first step in the evaluation process is the check for cheating. In the past any interviewer found to be falsifying questionnaires was immediately dropped. This may still be desirable in most cases. Some fieldwork managers are now checking these cases to determine if the character of the job was a significant factor in the cheating. Questions which are embarrassing or awkward for respondents lead some interviewers to skip them and to enter fictitious answers. If instructions are unclear, some interviewers will proceed as they understand, and as a result obtain incorrect and seemingly false responses. A significant portion of what has been considered cheating may have been the result of job situations of these types which destroyed interviewer morale. In any case, a record of problems in this area should be made on the interviewer's card.

Completed questionnaires are the only practical basis on which to evaluate the quality of an interviewer's work. Theoretically, expert interviewers could reinterview a sample of each interviewer's respondents to see if they obtained the same results, but this is too expensive and, because of the respondent's prior exposure, does not provide a completely reliable base for comparison.

An interviewer can be rated on several factors. The more important ones are cost, refusals, and following instructions.

Cost. Total cost (expenses and salary) per completed interview is a basis for comparison of interviewers. In personal interviews costs differ by city size so comparisons should be made only among interviewers working in

---

[17] Groves and Kahn, *Surveys,* pp. 44 and 193.

similar locations. Since some interviewers cover city, suburban, and rural areas in the same assignment, it may be necessary to tabulate the costs by interviewing site within each interviewer assignment in order to make a realistic analysis. The detailed cost data necessary for such an analysis, however, are seldom obtained.

Refusals.　The percentage of refusals can be compared among interviewers. This comparison should also be limited to interviewers working in similar areas.

Following instructions.　Each interviewer can be graded on the basis of the number of mistakes made. It is usually desirable to weight the various kinds of mistakes since some are more serious than others. Thus, the interviewer's performance on open-ended questions, as evidenced by the relevance of the responses recorded, should receive a heavier weight than many other types of work performance. The acceptance of an unsatisfactory answer, such as an ambiguous or partial answer, is more important than failure to date or sign the questionnaire. After totaling the number of points "off" for each interviewer, a rating can be assigned; for example, the number 10 can be assigned to those interviewers who on the basis of their score fall into the upper 10 percent of all interviewers. This would mean that such individuals had fewer mistakes than 90 percent of all interviewers.

The National Opinion Research Center supplies its coders with error sheets which are used to note the following types of interviewer error:[18]

Type of error	Error weight
Answer missing	3
Irrelevant or circular answer	3
Lack of sufficient detail	2
"Don't know"—with no probe	2
Dangling probe	1
Multiple codes in error	1
Superfluous questions asked	1

The interviewer's rating on each project should be made part of the records maintained for each interviewer. Results on a particular study may fit a trend and indicate what should be done about rehiring or retraining a particular interviewer. Upon the completion of a survey, interviewers should receive a report which indicates their completion and refusal rate, grade, and how well they did relative to interviewers working in comparable areas.

The entire procedure outlined above suffers in that only a relative rating is obtained and, if the results are uniformly bad, it will only reveal that some interviewers were worse than others. It is not a completely satisfactory

[18] Seymour Sudman, "Quantifying Interviewer Quality," *Public Opinion Quarterly* (Winter 1966–67):664–67.

method, since it lacks objective standards; however, since absolute standards are usually not available and since each study is likely to differ from the next, a relative comparison is of considerable value.

SUMMARY

Errors orginating with interviewers are undoubtedly a major source of error in most surveys. These interviewer errors can be classified in five major groups: (1) nonresponse errors, (2) respondent selection errors, (3) errors in stimulating responses, (4) errors in interpreting and recording answers, and (5) cheating.

Research directors differ as to the relative importance of the cheater problem, but they agree generally that the problem is serious in personal interview projects. Proper management can reduce this error to a relatively low level, but many door-to-door surveys probably have a significant bias because of cheating.

Personal field supervision is the best way of controlling the field force. Another control method—and one which should be used in addition to personal supervision—is to maintain a continuous preliminary edit. Such a procedure keeps a control on whether interviewers are keeping to the schedule and whether their work is generally satisfactory.

Completed questionnaires are the basis for evaluation of interviewers. The first step in the evaluation process is to determine whether the interviews were actually made. Interviewers should then be rated on a number of factors, including cost per completed interview, percentage of refusals to the total number of interviews assigned, and mistakes made. If such data are made part of the interviewer's permanent record, a basis exists for deciding what interviewers should be rehired and what additional training is needed.

Telephone interviewing has replaced personal interviewing as the most widely used survey communication method. One of the important reasons for this is the simpler, better controlled, cheaper fieldwork that is possible.

Case 12–1
QUALITY INTERVIEWS, INC.*

Quality Interviews, Inc., was one of the leading organizations in England which specialized in doing the fieldwork for marketing surveys and other public polling activities. Its reputation had been built on high quality service at a reasonable price. Nancy Borthwick, the owner and president, emphasized careful selection, training, and supervision of the interviewers used by

---

* Basic data in this case are provided by R. King and P. Trotman in a paper first presented at the ESOMAR Seminar, *Fieldwork, Sampling and Questionnaire Design.* Full proceedings of this seminar (vols. 1 and 2) may be obtained from the ESOMAR Central Secretariat, Raadhuisstraat 15, Amsterdam, The Netherlands, at a price of Sw. Frs. 80–per set.

Quality Interviews, but price competition was intense and it was not feasible to do the kind of job that would have "guaranteed" that all the firm's work was completely accurate. Ms. Borthwick was looking for new, simple ways to improve the quality of the work done by her interviewers.

Quality Interviews did fieldwork for many of the major manufacturers, advertising agencies, and marketing research firms in England. These other organizations typically developed the research design for a given project. But then they consulted with Quality Interviews on some aspects of questionnaire design and turned over to Quality the entire job of collecting data in the field.

Most interviewers were part-time workers, typically homemakers who worked on an hourly basis, one job at a time. Quality maintained a roster of over 2,000 such individuals throughout the country. Interviewers were used in their home territories so that on any given project each interviewer's territory tended to be separate from others. Within the bounds of these geographical contraints. Quality would always use the best interviewers it had available and would try to concentrate work with the best workers so that they would gradually become better trained, more experienced and, hence, better fieldworkers.

Errors in fieldwork could be classified in the following categories:

1. Errors resulting from lack of necessary abilities or from interviewer bias.
2. Interviewer mistakes—usually resulting from a failure to learn or understand directions.
3. Interviewer cheating—usually taking shortcuts to speed up the interview.

Ms. Borthwick thought she could use the low cost of computer information systems to retrieve data on the performance of her field staff in a way that would enable her to identify those who were cheating and those who did not understand their directions. She realized that fieldwork problems varied by the type of project and by individual questions. Accordingly, she began testing a system of quality control for specific types of questions. Two examples are shown below.

In a survey to monitor the acceptance of a new brand of instant coffee, Fine Blend, a precoded question was asked to determine the awareness of consumers of new brands in the market. *"Certain new brands of instant coffee have recently appeared in the shops. Can you tell me what brands there are?"* Interviewers were told to probe: *"What others?"* But they were not to prompt. Answers were to be recorded by circling the appropriate numbers(s) on a list as follows:

> Fine Blend 1
> Birds' 2
> A "new" Nescafé 3
> Other brands 4
> Don't know 5

TABLE 1. Awareness of new brands on the market (percentages)

Inter-viewer	Fine Blend	Birds'	A new Nescafé	Others	Don't know	Number of interviews
14	13	53	27	20	20	15
27	25	44	50	44	0	16
46	0	20	7	20	53	15
58	19	25	6	25	38	16
68	6	50	25	6	38	16
87	6	50	13	13	31	16
94	13	19	25	13	50	16
112	19	28	13	0	44	32
113	27	60	20	13	13	15
160	6	56	25	25	25	16
182	31	44	19	13	19	16
190	19	69	13	19	25	16
207	88	75	25	38	0	16
223	20	47	40	47	7	15
236	25	38	13	19	44	16
252	19	44	6	19	38	16
257	0	50	13	31	31	16
287	14	43	43	14	21	14
310	6	38	13	50	25	16
325	6	38	44	31	13	16
345	13	50	0	6	38	16
351	25	25	25	13	44	16
365	6	13	6	6	69	16
407	19	56	6	13	19	16
412	23	31	0	23	38	13
420	0	33	13	20	53	15
432	19	31	6	19	38	16
435	0	47	27	27	27	15
437	25	31	0	13	44	16
438	6	44	13	13	56	16
458	33	47	20	33	27	15
479	7	27	0	20	47	15
487	15	54	31	8	23	13
492	0	38	0	0	63	16
497	13	31	6	6	56	16
498	13	44	19	19	25	16
504	43	50	14	21	14	14
512	29	47	29	6	18	17
513	27	53	7	20	27	15
526	56	75	13	13	13	16
542	8	31	8	23	38	13
556	7	67	13	27	33	15
557	31	56	6	31	19	16
564	13	13	7	20	53	15
575	38	38	13	0	31	16
611	19	56	13	19	25	16
615	25	63	6	31	19	16
617	20	53	7	13	27	15
624	27	53	7	0	33	15
630	6	38	0	6	50	16
638	7	64	21	0	21	14

TABLE. 2. Average number of times each score reported by individual interviewers (per interview)

Inter-viewer	Number of interviews	Score								
		1	2	3	4	5	1+5	2+4	1+2	4+5
24 21		4.2	3.3	2.3	3.2	13.0	17.2	6.5	7.5	16.2
30 24		3.7	4.9	2.5	6.3	8.7	12.4	11.2	8.6	14.9
40 24		3.8	4.1	0.9	4.6	12.6	16.4	8.7	7.9	17.3
66 22		7.2	1.8	0.5	2.5	14.1	21.3	4.3	9.0	16.5
68 24		6.3	2.5	0.6	3.4	13.3	19.5	5.9	8.7	16.7
69 24		3.0	4.1	1.0	8.8	9.1	12.1	12.8	7.1	17.8
94 22		4.9	3.8	1.2	6.1	10.1	15.0	9.9	8.6	16.2
100 23		5.0	3.0	0.3	5.6	12.0	17.0	8.7	8.0	17.6
160 24		5.3	3.0	1.5	5.2	11.0	16.4	8.1	8.3	16.2
177 21		2.9	3.7	1.7	4.0	13.7	16.6	7.8	6.6	17.7
184 23		5.4	3.1	1.0	6.4	10.1	15.5	9.6	8.5	16.5
190 22		4.9	2.5	1.0	4.9	12.7	17.6	7.4	7.4	17.6
206 24		4.9	2.4	0.9	4.2	13.7	18.6	6.5	7.3	17.8
238 23		8.1	1.8	1.3	2.0	12.8	20.9	3.8	10.0	14.7
260 22		3.4	5.3	1.0	8.2	8.2	11.6	13.5	8.6	16.4
263 24		5.0	4.4	0.9	6.0	9.7	14.7	10.4	9.4	15.7
268 23		3.6	5.1	2.7	8.9	5.7	9.3	14.0	8.7	14.6
312 24		3.3	3.8	1.5	5.3	12.0	15.4	9.1	7.2	17.3
325 24		5.8	4.3	0.5	5.0	10.5	16.3	9.3	10.1	15.5
344 19		6.4	4.9	0.7	5.4	8.5	14.9	10.3	11.3	13.9
376 24		4.0	4.0	1.8	6.7	9.5	13.5	10.7	8.0	16.2
430 24		0.9	7.1	2.5	11.3	4.3	5.2	18.4	8.0	15.5
435 24		6.3	2.7	0.7	4.6	11.6	18.0	7.3	9.0	16.3
437 24		5.3	3.8	0.5	4.2	12.3	17.6	8.0	9.0	16.5
458 21		4.0	3.4	0.3	4.0	14.3	18.3	7.4	7.4	18.3
473 24		6.0	3.4	0.1	3.4	13.0	19.0	6.8	9.4	16.5
479 23		3.8	3.3	0.8	6.3	11.7	15.6	9.6	7.2	18.0
500 23		3.2	5.3	1.0	8.6	8.0	11.2	13.8	8.4	16.6
520 24		5.6	3.3	0.5	4.4	12.2	17.8	7.6	8.9	16.6
552 22		5.7	3.3	0.8	5.1	11.1	16.8	8.5	9.0	16.2
554 23		3.3	3.1	0.3	5.9	13.5	16.7	9.0	6.4	19.3
576 24		3.6	3.7	0.4	6.1	12.3	15.9	9.8	7.3	18.3
580 24		3.8	4.3	0.2	7.1	10.6	14.4	11.4	8.2	17.7
594 20		5.3	2.6	0.2	6.0	12.0	17.2	8.6	7.9	18.0
603 24		3.2	6.6	0.5	9.8	6.0	9.1	16.4	9.8	15.7
604 23		3.8	4.7	0.3	9.1	8.1	12.0	13.8	8.5	17.2
617 25		5.3	3.6	0.7	4.4	12.0	17.3	8.0	8.9	16.4
618 23		5.7	3.2	0.9	4.9	11.3	17.0	8.1	8.9	16.2
620 20		5.7	3.5	0.4	3.3	13.2	18.9	6.8	9.2	16.5
626 21		5.5	2.1	0.6	3.7	14.1	19.6	5.8	7.6	17.8
627 20		0.2	9.2	3.0	9.8	3.9	4.1	19.0	9.4	13.7
630 24		5.5	3.4	0.4	4.3	12.5	17.9	7.7	8.9	16.7
631 21		5.0	4.6	0.9	8.7	6.8	11.9	13.3	9.7	15.5
632 23		5.5	5.3	1.0	7.0	7.1	12.6	12.3	10.8	14.2
634 20		5.4	3.4	0.7	5.5	11.1	16.5	8.9	8.7	16.6
644 22		3.6	3.5	1.6	5.7	11.6	15.2	9.2	7.1	17.3
648 23		5.0	2.9	1.1	3.8	13.2	18.2	6.7	7.9	17.0
651 15		5.5	3.1	0.5	4.1	12.8	18.3	7.2	8.6	16.9
665 22		5.8	3.3	0.2	5.6	11.1	16.9	8.9	9.1	16.7
672 23		4.2	3.7	1.2	9.8	7.1	11.3	13.5	7.9	16.9

Fifty-one interviewers made approximately 16 interviews each. The computer print-out in Table 1 shows the results for each interviewer on the above question.

In another survey, consumers who used instant coffee were read 26 statements about brands tested in a product test. The question was:

> *I am going to read out some statements about Brand _____. I would like you to tell me whether you agree or disagree with each statement.*
>
> IF RESPONDENT REPLIES "AGREE" ASK: *Do you strongly agree or slightly agree?*
>
> IF RESPONDENT REPLIES "DISAGREE" ASK: *Do you strongly disagree or slightly disagree?*

The scale on the questionnaire was coded for the interviewer to circle the appropriate number:

1. Agree strongly.
2. Agree slightly.
3. Neither disagree nor agree—don't know.
4. Disagree slightly.
5. Disagree strongly.

Fifty interviewers made approximately 24 interviews each. The average number of times each interviewer reported each score per interview is shown in Table 2.

> *What can be determined about the quality of work done by interviewers from Tables 1 and 2?*
>
> *Is there evidence of misunderstanding or cheating?*
>
> *What action should Ms. Borthwick take?*
>
> *Does this method of quality control on fieldwork appear to be useful for long-term improvement of fieldwork service?*

CASE 12–2
SCHANZ AND ASSOCIATES

Schanz and Associates was a medium-sized marketing research firm located in a large midwest city. William Schanz was founder and president of the company, which had been in existence for 12 years and had grown steadily. The firm was able to offer clients a variety of marketing research services, but it specialized in field surveys involving personal and telephone interviews.

Over the years, Schanz and Associates had established good relationships with a number of clients, most of whom were manufacturers of consumer packaged goods. Mr. Schanz believed that the company's success was due, to a large extent, to its growing reputation for good study designs and to its personal interviewing capabilities. He felt the latter was especially important to the company's packaged goods clients, who frequently requested research on new products, on new forms or flavors of established products, on new uses for established products, on reformulated products, and on new packages. Almost all research of this type required that information be obtained through personal interviews with consumers in their homes. For these reasons, Schanz and Associates had developed a lengthy roster of field interviewing personnel located in most of the larger cities throughout the country. Schanz and Associates called on these people whenever the company received a job which required interviewing in their communities.

One day Mr. Schanz came across an article describing some of the problems encountered by field interviewers (see Exhibit 1). He found it especially interesting because it caused him to think about some things which had been bothering him for some time. The article implied that many of the problems associated with field interviewing were caused by the marketing research firm hiring the field interviewers, and that they could be minimized or eliminated if the firm hiring the fieldworkers made a serious attempt to do so. Mr. Schanz sent the article to the company's manager of field operations, John Vukovich, and asked him to schedule a meeting after he had had a chance to read and study the article.

The following day Mr. Vukovich met with Mr. Schanz and indicated to him that the article was probably quite realistic in most respects. He also indicated that some of the problems described in the article applied to the field interviewers used by Schanz and Associates. This revelation disturbed Mr. Schanz, who felt that the continued success of the firm was dependent upon its ability to obtain high quality information from its field interviewing operations.

"Is it not true," Mr. Schanz asked, "that in some eight or ten cities we regularly run one, and sometimes two, field studies each month, and in another dozen or so cities we run a study every month or two?" Mr. Vukovich indicated that that was the case. Mr. Schanz went on to inquire of Mr. Vukovich if quality was suffering as a result of the kinds of things discussed in the article. When Mr. Vukovich replied that there probably was some loss in quality, Mr. Schanz asked if it might be appropriate in some cities to hire a small interviewing force with a guarantee of some regular employment each month, say, to average out to 10–15 hours per week. These interviewers could be paid monthly, even if they did not work 10 or 15 hours each week during the month. Excess wage payments could be credited to other months when the interviewers worked more than 10–15 hours per week. Such a field force would not be expected to cover 100 percent of the firm's field interviewing needs. Rather, they would form a core of field interviewers in those cities, and additional temporary interviewers could be hired as needed, as was currently the practice.

Mr. Schanz indicated that another possibility might be to have field supervisors select the five or ten best and most experienced interviewers and to guarantee them a certain minimum amount of work for each three- or six-month period. Those interviewers would be paid even if they did not work that much during the stated period. There may be times, Mr. Schanz thought, when interviewers would not work the minimum stated hours, but if such a plan were to keep the best interviewers in the employ of Schanz and Associates, the small added expense might be more than offset by the higher quality of information obtained.

Mr. Schanz also wondered if they could find a way to improve the scheduling of their field studies, or if it would be possible to involve the more experienced supervisors in planning projects and in providing feedback on completed projects. By doing so, it might be possible to improve further the quality of information obtained from field studies. Mr. Schanz closed the meeting by asking Mr. Vukovich to study carefully how the firm's field operations might be improved, and to prepare a report on the various courses of action which might be taken, including the advantages and disadvantages of each.

What alternative courses of action should Mr. Vukovich consider?

What are the advantages and disadvantages of each?

What courses of action do you recommend?

EXHIBIT 1

The Lonely Field Interviewer: Why and How Your Research with Her Is Going Wrong*

By Shirley Colby

A crisis is brewing, and it is serious enough to suggest that you open your eyes and pay attention to the plight of the consumer research field supervisors and their armies of interviewers, for we are an endangered species.

I am concerned about the future of the face-to-face, personal form of interviewing essential to obtaining consumer reactions and evaluation of new concepts and products. We are plagued with such problems as delayed payment, feast or famine syndrome, low pay scale and poor communication with our market research suppliers and their clients.

I do not presume to speak for all supervisors. I assumed the title of field supervisor two years ago after a long stint as a new products specialist and

* Reprinted with permission from *Advertising Age*, June 30, 1975, pp. 33–36. Copyright © 1975 by Crain Communications, Inc.

EXHIBIT 1 *(continued)*

then as a consultant in new product development for several manufacturers. My partner, Jackie Acorn, conducted a successful field interviewing service from her home for many years after herself being an interviewer. Our business fits between the "little old lady" cottage industry and the large field agency.

Door-to-door, telephone, central location intercepts, home placement and concept tests, and attitude and usage surveys all require interviewers with special skills to establish rapport with the respondent whose opinions they record. This is the most interesting and vital service we handle. Unfortunately, it is also the most frustrating and unprofitable.

The chief characters in this field operation are these:

The *field supervisor* is a buffer between business and humanity, between the client and the field interviewer. The field supervisor relays the assignments to individual interviewers who gather crops of data from other human beings called respondents. (There are male supervisors and interviewers, but I use the feminine to conform with "little old ladies" and "girls," a field director's synonym of "interviewer.")

We start with a "job alert," usually given by phone by a field director. This includes specifications of the kind of study (home placement, telephone, probability, etc.), number of girls, interviewing dates and hours, and quota. We immediately line up the girls, set the time for the briefing and start to pray that the materials arrive in time. Once in the field, each girl reports on her day's accomplishment for consolidation into our report to the field director the following morning—early.

If a girl drops out before completing her quota, we must find an instant replacement and brief her immediately. The supervisor edits every completed questionnaire (this is generally night work) and validates a designated number by telephoning the respondents. She assembles the call record sheets, maps and other materials for return with the quota of completed questionnaires.

The *interviewer* comes in all ages and backgrounds. Our roster includes graduate students, retired military and other gentlemen, widows, divorcees, maiden ladies, brides, young mothers, grandmothers and retired career women. Most are women; some are men. Most have at least some college education. A few depend on interviewing earnings for their livelihoods. Others prefer interviewing to housework and turn their earnings over to a maid, houseworker or sitter.

The *respondent* usually has shown a kindness and cooperation that are a constant source of pleasure. When we validate, respondents often thank us for sending over "that nice lady" or "that delightful young man." Of course, we run into a few irrational or abusive types, but on the whole, people are very human.

The *field director,* like the supervisor, is usually a woman and is our *only* contact with our supplier. Often we never learn even the name of the client.

Some field directors began as interviewers and their empathy is loud and clear. Others totally lack that quality; their only concern is to get the most for the least possible expenditure.

The *research supplier* is the middleman, torn between meeting the demands of the client and obtaining quality statistics on a short budget.

I do not know how much communication, if any, now exists between field directors and their clients, but my past experience suggests there should be more. I recall some research we did, through a reputable research supplier, for children's cereals. Several products were placed in the home, and each

EXHIBIT 1 (continued)

child received a diary in which to record daily his consumption and reactions to each cereal in the test. He was asked to eat a specific cereal each day.

I accompanied an interviewer on her callbacks and observed several mothers filling in the diaries because the children had not done so. When I asked the interviewer about this she told me that nearly half the diaries were completed by the mothers despite her calling the previous day to remind the children to have them ready before they left for school. Few children kept the diaries current after the novelty of the first few days of the test wore off.

The supervisor told me she had complained many times to the field director of the infeasibility of using such diaries with children, and the field director promised to bring the problem to the attention of her superior, but somewhere along the way, either within the supplier's house or between supplier and client, her complaints were lost. New jobs kept coming with more diaries for children.

We used this particular kind of research for new products in advanced stages of development. I shudder to think of the go-no go decisions that were based largely on the data obtained from those diaries.

The *client* is the entity who pays the bills, ultimately. There are many links (some tenuous) in the chain from him to field supervisor.

At my first exposure to a briefing of field interviewers, the women sitting around the briefing table were awed by "the client" and bestowed their most business-like, rapt attention on me. I wanted to cry, "Relax, ladies, I'm really one of you."

But I was not; I was on the side of business. In fact, I was so much *not* one of them, I had no qualms in directing that research supplier to use a different supervisor in the future. I decided this after I observed an interviewer in the field and discovered that, instead of random door-to-door selection as had been requested, the girls were resorting to referrals among their friends to fill difficult quotas. Nearly all the respondents were children of upper-income families, products of the best summer camps, of one ethnic group, and had an average I.Q. of at least 140.

After this experience I tried to attend briefings and observe interviewers as frequently as I could. On one visit to a large city where we conducted broad-scale tests, the supervisor told me that I was the first representative of either the client or the supplier she had met in her seven years on our jobs. Such a statement would not surprise me today, but it did then.

Scheduling and how it can foul up

After numerous phone calls, we assemble the required girls, who agree to attend the briefing. Before this time arrives, we may get a call to tell us the job will be delayed because the client decided to make a last-minute change in the questionnaire, or the product has not been approved, or the material just did not get out in time. Perhaps the material is delayed in transit. Whatever the reason, we must realign the girls who can work on the study. More hours are spent on the phone—time for which we receive no compensation.

And there are the cancellations. In addition to the time wasted alerting the girls and rearranging lineups of pending jobs, we suffer serious loss of income. We recently had an alert for eight interviewers for a concept study. The supplier requested our very best girls because this was a job for a new client. The following day we had to turn down an alert for seven interviewers for a product placement with two callbacks because all available girls were

EXHIBIT 1 *(continued)*

tied up. And two days later we had a call informing us that the first concept study with eight girls was canceled because the client had a last-minute change of heart and decided to use a different city. By then, the product placement job we had refused had been placed elsewhere. Not only did we lose two jobs, but eight interviewers—among our best—were out of a week's work after rearranging their households to free them to work.

Delayed payment hurts us all

It is common practice to pay market research interviewers when the supervisor receives payment from the supplier. A new girl must sometimes wait several months for her first paycheck. She then sets up her own revolving fund if she continues to work regularly. This practice imposes an additional handicap on the acquisition of reliable interviewers. In fact, it forced us to borrow funds to pay our girls semimonthly. Interest comes out of our fee.

Pay scales penalize the skilled

Every interviewer receives the same rate of pay. This is obviously unfair, because good interviewers are penalized for their competence. Each girl has the same number of questionnaires to complete among qualified respondents. The girl who is skilled in obtaining cooperation of respondents and in administering her questionnaires will fill her quota faster than one who dawdles between houses and wastes time visiting with respondents. The first girl might complete her quota in half the time of the second, but since payment is made on an hourly basis, she will receive only half the pay for the job, although the quality of her work may be far superior.

The number of questionnaires assigned to one girl is generally limited; so we cannot give the more efficient girl a larger quota.

Our girls divide themselves into "street walkers" and "call girls." The walkers earn somewhat more than the telephone girls who work at home. The latter receive \$2.25/2.50 per hour for day/evening and weekend calling. Field interviewers, whether door-to-door or at central locations, receive a little more.

Feast or famine depletes our crew

It would be to everybody's advantage—client, supplier, interviewer and ours—if we could choose perhaps 25 of our best girls for a working crew and assure them steady employment with a minimum fixed salary. But this is impossible under the present piece-meal system; so we must sit back and relinquish one good interviewer after another who locates a regular parttime job elsewhere.

On the other side of the coin, we have been forced to refuse jobs because their timetables and/or deadlines could not be postponed one day. It is especially painful to refuse a job, because we need them to hold on to our girls. (Also, we need the money.) We might have 30 girls in the field one week, and five the next.

Arbitrary demands run us amok

Interviewing areas are usually assigned by the client or the research supplier. The field director sees only the outlines on a map; we see schools, industrial areas, parks, stretches of open desert, senior citizen trailer parks, barrios, and fenced-in condominiums. Most field directors allow us some judgment in changing to workable areas, but occasionally we are not allowed to change. This can be costly.

EXHIBIT 1 *(continued)*

Recently we fielded a probability survey involving a very long, tedious questionnaire, plus a worse self-administered one. Our sample area covered a large barrio (Spanish ghetto) that was 90 percent Mexican-American, bounded by a river, large state school and an interstate highway. Many residents did not speak English, and those who did *thought* in Spanish.

After two days of unproductive canvassing, we asked the field director to give us a different area, but she reminded us that this was a probability and there could be no changes. (We could expand, she said, but how do you interview in a river?) It took three times longer than anticipated to find qualified respondents. When we billed for the job the supplier asked us to lower our cost since our time was higher than the other cities in the survey. Had we dropped the job after the first two days, we would not have been compensated for our payment to our girls. Incidentally, this happened four months ago, and we have not yet received payment for our adjusted billing although we paid our girls for the entire job three months ago.

Field directors generally expect girls to work full, seven-hour days. Some of our girls do not have the stamina for performing the physical labor of carrying the products and papers for blocks on end. Others cannot remain away from home for that long. It would relieve pressure if they could work 5½ hours for four days instead of seven hours for three days. The saving of the travel time and mileage involved in that one extra day of work would be more than made up by better production from less weary, more alert interviewers.

Block those lengthy questionnaires

Some of the questionnaires we receive are unreasonably long and dull. Terminations during the interview are becoming more frequent—in fact, we have had several situations where the respondent fell asleep during the questioning. Some of our most promising new interviewers quit this profession after a few days spent administering such questionnaires. Respondents feel put-upon and refuse all further interviews. Some suppliers offer incentives in the form of gifts or cash, and some expect respondents to give a strange girl one or two or more hours with no compensation at all, or for little gifts our girls are embarrassed to offer.

Most interviews that require more than 30 to 45 minutes waste both the respondent's and the interviewer's time. The respondent wearies of reading, or listening to the interviewer read concept descriptions, lists of brands and products, and countless statements to be rated.

Why validation is a problem

Field directors tell us there has been a rise in the number of invalid questionnaires they receive. I attribute this mainly to turnover of interviewers.

Supervisors are expected to validate from 10 percent to 15 percent of each girl's work. We ask the qualifying questions spelled out in the instructions, such as: "Are you the female head of the household?" "What do you feed your dog?" "Do you own a clothes dryer, and how many loads of wash do you dry in an average week?" "How many cups of instant coffee do you yourself drink in an average week?" Each survey has a different set of qualifications. The supplier also validates, and some clients (with WATS lines) may validate 100 percent of the questionnaires.

Very rarely does an interviewer cheat by inventing respondents and answers. Most of the problems come from inexperienced girls who do not understand the instructions or the importance of strictly following instructions. Another reason for improper selection of respondents is pressure to meet quotas. To hold down costs, we may be limited to too few girls and/or

EXHIBIT 1 (*concluded*)

too little time. So, to meet her quota, an interviewer might stretch a point to obtain qualified respondents.

Quit the baloney on quotas

A major factor in setting quotas and deadlines is incidence. If the client is overly optimistic, it is impossible to complete the field work on time. For example, if a qualification is previous purchase of the client's brand of soap, and the client claims that 10 percent of consumers use that brand, we should find a respondent at every tenth house on average. But if the actual incidence is 5 percent, our girls will need to knock on twice as many doors to fill their quotas of interviews with qualified respondents.

Better pretesting would assure more reasonable timetables. When we are told that a girl is expected to complete five interviews a day and that each interview will take less than one hour to administer, it upsets not only our schedule, but also our girls' morale when they find it impossible to finish an interview in less than two hours.

13

Tabulation of collected data

Data tabulation is the process whereby raw data are transformed into the "list of needed information" which was established in step two of the marketing research process. Research design, sample design, and fieldwork are undertaken solely for the purpose of obtaining data which, when tabulated and analyzed, will yield this "needed information." That information should lead to conclusions, recommendations, and decisions. The reader should note that this observation supports what was stated in Chapter 7, namely, that the marketing research process consists of a number of interrelated steps. This was illustrated in the community bicycle path study discussed at the end of Chapter 7, which showed how the steps of "problem formulation", "listing the needed information", "designing the data collection form", and "tabulation", were interrelated.[1] Thus, a framework for tabulation and analysis procedures is established in the first three steps of the marketing research process.

While there are no standardized tabulation and analysis procedures which should always be followed, it is quite common for researchers to proceed through the following five steps:

1. Preparing and organizing the raw data. Each completed data collection form must be prepared to assure that the data contained therein are legible and accurate. Then the data must be organized, that is, categories and classes have to be established. For example, in a nationwide study to determine household uses of detergents, categories might consist of various types of detergents (liquid versus powder, heavy duty versus light duty, and so on), geographical regions, city sizes, ages of consumers, family incomes,

---

[1] See pages 210–11.

family sizes, and occupations. After these categories are established, the data collection forms are edited, and individual answers are classified into the appropriate categories. The number of responses in each category are then counted.

2. Summarizing the data contained in the categories. Frequently the raw data within a category will be too numerous or too bulky for researchers to analyze in a meaningful way. In such cases, the raw data in a category may be described with summary measures such as ranges, percentages, means, modes, and frequency distributions. Such summary figures will facilitate the researchers' understanding of the data and may suggest further tabulations and comparisons.

3. Determining whether significant differences exist between categories. Typically, researchers will observe differences among the data in different categories. Researchers will determine if these differences are too large to have occurred by chance due to sampling variations and, if so, will conclude that they reflect true differences between the categories. Statistical tests of significance are used for this purpose.

4. Explaining "why" differences exist. It is often assumed that the analysis function stops with the determination of whether or not differences are significant. It is imperative, however, that an attempt be made to explain *why* there are significant differences. Researchers who do not attempt to explain the differences may be overlooking important findings. This, in turn, may cause them to draw unwarranted conclusions.

This "why" information may require that hypotheses—tentative explanations—be set up and tested through a comparison of the survey data with other information. The importance of using other information cannot be overstressed, since it may help to explain more clearly the results obtained from a single research study. If this "why" information cannot be obtained either from the specific project or from other data, further research may be needed. However, it is unwise to contemplate additional research until the possibility of getting answers from the project at hand has been exhausted.

5. Making recommendations. After drawing statistical conclusions, the analyst needs to translate them into recommendations. Making recommendations usually requires an understanding of the practical details surrounding a given operation and so may not be the responsibility of researchers. In general, however, when researchers are qualified by their general knowledge of the operation, they should make recommendations.

It would be a mistake to infer that the analysis function *always* follows precisely the five-step procedure outlined above. In many projects the steps will tend to overlap since at any time the analyst may generate new hypotheses which require a recycling of earlier steps. All of the steps, however, are involved to some degree in each analysis.

Errors introduced in tabulation and analysis. Researchers must recognize that tabulation and analysis procedures may be another source of error in the research process. Errors can occur if the established categories are not as meaningful as they might be, if some of the data are not placed in the proper categories, or if the summary measures of a category are not properly calculated. Errors can also occur in interpreting the data and in attempting to explain why significant differences exist. Researchers should be aware of these possible sources of error and attempt to minimize the effect they can have on research findings. The procedures and analytic methods presented in the remainder of Part III can help researchers in this regard. The remainder of this chapter is devoted to the first two steps discussed above.

PREPARING RAW DATA

When the fieldwork is completed and all the data collection forms gathered in one place, researchers have a great deal of data, but little or no information. Researchers may have 300 completed questionnaires, but until they have been tabulated and analyzed, they represent only raw data. What is needed to transform these data into information is a procedure for organizing and compiling the bits of data contained in each of the 300 questionnaires.

Much of the data tabulation activity consists of counting the number of responses to a specific category of a specific question; for example, how many households which use a heavy-duty detergent prefer the liquid form over the powder form? On the surface, this may seem to be a relatively simple task. Yet, when researchers are going through 300 questionnaires, they will encounter questionnaires in which the recorded responses are not entirely clear. As a result, the tabulations made by researcher A could be different from those made by researcher B. Such "countings" would not be accurate or reliable. Tabulating is more than "just counting." If accurate and reliable information is to be obtained, it is necessary to establish a set of procedures to guide the tabulation. These include editing and coding individual questionnaires, establishing categories into which different responses can be classified and, when machine tabulation is to be used, keypunching the data onto computer cards. Each of these preparatory activities is discussed below.

Data collection forms.   The following discussions on data preparation and tabulation apply to all types of data collection forms—questionnaires, panel diaries, and forms used in observation studies. All such forms are similar in that they record some kind of "response." If the form is a questionnaire, the response is recorded on the questionnaire. If the form is a panel diary, the panelist records something which is a response to a question or instructions, for example, the television program being viewed or the brand of cake mix purchased on the last shopping trip. If the form is from an observation study, observers may have recorded what the shopper did, for example, the shopper compared the unit prices of several brands, but did not pick up any packages. To simplify the presentation in the following discussion, reference will be made to questionnaires, even though the discussion applies equally to all data collection forms.

Editing and coding

The primary purposes of editing and coding are to eliminate errors in the raw data and to process the data into categories so that tabulation may take place. The essential difference between the two is that editing is required to eliminate errors or points of confusion in the raw data, whereas coding assigns the data to pertinent categories, thereby expediting the tabulation. These functions are usually accomplished by the same individuals and often in the same operation.

There are a number of important reasons for studying these subjects. One is that the effectiveness of the entire analysis function may be hampered because of poor editing and coding. Another is that editing plays an important role in helping to evaluate the field force, the effectiveness of the questionnaire, and the survey operation in general. Thus, editing provides information about how the research procedure can be improved in the future. Also, the time and cost involved in editing and coding are sufficient reasons alone to warrant intensive study of the process. The authors have participated in a number of studies in which the editing and coding costs were more than 25 percent of the total survey costs.

Planning the editing and coding.   The design of the questionnaire should anticipate the editing and coding work, since the physical arrangement of the form must allow editing and coding space. If the data are to be machine tabulated, codes are assigned to the alternative answers, where possible, and included in the questionnaire format. This is referred to as precoding.

The persons who are to do the editing and coding work should be familiar with field interviewing procedures. If at all possible, they should be exposed to the interviewer training program and participate in the interviewer control work.

Editing and coding procedures must be written and must explain, in detail, how the answers to each question are to be handled. These instructions are prepared only after a sizable number of questionnaires have been studied and considerable thought has been given to what tabulations will be required. The instructions must be specific about the categories to use for general answers and for those answers involving such units of measurement as time, distance, and weight. Examples of how to edit and code the raw data should be included. These examples must be typical and of such a nature as to distinguish between the alternate categories in which answers might be placed.

The instructions pertaining to the handling of difficult questions, for example, open questions, should be discussed in detail and illustrated with examples taken from the particular study. Following this, the editors "practice" on a sample of questionnaires and their work is reviewed critically. The results of the practice work indicate whether it is necessary to revise the editing and coding instructions.

Adequate checks must be built into the editing and coding procedures. These checks are more intensive during the early stages of the work when the editing and coding personnel are still learning their work. Only rarely can the editing and coding instructions anticipate all the problems which will arise. Therefore, the survey leader must maintain constant contact with the work in progress.

All editing is done using a writing instrument with a color other than the one used by the interviewers. Unless this is done there is no way to distinguish between "original" and "edited" data. Editors must not destroy original data by erasure. Rather, where necessary, original entries are deleted by drawing a light line through them.

Making a preliminary check. After receiving all questionnaires from the field, a preliminary check is made before they are subjected to the detailed editing and coding work. Even though the questionnaires have been checked as part of the procedure for controlling the field force, they are rechecked for the following:

1. Adherence to sampling instructions. If the interview was not made with the proper respondent, it is rejected. For example, if the sampling universe consisted of homeowners, only interviews with such respondents are acceptable. Other interviews must be eliminated. To the extent that they can, editors make sure that the sampling requirements have been met. In many cases they can do little since there is no way of determining whether the fieldworker followed precisely the sampling instructions. In random sampling with the interviewers identifying households by a set procedure, it is impossible to determine if the "right" households were selected. But if households were selected from prepared lists, editors can verify the sampling procedure.

2. Legibility. If the handwriting is not clear, editors can do nothing to make the questionnaire usable. Where time permits, questionnaires may be returned to the interviewers for "translation." In any case, editors decide what the recorded information is or what action to take.

3. Completeness. All questions are expected to be answered since "blanks" can mean different things—no answer or refusal; the question was not applicable and, therefore, was not asked; or the interviewer failed to record the answer. When possible, interviewers may be asked to review such "blanks," but it is dangerous to let interviewers insert what they think should have been the entry. Except in unusual situations, interviews are too similar to permit accurate memory of a given one at a later date. Again, editors must decide to tabulate the question as a "no answer," to drop the entire questionnaire, or to attempt to find the correct information.

4. Consistency. Each questionnaire is examined to determine if it is internally consistent. An example of inconsistency would be on a travel questionnaire where the respondent reports not using a car and later, in answer to another question, mentions driving to a particular site. If inconsistencies exist on any questionnaire which cannot be "edited," editors must decide to eliminate the applicable questions from tabulation, to reject the entire questionnaire, or to attempt to reinterview the respondent.

5.   *Understandability.*   Answers to open-ended questions are often difficult to understand. The interviewer may have abbreviated the answer to such an extent that it is not clear what the respondent meant. Or, the answer may have been recorded verbatim and still not be clear. It is often impossible to know what such words as "this" or "it" refer to. It may be that the interviewer can interpret these ambiguous answers, but such a way of correcting the data is dangerous since the interviewer may try to cover up the ambiguities. The editors must determine what shall be done.

Preliminary inconsistency and understandability checks will not reveal all such errors; some may be detected only at the time detailed editing and coding take place. However, a preliminary check often makes it possible to obtain missing data or to clear up other difficulties while the field force is still intact and the survey fresh in the interviewers' minds.

Detecting incorrect answers.   It is sometimes possible to detect incorrect answers when answers to two or more questions are inconsistent. The handling of such answers depends upon the nature of the inconsistency. For example, a survey was conducted to find out what percent of those families owning a television set had purchased it below list price. After finding out whether a television set was in the home, the interviewer asked the brand and model. The answers were verified by observation. A later question asked the price at which the set had been purchased. A number of answers were received which indicated a price *substantially higher than* the known retail list price. Such answers were deleted, since the answer was obviously incorrect and there was no way it could be "edited in." In another study, respondents were asked whether they bought a majority of their groceries at a chain or at an independent store. Later in the questionnaire, they were asked the name of the grocery store they patronized "more than any other." A number of respondents who had answered earlier that they bought primarily from a chain store gave the name of an independent store. After this fact had been verified in the central office (the study covered only the Chicago area, so store type verification was not difficult), the earlier chain store answer was altered to independent.[2]

Completing incomplete answers.   Very little can be done with many incomplete answers. Only where a question ties in with other questions is it

---

[2] Had this study been designed to determine the extent of confusion existing in the consumer's mind about the type (chain versus independent) of store patronized, then no editing problem would have existed. This indicates how the objectives of the study can affect the editing process.

possible to fill in the missing data. For example, a study determined what brands of refrigerators respondents could name without help from the interviewer. When a later question in the study asked what brand of refrigerator the respondent owned, a number of respondents had not mentioned the brand they owned when they were asked the initial brand awareness question. These brands were added to those mentioned in the earlier question, although it could be argued that the association is not precisely the same.

It is impossible to specify rules for handling incorrect and incomplete answers. Each survey is different and the only safe editing rule to follow is that of being conservative. Only where one is absolutely certain as to the intent should the raw data be altered.

Establishing categories

While answers to some questions fall into obvious response categories, there are other questions which are more difficult to tabulate. Dichotomous and multiple choice questions have a specified response category, but open questions can elicit answers which fall into many different, and some unforeseen, response categories. Because of this characteristic the researcher must establish response categories for all open questions. After the completed questionnaires have been carefully edited, the next task is to review the answers to specific questions and to establish meaningful categories which will effectively report the findings of these questions.

The objectives of the survey should serve as the major guide in the selection of tabulation categories. Without reference to these objectives, it is impossible to select the most appropriate categories. For example, a variety of answers would be given in response to the question, *"What do you dislike about the car you drive most frequently?"* The answers to this question might be grouped according to the various parts of the car, such as engine, body, and interior, or according to what these dislikes mean to the respondent, such as inconveniences, discomfort, expense, pride, and fear. These are but two of the many classifications which might be set up. The classification to use depends on which is most relevant to the purpose of the inquiry.

It is extremely difficult to establish categories for data obtained through the use of open-ended questions. This is especially true with exploratory studies, since such studies do not typically start with well-stated hypotheses. The first step in setting categories, regardless of the type of study involved, is to develop a set of working hypotheses that indicate what factors are most relevant. If, for example, researchers are trying to find out why women buy a certain brand of hand lotion, they should first develop a set of hypotheses as to the "why" aspects of the problem. This does not mean that they would not be sensitive to data which suggest other hypotheses, but rather that they would start with some hypotheses as the rationale for the study.

Researchers must also concern themselves with establishing categories which deal satisfactorily with the different dimensions of the problem. In a hand lotion problem, the researchers involved were concerned with the following dimensions: (1) product qualities; (2) specific problems which led respondents to use the particular brand; (3) the image of the product with respect to what types of individuals were thought to use it; (4) what source induced respondents to try the product; (5) the regularity of use by respondents; and (6) the use of the product by other members of the household. Within these generalized dimensions, specific categories were established.

In classifying data with regard to any specific objective, it is essential that the categories established be mutually exclusive and at the same time cover all possible answers. Ideally, each category should contain similar responses so that overall there will be homogeneity *within* categories and differences *between* categories.

Coding individual responses

After categories have been established for those questions which require them, each questionnaire must be reviewed for the purpose of identifying the category into which a particular response falls. For example, assume that the categories of (1) inconvenience, (2) discomfort, (3) expense, and (4) safety were established for the question, *"What do you dislike about the car you drive most frequently?"* The response on one questionnaire may be "the lack of leg room in the rear seat," while the response on another questionnaire may be "the doors can only be locked from the outside with a key." The editor may decide that the first response belongs in the "discomfort" category and the second one in the "inconvenience" category. Codes of "2" and "1" should thus be written in the margins of the respective questionnaires. The editors must review the individual responses to all questions requiring coding and assign each response to a category. Those codes will then be available when the data on the completed questionnaires are to be put onto computer cards or tapes.

As indicated above, the person doing the editing usually does the coding. Because such a person must be familiar with the study, the coding activity is likely to be carried out with a minimum of error. Nevertheless, coding errors do occur, and researchers can best safeguard against such errors by establishing categories which are unambiguous, exhaustive, and nonoverlapping.

Keypunching

Since tabulations can be done either manually or with machines, the researchers will have to decide on which method to use. Both manual and machine methods possess unique advantages and disadvantages. Manual tabulation is applicable only when small samples are used (100 or less) or when only a few complex tabulations are planned. In comparing the two methods (machine versus manual), it is important to remember that machine tabulation requires additional preparatory work—that data have to be keypunched and extensive time may be required to program the operations.

In general, the most important determinant in selecting between the two methods is the number of tabulations to be made. When a large number of questionnaires is involved (100 or more) and each contains many questions, the speed of the electronic machines more than offsets the additional preparatory work required. If retabulations are required, they will be cheaper and faster if the data have been put on cards or tapes at the beginning.

Virtually all studies and certainly all large studies are now machine tabulated. Simple electronic machines are used to sort, count, and perform various arithmetic operations such as adding and subtracting. Computers are used for more sophisticated manipulations. Computers are important for speed and economy and because results are more accurate than work done by hand. "Extensive analysis has shown that the human will make at least 5 errors in 100 hand calculations, making the human at best 95 percent effective. The computer closely approaches 100 percent accuracy (99.99 percent). When an error does occur, it is usually sensed and its presence is indicated to the operator."[3]

In order to tabulate by machine, the data must be put onto computer cards or tapes. The keypunching operation occurs after each of the questionnaires has been edited and coded, and usually it is performed by a person other than one who did the editing and coding. When cards are used, the editor must indicate specifically what position on the card is to be punched for each answer. The keypunch operator's function is simply to convert the specified codes into a number of holes punched in a computer card.

The end result of keypunching is a deck of computer cards. Each respondent is represented by one card (or more, if the questionnaire is lengthy), and each card is coded to a specific questionnaire. One or more *columns* of a card are assigned *to each question,* and a respondent's answer to that question is then indicated by *a punched hole in that column.*

For example, Figure 13–1 shows a computer card set up for use in tabulating a dichotomous question (in column 20), a multiple choice question (in column 40), and an open question (in columns 60 and 61). For example, if a respondent answered "yes" to the question, *"Do you have a driver's license?"* the editor would indicate column 20, row 1 and a hole would be punched in the first row of column 20. The second row of column 20 would be punched if the respondent answered "no." Similarly, the first, second, third, or fourth row, and so on, in column 40 would be punched, depending on how the respondent answered the multiple choice question, *"What make of automobile do you drive?"* Columns 60 and 61 would be

---

[3] Daniel N. Leeson and Donald L. Dimitry, *Basic Programming Concepts and the I.B.M. 1620 Computer* (New York: Holt, Rinehart & Winston, 1962), p. 1.

FIGURE 13–1. Keypunching responses to questions

Column number ⟶	20		40		60	61	
	1		1		1	1	
	2		2		2	2	
			3		3	3	
			4		4	4	
					5	5	
					6	6	
					7	7	
					8	8	
					9	9	
					0	0	

punched to indicate the respondent's answer to the question, *"How many thousands of miles did you drive your automobile last year?"*

In spite of its advantages, machine tabulations do introduce another possible source of error. The keypunch operator may make visual or manual mistakes while transfering the data from questionnaires to punched cards. When using machine tabulations, the researcher should use procedures which minimize errors caused by keypunching. Such procedures consist primarily of having a second keypunch operator punch the same data on a machine which indicates if a punch different from the first one is made.

TABULATING THE DATA

Before tabulation can take place, the plan of analysis must be thought through. A tabulation plan which specifies the precise counts to be obtained must be prepared. Usually the plan consists of setting up dummy tables complete with column and row headings, plus a description of the data to be included. In effect, this means that the researchers must organize and summarize the findings in a manner compatible with the study's objectives and with the "list of needed information" established at the outset of the study.

After the raw data have been fully prepared, the tabulation work can begin. It consists of sorting the data into categories and classes and counting the number of "responses" associated with each. These results are then summarized in order to present the findings in a more compact and more easily understood format.

In the discussions which follow, the three activities of sorting, counting, and summarizing are presented as occurring almost simultaneously. This is due to the fact that these activities do occur together and are difficult to separate. Since those topics are discussed together, the reader should first be reminded of the character and use of summary statistics.

Using summary statistics

In presenting survey findings, researchers frequently employ statistical measures which attempt to typify the data. These are called *summary statistics,* the most common of which are the arithmetic mean, the median, the mode, the range, standard deviations, and percentages. All of these measures can be effectively utilized by researchers reporting study findings, but they can also be misleading if used improperly. It is often forgotten that the various "averages" are summary statistics and only substitutes for more detailed data. In effect, these statistics enable researchers to generalize about the sample surveyed, but they are helpful only if they reflect the sample accurately.

Each summary statistic suffers certain deficiencies when used to describe large bodies of data. For example, two sets of data may have the same mean, but different ranges. Or, they may have the same median, but different standard deviations. Under either of these circumstances, presenting the two sets of data as being similar—based only on their means or medians— could be very misleading. Researchers should remember that summary statistics only "summarize" the data and that presenting "summaries" to the manager can be a disservice if they inadequately describe the data.

Percentages

Because they are a special kind of summary statistic, percentages are discussed separately. *Percentages* are ratios which are highly useful when comparing two or more series of data. Their more common uses are for describing relationships and comparing distributions.

Describing relationships. Often a figure is obtained which has significance only when it is related to another figure. In all sampling situations the number of cases falling into a category is meaningless unless it is related to some particular base. If, for example, 1,000 households are interviewed and it is determined that 642 have a television set, the figure of 642 is more meaningful if it is related to the base of 1,000. By doing so, the figure is transformed into 64.2 percent.

Comparing in relative terms the distribution of two or more series of data. For example, assume the distribution of the sales of Car A and Car B in four separate metropolitan markets shown in Table 13–1. The analyst would have difficulty interpreting the absolute differences in the sales of the two makes of cars, but when relative differences are shown by the use of percentages the distribution pattern of car A versus car B is more clearly seen.

TABLE 13–1. Sales of two cars in four metropolitan areas

Metropolitan area	Car A	Percent	Car B	Percent
A	3,742	21.1	1,596	13.7
B	1,006	5.6	2,711	23.1
C	12,231	69.1	6,201	52.9
D	732	4.2	1,214	10.3
Total	17,701	100.0	11,722	100.0

Misuse of percentages. Confusion often exists in the use of percentages; it is important to describe briefly the more common types of such confusion.

Averaging percentages. Percentages cannot be averaged unless each is weighted by the size of the group from which it is derived. Thus, in most cases, a simple average will not suffice and it is necessary to use a weighted average.

Use of too large percentages. This often defeats the purpose of percentages, which is to simplify. A large percentage is difficult to understand and tends to confuse. If a 1,000 percent increase has been experienced, it is better to describe it as a ten-fold increase.

Using too small a base. Percentages hide the base from which they have been computed. A figure of 60 percent when contrasted with 33 percent would appear to indicate a sizable difference. Yet if there were only five cases in the one category and three in the other, the differences would not be as significant as it had been made to appear through the use of percentages.

Percentage decreases can never exceed 100 percent. This is obvious, but this type of mistake occurs frequently. The higher figure should always be used as the base. For example, if a price were reduced from $1.00 to 25¢ the decrease would be 75 (75/100) percent.

Sorting and counting the data

The sorting and counting of data collected with questionnaires and observation forms can be accomplished in a number of ways. The most simple way is to tabulate responses to *only one question* at a time. This is frequently referred to as univariate tabulation. Another way is to tabulate simultaneously responses to *two or more questions,* which is called bivariate or multivariate tabulation. Both approaches are employed in many marketing research projects today, and both are discussed in the following paragraphs.

Univariate tabulation

Some questions contain information which is so useful that these questions are tabulated individually. These cases usually involve one or more of the following four situations.

Dichotomous or multiple choice questions which allow only one answer. Each of these question types has predetermined response categories which should be established in accord with the overall objectives of the study. As a consequence, the tabulation of responses to such questions is predetermined and consists merely of counting the number of responses falling into each category. Table 13–2 illustrates the two most common

---

TABLE 13–2. Approaches to the tabulation of responses to multiple choice questions

QUESTION: *Are you in favor of, indifferent toward, or opposed to recent Food and Drug Administration attempts to test the long-term health effects of artificial food colorings?*

	Approach A		Approach B
	Number	Percent	Percent
In favor of	55	34.4%	34.4%
Indifferent toward	31	19.4	19.4
Opposed to	74	46.2	46.2
	160	100%	100%
			(Base = 160.)

---

approaches to tabulating the responses to multiple choice questions: (*A*) showing both quantities and percentages for each response category and (*B*) showing percentages for each response category, but only total quantity. The two approaches can be applied to both scale and dichotomous questions as well.

Open question with only one response. As mentioned above, categories must be established for responses to open questions, and individual responses to such questions must be read and coded according to these pre-established categories. If an open question elicits only a single answer, tabulation procedures will be similar to those described in the previous paragraph. An example of such a question is, *"What one characteristic is most important in deciding which brand of aluminum foil you purchase?"* (If the question asked, *"What characteristics are important in deciding which brand of aluminum foil you purchase?"* more than one response would be possible. Tabulating responses to such questions is discussed below.)

"Don't know" and "no answer" responses. Frequently a question will elicit responses which can only be classified as "don't know" or "no

answer" responses.[4] Such responses are even encountered when using multiple choice and dichotomous questions. Researchers should expect to encounter such responses and be prepared to cope with them in the tabulation procedure.

Some projects may contain so few "don't know" and "no answer" responses that they are included only to show complete statistical tables. In other studies, it might not be possible to state what the most prevalent or common answer was if a large number of "don't knows" was received. For example, in the situation shown in Table 13–3 the "don't knows" are so

---

TABLE 13–3. Percent of respondents purchasing television sets at types of outlets

Type of outlet	Percent of respondents
Appliance store	26%
Furniture store	16
Mail-order house	6
Department store	6
Discount house	3
All others	15
Don't know	28
Total	100%

(Base = 231.)

---

numerous as to prevent the analyst from drawing any sound conclusions as to which type of outlet is most important in the purchase of a television set. The data were obtained from the question: *"At which type of outlet did you purchase your TV set?"* (*Check one of the following store types.*) In this illustration, the high percentage of "don't knows" may be due to poor questionnaire construction. Many individuals did not know what was meant by the different outlet terms and, therefore, replied they did not know the type of outlet at which they purchased their television sets.

Legitimate "don't know" answers.   Not all "don't know" answers represent a problem. Such a thing as a legitimate "don't know" can exist if the question is aimed at finding out if a respondent possesses certain information or has made a decision relevant to a certain event. The questions below could produce legitimate "don't know" answers.

What products are advertised on the television program "M*A*S*H"?

What are the names of some automobiles made in England?

Do you plan on buying a new refrigerator in the next twelve months?

---

[4] The contents of this section were suggested by Hans Zeisel, *Say It with Figures*, 5th ed. (New York: Harper & Row, 1968), pp. 40–58.

In these examples, it would be safe to assume that most, if not all, of the "don't know" answers were legitimate. However, in other situations, considerable difficulty is experienced in determining whether the "don't know" answer is a function of the respondent's lack of information or the wording of the question. Thus, a "don't know" received from the question, *"Should Congress vote to broaden the laws concerning financing of congressional and presidential campaigns?"* could have been caused by the respondent not being familiar with current laws, or the respondent not having formulated a definite attitude.

Other reasons for "don't know" answers. In addition to the legitimate and "I'm confused" "don't knows," there are two other types, as follows:

1. Respondents really mean, "I don't want to answer this question" when they say, "I don't know." In questions dealing with personal matters or with socially unacceptable symbols, respondents may evade the necessity of giving an answer by hiding behind a "don't know."

2. Respondents by their "don't know" answer mean "too unimportant to warrant a specific answer." If a question dealing with a subject which the respondent thinks unimportant is asked, some respondents will give a "don't know" answer. It is a natural tendency for some individuals to answer a product comparison question with "I don't know," and then perhaps to add "They're about the same." The interpretation of a "don't know" answer as meaning "of little significance" should be used with caution.

Ways of handling "don't know" answers. There are three ways of handling the illegitimate "don't know" problem—none of which represents a fully satisfactory solution.

1. Distribute the "don't knows" proportionately among the other categories. This is the simplest way of dealing with the "don't know" problem. This procedure assumes that the remainder of the sample (those who gave an answer other than "don't know") will be representative of the universe. This assumption may not be correct, and, therefore, if the extent of the "don't knows" is not shown, the reader may be misled.

2. Show the "don't knows" as a separate category. This is the best procedure since it does not mislead anyone as to what happened.

3. Estimate answers from other data contained in the questionnaire. Occasionally the "don't know" answer can be inferred by studying other information contained in the questionnaire. For example, family income might be estimated by referring to the number of individuals in the family who are working and the occupations of each.[5]

Regardless of what efforts are made, the "don't know" and "no answer" categories will always be present to some degree. The best approach to this problem is to recognize it as an important one and to anticipate it at the time the questionnaire is prepared and the field force selected and trained.

Multiple responses to open and multiple choice questions. Some

---

[5] See the example in Zeisel, *Say It,* pp. 53–55.

open and multiple choice questions allow respondents to give more than one answer. Such questions present a somewhat different tabulation problem because the response percentages need not sum to 100 percent. For example, an open question such as *"What magazines did you read during the past week?"* will result in multiple answers from some respondents. They may be tabulated in four ways depending on the objectives of the study.

Share of respondents. In analyzing answers to the question, *"What magazines did you read during the past week?"* one might be interested in the percent of respondents reading any given magazines during this specified time period. The tabulation might be set up as shown in Table 13–4.

TABLE 13–4. Percentage of persons reading each magazine

Magazine	Percent of persons
1	20.1
2	18.3
3	14.7
4	13.5
5	18.8
6	10.4
All other	23.2
None	9.7
	(Base = 1,810.)

Note that no total is given for the percentage column because it would be meaningless. It obviously exceeds 100 percent because of multiple answers.

Number per respondent. The researcher might also want to know the percentage of persons reading none, one, two, three, and so on, magazines. Table 13–5 shows this information. Note that the percentage column adds to 100 percent because each respondent is counted only once.

TABLE 13–5. Number of magazines read

Number of magazines	Percent of persons
Zero	9.7
1	28.2
2	16.7
3	15.4
4	10.8
5	9.2
6 and over	10.0
Total	100.0
	(Base = 1,810.)

Duplication analysis. The answers to the magazine question could be tabulated to determine what combinations of magazines were read by respondents. Such an analysis would answer the question, *"How many respondents who read magazine 1 also read magazines 2, 3, 4, and so on?"* Such a tabulation is often referred to as a duplication analysis. From this kind of tabulation, the *overlap* or duplication between various magazines is ascertained. The results could help an analyst determine the number of additional or unduplicated respondents who might be reached if other magazines were added to an advertiser's media list.

Distribution of items (answers.) Here the distribution of answers (not respondents) is tabulated. For example, on a radio-brand ownership study, the percent (or share of each brand to the total) would be determined. Table 13–6 presents this type of information. Note that the number of sets

TABLE 13–6. Distribution of radio brands in metropolitan area X (based on replies from 427 respondents)

Brand	Number of sets	Percent of all sets
1	110	18.3
2	93	15.5
3	83	13.8
4	70	11.7
5	48	8.0
6	36	6.0
7	28	4.8
8	21	3.5
All other brands	21	15.2
Made by hand	19	3.2
Total sets	600	100.0

exceeds the number of respondents, since many respondents reported owning two or more.

Bivariate and multivariate tabulation

Frequently, the analysis of data will involve the simultaneous tabulation of responses to two or more questions. All of the points discussed above relative to univariate tabulation apply also to single questions used in a bivariate or multivariate tabulation. That is, before two or more questions are combined in a single analysis, proper attention must be given to the "don't know" and "no answer" responses and to the treatment of the multiple responses questions. After each question has been properly prepared, the tabulation of combinations of questions can be considered. Perhaps the main issue in bivariate and multivariate tabulation is deciding which combinations of questions should be tabulated?

If a questionnaire contains four multiple choice questions, there are six possible combinations of two questions (questions 1 and 2, 1 and 3, 2 and 3 and so on) which can be tabulated simultaneously. With six multiple choice questions, there are 15 possible bivariate tabulations. The number of possible bivariate tabulations increases more than proportionally with the number of questions. In order to determine which combinations of questions to tabulate, researchers should refer to step 2 in the marketing research process—"listing the needed information". That step should be used to identify the tabulations that are needed.

An illustration. The marketing manager of a margarine brand authorizes a study of households which use margarine. An item on the list of needed information is "product consumption patterns by size of household." One question asks consumers to estimate the pounds of margarine consumed by the family in the previous 30 days. Another question records the number of individuals in the household. The needed information is contained in the responses to these two questions.

As part of the tabulation procedure, three household size categories are established—households consisting of one or two individuals, households of three or four individuals, and households of five or more individuals. Four consumption categories are established—nonusers of margarine, light users (fewer than 2 lbs. per month), moderate users (between 2 and 5 lbs. per month), and heavy users (more than 5 lbs. per month). Thus, there are a total of 12 categories of household size and consumption patterns, as illustrated by the left side of Figure 13–2. After the responses are edited and coded, the needed information can be obtained *by counting* the number of questionnaires representing each specific (household size—consumption pattern) combination.

The above is a fairly typical example of a bivariate tabulation—tabulating the combined responses to two questions. Another item on the list of information needed from the margarine survey is one which involves responses to three questions—"margarine consumption patterns broken down by size of household and by income class." Since consumers are asked in the survey to identify their income class, answers to that question can be tabulated in conjunction with the household size and consumption questions referred to above. This has the effect of creating 12 categories of household size and consumption patterns *for each income class*. The right side of Figure 13–2 illustrates these categories for the overly simplified case of only two income classes. In order to obtain this information, it will be necessary *to count* the number of questionnaires falling into each of the 24 (income class—household size—consumption pattern) categories. Since this involves responses to three questions, it is a multivariate tabulation.

If still another item on the list of needed information is "the most favored television program of high income families, broken down by family size and consumption," the number of categories would be further increased. Additional sets of the 12 main categories are needed, one set for each of the tele-

FIGURE 13-2. Bivariate and multivariate tabulations

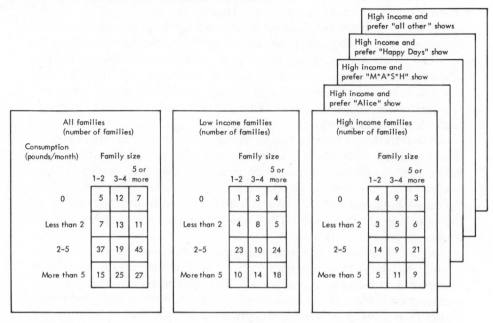

vision programs which high income families rate as "most favored." Such a breakdown of responses to four questions—family size, margarine consumption, income class, favorite television program—might be viewed in the manner suggested by the "layers" of tables portrayed on the right side of Figure 13-2. Obviously, the same type of multivariate tabulation can be performed for "low income families" and "all margaine users."

The purpose of this phase of the tabulation is to obtain the *number of respondents falling into each of the established categories.* Two advantages are gained if the tabulated data are kept as numbers and *not converted to percentages.* First, it is possible to obtain more aggregate tabulations by summing certain less aggregate tabulations. Thus, in Figure 13-2, the tabulation of "all margarine users, broken down by family size and consumption" can be obtained by summing the numbers in equivalent cells in the "high income" and "low income" tabulations. Similarly, "consumption among high income families, broken down by family size" can be obtained by summing the tabulations broken down by favorite television show, that is, by summing the tabulations for the "Alice" show with those of the "M*A*S*H" show with those of the "Happy Days" show with those of "all other" favorite television shows.

The second advantage of retaining the *number* of respondents falling into each of the established categories is that such data allow the researchers *to create other tabulations easily.* For example, if the researcher were interested in "family-size differences of heavy margarine users, broken down by income classes," Figure 13–2 shows that the number of respondents falling into those categories are (5, 11, 9) and (10, 14, 18) for the two income classes, respectively. Similarly, if the researcher were interested in knowing if the favorite television programs of high income heavy users differ from the favorite television programs of high income moderate users, those data are easily obtained from Figure 13–2. Still other tabulations can be obtained from Figure 13–2 if they are based upon one or more family-size categories, one or more consumption patterns, one or more income classes, and one or more favorite television programs.

The above discussion demonstrates how only four questions can result in a large number of tables. As more questions are added, the number of possible tables increases more than proportionally. This presents a frequently encountered marketing research problem; namely, with a large questionnaire it is possible to develop literally thousands of tables, especially if the data can be tabulated by machine. When large numbers of tables are prepared, many of them contain little or no relevant information; consequently, they tend to have a confounding rather than an enlightening effect. Thus, if tabulations are to be done on a machine, the researcher should plan very carefully which bivariate and multivariate tabulations are to be made. Only those which will yield information in the "list of needed information" should be tabulated initially. If desirable, other tabulations can be performed later.

Computer program.   No reference to either manual or machine tabulation has been made in the above discussion because the comments are equally applicable to both methods of tabulation. However, Appendix D presents and describes a simple SPSS computor program which can be used to perform univariate and multivariate tabulations of the type discussed above. Readers interested in the details of that computer program are referred to that appendix.

SUMMARY

The analysis function is divided into five parts: (1) ordering the data into meaningful categories, (2) summarizing the data contained in the categories, (3) determining whether significant differences exist between categories, (4) explaining "why" differences exist, and (5) making recommendations. The first step covers the editing, coding, and tabulation of the data.

The purpose of editing is to eliminate errors in the raw data prior to coding and tabulation. This requires uniform handling of incomplete and incorrect answers. Editing instructions should be prepared carefully and the personnel assigned to this work trained thoroughly. Written editing instructions should explain how to handle each question. Another part of the editing process consists of establishing mutually exclusive and exhaustive categories for the raw data. In doing this the analyst must consider the objectives of the study.

Coding is the process whereby the data are assigned numerical designations so that they may more easily be fitted into the appropriate categories. Coding is necessary where machine tabulation is used.

Tabulation consists of counting the number of cases which fall into the established categories. Tabulation may be accomplished using manual or machine methods. Both possess unique advantages and disadvantages. Machine tabulation is preferable when a large number of questionnaires is involved and where complex tabulations are planned.

CASE 13–1
INTERNATIONAL HARVESTER COMPANY (B)

International Harvester is a manufacturer of trucks, farm machinery and construction equipment. Until recently, the truck line included a number of pickup trucks, a heavy-duty station wagon (the Travelall), and all-purpose vehicles (the Scout II travel top and pickup truck) which were on-and-off highway vehicles with part-time four-wheel drive. Of all these vehicles, only the Scout II travel top (hereafter referred to only as the Scout) was still in the line. All the other vehicles had been discontinued and replaced by a Scout II station wagon (the Traveler) and a Scout II pickup (the Terra). Both of these new vehicles had a longer wheelbase than the Scout—118 inches compared with 100 inches. Both were also available with four-wheel drive.

Because of the significant changes made to this line of vehicles, management asked an independent marketing research firm, Marketing Analysts, Inc., to undertake a study which could help International Harvester identify the optimal marketing strategy to use on the Scout, Traveler and Terra. Management was especially interested in identifying (*a*) those segments of the market with the highest probability of purchasing the new line, and (*b*) a creative advertising strategy which would position the line optimally.

Marketing Analysts, Inc. undertook a three phase research project utilizing the members of a large consumer panel which they maintained. This panel consisted of approximately 100,000 households which had agreed to cooperate in research projects undertaken by the firm. In the first phase of the study, a mail questionnaire was used to screen these households in order to locate qualified prospects for the three vehicles. International Harvester was especially interested in panelists who owned the following types of vehicles—a Scout, other brands of all-purpose vehicles, heavy-duty station wagons, large station wagons, pickups, and medium and small station wagons. Qualified prospects were owners of these six types of vehicles who also reported in the first phase of the study that they were "likely" to buy an all-purpose vehicle or pickup within the next few years. More than eight thousand such respondents were identified, including both those who used their vehicles for personal use and those who used their vehicles for business use.

In phase two of the research, three hundred qualified respondents were mailed information, line drawings and pictures of International Harvester's vehicles (disguised) and competing vehicles (undisguised). Later, the respondents were interviewed in depth over the telephone to obtain their reactions to the International Harvester vehicles. The respondents' reactions were recorded verbatim, and these were then studied to identify themes which might be considered for use as creative strategies in advertising the new line. Four potential themes were identified: outdoor life (the vehicle for real outdoorsmen); for women too (a vehicle that women enjoy too); all family use/all purpose use (the vehicle for all the family/for all purposes); self-reliant complete life (the vehicle for living life as it should be lived, both on- and off-road).

Six groups of qualified respondents were selected for the third phase of the study—each group consisting of owners of one of the six types of vehicles used to identify qualified respondents. These respondents were mailed information, specifications, line drawings and pictures of the International Harvester vehicles and competing vehicles. Each of the six groups was randomly split into four sub-groups. One, and only one, of the four creative advertising themes identified in phase two of the study was sent to the respondents in a subgroup. That is, one subgroup was given information indicating that the International Harvester vehicles were for people who enjoyed outdoor activities, a second subgroup was given information indicating that the International Harvester vehicles would be enjoyed by women too, and so on. In all, there were 24 subgroups, based upon six types of vehicle ownership and four themes. In addition, half of each subgroup was given information that the price of the International Harvester vehicles was on a par with competitive vehicles, while the other half was informed that prices would be slightly higher than competitive vehicles.

Approximately 2,400 respondents participated in the third phase of the study. After reading the materials sent to them, respondents filled out a questionnaire designed to measure their reaction to both the International Harvester vehicles and the competing vehicles. Respondents were also asked to identify (*a*) the vehicles they found most appealing, (*b*) the vehicles which they'd go see at a dealership, and (*c*) the one vehicle they'd be most likely to purchase. These three questions were the main ones used when the survey results were tabulated. The responses to them were combined with equal weight and used as a single criterion for evaluating each subgroup's reaction to the advertising theme to which it had been exposed. This criterion was called the advertising theme's "basic appeal". For example, if the findings from one subgroup were that 30 percent reported they found the Scout to be one of the most appealing vehicles, that 20 percent reported they would go to a dealer to see it, and that 10 percent reported it to be the one vehicle they'd be most likely to purchase, the advertising theme which that subgroup was exposed to would be given a "basic appeal" of 60 (30+20+10) on the Scout.

From past sales records, International Harvester also knew that certain demographic groups and geographic markets were above-average buyers and users of all-purpose vehicles. Thus, states in the South, the Southwest and Rocky Mountain regions were considered prime markets, as was California. Certain types of households were considered to be prime prospects: households with annual incomes in excess of $20,000; rural nonfarm households; households in cities of less than 50,000 inhabitants; and suburban residents of larger cities. International Harvester also wished to know how these prime markets and prime prospects reacted to the four advertising themes.

Marketing Analysts, Inc. tabulated the "basic appeal" of the four advertising themes for each of the three International Harvester vehicles, for both the total sample and for "prime markets and prospects" (see Table 1). The "basic appeal" of the three International Harvester vehicles among different commercial and personal use market segments was also tabulated (see Table 2). Similar tabulations were made for different geographic regions (Table 3) and different demographic classes (Table 4). The effects of the two different price level treatments on the reactions of respondents was also tabulated (Table 5).

TABLE 1. "Basic appeal" of four advertising themes

Vehicle and sample	Advertising theme			
	Outdoor life	For women too	All family/ all purpose	Self-reliant complete life
Scout				
Total sample 53		65	51	49
Prime markets/prospects 51		69	55	50
Traveler				
Total sample 78		92	71	76
Prime markets/prospects 72		90	73	79
Terra				
Total sample 82		76	68	71
Prime markets/prospects 87		77	64	69

TABLE 2. "Basic appeal" of vehicles to different users

	Basic appeal of this vehicle to specified user segments		
	Scout	*Traveler*	*Terra*
Commercial use segments			
Farm	43	82	44
Construction	41	83	64
White-collar services	54	67	137
Blue-collar services	36	57	85
Wholesale/retail	38	71	83
Full-size pickup	44	71	61
Other pickup	72	72	92
Personal-use segments			
Intermediate, large station wagon owners	34	62	118
Heavy-duty station wagon owners	50	86	59
Car, station wagon owners intending to buy all-purpose vehicle, pickup, heavy-duty station wagon	71	101	53
All-purpose vehicle owner	82	95	112
Car, small station wagon owner	50	81	85
Average "basic appeal" of all four advertising themes to the total sample	54	79	74

TABLE 3. "Basic appeal" of vehicles to different geographic regions

	Basic appeal of this vehicle to specified geographic regions		
	Scout	*Traveler*	*Terra*
Geographic region			
Rocky Mountain	67	79	69
South, Southwest	64	71	76
California	63	89	81
New England	40	87	98
Middlewest	53	72	68
Other	44	91	73
Average "basic appeal" for all four advertising themes to the total sample	54	79	74

TABLE 4. "Basic appeal" of vehicles to different demographic classes

	Basic appeal of this vehicle to specified demographic classes		
	Scout	Traveler	Terra
Live in			
City of over 100,000	57	78	84
City of 50–100,000	55	100	84
City under 50,000	51	77	86
Suburb of major city	58	76	83
Rural, nonfarm	62	80	70
Farm	42	76	53
Annual income			
$20,000 or over	46	75	74
$15,000–19,999	59	82	73
$12,000–14,999	47	81	83
Under $12,000	71	83	70
Age			
Under 35	62	80	81
35–44	51	76	74
45–54	59	78	73
55 or over	49	84	72
Sex			
Men	54	80	71
Women	54	76	98
Average "basic appeal" for all four advertising themes to the total sample	54	79	74

TABLE 5. "Basic appeal" of vehicles to different price levels

	Basic appeal of this vehicle at different price levels		
Price level	Scout	Traveler	Terra
Lower price	50	74	79
Higher price	60	86	70
Average "basic appeal" for all four advertising themes to the total sample	54	79	74

What advertising theme(s) should International Harvester use for its vehicles?

Toward which markets and prospects should International Harvester direct its advertising and marketing efforts?

What additional tabulations, if any, should be performed prior to making recommendations?

Case 13–2
THE McCORMICK COMPANY

Kathy Braun, a marketing research analyst for The McCormick Company, had just completed a revision of a questionnaire she was planning to use in a field study involving personal interviews with approximately 200 respondents. The questionnaire had been pretested, revised, and pretested again. She felt that the latest version of the questionnaire (see Exhibit 1) would gather the information that was needed.

The McCormick Company was in the process of introducing a new fabric softener, Soft and Fluffy, which could be used in any kind of washing machine. The introduction was on a market-by-market basis, as permitted by the build-up of production capacity and the availability of the cash needed for introducing Soft and Fluffy into the next market. Soft and Fluffy was currently being introduced into a medium-sized city in the southeast portion of the United States. Advertising support for Soft and Fluffy was a "normal" level of daytime television commercials and newspaper advertisements. The marketing program introducing the new product also included a distribution of free samples to approximately one-half of the households in the city. The questionnaire being designed would be used in the next four to six weeks in a field study the objective of which was to measure the effectiveness of the free sampling program then being used in the city where Soft and Fluffy was being introduced.

After having reviewed the revised questionnaire once again, Ms. Braun felt that its use would result in accurate measures of awareness (using both unaided recall and aided recall) of Soft and Fluffy, of trial of Soft and Fluffy, and of adoption or intention to adopt Soft and Fluffy. These measures would be obtained from respondents who had not received the free sample, as well as from those who had. The questionnaire also included a question designed to measure how awareness was influenced by the free sampling, relative to other factors. By identifying trial and adoption among respondents whose awareness was influenced by free sampling and comparing those figures with trial and adoption among respondents who had not received the free sample, it would be possible to determine the effectiveness of the free sampling.

Ms. Braun then turned to the task of setting up tabulation and analysis procedures to be used on the completed questionnaires when they were returned from the field. She decided that she had to do two things. First, she had to develop step-by-step procedures which would summarize the responses to various questions and combinations of questions, in a manner which would allow her and the McCormick management to understand how effective the free sampling program had been. Second, she had to design dummy tables and charts which would be used in presenting the survey results to management. That is, she would have to design tables and charts with row and column headings which were specified both by name and units.

Where necessary, she would have to describe the data which would be contained in the various cells in the tables and charts. These charts would have to be self-explanatory, and clearly portray to management the key information showing how effective the free sampling program had been.

EXHIBIT 1

Good (morning, afternoon, evening—Ma'm, Madam, Sir). I represent The McCormick Company and am doing a survey on the use of certain laundry products. May I speak to the lady of the home? (Respondent acknowledges.) Could you please take a few minutes of your time to answer some questions? Thank you.

1. Do you do your own laundry, or do you have it sent out?
   _____ Do own laundry _____ Sent out (GO TO Q. 12.)
   _____ Someone else does laundry (ASK FOR THAT PERSON)

2. Do you use a fabric softener when you do laundry?
   _____ Yes, or sometimes _____ No (GO TO Q. 12.)

3. What brand or brands of fabric softener have you used most often in the last month? (ASK AS AN OPEN QUESTION.)
   _____ Soft and Fuffy
   _____ Other (GO TO Q. 7.) _____ Don't know (GO TO Q. 7.)

4. How did you first become aware of Soft and Fluffy? (ASK AS AN OPEN QUESTION.)
   _____ Rec'd free sample _____ Saw in store
   _____ Saw ads _____ Neighbors _____ Other

4a. (ASK ONLY IF "REC'D FREE SAMPLE" NOT INDICATED IN Q. 4.)
   Did you receive a free sample of Soft and Fluffy?
   _____ Yes _____ No (GO TO Q. 6.)

5. Are you still using the free sample or have you purchased the package currently being used?
   _____ Still using free sample _____ Purchased package being used

6. Do you plan to continue using Soft and Fluffy in the future?
   _____ Yes (GO TO Q. 12.) _____ No (GO TO Q. 6a.)
   _____ Maybe, or don't know (GO TO Q. 6a.)

6a. Why? _____
   _____
   _____ (GO TO Q. 12.)

7. Do you know of any new brands of fabric softeners on the market? (ASK AS AN OPEN QUESTION.)
   _____ Soft and Fluffy (GO TO Q. 8.) _____ Other, or none (GO TO Q. 7a.)

7a. Here is a list of fabric softener brands. (HAND LIST TO RESPONDENT.)
   Can you tell me if you recognize any new brands on this list?
   _____ Soft and Fluffy (GO TO Q. 8.) _____ Other, or none (GO TO Q. 9.)

EXHIBIT 1 (continued)

8. How did you first become aware of Soft and Fluffy? (ASK AS AN OPEN QUESTION.)

_____ Rec'd free sample   _____ Saw ad
        (GO TO Q. 10.)   _____ Saw in store
                                _____ From neighbor } (GO TO Q. 9.)
                                _____ Other

9. Did you receive a free sample of Soft and Fluffy—a new brand of fabric softener recently placed on the market?
    _____ Yes _____ No, or don't know

10. Have you tried using Soft and Fluffy?
    _____ Yes _____ No (GO TO Q. 12.)

11. Why did you discontinue using Soft and Fluffy? (ASK AS AN OPEN QUESTION.)

12. Classification
    Name _____
    Address _____
    Size of household _____
    Number of children _____
    Frequency of purchase _____
    Size of purchase _____
    Frequency of wash _____
    Income: $25K+ $15K–25K   Less than $15K   (CIRCLE ONE.)
    Education of household head: more than 16 years   16 years
        12–16 years   12 years   Less than 12 years   (CIRCLE ONE.)
    Age of respondent _____ (INTERVIEWER ESTIMATE.)
    (INTERVIEWER THANK RESPONDENT.)

Develop a step-by-step procedure which Ms. Braun can use to tabulate and summarize the data which will be contained in the completed questionnaires.

Design the dummy tables and charts which should be used to present the survey findings to The McCormick Company management.

Explain how you would get the data which would be contained in each table and chart.

Explain how you would use each of the tables and charts you design.

14

Data analysis I: Tests of significance—Sampling statistics, Chi-square, and analysis of variance

When the research data have been organized, summarized, and presented in tables and charts, the researchers will proceed with an interpretation of the findings. Since the data were obtained from a sample rather than from a complete census, researchers must ask whether the differences observed between two categories represent true differences found in the universe, or whether they could have resulted by chance due to the use of a sample.

For example, data obtained from a large sample might show that 44 percent of the households in New England serve cheese one or more times a week, but that only 39 percent of southern households do so. The researcher may well ask whether there really is a difference in cheese consumption between New England and the South, or whether the observed 5 percent difference can be attributed to sampling variations.

The above example represents a situation commonly encountered by researchers after data from a survey have been tabulated. Do the observed differences represent true differences, or could they have occurred by chance because of the variation possible when a sample is used? If it is highly unlikely that the observed differences could have occurred by chance—say, less than 1 chance in 10 or less than 5 chances in 100—researchers may decide that the differences are significant differences. If the chance of the observed differences occurring because of sampling variations is as high as 1 out of 6 or 1 out of 3, researchers may feel that the observed differences could easily be chance occurrences only and, therefore, should not be judged as significant differences. In judging the significance of differences, researchers must decide on the level of chance they will accept.

A variety of statistical methods has been developed to help researchers test the significance of differences in sample data. This chapter discusses some of the more commonly used tests and the situations to which they apply. The procedures used in testing the significance of observed differences require an understanding of standard error and confidence limits, both of which have been discussed in the sampling chapters. It is assumed here that the reader has a working understanding of these terms and concepts.

Categorical and continuous variables

Research data frequently include variables which are either categorical or continuous.

Categorical variables are ones which are not quantifiable, or which can only be measured in terms of classes or categories, or which are more conveniently measured in categories than on a continuum. A respondent's sex (male/female) and voter status (registered to vote/not registered to vote) are two examples of variables which can only be measured in categories. A person's readership of a magazine (never reads *Time*/occasionally reads *Time*/regularly reads *Time*) is more conveniently measured in categories than on a continuum. A household's annual income is a variable which can be measured on a continuum. However, it may be more convenient to measure this variable categorically (less than $10,000/$10–25,000/more than $25,000).

Continuous variables are ones which can be quantified or measured on a continuum, rather than in classes or categories only. A respondent's age (in years) and the number of miles he or she drives annually are two examples of continuous variables. Percentages are also continuous variables, as are a household's annual expenditures on all types of insurance and the pounds of coffee consumed annually.[1]

It is important to recognize the difference between continuous and categorical data, because the first method of analysis discussed in this chapter (sampling statistics) applies only to continuous variables, while the other two methods discussed in this chapter (Chi-square analysis and analysis of variance) apply only to data which have been placed into categories.

SAMPLING STATISTICS

Testing differences between two percentages. A common research finding reports the percentage of a group of respondents who behave or think in a certain way—such as owning a second automobile or feeding their pets a semi-moist food. Such findings lead researchers to ask whether one group of respondents behaves or thinks differently than some other group—

---

[1] In terms of the types of scales discussed in Chapter 9, categorical variables are equivalent to nominal scales, and continuous variables are equivalent to interval scales. Ordinal scales, which result in ranked data, represent a different type of variable which is not treated in this chapter.

large families versus small families, those with pedigreed pets versus those with mongrels, and so on. These are situations in which researchers are likely to observe differences in the sample data and to inquire whether these differences reflect true differences in the universe (that is, are the differences significant?).

The two situations to which sampling statistics are most commonly applied involve comparisons of (1) an observed percentage with an hypothesized percentage or (2) observed percentages in two different subpopulations. These are illustrated in the following examples.

Comparing observed percentage with hypothesized percentage. The Holmes Food Company, a large manufacturer of grocery products, is interested in acquiring a manufacturer of bottled meat sauces, the MS Company. The MS Company claims that its brand is used by 30 percent of the households using bottled meat sauces. To check the validity of this claim, the Holmes Food Company selects a large random sample of all U.S. households. The results show 920 households using bottled meat sauces, of which 25 percent (230 households) use the MS brand. Holmes would like to know if the difference—between the observed 25 percent and the hypothesized 30 percent—is large enough to conclude that the MS brand's usage rate is less than 30 percent? If it is, they may reevaluate their interest in the MS Company.

In order to answer this question, it is useful to assume that the hypothesis is true—that is, 30 percent of the bottled-meat-sauce-using households do use the MS brand—and to ask how probable it is, under this assumption, for a random sample to show that 25 percent of the 920 such households use the MS brand. If a 25 percent finding could be easily obtained when a sample of 920 units is drawn from a universe with a mean of 30 percent, there would be little reason to doubt the claim that the MS brand has a 30 percent market share. On the other hand, if the chance of getting a result as small as 25 percent is an unlikely one, researchers will conclude that the difference between the observed level (25 percent) and the hypothesized level (30 percent) is a significant one. They would, then, reject the MS Company's claim that the MS brand is used by as many as 30 percent of the households using bottled meat sauces.

The researchers' conclusion hinges on the chance, or probability, of obtaining a 25 percent sample result if the true universe share is 30 percent. The following analysis shows how often a sample result of 25 percent or smaller could be expected if the true universe percentage were 30 percent. It is based on the standard error of a percentage, which can be calculated as shown below.

$$s_p = \sqrt{\frac{pq}{n}}$$

$$= \sqrt{\frac{(30)(70)}{920}} = \sqrt{\frac{2100}{920}} = \sqrt{2.2826}$$

$$= 1.51\%$$

where

s_p = Standard error of a percentage.

p = Hypothesized percentage of the universe with the characteristic being studied.

$q = (100\% - p)$.

n = Size of sample.

Having calculated the standard error (s_p), researchers can translate the observed difference (between the hypothesized 30 percent and the sample result of 25 percent) into an equivalent number of standard errors by using the relationship

$$Z = \frac{\text{hypothesized \% } - \text{ observed \%}}{s_p} = \frac{30\% - 25\%}{1.51\%} = 3.3$$

where Z is the observed difference expressed in numbers of standard errors. Thus, with a sample size of 920, the observed difference is equal to 3.3 standard errors. How likely is it that a difference this large could have occurred by chance due to sampling variation?

In this example, Holmes is interested primarily in knowing if the MS brand has *as much as* 30 percent usage among meat sauce users. If usage is larger than 30 percent, they will acquire the company regardless of how much larger than 30 percent the usage actually is. If usage is less than 30 percent, they may not do so. Consequently, Holmes is only interested in testing findings *on one side*—the lower side—of the assumed 30 percent usage level. The one-sided nature of this testing causes it to be referred to as a "one-tail test."

A table of the area under the normal curve can help the researcher determine if a difference of $Z = 3.3$ could have occurred by chance. Such a table is shown in Appendix A. Specifically, it is the area under *one tail* of this curve which is representative of the observed difference and the possibility that it might have occurred by chance. The third column of Appendix A shows the area under one tail of the normal curve for different values of Z. It shows that an observed difference equivalent to 3.3 or more standard errors can occur by chance only about once in 2,000 times.[2] Confronted with this result, the Holmes Food Company would almost certainly conclude that the MS brand did not have 30 percent usage among households using bottled meat sauces. In arriving at this conclusion, however, Holmes should recognize that it is not possible to be 100 percent certain that the MS brand's share is not as large as 30 percent—there is a chance of one in 2,000 that it is.

Special note should be given to the role of sample size in the above

---

[2] The appendix shows that only 0.05 percent of the sample means will be 3.3 or more standard errors below the hypothesized universe mean. This is equivalent to a chance of 5 out of 10,000 or 1 out of 2,000.

analysis. The key factor is a standard error of only 1.51 percent, which is due to the large sample size of 920. If the sample size had been only 100, the standard error would have been 4.58 percent. As a result, Z would equal 1.09 [(30–25)/4.58)] and the third column of Appendix A shows that the chance of getting a sample result of 25 percent or smaller would be about one in seven.[3] Under such conditions, the observed difference might not be considered "significant" by the Holmes Food Company managers. Instead, they might view the result as evidence supporting the claim that the MS brand enjoys about 30 percent usage. This illustrates that the determination of "significant differences" is a subjective judgment, and that it can be influenced by the size of the sample used when obtaining the data.

Comparing two observed percentages.   At times researchers will observe two different percentages and be concerned with the significance of the difference between them. Although the principles underlying the analysis of two observed percentages are similar to those described above, the procedure is slightly different. Consider the following example.

The Snack Company decided to use a test market to evaluate the effectiveness of a special coupon promotion. In a random sample of 100 households taken *before* the promotion, 18 percent reported that they had tried at least one of the company's products. A random sample of 120 different households in the test market was taken two months *after* the special coupon promotion had been completed. Twenty-two percent of these households reported using at least one of the company's products. Did the special promotion bring about a real increase in product trial, or could the observed difference be attributed to the use of sample data?

As in the previous example, the first step in evaluating the significance of the observed difference is the calculation of the standard error. The standard error formula for the difference between two sample percentages is

$$s_{\text{difference}} = \sqrt{s_a^2 + s_b^2}$$

where

$s_{\text{difference}}$ = Estimated standard error of the difference.

s_a = Estimated standard error of percentage a.

s_b = Estimated standard error of percentage b.

The formula for the estimated standard error of a percentage is

$$s_p = \sqrt{\frac{pq}{n}}.$$

Substituting this formula into the previous equation results in:

---

[3] The appendix shows that about 14 percent of sample means will be 1.09 or more standard errors away from the hypothesized universe mean. This is equivalent to about 1 chance in 7.

$$S_{\text{difference}} = \sqrt{\left(\sqrt{\frac{p_a q_a}{n_a}}\right)^2 + \left(\sqrt{\frac{p_b q_b}{n_b}}\right)^2}$$

$$= \sqrt{\frac{p_a q_a}{n_a} + \frac{p_b q_b}{n_b}}$$

$$= \sqrt{\frac{(18)(82)}{100} + \frac{(22)(78)}{120}}$$

$$= \sqrt{29.06} = 5.4\%.$$

As before, the observed difference can be translated into an equivalent number of standard errors using the relationship

$$Z = \frac{\text{after } \% - \text{before } \%}{S_{\text{difference}}} = \frac{22\% - 18\%}{5.4\%} = 0.74$$

where Z is as defined earlier.

The researcher must now determine whether an observed difference of approximately 0.75 standard errors could have occurred by chance. Column 2 of Appendix A shows that there is a two-out-of-three chance that the observed difference will fall within plus or minus 1 standard error if there is no difference between the *before* and *after* samples. Since the observed difference in this case is less than 1 standard error, this result could easily have occurred by chance due to sampling variation. Therefore, evidence does not allow researchers to conclude that the observed difference is significant. While there is some chance that the special coupon promotion caused a change in the percentage of households that had used the Snack Company's products, the probability is only about 0.50 that this is the case.

As before, the reader should note the effect of sample size. In this case, if both the *before* and *after* samples number 1,600, the standard error of the difference would be about 1.4, and Z would be about 2.8 [(22 − 18)/1.4] standard errors. Column 2 of Appendix A shows that only about 0.52 percent (100.00–99.48) of the sample results will be as far away as 2.8 or more standard error from the universe mean. Thus, if samples of 1,600 had been used, there would be only a 52/100 of 1 percent chance that the difference between the two samples (Z = 2.8) could have occurred by chance due to sampling variation. This would almost certainly cause the researcher to conclude that the two percentages reflect real differences; that is, the product trial rate was significantly increased as a result of the special promotion.

Testing differences between continuous variables.   When survey results are summarized as percentages, the foregoing formulas are used to calculate the estimated standard error. When survey data are continuous variables *other* than percentages, the analysis procedures must be modified slightly. For example, the number of miles a respondent drives annually, or a household's annual expenditures on all types of insurance or entertainment are data which might be collected in a marketing research project. When researchers have such data and wish to test the significance of the differences observed between two groups, they must estimate the standard error of the mean $(s_{\bar{x}})$ *from the sample data* using the relationship

$$s_{\bar{x}} = \frac{s}{\sqrt{n}}$$

where

$s_{\bar{x}} =$ Estimated standard error of the mean.
$s =$ Standard deviation of the sample.[4]
$n =$ Number of observations in the sample.

For example, a survey of the monthly milk consumption of 50 households showed one household consumed 8 quarts; another, 14 quarts; another, 7 quarts; still another, 18 quarts; and so on. Average consumption for all 50 households was 10 quarts per month. The standard deviation of the sample (s) was

$$s = \sqrt{\frac{(8-10)^2 + (14-10)^2 + (7-10)^2 + (18-10)^2 + \cdots}{50-1}} = 2.8 \text{ quarts.}$$

Using the formula in the above paragraph, the estimated standard error of the mean $(s_{\bar{x}})$ was calculated as

$$s_{\bar{x}} = \frac{2.8}{\sqrt{50}} = \frac{2.8}{7.07} = 0.39 \text{ quarts.}$$

This estimated standard error is used in the same manner as s_p and $s_{\text{difference}}$ were used in the two foregoing examples.

Using sampling statistics when the samples are small

When a large sample is taken—say, of 100 or more respondents—a table of the area under a normal curve (similar to that of Appendix A) is used to estimate whether the sample results could easily have occurred by chance. Such a table is not accurate when small samples are used to collect the data.

If the sample is small—say, 30 or fewer respondents—the results can be easily affected by atypical items. Thus, the theory of normal distribution cannot be used, since it is based on a sample sufficiently large to balance out the extreme cases. The means of small samples follow the t distribution. This distribution increases the number of standard errors needed to obtain a certain level of confidence.

Table 14–1, an abbreviated table of the t distribution, can be used to illustrate. The table shows that when samples are very large, researchers use 1.64 standard errors for a 90 percent confidence level, 1.96 standard errors for a 95 percent confidence level, and 2.58 standard errors for a 99 percent confidence level. (These figures can be confirmed in Appendix A.) If the

---

[4] The standard deviation formula is presented in footnote 8, Chapter 10.

TABLE 14–1. Number of standard errors needed for selected confidence levels and sample sizes (n)

n	Confidence level		
	90%	95%	99%
5	2.02	2.57	4.03
10	1.81	2.23	3.17
15	1.75	2.13	2.95
20	1.72	2.09	2.84
25	1.71	2.06	2.79
30	1.70	2.04	2.75
∞	1.64	1.96	2.58

Source: Rounded values from R. A. Fisher and F. Yates, *Statistical Tables for Biological, Agricultural and Medical Research* (New York: Hafner Publishing Co., 1963).

sample size is small, a larger number of standard errors is needed for a given level of confidence. Thus, if the sample size is 20 ($n = 20$), 1.72 standard errors are needed for a 90 percent confidence level (instead of only 1.64), and 2.09 standard errors are needed for a 95 percent confidence level (instead of only 1.96). Table 14–1 shows that as the sample size gets even smaller, the number of standard errors needed for a given level of confidence grows even larger. Whenever the sample is a small one, researchers should use a table of the *t* distribution rather than the normal distribution.[5]

DIFFERENCES BETWEEN SETS OF DATA

The foregoing discussions were concerned with the significance of differences between only two numbers which were summary measures of continuous variables. Frequently, marketing research data are tabulated in column and row form, where the different columns and rows represent different categories. Researchers often make comparisons of the numbers they see in the different columns, rows, and tables, that is, which they see in the different categories. When researchers have such categorical data, they can use statistical tests of significance especially designed for sets of data to determine whether the two sets of data are really different, or whether the differences could easily be attributed to sampling variation. The two tests most com-

---

[5] More detailed discussions can be found in Thomas H. Wonnacott and Ronald J. Wonnacott, *Introductory Statistics for Business and Economics*, 2d ed. (New York: John Wiley & Sons, 1977); Lawrence Lapin, *Statistics for Modern Business Decisions*, 2d ed. (New York: Harcourt Brace Jovanovich, Inc., 1978); John E. Freund and Frank J. Williams, *Elementary Business Statistics: The Modern Approach*, 3d ed. (Englewood Cliffs, N.J.: Prentice-Hall, Inc., 1977). Readers interested in computerized versions of these statistical methods will want to be aware of the SPSS and BMD packaged programs. See N. H. Nie, C. H. Hull, J. G. Jenkins, K. Steinbrenner, and D. H. Bent, *Statistical Package for the Social Sciences*, 2d ed. (New York: McGraw-Hill, 1975); and W. J. Dixon and M. B. Brown, *Biomedical Computer Programs, P-Series*, (Berkeley: University of California Press, 1979).

monly used for these purposes are the *Chi-square analysis* and the *analysis of variance.*[6]

Chi-square analysis: Testing differences between two sets of data

The objective of Chi-square analysis is to determine if the differences observed in two sets of data can be attributed to sampling variation. If the Chi-square analysis indicates that the observed difference could easily have occurred by chance, then the observed difference is considered likely to be the result of sampling variation. If the analysis indicates that the chance of the difference occurring because of sampling variation is very small, then the observed difference is considered likely to be a real one, and the two sets of data are judged to have come from two different populations.

A Chi-square analysis can be used when the data satisfy four conditions.

1.   There must be two observed sets of sample data *or* one observed set of sample data and one hypothetical set of data. Typically these data sets are in table form (*R* rows and *C* columns), or in frequency distribution form (one row and *C* columns, or *R* rows and one column).
2.   The two sets of data must be based on the same sample size.
3.   Each cell in the data contains an observed or hypothetical count (not a percentage or proportion) which is five or larger.
4.   The different cells in a row or column can represent either categorical variables or continuous variable data which have been placed into classes or categories.

The application of Chi-square analysis involves (1) calculating a statistic (called the Chi-square statistic) which *summarizes the differences* between the two sets of data, (2) determining the degrees of freedom associated with the data set, and (3) using those two values and a table of the Chi-square distribution to determine if the calculated Chi-square statistic falls within the range which could easily have occurred by chance due to sampling variation. If it does not, the differences between the two sets of data are judged to be significant. The examples below will illustrate this three-step procedure for some common applications.

Comparing two frequency distributions. Assume that in the past a large survey showed that households could be classified on the basis of cottage cheese consumption as follows: 25 percent heavy consumers, 30 percent moderate consumers, 20 percent light consumers, and 25 percent nonconsumers. In an attempt to determine if consumption patterns were changing, the Howard Company sampled 1,000 households nationwide. This study showed that 220 households were heavy consumers of cottage cheese, 270 were moderate consumers, 230 were light consumers, and 280 were nonsumers. Table 14–2 shows that most recently observed data (left column),

---

[6] Ibid.

TABLE 14–2. Cottage cheese consumption patterns

	Number of households in each consumption category		
Consumption category	Recent study	Old study scaled to 1,000	
Heavy	220	250	(25% × 1,000)
Moderate	270	300	(30% × 1,000)
Light	230	200	(20% × 1,000)
Nonusers	280	250	(25% × 1,000)
	1,000	1,000	

as well as *the old data after it has been scaled to a sample size of 1,000* (right column).[7] The right column is considered the "expected" distribution, in the sense that it shows the results one would "expect" if there has been no change in cottage cheese consumption since the earlier study.

A Chi-square analysis can be used to test whether the differences between the two columns of figures are significant. When applying a Chi-square analysis, it is necessary first to calculate the value of the statistic which summarizes the differences in the data. This is the Chi-square statistic (χ^2), and it is calculated using the formula

$$\chi^2 = \sum_{i=1}^{k} \frac{(f_i - F_i)^2}{F_i}$$

where

k = The number of cells.
i = The ith cell (where i = 1, 2, ... , k).
f_i = The observed count in the ith cell.
F_i = The "expected" count in the ith cell.

The summation sign after the equal sign means that the equation following must be added for all the cells in the table. This can be demonstrated using the left column in Table 14–2 as the observed data and the right column as the "expected" data. The Chi-Square value is the sum of four terms (one for each pair of observed and "expected" cells) and is calculated as follows:

$$\chi^2 = \frac{(220-250)^2}{250} + \frac{(270-300)^2}{300} + \frac{(230-200)^2}{200} + \frac{(280-250)^2}{250}$$

$$\chi^2 = \frac{(-30)^2}{250} + \frac{(-30)^2}{300} + \frac{(30)^2}{200} + \frac{(30)^2}{250} = 14.7$$

---

[7] Since the earlier study was based on a sample larger than 1,000, its results must be scaled down to "match" the sample size used in the recent study.

The second step in the analysis is the determination of the number of degrees of freedom *associated with the observed set of data*—in this case, a column of data consisting of four cells. When there are four cells in the observed data, there are three degrees of freedom associated with the data. In general, the degrees of freedom (*d.f.*) associated with column or row data consisting of *k* cells is

$$d.f. = k - 1$$

Next, researchers use a table of critical Chi-square values to determine if the observed difference—represented by a Chi-square value of 14.70 and 3 degrees of freedom—could have occurred by chance. Appendix B is such a table. Column 2 shows the Chi-square values associated with a 90 percent confidence level, that is, *if the observed and expected data were drawn from the same universe,* nine times out of ten the Chi-square value will not exceed the figures shown in column 2. When a Chi-square value does exceed the figures shown in column 2, researchers will be 90 percent confident that the observed and expected data were not drawn from the same universe, and so conclude that the two distributions are significantly different.

For 3 degrees of freedom, 90 percent of the Chi-square values will not exceed 6.25 if the two sets of data are from the same universe. If the Chi-square value calculated in the example above did not exceed 6.25, researchers would not conclude that the two sets of data were significantly different. On the other hand, column 4 shows that Chi-square values *larger than* 11.34 can occur by chance only once in 100 tries. When such values occur, the observed difference is said to be statistically significant. Therefore, with a Chi-square value of 14.70, it is unlikely that the two sets of data could have been drawn from the same universe. The Howard Company could conclude, with more than 99 percent confidence, that there had been a downward shift in the pattern of cottage cheese consumption.

Comparing an observed frequency distribution with a hypothetical one. A detergent manufacturer has information showing that 42 percent of the households nationwide use heavy-duty detergents. Because the company wishes to know if there are regional variations in the consumption of this product type, it surveys 100 households in each of the company's five sales regions. Survey results show that the number of households (out of 100) using heavy-duty detergents in the five regions are 50, 41, 35, 47, and 39, respectively. If the hypothesis is that there is no regional variation in usage, one would "expect" 42 households (out of 100) in each region to use heavy-duty detergents. Thus, the observed counts are 50, 41, 35, 47, and 39, and the expected counts are 42, 42, 42, 42, and 42. A Chi-square analysis can be applied to these data to determine if the observed data differ significantly from the "expected" hypothetical data.

Such an analysis (left to the reader as an exercise) results in a Chi-square value of 3.52, which has associated with it four degrees of freedom. Referring to the values of Chi-square associated with four degrees of freedom in Appendix B, one sees that there is only one chance in ten of obtaining a Chi-square value larger than 7.78 if the two samples were drawn from the same universe. Since in this case the calculated Chi-square value (3.52) is much smaller than 7.78, it is one of the values which can easily occur due to sampling variations. The company would conclude, therefore, that the observed data are not significantly different from the "expected" data. Stated another way, the company does not have enough evidence to conclude with confidence that there are regional variations in the usage of heavy-duty detergents. (If, in this example, the calculated Chi-square value were 12.08, the company could conclude that there were regional variations in heavy-duty detergent usage, and be 95 percent confident that such a conclusion was correct.)

Comparing two large tables of data. Occasionally research findings are reported in two tables which are compared for similarities and differences. For example, Table 14–3a shows the number of households falling into each of 12 different product consumption and household income categories. These data are for a representative nationwide sample of 2,000 households. Table 14–3b shows similar data for a separate sample of 300 households which identified television program A as their favorite. The researcher can ask: *"Are households which prefer television program A different, with respect to income and product usage, when compared with the nation as a whole?"*

To analyze these data, researchers must identify an "expected" set of data with which they can compare the observed set of data shown in Table 14–3b. The nationwide data in Table 14–3a can be used for this purpose, if they are scaled down to a base of 300 households—to "match" the sample size used in Table 14–3b. This can be accomplished by multiplying each number in Table 14–3a by the factor 0.150 (300/2,000). The result is Table 14–3c, which represents the "expected" F_i counts needed for the calculation of Chi-square. Tables 14–3b and 14–3c are then used to calculate Chi-square.

$$\chi^2 = \frac{(44-15)^2}{15} + \frac{(55-38)^2}{38} + \frac{(18-8)^2}{8} + \frac{(42-30)^2}{30} + \frac{(48-53)^2}{53}$$
$$+ \frac{(12-15)^2}{15} + \frac{(15-8)^2}{8} + \frac{(18-34)^2}{34} + \frac{(11-38)^2}{38} + \frac{(12-8)^2}{8}$$
$$+ \frac{(15-26)^2}{26} + \frac{(10-30)^2}{30} = 134.7.$$

The number of degrees of freedom associated with the observed data must also be determined. When the observed data are in a table consisting of R rows and C columns, the degrees of freedom are calculated with the following formula:

$$d.f. = (R-1)(C-1).$$

In this case,

$$d.f. = (4-1)(3-1) = 6.$$

TABLE 14–3. Product consumption by household income

a.   Nationwide sample of 2,000

	Household income High	Medium	Low	Total
Heavy consumers	100	250	50	400
Moderate consumers	200	350	100	650
Light consumers	50	225	250	525
Nonusers	50	175	200	425
Total	400	1,000	600	2,000

b.   300 households whose favorite television program is A

	Household income High	Medium	Low	Total
Heavy consumers	44	55	18	117
Moderate consumers	42	48	12	102
Light consumers	15	18	11	44
Nonusers	12	15	10	37
Total	113	136	51	300

c.   Nationwide sample scaled down

	Household Income High	Medium	Low	Total
Heavy consumers	15	38	8	61
Moderate consumers	30	53	15	98
Light consumers	8	34	38	80
Nonusers	8	26	30	64
Total	61	151	91	303*

* Figures do not add to 300 because of rounding.

Researchers can now address the question posed above; namely, *"Are households which prefer television program A different, with respect to product consumption and income, from the nation as a whole?"* In looking at the observed and "expected" data in Tables 14–3b and 14–3c, researchers believe that households favoring television program A have higher incomes and are heavier consumers of the product class. They can use the Chi-square analysis to test if the differences are significant. The Chi-square value and degrees of freedom associated with the data are 134.7 and 6, respectively. Referring to the values of Chi-square associated with 6 degrees of freedom, one sees that there is only 1 chance in 100 of obtaining a Chi-square value larger than 16.81 if the two samples were drawn from the same universe (see column 4 in Appendix B). Since the chance of a Chi-square value of 134.7 occurring is even smaller, researchers will conclude that there is a significant difference between the two sets of data and that households which prefer television program A have higher incomes and are heavier consumers than the universe as a whole.

Testing the independence of two variables in a table. A researcher may wish to investigate whether the two variables associated with a table of data are independent of each other. For example, the hypothetical data in Table 14–4 show usage and nonusage of electric razors by males in different age categories. In order to use a Chi-square analysis to determine if the variable of electric razor usage is independent of the variable of age, the researcher must create an "expected" table which reflects the situation where the two variables are independent of each other. The count associated with each cell i in such an "expected" table can be determined with the following relationship.

$$\text{"Expected" count in cell } i = \frac{\begin{bmatrix} \text{The total number of} \\ \text{observations in the} \\ \text{row in which cell } i \text{ is} \\ \text{located} \end{bmatrix} \times \begin{bmatrix} \text{The total number of} \\ \text{observations in the} \\ \text{column in which cell } i \\ \text{is located} \end{bmatrix}}{\text{The total number of observations in all cells}}$$

Applying this relationship to the data in Table 14–4, the "expected" count in the upper left cell is calculated to be 23 ((100 × 46)/200). Applying this relationship to the other three cells in the top row results in "expected" counts of 27, 26 and 24 for the second, third and fourth cells, respectively. Since the total number of observations in the second row is also 100, the "expected" counts in the second row are also 23, 27, 26, and 24.

TABLE 14–4. Electric razor usage by males in different age categories

	Age category				
	Under 25	25–39	40–54	Over 54	Totals
Use electric razors	20	30	38	12	100
Don't use electric razors	26	24	14	36	100
Totals	46	54	52	48	200

The researcher can use a Chi-square analysis to determine if there is a significant difference between the data in Table 14–4 and a similar table which represents the situation where the two variables are independent of each other, that is, a table with left-to-right counts of 23, 27, 26, and 24 in both rows. Such an analysis (left to the reader as an exercise) results in a Chi-square value of 24.5, with three degrees of freedom. Since Appendix B shows that, for 3 degrees of freedom and 99 percent confidence, the critical Chi-square value is 11.34, the researcher will conclude that with a Chi-square value of 24.5 there is a significant difference between the observed and "expected" sets of data. Stated another way, this means that the variable of electric razor usage is probably related to age, and the two are not independent of one another as was originally hypothesized. Chi-square analysis can be used in this manner to test the independence of the variables associated with tables of data.

Closing comments on Chi-square analysis.   Chi-square analysis applies to data which have been placed in different cells, such as are found in frequency distributions and tables. In such sets of data, each cell typically represents a unique category based upon one or more characteristics. The cells in Table 14–2 represent unique categories of consumption, while the cells in Table 14–3 represent unique categories of income and consumption. Thus, the Chi-square analysis can be applied to many of the different types of categorical data frequently found in marketing research. Examples would include data relating to different sales territories, market segments, packages, advertising copy, and colors. To use a Chi-square analysis, researchers need only have a count of the number of items falling into each unique category, that is, the number of customers located in each sales territory, the unit sales made to each different market segment, the number of respondents indicating preference for each different package or color, and the number of product users who remember each different advertising copy. In short, a Chi-square analysis is an easy-to-apply, versatile, statistical technique which marketing researchers can use to test the significance of the differences observed between two sets of categorical data.

Analysis of variance: Analyzing a large set of experimental data

The analysis of variance is a technical subject which cannot be fully treated here. The following discussion is designed to help the reader gain an understanding of the basic concepts of analysis of variance, and for the most part, avoids the complex calculations which form an integral part of the technique. Interested readers should refer to a more detailed treatment of the analysis of variance, which can be found in many statistical textbooks.[8]

A comparison of the analysis of variance with the Chi-square analysis will help the reader understand when to use one rather than the other. There are two important differences.

The first difference reflects the fact that Chi-square analysis can be applied to survey data placed into categories and classifications which are determined *after* the data have been collected. In contrast, analysis of variance is most commonly applied to a set of *categorical data collected in an experimental setting.* Such data are usually arranged in a table consisting of a predetermined number of rows and columns.

---

[8] See the references listed in footnote 5.

Table 14–5 is an example of such a table. The data resulted from an experiment in which four different advertising copy platforms and five different package labels were tested under similar conditions to evaluate their effectiveness. Each copy platform was tried with each label, with only one copy approach being used with one label at a time. Each row of the table represents a different treatment of one categorical variable (advertising copy platforms). The columns represent different treatments of some other categorical variable (labels). The number in each cell shows the sales (in dozens of cases) resulting from each copy platform-label combination used in the experiment. (When copy platform 2 was used with label D, 48 dozen cases of the product were sold.)

TABLE 14–5. Sales of product X in dozens of cases when given labels and advertising copy platforms were used

Copy platform	Label				
	A	B	C	D	E
1	62	46	56	55	37
2	59	41	59	48	33
3	58	40	61	51	32
4	63	43	58	54	34

The second important difference between analysis of variance and Chi-square analysis is that the latter is always applied to *two sets of data* in an attempt to determine whether they are significantly different. In contrast, analysis of variance is applied to only *one set of experimental data* typically arranged in rows and columns. In such a set of data, researchers usually will observe differences *down the rows* or *across the columns*. In looking at Table 14–5, researchers will note that there are differences in the sales figures for copy platform 1 when used with different labels, and that there are differences in the sales figures for label D when used with the different copy platforms. Researchers can ask: "Are the column to column sales differences due to the different labels used in the experiment, or only due to sampling variation? Are the row to row sales differences due to the different copy platforms used in the experiment, or only due to sampling variations?" Researchers can use the analysis of variance to determine if the variation observed down the rows or across the columns could easily have occurred by chance due to the sampling process. If researchers believe it is unlikely that the observed variation could have occurred by chance, then they can conclude that the differences are probably real, that is, the variation can be attributed to the effects of the different treatments associated with the rows or columns. Thus, analysis of variance is concerned with significant differences *within one set of data,* rather than with significant differences between two sets of data.

The data in Table 14–5 could have been obtained from any of a number of different experiments. For example, instead of representing different labels, the five columns might represent different shapes of containers or different prices. The four rows might represent different promotional programs instead of different advertising copy platforms. In other words, data similar to that shown in Table 14–5 can be obtained from many different marketing experiments. The analysis of variance can be used to test whether the observed differences in the data can be attributed to either or both of the experimental variables.

Analysis of variance can be applied to data resulting from experiments using only one test variable, or it can be applied to experiments using two or more test variables. If only one test variable is used, the analysis of variance is called a one-way analysis of variance to reflect the single test variable. If two test variables are used, the analysis of variance is called two-way analysis of variance due to there being two test variables. Although two-way analysis of variance is more commonly encountered, the discussion will begin with one-way analysis of variance because it will lay the foundation for understanding two-way analysis of variance.

One-way analysis of variance. The Bell Baking Company was interested in evaluating the sales effect of two different colors (the test variable) for the package of one of its cookie products. The firm selected ten stores with similar monthly sales of cookies, and randomly split them into two groups of five stores each. One group of stores was stocked only with red packages, while the other group of stores was stocked only with blue packages. All stores were monitored for two weeks to make certain that the packages were properly displayed and that no stock-outs occurred. Table 14–6a shows the

TABLE 14–6. Sales test of package colors

a.   Sales results (number of packages)

	Sales by store	
	Red package	*Blue package*
	6	16
	8	18
	10	20
	12	22
	14	24
Total	50	100
Mean	10	20

b.   Analysis of variance summary

Variation source	Variation	Degrees of freedom	Estimated variance
Between columns	250	1	250
Unexplained	80	8	10
Total	330	9	

number of test packages which were sold in each store for the two week period.

To proceed with the analysis the researcher needs a measure which summarizes the differences in Table 14–6a. Recall that the Chi-square statistic is a measure that summarizes the observed differences *between two sets of data*. In this case, the measure which is used to summarize the differences *in one set of data* is called "variation."

Variation in a set of data is calculated by summing the square of the deviation of each item from the mean of all items.

$$\text{Variation} = \sum_{k=1}^{t} (x_k - \bar{x})^2$$

where

$t = $ The number of items in the set of data.
$k = $ The kth item $(k = 1, 2, \ldots, t)$.
$x_k = $ The value of item k.
$\bar{x} = $ The mean of all t items.

Since the total mean of all the data in Table 14–6a is 15, the variation in the data is the sum of $(x_k - 15)^2$ for all the ten items. That is:

$$\begin{aligned}
\text{Variation} = &(6 - 15)^2 + (8 - 15)^2 + (10 - 15)^2 + (12 - 15)^2 \\
&+ (14 - 15)^2 + (16 - 15)^2 + (18 - 15)^2 + (20 - 15)^2 \\
&+ (22 - 15)^2 + (24 - 15)^2 = 330
\end{aligned}$$

An important property of variation in a set of data is that total variation must equal the sum of the variation components. The above calculation shows total variation to be 330. It is also possible to calculate the variation associated with two components of the data—that is, the variation existing *between* the two column means relative to the toal mean, and the variation existing *within* the two columns of numbers relative to the column means.

The variation *between* the two column means relative to the total mean is of interest to the baking company because *it represents the different sales effects which can be attributed to the experimental variable* (in this case, the red and blue packages). The variation between the total mean and the two column means is calculated as

$$\text{Between-column variation} = n_1 (\bar{x}_1 - \text{total mean})^2 + n_2 (\bar{x}_2 - \text{total mean})^2$$

where n_1 and n_2 are the number of observations associated with columns 1 and 2, respectively, in Table 14–6a and $\bar{x}_1$ and $\bar{x}_2$ are the means of columns 1 and 2, respectively. In this example,

$$\text{Between-column variation} = 5(10 - 15)^2 + 5(20 - 15)^2 = 250.$$

Thus, the variation due to the different color packages is 250.

Note that the figures in a given column represent unit sales of the same type of cookie in the same color package and in stores with similar historical sales of cookies. For these reasons the variation *within each column* is considered to be unexplained variation because it cannot be attributed to different color packages or different cookies or to dissimilar stores. It can only be attributed to random or unexplained factors. However, it is a component of total variation, and it can be determined by calculating *the variation of the numbers in each column around the column mean,* and adding up this variation for all columns. In Table 14–6a

$$
\begin{aligned}
\text{Within-column variation} = &\ (\ 6 - 10)^2 + (\ 8 - 10)^2 + (10 - 10)^2 \\
&+ (12 - 10)^2 + (14 - 10)^2 + (16 - 20)^2 \\
&+ (18 - 20)^2 + (20 - 20)^2 + (22 - 20)^2 \\
&+ (24 - 20)^2 = 80.
\end{aligned}
$$

Thus, the unexplained variation observed within the columns is 80.

Since the total variation within a set of data must equal the sum of the components of variation, total variation can be shown as:

Total variation = Variation of column means from total mean
+ Variation within columns (unexplained)

Thus, the total variation in Table 14–6a can be summarized as shown in the first two columns of Table 14–6b. This summary shows that about three fourths of the total variation in the data can be attributed to the differences between the columns, rather than to differences within the columns. This suggests to the researchers that most of the variation is associated with the different color packages and that, therefore, one of the colors must be more effective than the other.

In order to complete the analysis, the number of degrees of freedom (*d.f.*) associated with the total variation and with each variation component must be determined. The total number of degrees of freedom associated with a set of data like Table 14–6a is one less than the total number of observations contained in the table. In Table 14–6a

$$\text{Total } d.f. = (\text{total number of observations}) - 1 = 10 - 1 = 9.$$

The number of degrees of freedom associated with the between-column variation is one less than the total number of columns (C) of data. In Table 14–6a

$$\text{Between column } d.f. = C - 1 = 2 - 1 = 1.$$

Just as total variation equals the sum of the variation components, so also do the total degrees of freedom equal the sum of the individual degrees of freedom. This means that the degrees of freedom associated with the unexplained variation can be determined from the relationship:

$$\text{Unexplained } d.f. = \text{Total } d.f. - \text{Between-column } d.f.$$

In Table 14–6a the unexplained $d.f. = 9 - 1 = 8$. The third column of Table 14–6b shows all the degrees of freedom associated with Table 14–6a.

The next step in the analysis is to calculate the estimated variance associated with each variation component in Table 14–6a. The relationship used for this calculaiton is

$$\text{Estimated variance} = \frac{\text{Variation}}{\text{Degrees of freedom}}.$$

Thus, the reader should note that the estimated variance is a measure of variation *per degree of freedom.* In other words, the estimated variance transforms each component's variation into an equivalent "per unit" variation which is more meaningful for comparison purposes. In this example, the between-column estimated variance is 250 (250/1), and the unexplained estimated variance is 10 (80/8). These figures are entered in the last column of Table 14–6b.

When using analysis of variance, the data are typically summarized as shown in Table 14–6b. This summarization helps researchers determine if the variation associated with the column treatments (different package colors, in this case) is large enough to have been caused by the different treatments rather than by chance sampling variations. To make such a determination, researchers must compare the between-column estimated variance with something that can be used as a standard. In one-way analysis of variance, researchers typically use the unexplained estimated variance as the basis for evaluating the between-column estimated variance. For example, in Table 14–6b the unexplained estimated variance is ten. This estimated variance can be thought of as the estimated variance that occurred randomly, or by chance, or which cannot be attributed to any specific factor. If the estimated variance due to the different package colors (the between-column estimated variance) is not larger than the unexplained estimated variance, researchers have no basis for claiming that the column treatment (different package colors) had a significant effect on the observed variation in the data. However, in this case, the between-column estimated variance is much larger than the unexplained estimated variance, so researchers have some evidence suggesting that the different package colors have had different effects on sales.

Table 14–6b provides researchers with all the data needed for the statistical test of significance employed in analysis of variance—the F test. This test calculates a statistic (called the F statistic) which is the ratio:

$$F = \frac{\text{Estimated variance the significance of which is being tested}}{\text{Unexplained estimated variance}}$$

As explained in the above paragraph, researchers typically use the unexplained estimated variance as a basis for evaluating the significance of the between-column estimated variance. For that reason, the unexplained estimated variance is used in the denominator. Associated with both the numerator and the denominator of this ratio are their respective degrees of freedom, but these do not enter into the calculation of the F statistic. Thus, the F statistic for evaluating between-column variation is:

$$F = \frac{\text{Between-column estimated variance}}{\text{Unexplained estimated variance}}$$

The F value used for testing the significance of the between-column estimated variance associated with different package colors is

$$F = \frac{250}{10} = 25.$$

The last step is to use a table of critical F values to determine the minimum value of F (for 1 *d.f.* in the numerator and 8 *d.f.* in the denominator) which is associated with statistical significance. Appendix C is such a table for tests of significance at the 95 percent confidence level. This appendix shows that when the F test has 1 *d.f.* in the numerator and 8 *d.f.* in the denominator, the critical F value is 5.32. Values of F *as large or larger* than 5.32 can occur by chance only about one time in 20 (95 percent confidence). Since the F value in this case (25) is much larger than the critical F value, the researchers would conclude (with 95 percent confidence) that the observed variation did not occur by chance and that the different package colors must have caused the different sales volumes.

Two-way analysis of variance. The basic procedures underlying one-way analysis of variance apply also to two-way analysis of variance, except for the fact that in two-way analysis of variance there are two test variables or treatments rather than only one. The addition of a second test variable requires some minor changes from the procedures described above. The following example will illustrate.

The Williams Candy Company was planning a test of three new candy flavors (A, B, C). In the test the company wished also to measure the effect of three different retail price levels—79 cents, 89 cents, and 99 cents. The company selected nine "matched," but geographically separated, stores as the sites for the test. These stores had similar levels of candy sales and were located in neighborhoods with similar demographic characteristics.

The company arranged to have the new flavors delivered to the stores, and to see to the proper displaying and pricing of the candy in all stores throughout a four week period. At the end of the four weeks the unsold candy was collected from the stores, and the company determined the number of cases of each flavor which was sold at each of the three prices. With the data from this experiment, the Williams Candy Company hoped to determine which of the new flavors had been most well received and what effect the different prices had, if any. In order to illustrate the basic concepts underlying two-way analysis of variance, three different possible sets of experimental results are discussed below.

Possible outcome 1. One possible result from this experiment would be that 10 cases of the new candy flavors were sold *in each of the stores used in the test*. This result is shown in Table 14–7a. These data show no variation at all. Each cell contains the number 10. In these data, the total mean, the mean of each of the three rows, and the mean of each of the three columns are all equal to 10. By observation, it is also seen that there are no differences down the rows and none across the columns. Since there are no observed differences in the data, no effect can be attributed to either the different flavors or the different prices.

TABLE 14.–7. Number of cases of new flavors sold at different prices

a. **Possible outcome 1**

Price	Flavor A	Flavor B	Flavor C	Row means
79¢	10	10	10	10
89¢	10	10	10	10
99¢	10	10	10	10
Column means	10	10	10	

Total mean = 10

b. **Possible outcome 2**

Price	Flavor A	Flavor B	Flavor C	Row means
79¢	10	10	10	10
89¢	4	10	16	10
99¢	16	10	4	10
Column means	10	10	10	

Total mean = 10

Possible outcome 2. A second possible result from the experiment would be that in five of the stores only 10 cases of the new flavors were sold, but in four of the stores the number of cases sold was different from 10. Such a result is shown in Table 14–7b. Researchers can observe differences in this set of data. However, the total mean, the three row means, and the three column means are all identical and equal to 10. (In this regard, Tables 14–7a and 14–7b are identical.)

As in one-way analysis of variance, the researchers must calculate all of the components of both variation and degrees of freedom in order to complete the analysis. Since the total mean of all the data in Table 14–7b is 10, the variation in the data is the sum of $(x_k - 10)^2$ for all of the nine items.

Total variation $= (10 - 10)^2 + (10 - 10)^2 + (10 - 10)^2 + (4 - 10)^2$
$+ (10 - 10)^2 + (16 - 10)^2 + (16 - 10)^2 + (10 - 10)^2$
$+ (4 - 10)^2 = 144.$

It is also possible to calculate the variation in Table 14–7b relative to the three row means and also relative to the three column means. For example, the variation associated with the rows can be calculated using the following formula:

$$\text{Row variation} = C\left[\sum_{i=1}^{R} (\text{row mean}_i - \text{total mean})^2 \right]$$

where C and R are the number of columns and rows in the table, respectively, and i is used to identify a specific row. In the case of Table 14–7b:

Row variation $= 3\,[(10 - 10)^2 + (10 - 10)^2 + (10 - 10)^2] = 0.$

This indicates there is *no variation due to the different prices*. The variation associated with the columns can be calculated using the formula:

$$\text{Column variation} = R\left[\sum_{j=1}^{C} (\text{column mean}_j - \text{total mean})^2 \right]$$

where R and C are as defined above, and j is used to identify a specific column.

Column variation $= 3[(10 - 10)^2 + (10 - 10)^2 + (10 - 10)^2] = 0.$

This shows there is *no variation due to the different flavors*. As indicated earlier, the total variation in a set of data must equal the sum of the components of variation. Yet, in this case, total variation is 144 and the variation due to rows (prices) and columns (flavors) are both zero. Since the row and column variations do not sum to 144, this indicates that there is still another component of variation.

A third component of total variation is *the variation which is unaccounted for by either the variation due to the rows or the columns*. Since it is unaccounted for, it is frequently called "unexplained" variation. (However, it is also called "interaction" variation, to indicate that perhaps the variation is due to the interaction of row treatments with column treatments, for example, due to specific combinations of flavors and prices being more or less effective. Thus, Table 14–7b suggests that flavor C might be more appealing when priced at 89 cents per package.)

Since the total variation in a set of data must equal the sum of the components of variation, total variation can be shown as:

Total variation $=$ Variation of row means from total mean
$+$ Variation of column means from total mean
$+$ Variation which is unexplained

Total variation in Table 14–7b was calculated as 144, and row and column variations were calculated as zero. The unexplained variation can be calculated by subtracting row and column variations from total variation (144 − (0 + 0)). Thus, the variation in Table 14–7b can be summarized as:

Component	Variation
Row	0
Column	0
Unexplained	144
Total	144

This summary shows that there is some variation in the data, but that none of it can be attributed to the rows or the columns. All of the variation is unexplained, that is, it is somehow distributed throughout the data, but not in a pattern which is clearly associated with rows or columns.

Possible outcome 1 illustrated the case where there were no differences in the data. Possible outcome 2 illustrated that differences in a set of data can be summarized by calculating total variation and each of the variation components. That summary information is then used in an analysis of variance, which is treated more fully in the discussion of possible outcome 3 which follows.

The summarized variation data from possible outcome 2 illustrates another aspect of two-way analysis of variance. After researchers have the summarized variation data, typically they will want to inquire if the variation associated with row treatments (different prices, in this case) or with the column treatments (different flavors) is large enough to have been due to those different treatments rather than to chance sampling variations. This implies that these variations must be compared with something which can be used as a standard. In two-way analysis of variance, researchers typically *use the unexplained variation as the basis for evaluating the variation in rows and columns.* For example, in the summarized variation data for possible outcome 2, row and column variation were both zero, while unexplained variation was 144. The variation associated with the columns (and the rows) is much less than *the variation which is unaccounted for,* that is, the unexplained variation. The general idea is that, if the column variation (or the row variation) is not as large as the unexplained variation, there is no basis for claiming that the column treatments—in this case, different flavors—have had a significant effect on the observed variation. The source or reason for the variation must lie elsewhere.

Possible outcome 3. A third possible set of results is shown in Table 14–8a. No differences are observed between the three price levels (all three row means equal 10), but it appears that flavor C is preferred over B, and B over A (see the column means of 13, 10, and 7 in Table 14–8a). In such a case, the researcher may well ask if the variation associated with flavors A,

TABLE 14–8. Number of cases of new flavors sold at different prices

a. **Possible outcome 3**

Price	Flavor A	Flavor B	Flavor C	Row means
79¢	8	8	14	10
89¢	4	14	12	10
99¢	9	8	13	10
Column means	7	10	13	

Total mean = 10

b. **Analysis of variance summary**

Variation source	Variation	Degrees of freedom	Estimated variance
Columns	54	2	27
Rows	0	2	0
Unexplained	40	4	10
Total	94	8	

B, and C is significant, that is, if the observed differences are due to the flavors rather than to sampling variation.

The four components of variation are calculated in the manner described in the discussion of possible outcome 2.

$$\text{Total variation} = (8 - 10)^2 + (8 - 10)^2 + (14 - 10)^2$$
$$+ (4 - 10)^2 + (14 - 10)^2 + (12 - 10)^2$$
$$+ (9 - 10)^2 + (8 - 10)^2 + (13 - 10)^2 = 94.$$
$$\text{Row variation} = 3[(10 - 10)^2 + (10 - 10)^2 + (10 - 10)^2] = 0.$$
$$\text{Column variation} = 3[(7 - 10)^2 + (10 - 10)^2 + (13 - 10)^2] = 54.$$
$$\text{Unexplained variation} = \text{total variation} - (\text{row variation} + \text{column variation})$$
$$= 94 - (0 + 54) = 40.$$

These variations are recorded in the first two columns of Table 14–8b.

In order to complete the analysis of variance, the number of degrees of freedom associated with total variation and with each variation component must be determined. If the analysis of variance is being applied to a table of data consisting of R rows and C columns, the number of degrees of freedom ($d.f.$) associated with total variation are $= (R \times C) - 1$. For Table 14–8a:

$$\text{Total } d.f. = (3 \times 3) - 1 = 8.$$

The number of degrees of freedom associated with R row means and C column means are, respectively:

$$\text{Row } d.f. = R - 1 = 3 - 1 = 2.$$
$$\text{Column } d.f. = C - 1 = 3 - 1 = 2.$$

Because total degrees of freedom equal the sum of individual degrees of freedom, the degrees of freedom associated with the unexplained variation can be determined from the relationship:

$$\text{Unexplained } d.f. = \text{total } d.f. - (\text{row } d.f. + \text{column } d.f.).$$

For the data in Table 14–8a:

$$\text{Unexplained } d.f. = 8 - (2 + 2) = 4.$$

The third column of Table 14–8b shows all of the degrees of freedom associated with Table 14–8a.

In order to complete the analysis, one must calculate the estimated variance (= variation/degrees of freedom) associated with each variation component in Table 14–8a. In this example, the column estimated variance is 27 (54/2), the row estimated variance is 0 (0/2) and the unexplained estimated variance is 10 (40/4). These figures are entered in the last column of Table 14–8b.

As in one-way analysis of variance, this summary information is analyzed by using the F statistic ratio:

$$F = \frac{\text{Estimated variance the significance of which is being tested}}{\text{Unexplained estimated variance}}$$

Since there is no variation associated with the rows (different prices), there is no reason to test the significance of row variation. However, there is variation associated with the columns (different flavors), and it can be tested for significance. The F statistic for evaluating the significance of the column estimated variance in Table 14–8b is:

$$F = \frac{\text{Column estimated variance}}{\text{Unexplained estimated variance}}$$

The F value used for testing the significance of the column variation associated with flavors A, B and C is

$$F = \frac{27}{10} = 2.70$$

The next step is to use a table of critical F values to determine the minimum value of F (for 2 degrees of freedom in the numerator and 4 degrees of freedom in the denominator) which is associated with statistical significance. Appendix C is such a table for tests of significance at the 95 percent confidence level. This appendix shows that when the F test has 2 degrees of freedom in the numerator and 4 degrees of freedom in the denominator, the critical F value is 6.94. Thus, values of F *as large or larger* than 6.94 can occur by chance only about one time in 20 (95 percent confidence). If the F value was as big as 6.94, researchers would conclude (with 95 percent confidence) that the observed variation was statistically significant, and that the observed difference in sales could be attributed to the different flavors used in the test. Since the F value in this case is only 2.70, researchers would not arrive at such a conclusion. Rather, they would conclude that the observed sales variation associated with the columns is not large enough to say that sales were affected by the different flavors used in the test.

Concluding comments on analysis of variance.   The foregoing examples serve the purpose of introducing the basic concepts of analysis of variance. It should be noted that the first example involved only two alternatives of one test variable (two package colors), while the second example involved three alternatives for each of two test variables (flavor and price). These examples suggest the flexibility of analysis of variance; namely, that it can be applied to sets of experimental data with any number of rows and any number of columns.

Many marketing tests and measurements are concerned with the effects of categorical variables—different cities, colors, flavors, packages, copy platforms, and so on. Frequently such tests and measurements involve two or more variables of this type. Analysis of variance is especially suited for analyzing such experimental data and, as a result, has proven to be a useful analytic tool for marketing researchers.

SUMMARY

After the tabluation has been completed, researchers typically attempt to determine whether any differences exist between groups and whether these differences are statistically significant. This requires the use of tests of significance, which indicate the probability that the difference is due to the use of sampling. If the data consist of two numbers, then sampling theory is used to test the significance of the difference. If the data consist of two tables, then Chi-square analysis is used to test for significant differences. If the data are from an experiment which tested the effect of a number of different treatments of one or more variables, then analysis of variance should be used.

These tests make use of the standard error and confidence limit concepts, and are based on probability sampling. If nonprobability samples are used, the tests are not pertinent. However, they are at times used with nonprobability samples to obtain some idea of the possible significance of differences.

Case 14–1
THE DELTA COMPANY

The Delta Company was a medium-sized food company which marketed a wide variety of prepared foods. Its products were mostly packaged in cans and, in the sense that they had been precooked, were ready to eat with little or no additional preparation. Among the products in the line were a group of ready-to-eat desserts, such as pudding and gelatin with a variety of fruit, nut, and cream ingredients.

Bill Ramsay was the marketing manager for three of the firm's dessert products. He was closely watching the test market results of a new product, Pudding Delight, a ready-to-eat pudding, fruit, and nut dessert which was packaged in cans and required no refrigeration or preparation. The product was considered an improvement over those already on the market in that its taste, appearance, and texture were almost identical to that of pudding prepared in the home.

Early results from the test market indicated that Pudding Delight was achieving the goals which had been established for it. If the product continued to perform as well as suggested by its early trend, it would reach sales levels normally achieved by other successful products. One aspect of the test market of special interest was an experiment testing the effectiveness of two forms of promotion—free samples and cents-off coupons, both of which were sent through the mail. Mr. Ramsay had had the experiment built into the test market in order to determine which promotional form was most effective in getting consumers to purchase the new product.

In order to set up the experiment, it was necessary to identify two sections of the test market city whose demographic characteristics were similar to each other and to the city as a whole. By using the most recent data from the U.S. Bureau of Census, Bill identified two census tracts which satisfied these conditions. Households in one census tracts were mailed a cents-off coupon, while a free sample was distributed to households in the other census tract. Households in the remainder of the city received neither, and thus were viewed as a control group useful in measuring the effectiveness of the promotion.

TABLE 1. Households which purchased Pudding Delight

Family size	Received free sample		Received coupon		Received neither sample nor coupon	
	Purchased	Did not	Purchased	Did not	Purchased	Did not
2	23	81	9	147	18	348
3–4	47	158	25	148	57	299
5 or more	50	162	57	153	54	151
Totals	120	401	91	448	129	798

One information source used in evaluating the test market results was a relatively large consumer panel whose members kept diaries of their supermarket purchases. That purchase diary information was broken down in such a way as to isolate the data in terms of whether the household received the free sample, the cents-off coupon, or neither. The data showing the households which had already purchased the product are shown in Table 1, broken down for different family sizes.

Analyze the results of the experiment.

What conclusion(s) do you reach? Be prepared to defend the test, or tests, of significance you used in your analysis.

Case 14–2
NIAGRA, INC.

Niagra, Inc. was a moderately large advertising agency whose list of clients included companies with well-known national brands. One of its clients had a deodorant brand which held a good position in the marketplace. However, the client felt that competitors were developing television commercials more and more like its own. This was disturbing to the client because, if the commercials were similar, consumers might come to believe that the different deodorant brands were similar. Because of this, the client requested that Niagra develop some new ideas and approaches for its product's television commercials.

The deodorant market was a highly competitive one, and most practitioners believed that effective television advertising was a very important ingredient to the success of any deodorant brand. Niagra's client also felt this way, and stressed that the new commercial ideas should have high memorability. That is, respondents who see the new advertisement should have a high recall of it, especially of the clients' brand name.

In response to the client's request, the Niagra television department produced six 30-second television commercials in photomatic form. Each such commercial consisted of a series of still photographs spliced together in a sequence which told the story the commercial was supposed to tell. When accompanied by an audio tape of the commercial's sound track, the series of pictures became somewhat of a crude motion picture with sound. These six commercials were then tested on customers in order to identify which one would be put into final production and eventually used over the air.

Personnel from Niagra's research department designed an experiment which was carried out in three cities, one each in the east, midwest and west. In each city, six separate samples of 100 deodorant users were recruited by a random selection process using the metropolitan telephone directories of the test cities. The respondents gathered in an auditorium where they were shown nine potential television commercials, all in photomatic form. Each sample of 100 respondents was shown only one of the new deodorant commercials, and it was always the fifth commercial in the series of nine commercials. The other eight commercials were not for deodorants or similar cosmetics, but were for a variety of products typically purchased in supermarkets and drugstores. These eight commercials, and their sequencing, were the same for every sample.

After having seen all of the commercials, the respondents were asked to recall the names of the brands they had seen in the commercials. The percentage of respondents who correctly recalled the brand name of the deodorant featured in the test commercials is shown in Table 1, broken down by test city and by each test commercial.

TABLE 1

	Recall (percent)		
Commercial	City A	City B	City C
1	21	12	22
2	36	24	30
3	36	21	20
4	39	28	23
5	28	24	25
6	46	15	31

Which commercial would you recommend be produced for over-the-air use?

What statistical test(s) of significance should be used to support your recommendation? Why?

15

Data analysis II: Explaining observed differences— Cross-tabulation, correlation, and regression

Chapter 14 introduced the topic of data analysis and discussed methods of determining whether observed differences are significant. If the observed differences in survey data are judged to be significant, the researcher may want to undertake further analyses in order to gain a better understanding of *why there are differences or variations in the data.*

Brand managers for convenience foods or gourmet products may believe that their products appeal more to prosperous single individuals or working couples. To determine whether their beliefs are realities, the managers undertake surveys in which heavy users, light users and nonusers of the product are identified and various economic and social measurements of them are made. To have a better understanding of the differences between those three types of users, the data are analyzed with respect to age, income, family size, and perhaps other variables. If the results show that prosperous single individuals or working couples are the heavier users of convenience foods or gourmet products, managers will have a better understanding of why some people are heavier users and why some people are light users. They are then able to direct their marketing programs to the heavier users of their products.

In the above situations, and in many similar ones as well, the researcher will have (1) data reflecting different attitudes, behavior, or opinions and (2) descriptive data, such as age, income, and education which may help explain why people have these different behaviors, attitudes, and opinions. The techniques used to analyze such data are multivariate techniques. In this chapter, cross-tabulation, the most simple of the techniques, will be discussed first, followed by correlation and regression analysis. To apply multivariate techniques to data in such situations, certain assumptions must be valid and the data must possess certain characteristics.

Assumptions

The statistical methods discussed in the remainder of this chapter are based on the following three assumptions:

1. The data to be analyzed are obtained from descriptive studies, not from experiments.
2. The data are from very large samples, usually in excess of 300 and frequently as large as 1,000.[1]
3. The data include measures on a number of variables *for each respondent,* such as monthly household consumption of coffee, television-viewing habits of adults in the household, coffee brand awareness, annual household income, education of adults, number of children, and so on.

Explaining variation with dependent and independent variables

A researcher is usually interested in understanding and explaining why sales are larger in some markets than in others, or why some people are heavy users of a product while others do not use it at all, or why some people prefer brand A while others prefer brand B. Large unit sales versus small unit sales, heavy product usage versus nonusage, and prefer brand A versus prefer brand B are differences or variations in survey data which are of great interest to researchers, and which they would like to understand better. Stated another way, researchers would like to identify characteristics which are common to heavy users of a given product, but which are not common to light users of the same product. Or, they would like to identify characteristics which are common to people who prefer brand A, but which are not common to people who prefer brand B.

Measures such as unit sales, rate of product usage, and brand preference can be influenced or affected by product quality, advertising, price, and other things, some of which are controlled by the manager. Since sales, product usage, and preference are dependent upon the marketing activities controlled by the manager, such variables are called *dependent variables.*

An *independent variable* is one which the researcher believes can help explain the differences or variations which occur in dependent variables. Changes in a brand's price, package, and advertising are thought to affect the brand's sales, rather than vice versa. Consequently, these three variables can be viewed as independent variables. If a product is believed to be consumed more by large families with moderate-to-high incomes, then family

---

[1] In Chapter 10 samples of 30 or more were defined as "large." *Very large* samples are necessary when applying multivariate statistics because of the way the data are broken down into many different cells, for example, "*heavy users* of a product who are from *small families* with *medium income* and living in *large northern cities.*"

size and income are considered to be independent variables which influence the dependent variables—family consumption of a product. Thus, changes in independent variables are believed to cause changes, or to explain variations, in dependent variables.

Methods of analysis

Cross-tabulation, correlation and regression analysis are methods of analysis which can help explain why there are differences or variations in a dependent variable. These methods are similar in the sense that they all analyze patterns of change which are common to *both* a dependent variable and one or more independent variables. These methods are different in that they are used on different types of data. Cross-tabulation is applicable to data in which the dependent variable and the independent variables are categorical variables or continuous variables which have been placed into categories. Correlation and regression analysis are commonly applied to situations where both the dependent variable and the independent variables are continuous.[2]

The following discussion describes these methods of analysis and indicates when and how they can be used. Some are complex and mathematical, but those aspects will be minimized.[3]

CROSS-TABULATION

Surveys are frequently undertaken to determine why some families use a product, while others do not; why some households are heavy users, while others are light users; why some prefer brand A, while others prefer brand B or C; or why some use only their favorite brand, while others frequently switch brands. Since marketing managers can be more successful if they know who are the heavy users of their products, if they know what causes preferences for a particular brand, or if they know which kinds of shoppers switch brands, they may use research to gain this understanding. In these cases, product consumption, brand preference, and brand switching represent *variations* in certain kinds of behavior and attitudes which the manager would like to understand better. These are likely to be the *dependent variables.*

If heavier consumption is believed to be caused by more people in the household and by larger income, family size and family income will be *independent variables.* Similarly, if brand switching is hypothesized as being practiced by shoppers who are especially "value-oriented," who shop at many stores to search out good bargains, and who use coupons extensively, these three factors will be *independent variables* in such a study.

---

2 Continuous and categorical variables were discussed in Chapter 14.

3 For more details on these methods of analysis, see sources in footnote 5, Chapter 14.

Perhaps the multivariate statistical method of analysis used most often in marketing research is cross-tabulation. Cross-tabulation can be used whenever the dependent variable (heavy user versus light user, prefer brand A versus prefer brand B vesus prefer brand C, and so on) and the independent variables (household size, household income, number of stores shopped at, use of coupons, and so on) *are both categorical.*[4]

An illustration.   When the U.S. Senate was debating the ratification of the Panama Canal treaties, a nationwide Gallup poll of some 1500 people showed that 36 percent favored ratification, 46 percent opposed ratification, and 19 percent were undecided.[5] While these figures showed the current attitudes of the public toward the issue, they didn't reveal any information as to why some citizens favored or opposed the treaties. In order to gain a better understanding of why respondents favored or opposed the treaties, additional questions were asked during the polling. These questions determined (1) whether respondents had read or heard about the debates, and (2) whether they were well informed about the debates, that is, whether they could correctly answer three questions relating to the canal and the treaties.

With this additional information, researchers were able to divide the total sample into three categories—those unaware of the treaty debates; those aware, but not well informed, of the debates; those well informed of the debates. Table 15–1 was obtained by cross-tabulating the attitude data with

TABLE 15–1. Attitudes toward Senate ratification of the Panama Canal Treaties

	Unaware		Aware, not well informed		Aware, and well informed	
	Number of persons	Percent	Number of persons	Percent	Number of persons	Percent
Favor	90	23%	390	39%	54	51%
Oppose	152	39	482	48	51	46
Undecided	148	38	130	13	3	3
Totals	390	100%	1002	100%	108	100%

Source: Derived from "Carter Thesis on Canal Treaties Basically Right: Better Informed More Likely to Favor Ratification," *The Gallup Opinion Index* Report 149 (December 1977): 1–14.

the data on debate awareness and knowledge. To gain a better understanding of why people favored or opposed the treaties, the data in that table can be compared with the findings that, of the total sample, 36 percent favored and

---

[4] Readers interested in a description of a computer program which performs cross-tabulations should see N. H. Nie et al., *Statistical Package for the Social Sciences* (New York: McGraw-Hill, 1975), chap. 16.

[5] "Carter Thesis on Canal Treaties Basically Right: Better Informed More Likely to Favor Ratification," *The Gallup Opinion Index* Report 149 (December 1977):1–14.

46 percent opposed ratification. For example, Table 15–1 shows that only one out of four unaware people were likely to favor the treaties, but that this ratio increases to four out of ten for people who were aware of the debates. Among people who were well informed of the issues, a majority were in favor of ratification. Thus, it appears that awareness and knowledge were factors which could help explain why different individuals favored or opposed the treaties.

Adding additional variables.   What should a researcher do if a cross-tabulation does not reveal a clear-cut relationship? One thing would be to try another cross-tabulation, but this time using one of the other independent variables hypothesized to be important by the researcher when designing the study. However, such alternative tabulations may be misleading. A preferred course of action is to introduce each additional variable simultaneously with, rather than as an alternative to, the other variable so that interrelationships between the dependent variable and *two or more independent variables* can be studied.

An example will illustrate this point. Assume that by a simple cross-tabulation a 20 percent ownership of electric razors (the dependent variable) is found among men under 40 years of age while only a 10 percent ownership is found among men 40 and over (here age is the independent variable). (See Table 15–2.)

TABLE 15–2. Ownership of electric razors by age

	Under 40	40 and over	Total
Own electric razor	20%	10%	15%
Do not own electric razor	80	90	85
Total	100%	100%	100%

The analyst may not be satisfied with this finding, and may look for a better relationship. The analyst may believe income is another factor which explains ownership of an electric razor. Rather than repeat the procedure which resulted in the data presented in Table 15–2 (except using income in lieu of age), the better procedure would be to show the variation in the dependent variable for different combinations of age and income. If two income groups were used along with the two age groups, a total of eight cells would result.

Table 15–3 presents the relationship of age and ownership for those individuals with an annual income of $20,000 and over and for those individuals with an annual income of less than $20,000. These additional breakdowns (as contrasted to those shown in Table 15–2) show that ownership is found three times as often among those with a higher income than for those

TABLE 15-3. Ownership of electric razors by age and income

	Income $20,000 and over		Income under $20,000	
	40 and under	*Over 40*	*40 and under*	*Over 40*
Own electric razor	30%	15%	10%	5%
Do not own electric razor	70	85	90	95
Total	100%	100%	100%	100%

with a lower income. Thus, the results of the initial cross-tabulation (which showed age and ownership) have been refined.[6]

Practical limit to the number of independent variables. The above example illustrates the better understanding of the variation observed in the survey data when two independent variables were analyzed at the same time. There is a practical limit, however, to the number of independent variables which can be used in a cross-tabulation. There are two reasons for this limit.

As researchers include additional independent variables in a cross-tabulation, they are creating more and more unique cells of data. For example, with only one independent variable to explain electric razor ownership (see Table 15–2), there are four cells. With two independent variables (see Table 15–3) there are eight cells. If 200 respondents were surveyed in the electric razor study, some of the cells in Table 15–3 might represent as few as 5 or less respondents. These numbers are so small that it would not be practical to reduce them further by the addition of a third independent variable to the cross-tabulation. For this reason, most cross-tabulations involve no more than three or four variables.

Another reason for a limit on the number of independent variables to use in a cross-tabulation has to do with the "logic" of the relationship between the dependent and independent variables. For example, family size and income appear to be "logically" related to household consumption of certain basic food products such as cereals, convenience foods, and meat. It may also be "logical" to relate fear of heart disease with the consumption of certain foods and the nonconsumption of others. However, it may not be logical to relate the number of automobiles owned with the brand of toothpaste preferred, or to relate the type of family pet with the occupation of the head of the family. If an independent variable is logically related to the dependent variable, the variation explanation resulting from the cross-tabulation is said to be valid. However, if the independent variable is not logically related to the dependent variable, the relationship which the num-

---

[6] An excellent example of the value of cross-tabulations is found in Tables 2–2 through 2–4 in Chapter 2.

bers seem to show is probably not a true cause-and-effect relationship and may be spurious.

Cross-tabulations—valid explanations. A simple cross-tabulation showed that a larger proportion of male drivers had an automobile accident (the dependent variable) than of female drivers.[7] This seems contrary to the general belief that males are better drivers than females. By adding a second independent variable—number of miles driven per year—the results shown in Table 15–4 were obtained.

The contents of Table 15–4 show that the relationship between sex and accident rate has, in effect, disappeared since for drivers who drove approximately the same distance, there is no difference between men and women. But drivers who "drive more" have a greater chance of having an accident. Because "driving more" is logically related to having an accident, this explanation is thought to be a valid one.

TABLE 15–4. Automobile accidents of male and female drivers by number of miles driven

	Male drivers		Female drivers	
	Drove more than 1,000 miles	Drove 1,000 miles or less	Drove more than 1,000 miles	Drove 1,000 miles or less
Had at least one accident while driving	52%	25%	52%	25%
Never had an accident	48	75	48	75
Total	100%	100%	100%	100%
Number of cases	(5,010)	(2,070)	(1,951)	(5,035)

Source: Hans Zeisel, *Say It With Figures*, 5th ed. (New York: Harper & Row, 1968), p. 133.

Cross-tabulations—spurious explanations. The example of attendance at university football games can be used to illustrate a spurious relationship. If the attendance data are broken down by multiple television set ownership, the results represented in Table 15–5 are obtained.

TABLE 15–5. Attendance at university football games by television ownership

	Multiple television set ownership	
Attendance	Owning more than one set	Owning one set
Yes	60%	52%
No	40	48
Total	100%	100%

[7] Hans Zeisel, *Say It with Figures,* 5th ed. (New York: Harper & Row, 1968), pp. 119–20 and 132–34.

This table shows that the proportion of attendance is greater among those owning more than one television set than it is among those owning only one. Assuming these differences to be significant, this appears to be a spurious relationship, since it does not seem logical to attribute causality to the ownership of more than one television set. It would likely be hypothesized that a third variable might be operating to affect both multiset ownership and attendance. Of course, it may be that only a combination of several other factors will explain the results.

For simplicity, assume that the results can be explained in terms of income. The data from Table 15–5 would be broken down by income as shown in Table 15–6.

TABLE 15–6. Attendance at university football games by television ownership and income

Attendance	Income over $20,000		Income $20,000 and under	
	Multiple television ownership	Single television ownership	Multiple television ownership	Single television ownership
Yes	70%	65%	40%	38%
No	30	35	60	62
Total	100%	100%	100%	100%

By controlling for income, the relationship between multiple television set ownership and football attendance is at least partially eliminated. Among persons with an income of over $20,000 (or among those having an income of less than $20,000) there are but slight differences in attendance between those having more than one television set and those not having more than one television set. Among the higher-income persons, attendance is high for both types of television owners. Among lower-income persons, attendance is low for both subgroups.

It is likely that other variables may also help to explain attendance. For example, whether the respondent attended a given university may be correlated with football attendance and, if such information is available, it could be tested for its effect on football attendance.

Concluding comments on cross-tabulation

Field studies frequently are undertaken because a manager or a researcher wishes to find out why sales are higher in some markets and lower in others, why some households use a product and others do not, and so on. A field survey can gather this type of data, along with other factors which are hypothesized to cause the variation in sales or consumption, for example, age, income, or family size. When both the dependent variable and the independent variables are in categorical form (or can be put in categorical form), cross-tabulations can be used to analyze the data to see if they support the hypotheses that led to the initiation of the research.

Cross-tabulation is a greatly used and highly flexible method of analyzing multivariate data. When researchers wish to understand the variation in a certain dependent variable (for example, consumption rates), it can be combined in a simple cross-tabulation with a single independent variable (for example, family size). Researchers can add a second independent variable (for example, income) to the cross-tabulation if it seems reasonable to do so. The addition of a second independent variable in the cross-tabulation may confirm, modify, or reject the relationship suggested by the simple cross-tabulation. In either case, analysts have learned more about the survey data and are in a better position to proceed with their investigation.

Theoretically, the introduction of additional independent variables can continue for as many variables as there are data, providing the sample is large enough so that the "breakdowns" remain meaningful. Practically speaking, most cross-tabulations do not use more than three or four variables. In addition, the objectives of the study must always be kept in mind when specifying what cross-tabulations to run. It is often a temptation to run numerous cross-tabulations because they might be of interest. But cross-tabulations of variables which are not logically related may show spurious relationships and should be avoided. They cost money and distract researchers from the main analysis.

Finally, there is no guarantee that cross-tabulation will identify useful relationships. This may be true for two reasons. If the variables which most effectively explain the variation in a dependent variable have not been measured, they cannot be included. Also, if the categories established at the outset of data collection were not wise choices, the data may not reveal the most important relationships.

CORRELATION AND REGRESSION ANALYSIS

One of the weaknesses of cross-tabulation is that the results must be evaluated subjectively by researchers. For example, when looking at Table 15–3 or Table 15–6, one can ask if the results are a complete representation of the relationship which exists between the dependent variable and the two independent variables. This question cannot be answered objectively, but only subjectively.[8] One should keep in mind, for example, that the eight cells in Table 15–3 are due to the two categories of age (40 and under, and over 40) and the two categories of income (under $20,000, and $20,000 and over). If each of these two independent variables were split into different categories (for example, using 30 years of age rather than 40, and $15,000 rather than $20,000), the results might be different from those shown. Yet,

---

[8] It is possible, however, to apply a Chi-square analysis to a cross-tabulation to determine if the data in the table indicate that the two variables are independent of each other. See Chapter 14.

researchers would still be studying the effect of age and income on electric razor ownership.

Because the boundaries between categories tend to be determined subjectively, and because results must be evaluated subjectively, cross-tabulation is not thought to be a very precise or very rigorous multivariate statistical technique. For this reason, some marketing research analysts prefer to use techniques yielding results which can be objectively evaluated. *Correlation* and *regression analysis* are two such techniques, and they can be used in situations where both the dependent and independent variables are of the *continuous* type.[9]

For example, in the cross-tabulation presented in Table 15–3, the dependent variable was categorical (own, or do not own, an electric razor), as were the two independent variables (under $20,000 income and $20,000 income or more, and over 40 and 40 and under). If, instead, the dependent variable were continuous (for example, annual household consumption of milk in gallons, or thousands of miles driven annually on business), and the independent variables were in continuous form (for example, age of head of household in years and annual household income in thousands of dollars), the researcher could use correlation and regression analysis to examine the relationship among variables. Generally speaking, the results from such analyses are judged to be (1) more accurate representations of the relationships between variables and (2) more objectively arrived at than similar results from cross-tabulations.

Correlation

A hypothetical example will illustrate the application of correlation analysis. Five households were interviewed in each of city A and City B for the purpose of identifying whether household wine consumption increases or decreases with increases in annual income. The data clearly show that wine consumption (the dependent variable) varied by household. Could the variation be explained by income?

Both the monthly wine consumption (in quarts) and the annual income (in thousands of dollars) for the ten households are shown in Table 15–7. These data are typical of those to which regression and correlation analysis can be applied: (1) they are continuous variables, (2) more than one variable is measured for each respondent, and (3) the number of respondents is greater than the number of variables.

A good way to start a correlation analysis is to construct scatter diagrams of the data. Scatter diagrams of the data for each city are shown in Figure 15–1. A dot's vertical (Y) location represents a household's monthly wine consumption and its horizontal (X) location represents the household's annual income. From the scatter diagram, one can see a clear-cut relation-

---

[9] Certain types of correlation and regression analysis can be applied to variables which are not the continuous type, but those methods of analysis are not discussed here.

FIGURE 15–1. Scatter diagrams of wine consumption and income

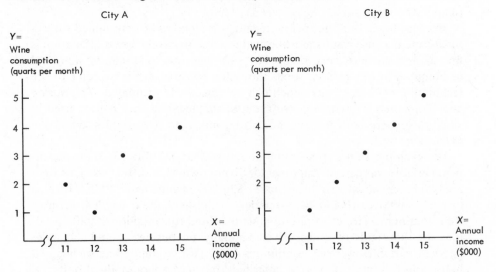

ship between wine consumption (identified as variable Y) and income (identified as variable X) for the five households in city B. The scatter diagram for city A does not show as clear-cut a relationship. Yet, it should be noted from Table 15–7, the average household wine consumption ($\overline{Y}$) and the average household income ($\overline{X}$) are the same for both cities.

TABLE 15–7. Household wine consumption and income

City A

Household	Monthly wine consumption in quarts	Annual income ($000)
$i = 1$	$Y_1 = 2$	$X_1 = \$11$
$i = 2$	$Y_2 = 1$	$X_2 = 12$
$i = 3$	$Y_3 = 3$	$X_3 = 13$
$i = 4$	$Y_4 = 5$	$X_4 = 14$
$i = 5$	$Y_5 = 4$	$X_5 = 15$
	Average ($\overline{Y}$) = 3	Average ($\overline{X}$) = $13

City B

Household	Monthly wine consumption in quarts	Annual income ($000)
$i = 1$	$Y_1 = 1$	$X_1 = \$11$
$i = 2$	$Y_2 = 2$	$X_2 = 12$
$i = 3$	$Y_3 = 3$	$X_3 = 13$
$i = 4$	$Y_4 = 4$	$X_4 = 14$
$i = 5$	$Y_5 = 5$	$X_5 = 15$
	Average ($\overline{Y}$) = 3	Average ($\overline{X}$) = $13

Correlation analysis can be applied to the data from each city to determine if a relationship exists between income and wine consumption. A positive relationship is said to exist between two variables when larger values of one variable are associated with larger values of the other variable. Thus, wine consumption and income are said to be *positively* related if *higher* levels of wine consumption tend to be associated with higher income. Wine consumption and income are said to be *negatively* related if *lower* levels of wine consumption tend to be associated with higher income.

A measure of the relationship between two variables is the correlation coefficient r. If there is perfect positive correlation $r = +1.00$; perfect negative correlation is indicated by $r = -1.00$; no relationship is shown by $r = 0.00$. The following equation is used to calculate r.

$$r = \frac{\Sigma[(Y_i - \overline{Y})(X_i - \overline{X})]}{\sqrt{[\Sigma (Y_i - \overline{Y})^2][\Sigma (X_i - \overline{X})^2]}}.$$

In this equation, $\overline{Y}$ and $\overline{X}$ are average wine consumption and average income respectively, and Y_i and X_i are wine consumption and income from individual households (see Table 15–7). $(Y_i - \overline{Y})$ is the wine consumption of household i expressed as a deviation from average household wine consumption. $(X_i - \overline{X})$ is the annual income of household i expressed as a deviation from average household income. These are shown in the fourth and sixth columns of Table 15–8. The summation signs (Σ) indicate that the calculations following the summation sign are to be made for each household, and then all such calculations are to be summed. For example, the individual calculations for the numerator of the correlation coefficient are shown in the eighth column of Table 15–8. The sum of the figures in the eighth column is the numerator of the equation for the correlation coefficient. Similarly, the two terms in the denominator of the correlation coefficient—$\Sigma(Y_i - \overline{Y})^2$ and $\Sigma(X_i - \overline{X})^2$—are the sum of the figures shown in the fifth and seventh columns of Table 15–8.

Applying the calculation for city A to the correlation coefficient formula:

$$r = \frac{\Sigma (Y_i - \overline{Y})(X_i - \overline{X})}{\sqrt{[\Sigma (Y_i - \overline{Y})^2][\Sigma (X_i - \overline{X})^2]}} = \frac{8}{\sqrt{[10][10]}} = \frac{8}{10} = +0.80.$$

For city B the calculations are:

$$r = \frac{10}{\sqrt{[10][10]}} = \frac{10}{10} = +1.00 \text{ (perfect positive correlation)}.$$

This very simple example illustrates the calculations used in a correlation analysis. When there is little data, it may be possible to interpret them visually. On the other hand, many marketing research studies use hundreds of respondents and collect information on more than two variables. In a less hypothetical study of wine consumption, for example, information concerning age, income, family size, education, media used, and other things may be

TABLE 15–8. Household wine consumption and income

City A

Household	Monthly wine consumption in quarts	Annual income ($000)	$Y_i - \bar{Y}$	$(Y_i - \bar{Y})^2$	$X_i - \bar{X}$	$(X_i - \bar{X})^2$	$(Y_i - \bar{Y})(X_i - \bar{X})$
$i = 1$	$Y_1 = 2$	$X_1 = \$11$	-1	1	-2	4	$(-1)\,(-2) = 2$
$i = 2$	$Y_2 = 1$	$X_2 = 12$	-2	4	-1	1	$(-2)\,(-1) = 2$
$i = 3$	$Y_3 = 3$	$X_3 = 13$	0	0	0	0	$(0)\,(0) = 0$
$i = 4$	$Y_4 = 5$	$X_4 = 14$	2	4	1	1	$(2)\,(1) = 2$
$i = 5$	$Y_5 = 4$	$X_5 = 15$	1	1	2	4	$(1)\,(2) = 2$
	Average $(\bar{Y}) = 3$	Average $(\bar{X}) = \$13$		10		10	8
				$= \Sigma (Y_i - \bar{Y})^2$		$= \Sigma (X_i - \bar{X})^2$	$= \Sigma [(Y_i - \bar{Y})(X_i - \bar{X})]$

City B

Household	Monthly wine consumption in quarts	Annual income ($000)	$Y_i - \bar{Y}$	$(Y_i - \bar{Y})^2$	$X_i - \bar{X}$	$(X_i - \bar{X})^2$	$(Y_i - \bar{Y})(X_i - \bar{X})$
$i = 1$	$Y_1 = 1$	$X_1 = \$11$	-2	4	-2	4	$(-2)\,(-2) = 4$
$i = 2$	$Y_2 = 2$	$X_2 = 12$	-1	1	-1	1	$(-1)\,(-1) = 1$
$i = 3$	$Y_3 = 3$	$X_3 = 13$	0	0	0	0	$(0)\,(0) = 0$
$i = 4$	$Y_4 = 4$	$X_4 = 14$	1	1	1	1	$(1)\,(1) = 1$
$i = 5$	$Y_5 = 5$	$X_5 = 15$	2	4	2	4	$(2)\,(2) = 4$
	Average $(\bar{Y}) = 3$	Average $(\bar{X}) = \$13$		10		10	10
				$= \Sigma (Y_i - \bar{Y})^2$		$= \Sigma (X_i - \bar{X})^2$	$= \Sigma [(Y_i - \bar{Y})(X_i - \bar{X})]$

obtained from 300 respondents. Rather than make a scatter diagram of wine consumption and age for all 300 respondents, another scatter diagram of wine consumption and income for all 300 respondents, and so on, the analyst can put the data on the computer to run a correlation analysis of the dependent variable (wine consumption) with each of the independent variables (age, income, and so on).

The advantages of correlation analysis can be identified by asking what has been learned about wine consumption in city A and in city B. Without the analyses, researchers know that average wine consumption and average income in the two samples are identical, and the scatter diagram for city B indicates a clear and direct relationship between wine consumption and income, while that for city A is less clear. Correlation analysis can help researchers be more precise about the relationship existing between two variables. It can do so in two ways.

First, a high correlation coefficient indicates that there is common variation between the dependent variable and the independent variable, that is, certain values of the dependent variable will tend to be associated with certain values of the independent variable. If the value of the correlation coefficient (disregarding its sign) is 0.8 or larger, there is a very strong or high relationship between variables. If r is between 0.4 and 0.8 (again disregarding sign), the relationship between the variables is considered moderate to high. For lower values of r, the relationship is small to insignificant. When a correlation analysis results in an r of less than 0.4, researchers do not have strong evidence which indicates that there is a relationship between the dependent and independent variables. If they wish to explain the observed variation in the dependent variable, they will want to try other independent variables.

When the correlation coefficient is large enough to indicate the presence of a strong relationship, the correlation analysis provides a second piece of information which helps researchers to be more precise about the relationship between the two variables. The sign ($+$ or $-$) on the correlation coefficient indicates whether the relationship is positive or negative. The plus ($+$) sign on the above coefficients indicates that there is a positive relationship between the variables—heavier wine consumption is associated with higher income. When a correlation coefficient has a negative ($-$) sign, the relationship is negative. If in the above calculations r proved to be -0.8 and -1.0, respectively, researchers would have evidence that wine consumption is lower among households with higher income. Thus, the second piece of information provided by a correlation analysis is the sign of the coefficient r, and it tells researchers whether the dependent variable is positively or negatively related to the independent variable.

Summary on correlation.   Correlation analysis, like cross-tabulation, attempts to identify patterns of variation common to a dependent variable and an independent variable. When both the dependent and independent variable are continuous, researchers can use correlation analysis to examine the relationship between the variables. This results in an objectively arrived at correlation coefficient, which indicates how strongly the two variables share a common pattern of change, and whether the pattern is positive or negative. In contrast, cross-tabulation is applicable to categorical variables, and must be evaluated subjectively rather than objectively.

Regression analysis

A correlation analysis may not describe the relationship between two variables as clearly as researchers may like. For example, the data for city B in Table 15–7 result in a r coefficient of $+1.00$. If, instead of the figures shown in Table 15–7, household income were $10, 12, 14, 16, 18, respectively, the r coefficient would still be $+1.00$. Or, if household income were $10, 13, 16, 19, 21, respectively, r would still be $+1.00$. The scatter diagrams for these three different sets of data (all with $r = +1.00$) would all lie on straight lines, but they would slope at different angles.

The correlation coefficient is a summary measure which indicates the relative strength of a relationship between two variables and the direction of the relationship. But it does not describe the underlying relationship. For example, it cannot be used to predict the size of change to expect in the dependent variable if the independent variable is changed by one unit— that is, how large a change in wine consumption would occur with a given increase in income. What is needed is a description of how one variable is related to the other, something like the following equation which shows a relationship between sales and advertising:

Sales ($ millions) $=$ $15 millions $+$ 3.5 (Advertising in $ millions).

This equation indicates that when advertising is $1.0 million:

Sales ($ millions) $=$ $15 million $+$ (3.5) ($1 million) $=$ $18.5 million.

If advertising were $1.1 million:

Sales ($ millions) $=$ $15 million $+$ (3.5) ($1.1 million) $=$ $18,850,000.

This equation tells researchers that sales are likely to increase by $350,000 if advertising is increased $100,000. An equation such as the above is more useful to the decision-maker than a correlation coefficient. The latter indicates the presence of a relationship, while the former describes the relationship in more detail.

When to use regression analysis.   When two variables in a set of data have a high correlation coefficient, researchers have evidence indicating the presence of a strong relationship between the variables. Wine consumption in city B, for example, seems strongly related to income. If a correlation of brand awareness and advertising expenditures resulted in an $r = +0.90$, researchers would have evidence of a strong relationship between advertising and awareness. If researchers wished to describe either of these relation-ships more clearly, they could undertake a regression analysis.

Regression analysis is a technique whereby a mathematical equation is "fitted" to a set of data. In order to understand regression analysis, it is necessary to understand (1) the set of data, (2) the mathematical equation, (3) the technique which "fits" the equation to the data, and (4) how the equation is evaluated to see how well it "fits" the data.

Data set.   The data must have the same characteristics as required for correlation analysis. They must consist of measures of two or more continu-ous variables, and the sample size must be at least two or three times as large as the number of measured variables, preferably even larger. In Table 15–7 there are two and a half times as many households as there are variables—wine consumption and income (two variables) were observed in five households.

To illustrate the application of regression analysis, assume that the data obtained on wine consumption and annual income in five households in city C are as follows:

Household	Monthly wine consumption in quarts	Annual income ($000)
1	2	10
2	1	12
3	3	14
4	5	16
5	4	18

For these data, r = +0.80, which indicates the presence of a strong relation-ship between the variables.[10]

Mathematical equation.   In most applications of regression analysis, the equation which is used is similar to the sales and advertising equation discussed above. The general form of that equation is

$$Y = a + bX,$$

where Y is the dependent variable, X the independent variable, and b is a coefficient which indicates the effect on Y of a one unit change in X. That is, if $b = +8.2$, a one unit increase in X will result in an 8.2 unit increase in Y. (The coefficient a is a structural coefficient needed to complete the equation, and is generally of little significance.) Because there is *only one independent variable* in this equation, and because the equation is that of a *straight line,*

---

[10] The correlation coefficient of +0.80 can be verified by the student using the pro-cedures described above.

it is called a *simple, linear regression equation.*[11] Linear regression equations are the most commonly used because they are easy to understand and easy to apply.

A simple, linear regression equation can be applied to the wine consumption data available from city C. This equation is

$$\overset{*}{Y} = a + bX$$

where

$\overset{*}{Y}$ = The predicted values of the dependent variable, that is, monthly household wine consumption in quarts.

X = The observed values of the independent variable, that is, annual household income in thousands of dollars.

b = A coefficient which indicates by how much household wine consumption (in quarts) is expected to increase with a $1,000 increase in annual household income.

a = Structural coefficient.

The regression analysis procedures use the observed data on wine consumption and income to arrive at estimates of a and b, that is, by estimating values for a and b, a mathematical equation is "fitted" to the data. After a and b have been estimated, researchers will have a regression equation which is a description of the relationship between wine consumption and income.

Fitting the equation to the observed data. If wine consumption and annual income data *from a very large sample* were plotted on a scatter diagram, they might appear as shown in Figure 15–2. (To enhance its visual appearance, only a limited number of dots are shown in the figure.) After all the data have been plotted, one can envision fitting a line through the points in some manner which results in "the best possible fit." Figure 15–2 illustrates a regression line fitted to the data—line *LL*.

The fitted regression line can be viewed as a "predictor line," in the sense that it "predicts" household wine consumption for each different value of annual household income. Thus, Figure 15–2 shows that if a household's income is X_i (measured horizontally), the regression line "predicts" its wine consumption to be $\overset{*}{Y_i}$ (measured vertically). For each and every observed value of annual household income (X_i), the regression line provides a predicted value of wine consumption ($\overset{*}{Y_i}$).

The difference between the wine consumption reported by household *i* (Y_i) and its predicted wine consumption ($\overset{*}{Y_i}$) is ($Y_i - \overset{*}{Y_i}$), and this dif-

---

[11] If a regression equation has more than one independent variable, it is called a *multiple* regression equation. If the independent variable is of the form $\sqrt{X}$ or X^2, rather than X, then the equation is called a nonlinear regression equation. Further discussion of these topics can be found in sources listed in footnote 5, Chapter 14.

FIGURE 15–2. Pictorial presentation of regression analysis

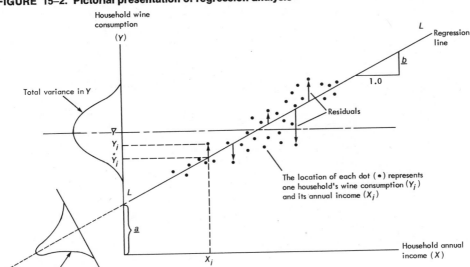

ference is called a "residual." The "residual" for the household with annual income of X_i is shown in Figure 15–2 by the upward pointing arrow from the regression line LL (which is the $\overset{*}{Y}_i$ value for household i) to the wine consumption reported by household i (Y_i). Some other residuals are illustrated in Figure 15–2 by the vertical arrows extending up and down from the regression line to the wine consumption figure reported by individual households.

The procedure commonly used to calculate the regression line which "best fits" a particular set of data is one called the least squares method. This procedure identifies the one equation which, when fitted to the observed data, *minimizes the sum of the square of all residuals.* That is, the procedure minimizes

$$\sum_{\text{all } i} (Y_i - \overset{*}{Y}_i)^2$$

where Y_i and $\overset{*}{Y}_i$ are as defined above.

Typically, the observed data (the X_i and Y_i values) are easily and quickly processed on a computer using procedures which are too complicated to present here.[12] Basically, those procedures calculate estimates of the coefficients a and b by using the two formulas presented below. The wine con-

---

[12] For an explanation of those procedures and a discussion of a computerized regression analysis program, see Nie et al., *Statistical Package,* chap. 20.

sumption and household income data obtained from the five households in city C can be used to illustrate those calculations.

The calculation of a and b estimates can be made easy by setting up a table similar to Table 15–9. The second column shows each household's

TABLE 15–9. Calculations needed for the regression analysis of wine consumption in city C

Household	Monthly household wine consumption (quarts) (Y_i)	Annual household income ($000) (X_i)	X_i^2	X_iY_i
1	2	10	100	20
2	1	12	144	12
3	3	14	196	42
4	5	16	256	80
5	4	18	324	72
	$\Sigma Y_i = 15$	$\Sigma X_i = 70$	$\Sigma(X_i)^2 = 1{,}020$	$\Sigma X_iY_i = 226$

$$\overline{Y} = \frac{\Sigma Y_i}{n} \qquad \overline{X} = \frac{\Sigma X_i}{n}$$

$$\overline{Y} = \frac{15}{5} = 3 \qquad \overline{X} = \frac{70}{5} = 14$$

monthly wine consumption in quarts (Y_i), and the third column shows each household's annual income in thousands of dollars (X_i). The figures in each of these columns are totaled to arrive at ΣY_i and ΣX_i, and each of these totals is divided by the sample size ($n = 5$) to calculate average household wine consumption $(\overline{Y})$ and average household income $(\overline{X})$.

Each entry in the fourth column of Table 15–9 is merely the square of each entry in the third column (X_i^2). The figures in column four are summed to arrive at $\Sigma(X_i^2)$.

Each entry in the fifth column is the product of each household's wine consumption (Y_i) and its annual income (X_i), or (X_iY_i). The figures in this column are summed to arrive at $\Sigma X_i Y_i$.

An estimate of the coefficient b is calculated from the following formula, which uses the terms described above.

$$b = \frac{n(\Sigma X_i Y_i) - (\Sigma X_i)(\Sigma Y_i)}{n\left[\Sigma(X_i^2)\right] - (\Sigma X_i)^2}.$$

By inserting into this formula the sample size ($n = 5$) and the totals at the bottom of the four columns of Table 15–9, one obtains:

$$b = \frac{5(226) - (70)(15)}{5(1020) - (70)^2} = \frac{1130 - 1050}{5100 - 4900} = \frac{80}{200}$$

$$b = +0.40.$$

An estimate of the coefficient a is calculated from the formula below.

$$a = \overline{Y} - b\overline{X}$$
$$a = 3 - (0.40)(14) = 3 - 5.6 = -2.60$$

These two estimates are then used to complete the regression equation.

$$\overset{*}{Y} = -2.60 + 0.40X.$$

This equation and a scatter diagram of the data are graphed in Figure 15–3. It should be noted that the regression line intersects the Y axis at -2.60, that is, at the value of the a coefficient. The b coefficient indicates that, for each $1,000 increase in annual household income, monthly wine consumption is predicted to increase by 0.40 quarts. This is demonstrated by setting the slope of the regression line at a value of $+0.40$, which takes it in a upward direction to the right. The regression line continues in that direction and passes through the point identified by $\overline{X}$ and $\overline{Y}$. Thus, with the estimates of the a and b coefficients and the point identified by $\overline{X}$ and $\overline{Y}$, the regression equation is easily located on a graph.

FIGURE 15–3. Scatter diagram and regression equation for wine consumption in city C

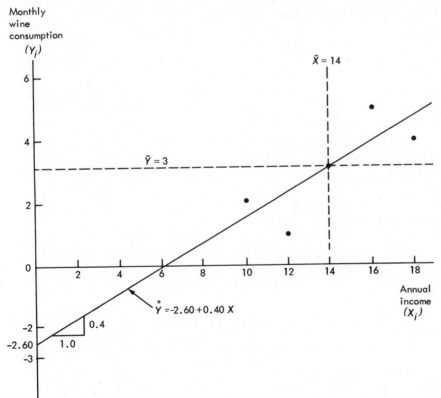

This result demonstrates the advantage of a regression analysis over a correlation analysis. With an $r = +0.80$, the correlation analysis only identifies the presence of a moderately strong positive relationship between wine consumption and income. The regression analysis leads to a more complete description of the relationship, for example, monthly wine consumption is likely to be 1–2 quarts for households with $10–12,000 annual income, 3–4 quarts for households with $13–15,000 annual income, and 4 or more quarts for households with more than $15,000 annual income. Because the b coefficient indicates by how much the dependent variable will change for a given change in the independent variable, a regression equation is a type of descriptive relationship which can help the researcher arrive at a better understanding of why there is variation in the dependent variable.[13] Such descriptive relationships can be obtained from a regression analysis, but not from a correlation analysis.

Evaluating the regression equation.   Whenever a regression analysis is performed, researchers will want to know how good it is, that is, how well the regression equation "explains" the variation observed in the dependent variable (Y). All regression procedures also calculate a measure called the coefficient of determination, which is identified as R^2. This coefficient takes on a maximum value of 1.00, but can be as small as zero. An R^2 value of 1.00 indicates that the regression equations "explains" 100 percent of the variation in the dependent variable *about its mean*. The observed variation in the dependent variable is shown pictorially in Figure 15–2 as the distribution centered on the Y mean $(\overline{Y})$ on the vertical axis. This variation would be explained perfectly *if every dot in the scatter diagram fell precisely on the regression line,* that is, if all of the residuals were equal to zero. When the regression equation does not fit the data perfectly, some of the residuals will be greater than zero, as shown in the figure. Those residuals form a distribution *around the regression equation,* and this distribution (shown at the lower left end of the regression line in Figure 15–2) can be used as a measure of *how much variation is "unexplained"* by the regression equation. These two distributions can be interpreted as representing total Y variance[14] and Y variance "unexplained" by the regression equation, and they are used to calculate R^2 as follows:

$$R^2 = \frac{\left(\begin{array}{c}\text{Total variance in} \\ \text{the dependent variable}\end{array}\right) - \left(\begin{array}{c}\text{Variance "unexplained" by} \\ \text{the regression equation}\end{array}\right)}{\text{Total variance in the dependent variable}}.$$

---

[13] The a coefficient should not be similarly interpreted. It is only a mathematical constant needed to complete the description of the equation. For example, Figure 15–2 shows that the constant a merely identifies where the regression line intersects the Y axis. This is the interpretation which should be given to a. In the wine consumption study, the regression line intersects the Y axis at 2.60 units (quarts) *below* the X axis.

[14] Variance = (Standard deviation)^2, and it is a measure of the variation in a set of data.

If the regression line *explains all* of the variation in Y, all the residuals will be zero, the variance "unexplained" by the regression equation will be zero, and the coefficient of determination will be

$$R^2 = \frac{\text{Total variance in the dependent variable} - 0}{\text{Total variance in the dependent variable}} = 1.00.$$

R^2 values in the 0.50–1.00 range are usually interpreted to mean that the regression equation does a good job of explaining the Y variation.

Wine consumption in city C can be used to illustrate the calculation of R^2. The exact formula for R^2 is

$$R^2 = \frac{\Sigma(Y_i - \overline{Y})^2 - \Sigma(Y_i - \overset{*}{Y})^2}{\Sigma(Y_i - \overline{Y})^2}$$

where each of the terms is as defined above. The calculation of R^2 can be simplified by setting up a table similar to Table 15–10. The first two columns

---

TABLE 15–10. Calculating R^2 for the wine consumption regression equation for city C

Y_i	X_i	$\overset{*}{Y_i} = a + bX_i$	$Y_i - \overline{Y}$	$(Y_i - \overline{Y})^2$	Residual $(Y_i - \overset{*}{Y_i})$	$(Y_i - \overset{*}{Y_i})^2$
2	10	1.4 = −2.6 + 4.0	−1	1	0.6	0.36
1	12	2.2 = −2.6 + 4.8	−2	4	−1.2	1.44
3	14	3.0 = −2.6 + 5.6	0	0	0	0
5	16	3.8 = −2.6 + 6.4	+2	4	1.2	1.44
4	18	4.6 = −2.6 + 7.2	+1	1	−0.6	0.36
15				10		3.60

$= \Sigma Y_i$ $= \Sigma(Y_i - \overline{Y})^2$ $= \Sigma(Y_i - \overset{*}{Y})^2$

$\overline{Y} = \dfrac{\Sigma Y_i}{n} = \dfrac{15}{5} = 3$

---

are household wine consumption (Y_i) and annual income (X_i). Column three is the predicted wine consumption for each household $(\overset{*}{Y_i})$, and it is calculated by using the regression equation $(\overset{*}{Y_i} = -2.6 + 0.40X_i)$. Column four is each household's wine consumption expressed as a deviation from average wine consumption $(Y_i - \overline{Y})$, and column five is the square of column four. The sum of the figures in column five is the total variance in the dependent variable, which is also the first term in the numerator and the only term in the denominator of the R^2 formula. The sixth column is the residual $(Y_i - \overset{*}{Y_i})$ associated with each household, and it is calculated by subtracting column three from column one. The seventh column is the square of the sixth, and the sum of all the figures in the seventh column is the variance "unexplained" by the regression equation. This sum is also the second term in the numerator of the R^2 formula.

Taking the sums from the bottom of columns five and seven of Table 15–10, and placing them in the R^2 formula, one has:

$$R^2 = \frac{10 - 3.6}{10} = \frac{6.4}{10} = 0.64.$$

The researcher can interpret this as indicating that the calculated regression equation ($\overset{*}{Y_i} = -2.60 + 0.40X_i$) is capable of explaining about 64 percent of the total variation observed in the dependent variable—monthly household wine consumption. Stated another way, the researcher can say that 36 percent of the total variation in household wine consumption is "unexplained" by the regression equation. As indicated above, a regression equation with an R^2 value of 0.50–1.00 is typically judged to do a good job of explaining the variation observed in a dependent variable. That judgment is appropriate for the regression equation evaluated in this example.

If the regression line *does not explain any* of the variation in Y, all the residuals will be large, and *the variance "unexplained" by the regression equation will be approximately equal to total Y variance.* The two terms in the numerator of the R^2 formula will be equal, the numerator will be zero, and R^2 will be zero. An R^2 value approximating zero indicates that the regression equation does not explain any of the variation observed in Y. In general, R^2 values of 0.25 or less indicate that the regression equation is of little use in explaining variation. Regression equations with R^2 values in the 0.25–0.50 range are typically judged to be of only moderate use in explaining the variation observed in a dependent variable.[15]

Summary of simple regression.   Many marketing research studies are undertaken for the purpose of studying the relationships between two or more variables: Why are sales larger in some markets than others? Why do some households consume more of product A or service B than others? If researchers are attempting to answer these types of questions, frequently a large sample survey is taken in which measurements are made on each of the variables of interest. As discussed in the previous section of this chapter, when those variables are of the *categorical type,* researchers are likely to use *cross-tabulations* to study the relationships between the variables. When the survey data consist of a *continuous* dependent variable and one or more *continuous* independent variables, researchers may want to use *correlation and regression analysis* to study the relationship between the variables.

Correlation analysis can tell researchers whether there is *common variation* between a dependent variable and an independent variable. When there

---

[15] Although R^2 is most commonly used, there are other statistical tests which can help researchers judge how well the equation fits the data. These are discussed in sources listed in footnote 5, Chapter 14.

is, such variables can be analyzed in a regression analysis *to identify more fully the relationship* existing between the variables. Regression analysis, using procedures which minimize the sum of the squares of the residuals, identifies the equation which "best describes" the relationship between the variables. The coefficient of determination (R^2) tells researchers how well the equation "fits" the data. R^2 values in the 0.50–1.00 range indicate that the regression equation fits the data very well and does a good job of "explaining" the observed variation in the dependent variable.

Multiple linear regression. The foregoing discussions placed emphasis on simple linear regression, that is, using *only one* independent variable. Frequently, data gathered in a field study include a number of independent variables, such as age of husband, age of wife, years of the husband's formal education, size of the family, and its annual income. Such variables are included because researchers have hypothesized that *both* age of husband and years of the husband's formal education can help explain why some households consume more of a particular product, or that the *three* variables of age of husband, size of family, and annual income are needed to explain annual expenditures on certain types of vacations. When *two or more* independent variables are used in a linear regression analysis, it is called a *multiple linear regression*. The linear equation commonly used for such regression analyses is

$$Y = a + bX_1 + cX_2 + dX_3 + \ldots,$$

where Y is the dependent variable, and $X_1, X_2, X_3, \ldots$ are independent variables. The additional coefficients (c, d) are similar to the b coefficient, except that they are associated with independent variables X_2 and X_3.

The four topics discussed above in relation to simple linear regression apply also to multiple linear regression (the data, the equation, fitting the equation, and evaluating it). The only difference is that the calculational procedures for a multiple linear regression are more complex due to the additional independent variable(s) and the need to calculate the values for c and d as well as for a and b.[16]

To illustrate, assume in the wine consumption study in city C that the researcher hypothesized that older people tend to consume more wine. Consequently, the age of the head of household could be the second independent variable (X_2) in a regression analysis. The first four columns in the top half of Table 15–11 show the data for such a regression. (The subscript i, which was used in Tables 15–9 and 15–10 to identify households, is omitted in Table 15–11 only to make the table appear less cluttered.) To facilitate the procedures used in calculating the coefficients a, b, and c, it is convenient to express the three variables as *deviations from their respective means*. That is, instead of using Y, X_1 and X_2 in the calculational procedures, the variables

---

[16] For discussions of multiple linear regression involving three or more independent variables, see sources listed in footnote 5, Chapter 14.

$$y = Y - \overline{Y}$$
$$x_1 = X_1 - \overline{X}_1$$
$$x_2 = X_2 - \overline{X}_2$$

will be used in their place. These transformed figures are shown in the three right-most columns in the top half of Table 15–11.

TABLE 15–11. Calculations needed for the multiple linear regression of wine consumption in city C

Household	Monthly household wine consumption in quarts (Y)	Annual household income ($000) ($X_1$)	Age of head of household (X_2)	$y = (Y - \overline{Y})$	$x_1 = (X_1 - \overline{X}_1)$	$x_2 = (X_2 - \overline{X}_2)$
1	2	10	25	−1	−4	−5
2	1	12	27	−2	−2	−3
3	3	14	30	0	0	0
4	5	16	36	2	2	6
5	4	18	32	1	4	2
	$\Sigma Y = 15$	$\Sigma X_1 = 70$	$\Sigma X_2 = 150$			
	$\overline{Y} = \dfrac{\Sigma Y}{n}$	$\overline{X}_1 = \dfrac{\Sigma X_1}{n}$	$\overline{X}_2 = \dfrac{\Sigma X_2}{n}$			
	$\overline{Y} = \dfrac{15}{5}$	$\overline{X}_1 = \dfrac{70}{5}$	$\overline{X}_2 = \dfrac{150}{5}$			
	$\overline{Y} = 3$	$\overline{X}_1 = 14$	$\overline{X}_2 = 30$			

Household	yx_1	yx_2	x_1x_2	x_1^2	x_2^2
1	4	5	20	16	25
2	4	6	6	4	9
3	0	0	0	0	0
4	4	12	12	4	36
5	4	2	8	16	4
	16	25	46	40	74
	$= \Sigma yx_1$	$= \Sigma yx_2$	$= \Sigma x_1x_2$	$= \Sigma x_1^2$	$= \Sigma x_2^2$

The transformed figures are then used to calculate the five columns of data (yx_1, yx_2, x_1x_2, x_1^2, and x_2^2) shown in the bottom half of table 15–11. Each column of figures is then summed to arrive at Σyx_1, Σyx_2, Σx_1x_2, Σx_1^2, and Σx_2^2. These five sums are substituted into the following formula to calculate the b coefficient.

$$b = \frac{(\Sigma yx_1)(\Sigma x_2^2) - (\Sigma yx_2)(\Sigma x_1x_2)}{(\Sigma x_1^2)(\Sigma x_2^2) - (\Sigma x_1x_2)^2}$$

$$b = \frac{(16)(74) - (25)(46)}{(40)(74) - (46)^2} = \frac{1184 - 1150}{2960 - 2116} = \frac{34}{844} = 0.0402.$$

By substituting the five sums into the formula below, c is calculated to be

$$c = \frac{(\Sigma yx_2)(\Sigma x_1^2) - (\Sigma yx_1)(\Sigma x_1 x_2)}{(\Sigma x_1^2)(\Sigma x_2^2) - (\Sigma x_1 x_2)^2}$$

$$c = \frac{(25)(40) - (16)(46)}{(40)(74) - (46)^2} = \frac{1000 - 736}{2960 - 2116} = \frac{264}{844} = 0.312.$$

The a coefficient is calculated with the following formula:

$$a = \bar{Y} - b\bar{X}_1 - c\bar{X}_2 = 3.0 - (0.0402)(14) - (0.312)(30) = -6.923.$$

Using these three coefficients, the regression equation is written as

$$\overset{*}{Y} = -6.923 + 0.0402X_1 + 0.312X_2.$$

From this equation, researchers see that a greater increase in wine consumption is associated with a one-year increase in age (0.312 quarts) than is associated with a thousand dollar increase in annual income (0.0402 quarts). As in simple linear regression, the a coefficient (-6.923) should be interpreted as a structural coefficient.

The coefficient of determination (R^2) for this mulitple linear regression is calculated using the procedures described in Table 15–10. Compared with the simple linear regression example used in that table, the only difference in this case is that each household's X_1 and X_2 values must be used in the equation

$$\overset{*}{Y} = -6.923 + 0.0402X_1 + 0.312X_2$$

to calculate $\overset{*}{Y}$ for each household. The procedure then uses $\bar{Y}$ and each household's Y and $\overset{*}{Y}$ value to calculate each household's $(Y - \bar{Y})^2$ and $(Y - \overset{*}{Y})^2$. As before, these are then summed for all households and the measures $\Sigma(Y - \bar{Y})^2$ and $\Sigma(Y - \overset{*}{Y})^2$ are used in the R^2 formula to calculate the coefficient of determination.

In the simple linear regression using annual income as the only independent variable, R^2 was calculated to be 0.64. In this example, R^2 is 0.848, an increase of 0.208 over the previous figure. This demonstrates that the addition of a second independent variable to a regression analysis can lead to a noticeable improvement in explaining the observed variation in a dependent variable. Because of this capability, multiple linear regression is a much more useful analytical tool than simple linear regression.

Some necessary conditions. This example is presented *only* for the purpose of demonstrating how the calculational procedure for a regression with two independent variables differs from that with only one independent variable. It should be noted, for example, that a regression with three variables (Y, X_1, and X_2) should be based on at least 10–15 respondents and preferably many more. If this condition is not satisfied, the estimates of the *b* and *c* coefficients will not be good ones; hence, the regression equation is likely to be of little use. Also, the two independent variables should be subjected to a correlation analysis to see if they are highly correlated. If they are, the two of them cannot be used in the same regression without violating some of the basic assumptions underlying this method of analysis.

Stepwise multiple linear regression.   In some studies the researcher may hypothesize that four or five independent variables can explain the variation in a certain dependent variable. However, in so hypothesizing, researchers may not know if all five independent variables are equally important, or if only three are very important, or if only one is very important and the remaining four of slight or no importance. In such cases, researchers believe they have identified the important independent variables, but they are not sure if all are equally important or if some combinations can more effectively explain the variation than others. To resolve this uncertainty, researchers must evaluate various combinations of independent variables used in different regression equations. They must decide on which, and how many, independent variables to include in each regression analysis. For example, in a study involving only three independent variables (X_1, X_2, and X_3), there are four different multiple linear equations which can be evaluated with a regular regression analysis—equations using X_1 and X_2 only, X_2 and X_3 only, X_1 and X_3 only, or X_1, X_2, and X_3. If researchers have five independent variables to work with, 26 different multiple linear regression equations are possible. Thus, when researchers hypothesize that a number of independent variables are important, many different multiple linear regression analyses are possible, and researchers must decide which are to be performed.

Another way of determining how many, and which, variables to include in a multiple linear regression analysis is to use a computer program which performs stepwise multiple regression.[17] For example, in the case where there are five independent variables (X_1, X_2, X_3, X_4, X_5), stepwise multiple regression first evaluates *each independent variable separately* to determine which one results in the largest R^2, that is, which one explains most of the variation in the dependent variable. If it is X_3, that independent variable is selected for the regression equation. Next, the stepwise regression exaluates *X_3 in combination with each of the remaining independent variables (one at a time)* to determine which one of the latter results in the largest increase in R^2. If it is X_5, that variable becomes the second independent variable selected for the regression equation. Using the same procedures, the remaining unselected independent variables (X_1, X_2, X_4) are evaluated one at a time (with the two already selected ones) to determine which one is to be the third independent variable. This procedure continues until R^2 can no longer be increased significantly by adding another independent variable to the regression equation. The independent variables which are not selected do not become part of the regression equation.

---

[17] For a discussion of a computerized stepwise regression program, see Nie et al., *Statistical Package*, pp. 345–47.

Problems in using regression analysis. When using regression analysis, it is possible to encounter problems and difficulties which can cause the results to be inaccurate and misleading. Four of the major problems and difficulties are listed below.

1. An inadequate sample size was used to collect the data. The sample size should be at least two or three times the number of variables used in the regression equation, and preferably much larger.
2. The independent variables measured during the study have been poorly measured, are in the wrong form, or are not the right ones, that is, they are not the ones which have a direct effect on the dependent variable.
3. The independent variables are highly correlated with each other. If two independent variables are perfectly correlated with each other (that is, $r = +1.00$), their effect will be the same as that of a single independent variable which has been used twice in the same regression analysis.
4. The true relationship between the dependent variable and the independent variable(s) is not linear, or it is an unusual shape which cannot be analyzed with regression techniques.

Prior to undertaking a regression analysis, researchers should assure themselves that their sample size is many times larger than the number of variables used, and that the variables are accurately measured and in the form identified by the researchers' hypotheses. When the data have been collected, correlation analyses should be applied to all pairs of independent variables to see if any are highly correlated and, if two are found to be so, researchers must select the most appropriate one to use in the regression analysis. Lastly, researchers may wish to use nonlinear multiple regression analysis on the data, to see if a nonlinear equation fits better than a linear one.

Another problem can stem from the fact that the regression equation applies only to the range within which observations have been made. For example, if the sales data used in a regression analysis range from $50–100 million, the regression equation derived from those data may not apply for sales figures as small as $10 million or as large as $200 million. The relationship at these lower or higher values may be quite different from the one developed from the $50–100 million sales data.

Finally, the mathematical calculations of regression analysis are based on a number of assumptions which are too complicated to be described here. Briefly, it may be said that regression analysis techniques assume that (1) each item of data is independent of the others, (2) the data measurements are unbiased, (3) the errors are randomly distributed throughout the data, and (4) the error variance is constant over the entire range of data, rather than larger in some parts of the data range and smaller in others.[18] If these as-

---

[18] For a complete discussion of the assumptions underlying regression analysis, see sources listed in footnote 5, Chapter 14.

sumptions are seriously violated, the results of the regression analysis may be misleading.

SUMMARY

This chapter discussed three methods of analysis which researchers can use to explain observed differences in survey data—cross-tabulation, correlation analysis, and regression analysis. These methods are similar insofar as all are concerned with explaining the variation observed in a dependent variable through the use of one or more independent variables. These methods differ in that they do not all use the same types of data.

Whenever researchers attempt to explain variation in a dependent variable, they should use only those independent variables which are logically related to the dependent variable, or which are hypothesized by researchers to have an effect on the dependent variable. If the dependent and independent variables are not logically related, their use in these techniques is little more than a manipulation of numbers which cannot lead to the discovery of useful marketing relationships.

Cross-tabulation is the most frequently used method for trying to explain or understand variation. It can be applied to data in which both the dependent variable and independent variables are categorical. The results of a cross-tabulation usually are presented in tables which will reveal relationships between the variables. However, those relationships must be interpreted and evaluated subjectively.

Correlation and regression analysis are used when both dependent variable and independent variables are the continuous type. Correlation is used to measure the relative strength of the relationship between a dependent and an independent variable. The result of a regression analysis is an equation expressing the relationship between the dependent variable and the independent variables, including coefficients which indicate the sensitivity of the former to a unit change in the latter. Also calculated is a coefficient of determination (R^2), which indicates how well the equation fits the data.

These methods of analysis offer no guarantee that observed variation will be explained. Their effectiveness depends upon the accuracy and appropriateness of the data used in the analysis and upon the degree to which certain assumptions underlying the method have not been violated. Therefore, researchers must take the proper precautions when using these methods of analysis.

Case 15–1
TOBART COMPANY

Tobart after-shave lotion had been one of the five major lotions on the American market for a number of years and was also one of the best advertised. In recent years, Tobart executives had grown more and more aware of their lack of knowledge as to the actual effect of their advertising expenditures on sales. Accordingly, they directed the marketing research manager to analyze advertising expenditures for the last two years to determine what effect, if any, advertising had had on sales.

The marketing research director decided to use data on the last two full years for which sales and advertising expenditures were available. He set up a table to show total sales for 1978 and 1979 and advertising expenditures broken down by type for the same two years (see Table 1). Both figures were computed on a "per 1,000 males" basis as well as in total dollars. Since by far the largest portion of advertising had been devoted to television, the research manager decided to make his analysis on that basis. Accordingly, he divided the United States into 38 areas based on 38 distributors who handled the Tobart after-shave lotion. Each of these distributors had an exclusive territory so that sales in each of these territories could be measured fairly accurately.

TABLE 1. Tobart Company sales and advertising expenditures—1978–1979

	1978	1979
Sales	$8,944,570	$10,310,318
Sales per 1,000 males over 15 years of age	125.46	144.46
Total advertising expenditures	5,072,724	6,379,180
Network television	3,249,480	4,289,824
Spot television	1,109,360	1,195,486
Consumer magazine	713,884	893,870
Total advertising per 1,000 males over 15	71.16	89.40

It was a much more difficult job to allocate advertising expenditures. The research manager set out to determine the actual coverage area of each television station over which Tobart commercials had been broadcast. Data were available on the approximate area covered by each station and on the approximate number of television sets within each of those areas. It was fairly easy to allocate the television advertising expenditures on spot television according to the areas, but there were still difficult problems because the television coverage areas did not fall entirely within individual distributor territories. Many of them overlapped two or more distributor areas. In such instances, the research manager distributed the expenditures between the two or more distributor areas on the basis of his best judgment. For example, if half a television station coverage area fell in each of two distributors' areas, he allocated half the advertising from that station to each of these distributor areas. When, as was usually the case, the television station coverage area was not split evenly between distributor areas, he used his judgment to determine the proportion of coverage that should be charged to each distributor. This was based upon an estimate of the percentage of the total coverage area with an adjustment being made for the assumption that the number of television sets available in a coverage area was concentrated toward the center and was thinner toward the outer edge of the station coverage area.

Network television expenditures were allocated among the stations carrying the network at the time of the particular Tobart commercials. If a given station had 1 percent of all the sets included in the network at the time of a particular commercial, it was charged 1 percent of the cost of that commercial. Consumer magazine advertising expenditures were allocated to distributor areas on the basis of circulation data furnished by the magazine publishers. These data were on a state by state basis and had to be broken down among distributor areas on the basis of judgment where distributor areas did not conform to state lines.

With the information thus computed, the research manager prepared another table to show the total advertising expenditures and sales by individual territories (see Table 2). The distribution of advertising among the distributor areas was approximately the same in 1979 as in 1978; however, sales changed. The percentage changed in sales for 1979 over 1978 is shown in a separate column.

TABLE 2. Tobart Company sales and advertising expense by distribution area—1979

	Advertising expense		Sales			
Area	Total ($000)	Per 1,000 males	Total ($000)	Per 1,000 males	Percent change over 1978	Percent homes with television
1	$312.1	$ 89.18	$528.1	$151.67	37.9	90
2	148.8	108.96	182.4	133.48	7.6	87
3	288.9	83.32	504.3	147.05	11.2	84
4	86.4	95.72	91.1	98.11	—18.6	91
5	81.6	87.80	153.6	162.91	45.7	87
6	288.3	88.66	337.9	104.82	40.8	92
7	321.6	84.68	595.2	156.07	11.7	91
8	153.6	56.54	345.5	128.19	— 6.5	75
9	220.8	87.40	532.8	212.21	42.7	94
10	168.7	79.58	388.7	183.25	22.6	83
11	264.5	87.68	309.9	102.41	40.8	92
12	187.2	111.02	263.7	159.40	36.1	88
13	292.8	101.76	441.6	152.64	17.6	91
14	72.5	69.26	139.1	132.85	11.3	64
15	57.6	58.56	138.9	142.36	—15.8	82
16	201.6	94.84	350.4	166.55	17.0	88
17	336.3	119.96	455.7	162.71	16.9	88
18	163.2	75.94	384.1	179.28	10.0	76
19	148.8	75.46	326.4	164.11	3.9	73
20	340.8	110.40	460.7	164.15	16.9	88
21 ..:..	177.6	77.66	326.3	143.86	— 1.3	77
22	$ 96.1	$ 90.14	$139.2	$132.91	— 9.0	80
23	14.2	40.26	33.6	108.56	—11.1	61
24	91.2	90.27	124.7	122.09	9.7	67
25	110.4	109.10	148.8	144.38	— 5.7	77
26	43.2	69.74	76.7	127.75	— 3.6	76

TABLE 2. (*continued*)

	Advertising expense		Sales			
Area	Total ($000)	Per 1,000 males	Total ($000)	Per 1,000 males	Percent change over 1978	Percent homes with television
27	168.1	82.28	302.4	147.11	15.5	72
28	52.8	92.34	81.5	144.92	12.7	71
29	230.4	84.82	369.6	136.13	39.3	79
30	326.4	101.27	460.7	142.45	74.0	86
31	196.8	96.85	254.3	134.76	−19.2	74
32	120.3	106.18	158.4	144.27	10.3	76
33	110.4	81.39	201.5	146.64	− 1.1	63
34	129.6	83.03	196.8	124.81	11.7	70
35	120.7	91.20	172.7	130.15	− 2.2	68
36	38.4	72.01	72.1	130.56	21.1	70
37	72.9	70.07	100.7	98.59	−10.5	71
38	148.8	97.69	158.4	105.50	13.4	73

What conclusions should the Tobart research manager draw relative to the effectiveness of the company's advertising expenditures on sales?

Case 15–2
THE DUPORT COMPANY

The Duport Company manufactured the concentrate for Genii, a bottled carbonated grapefruit drink. The company had franchised bottlers in 44 states but had varying coverage of the population of these states. In planning future expansion and franchising of new bottlers, Herbert Walker, president of Duport, felt that the company should have some idea of the potential of each state. By concentrating on those areas where the potential was the greatest, Mr. Walker felt that Duport could make the greatest gains at the least cost.

The Duport Company was not a bottling company. It manufactured concentrated flavors which were used in making carbonated soft drinks. Bottlers purchased the concentrate and mixed it with carbonated water to produce a soft drink. This was then bottled for distribution. Besides the Genii concentrate, Duport also sold assorted flavors, ginger ale, root beer, orange, and so on, for bottling in 24-ounce bottles under the Walker label. The Walker brand was not nationally advertised but had a strong following in several of the major metropolitan markets.

Duport had 150 bottlers franchised to bottle Genii in the United States. The company also had bottlers in South America, Canada, and Western Europe. Duport had established a distinctive bottle design and labels which all bottlers used. An 8-ounce bottle was used for Genii. The terms of the franchise required bottlers to use only concentrate purchased from Duport for bottling Genii, to use the bottle and label specified for Genii by Duport, and to maintain certain standards of quality. The bottlers were required to send periodic samples of bottled Genii to Duport for quality checks. The franchise granted the bottlers an exclusive territory.

The bottlers were also expected to promote Genii in their area through sales and advertising. Duport participated in cooperative advertising with the bottlers. Most of the franchised bottlers had an advertising account with Duport. The bottlers paid an extra charge of one dollar for each gallon of concentrate. This was matched by Duport and set aside in the advertising account. The bottlers would then forward any bills for advertising Genii to Duport for payment out of their advertising accounts. Also, the cost of displays and other promotional materials provided the bottler by Duport were deducted from this account. Duport allowed the bottlers, particularly newly franchised bottlers, some latitude in drawing against future accruals in their advertising accounts.

Duport regularly conducted national advertising campaigns for Genii using magazine and spot television. Regional campaigns were conducted from time to time, primarily through newspapers. Duport provided bottlers with mats and ideas for local advertising.

The first step in determining potentials was to attempt to isolate those factors which affected soft drink sales. Mr. Walker had learned of studies by other soft drink companies which had found that temperature and income were factors that affected soft drink sales. He also felt that an important factor as far as the Duport Company was concerned was the proportion of the population which was able to buy Genii in a local grocery store. Accordingly, he asked his marketing research department to collect and analyze such data for the purpose of measuring market potentials. Table 1 shows the data collected for the 48 contiguous states.

TABLE 1. Selected data related to soft drink sales

State	Bottles of all soft drinks consumed per capita*	Mean annual temperatures†	Income per capita‡ ($100s)	Bottles of Genii consumed per capita§	Percent of state population under franchise by Duport
Alabama	200	66	$13	1.8	63.9%
Arizona	150	62	17	9.4	18.8
Arkansas	237	63	11	3.3	55.9
California	135	56	25	8.2	8.4
Colorado	121	52	19	3.3	83.4
Connecticut	118	50	27	2.1	4.9
Delaware	217	54	28	—	—
Florida	242	72	18	3.7	23.4
Georgia	295	64	14	1.3	18.0
Idaho	85	46	16	5.5	70.8
Illinois	141	52	24	3.0	75.8
Indiana	184	52	20	2.2	28.9
Iowa	104	50	16	3.0	30.3
Kansas	143	56	17	3.7	18.6

TABLE 1. (*continued*)

State	Bottles of all soft drinks consumed per capita*	Mean annual tempera- turest	Income per capita‡ ($100s)	Bottles of Genii consumed per capita§	Percent of state population under franchise by Duport
Kentucky	230	56	13	5.1	66.4
Louisiana	269	69	15	3.1	33.9
Maine	111	41	16	2.4	88.3
Maryland	217	54	21	14.4	5.4
Massachusetts	114	47	22	2.8	38.6
Michigan	108	47	21	1.0	75.6
Minnesota	108	41	18	4.2	85.6
Mississippi	248	65	10	4.8	57.2
Missouri	203	57	19	3.6	35.2
Montana	77	44	19	4.0	89.0
Nebraska	97	49	16	2.7	39.0
Nevada	166	48	24	2.8	16.3
New Hampshire	177	35	18	3.7	67.9
New Jersey	143	54	24	.9	66.2
New Mexico	157	56	15	—	—
New York	111	48	25	4.0	30.2
North Carolina	330	59	13	6.4	42.3
North Dakota	63	39	14	2.5	68.7
Ohio	165	51	22	1.9	24.3
Oklahoma	184	62	16	1.0	66.1
Oregon	68	51	19	2.4	74.3
Pennsylvania	121	50	20	1.8	28.1
Rhode Island	138	50	20	—	—
South Carolina	237	65	12	3.3	73.0
South Dakota	95	45	13	7.8	44.5
Tennessee	236	60	13	4.0	96.6
Texas	222	69	17	3.7	36.6
Utah	100	50	16	5.7	81.3
Vermont	64	44	16	—	—
Virginia	270	58	16	5.8	26.7
Washington	77	49	20	3.4	38.6
West Virginia	144	55	15	1.2	65.2
Wisconsin	97	46	19	2.2	55.2
Wyoming	102	46	19	2.5	18.6

* Source: "The Soft Drink Industry—A Market Study," *National Bottler's Gazette.*
† Source: U.S. Weather Bureau, *Climatological Data—National Summary.*
‡ Source: U.S. Department of Commerce, Office of Business Economics, *U.S. Income and Output,* a supplement to the *Survey of Current Business.*
§ Based on percentage of population under franchise in each state.

What procedure(s) should be used to analyze the data?

What states have the highest market potential?

Where should Duport plan to locate new franchises?

If you could start all over, would you take a different approach to esti- mating each state's market potential? If so, describe it in detail, includ- ing the analytical procedures you would use.

16

Data analysis III: Explaining observed differences— Linear discriminant analysis and automatic interaction detector

Chapter 15 described three methods of analysis frequently applied to multivariate data—cross tabulation, correlation and regression. The purpose of Chapters 16 and 17 is to introduce some more advanced multivariate methods of analysis the use of which has been growing in recent years. Many research projects result in complex sets of data which cannot be easily or adequately analyzed with the methods discussed in Chapter 15. If researchers wish to analyze such complex data, they should have an understanding of these more advanced methods in order to know which can be useful in what situations.

Before proceding with the description of these methods, it will be helpful first to discuss briefly (1) the character of multivariate data, (2) the use of the computer in multivariate analysis, and (3) the main points to be made during the discussions of these methods.

Multivariate data and multivariate analysis. The following discussions will be easier to understand if the reader will first attempt to visualize a large set of multivariate data. For example, Figure 13–2 on page 414 graphically displays multivariate tabulations involving four variables (or dimensions). Readers should try to visualize such a data set involving five or six or more variables. The data set would be similar to that shown in Figure 13–2, except that there would be a fifth variable and a sixth variable and so on. Similarly, Figure 15–1 on page 464 shows a scatter diagram of data consisting of two variables (or dimensions). Readers should have little trouble visualizing a scatter diagram of data involving two variables; it is more difficult with three variables; it is almost impossible with four or more variables. They are impossible to draw on paper.

Assume now that a researcher is trying to analyze a set of multivariate data. In such a situation, the researcher may very well be trying to determine:

> If large families with high income are heavy consumers of margarine and, if so, what are their favorite television programs? If there are not too many variables, the researcher can set up a cross-tabulation to analyze the data (see Figure 13–2).

> If older and wealthier people are heavier users of wine. In such a case, the researcher may wish to *"best fit" a line to the data* in such a way that the line is *a good fit* of the data and so can be used to measure how wine consumption changes with increases in age and income (see Figure 15–3 and Table 15–11).

> If successful salesmen make more sales calls, spend more time selling, and travel more miles than unsuccessful salesmen. The researcher may do this by trying to *fit a line through the data* in such a way that the line *accurately separates* one category of data (successful salesmen) from another category of data (unsuccessful salesmen).

> If the activities, interests and opinions of housewives differ in such a way that those things can be used as the basis for identifying different market segments. The researcher hopes to identify similar respondents (ones who have given similar answers to certain sets of questions) within the large set of data by *locating densely compacted clusters* or subsets of the data.

In other words, the researcher will typically be trying to "see patterns,"or to "fit" a line to the data, or use a line to "split" the data into two subgroups, or to "identify subsets" of the data which are highly correlated. This is why researchers use these more advanced methods of analysis—to make sense out of very large scatter diagrams or multivariate tabulations which usually involve more than three or four variables and which, as a result of their complexity, cannot be analyzed visually.

Use of the computer: A blessing or a curse?   When a marketing research project involves a large sample of respondents who are measured on more than three or four variables (and perhaps on as many as 50–100), a multivariate analysis cannot be performed without the use of the computer. There are just too many variables and too many respondents for it to be done manually. Most multivariate methods also require numerous complex calculations which cannot be performed without the computer. In fact, without the computer, these methods would be little used, if at all. The growing use of multivariate methods is due in large part to the availability of computer programs which can analyze data representing a large number of respondents and variables.[1] On the one hand, these programs make it con-

---

[1] Descriptions of some of these computer programs can be found in the SPSS and BMD references listed in footnote 5, Chapter 14.

venient for researchers to use multivariate methods. On the other hand, this convenience can be a curse if the proper precautions are not taken. Many highly qualified experts feel that this convenience is abused by researchers who include in their analyses all of the variables they can get their hands on, even ones which have no logical basis for being included. This can lead to numerical relationships which have no real meaning. The point of view taken here is that multivariate methods of analysis should only be used on variables which are logically related to the problem being studied.

Four main points.   In Chapters 16 and 17 the discussion of each of several methods of analysis will be oriented toward answering the four questions listed below. These four questions are also integrated into Table 16–1, which shows how the questions are answered for different multivariate methods of analysis. Readers should make frequent reference to the table as they progress through the chapter, as this will help them distinguish between the different methods and their uses and applications.

1.   What is the typical problem or situation which can be studied with the method?   Answering this question will help the reader gain an understanding of the problems and situations to which the method can be applied.

2.   What does the method do?   The above discussion on the character of multivariate data indicated that various methods may try to "see patterns" in the data, or "best fit" a line to the data, or use a line "to split" the data into different categories, or to "identify clusters" within the data. If the reader knows both the typical problem to which each method can be applied (question (1) above), and what each method does, he or she will have a better understanding of the different methods and when one method should be used rather than another.

3.   What types of variables can be analyzed?   Chapter 15 pointed out that cross-tabulation can be applied to categorical variables and that regression analysis can be applied to continuous variables (see Table 16–1). The different methods discussed here cannot all be used with the same kinds of variables. By knowing which kinds of variables can be analyzed by a given method, readers will gain further understanding of when to use the different methods.

4.   Does the method use independent variables to characterize respondents falling into different categories defined by the dependent variable, that is, does it use independent variables to explain the variation in a dependent variable? Or does the method identify interdependencies among a number of variables without treating any of them as dependent or independent?   All of the methods discussed in Chapter 15 used independent variables to analyze or explain the variation in a dependent variable. That is also true for the methods discussed in this chapter. However, the three methods discussed in the next chapter are different in the sense that they don't treat some of the variables as independent and some as dependent. Rather, they treat all of the variables as somehow being interdependent, and they attempt to identify how the variables are related to each other. Thus, this fourth question can

TABLE 16-1. Distinguishing characteristics of selected multivariate methods of analysis

A. Using independent variables to characterize respondents falling into different categories defined by the dependent variable

Method of analysis	Typical problem studied	What the method does	Dependent variable	Independent variable
Cross-tabulation	Is heavier consumption of margarine associated with large families of high income? (See Figure 13–2)	Establishes tables with cells of data	Categorical	Categorical
Regression	By how much does usage of wine increase with given increases in income and age? (See Figure 15–3 and Table 15–11)	"Best fits" a line to a scatter diagram of data	Continuous	Continuous
Linear discriminant analysis (LDA)	What characteristics are possessed by salesmen who fall into one category (successful) but are not possessed by salesmen who fall into the other category (unsuccessful)? (See Figure 16–1)	Finds a straight line through a scatter diagram which accurately discriminates one category of respondent from the others	Categorical	Continuous
Automatic interaction detector (AID)	Of the many characteristics measured, which ones are associated with people who are very heavy users, heavy users, moderate users, light users, etc. of advertising and other information sources when purchasing an appliance? (See Figure 16–2)	Uses analysis of variance to search out important characteristics and to split the total sample into subsamples of heavy, average, and light users	Continuous	Categorical

B. Identifying interdependencies among a number of variables

Method of analysis	Typical problem studied	What the method does	Variables
Cluster	What are the different segments that exist in the total market for sporting goods? (See Figure 17–1)	Identifies clusters of respondents who have given the same answers to a certain combination of questions	Interval scales, continuous, or categorical
Factor	What are the main characteristics ("factors") of compact cars which potential buyers consider to be very important?	Identifies sets of statements which result in highly correlated responses (see Table 17–2), each such set representing a different factor	Interval scales, or continuous
Conjoint	What combination of features should be designed into a new household upholstery cleaner?	Calculates the value (utility) of each feature being considered for the product (see Table 17–5 and Figure 17–5)	Categorical

also help readers have a better understanding of when to use the different methods.

Two other aspects of this presentation must be mentioned before proceeding into the chapter. First, typically there are available a number of different versions of each of the methods discussed here. Only the more basic versions of these methods are described. Second, in order to keep the exposition both clear and simple, the examples discussed here employ only a few variables, rather than many variables. As noted above in the discussion concerning the computer, these methods can be applied to data consisting of many variables.

LINEAR DISCRIMINANT ANALYSIS (LDA)

Typical problem.   Linear discriminant analysis (LDA) is typically used to identify the characteristics which can accurately discriminate between the respondents who fall in one category from those who fall in another category. For example, LDA can be used to study successful salesmen and unsuccessful salesmen in order to determine the characteristics which are possessed by successful salesmen but not possessed by unsuccessful salesmen. (See Table 16–1). Once the characteristics of successful salesmen have been identified, the information can be used to recruit individuals with characteristics similar to those possessed by successful salesmen. LDA can also be used to study owners and nonowners of videotape recorders, or to study beer drinkers who prefer different brands of beer (Budweiser versus Miller versus Schlitz), or to study motorists with different attitudes toward the rationing of gasoline (those in favor versus those opposed versus those undecided). In each of these situations, a researcher can use LDA in an attempt to determine the characteristics which are possessed by one category of respondent but not possessed by the other categories of respondents.

What the method does.   LDA is applied to a large scatter diagram of data like Figure 16–1 which represents the characteristics of individual salesmen (e.g., education, experience, etc.). Some of the data points in the scatter diagram belong to salesmen who fall into one category (e.g., successful), while the rest of the data points belong to salesmen who fall into another category (e.g., unsuccessful). LDA attempts to find a straight line which, when placed in the scatter diagram, accurately discriminates or separates one category from the other. In this example, all or most of the respondents on one side of the line will be successful salesmen who possess certain characteristics, and all or most of the respondents on the other side of the line will be unsuccessful salesmen who possess different characteristics. (See Figure 16–1.)

Types of variables.   A researcher can use LDA whenever the dependent variable of interest is a categorical one and when all of the independent variables to be used in the analysis are continuous. This is quite different

FIGURE 16–1. LDA for Alloy Steel Company Salesmen

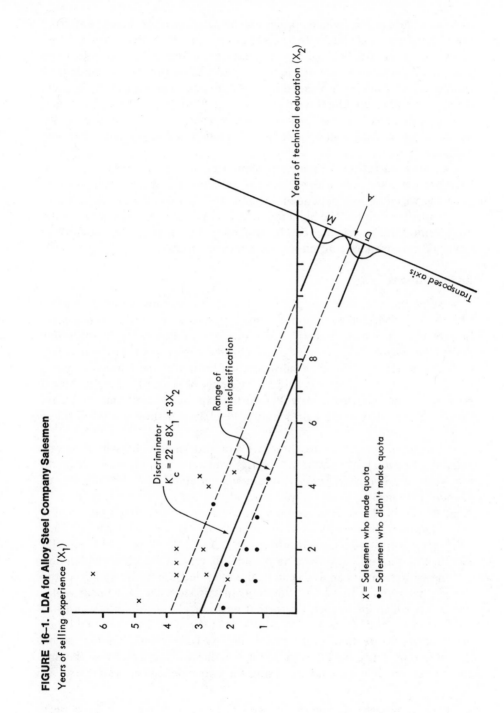

x = Salesmen who made quota

● = Salesmen who didn't make quota

from cross-tabulation (which applies only to categorical variables) and from regression (which applies only to continuous variables). Because LDA can be used on a set of data consisting of a categorical dependent variable and a number of continuous independent variables, LDA provides a method of analysis which can't be duplicated by cross-tabulation or regression. Readers should carefully study the three methods listed at the top of Table 16–1, and recognize that the three methods compliment each other insofar as each aplies to a set of data which can't be analyzed by either of the other two methods.

Explains variation.   Finally, it should be noted that researchers use LDA for the same reason they use cross-tabulation and regression—to explain the variation in a dependent variable through the use of one or more independent variables. The big difference, as noted above, is that LDA is the only method of analysis that can be applied to a categorical dependent variable and two or more continuous independent variables.

An illustration

Assume the sales manager of the Alloy Steel Company is trying to identify what it is that makes a good salesman, that is, why some salesmen meet or exceed their quotas, and why some do not.[2] In attempting to study this matter the sales manager compiles data on the company's twenty salesmen, including whether or not each salesman met his quota, the number of years of experience selling alloy steel, and the number of years of formal technical education. The sales manager collected the experience and education data because he felt they could help identify the characteristics of a good salesman.

In this set of data, there are three items of information on each salesman: a *dependent categorical* variable, which is whether or not he made his quota that year, and two *independent continuous* variables—(1) the number of years of experience selling alloy steel, and (2) the amount of formal technical education. These data are presented in Figure 16–1. Each salesman is located graphically according to the number of years of selling experience (X_1) and formal technical education (X_2). The 11 salesmen who actually met their quotas are shown with an x, and 9 that didn't are shown with a dot.

Linear discriminant analysis can be used to select the linear equation (the straight line) which best "fits" the data. In this case, the best linear equation is one which fits in such a way that most, or all, of the observations in one category (made quota) *fall on one side* of the linear equation and most, or all, of the observations in the other category (didn't make quota) *fall on the other side*. Thus, the linear equation is a discriminator. Because the line can be expressed as an equation using the two independent variables $(X_1$

---

[2] This is a hypothetical example, but one which is based on the much larger study reported in Ronald E. Turner, "Perceptual Dimensions of Salesmen: A Multidimensional Analysis of Call-Allocating and Sales-Response Behavior," unpublished dissertation, Northwestern University, 1970.

and X_2), the discriminator tells the researcher what combinations of X_1 and X_2 are associated with each category. With such a discriminator, the sales manager has a better understanding of how years of selling experience (X_1) and years of formal technical education (X_2) are related to a salesman's making or not making quota.

Like regression analysis, the concepts underlying LDA are not complex, even though its procedures are. In order to understand how LDA can be used, the reader must have some knowledge of (1) the linear discriminating equation, (2) how it can be used, and (3) how to evaluate the equation in terms of how well it fits the data.

The discriminating equation. Using procedures much like those used in regression analysis, LDA determines a "best fit" linear equation of the form

$$K = aX_1 + bX_2 + cX_3 + \ldots$$

where the $X_1, X_2, X_3, \ldots$ are independent variables (in the example, years of selling experience and technical education), the $a, b, c, \ldots$ are coefficients determined in the LDA during the "best fit" procedures, and K is a constant (a number) which is also determined during the LDA procedures.[3] (K is needed to complete the equation: it does not represent any of the variables.) In the Alloy Steel Company example, the LDA procedures calculate the a and b coefficients to be 8 and 3, respectively, and these result in a discriminating equation of

$$K = 8X_1 + 3X_2$$

where X_1 represents years of selling experience and X_2 represents years of formal technical education. (If four independent variables had been used in this analysis, the discriminating equation would have had cX_3 and dX_4 terms as well.) The LDA procedure also calculates a critical value for K (designated K_c). The K_c calculated in the salesmen example is 22. (The value of K_c has the effect of raising or lowering the discriminating line in Figure 16–1. Thus, if K_c were 40 instead of 22, the discriminating line would intersect the X_1 axis at 5 and the X_2 axis at 13.3, with the slope of the line remaining unchanged.) These two things—the linear equation and the K_c value—are the major outputs of a LDA, and they combine to form the discriminator.

The discriminator is formed by substituting the calculated K_c value for K in the linear equation. Thus, by replacing K in the above equation with 22 ($= K_c$),

$$22 = 8X_1 + 3X_2$$

---

[3] Explanations of the procedures used in calculating the coefficients can be found in William F. Massy, "Statistical Analysis of Relations between Variables," in R. E. Frank, A. A. Kuehn, and W. F. Massy (eds.), *Quantitative Techniques in Marketing Analysis* (Homewood, Ill.: R. D. Irwin, 1962), pp. 95–100. For a description of a computerized LDA program, see pp. 434–67 of the N. H. Nie et al., *Statistical Package*.

the discriminator for the Alloy Steel Company case is formed. This equation is shown as the downward sloping line in Figure 16–1. The space above and to the right of the discriminator represents combinations of years of experience selling alloy steel (X_1) and years of formal technical education (X_2) which are associated with "making quota"; the space below and to the left of the discriminator represents combinations of X_1 and X_2 which are associated with "not making quota." The two coefficients in the discriminator (8 and 3) imply that a year of selling experience is much more important than a year of formal technical education in explaining why a salesman did or did not make quota.

The following is a greatly simplified discussion of how the discriminator is determined. To best understand the discussion, the reader should look at the data from point A at the lower right end of the discriminator (see the arrow in Figure 16–1). If a new axis (the "transposed axis" in Figure 16–1) is drawn perpendicular to the discriminator, it is possible to plot on the transposed axis the frequency distributions of salesmen who met quota and also of salesmen who didn't meet quota as they are seen from point A. These are shown as the two distributions on the transposed axis appearing in the lower right portion of Figure 16–1. These two distributions have means of $\overline{M}$ (for "made quota") and $\overline{D}$ (for "didn't make quota"). Next, these two frequency distributions are subjected to a calculation very much like a one-way analysis of variance which determines the ratio of ("between group" variation ÷ "within group" variation).[4] Note that if many different lines were drawn through the data in Figure 16–1, each line would result in different "made quota" and "didn't make quota" frequency distributions on its transposed axis, and therefore the ratio of ("between group" variation ÷ "within group" variation) would be different for different lines. The line which is selected as the discriminator by the LDA procedures is the one which maximizes the ratio of ("between group" variation ÷ "within group" variation)—that is, the one which maximizes the "between group" variation while minimizing the "within group" variation. That line is the best possible discriminating line among all the possible lines that can be drawn through the data.

Using the discriminator.   The discriminator can be used as a predictor in the following manner. The independent variables (years of selling experience and education) associated with a salesman are placed in the linear equation to calculate a K value for each salesman. For example, if a salesman had two years of experience and four of education ($K = (8)(2) + (3)(4) = 28$), or seven of experience and one of education ($K = (8)(7) + (3)(1) = 59$), the K value associated with the salesman is larger than the critical K value ($K_c = 22$), and thus the discriminator predicts that the salesman belongs in the "made quota" category. If a salesman has one year of experience and four of education ($K = (8)(1) + (3)(4) = 20$), the salesman's K value is less than 22 and so the discrim-

---

[4] One-way analysis is described in detail in Chapter 14.

inator predicts that the salesman belongs in the "didn't make quota" category. Thus, the linear equation and K_c are used to classify salesmen into different categories (dependent variable), based only upon their years of experience and technical education (independent variables).

Evaluating the discriminator. The sales manager of the Alloy Steel Company can ask, "How well does the discriminator fit the data? How good is it as a predictor?" Unlike regression analysis, the "fit" of a discriminator cannot be evaluated through the calculation of something equivalent to R^2. A discriminator must be evaluated more subjectively, in the manner described below.

The linear equation uses the independent variables associated with each salesman to determine K. By comparing K with K_c, each salesman is classified in one category or another. If this classification agrees with the salesman's actual performance (did or did not make quota), the discriminator is accurate *for that salesman*. If the discriminator is an accurate predictor for *all or most* of the 20 salesmen, it could be judged to fit the data well and to be an accurate predictor.

For example, the sales manager can use Figure 16–1 to judge the classification ability of the discriminator. In this case, the discriminator has misclassified 2 of 20 salesmen (one dot is above the line while one x is below the line). Alternatively, one can say that the discriminator correctly classified, for 90 percent of the salesmen, the category (met quota/did not meet quota) in which the salesman was actually observed. An LDA which correctly classifies 70–100 percent of the observations is generally thought to be good.

Another way of judging the utility of the discriminator is to look at the *range of misclassification* (shown in Figure 16–1). It can be defined as the range on both sides of the discriminator which just encompasses all of the misclassified salesmen. Within this range the classification ability of the discriminator is less than 100 percent (Figure 16–1 shows that only five of the seven salesmen within the misclassification range have been correctly classified.) But outside of this range, 100 percent of the salesmen are correctly classified. Therefore, the discriminator is less useful when the misclassification range is wider and includes more incorrectly classified salesmen. When this occurs, the LDA must either be judged unsuccessful, or it must be repeated with additional independent variables in an attempt to arrive at a more accurate discriminating equation.

Problems in using LDA. As with regression analysis, one may encounter problems and difficulties when using LDA.[5] The four difficulties listed at the end of the regression analysis discussion—too few observations, the

[5] A critical evaluation of the application of LDA to marketing research can be found in William R. Dillon, Matthew Goldstein, and Leon G. Schiffman, "Appropriateness of Linear Discriminant and Multinomial Classification Analysis in Marketing Research," *Journal of Marketing Research* 15 (February 1978):103–112. See also Melvin R. Crask and William D. Perreault, Jr., "Validation of Discriminant Analysis in Marketing Research," *Journal of Marketing Research* 14 (February 1977):60–68.

wrong independent variables, highly correlated independent variables, and a true relationship which is not linear—also apply to LDA. In addition, the dependent variable data used in the LDA may be of poor quality, especially if the categories were established subjectively (for example, good/bad, or comfortable/uncomfortable) rather than objectively. In the salesman's study, for example, the observed dependent variable (made quota/didn't make quota) for each salesman will also reflect whether a salesman's quota was set unreasonably high or low. If the quotas are unrealistic, the dependent variable data will be poor, and it will not be possible to interpret the LDA results in a meaningful way.

AUTOMATIC INTERACTION DETECTOR (AID)

Typical problem. Researchers typically use automatic interaction detector (AID) in studies where a firm is trying to identify the characteristics of heavy users, of moderate users, of light users, and of nonusers of a product or service. For example, many marketing studies measure the rate at which consumers use a certain product, service or advertising medium, while other studies measure the amounts consumers spend on insurance, vacations, or entertainment. Frequently the purpose of such studies is to identify how the characteristics of heavy users are different from the characteristics of average or light users (see Table 16–1). Such information can be very useful in more effectively directing marketing programs to specific target markets.

If a large number of other variables (age, income, etc.) have also been measured, it is impractical for researchers to attempt to analyze the data using cross-tabulation. Instead, researchers will find it more efficient to use AID to identify the characteristics of very heavy users or spenders, to identify the characteristics of moderately heavy users or spenders, to identify the characteristics of average users or spenders, and so on. AID is useful because it *helps researchers identify which of the many variables studied can be used to characterize the individuals falling into the different consumption categories.* In effect, AID assists the researchers by systematically searching through the many variables which were measured and by selecting only the ones which are important.

What the method does. AID is a searching procedure which uses one-way analysis of variance to split a sample into two subsamples in such a way (*a*) that the difference between the means of the two subsamples is the largest possible difference that can be found, and (*b*) that the difference is statistically significant.

For example, if a researcher is trying to identify the characteristics of heavy users versus light users, AID searches out the one variable (among those available) which does the best job of splitting the total sample into two subsamples which are different with respect to usage. One subsample (subsample A) will have a "high average" while the other subsample (subsample B) will have a "low average." That is, the average usage rate of the respondents in each subsample will then be different from the average usage rate of the total sample of respondents. Subsample A is then separately analyzed by the AID procedures. The procedures will search out a second variable (among those still available) which does the best job of splitting subsample A into two smaller subsamples. One of these subsamples (call it AA) will consist mostly of respondents who use the product or service at a rate greater than the "high average," while the other subsample (call it AB) will consist mostly of respondents who use the product or service at a rate below the "high average." This procedure is applied also to subsample B to identify a third variable which can be used to create two additional subsamples (call them BA and BB). Thus, there will be four subsamples, one of which (subsample AA) will include mostly respondents who are *well above average* in their usage and one of which (subsample BB) will include mostly respondents who are *well below average* in their usage. The three variables which were used to split the total sample into four subsamples are then used to identify the characteristics associated with very heavy users and with very light users of the product in question. This procedure is continued to create even more subsamples if the total sample size is large enough to permit.

Types of variables.   As Table 16–1 shows, a researcher can use AID if the main variable of interest (e.g., consumption or usage rates) is a continuous variable, and all the other variables are categorical. That is, AID can be applied to a set of data consisting of a *continuous dependent variable* and *categorical independent variables*. This is different from the types of variables needed for cross-tabulation, regression or LDA. The reader should note in Table 16–1 that with the addition of AID, a researcher has available a method of analysis for every possible combination of categorical and continuous dependent and independent variables.

Explains variation.   AID is like cross-tabulation, regression, and LDA in that AID is used to understand and explain the variation in a dependent variable (see the upper half of Table 16–1). However, as noted above, AID is different from those three methods in that it is the only method that can be applied to data consisting of a continuous dependent variable and categorical independent variables.

An illustration

A manufacturer of consumer appliances wanted to learn more about appliance owners, especially about the advertising and other information sources they used when making an appliance purchase decision.[6] Among other things, the manufacturer wanted to know how many different sources of information they used, as well as what those sources were. Such information would enable the manufacturer to do a better job of selecting media and preparing advertising materials.

---

[6] This illustration is a greatly oversimplified adaptation of the research reported in Joseph W. Newman and Richard Staelin, "Information Sources of Durable Goods," *Journal of Advertising Research* 13 (April 1973): 19–29.

Researchers for the manufacturer selected a sample of 653 households which had recently purchased an appliance. Respondents were asked to indicate the number and types of advertising and other information sources they used when they were making their purchase decisions. Possible sources of information included friends and neighbors, books and magazines, media advertising, advertising pamphlets and brochures, and retail store personnel. Researchers also collected information on 25 other variables such as the number of appliances the household was expecting to buy at the time, cost of the appliance, number of different brands considered, whether the respondent bought the same brand as previously owned, the age and education of the head of household, family income, number of children, and others.

The survey showed that usage of advertising and other information sources varied a great deal among the respondents. Fourteen percent of the households used no information sources at all when making their purchase, and none of the households used as many as five sources of information when making their decision. On the average, each household used 1.84 information sources when purchasing an appliance. Table 16–2 shows these results.

TABLE 16–2. Number of information sources used when purchasing an appliance

Number of information sources used	Percent of households
0	14%
1	30
2	26
3	18
4	12
5	0
	100%

Source: Joseph W. Newman and Richard Staelin, "Information Sources of Durable Goods," *Journal of Advertising Research* 13 (April 1973): 19–29.

The manufacturer wanted to know if appliance purchasers who made above-average use of advertising and other information sources had characteristics different from purchasers who made average use or below-average use of the various sources of information. If there were differences, the manufacturer could use that knowledge to direct his advertisements toward consumers who used such sources when making a purchase decision.

The researchers could have used either cross-tabulation or AID to analyze the data. (They would first have had to convert the dependent variable into categorical form in order to use cross-tabulation.) The researchers did not use cross-tabulation because there were 25 variables which could be used to describe the characteristics of respondents. They knew that cross-tabulation becomes quite cumbersome with so many variables. Instead, the researchers used AID because it would systematically search through all of the many variables and identify only the important ones.

What characteristics did heavy users of information sources possess which average and light users did not? In order to set up an AID analysis to help answer this question, the researchers selected the number of information sources used by each respondent (a continuous variable) as the dependent variable in their AID analysis. The researchers used the 25 other variables collected in the study as the independent variables in their AID analysis. This was possible because all of these variables were in categorical form. The data from the 653 respondents on these variables were then subjected to the AID procedures, which are described below. These procedures consist of (1) a basic analysis, (2) a complete enumeration of all possible binary splits, (3) selecting the best split, and (4) repeating steps 1, 2, and 3 to create additional splits.[7]

Basic analysis.   The basic analysis is essentially a one-way analysis of variance applied to two subsamples of the original data in order to see if there is a statistically significant difference between the average number of information sources used by the two subsamples.[8] Any one of the 25 categorical independent variables can be used as the basis for splitting the total sample into two subsamples.

For example, the total sample might be broken down into two groups consisting of households with $10,000 or more annual income, and households with less than $10,000 annual income. The basic analysis calculates the average number of information sources used by each of the two subsamples and applies a one-way analysis of variance to the two subsamples. If the one-way analysis of variance does not indicate that the difference between the two subsamples is significant, the researcher has no basis for saying that households with larger annual incomes use more (or fewer) information sources when purchasing an appliance. Thus, the researcher would not use income to describe how heavy users of information sources differ from light users of information sources. However, if the one-way analysis of variance shows that the difference between the two subsamples is significant, the researcher has some evidence indicating that household income is useful in describing how heavy users of information sources differ from light users of information sources. This is why the basic analysis is part of the AID procedures. This basic analysis is used in the manner described below.

---

[7] A complete description of AID procedures is found in J. A. Sonquist, E. L. Baker, and J. N. Morgan, *Searching for Structure (Alias, AID-III)* (Ann Arbor: Survey Research Center, University of Michigan, 1971).

[8] One-way analysis of variance was described in Chapter 14.

Complete enumeration of all possible binary splits. Because all of the independent variables used in the AID analysis are categorical, each category of each independent variable can be used to split the total sample into two subsamples. For example, the above paragraph illustrated how annual household income of (less than $10,000/$10,000 or more) could be used as the basis for dividing the total sample. Note that if annual income was recorded in the categories of (less than $10,000/$10,000–15,000/more than $15,000), annual household income of ($15,000 or less/more than $15,000) also could be used as the basis for dividing the total sample, as could incomes of ($10–15,000/other than $10–15,000).[9] Age of the head of the household is another independent variable which could be used to divide the total sample. For example, the total sample might be broken into two groups using 45 (or 25) years of age as the basis for the split. This breaking down of the total sample (or of a subsample) into two parts is called a *binary split,* and each such binary split uses a categorical independent variable as the basis for the split. This is an important aspect of AID, because the AID procedures *determine every possible binary split of every independent variable included in the analysis.*

In order to determine how the total sample should first be split, the AID procedures apply the basic analysis to every possible split of the total sample which can be made using the categorical independent variables. For each possible split, a one-way analysis of variance is used to determine if the difference between the two subsamples is statistically significant. Each binary split which results in a significant difference is listed for possible use as the basis for making the first AID split. For example, Table 16–3 shows a representative (but much abbreviated) list of the type of information available from a complete enumeration of all possible binary splits. The table shows that when the independent variable "cost of product" was used to

---

TABLE 16–3. Significantly different splits identified in the complete enumeration of all possible binary splits

Independent variable	Binary split	Average number of information sources used by each group
Age of head of household	45 years or less/over 45 years	1.98/1.62
Cost of product	$200 or more/less than $200	1.95/1.68
Education of head of household	high school diploma or more/ no high school diploma	2.13/1.61

---

9 This income variable indicates that the basis for a split need not be in order or in sequence. For example, identify the three income categories discussed above as simply A, B, and C. "Ordered" splits can be based on (A/BC) and AB/C), but the split can also be an "unordered" or out-of-sequence one, such as (B/AC).

divide the total sample on the basis of ($200 or more/less than $200), the average number of information sources used by the two subgroups was 1.95 and 1.68 respectively, which was judged to be statistically significant on the basis of a one-way analysis of variance.

Selecting the best split.   Next, the AID procedures compare all of the significantly different binary splits uncovered in the previous step and select the one independent variable and binary split of that independent variable which results in the two subsamples with the largest difference between their means. For example, Table 16–3 indicates that the greatest difference in the average number of information sources used occurred when the total sample was divided into one group where the head of household had at least a high school education, and a second group where the head of household did not finish high school.

The AID procedures selected that split as the best one because, of all the possible ways the total sample can be divided into two subsamples with the available categorical independent variables, that split resulted in the largest difference between the two subsamples. That split is shown pictorially in the tree diagram in Figure 16–2. The left-most box symbolizes the total sample of 653 households (recorded in the lower right corner of the box) which used an average of 1.84 information sources when purchasing an appliance (recorded in the lower left corner of the box). The first AID split created a subsample of 283 where the head of household was a high school graduate (subgroup A), and another subsample of 370 where the head of household did not complete high school (subgroup B). The two boxes to the right of the total sample box in Figure 16–2 portray this split, and show that subgroup A used an average of 2.13 information sources, while subgroup B used an average of only 1.61 information sources. Thus, the analysis to this point gives the researchers some evidence which allows them to characterize heavier users of information sources as people with a high school education.

Additional splits.   As indicated earlier, AID is a stepwise method of analysis. Using the procedures described above, the total sample was divided into subgroups A and B. Since the researchers have 24 more categorical independent variables which they can use to study the characteristics of heavy and light users of information sources, they could carry their AID analysis further. To do so, the same procedures described above are applied to each of the subgroups individually in exactly the same manner, except that the education of the head of household cannot be used again in the analysis. For example, each of the two subgroups (A and B) resulting from the first split were further analyzed with AID. Figure 16–2 shows the results of this analysis. Subgroup A was split on the basis of number of brands initially considered, and subgroup B on the basis of product cost. This resulted in the four subgroups (A_1, A_2, B_1, B_2) in the middle of Figure 16–2. These four subgroups were then split once again, creating a total of eight subgroups, shown on the right side of Figure 16–2. The AID stepwise procedure allows the splitting process to continue as long as the resulting splits (a) are statis-

FIGURE 16–2. AID tree diagram for a study of the information sources used when purchasing a major appliance*

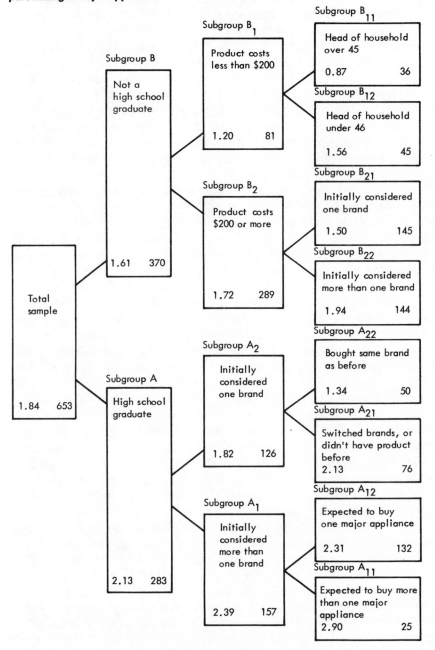

* Average number of information sources used appears in the lower left-hand corner and number of households in the lower right-hand corner of each box.
    Source: Adapted from Joseph W. Newman and Richard Staelin, "Information Sources of Durable Goods," *Journal of Advertising Research* 13 (April 1973): 22.

tically significant in a one-way analysis of variance test and (b) the resulting sample size in any subgroup does not fall below 20.[10]

Usefulness of AID. Figure 16–2 shows the final tree diagram resulting from the AID analysis. A careful analysis of the tree diagram will show that the AID procedures used 6 of the 25 categorical independent variables which were available to split the total sample into 8 subgroups which utilized information sources with differing levels of intensity. The group (A_{11}) using the most information sources (an average of 2.90) can be characterized as high school graduates who initially considered more than one brand, and who expected to buy more than one major appliance. The group (B_{11}) using the fewest information sources (an average of 0.87) can be characterized by a head of household who didn't finish high school, who was over 45 years of age, and who considered the purchase of a product costing less than $200. Thus, the researchers used an AID analysis to identify eight groups whose average use of information sources ranged from 0.87 to 2.90. When the researchers compare those averages with the total average of 1.84, they can begin to identify the characteristics of appliance purchasers who make above average use of advertising and other information sources. This information can help the appliance manufacturer prepare more effective marketing programs.

Many marketing studies are concerned with identifying the characteristics of the heavier users of a product or brand, of the more frequent readers of a newspaper or magazine, or of the individuals with a more favorable attitude toward dining out and going to the theatre. These things can be the dependent variables in AID analyses if they are measured as continuous variables. Most studies of this type can be analyzed with AID if the researchers have also collected ten or more categorical independent variables. When such studies have many independent variables, researchers will find that it is too cumbersome to analyze the data with cross-tabulations. Rather, AID can be used instead, and it is a more efficient method of analysis in three ways.

First, AID will select only those variables which can split the total sample into two subsamples in such a way that the difference between the subsample means on the dependent variable in question is statistically significant. Second, AID identifies the independent variables in the order of their ability to select groups with the largest differences—the first independent variable creates two groups with the largest possible significant difference, the second independent variable creates two new subgroups which again have the largest possible difference, and so on. Third, AID can help researchers detect the interaction which exists between variables. For example, Figure 16–2 shows that being a high school graduate (average use = 2.13) becomes much more important if the individual also is considering more than one brand *and* is expecting to buy more than one major appliance (average use = 2.90).

---

[10] Because AID procedures use the sum of squares calculation (see the discussion of one-way analysis of variance), and because small samples can have some "extreme" observations which bias the sum of squares calculation, a generally accepted practice to avoid such bias is to not allow any split which results in a subsample smaller than 20.

Because of these advantages, if a researcher is working with many independent variables (say, ten or more), the AID tree diagram can be very helpful in identifying the characteristics associated with heavy or light users. It is even possible that an AID analysis will uncover certain interactions between variables which would go undetected if the researcher only used cross-tabulations.

Problems in using AID.[11]   Researchers can encounter a serious problem when using AID if they include in their analysis certain independent variables that are not logically related to the dependent variable. It is worth remembering that AID is a stepwise analysis and that, if the first split is a spurious one, the remaining splits on the tree diagram will probably reflect useless findings. This suggests that AID should not be used as a "fishing expedition"—analyzing all possible independent variables and hoping for "good" results. Rather, the independent variables used in the analysis should be carefully selected.

Another problem with AID is that the researchers can't tell how well the tree diagram fits the data. Unlike regression analysis which calculates an R^2 value, or LDA which provides a "Range of Misclassification," the AID procedures are unable to measure how good the results are. There are no statistical or other tests which can help the researcher with this problem. In order to have confidence in the results obtained from an AID analysis, many researchers argue that a very large sample should be taken and then randomly split into two sets of data. A separate AID analysis should then be applied to each set of data. If similar results are obtained from the two separate analyses, researchers will have greater confidence in the validity of the findings.

SUMMARY

This chapter discussed two additional methods of analysis which can be used to explain the variation observed in survey data—linear discriminant analysis (LDA) and automatic interaction director (AID). These two methods are different from cross-tabulation and regression in that LDA is applied to data consisting of a categorical dependent variable and continuous independent variables, while AID is applied to data consisting of a continuous dependent variable and categorical independent variables. Cross-tabulation, regression, LDA, and AID form a combination of methods of analysis which allow the researcher to analyze any combination of categorical and continuous dependent and independent variables.

Cases

See cases following Chapter 17.

---

11 See Peter Doyle and Ian Fenwick, "The Pitfalls of AID Analysis," *Journal of Marketing Research* 12, (November 1975):408–13.

17

Data analysis IV: Identifying interdependencies—Cluster analysis, factor analysis, and conjoint analysis

Readers should consider Chapter 17 to be a continuation of Chapter 16, in the sense that the chapter presents additional methods of analyzing multivariate data—cluster analysis, factor analysis, and conjoint analysis. To help the reader have a better understanding of when cluster analysis, factor analysis, and conjoint analysis should be used instead of cross-tabulation, regression, LDA, or AID, the discussion here will follow the main four points used in the last chapter (that is, what is the typical problem that can be studied with the method? What does the method do? etc.). This same information is also summarized in Table 16–1, to help readers make an easy visual comparison of all the multivariate methods discussed in this book.

The methods discussed in this chapter are different from those discussed in Chapters 15 and 16 in one important way. Cross-tabulation, regression, LDA and AID all attempt to explain the variation observed in a dependent variable through the use of one or more independent variables. That does not hold true for cluster analysis, factor analysis, or conjoint analysis. These methods are different in the sense that they do not treat some variables as independent and some as dependent. Instead, these methods try to identify interdependencies among a number of variables without treating any of them as dependent or independent.

CLUSTER ANALYSIS

Typical problem. Probably the most typical applications of cluster analysis are found in market segmentation studies. Many firms try to identify and describe the different segments which exist in a given market, and to determine the size of each. The market segmentation information can be used by the firm to develop better advertising appeals, to select more effective media and to direct their marketing activities more precisely at selected market segments. For example, a sporting goods manufacturer may wish to identify the various market segments which constitute the total market for sporting equipment (see Table 16–1). A large sample of users of all kinds of sporting equipment are asked many questions such as how often they participate in sports, whether they prefer indoor or outdoor sports, which sports they participate in, whether they prefer rugged or easy sporting activities, and others. This data will be analyzed to see if the total market consists of a number of different segments. Cluster analysis is probably the most widely used method for analyzing data collected in such surveys when the purpose is to identify the different market segments which exist in a market.

What the method does. Cluster analysis identifies different groups (or clusters) of respondents, such that the respondents in any one cluster are all similar to each other, but different from the respondents in the other clusters. Cluster analysis is typically applied to a large sample of data consisting of many variables. The cluster analysis procedures search through the data and identify respondents *who have given identical, or at least very similar, answers to a certain combination of questions.* These respondents are formed into one cluster. Because, in a large study, *different groups* of respondents are likely to give the same answers to *different combinations of questions,* it is possible to identify a number of different clusters in which the respondents in each cluster are different from the respondents in the other clusters. Thus, by applying cluster analysis to the sporting goods segmentation study, researchers would hope to identify different segments of the market on the basis of answers given to different combinations of questions.

Types of variables. Cluster analysis is typically applied to data which have been recorded on scales such as 5-, 7-, or 10-point scales, but it can also be applied to continuous variable data and to categorical variable data. (See Table 16–1.) However, there tend to be fewer applications of cluster analysis to continuous variable data than to scaled data, and applications of cluster analysis to categorical data are encountered even less frequently.

Identifies interdependencies. Each of the previously discussed multivariate methods (cross-tabulation, regression, LDA, and AID) was concerned with a single variable that in some way was important to marketing decision-makers. For example, in the LDA illustration the single variable of interest was the salesman's success, and in the AID illustration the single variable of interest was the number of advertising and other information sources used when purchasing appliances. In those cases the researcher was using *a single variable* to identify a class or a category into which a respondent belonged.

There are situations in which a researcher may wish to use *more than one variable* to identify the class or category into which a respondent belongs.

If the researcher *does not know which and/or how many variables are best to use for this purpose,* it will be necessary to analyze the variables in some way. When researchers encounter such situations, they will want to use cluster analysis, or one of the other two methods yet to be discussed in this chapter. A multiple variable classification is used because, presumably, in those situations it is more useful to marketing decision-makers than a single variable classification. This is indicated in the bottom half of Table 16–1, which shows that cluster analysis is concerned with finding interdependencies among a number of variables which were measured in the study, especially within different subsets of respondents. Readers should note this because it will help them better understand when cluster analysis can be used rather than some other method.

An illustration

A sporting goods manufacturer attempted to identify the market segments which existed for sporting equipment. A large number of sports-active individuals were asked to respond to questions regarding their sporting activities and interests. These individuals used a 10-point scale to report their preference for indoor versus outdoor sports (variable X_1), another 10-point scale to report their preference for rugged and heavy versus easy and light activities (variable X_2), and other 10-point scales for still other questions (X_3, X_4, . . .). Figure 17–1 illustrates the data obtained from 12 of the respondents on variables X_1 and X_2 only. Each dot represents a respondent's scores on X_1 (vertically) and X_2 (horizontally).

Researchers can use Figure 17–1 to see if there are any patterns of responses in the geometrical space defined by variables X_1 and X_2. Specifically, the researchers would look to see if a number of respondents have answered the two questions in about the same way. For example, one sees in Figure 17–1 that there are three different sets of respondents who have given similar answers to the two questions: individuals 9, 11, and 12 in the upper right portion of the figure; individuals 6, 7, 8, and 10 in the upper left portion; individuals 2, 3, and 4 in the lower center portion.

This clustering of different sets of respondents suggest that the market for sporting equipment might be segmented on the basis of indoor versus outdoor *and* on the basis of rugged versus light activities. For example, individuals 9, 11, and 12 are interested in hunting, backpacking and offroading, and so indicate a preference for rugged outdoor activities. Because individuals 6, 7, 8, and 10 are interested in hiking, fishing and camping, they have a preference for easy outdoor activities. Individuals 2, 3, and 4 enjoy racquetball, indoor tennis and gymnastics. These individuals prefer indoor activities which are not too easy but also not too rugged. One bowling enthusiast (1) preferred easy indoor activities, and another all-round sports activist (5) preferred fairly rugged activities which could be either indoors or outdoors.

Because the example in Figure 17–1 involves only two variables, it is easy to lay out the data graphically and to identify visually any clusters which may exist. If another variable (X_3) were included in this example, the only difference would be that Figure 17–1 would have to be presented in three-

FIGURE 17–1. Plot of data from sporting activities and interests study

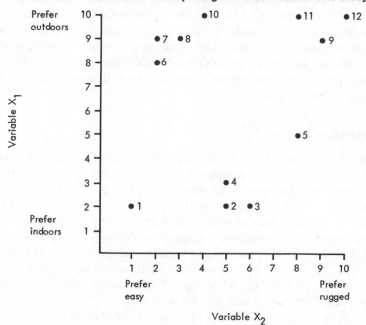

dimensional space (which is difficult to illustrate on paper). If four or more variables were included in the example, the idea of laying out the data in a manner similar to Figure 17–1 remains unchanged, except that the data would have to be laid out in what mathematicians call "n-dimensional space," where $n = 4, 5, 6, \ldots , n$. Obviously, if a study involves many respondents and more than two or three variables, researchers will not be able to "visualize" the clusters which may exist in the data. Some kind of procedure is needed to analyze the data to determine if clusters do exist.

To fill this need, researchers have developed procedures which have come to be known as cluster analysis. In order to understand what goes on within the cluster analysis procedures, readers must first be familiar with the two steps always found in cluster analysis: (1) developing a "measure" to identify similar respondents, and (2) developing a procedure for grouping similar respondents. These are discussed below.

Similarity measure. Because the first step in a cluster analysis is to identify similar respondents, the researcher must use some measure to identify the "similarity" between two respondents. While there is no ideal way to measure similarity, "distance" between two respondents is a commonly used measure of similarity when continuous or intervally scaled variables were used in the study. The distance separating any two respondents can be seen in Figure 17–1. For example, the distance separating respondents 7 and 8 is only one unit of variable X_2, while the distance separating respondents 7 and 9 is seven units of variable X_2. Thus, because the distance between respondents 7 and 8 is small, these two respondents can be judged to be more similar than respondents 7 and 9, who can be judged to be not very similar because of the large distance separating them.

The most commonly used distance measure is the measure used in Euclidean geometry. In general, the distance (D_{12}) between respondents 1 and 2 in a study where continuous or intervally scaled variables X_1, X_2, X_3, ..., X_n have been measured is calculated with the formula

$$D_{12} = \sqrt{(X_{11} - X_{12})^2 + (X_{21} - X_{22})^2 + (X_{31} - X_{32})^2 + \ldots + (X_{n1} - X_{n2})^2}$$

where the second subscripts 1 and 2 are used to identify each respondent's data on the variables.[1] For example, the distance between respondents 1 and 4 in Figure 17–1 is

$$D_{14} = \sqrt{(2 - 3)^2 + (1 - 5)^2} = \sqrt{1 + 16} = 4.1.$$

This distance measure must be calculated for every possible pair of respondents in the study, with the resulting set of distances being placed in a matrix of inter-respondent distances. Table 17–1 is a table of such distances calculated for the 12 respondents shown in Figure 17–1. For example, the first row and fourth column of the table show that respondents 1 and 4 are separated by a distance of 4.1 units of the space represented by the two dimensions shown in Figure 17–1. Row 2 in column 9 shows that respondents 2 and 9 are separated by a distance of 8.1 units. Every intersection of a row and column is given the same interpretation.

Grouping procedures.   In order to form clusters of respondents, there must be a procedure whereby each respondent is evaluated to determine if he or she should be placed with a particular group or cluster. This procedure must include a "rule" for placing a respondent into a given group. One such rule is called the "single linkage" rule, and it simply states that a respondent will be placed into a group *if the distance between that respondent and any single respondent already in the group is smaller than some pre-established minimum distance (designated as* MD *in this discussion).* (The implication

---

[1] If the variables are categorical rather than continuous or intervally scaled, the "distance" between two respondents can be measured by the number of questions on which the two respondents give the same answers. For example, in a study involving three categorical questions (prefer indoor or outdoor sports, prefer rugged or easy sports, prefer summer or winter sports), if two respondents picked exactly the same categories on all three of the questions, they could be judged to be similar. Thus, cluster analysis can be applied to categorical data as well, but the similarity measure is somewhat different from those discussed here.

TABLE 17–1. Inter-respondent distance matrix for data shown in Figure 17–1

		1	2	3	4	5	6	7	8	9	10	11	12
							Respondent						
Respondent	1		4.0	5.0	4.1	7.6	6.1	7.1	7.3	10.6	8.5	10.6	12.0
	2			1.0	1.0	4.2	6.6	7.6	7.3	8.1	8.1	8.5	9.4
	3				1.4	3.6	7.2	8.1	7.6	7.6	8.2	8.2	8.9
	4					3.6	5.8	6.7	6.3	7.2	7.1	7.6	8.6
	5						6.7	7.2	6.4	4.1	6.4	5.0	5.4
	6							1.0	1.4	7.1	2.8	6.3	8.2
	7								1.0	7.0	2.2	6.1	8.1
	8									6.0	1.4	5.1	7.1
	9										5.1	1.4	1.4
	10											4.0	6.0
	11												2.0

of setting *MD* at various values is discussed later, when it will be more meaningful to the reader.) Using the single linkage rule, the grouping procedure then searches through the matrix of inter-respondent distances, first to form groups of respondents who are very close together, then to form groups of respondents who are moderately close together, then to form groups of respondents who are still further apart but within *MD*.[2] This grouping procedure, using the single linkage rule, is described below using the data in Table 17–1.

The procedure for forming clusters can be illustrated with a tree diagram called a dendogram, like the one shown in Figure 17–2. The 12 respondents are listed along the vertical axis, while the horizontal axis represents inter-respondent distances. The horizontal lines, originating at each respondent and extending to the right, indicate that if *MD* is set at any number below 1.0, no two respondents are as close together as the minimum distance (see Table 17–1), so no groups can be formed. If *MD* is set at 1.0, the researchers see in Table 17–1 that there are four inter-respondent distances of 1.0 (respondents 2 and 3, 2 and 4, 6 and 7, 7 and 8). Therefore, when *MD* equals 1.0, respondents 3 and 4 join with respondent 2 to form a group, and respondents 6 and 8 join with respondent 7 to form a second group. The dendogram shows this forming of groups by merging the three horizontal lines associated

---

[2] In a study involving the three categorical questions listed in footnote 1, the grouping procedure would first form groups of those respondents who prefer rugged outdoor summer sports, then form groups of respondents who prefer easy outdoor summer sports, then form groups of respondents who prefer rugged indoor summer sports, and so on. Thus, categorical data can be cluster analyzed, but the grouping procedures are different from those discussed here.

FIGURE 17–2. Dendogram for data shown in Figure 17–1 and Table 17–1

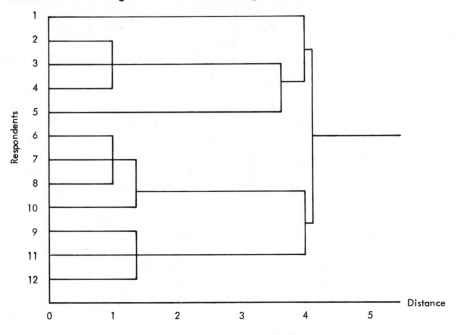

with respondents 2, 3, and 4 into only one horizontal line. The grouping of respondents 6, 7, and 8 is also identified in the same manner. Thus, if the researcher had set *MD* equal to 1.0, this cluster analysis would result in two groups being formed, but also with half the respondents (6 out of 12) not being included in either group.

Suppose the researcher had used a *MD* value of 2.0 instead of 1.0. Table 17–1 shows that respondent 10 is only 1.4 units away from respondent 8 and so respondent 10 can join the group already consisting of respondents 6, 7, and 8. This is shown in the dendogram by the merging of respondent 10's horizontal line with the horizontal line representing the group of respondents 6, 7, and 8. Table 17–1 also shows that respondents 11 and 12 are only 1.4 units away from respondent 9, so they form into a group (also shown in the dendogram at the distance of 1.4). Thus, if *MD* is set at 2.0, the cluster analysis would result in three "tight" or compact groups being formed (respondents 2, 3, and 4; respondents 6, 7, 8, and 10; respondents 9, 11, and 12), with only two of the respondents not being included in any group (respondents 1 and 5). As discussed at the beginning of this illustration, these groups represent one cluster which prefers rugged outdoor activities, one which prefers easier outdoor activities, and one which prefers indoor activities which are not too rugged or too easy.

The procedures described in the two foregoing paragraphs are essentially the procedures used in a cluster analysis; namely, respondents who are close together are the first ones formed into groups; then respondents who are a little further apart are the next groups formed; then respondents who are still futher apart (but less than MD apart) are the last groups formed. The procedure continues until all inter-respondent distances less than or equal to MD have been identified and all such respondents placed into groups.

What would happen if still larger values of MD were used? Figure 17–2 shows that respondent 5 would join with respondents 2, 3, and 4 at an MD value of 3.6, thus placing 11 of the 12 respondents into groups. If MD were set at 4.0, all respondents would be placed into groups, but the two groups at the top of Figure 17–1 would merge into one, and all of the respondents in the bottom half of the figure would form a second group. Thus, by letting MD get as large as 4.0, all respondents would be placed into groups, but in essence the groups have become so large that the cluster analysis has only grouped those who preferred outdoor activities compared with those who preferred indoor activities. Finally, as Figure 17–2 shows, if MD is set as high as 4.1, all respondents form one single group. This suggests that MD should be set at a small value rather than a large value, say, 1.5 or 2.0 when the data are recorded on a 10-point scale. (It should be noted that when MD is set at 1.5 or 2.0, the cluster analysis forms the three "tight" groups discussed above.) If a 5 or 7 point scale were used instead, MD should be set even smaller, say, at 1.0 or 1.5.

Because it is simple and easy to understand, the "single linkage" rule was used in the foregoing discussion. However, that rule is not heavily used in practice because it allows the formation of odd-shaped clusters. (It should be noted that when MD is set at 4.0, Figures 17–1 and 17–2 show that long, stringy clusters are formed—one stretching between respondents 1 and 5, and another stretching between respondents 6 and 12.) Because the purpose of a market segmentation study is to locate similar respondents, it is preferable to have the cluster analysis locate compact clusters. Researchers can obtain more compact clusters by replacing the "single linkage" rule with the "average linkage" rule, which is discussed below.

The "average linkage" rule first calculates an average location for each group that is formed during the grouping procedure and, then, *any additional respondent which joins with the group must be within the distance* MD *of the group's average location*. This can be illustrated with Figure 17–2. If MD is set at 2.0, the first group formed will occur when the cluster analysis evaluates the inter-respondent distance matrix (Table 17–1) at the distance of 1.0. At that point in the procedure, respondents 2, 3, and 4 form into a group, and their average location along the X_1 dimension is 2.33 [(2 + 2 + 3)/3] and their average location along the X_2 dimension is 5.33 [(5 + 6 + 5)/3]. That is, this group of respondents 2, 3, and 4 is considered to be centered on their average location of $X_1 = 2.33$ and $X_2 = 5.33$ in Figure 17–1. With the "average linkage" rule, no respondent can join this group unless he or she is within $MD = 2.0$ units of the point identified by $X_1 = 2.33$ and $X_2 = 5.33$. Except for this, a cluster analysis using the "average linkage" rule is essentially the same as described above for the "single linkage" rule.[3]

Usefulness of cluster analysis.   Cluster analysis is probably the most useful method available when a researcher is attempting to identify different segments in a market on the basis of a number of attitudinal or behavioral variables of the type used in the foregoing example. There are many potential applications of cluster analysis to market segmentation situations. For example, a cosmetics manufacturer may wish to study how female users of cosmetics perceive themselves on a number of lifestyle variables and to use cluster analysis on those variables to determine if the total market can be broken down into different market segments on the basis of self-perceptions. Chapter 19 reports the application of cluster analysis to a large sample of males who were asked over a hundred attitudinal and behavioral questions. The cluster analysis identified eight different segments within the male population (see page 566). Such situations are quite different from the ones where researchers are trying to identify different market segments on the basis of *one variable only* (e.g., heavy users/average users/light users, or prefer brand A/prefer brand B). When researchers are segmenting on the basis of only one variable (typically a dependent variable), they will not use cluster analysis, but rather will use the four methods listed in the top half of Table 16–1.

Problems in using cluster analysis.   Researchers can encounter certain problems when using cluster analysis, even if clusters do exist in the population being studied. Careful thought must be given (1) to the variables to be measured, (2) to the similarity measure to be used, and (3) to the grouping procedure to be used. The same applies to (4) the selection of the MD value to be used in the grouping procedure, for if the MD value is too large, the analysis is likely to identify only a few "spread out" clusters, each of which will include some respondents who are rather different from some of the other respondents in their cluster. On the other hand, if MD is too small, the respondents in each cluster are likely to be quite similar, but there may be many respondents who are not included in any of the clusters. Probably the clusters in the data can be better understood by trying a few

---

[3] The use of the "average linkage" rule requires that a new inter-respondent distance matrix be calculated every time a new group is formed or a new respondent is added to an already formed group. The new matrix is similar to the one shown in Table 17–1 except that (in the above illustration) respondents 2, 3 and 4 are combined and treated as one respondent, and all distances with other respondents are recalculated using the average location of 2.33 and 5.33 for the group consisting of respondents 2, 3, and 4. For example, respondent 1 is (2.33–2.00) units and (5.33–1.00) units away from this group along the X_1 and X_2 dimensions, respectively, and so respondent 1 is $\sqrt{(0.33)^2 + (4.33)^2} = 4.34$ units away from this group. Since cluster analysis is always performed on a computer, the recalculation of the distance matrix is routine.

"reasonable" values of *MD* to see which lead to "reasonable" results.[4]

Finally, there is (5) the problem of "how good is the cluster analysis?" If four different clusters are formed, how does the researcher know if four is the proper number of clusters, or if there should really be three or five or some other number. There are no statistical or other tests which can help the researcher with this problem. Two courses of action are available to the researcher who wishes to have greater confidence in the results of a cluster analysis. One is to take two separate samples or randomly split the one sample into two subsamples, and then to cluster analyze each to see if similar results are obtained. The second is to analyze the data using two or more "appropriate" cluster analysis programs to see if the results are similar. The idea is, if clusters really do exist in the data, they should show up as being similar regardless of which "appropriate" cluster analysis program is applied to the data.

FACTOR ANALYSIS

Typical problem.   Factor analysis is typically applied to intervally scaled responses to questions about a particular product or service in order to identify the major characteristic or factors considered to be important by consumers. For example, researchers for an automobile company may ask a large sample of potential buyers to report (using a 7- or 10- or 11-point scale) the extent of their agreement or disagreement with a number of statements such as "The side profile of a car should be sleek," and "A car's brakes are its most critical parts." Researchers apply factor analysis to such a set of data to identify which factors—such as "safety," "exterior styling," "interior roominess," or "economy of operations"—are considered to be important by potential buyers (See Table 16–1.) Once this information is available, it can be used to guide the overall characteristics to be designed into the product or to identify advertising themes which potential buyers would consider important.

What the method does.   Factor analysis applies an advanced form of correlation analysis to responses to a large number of statements to identify those which are similar, that is, to identify one or more sets of statements which result in highly correlated responses. The idea is, if the responses to a set of three or more statements are highly correlated, then it is believed that the statements measure some factor which is common to all of them. Since such studies usually involve many statements, there are likely to be three or more sets of such correlated statements. The statements in any one set are highly correlated with each other, but not highly correlated with the statements in any of the other sets. For each such set, the researchers use their

---

[4] Practically speaking, since all cluster analysis procedures are computerized, problems 2, 3 and 4 require that researchers carefully study a number of cluster analysis programs to see how they operate, and then to select that program which is most logically applicable to the project at hand.

own judgment to determine what the single 'theme" or "factor" is that ties the statements together in the minds of the respondents. For example, regarding the automobile study mentioned above, researchers may find high correlations among the responses to the following three statements: A car's brakes are its most critical parts; I want my next car to be equipped with an "air bag" and seat belts; A collapsable steering column should be standard equipment on all new cars. Researchers may then make the judgment that agreement with the set of statements indicates an underlying concern with "safety," although other researchers might decide the basic concern was with "modern technology" or "up-to-date engineering."

Type of variables.   Factor analysis can only be applied to continuous or intervally scaled variables. Thus, it is less versatile than cluster analysis, which can also be applied to categorical variables.

Identifies interdependencies.   Factor analysis, like cluster analysis, uses more than one variable to identify a class or a category (e.g., "economy of operation") which is important from a marketing standpoint. (See the bottom half of Table 16–1.) Recall that cluster analysis identifies respondents who gave the same answers to a number of questions. Factor analysis identifies a number of questions which result in highly correlated responses. In these ways, both methods look for interdependencies or interrelationships among the data, and so are different from the four methods of analysis listed in the top half of Table 16–1. An awareness of this characteristic can help the reader better understand when to use factor analysis rather than some other method.

An illustration

An automobile manufacturer wanted to know which automobile characteristics ("factors") were considered to be very important by potential buyers of compact cars.[5] Company researchers chose not to ask undisguised multiple choice questions about the importance of horsepower, interior roominess, luggage space, and so forth, because they felt consumers could not report accurately the importance of these items in their buying decisions. They also chose not to ask open questions as to what characteristics were important, because they felt respondents could not verbalize the automobile characteristics which were important to them. Instead, the researchers prepared 100 statements that related to all characteristics of automobiles they believed were important, and respondents were asked to report on a 7 point scale the extent to which they agreed or disagreed with each statement. The researchers could then use factor analysis to identify what basic automobile characteristics were important to consumers. In other words, the researchers felt that they couldn't get the information they wanted through direct questioning, but that they could get it through an indirect way utilizing factor analysis.

---

[5] A hypothetical example.

Three hundred potential buyers of compact cars were selected on a probability basis. They were asked to read 100 statements of the type listed below, and to record on a 7-point scale the extent to which they agreed or disagreed with each statement. (See the 7-point Likert scale described in Chapter 9.)

The side profile of a compact car should be sleek.

A compact car's brakes are its most critical parts.

Interior appointments in a compact car should be attractive.

Four adults should be able to sit comfortably in a compact car.

Gasoline mileage in a compact car should be at least 30 miles per gallon.

This resulted in a set of data in which each of 300 individuals gave a response to each of 100 statements. For any given statement, some individuals were found to agree strongly, some were found to disagree slightly, some neither agreed nor disagreed with the statement, and so on. Thus, for each statement, there was a distribution of 300 responses on a 7-point scale, and there were 100 such distributions, one for each of the 100 statements.

The following is a description of how researchers applied factor analysis to the data to identify the major characteristics ("factors") which potential buyers of compact cars considered important. This description treats five factor analysis topics: (1) three important measures; (2) the role of correlation; (3) the determination of factors; (4) the output of a factor analysis; (5) evaluating the results.

Three important measures. An understanding of factor analysis requires knowledge of the three measures that are used in the procedures. The first measure is the *average variation* (called *variance*) associated with the distribution of the 300 responses obtained to each of the 100 statements.[6] A factor analysis is somewhat like regression analysis in that it tries to "best fit" factors to a scatter diagram of the data in such a way that the factors explain the variance associated with the responses to each statement. Figure 15–2, which will help the reader recall the "best fit" concept, shows how a regression equation fitted to a scatter diagram of responses to variables Y and X helps explain the variance observed in the responses to variable Y. Just as a user of regression analysis would like to explain 100 percent of the variance in a dependent variable—that is, get an $R^2 = 1.00$—so also would a user of factor analysis like to explain 100 percent of the variance associated with each statement used in the study.

The second measure is a *standardized score* of each individual's response to a given statement. Since there are 300 responses to each statement, it is possible to calculate the mean and standard deviation of the responses to

---

[6] The reader will recall from the Chapter 14 discussion of analysis of variance that, for any question, the variation in a sample of responses is equal to the sum of the squares of the difference of each response from the mean of all responses [Σ(response − mean)^2]. Variance is equal to the variation divided by the number of responses.

each statement. An individual's actual response to a statement is "standardized" by using the relationship:

$$
\begin{array}{l}
\text{Individual's standardized} \\
\text{score on the statement}
\end{array}
=
\dfrac{
\left[\begin{array}{l}\text{Individual's actual} \\ \text{response to the} \\ \text{statement}\end{array}\right]
-
\left[\begin{array}{l}\text{Mean of all 300} \\ \text{responses to} \\ \text{the statement}\end{array}\right]
}{
\begin{array}{l}\text{Standard deviation of all 300 responses} \\ \text{to the statement}\end{array}
}
$$

Thus, an individual's standardized score is nothing more than an actual response which is measured in terms of the number of standard deviations ($+$ or $-$) it lies away from the mean.[7]

It should be noted that standardized scores are the raw data used in a factor analysis. For example, in the automobile study, each of the 100 statements is treated as a variable (X_1, X_2, X_3, ... X_{100}) and for each variable there are 300 standardized scores.

The third measure used is the *correlation coefficient associated with the responses to each pair of statements*. For example, the 300 standardized responses to the first and second automobile statements could be plotted on a scatter diagram, and the correlation coefficient associated with the data could be calculated. This could also be done for the responses to statements 1 and 3, 1 and 4, 1 and 5, 2 and 3, 2 and 4, and so on, for every possible pair of statements. This results in a matrix of correlation coefficients which is a very important part of a factor analysis.[8]

The role of correlation. The role of correlation in factor analysis can be more easily explained by using fewer than the 100 statements mentioned above. For simplicity, assume that only six statements are used in the study. Assume also that correlation coefficients are calculated for the responses to all possible pairs of statements. Table 17–2 shows two possible matrices of correlation coefficients for all pairs of the six statements. Again, for simplicity, only perfect correlation (1) or zero correlation (0) are shown. These tables will illustrate how correlation can suggest to researchers if any factors exist in the data and, if so, how many factors there are.

The correlation coefficients in Table 17–2a show that the responses to statements 1, 2, and 3 are perfectly correlated with each other, but are completely uncorrelated with the responses to statements 4, 5, and 6. Similarly, the responses to statements 4, 5, and 6 are perfectly correlated with each other, but are completely uncorrelated with the other three statements. With these results, researchers have evidence suggesting that two factors exist in the data—one associated with statements 1, 2, and 3 and another associated

---

[7] Standardized scores are used because responses to different statements or questions may be recorded using different units of measurement. Standardizing the scores eliminates the effects of the different units of measurement.

[8] Since none of the three measures discussed here can be obtained if the data are categorical, factor analysis cannot be applied to categorical data.

with statements 4, 5, and 6. The example in Table 17–2a also reveals something very important about the character of the two factors identified, namely, that one factor is unrelated to the other factor. (Note in the table that none of statements 1, 2, and 3 show any correlation at all with any of statements 4, 5, and 6, and vice-versa.) Thus, each of the two factors is assumed to be measuring a different characteristic of automobiles.

TABLE 17–2. Matrices of two possible correlation coefficients between pairs of statements (both axes of each matrix should be labeled "statement")

a.

	1	2	3	4	5	6
1	1	1	1	0	0	0
2		1	1	0	0	0
3			1	0	0	0
4				1	1	1
5					1	1
6						1

b.

	1	2	3	4	5	6
1	1	1	0	0	0	0
2		1	0	0	0	0
3			1	1	0	0
4				1	0	0
5					1	1
6						1

Following this line of reasoning, one sees from the example in Table 17–2b that statements 1 and 2, 3 and 4, and 5 and 6 are perfectly correlated with each other, but each pair is completely uncorrelated with the other four. Such results suggest that, perhaps, three factors exist in the data.

The purpose of these examples is to help the reader gain an understanding of two basic concepts underlying factor analysis. The first is that a factor analysis searches through a large set of data to locate one or more sets of highly correlated statements, where the statements in any one set are highly correlated with each other, but are relatively uncorrelated with statements in other sets. The statements in any one set need only be highly correlated, say, $r = 0.6$ or larger. They do not have to be perfectly correlated. The second basic concept underlying factor analysis is that, since the different sets of statements are relatively uncorrelated with each other, a separate and distinct factor relative to automobiles is associated with each set. (However, it should also be made clear that these examples are meant to provide insight into factor analysis, and that factors are not determined directly from matrices such as those shown in Table 17–2.)

Determining factors. Factors are weighted, linear combinations of the variables used in a factor analysis (the standardized responses to the 100 statements in the automobile study). This concept of factors can be illustrated with Figure 17–3, which shows a scatter diagram of the standardized scores on two factor analysis variables (X_1 and X_2). The figure also shows two factors fitted to the data. The first factor can be written as the equation

FIGURE 17–3. Illustration of the concept of factors

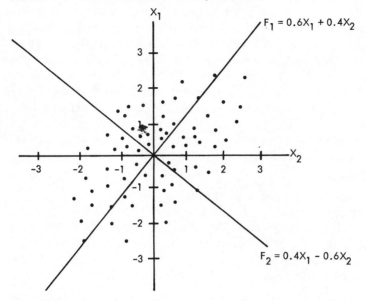

$F_1 = 0.6X_1 + 0.4X_2$, while the second factor can be written as the equation $F_2 = 0.4X_1 - 0.6X_2$. Thus, each factor is a weighted, linear combination of the variables being analyzed. Because 100 variables are being factor analyzed in the automobile study, factor equations there would consist of weighted combinations of all 100 variables.

Factors are identified through the use of extremely complex calculations. One of the more well-known procedures used to factor analyze data is called "principal components analysis," and it is described below in a very over-simplified manner.

Recall that one of the important measures used in factor analysis is the *variance* associated with the responses to each statement used in the factor analysis study. Principal components analysis selects factors one at a time using procedures which "best fit" each factor to the data. (Readers may find it helpful to think of this "best fit" procedure as being somewhat akin to the "best fit" procedures used in regression analysis. See Figure 15–2 and the discussion of stepwise multiple regression in Chapter 15.) The first factor selected is one which fits the data in such a way that it explains more of the variance in the entire set of standardized response scores than any other pos-sible factor. The second factor to be selected will be concerned with explain-ing the residual variance, that is, the variance in the entire set of data which the first factor did not explain. The second factor must also be uncorrelated with the first factor. (Figure 17–3 shows that factors F_1 and F_2 have equation lines which are perpendicular to each other, and hence are uncorrelated.) Subject to this condition, principal components analysis selects as the second factor the one which explains more of the residual variance than any other possible factor. The third factor selected attempts to explain the variance unaccounted for by the first two factors, subject also to the condition that the third factor is uncorrelated with either of the first two factors. This selection process continues, with each selected factor typically explaining less of the variance than its predecessors, and each being uncorrelated with all of its predecessors. Thus, principal components analysis uses a "best fit" type of procedure in a stepwise manner to select factors which explain the largest amount of residual variance in the entire set of standardized response scores.

Output of factor analysis.   For simplicity, only the following six statements from the automobile study will be used to explain the output of a factor analysis.

1.   A compact car should be built to last a long time.
2.   Gasoline mileage in a compact car should be at least 30 miles per gallon.
3.   A compact car should be easily maintained and serviced by its owner.
4.   Four adults should be able to sit comfortably in a compact car.
5.   A compact car should have adequate leg and head room for all riders.
6.   A compact car's brakes are its most critical parts.

The results of a factor analysis of these six statements will appear in the form shown in Table 17–3, which can be used to illustrate the three important output measures from a factor analysis.

TABLE 17–3. Factor analysis output of the compact car study

		Factors			Commu-
		F_1	F_2	F_3	nalities
	1	0.86	0.12	0.04	0.76
	2	0.84	0.18	0.10	0.75
Statement	3	0.68	0.24	0.15	0.54
Number	4	0.10	0.92	0.05	0.86
	5	0.06	0.94	0.08	0.89
	6	0.12	0.14	0.89	0.83
Eigenvalues		1.9356	1.8540	0.8351	
$\dfrac{\text{Eigenvalues}}{\text{Number of statements}}$		0.3226	0.3090	0.1391	

The six rows of the table are associated with the six statements listed above. The table shows that the factor analysis has identified three factors (F_1, F_2, F_3), and the first three columns of the table are associated with those factors. The 18 numbers located in the 6 rows and 3 columns are called *factor loadings,* and they are one of the three useful output measures obtained from a factor analysis.

As shown in Table 17–3, each statement has a factor loading on each of the three factors. Recall that a factor is a weighted, linear combination of the variables being studied, and so can be drawn on a scatter diagram of the variable data (as shown in Figure 17–3). The factor loading associated with a specific factor and a specific statement is simply the correlation between that factor and that statement's standardized response scores. This concept is illustrated in Figure 17–4. Figure 17–4a shows the case where a factor is highly correlated with the variables in a scatter diagram, while Figure 17–4b

FIGURE 17–4. Illustrations of high and low factor loadings

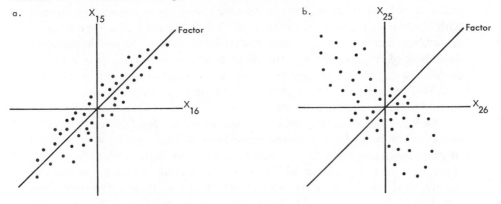

shows the case where a factor is not highly correlated with the variables in a scatter diagram. Thus, a "factor loading" is a measure of how well the factor "fits" the standardized responses to a statement—a high factor loading means the factor fits the data well, while a low factor loading indicates a poor fit.

Applying this notion to the factor loadings in Table 17–3, one sees that factor F_1 is a good fit on the data from statements 1, 2, and 3, but a poor fit on the other statements. This indicates that statements 1, 2, and 3 are probably measuring the same basic attitude or value system, and so can be used as evidence that a factor exists. Using their own judgment, researchers from the automobile company concluded from these results that "economy of operation" was the factor that tied these statements together in the minds of the respondents.

Next, the researchers asked if the study's 300 respondents felt that "economy of operation" was an important factor. In order to answer this question, the researchers had to look at the 300 responses to each of statements 1, 2, and 3. They found that the means of these responses were +0.97, +1.32 and +1.18, respectively, for statements 1, 2, and 3, indicating that most respondents agreed with the three statements. (See the above discussion of "standardized scores.") Since a majority of respondents had agreed with these statements, the researchers also concluded that this factor was very important in the minds of potential compact car buyers.

Table 17–3 also shows that Factor F_2 is a good fit on statements 4 and 5, but a poor fit on the other statements. This factor is clearly measuring something different than statements 1, 2, 3, and 6. Factor F_3 is a good fit only on statement 6, and so is clearly measuring something not being measured by statements 1–5. Again, using their own judgment, researchers concluded that the two factors underlying statements 4 and 5 were "interior roominess" and that statement 6 was related to "safety." Since there are only two and one statements, respectively, associated with these factors, the researchers had fewer statements on which to base their identification of the factors and, hence, were less confident of them. Because a majority of respondents agreed with statements 4 and 5 (with means of $+0.91$ and $+1.22$, respectively), researchers concluded that "interior roominess" was an important factor in the minds of respondents. On the other hand, because there was no clear pattern of agreement or disagreement with statement 6 (its mean was $+0.07$), researchers were unable to conclude that "safety" was also considered to be an important factor.

Of course, the above example is a much simplified one. Typically a factor analysis will be applied to many more than six statements, with 50–100 or more being common. In such cases, researchers hope to identify at least three statements associated with each of the identified factors. When this occurs, they have more information on which to base their judgmental identification of the factors, and so are likely to have greater confidence in their identification of the factors derived from the factor analysis.

Evaluating the results.   The second output measure from a factor analysis indicates how well the identified factors fit the response data obtained from each statement. The figures in the rightmost column in Table 17–3 are called *communalities,* and for each statement they indicate the proportion of the statement's variance which is explained by the three factors.[9] For example, the table shows that the three factors explain 0.89 (or 89 percent) of statement 5's variance but only 0.54 (or 54 percent) of statement 3's variance. The communalities associated with the other statements are similarly interpreted. The table shows that the three factors explain 75 percent or more of the variance associated with statements 1, 2, 4, 5, and 6, but only about half of statement 3's variance. Researchers can use these communalities to make a judgment about how well the factors fit the data. Since the three factors account for most of each statement's variance in this example, the three factors fit the data quite well.

The third factor analysis output measure can be used to indicate how well all of the identified factors fit the response data from all the statements. This

---

[9] A statement's communality is merely the sum of the squares of its factor loadings. For example, statement 5's communality = $(0.06)^2 + (0.94)^2 + (0.08)^2 = 0.89$.

output measure consists of figures called *eigenvalues,* and there is an eigen-value associated with each of the factors. These are shown at the bottom of Table 17–3.[10] When a factor's eigenvalue is divided by the number of statements used in the factor analysis, the resulting figure is the proportion of the variance in the entire set of standardized response scores which is explained by that factor. This calculation is shown at the bottom of Table 17–3, where each eigenvalue is divided by 6—the number of statements.[11] For example, the table shows that factor F_1 explains 0.3226 (or 32.26 percent) of the variance in the standardized response scores from all six statements. By adding these figures for the three factors, one sees that the three factors together explain $0.3226 + 0.3090 + 0.1391 = 0.7707$ (or 77.07 percent) of the variance in the entire set of response data. This figure can be used as a measure of how well, overall, the identified factors fit the data. In general, a factor analysis which accounts for 60–70 percent or more of the total variance can be considered a good fit to the data.

Uses of factor analysis.   Readers should easily recognize that the foregoing discussion can apply to any product or service which possesses many traits or characteristics, the consequences of which are that users of the product or service frequently are unable to identify the characteristics of importance to them. For example, researchers could ask about the important characteristics one considers when buying fine furniture or a house, or when selecting a bank, an insurance company, a stock brokerage firm, or a favorite retail store. When studying such things, the researchers need to locate a large number of qualified respondents, to ask them to indicate their agreement or disagreement with a large number of appropriate statements, and to apply a factor analysis to the data. Thus, factor analysis can be applied to many problems of this type. Its strong point is that it can help researchers identify the really important characteristics of products or services which are so complex that frequently the users of those products and services have difficulty identifying those characteristics which are important to them.

Problems in using factor analysis.   Researchers can encounter four potential problems when applying factor analysis. First, as with other methods of analysis, a factor analysis will be of little use if the appropriate variables have not been measured, or if the measurements are inaccurate, or if the relationships in the data are nonlinear.

A second difficulty is concerned with deciding on how many of the identified factors one should use. For example, the bottom of Table 17–3 shows

---

[10] A factor's eigenvalue is merely the sum of the squares of its factor loadings. For example, factor F_1's eigenvalue $= (0.86)^2 + (0.84)^2 + (0.68)^2 + (0.10)^2 + (0.06)^2 + (0.12)^2 = 1.9356$.

[11] Because the responses to the statements are standardized, the variance associated with the responses to any statement equals 1.0, and the variance associated with all six statements equals 6.0. Since the eigenvalue of 1.9356 is the variance accounted for by factor F_1, dividing that figure by the total variance (which is also equal to the number of statements) yields the proportion of the total variance explained by F_1.

that the first two factors explain 63.16 percent (32.26% + 30.90%) of the total variance in the data. The third factor explains an additional 13.91 percent of the total variance. Because the addition of this factor represents a substantial increase in the explained variance—an increase from 63.16 percent to 77.07 percent, or an increase of almost one-fourth—it is reasonable for researchers to use this third factor along with the first two. But should another factor (say, a fourth factor) be used if it only explains 2–3 percent of total variance. This is a problem that has not been solved in an objective manner.

A third difficulty has to do with identifying and naming the factors. It seems clear that the first factor in Table 17–3 is concerned with "economy .of operation," but just exactly what it is that is being measured by this factor is not known with certainty. In some cases, the 3–5 statements associated with an identified factor may not give a clear indication as to how the factor should be named. The naming of factors then becomes quite subjective, and this subjectivity is disturbing to many researchers.

Another difficulty is that some factor analysis procedures allow researchers to "rotate," or move around, the set of factors in the scatter diagram to see if they can arrive at better factor loadings than the ones originally obtained. Consequently, it is possible for two different researchers to arrive at different factor loadings when working with the same data. This difficulty, along with the second, causes some researchers to raise doubts about the reliability and validity of factor analysis results.

CONJOINT ANALYSIS

Typical problem.   Conjoint analysis is typically used to identify the most desirable combination of features for a new product or service (e.g., what features should be offered in a new public transportation system?). In such studies, respondents are told about the various combinations of new features under consideration and are asked to indicate the combination which they most prefer, to indicate the combination which they next most prefer, and so on. Conjoint analysis uses such preference data to identify what respondents consider to be the product or service's most important features and most important combinations of features. (See Table 16–1.)

What the method does.   A conjoint analysis applies a complex form of analysis of variance to the preference data obtained from each respondent. This analysis calculates a value (or utility) for each feature. Features with the highest values are judged to be the most important to respondents.

Type of variables.   Conjoint analysis is applied to *categorical* variables which reflect different features or characteristics of the product or service under consideration. For example, some new product characteristics of interest to researchers could include color (red or blue), size (large, medium, or small), shape (square or cylindrical), price ($1.00, $1.50, or $2.00), and so on. Because it is applied only to categorical variables, conjoint analysis is different from both factor analysis and cluster analysis. (See Table 16–1.)

Identifies interdependencies. Conjoint analysis differs from cross-tabulation, regression, LDA, and AID in that it is not concerned primarily with a single dependent variable. Rather, conjoint analysis is like cluster analysis and factor analysis in the sense that those methods try to identify the interdependencies which exist between a number of variables. In this case, conjoint analysis tries to measure the relative importance of the various combinations of features and characteristics (variables) which can be designed into a product or service.

A simple illustration

Assume that a medium-size southern city was planning to improve its outdated public transportation system, and that city officials wanted to identify the characteristics of the system which potential users would find attractive. City officials were concerned with the relative desirability of the three main system attributes of fare, frequency of service, and comfort (identified as the presence or absence of air conditioning and recorded music). Each of these attributes could be offered in three or four different ways or levels. For example, city officials were considering three fare levels (40 cents, 60 cents, 80 cents), three levels of frequency of service (every 10 minutes, every 15 minutes, every 20 minutes), and four different comfort features (both air conditioning and recorded music; air conditioning only; recorded music only; neither air conditioning nor recorded music).

City researchers selected a representative sample of 500 adults interested in using public transportation if it were available. Each of these adults was shown the 12 combinations which resulted from the three frequency of service levels and four comfort features under consideration. (See Table 17–4.) They were then asked to identify which combination of service and comfort was their first preference, which combination of service and comfort was their second preference, and so on until they rank-ordered all 12 combinations. These adults were asked to repeat this procedure two more times —once for all possible combinations of fares and comfort, and once for all possible combinations of fares and frequency of service. In other words, respondents were asked to rank order their preferences for *all possible pairs of attributes and for each level or feature being considered for each attribute.* These preference rankings were used in a conjoint analysis to calculate values (called "utilities") which could help managers decide on the best combination of features to offer.

To obtain a good understanding of how conjoint analysis can be applied to the public transportation system project, readers must have an understanding of (1) utilities, (2) how the utilities correspond to preferences,

TABLE 17–4. Two respondents' preference rankings on the frequency of service and comfort attributes

a. Jane Smith

		Comfort			
		AC and music	AC	Music	Nothing
Service every	10	1	2	3	4
_____ minutes	15	5	6	7	8
	20	9	10	11	12

b. Bill Jones

		Comfort			
		AC and music	AC	Music	Nothing
Service every	10	1	4	7	8
_____ minutes	15	2	5	9	10
	20	3	6	11	12

and (3) how the utilities can be used. It should be noted that the following discussions of these three items *pertain to a single respondent,* and that what applies to a single respondent applies also to every other respondent.

Utilities.   Conjoint analysis applies a complex form of analysis of variance to a respondent's preference rankings to calculate a utility for each level or feature of each attribute. These are basically index numbers which reflect the relative value or desirability to a respondent of a particular feature. The idea is that each respondent's preference rankings reveal something about the relative utility which he or she has for each feature. Features which a respondent is *reluctant to give up* from one preference ranking to another are judged to be of *high utility* to that respondent. This can be illustrated with the preference rankings shown in Table 17–4.

Table 17–4a shows that Jane Smith's first choice is service every 10 minutes with both air conditioning and music. However, the table also shows that she has a high utility for frequent service, that is, she wants service every ten minutes even if it means doing without both air conditioning and recorded music (giving up her first choice), or doing without air conditioning only (giving up her second choice), or doing without recorded music only (giving up her third choice). This same pattern of preference holds true for the second row of the table and again for the third row. Clearly, frequency of service is of higher utility to this respondent than comfort.

On the other hand, Table 17–4b shows that Bill Jones has a higher utility for comfort than for frequent service. The table shows that Bill wants both air conditioning and recorded music, and will "give up" or "trade off" more frequent service for this greater comfort. If he can't have both air conditioning and recorded music, Jones prefers to have air conditioning regardless of the frequency of service. It is only when he can't have air conditioning that Jones shifts his preference pattern. The table shows that, if he can't have air conditioning, he will prefer frequent service over recorded music. Such a pattern of preferences implies that air conditioning has a higher utility than frequency of service, and that frequency of service has a higher utility than recorded music.

Utilities correspond to preferences. A conjoint analysis will use such preference rankings to calculate a set of utilities for each respondent—one utility for each attribute feature or level.[12] The utilities display the following characteristic: When a utility of one attribute feature or level is added to the utility of some other attribute's feature or level, *the sum for that combination will show a good correspondence with that combination's position in the respondent's original preference rankings*. This can be illustrated with the preference rankings obtained from one respondent on the attributes of service frequency and comfort.

For example, using the preference rankings shown in Table 17–5a, conjoint analysis may calculate the utilities of 1.6, 1.2, and 0.4 for service frequencies of every 10, every 15, and every 20 minutes, respectively, and utilities of 1.2, 1.1, 0.6, and 0.4 for the comfort features of air conditioning and recorded music, air conditioning only, recorded music only, and neither

TABLE 17–5. One respondent's preference rankings and combined utilities for frequency of service and comfort attributes

a. Preference rankings

		Comfort			
		AC and music	AC	Music	Nothing
Service every	10	1	2	5	6
_____ minutes	15	3	4	7	9
	20	8	10	11	12

b. Combined utilities

		Comfort			
		AC and music	AC	Music	Nothing
Service every	10	2.8	2.7	2.2	2.0
_____ minutes	15	2.4	2.3	1.8	1.6
	20	1.6	1.5	1.0	0.8

[12] For a discussion of the calculational procedures used in conjoint analysis, see Richard M. Johnson, "Trade–Off Analysis of Consumer Values," *Journal of Marketing Research* 11 (May 1974):121–27.

air conditioning nor recorded music, respectively. These are shown in Figure
17–5. By adding the various combinations of utilities, one can obtain the
utilities shown in Table 17–5b. For example, for this respondent, the com-

**FIGURE 17–5. Utilities calculated from preference rankings, for frequency of service and
comfort attributes**

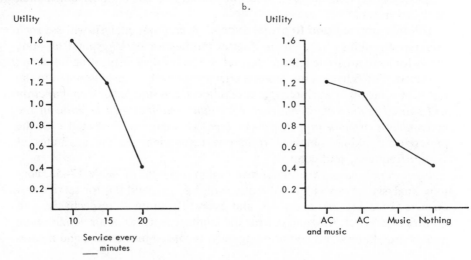

bined utility for service every 10 minutes and air conditioning only is 2.7
(1.6 + 1.1), while the combined utility for service every 15 minutes and
recorded music only is 1.8 (1.2 + 0.6). A close inspection of the table
reveals that the respondent's first preference has the largest combined utility
(2.8), and that the respondent's second preference has the next largest combined utility, and so on. The only combined utilities which are not quite in
correspondence with the respondent's preference rankings are those associated with the respondent's eighth and ninth preferences, which both have a
combined utility of 1.6.

This simple example serves to illustrate that conjoint analysis procedures
calculate combined utilities which show a good correspondence with the
respondent's original preference rankings. It is this characteristic which gives
researchers confidence that the calculated utilities are useful representations
of how a particular respondent views the relative importance of each attribute level or feature.

Usefulness of utilities. Utilities are useful in two ways. First, they
identify the more important attributes. For example, attributes with highly
fluctuating utilities (such as frequency of service) are judged to be more
important to the respondent than ones with slightly fluctuating utilities. The
importance of an attribute can be gauged by the range of its utilities. Fre-

quency of service has a utility range of $1.6 - 0.4 = 1.2$ and comfort features have a utility range of $1.2 - 0.4 = 0.8$. These ranges indicate what is visually perceived in Figure 17–5, namely, that the respondent is much more sensitive to the different frequency of service offerings than to the different comfort feature offerings; therefore, the former is more important.

The second use of utilities is to indicate the importance of each attribute level or feature. For example, Figure 17–5 shows that service every 10 minutes has a much higher utility than service every 15 minutes. The figure also shows that the utility of air conditioning only is much larger than the utility of recorded music only, and only slightly below the utility of air conditioning and recorded music.

A product design illustration

An interesting application of conjoint analysis is one concerned with the design of a spot remover for upholstery.[13] The product design involved the following five attributes and their levels: three package alternatives, three price levels, three brand names, a money-back guarantee or no such guarantee, and a *Good Housekeeping* seal of approval or no such approval. There were $3 \times 3 \times 3 \times 2 \times 2 = 108$ combinations in all.

Because it would be impractical to ask respondents to rank order all possible combinations of all possible pairs of attributes, only a representative sample of the 108 combinations was used. Researchers selected 18 combinations as ones they believed respondents would find most attractive. Respondents were shown 18 cards, each of which described a different product configuration, that is, on each card was written one package design, one brand name, one price, whether or not the product would have a money-back guarantee, and whether or not it had the *Good Housekeeping* seal of approval. Thus, the 18 cards represented 18 different product configurations in which no attribute level or feature was given preponderance. Respondents were then asked to study the 18 cards and to rank them according to their preferences.

Because each of these preference rankings involved five features (rather than only two, as in the previous example), procedures slightly different from those described above were performed on the data. However, the end result of the analysis was a set of utilities for each respondent and for each attribute, similar to those shown in Figure 17–5. These five sets of utilities for one respondent are shown in Figure 17–6. The relative importance of each attribute is determined by calculating the ranges, as is shown in Table 17–6. This table indicates that price and package design are by far the most important attributes. The money-back guarantee seems to be about half as important as price and package. Brand name and the Good Housekeeping seal of approval are clearly of less importance.

---

[13] See Paul E. Green and Yoram Wind, "New Way to Measure Consumers' Judgment," *Harvard Business Review* 53 (July–August 1975):107–17.

FIGURE 17–6. One respondent's utilities for attributes of an upholstery spot remover product

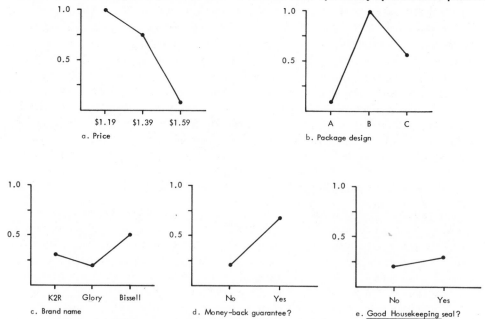

a. Price

b. Package design

c. Brand name

d. Money–back guarantee?

e. Good Housekeeping seal?

TABLE 17–6. Importance of each attribute for one respondent

Attribute	High utility		Low utility		Difference	Percent of total
Price	1.0	—	0.1	=	0.9	33
Package design	1.0	—	0.1	=	0.9	33
Money-back guarantee	0.7	—	0.2	=	0.5	19
Brand name	0.5	—	0.2	=	0.3	11
GH approval	0.3	—	0.2	=	0.1	4
Total				=	2.7	

Management can use these utilities to study how alternate product designs compare with one another. For example, Figure 17–6 shows that the combination of package design B, price of $1.19, the Bissell name, no money-back guarantee, and no *Good Housekeeping* seal of approval would result in a total utility value of 2.9 (1.0 + 1.0 + 0.5 + 0.2 + 0.2). However, the figure also shows that a money-back guarantee would increase total utility by 0.5, and that the combination of a money-back guarantee and a $1.39 price would increase total utility by 0.2 (+0.5 from the money-back guarantee and -0.3 from increasing the price to $1.39). This indicates that management might increase consumer acceptance by including both a money-back guarantee and the $1.39 price, and that doing so could result in both greater sales and a higher price. Note that if management wanted the combination with the largest total utility value regardless of price, it would be the combination of package design B, price of $1.19, the Bissell name, a money-back guarantee, and the *Good Housekeeping* seal of approval.

The utilities shown in Figure 17–6 are derived from a single respondent's preference rankings. Such a set of utilities is calculated for each of the 100 respondents who participated in the study, but of course the utilities differ for each respondent. For example, in the spot remover study there would be 100 sets of the five different utilities illustrated in Figure 17–6. These could be used to study the relative sales volumes, revenues, and profitability associated with some or all of the 18 different product configurations.

The general approach would be to identify the two or three most important attributes for all respondents combined (say, price, package design, and money-back guarantee) and the one or two best levels or features of each.[14] For example, researchers might identify as the most important possible configurations the four designs based on package B used with the four combinations resulting from $1.19 and $1.39 prices and the presence or absence of the money-back guarantee (i.e., one design would consist of package B at $1.19 with no money-back guarantee, another design would consist of package B at $1.39 with a money-back guarantee, and so on). A search through the 100 sets of utilities would determine the number of respondents who had high utilities on each of the four best design combinations. The relative sales volume, revenues, and profitability of each of the four combinations could be estimated from these data, and management could use this information to select the design combination to be used in the new product.

Problems in using conjoint analysis. Although conjoint analysis has been widely applied to projects concerned with the design of products and services, researchers can encounter problems with its use. Conjoint analysis assumes that the attributes being used in the study are the most important ones. This means that researchers should have some confidence, or evidence, that they have identified the important attributes. For example, a previous factor analysis study may have been used to identify the important features or attributes. A second possible problem is with the appropriateness of the levels or features used for each attribute in the study. For example, if two important comfort features of public transportation facilities were "comfortable seats" and "clean interiors," the results from the previously described conjoint analysis study would not have reflected those important features. The exclusion of those two features from the study might have led management into making a poor decision. As with the first difficulty, this one can be overcome if the researchers take the precaution of first identifying

---

[14] For a more detailed discussion, see the Johnson article cited in footnote 12.

the proper attribute features or levels. A third difficulty may exist because conjoint analysis procedures require that the researcher make an assumption on how the utilities are to be combined. In the foregoing example it was assumed that the utilities should be added. While this assumption seems reasonable, it is not known for certain that it is valid.[15]

PROCEED WITH CAUTION

Readers should note that each of the foregoing sections ended with a discussion of the problems a researcher may encounter when using multivariate methods. It is important, therefore, to proceed with caution when using these methods.

The Oscar Mayer Company did just that when it found that two different studies concerned with the same objective had quite different results. The two research projects were carried out by different research suppliers, but both covered the same product category and both used multivariate methods.[16] One study concluded that the market consisted of four different segments based upon the two factors of flavor and quality. These findings suggested that the best course of action would be for the company to reposition its brand by emphasizing the high quality of its ingredients in its advertising. The second study indicated that the market was not segmented in any way, but that the three most important product factors were color/appearance, ingredients, and versatility. These findings suggested that the company reposition its brand by emphasizing color/appearance in its advertising, and perhaps also that the company's brand might be in need of reformulation to improve its color/appearance. Needless to say, these two studies caused a dilemma among company managers. This dilemma was resolved by comparing the results of both studies with a great deal of information which had been previously gathered regarding the specific product category. This comparison showed that one of the studies had findings which were much more in agreement with the larger set of previously gathered information. This experience led the company's marketing research manager to comment:

> "We have been using methods and models without sufficient documentation of their validity. And, we have paid little attention to whether or not there is even any utility to be derived from the various methods."[17]

An experienced user of multivariate methods has offered a number of guidelines to consider, three of which are:[18]

---

[15] For an in-depth discussion and evaluation of a number of aspects of conjoint analysis, see Paul E. Green and V. Srinivasan, "Conjoint Analysis in Consumer Research: Issues and Outlook," *Journal of Consumer Research* 5 (September 1978):103–23.

[16] "A Tale of Two Studies—Disturbing: Struse," *Marketing News* (May 18, 1979): 7 and 18.

[17] Ibid., p. 18.

[18] "Venkatesh Offers Caveats in Use of Multivariate Methods," *Marketing News* (May 4, 1979):8.

1. Do not blindly crank the data through canned programs without fully understanding the implications of the various options and assumptions.
2. Fit the technique to the problem, not vice-versa.
3. Regard the multivariate techniques as a means to an end, not the end itself.

Perhaps the Oscar Mayer dilemma is a good example of putting the third guideline into practice. It is wise to use multivariate methods of analysis in conjunction with other information already available to the firm, and to use the findings from these methods if they support previously available information, or are logical and in agreement with management's beliefs concerning the topic studied. If the firm has little information available on the subject, or if management has no beliefs or convictions about the subject, it is probably best to use multivariate methods only for exploratory purposes—to help management gain some understanding of the phenomenon being studied, and perhaps to identify some hypotheses which might be investigated in further studies.

SUMMARY

Chapters 16 and 17 have presented five complex multivariate methods of analysis which are finding increasing use in marketing research. The discussions have focused on four points, all of which are illustrated in Table 16–1. These four points can help researchers make proper use of these multivariate methods. (1) What is the typical kind of problem which can be studied with each method? This can help readers identify situations to which the various methods can be applied. (2) What does the method do? Researchers will be better prepared to use these methods by knowing whether a specific method determines a discriminating line, forms clusters of similar respondents, or does something else. (3) Is the method concerned with explaining the variation in a dependent variable through the use of two or more independent variables, or is it concerned with identifying if and how a number of variables are interrelated or interdependent? Researchers will know that LDA and AID can be useful in the former situation, while cluster analysis, factor analysis and conjoint analysis can be useful in the latter situation. (4) What types of variables are available for analysis? Most of the methods discussed here are applicable only to a certain kind of variable (categorical, continuous, or intervally scaled), or to certain combinations of variables (for example, a categorical dependent variable and continuous independent variables). By knowing the types of variables which are to be analyzed, researchers can identify the method(s) of analysis which can be used.

Case 17–1

FENTON'S, INC.

Fenton's, Inc. was a large department store chain located in an east coast city. Fenton's had a good reputation for providing quality merchandise and good service. Annual sales exceeded $400 million, but were growing only at a moderate rate.

Jane Lamp, manager of marketing research, was asked by the vice president of planning and development to investigate the size and character of the market for merchandise purchased by mail, either through catalogs or through direct mail solicitations. The vice president wondered if Fenton's could improve its sales growth by developing a successful mail-order business. He felt that Fenton's good reputation might be able to support sizable mail-order sales from its own market area and perhaps even from the surrounding regions.

A review of past research findings from projects carried out by Fenton's and from numerous secondary sources revealed two important aspects of mail-order business. Reportedly, it didn't have a good reputation. People thought of it as old-fashioned, as a way to sell to farmers. Some people didn't trust the mail-order business, believing it to consist of numerous operators whose business practices might often be questionable. Many people considered the mail-order business to be inconvenient due to the uncertainty as to when the merchandise would be delivered or even if it was in stock, due to uncertainty as to the condition and quality of the merchandise when it arrived, and due to the need to pay in advance in many cases.

The second important aspect of the mail-order business was that it was big business—estimates were that mail-order sales exceeded $25 billion a year, which amounted to 10–12 percent of all general merchandise sales. Reports also indicated that it was growing and was highly profitable. It was estimated that mail-order sales per capita exceeded $100 per year, and that well over half of all adults made purchases through the mail. There was some evidence that as few as 25 percent of all adults accounted for the bulk of all mail-order sales. Some of the most popular items being sold by mail, which were also of interest to Fenton's, were shoes and clothing, housewares and home furnishings, sporting goods and equipment, books and records, and specialty and gourmet foods.

The size and growth of mail order sales appeared to be related to a number of social and economic changes: people were probably making fewer shopping trips because of the rising cost of gasoline; population had been shifting out of the cities to far suburbs and even to rural areas, where there were fewer shopping facilities; and more households had two adults working full time, so it wasn't easy for them to shop. The growth in mail-order sales may have been encouraged also by such developments as the increasing difficulty in obtaining good store personnel, more attractive and more informative catalogs, an improvement in service by a number of mail-order businesses, and the ready availability of numerous mailing lists.

Lamp also found that certain factors tended to limit the future growth of mail-order sales. Research had shown that, for many, shopping was a social experience in which the item purchased was often of secondary importance. To such people, shopping by mail would be an unacceptable substitute. Other shoppers must see and touch the merchandise they're buying, and often shoppers want the assistance of a sales clerk when making a purchase decision. In addition, stores offer supplemental services which shoppers want and which cannot be offered by mail order.

When Lamp reported her findings to the vice president of planning, he was impressed with the size of the mail order market and the fact that it represented 10–12 percent of all general merchandise sales. He even remarked that if Fenton's could build a mail-order business to about 10–12 percent of its retail store sales, it would represent approximately $50 million per year. He then gave Lamp approval to develop specifications for research to identify the extent to which a mail-order business would represent an opportunity to Fenton's, who the target market(s) would be, what products they would purchase by mail, and what characteristics they would like in the mail-order service they would patronize. The vice president stressed that the mail-order service should be designed to bring in new business and not take business away from Fenton's regular retail sales. He also indicated that Lamp would have a budget of about $50,000 for the research.

Lamp's first step was a review of past efforts at identifying different types of shoppers. One approach classified all shoppers into four groups: those who find shopping a pleasure, shoppers who are conservative buyers, impulse buyers, and shoppers who find it difficult to get to a store. Lamp judged that shoppers in the first two groups would have little interest in purchasing by mail because either the act of shopping or the need to actually see the product was very important to them. On the other hand, she reasoned, that impulse buyers might be good mail-order customers if the sales catalogs and brochures sent to them were eye-catching and attractive. She also felt that the last group—shoppers who find it difficult to get to a store—would be potential mail-order customers either because both adults were working, or they lived far from good shopping facilities, or there was a parent with an infant and other very young children.

Lamp also found a source that classified shoppers according to those who preferred to shop by mail and did so, those who would like to shop by mail but didn't, those who didn't prefer to shop by mail but did so for one reason or another, and those who preferred not to shop by mail and in fact didn't. While the first and third groups were important to her research, the second group could be important if the research could identify what it would take to actually get them to shop by mail.

Lamp concluded that there might be five types of shoppers to be identified by the research. Both impulse shoppers and shoppers who had difficulty in getting to a store should be studied to determine their potential as mail-order shoppers. In addition, people who did shop by mail, both those who preferred to and those who didn't, would also have to be studied to find out who they were, what they purchased by mail, and what kind of mail-order service they preferred. The group which would like to shop by mail but didn't would also have to be studied to determine how it might be motivated to do so.

Jane Lamp then listed seven items which, she felt, should guide whatever research would be undertaken. The study should: (1) be representative of shoppers in the surrounding regions, as well as in Fenton's retail market area; (2) determine the number who purchased by mail in the last 6–12 months, how much they purchased, and what they purchased; (3) identify the different types, or market segments, of shoppers in terms of their lifestyles, attitudes and opinions, and how the total population of shoppers breaks down into the various segments; (4) obtain demographics that can be used to identify the different market segments (e.g., age, income, education, number of working adults, location of residence); (5) identify the segments which are the best current and potential mail-order markets; (6) identify the product categories which they purchase by mail; (7) identify the characteristics of a mail-order service which will encourage present mail order shoppers to increase their mail-order purchases, and which will motivate prospective mail order shoppers to begin purchasing by mail.

> *Describe in detail the research design you would recommend for use by Fenton's, Inc.*
>
> *Specify (give examples) how your questionnaire would be constructed so as to obtain the required information.*
>
> *Present your plan of analysis, that is, describe each of the analyses you would make and the data you would use in each. Also indicate how the output of each analysis would be of use to Fenton's.*

Case 17–2
SHAFFER COMPANY

The Shaffer Company produced a line of popular priced men's toiletries, including colognes, shaving creams, and deodorants. Shaffer sold its line nationally through such outlets as drugstores, supermarkets, and department stores. Early in 1978 the agency which had handled the Shaffer advertising account for ten years was replaced because the new marketing director of Shaffer felt a new advertising approach was needed.

After evaluating the company's advertising history and what research was available, the new agency proposed that a lifestyle or psychographics study be undertaken in an effort to learn more about what kinds of men represented the potential for the Shaffer line of products. In commenting on this request, the agency account executive stated that such a study, if properly conducted, could have far-reaching significance in helping to segment the market, to provide a direction for the agency's copy and media strategies, and to identify the strengths and weaknesses of competitors.

More specifically, the agency proposed that this research attempt to relate buyer behavior regarding the different product categories to a variety of activity and attitude factors, to obtain product usage and brand preference data, and to collect information about individuals' ideal brand choice criteria and determine how various brands of men's toiletries rated against these criteria. It was suggested that the data be obtained from a sample of 1,500 using an existing consumer mail panel. Data collection costs, including pretesting the questionnaire, were estimated at $25,000.

In discussions between the research directors of the agency and the Shaffer Company, it was determined that it was possible to obtain a tested list of some 300 life-style statements. These could serve as a starting point in the development of the specific activity factors to be used. These 300 statements had been developed over time and, while essentially concerned with female activities, could help in suggesting life-style factors to be studied for men. Thus, it was planned to include "statements" dealing with how males spent their time; that is, work, hobbies, sports, vacations, community activities, and social events; what their interests were in terms of the relative importance of the family, home, work, sports, social activities, reading, television viewing, and so on; their opinions and thoughts about themselves relating to business, culture, social issues, politics, and education; and their demographic characteristics. Respondents would be asked to rate (using a five-point scale) the extent to which they agreed with such statements as "I often try new brands before my friends do" and "I like to go to parties where there are lots of music and talk."

Media usage information would be obtained by providing respondents with a list of magazines (for example, *Esquire, Playboy,* and *Reader's Digest*) and specific television shows (for example, "Kojak," "CBS News," and "Monday Night Football"). For each such vehicle respondents would be asked to indicate whether they read (or viewed) almost every issue, most issues, about every other one, less than half, a few, or almost none. The idea here was to get information which would classify the extent to which a given magazine or television show was patronized.

Regarding product usage and brand preference, the intent was to determine present brand(s) in use by product type (colognes, deodorants, and shave creams), whether purchased or received as a gift (if gift, from whom and for what occasion), where purchased (type of outlet), and brands purchased before the present one. Respondents would also be asked to indicate the relative importance of a number of different product characteristics on a scale of zero to ten for each of the three product types. They would then be asked to rate the brands they were familiar with on the same characteristics.

It was estimated that the final questionnaire would probably contain 250 to 300 questions, including demographic and classification information. Before turning to a formulation of the questionnaire, the two directors thought it advisable to develop a detailed analysis plan since the handling of such a large amount of data, much of it involving scaling, posed real problems. Without a rather precise plan, tabulating costs and the time devoted to analysis could quickly get out of control. Since neither director had prior experience in dealing with the analysis of such a study, it was decided to turn the problem over to a research consultant.

After several discussions with consultants, it was agreed that they should present a plan of analysis which would set forth the decision areas of primary concern to the agency and its client and the data needed to classify each such area. For example, the agency wanted to know what media vehicles were used, and to what extent, by heavy versus light users of men's toiletries. It wanted to use the data in the development of media schedules, taking into account reach, frequency, and cost.The client, on the other hand, was extremely interested in using the data to specify market segments on the basis of brand choice criteria and the perceptions of the various brands.

What "problem" or "decision" areas should be specified for the agency? For Shaffer?

How should the two sets of requests be integrated and sequenced?

In general, what data can be used, and in what combinations, to shed light on each of the decision areas?

How should the data be analyzed in order to satisfy both the agency and Shaffer?

Case 17–3
CONSOLIDATED NATIONAL BANK

Consolidated National Bank was a moderate-sized franchisee for a major bank credit card program. Despite a decade and a half of growth, the credit card program had not been as profitable as management's original expectations. Initially, losses were caused by the bad debt experience resulting from indiscriminate mass issuance of cards, a step management thought necessary to build volume rapidly. Later, these losses were eliminated when policy was changed to require that an application form be completed prior to issuing a card. The application revealed the applicant's age, income, job stability, and credit experience, which were the standard characteristics used to evaluate credit worthiness.

Although bad debt expenses were reduced by this procedure, profits from

---

* Adapted with permission from cases prepared by Conway Rucks, Associate Prof. of Marketing, University of Arkansas at Little Rock, from materials originally appearing in Elick E. Maledon and Conway T. Rucks, "Bank Card Profitability: User Characteristics," *Journal of Consumer Credit Management* 6 (Summer 1974):22–32.

the program were still far below expectations even though actual volume remained high. To explore the nature of the profit problem, the bank hired a consultant.

The consultant first identified the source of both revenue and costs in the credit card program. The two basic sources of revenue were (1) service charge revenue from participating merchants—normally 5 percent of each sale—and (2) interest revenue—1.5 percent per month on the credit card holder's unpaid balance. The two basic types of costs were bad debt losses and processing costs, which increased directly with the number of trans-actions for each credit card holder.

From these insights, the consultant profiled the "ideal" customer from the standpoint of card program profits. The "ideal" customer:

1. Used the card extensively for purchasing merchandise and services, thus generating service charge revenue.
2. Made use of the credit aspect of the card, ideally by perpetually keeping his credit limit near maximum, thus generating interest revenue.
3. Made large and infrequent purchases, thus reducing processing costs per transaction.
4. Was not delinquent in making the minimum monthly payments and did not default, thus reducing bad debt losses.

The consultant concluded that the cardholders' *total pattern* of usage de-termined card program profit, while the customer "selection" process (the application review) emphasized only one part of that pattern, credit worthi-ness. He then set out to analyze the patterns of usage of present cardholders to determine the degree to which their actual patterns of usage conformed to the "ideal" pattern. To determine these patterns, he decided to cluster analyze all the usage data that the bank had about its cardholders.

One hundred cardholders' records were selected by systematic sampling. The data on the cardholders' application forms were recorded, as were their payment records for the most recent 15-month period. For each cardholder, these variables were believed to represent the "extent of usage" of the credit card, how much use was made of the credit aspect of the card ("credit usage"), and characteristics of the user. (See Table 1.)

It was these variables which were cluster analyzed. Prior to cluster anal-ysis, however, each of the variables was correlated with each of the other variables. Because cardholders' average opening balance and their average interest were highly correlated ($r = .96$), interest was not used as a variable in the cluster analysis program.

A cluster analysis showed that three groups of highly differentiated usage patterns existed in the data. (See Table 2.) Tests also showed that the differences among the three groups' usage patterns were statistically sig-nificant. The three groups could be described as infrequent users (group II), high average charge, moderate credit users (group I), and small average

---

TABLE 1. Variables utilized for analysis

I. Usage patterns
    A. "Extent of usage" variables
        1. Average opening balance (15-month period)*
        2. Average charges (15-month period)
        3. Average payments (15-month period)
        4. Number of months (out of 15) card was used
        5. Months from application approval to present
        6. Percentage of months since application approval that card was used
        7. High balance (15-month period)*
    B. "Credit usage" variables
        1. Average interest charges
        2. Number of months (out of 15) card was used that cardholder had a past-due balance
        3. Percentage of times past due (15-month period)
        4. Number of months past due five days or less (15-month period)
        5. Number of months past due 6–30 days (15-month period)
        6. Number of months more than 30 days past due (15-month period)

II. User characteristics
    A. Age of applicant
    B. Number of dependents
    C. Months at current address
    D. Applicant's monthly income
    E. Applicant's months with current employer
    F. Spouse's monthly income
    G. Spouse's months with current employer
    H. Family income

---

* Also indicates "credit" usage.

charge, high credit users (group III). The usage patterns displayed by groups I and III were ones that were more likely to be profitable to the bank.

Because the application form data were supposedly predictive of card usage tendencies, the consultant attempted to determine the ability of that data to "predict" the usage patterns revealed by the cluster analysis. Table 3 shows, for each of the three groups, the means of the eight user characteristics employed in the analysis. Only one of these variables, when taken alone, contributed significantly to overall group differentiation—"months at current address."

The consultant also applied discriminant analysis to the data. To do so, he used groups I, II, and III as the categorical dependent variable, and the eight user characteristics as continuous independent variables. The outcome of this analysis did not prove helpful, that is, it did not appear that the data available from the credit card application form would help bank personnel identify whether an applicant was most likely to fall into group I or II or III. Table 4 shows the number of users which the discriminant analysis cor-

TABLE 2. Usage pattern of user groups

Usage variables	All groups (N = 100)	Group I (71 percent)	Group II (21 percent)	Group III (8 percent)
1. Average opening balance ...	$177.75	$216.13	$9.20	$292.04
2. Average charges	$30.90	$40.46	$5.88	$11.70
3. Average payment	$28.79	$37.10	$4.57	$18.44
4. Average interest	$1.85	$2.06	$0.05	$4.70
5. Number of months (out of 15) card was used	11.87 mos.	14.01 mos.	3.48 mos.	14.87 mos.
6. Average high balance (15 months)	$350.56	$377.75	$207.48	$406.20
7. Months from application approval (including 15 months)	25.51 mos.	25.06 mos.	25.04 mos.	30.75 mos.
8. Percentage of months card was used since application approval	71%	84%	22%	90%
9. Percentage of months card was used that cardholder had a past-due balance	11%	6%	1%	71%
10. Percentage of months past due	10%	6%	0.3%	70%
11. Number of months (out of 15) balance past due 5 days or less	1.91 mos.	1.37 mos.	0.10 mos.	11.50 mos.
12. Number of months (out of 15) balance past due 6–30 days ..	0.39 mos.	0.10 mos.	0.00 mos.	4.00 mos.
13. Number of months (out of 15) balance more than 30 days past due	0.10 mos.	0.00 mos.	0.00 mos.	1.25 mos.

TABLE 3. Mean user characteristics of three groups of bank card-users classified on the basis of similar usage patterns

Characteristic	All groups	Group I	Group II	Group III
1. Age	35.19	33.94	38.57	37.37
2. Number of dependents	2.29	2.35	2.19	2.00
3. Months at current address	72.35	57.31	73.67	202.37
4. Monthly income	$928.80	$910.98	$1,057.14	$750.00
5. Months with employer	78.45	71.46	89.95	110.25
6. Spouse's monthly income .	$151.20	$177.46	$97.14	$60.00
7. Spouse's months with employer	7.72	9.26	4.81	1.62
8. Family monthly income	$1,080.00	$1,088.44	$1,154.28	$810.00

rectly classified into the group to which they actually belonged. Thus, 45 of the 71 group I users were correctly classified, 8 of the 21 group II users were correctly classified, and 5 of the 8 group III users were correctly classified.

TALE 4. Classification table for usage-pattern groups by user characteristics

Actual group membership	Predicted group membership		
	Group I	Group II	Group III
Group I	45	21	5
Group II	10	8	3
Group III	1	2	5

Study the characteristics of each of the three groups resulting from the cluster analysis, and give each a name which is descriptive of its usage pattern. How appropriate and useful was the application of cluster analysis? Of discriminant analysis?

Should some other method(s) of analysis have been used? If so, which one(s), and why?

Given the consultant's findings, can you recommend research which would help the bank make its credit card program more profitable?

18

Research presentation and research process evaluation

No matter what the quality is of the research undertaken, much of the acceptance of the results depends on the way they are communicated to the relevant audiences. Standards for researchers are apt to be different from those of executives to whom they wish to communicate. Executives are not much interested in methodology—they want the "results." While the written or oral presentation may be an anticlimax to researchers, it is frequently all executives hear or see of the project. If executives are to act on the basis of the results, they must be convinced of their value. Researchers must make their presentation technically accurate as well as understandable and useful.

Proper execution of the research steps makes the research presentation easier to prepare. All steps, in one way or another, anticipate the presentation. If the overall problem is clearly understood, and if the information needed to achieve the objectives has been specified, then the framework of the presentation has been largely predetermined. Several sections of the presentation may be partially written during the conduct of the research; for example, it is customary to begin a presentation with a statement of the study objectives and to point out how the attainment of these will help "solve" the overall problem. This part of the presentation can be taken directly from earlier work.

Each project is different and, thus, the process of communicating the results is never automatic. Each requires originality. If the earlier steps in the research process have been well executed, however, it is more likely that a good presentation will result. It is difficult to visualize a successful presentation originating from a study in which the objectives were not clearly defined.

Frequently researchers will be required to make both an oral and a written presentation. Only the written presentation is discussed here.

WRITTEN RESEARCH REPORT

No two people will prepare a written report in exactly the same way. Situational differences in the personality, background, and responsibility of the researcher and the manager to whom the report is addressed should conspire to give each report a unique flavor. But even so, most agree that the following principles should be kept constantly in mind.

Many reports fail to achieve their objectives because the writers do not consider their "market"—the individuals who will read the report. Failure to understand the nature and capacity of these individuals, their interest, or lack thereof, in the subject area, the circumstances under which they will read and evaluate the report, and the uses they will make of the report may doom the report before it is written.

Being technical people themselves, researchers often tend to write reports as if they were intended for other technical persons. They tend to discuss the research problems involved in the project and to use the technical terms which are common to them, but not to the reader. The result is often misunderstanding, suspicion, and even hostility.

Executives have individual preferences which must be considered. Some executives demand a minimum report; they want only the results—not a discussion of how the results were obtained. Others want considerable information on the research methods used in the study. Many executives place a premium on brevity, while others demand complete discussion. Some are interested only in the statistical results and not in the researcher's conclusions and recommendations.

Thus, the audience determines the type of report. Researchers must make every effort to acquaint themselves with the specific preferences of their audiences. They should not consider these preferences as unalterable, but any deviations from them should be made with reason and not from ignorance.

Different readers may present conflicting demands. For example, some persons may want more data on the technical aspects of the research process than others. These different interests are often hard to reconcile and may, in extreme cases, require the preparation of more than one report. In other cases, the basic report may include a minimum of detail but have appendixes which cover the technical details for the benefit of those who are interested. Obviously, this problem of conflicting demands has no easy solution. Researchers have to be aware of such conflicts and use their ingenuity in reconciling them.

Adhere to the study objectives

A good report seeks to achieve certain results which consist primarily of answering the questions which derive from the statement of objectives. Merely to report the findings without reference to the objectives is to produce a sterile piece of writing. This requires researchers to be on "intimate" terms with the problem. If the management group has not permitted the researchers to participate in formulating the problem and has either handed down the problem or, worse still, merely demanded certain information, then there can be no definite goal for the report and it will suffer. Under such conditions it will be difficult, if not impossible, for report writers to draw conclusions and make recommendations.

Be selective

No report was ever written that contained all that was known on the given subject. If an attempt is made to include too much, there is always danger that the important points will be lost in the detail. Therefore, it is important to exclude anything that is not necessary. Since necessity in this sense is a matter of degree, researchers must use their judgment in deciding what things can be omitted. Such judgments are particularly difficult in relation to explanatory material. The reasons for using certain techniques or the logic leading from findings to conclusions to recommendations for action often take a lot of space to explain. Such explanations can obscure what was done or the specific recommendations made; however, if explanations are not given, the reader may conclude that the research was not conducted carefully. Somehow a satisfactory compromise must be reached. One solution is to mention that certain details have been omitted but are available upon request.

Be objective

Writers must at all times retain their objectivity. Often researchers will become so enamored of a study that they overlook their scientific role. This is a natural temptation since much marketing research is done within a sales environment. It is one thing to sell objective results and quite another to present results which have been "slanted" in such a way as to make them salable. Writers do neither themselves nor their company any favors if they lose their objectivity.

All researchers have experienced situations in which specific studies were condemned by management because the results did not agree with management's judgment or, perhaps, a previous position taken on the subject. A few experiences of this type may tend to cause researchers to slant their results toward the answers that they believe management is hoping to find. Advertising managers will receive with enthusiasm a report that shows an expensive campaign has been successful, when they may be hostile to the same study if it indicates the advertising funds have been wasted. Obviously, researchers must have enough courage to present and to defend their results if they are convinced the results are sound. Occasional kudos may be obtained for providing what managers want to find, but it is hard to conceive of a solid research reputation being established on such a basis.

Have a purposeful organization

Mere recording of facts without purpose or organization inevitably results in confusion which leads to loss of interest. The objective of the report
is to give the reader the overall "picture" in the shortest possible time.
Therefore, each paragraph should be written with the thought of its position
in the entire report in mind. Readers should be conscious of the organization
so that at any one time they know where they are in the report and where
they are going. A working outline helps readers comprehend the organization and helps the writer make certain that every point is covered without
duplication.

Write clearly

It is easy to say "write clearly," but this is difficult for most people to
accomplish. Clarity has many facets and is highly subjective. Despite this subjectivity, some basic principles can be itemized which, if followed, help to
produce better reports.

1.   Use short, to-the-point sentences—avoid sentence structures which are
     too elaborate. Always prefer the simple to the complex.
2.   Use words the reader will be familiar with, but which will provide
     variety and change in pace to the report. Avoid too many difficult
     words. The prime purpose of the report is to communicate the results
     of the study—not to impress the reader with the erudition of the writer.
     Avoid slang and clichés.
3.   Make certain the words express *precisely* what the writer wants to say.
4.   Avoid mechanical flaws such as incorrect grammar. Too often a worth-
     while report is discredited because of such flaws.
5.   Be sure that the report has uniform style and format. It is usually de-
     sirable to write a first draft and then allow a day to elapse before
     rewriting it. It is wise to submit the revised draft to another researcher
     for review and comment before the final report is prepared.

The report format

There is no one *best* format for all reports. However, the physical format
can be employed to create desirable emphasis and clarity. The use of widely
spaced paragraphs, varied margins, separated headings, different type sizes
and colors—all make it possible to emphasize major points and to clarify
the sequence and relationship of ideas. A report must use the format that
best fits the needs and wants of its readers. The following format is suggested as a basic outline which has sufficient flexibility to meet most situations. It should *not* be thought of as a rigid outline which must always be
followed.

   I.   Title page.
  II.   Table of contents.
 III.   Foreword (introduction).
  IV.   Statement of objectives.
   V.   Methodology.
        A.   Research design.
        B.   Data collection method.
        C.   Sampling.
        D.   Fieldwork.
        E.   Analysis and interpretation.
  VI.   Limitations.
 VII.   Findings.
VIII.   Conclusions and recommendations.
  IX.   Appendix.
        A.   Copies of forms used.
        B.   Details of sample with validation.
        C.   Tables not included in findings.
        D.   Bibliography, if pertinent.

Each of these items is discussed briefly in the following paragraphs.

Title page.   The title page should indicate the subject, date the report is prepared, for whom prepared, and by whom prepared. Sometimes it is not necessary to specify for whom the report is prepared, while at other times it is wise to indicate this precisely and to show who actually receives copies. Some research reports are confidential and for limited distribution; in such cases, it is particularly desirable to indicate on the title page who will receive a copy.

Table of contents.   If the report is lengthy or if it is divided into numerous parts, it is usually desirable to have a table of contents. If the report includes numerous charts, graphs, and tables, it is desirable to include a list of them immediately following the table of contents.

Foreword.   This section serves to introduce the reader to the research project. It should give the background of the problem (for example, how and when it came into existence), the importance of the problem, the various dimensions of the problem, and whether any previous research was done which is pertinent to the specific project being reported.

Statement of objectives.   The specific objectives of the report need to be set forth clearly. The reader must know exactly what the report covers. If the particular project is part of a large problem, it is desirable to state the overall problem and the problem solution process. Sometimes it may even be wise to provide some background information as to how the problem arose and what previous research work, if any, has been carried out. If such information will help in understanding the report, it should be furnished, but it should be kept as brief as possible.

Methodology. The purpose of the methodology section is to describe the research procedure. This includes the overall research design, the sampling procedures, the data collection method, the field methods, and analysis procedures. This section is difficult to write because it is hard to discuss methodology without using technical terms, yet much of the audience for the report will not understand technical language.

Research design. A description of the research design should make it clear whether the study is exploratory or conclusive in nature and whether it is case, statistical, or experimental in design. In addition to describing the research design, the researcher must explain why the particular design was used—what its merits are for the project at hand.

Data collection methods. Were data collected from secondary sources or from primary sources; were results collected by survey or observation? Again the researcher must explain why the method selected was appropriate for the project. A copy of the questionnaire or form for recording observational data may be included here. If the form is at all lengthy, however, it will probably be better in the appendix, where it will not break the continuity of the report.

Sampling. In describing the sampling procedure, it is first necessary to indicate the nature of the universe studied. The exact sampling units, such as stores, consumers, or business executives, must be defined and the geographical limits specified. If there were any difficulties in identifying the sampling units in the field, the procedure used for overcoming such difficulties must be explained. If the sampling unit definition used differed from the commonly accepted one, this fact should be noted and the differences pointed out to avoid possible confusion.

Next, the researcher should describe the size of the overall sample and of each subsample and should explain the reasons for their sizes. In describing the sampling design employed, the writer must be careful not to use terms which will confuse readers. Every effort must be made to describe the selection process adequately. Analogies may be useful. For example, if a probability sample were used, it might be best to describe it as a process "which is equivalent to putting the names and addresses of all women over 21 years of age, living in the state of Illinois, in a drum, stirring them around, and drawing out the names of 200. Such a process insures that every respondent has an equal chance of selection for the sample." Naturally, if complex designs have been used, the description will be more difficult. If the study covers a number of cities and counties, it is often desirable to include, as an exhibit, a map showing the distribution of the sample or a table indicating the sampling sites by regions, states, and counties.

Fieldwork. In describing fieldwork methods, the researcher needs to tell readers enough to give some idea of the accuracy with which the work was done. This will usually include a description of the number and type of fieldworkers used; how they were selected, trained, and supervised; and how their work was verified. A general summary of the degree of competence shown by the fieldworkers is helpful to readers. Copies of instructions or other forms used in the field operation can be included here or in the appendix.

Analysis. Relatively little can be said about the analysis and interpretation methods. The findings tend to show what has been done in this regard. If any special, statistical techniques have been used, they should be mentioned. If various executives have assisted in interpretation, this fact should be noted. This may help gain acceptance of the report, and, since interpretation is at least partially subjective, it helps readers appraise the interpretation given.

Limitations. A good report "sells" the results of the study, but it should not "oversell." Every project has limitations. The competent researcher does not attempt to gloss over these points but instead calls them to the attention of the readers. This helps readers form a more accurate interpretation of the results than they would otherwise do. It has the added advantage, from the researcher's standpoint, of giving confidence in the results presented. If readers find limitations which the report does not point out, they are apt to wonder how carefully the research was done.

Limitations may be of several types. One that should always be emphasized is the degree to which one may generalize from the results. If the universe studied is Cleveland, Ohio, readers should be cautioned not to generalize about the United States at large. If the study is an exploratory one designed to find new hypotheses, readers should be warned not to conclude that the results are an accurate measure of the phenomenon studied.

If particular questions in a survey seem to have confused respondents, the readers should be warned to use particular care in interpreting the results of these questions. If many not-at-homes were encountered in the fieldwork and substitutions were made, readers should be cautioned as to the effect this could have on the results. In short, researchers should note any weaknesses in the research methods used.

In describing the limitations of the study, researchers should point out the degree to which they could affect the results. If limitations are over-emphasized and not put in their proper perspective, they may tend to destroy confidence in the valuable parts of the study instead of increasing confidence.

Findings. Findings are the results of the study. This section makes up the bulk of the report. It is not just an assortment of statistical tables and charts, but an organized narrative of the results. Summary tables and graphic methods of presentation should be used liberally. Highly detailed tables should be relegated to the appendix. The specific objectives of the study should be kept in mind and the findings presented with them in view. Too often, writers feel they must present *all* the findings regardless of their bearing on the objectives of the study. The list of information needed to achieve the objectives, which was prepared in the problem formulation step, should limit the scope of the findings presented.

Conclusions and recommendations.   Conclusions should be drawn with direct reference to the objectives of the study. The readers should be able to read the objectives, turn to the conclusions section, and find specific conclusions relative to each objective. If, as sometimes happens, the study does not obtain satisfactory data from which to draw a conclusion relative to an objective, this should be acknowledged rather than disguised.

While it is almost always necessary for the researchers to draw conclusions, it is not always possible or advisable for them to make recommendations. On occasion the researchers may be specifically asked not to make recommendations. In other situations where the researchers have worked on one problem but have limited knowledge of the company's background and general operating policies, they would be unwise to recommend definite courses of action even if asked to do so. Making recommendations assumes considerable knowledge of the total "picture," including the resources of the firm and all the alternative courses of action. Often research workers do not have this knowledge.

Appendix.   The purpose of the appendix is to provide a place for those report items which do not fit in the research report proper because they are either too detailed or are too specialized. For example, the appendix may contain a detailed statement of the sample design, the formulas used to determine the sampling error, detailed statistical tables, and the various research forms used, such as the questionnaire and the written interviewer instructions. Nothing should be relegated to the appendix if its absence from the report proper will make it difficult for the readers to understand the results. If certain data are discussed in any detail, the tables containing such data should be included in the report at that point. In many cases the main ideas can be presented graphically in the findings section. In this case the tables on which the charts are based should be included in the appendix. This permits anyone who wishes to check the details to do so.

Summary report.   The report format suggested above does not contain any summary section. This exclusion is deliberate. The summary should not be prepared until the full report is written. Once the report is completed, a summary can be prepared quickly and efficiently. A summary, however, is usually prepared. Its objective is to present the highlights of the complete report so that executives can get the main ideas quickly. Some companies treat the summary as a separate report and send it to certain executives instead of the full report. In other instances, the summary is attached to the full report.

Report writers often place the summary at the beginning of the findings section, in which case the summary covers only the findings—it does not include any mention of the other sections in the report. If this is done the findings section is broken into two parts: (1) the summary and (2) the detailed account of the findings. Other writers prefer to make the summary a separate section at the start of the report. This latter method makes it easy for busy executives to read the summary and decide whether to go further.

It also permits them to determine quickly who else in the organization should read the report. When the summary is made the first part of the report, the objectives, findings, conclusions, and recommendations are included in it.

EVALUATION OF THE RESEARCH PROCEDURE

Immediately following the writing of the report, the efficiency of the research project should be evaluated. Inevitably, certain research decisions have to be made with the benefit of little, if any, evidence. For example, the allocation of the sample between regions and city size groups may be based, in part, on some estimate of the homogeneity of the groups being studied. If the assumption is that people on the West Coast are more homogeneous with regard to the characteristic being studied than, say, persons living in New England, then, all other factors being equal, more interviews would be scheduled in the latter region. An analysis of the findings would give some indication of the accuracy of this assumption. Such data on variance—even if only a rough approximation—will help in the planning of future studies and will enable the research workers to obtain greater efficiency.

Even though the questionnaire was thoroughly pretested before adoption, a "postmortem" study will probably reveal certain ways in which it could have been improved. Closely tied with this is the possibility that the fieldwork could have been improved through changes in the interviewer selection, training, and control procedures. Evaluation of the individual fieldworkers is in order. What interviewers need to be dismissed?

The above discussion suggests only a few ways in which the evaluation process can be of benefit to the research department and the firm. Through such a process, better research work can be developed in the future.

Research work lends itself to experimentation, and researchers usually have an opportunity to do some experimentation in each study they conduct. They can test a number of alternative decisions by designing experiments within the main project. Naturally, the experiments must not interfere with the main objectives of the study. For example, a test might be run to determine whether the use of an interviewer's quiz on field instructions resulted in better fieldwork. On a random selection basis, half the interviewers could receive the quiz and half not. Interviewers could then be graded on the basis of how well they followed the instructions, the number of completed interviews, cost per completed interview, and the number of unsatisfactory returns. The two groups of interviewers would then be compared to determine whether any significant differences resulted. Since the two groups were equated in advance by the use of a random selection method, any differences would be due to either the quiz or to random sampling fluctuations. Significance tests would then determine whether the differences could be explained entirely by sampling variations.

This is but one of many ways that the research workers can build into their research designs tests which will help them to improve research technique.

SUMMARY

Excellent research is sometimes wasted because research workers did not prepare a good research presentation. One common cause of this failure is that the writers did not consider the wants and needs of the relevant audience. Frequently researchers use technical terms and turn out a presentation which is over the heads of their audience. They should not hesitate to use honest salesmanship to put over the results of their work.

The methodology used in a study should be evaluated immediately after completion to discover more efficient procedures. A careful review of the sample design, the questionnaire, and the field methods will almost always pay dividends. Research work lends itself to experimentation so most studies offer an opportunity to test new ideas.

PART **IV**

SELECTED APPLICATIONS OF MARKETING RESEARCH

Part III presented the individual steps used when developing a marketing research project. In Part IV attention turns to the use and applications of marketing research. It was pointed out in Chapter 1 that marketing research can help provide the information needed by managers during different phases of the administrative process; that is, when setting goals and establishing strategies, when developing a plan, when putting the plan into action, and when devising control and reappraisal procedures (see Table 1–2). Regularly planned marketing research should occur in each of these phases, and this research will constitute management's regular information system.

Part IV consists of four topics which follow the sequence of the administrative process: defining markets, developing a product, designing advertising, and establishing methods of reappraising and controlling marketing activities and expenditures. Over a period of time, managers will encounter each of these administrative tasks. Part IV shows how marketing research can provide useful information inputs to managers when they are faced with each of these tasks.

19

Identifying market segments

Most marketers of goods and services are aware that not all individuals, households, or companies use or consume products in the same way or at the same rate. Sometimes different consumption patterns are observed geographically, that is, Westerners and Southerners consume more bourbon than Northerners and Easterners. Rural families consume more hot cereal than urban families. Households with different demographic characteristics consume differently; large families consume more snacks and sweets than small families, and wealthy families buy more expensive stereo and audio equipment than families of more modest means. People with more education tend to be more worldly oriented, and they travel more often and farther than less educated individuals. Marketers are concerned with knowing more about the heavy users of a product or service because, frequently, heavy users account for as much as 60–70 percent of total consumption of that product or service, even though they may constitute no more than 30 percent of the total population.

It is typically not possible for marketers to try to sell a single product to all consumers. A product that is promoted as one that is cheaper than competitive brands will attract some customers who favor the least expensive item, but it will lose others who will seek satisfaction from buying the more expensive (and presumably) better brands.

The essential research question addressed in this chapter is how to identify groups of consumers who are relatively homogeneous with respect to their responses to marketing inputs. These groups are referred to as *market segments*. The less variation in response within a given segment and the greater the variation between segments, the better will be the segmentation scheme. Most segmentation studies have been concerned with consumer goods. Yet the concept and a goodly portion of the techniques involved can apply to industrial goods.

TWO GENERAL APPROACHES

There is probably no greater problem area in marketing than how to effect a successful market segmentation scheme for a given product or service. When done properly, a segmentation scheme provides quantitative measurement of the size of different "parts" of the market and, by describing characteristics of each "part," such a scheme helps managers make decisions about product modifications, price, advertising copy, advertising media, personal selling, and merchandising. Thus, market segmentation provides strategy guidelines for the firm by helping to answer the question "In what product-market relationships should the firm engage?" In so doing it is concerned with the problem of how the firm's resources will be allocated across those relationships. In addition, market segmentation provides the basis for the development of the marketing plan.

There are two approaches one can take to identify and measure market segments. One approach starts with a basis for segmentation such as kinds of consumers and/or their purchase behavior in terms of, for example, usage and loyalty. The research typically seeks to describe the segments in terms of their demographics and to show how they vary with respect to their purchase rates, brand loyalties, and sometimes their media exposure habits. This type of research uses an *a priori* segmentation design.[1]

In contrast, the other type of segmentation research study employs a *cluster-based* design which "defines" segments on the basis of a grouping (clustering) of respondents on a set of relevant variables. Attitudes towards product characteristics as well as benefits sought and use situations serve as the more common bases for clustering. Such studies also obtain demographic data in an effort to describe the membership of each cluster.

Regardless of type of research design employed, it is necessary to select a basis for the segmentation and the descriptors used to identify the various segments. As noted above, the variables can be of two types: (1) "*general customer characteristics,* including demographic and socioeconomic characteristics, personality and life style characteristics, and attitudes and behavior toward mass media and distribution outlets, and (2) *situation specific customer characteristics,* such as product usage and purchase patterns, attitudes towards the product and its consumption, benefits sought in a product category, and any responses to specific marketing variables such as new product concepts, advertising, and the like."[2]

---

[1] The classification system used here is taken from that proposed by Yoram Wind in his article "Issues and Advances in Segmentation Research," *Journal of Marketing Research* (August 1978):317–37.

[2] Ibid., p. 319.

A PRIORI SEGMENTATION

The oldest approach to segmentation starts with established groups of consumers who differ as to their purchase of the product in question. Demographics, social class, and, more recently, life-style variables are then used as the basis for establishing market segments.

Demographic measures

An example of the results of an a priori type of market segmentation study based on demographic measures is shown in Figure 19–1. This study used economic class, occupation of family head, and age of homemaker as bases for segmentation. The percentage of families in each segment which bought the product and each segment's annual purchase rate (expressed as

FIGURE 19–1. Consumption of a household product by different consumer segments

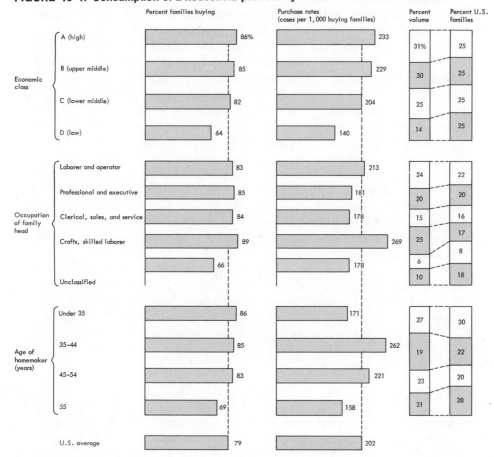

Source: Market Research Corporation of America.

the number of cases purchased per 1,000 buying families) are shown. While consumption of this product was not heavily concentrated in any one segment, upper income families, families of craftspeople and skilled laborers, and families in which the homemaker was 35–44 years old were clearly the largest buyers. With this information as a guide, product manufacturers would concentrate their marketing efforts on these segments.

Market segmentation studies of this type are usually based on large sample studies using structured, nondisguised data collection forms. The data may be collected from field studies using personal interviews, telephone interviews, or mail questionnaires or from purchase diary reports from a consumer panel service. The development of computer based telephone interviewing has made the telephone a highly desirable way of collecting the needed data. The measures needed for such a study are demographic characteristics, product or brand purchases, and consumption rates for each household.

Comments on a priori market segmentation using demographic measures.   After reviewing the rather substantial research literature on this subject, one researcher concluded that "Household demographic, socioeconomic and personality characteristics appear to have, at best, a relatively low degree of association with total household purchases of any particular grocery product."[3] This researcher also concluded that much the same can be reported with respect to household differences in purchase rates (for example, heavy versus light buyers), in response to promotional programs (for example, coupon users versus those who do not use coupons), and in brand loyalty (for example, consumers loyal to one brand versus consumers who use several brands). However, other researchers disagree with the conclusion that these measures cannot be used effectively in defining market segments.[4] Perhaps because they intuitively agree with the latter researchers, most consumer goods sellers have long used this type of market segmentation. There is no doubt they have found it useful—especially in making advertising decisions.

It is true that market segmentation based on demographic measures does not discriminate perfectly between users and nonusers or between heavy users and light users. Nevertheless, in most cases, such information is relatively useful, easy to obtain, easily understood, and helpful to advertising managers when identifying media which can be used in communicating with the firm's more promising customers.

---

[3] Ronald E. Frank, "Market Segmentation Research: Findings and Implications," in Frank Bass, Charles King, and Edgar Pessemier, eds., *Application of the Sciences to Marketing Management* (New York: John Wiley & Sons, 1968), pp. 39–68.

[4] Frank M. Bass, Douglas J. Tigert, and Ronald T. Lonsdale, "Market Segmentation: Group versus Individual Behavior," *Journal of Marketing Research* (August 1968): 264–70.

Usage rate measures

This segmentation scheme classifies the consumers of a particular product type or a brand on some bases such as the following: (1) heavy users, light users, and nonusers, or (2) heavy users and light users, or (3) users and nonusers. After respondents have been classified according to their usage or consumption rates, the different usage groups are analyzed on either demographic measures or psychographic measures, as demonstrated by the two examples below.

Demographic measurements. The results from one study which analyzed heavy and light buyers demographically are shown in Table 19–1. The findings demonstrate that purchase rate data, when correlated with selected demographic variables, can be helpful in identifying market segments. For example, the data in Table 19–1 would be of value to sellers of catsup, frozen orange juice, candy bars, and cake mixes in planning their marketing programs. These results show that heavy and light users are clearly different on such demographic variables as marital status, number of children, age, education, and income.

Psychographic measurements. One study, concerned with differences between heavy users of shotgun ammunition and nonusers, gathered both demographic and psychographic data from more than 500 respondents.[5] The demographic data indicated that, compared with nonusers, heavy users of shotgun ammunition tended to be younger, to have less income, to be blue-collar workers or craftpeople rather than in the professional or managerial ranks, and to live in rural areas of the South and the West. The full demographic profiles of heavy users of shotgun ammunition and of nonusers are shown in Table 19–2.

Psychographic data obtained from the same respondents demonstrate how it is possible to arrive at a better description of the differences between users and nonusers of a particular product type. Heavy users of shotgun ammunition are more active and more oriented to the out-of-doors than are nonusers (see the first eight items in Table 19–3). Users are more attracted to violence and danger and tend to be less risk-averse than nonusers (see the next ten items in Table 19–3). Users are also more self-indulgent than nonusers and less easy to reach through newspaper advertisements (see the last four items in Table 19–3).

This example demonstrates how a psychographic profile can supplement a demographic profile when attempting to arrive at a better description of one or more market segments. Some of the insights available from the psychographic profile might have occurred to the researchers from the demographic profile alone, but not all of them, and certainly the researchers would have had less evidence of the validity of those insights.

---

[5] Psychographic (life-style) classifications are based on measures of an individual's activities, attitudes, interests, beliefs, and opinions.

TABLE 19–1. Light and heavy buyers by mean purchase rates for different socioeconomic cells

Product	Description		Mean consumption rate ranges		Ratio of highest to lowest rate
	Light buyers	Heavy buyers	Light buyers	Heavy buyers	
Catsup	Unmarried or married over age 50 without children	Under 50, 3 or more children	0.74– 1.82	2.73– 5.79	7.8
Frozen orange juice	Under 35 or over 65, income less than $10,000, not college grads, 2 or less children	College grads, income over $10,000, between 35 and 65	1.12– 2.24	3.53– 9.00	8.0
Pancake mix	Some college, 2 or less children	3 or more children, high school or less education	0.48– 0.52	1.10– 1.51	3.3
Candy bars	Under 35, no children	35 or over, 3 or more children	1.01– 4.31	6.56–22.29	21.9
Cake mix	Not married or under 35, no children, income under $10,000, TV less than 3½ hours	35 or over, 3 or more children, income over $10,000	0.55– 1.10	2.22– 3.80	6.9
Beer	Under 25 or over 50, college education, nonprofessional, TV less than 2 hours	Between 25 and 50, not college graduates, TV more than 3½ hours	0–12.33	17.26–40.30	∞
Cream shampoo	Income less than $8,000, at least some college, less than 5 children	Income $10,000 or over with high school or less education	0.16– 0.35	0.44– 0.87	5.5
Hair spray	Over 65, under $8,000 income	Under 65, over $10,000 income, not college graduates	0– 0.41	0.52– 1.68	∞
Toothpaste	Over 50, less than 3 children, income less than $8,000	Under 50, 3 or more children, over $10,000 income	1.41– 2.01	2.22– 4.39	3.1
Mouthwash	Under 35 or over 65, less than $8,000 income, some college	Between 35 and 65, income over $8,000, high school or less education	0.46– 0.85	0.98– 1.17	2.5

Source: Frank M. Bass, Douglas J. Tigert, and Ronald T. Lonsdale, "Market Segmentation: Group versus Individual Behavior," *Journal of Marketing Research* (August 1968): 267.

TABLE 19–2. Demographic profiles of heavy users and nonusers of shotgun ammunition*

	Heavy users (141)	Non-users (395)
Age		
Under 25	9%	5%
25–34	33	15
35–44	27	22
45–54	18	22
55+	13	36
Occupation		
Professional	6	15
Managerial	23	23
Clerical-sales	9	17
Craftperson	50	35
Income		
Under $6,000	26	19
$6,000–10,000	39	36
$10,000–15,000	24	27
$15,000+	11	18
Population density		
Rural	34	12
2,500–50,000	11	11
50,000–500,000	16	15
500,000–2 million	21	27
2 million+	13	19
Geographic division		
New England–Mid-Atlantic	21	33
N.W. Central	22	30
South Atlantic	23	12
E. South Central	10	3
W. South Central	10	5
Mountain	6	3
Pacific	9	15

* Figures shown are percent of each user group in the different age, occupation, income, population, and geographic classes.
Source: W. D. Wells, "Psychographics: A Critical Review," *Journal of Marketing Research* 12 (May 1975): 197.

Methods of collecting data. Data for usage rate types of market segmentation studies are derived from large samples obtained from consumer diary panels or field surveys. Structured, nondisguised data collection forms are most likely to be used if segmentation is to be based on demographic data only. If psychographic data are to be collected, a structured, disguised or semidisguised questionnaire will be used. As shown in the three tables above, data analysis usually consists of basic cross-tabulations.

Comments on usage rate market segmentation. In many product categories, a relatively small proportion of the total population accounts for a large proportion of total consumption. In such cases, the soundness and

TABLE 19–3. Psychographic profiles of heavy users and nonusers of shotgun ammunition*

Statement	Heavy users (141)	Non-users (395)
I like hunting	88%	7%
I like fishing	68	26
I like to go camping	57	21
I love the out-of-doors	90	65
A cabin by a quiet lake is a great place to spend the summer	49	34
I like to work outdoors	67	40
I am good at fixing mechanical things	47	27
I often do a lot of repair work on my own car	36	12
I like war stories	50	32
I would do better than average in a fist fight	38	16
I would like to be a professional football player	28	18
I would like to be on the police force	22	8
There is too much violence on television	35	45
There should be a gun in every home	56	10
I like danger	19	8
I would like to own my own airplane	35	13
I like to play poker	50	26
I smoke too much	39	24
I love to eat	49	34
I spend money on myself that I should spend on the family	44	26
If given a chance, most men would cheat on their wives	33	14
I read the newspaper every day	51	72

* Figures shown are percent of each user group answering "Yes" to each statement.

Source: W. D. Wells, "Psychographics: A Critical Review," *Journal of Marketing Research* 12 (May 1975): 198.

logic of the usage rate approach are especially appealing. The entire procedure is simple and straightforward and is, therefore, easily understood and used by both managers and researchers. Both demographic and psychographic data can be used to differentiate between the users and nonusers. But the approach has its shortcomings and especially so in applying the findings to a given brand. Thus, not all "heavy" or "light" buyers want the same product benefit or use it for the same reason (e.g., the use of a mouthwash to prevent sore throats versus to eliminate bad breath.)[6]

CLUSTER BASED SEGMENTATION

In contrast to the *a priori* method of segmentation, in cluster based segmentation the number and type of segments are not known in advance.

6 See Nariman K. Dhalla and Winston M. Mahatoo, "Expanding the Scope of Segmentation Research," *Journal of Marketing* (April 1976):35.

Rather, the segments evolve from a clustering of respondents based on their similarities with respect to a set of variables such as those having to do with life-style (psychographics), product benefits sought, and attitudes towards both new and established products. There are a great many different clustering models available, although not enough is known to prove what models are best for what purposes.[7]

Psychographic/life-style measures. Psychographic measures can be used to classify consumers with respect to activities, attitudes, interests, beliefs, and opinions. The idea is similar to that underlying the use of demographics to identify different segments, except that psychographics are used instead. To obtain psychographic data, consumers are usually asked to indicate the extent to which they agree or disagree (typically on a three-, four-, five-, six-, or ten-point scale) with a series of statements. The statements are listed in random order on the questionnaire, so that when they are read the respondents are not likely to discern any meaningful pattern. However, the statements are designed to measure specific attitudes, opinions, or beliefs. Table 19–4 shows some sample statements which might be used to measure

---

TABLE 19–4. Psychographic variables and sample statements

Psychographic variable	Sample statement
Price conscious	I shop a lot for "specials."
Fashion conscious	My outfits are usually of the latest style.
Self-confidence	I am more independent than most people.
New brand trier	Often I buy a new brand just to see what it is like.
Arts enthusiast	I enjoy ballet.

Source: Adapted from William R. Darden and William D. Perreault, Jr., "Identifying Interurban Shoppers: Multiproduct Purchase Patterns and Segmentation Profiles," *Journal of Marketing Research* (February 1975):51–60.

---

such things as price consciousness, fashion consciousness, self-confidence, new brand trying, and enthusiasm for art. For each attitude, activity, belief, and so on, which the researchers are trying to measure, there will be several statements on the questionnaire. Consumers who agree strongly with statements of the type shown would be judged to be price conscious, fashion conscious, self-confident, triers of new brands, and art enthusiasts. Consumers are also asked to report their usage of the product or brands in question and of various advertising media. The responses are analyzed (1) to identify groups of consumers who demonstrate different activities, attitudes, interests, and opinions and (2) to identify how these groups differ with respect to their product, brand, and media usage.

One psychographic study involved a national sample of approximately

---

[7] See discussion of cluster analysis in Chapter 17.

4,000 men who were asked to respond to several hundred psychographic questions, as well as to questions concerned with product and service usage and exposure to media. A cluster analysis was applied to the responses to the psychographic questions. It indicated that the sample could be divided into eight relatively homogeneous groups; that is, there were eight groupings of respondents, and each group consisted of consumers who tended to answer most of the questions in the same way. After carefully studying the characteristics of each group, the researcher gave them the labels shown in Table 19–5.

TABLE 19–5. Eight male psychographic segments

Group 1. *"The quiet family man"* (8 percent of total males)
   He is a self-sufficient man who wants to be left alone and is basically shy. He tries to be as little involved with community life as possible. His life revolves around the family, simple work, and television viewing. He has a marked fantasy life. As a shopper he is practical and less drawn to consumer goods and pleasures than other men.
   With low education and low economic status, he tends to be older than average.

Group 2. *"The traditionalist"* (16 percent of total males)
   He is a man who feels secure, has self-esteem, and follows conventional rules. He is proper and respectable, regards himself as altruistic and interested in the welfare of others. As a shopper he is conservative, likes popular brands and well-known manufacturers.
   With low education and low or middle socioeconomic status, he is a member of the oldest age group.

Group 3. *"The discontented man"* (13 percent of total males)
   He is a man who is likely to be dissatisfied with his work. He feels bypassed by life, dreams of better jobs, more money, and more security. He tends to be distrustful and socially aloof. As a buyer, he is quite price conscious.
   He is a member of the lowest education and lowest socioeconomic group and is generally older than average.

Group 4. *"The ethical highbrow"* (14 percent of total males)
   This is a very concerned man, sensitive to people's needs. Basically a puritan, he is content with family life, friends, and work and is interested in culture, religion, and social reform. As a consumer he is interested in quality, which may at times justify greater expenditure.
   He is well educated, of middle or upper socioeconomic status, and is middle-aged or older.

Group 5. *"The pleasure oriented man"* (9 percent of total males)
   He tends to emphasize his masculinity and rejects whatever appears to be soft or feminine. He views himself a leader among men. Self-centered, he dislikes his work or job and seeks immediate gratification for his needs. He is an impulsive buyer, likely to buy products with a masculine image.
   He has a low education, is of the lower socioeconomic class, and is middle-aged or younger.

TABLE 19–5 (continued)

Group 6. *"The achiever"* (11 percent of total males)

This is likely to be a hardworking man, dedicated to success and all that it implies, social prestige, power, and money. He is in favor of diversity and is adventurous about leisure time pursuits. He is stylish, likes good food, music, and so on. As a consumer he is status conscious and a thoughtful and discriminating buyer.

He has a good education, high socioeconomic status, and is young.

Group 7. *"The he-man"* (19 percent of total males)

He is gregarious, likes action, seeks an exciting and dramatic life. He thinks of himself as capable and dominant and tends to be more of a bachelor than a family man, even after marriage. The products he buys and brands preferred are likely to have "self-expressive value," especially a "man of action" dimension.

He is well educated, mainly middle socioeconomic status, and a member of the youngest of the male groups.

Group 8. *"The sophisticated man"* (10 percent of total males)

He is likely to be an intellectual, concerned about social issues, admires men with artistic and intellectual achievements. He is socially cosmopolitan with broad interests and wants to be dominant and a group leader. As a consumer he is attracted to the unique and fashionable.

He is the best educated and of the highest economic status of all groups. He is younger than average.

Source: Adapted from W. D. Wells, "Psychographics: A Critical Review," *Journal of Marketing Research* 12 (May 1975): 201.

In this case researchers were interested in several different products and services. The consumption of each of these and the use of a number of magazines by the individuals in each of the eight psychographic groups are shown in Table 19–6.

As expected, the results showed that users of each product (for example, beer) were found in all of the eight market segments. However, men in Groups 5, 7, and 8 were more apt to drink beer than were men in the other groups, and they tended to be the heaviest readers of *Playboy*. Similarly, those identified as "sophisticated men" were the heaviest users of air travel and were among the heaviest readers of *Playboy, Time, National Geographic,* and *Newsweek.* This example illustrates how a firm can use psychographics to identify two or more relatively homogeneous segments of consumers of specific products and to find media which will be effective in reaching those market segments. Psychographic market segmentation studies are usually based on large sample field surveys using structured, disguised, self-completion questionnaires which are delivered either personally or by the mail to respondents. The data collection forms are disguised, in the sense that there are a large number of psychographic statements with little

TABLE 19–6. Product and media use by psychographic group

	Psychographic group percentages							
	1	*2*	*3*	*4*	*5*	*6*	*7*	*8*
Drink beer	45	56	57	51	75	59	80	72
Smoke cigarettes	32	40	40	29	54	42	51	38
Air travel outside United States	4	4	6	7	5	8	12	19
Air travel, domestic	14	15	14	26	19	32	20	42
Use brand X deodorant	7	7	6	8	14	10	9	12
Used headache remedy in								
past four weeks	53	60	66	61	61	64	65	67
Read current issue of:								
Playboy	8	11	8	13	25	27	36	30
National Geographic	21	13	11	30	13	28	16	27
Time	17	8	7	16	9	26	17	29
Newsweek	17	14	8	20	11	18	13	22
Field & Stream	10	12	14	8	12	9	13	3
Popular Mechanics	11	6	9	9	9	9	8	6

* Described in Table 19–5.
  Source: W. D. Wells, "Psychographics: A Critical Review," *Journal of Marketing Research* 12 (May 1975): 202.

or no apparent organization and with no clear meaning to the respondents. Questions about brand and media usage are of a nondisguised nature.

The general feeling among marketing people is that psychographic research provides useful insights into market segmentation on the basis of attitudes, activities, interests, and so on. When compared with the demographic approach, psychographic segmentation is especially advantageous in helping managers and researchers infer how different segments may respond to advertising messages placed in selected media.

It must be pointed out, however, that there are problems in using psychographics. Given the large number of variables which may be involved and the lack of any theory dealing with how they should interrelate, the analysis of psychographic data is both subjective and complex. There is always the problem of whether a psychographic measure is related to a particular product or brand: for example, does being a "new brand trier" imply a tendency to try both inexpensive household products *and* expensive new consumer durables?

There is considerable question also about the reliability of psychographic measurements. A recent study involving a test-retest to determine the reliability of 36 life-style measures after a one year time interval concluded there was a lack of precision associated with these measures. Of the 36 items, 12 appeared to identify psychographic variables that were consistent over the two years, 6 identified variables that had changed over the year's time, and 12 did not seem to identify any variable that existed over the period.[8]

---

[8] Alvin C. Burns and Mary Carolyn Harrison, "A Test of the Reliability of Psychographics," *Journal of Marketing Research* (February 1979):32–37.

Benefit structure analysis.[9]   Benefit structure analysis (BSA) is designed to help find new product opportunities within very broad existing product categories and to help with product modifications and repositioning. There are typically two stages to a BSA study. The first consists of in-depth interviews with 25–50 respondents to build a data bank consisting of tasks or needs, products used for each task or need, the benefits sought from using the products, and the physical attributes of products used. This data bank is then used to formulate a large-scale study designed to determine for each type of usage the extent to which each benefit and product characteristic is desired *and* the extent to which they are provided. The goal is to identify the gap or deficiencies between what was wanted and what was "delivered."

An example with household cleaning products will illustrate the use of the BSA technique. Table 19–7 contains examples of benefits sought and the

---

TABLE 19–7

Examples of benefits sought

Bleaches	Doesn't dull
Removes stains	Doesn't hurt hands
Removes grease	No streaking
Cleans tub ring	Seals porous floors
Kills mildew	Dissolves grease
Disinfects	No rinsing necessary

Examples of product characteristics desired

Strong smell	Concentrated
Low suds	Self-polishing
Quick drying	Can spray on
Dark color	Contains deodorant
Contains wax	Little odor
Biodegradable	Contains ammonia

Source: James H. Myers, "Benefit Structure Analysis: A New Tool for Product Planning," *Journal of Marketing* (October 1976):25. Reprinted from *Journal of Marketing* published by the American Marketing Association.

---

product characteristics desired. Central to the BSA technique is the question of how much *each* benefit is wanted and the extent to which this want has been satisfied. The results are called a Benefit Deficiency Matrix (see Table 19–8). Given a sample size of 500, the table shows that 34 respondents wanted to remove grease (the benefit) "a whole lot," but that the product used did so "not at all," another 26 wanted the same benefit, but their product did so only "somewhat," and so on. In all, Table 19–8 shows that 294 respondents wanted the benefit "removes grease" "pretty much" or "a

---

[9] This discussion is based on James H. Myers, "Benefit Structure Analysis: A New Tool for Product Planning," *Journal of Marketing* (October 1976):25.

TABLE 19–8. Benefit deficiency matrix

Benefit: "Removes grease"

	Received				Marginal sums	
Wanted	"Not at all"	"Some-what"	"Pretty much"	"A whole lot"	Wanted	Got
"A whole lot"	34	26	27	109	196	147
"Pretty much"	23	30	25	20	98	75
"Somewhat"	22	15	13	6	56	84
"Not at all"	108	13	10	12	143	187
Total	187	84	75	147		

Source: James H. Myers, "Benefit Structure Analysis: A New Tool for Product Planning," *Journal of Marketing* (October 1976):27. Reprinted from *Journal of Marketing* published by the American Marketing Association.

whole lot," but only 222 respondents believed they got the benefit to the extent they desired.

Next, market segments are formed by identifying benefits wanted, but not received, when doing a specific task. By counting the number of respondents in each such segment, the researcher can estimate whether or not it is large enough to identify a new product opportunity. For each target benefit segment the study reveals what product characteristics are "wanted" and what types of products are judged best at delivering the benefit.

There are a number of problems with the BSA approach to defining segments. The biggest problem is its failure to consider the multivariate nature of the relationships between benefits wanted and benefits received as well as between benefits wanted and product characteristics. There is also the problem of the need to use a large sample given the number of subsets involved in the analysis.

Product attributes. In recent years increasing attention has been paid to segmentation based on the perceptions prospective consumers have of the characteristics of various new product concepts and existing brands. Essentially, this procedure for predicting purchase behavior is based on a theory which holds that an attitude toward a brand is comprised of beliefs about the brand's attributes combined with the importance given to those attributes. Thus, "a consumer's attitude toward a particular brand in a certain product category is . . . hypothesized to be a function of the relative importance of each of the relevant product attributes and the consumer's beliefs about the brand on each attribute."[10] A score is obtained by scaling the extent to which each brand possesses certain characteristics *and* the importance attached to each by the consumer. Based on the scores for each brand, a prediction is

---

[10] Martin Fishbein, "A Consideration of Beliefs and Their Role in Attitude Measurement" and "A Behavior Theory Approach to the Relations between Beliefs about an Object and the Attitudes toward an Object," in Martin Fishbein, ed., *Readings in Attitude Theory and Measurement* (New York: John Wiley & Sons, 1967).

made of the individual's preference ranking. The results to date of such an approach have been encouraging.

If the above can be accomplished for the various brands of a given product, insights into buying behavior may follow. The marketers will know the product characteristics different consumers want and how various brands are perceived with regard to these characteristics. If the consumer's "ideal" with regard to these characteristics is also found, the data can help in positioning new products, deciding upon new product entries, repositioning old products, targeting research and development funds, forecasting market-share trends, and allocating promotion funds among brands. If the marketers can then distinguish between the individuals or households comprising the various product segments, they can often infer why certain product or brand preferences exist, as well as how and why consumers may respond to advertising messages as they do.

There are also drawbacks to this segmentation approach. The analysis and interpretation of multiattribute rating data for a number of real brands as well as an "ideal" brand are among the more difficult undertakings in marketing research. Not only is considerable skill needed to manipulate the large quantities of data involved, but the resultant relationships are apt to be more descriptive than causal. This, in turn, often forces analysts to rest their conclusions more on their assumptions and inferences than they would like.

Multidimensional scaling. Multidimensional scaling can be used to group respondents on the basis of a number of different dimensions, for example, the perceived relative importance of a number of different product characteristics. Thus, the "market" is divided into a number of relatively homogeneous segments based on responses to a number of direct questions.

To illustrate, assume that respondents in a sample are asked to describe their ideal brands of beer by rating the importance of a number of different attributes which collectively serve to explain differences between brands. Each beer brand is rated using the same set of attributes. Given such data and using multiple discriminant analysis, it is possible to determine the weighted combinations of attributes which best distinguish respondents' ideal brands from actual brands. The above procedure was actually used on 500 male beer drinkers to study how they compared eight brands on 35 attributes. The results showed that two dimensions accounted for 90 percent of the discrimination among the eight brands.[11] Figure 19–2 shows the spatial location of each brand relative to these two major dimensions. The vertical dimension portrays relative lightness while the horizontal dimension deals with quality. Figure 19–2 also shows the distribution of respondents' "ideal" ratings. These tend to form clusters which are represented by circles. All ideal ratings do not fall within the circles since they are dis-

---

[11] Richard M. Johnson, "Market Segmentation: A Strategic Management Tool," *Journal of Marketing Research* (February 1971):15.

**FIGURE 19–2. Distribution of selected beer brands and ideal
points in product space**

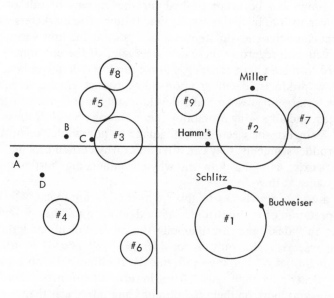

Source: Richard M. Johnson, "Market Segmentation: A Strategic Management Tool," *Journal of Marketing Research* (February 1971): 16.

tributed throughout the entire map. The size of the circles indicates the relative importance of that segment. The letters and names indicate specific
brand locations.

In commenting on how such an analysis can aid a company in determining the best product strategy, the author of the study notes that a brand's
share ". . . should be increased by repositioning: (1) closer to ideal points
of sizable segments of the market, (2) further from other products with
which it must compete, and (3) on dimensions weighted heavily in consumers' preferences."[12]

Conjoint analysis. Representing a relatively new way of segmentation,
conjoint analysis permits management to develop a number of alternative
segments and decide which ones are most appropriate. This approach is
particularly useful in new product development work where different new
products (each based on a different combination of product attribute levels)
can be tested to determine which is preferred by the largest number of respondents, and to identify the characteristics of the market segment pre-
ferring that product.[13]

[12] Ibid.

[13] Additional detail is provided in the discussion of conjoint analysis in Chapter 17.

SEGMENTATION AND THE RESEARCH PROCESS

Segmentation studies are among the most difficult ones to undertake regardless of which segmentation model is used. There are difficulties in terms of the sample design, the reliability of the data collected, data collection methods, and data analysis as well as in the interpretation of the results.

Segmentation studies seek not only to segment a sample on the basis of "differences," but also to project the findings to the appropriate universe. The latter often poses a difficult problem in that the unit of analysis is not always clearly specified. In studies involving consumer goods, respondents are typically housewives despite the fact that much household purchasing involves other members of the family to varying degrees. This unit-of-analysis problem is also a problem in the study of purchase behavior relating to industrial goods where multiple purchase influences abound.

In addition to the above problem, there is usually a sampling problem because quota samples are used despite their obvious limitations. Most segmentation studies also ignore the nonresponse problem, although there is every likelihood that there are significant differences between respondents and nonrespondents. The increasing costs of doing research encourage the use of quota samples and the ignoring of the nonresponse problem. Under such conditions, it can be argued that the researcher would be well advised to use a small probability sample which is well controlled with respect to call backs and includes a study of nonrespondents.

Every segmentation study has the problem of defining, in an operational sense, the dependent and independent variables. In product attribute studies there is the question of how to define or describe product characteristics in a way which will mean the same to all respondents. Should these be presented verbally, pictorially, or how? How should importance be measured? If a scale is used, how many points should be used and how should the scale be anchored? Should variables be ranked using verbal descriptions ("very important") or rank ordered in sequence of importance? These kinds of decisions will impact on the number and type of segments which emerge from such studies, and yet there are no ready answers to these questions.

Few segmentation studies have concerned themselves with the question of data reliability. Much the same can be said to apply to segment stability: How stable will the segment be over time? The latter is a more difficult subject to come to grips with since stability is a function of changes in the marketplace as well as in the consumer's perceptions of the relevant products. Because of these problems, it is difficult to know the validity of a segmentation study.

Segmentation studies have used a variety of data collection methods, including personal interviews, mail, and telephone. Which one is best in terms of a balancing of reliability and costs is a moot question. Much, of course, depends on the situation and what kinds of data are sought. If pictures are used to portray a new product concept, then the telephone method is ruled out. If it is thought necessary to obtain the uncontaminated views of a respondent, then the use of a mail survey is precluded. Computer-based telephone interviewing systems have increased the efficiency of telephone studies so that the telephone may be used even when it may not provide the greatest data reliability.

An ever-increasing number of models are available to analyze data derived from market segmentation studies. Typically, one has to understand a variety of techniques in order to decide which are most appropriate to classify respondents into segments (techniques ranging from simple cross-tabulations to multidimensional scaling) and then to discriminate between segments on the basis of respondent profiles.

In his discussion of the problems associated with the selection of appropriate techniques, one author sums up the situation as follows:

> Unique to segmentation studies is the need to apply a variety of analytical procedures in tandem. Most segmentation studies involve complex designs . . . revolving around several hybrid bases for segmentation. . . . However, because one cannot know in advance which basis for segmentation will lead to the identification of meaningful segments, segmentation studies should be *flexible,* allowing diverse analyses aimed at the identification of relevant segments. This need creates special demands for researchers with knowledge of a large number of analytical procedures, good conceptual understanding of alternative segmentation models, and a high level of research creativity.[14]

INDUSTRIAL BUYER BEHAVIOR AND MARKET SEGMENTATION

Most of the work done in connection with industrial buying behavior has centered on lists of factors which are important to consider in selecting a supplier and on modeling the typical behavior of a buying organization. There have been studies dealing with specific buying situations. But, generally speaking, the concepts discussed above as they relate to consumer goods have found scant application to industrial marketing. There seems to be considerable opportunity for buyer behavior research in the industrial goods area even though it represents a substantially different purchasing environment.

Most of the industrial buyer behavior models recognize the organizational constraints which impinge on the buying process. These include such "influences" as the presence of individuals who support certain suppliers, organizational preferences for certain kinds of suppliers, the purchasing agent's background, the willingness to accept risk, and position within the organization."[15]

---

[14] Wind, *"Issues and Advances,"* p. 332.

[15] See, for example, Jagdish N. Sheth, "A Model of Industrial Buyer Behavior," *Journal of Marketing* (October 1973):50–56; for a discussion of risk acceptance, see David T. Wilson, "Attitude Referents and Perceived Risk: Influences in Organizational Buyer Choice," in Ronald C. Curhan, ed., *1974 Combined Proceedings* (Chicago: American Marketing Association), pp. 75–79.

Studies dealing with the criteria by which supplier decisions are made are of considerable value. These employ essentially the same techniques as are used with consumer goods. One of the earliest buyer behavior models dealt with how physicians selected various pharmaceutical products. It centered on how doctors perceived alternative products in terms of their product characteristics and compared these ratings against a set of ideal criteria.[16] It should be noted that industrial products are perceived not only on their physical characteristics, but also on organizational features such as delivery promptness, billing procedures, and post purchase service. Multidimensional scaling techniques can be used to determine what market segments exist.

In addition to the use of product perception as a basis for segmenting the industrial market, the following bases can be used: (1) type of buying situation—new task, modified rebuy, or straight rebuy, (2) the phase of the buying or decision process, (3) the primary role of the buyer, (4) purchasing strategies, (5) problems faced by different buyers, and (6) self-confidence of buyers. These could be combined in a variety of ways to establish more precise segments.

In conclusion it should be noted that, while there are obvious differences in the study of industrial versus consumer buyers, there are also substantial similarities. This is particularly true with respect to the data gathering and analytical techniques used. The difficulty of applying these techniques may be greater when several members of an organization are respondents than when individual consumers are involved.

SUMMARY

Because different individuals, households, and organizations consume products and services at different rates, marketers try to identify groups which represent the greatest sales potential. By directing their marketing efforts toward these markets rather than toward the population as a whole, they can employ their marketing resources more efficiently. Reasearch used to identify these groups is called market segmentation research. The problem can be approached from either of two directions: (1) classifying respondents on an *a priori* basis based on the kinds or types of consumers and/or their purchase behavior or (2) clustering respondents on the basis of their similarities in regard to a set of relevant variables.

A priori segmentation starts with established groups of consumers and proceeds to see how they differ with respect to their purchases of a given product and exposure to different advertising media. Usage rate segmentation classifies consumers on the basis of some measure of purchase behavior such as heavy versus light users. The resulting groups are then

---

[16] See A. E. Amstutz, *Computer Simulation of Competitive Market Response* (Cambridge, Mass.: M.I.T. Press, 1967).

described using demographic and psychographic measures. Despite the fact that these measures are not always strong in their ability to discriminate among the numbers of the various groups, such research is often helpful, particularly in making advertising decisions.

Cluster based segmentation groups respondents on the basis of their similarities with respect to a set of variables such as those having to do with product benefits, product attributes, and demographics/life-style. Benefit segments are formed by clustering those respondents who want similar benefits and report present products are unable to satisfy their needs. This type of segmentation research fails to consider the multivariate nature of the relationships between benefits wanted and benefits received.

Segments based on product attributes have become increasingly popular, particularly in the case of new products. Such segmentation research can use product concepts or actual products as the stimuli. There are a great variety of techniques which can be used to cluster respondents into relatively homogeneous groups, including multidimensional scaling and conjoint analysis.

Segmentation studies are difficult ones to undertake. Since they need to be projected to the appropriate universe, a probability sample should be used, but seldom is. Most studies pay little attention to the nonrespondent problem. There is always the difficulty of defining operationally both the dependent and independent variables and few segmentation studies have concerned themselves with the question of data reliability.

Generally speaking, the concepts and techniques discussed in this chapter have been used primarily in studies involving consumer goods. To date little attention has been paid to industrial products. A number of bases can be used to model industrial buyer behavior as it relates to segmentation, including type of buying situation, phase of buying process, problems faced by the buyer, and buyer self-confidence.

Case 19–1
MORNING TREAT COFFEE BAGS

William Brandt, marketing manager to the Morning Treat Coffee Company, was trying to decide if the company's newest product was ready for a test market. The product—real, fresh coffee in a bag similar to a tea bag—had been tested by a consumer panel for several months. The results were encouraging, and suggested that the product would have appeal because it offered the convenience of instant coffee combined with the aroma and flavor of fresh coffee. Mr. Brandt was concerned about going into test marketing without a better understanding of the types of coffee drinkers most likely to use the new coffee bag.

Background

Approximately 2 billion pounds of coffee were sold annually through food stores in the United States. About 35–40 percent of total coffee sales were in the instant or freeze-dried form, which was a growing segment of the coffee market. This growth in instant and freeze-dried coffee was due to the increased popularity of convenience foods. The demand for convenience in beverages was reflected in the fact that over 90 percent of the loose tea sold in the United States was packaged in individual bags.

It had taken more than 20 years to develop a process for packaging coffee in individual bags. Tea can be packaged in a cellulose fiber bag placed inside an individual paper bag because it is an organic material that is relatively unaffected by exposure to air. However, coffee is a more complex substance, consisting of oils, solids, and gases that are affected by oxygen. Because of its complex chemical composition, fresh ground coffee cannot be packaged in a tea bag. The newly developed coffee bagging process used a specially developed synthetic fabric which sealed freshly ground coffee in a bag containing no oxygen. The shelf life of the coffee in the new bag was in excess of one year.

Issues

Mr. Brandt and other members of the marketing staff believed that Morning Treat Coffee Bags would appeal to convenience-oriented consumers. It was felt that heavy drinkers of fresh coffee were not likely to be included in this group because of the ingrained habit of brewing a large pot of coffee. The target groups were thought to be moderate and light drinkers of fresh coffee and all drinkers of instant and freeze-dried coffee. The marketing staff believed that many users of instant and freeze-dried coffee liked the convenience, but that they were less than satisfied with the flavor, taste, and aroma of that beverage. Heavy users of instant and freeze-dried coffee were considered to be the main market for the new product. Some staff members were concerned, however, that the coffee bags might appeal most to a relatively unimportant market segment—households of only one, two, or three individuals who consumed small quantities of fresh coffee.

Identifying the best market segments for coffee bags and the reasons why some segments would be attracted to coffee bags were thought to be critical issues which had to be resolved before going into test markets. The J. M. South Company, a marketing research firm, was invited to propose research that would clarify these issues. An abbreviated version of its proposal is shown in Exhibit 1.

EXHIBIT 1. Proposal

Purpose

The purpose is to identify the market segment or segments which include the most potential users of the new coffee bags and also to identify the basic reasons for the product's appeal to those segments. Specific measures of respondent identification will include whether they drink fresh or instant/freeze-dried coffee, and the amount of coffee consumed. Because of the convenience aspect, coffee bags may appeal most to single persons and families with two working parents. Therefore, potential users will also be identified relative to the number of adults in the household and their employment status.

Design

The following four-point research design is proposed.

1. Use the U.S. Postal Service to distribute free packages containing three coffee bags to households on selected blocks in selected zipcode areas in the same city or cities to be used as test markets. Each package of sample coffee bags will include a cover letter explaining that the product is new, the samples are free, and that the respondents are invited to try them at their convenience.
2. Follow-up personal interviews will be made three to six weeks after the sample mailing. Persons selected as respondents will be adults who received and tried the new coffee bags.
3. Respondents will be identified as potential users or potential nonusers, depending upon how they score on the product-attitude rating scale to be used in the proposed questionnaire. (That scale is described below.)
4. All respondents (both potential users and potential nonusers) will be classified according to three descriptive measures (*a*) amount of coffee consumed—three or more cups daily (heavy), or less than three cups daily (light); (*b*) form of coffee consumed—fresh only, instant/freeze-dried only, or both; and (*c*) number of working adults in the household—single adult, one working parent, two working parents, or others. Thus, respondents will be classified according to amount and form of coffee consumed and number of adults in the household and their employment status. Tabulation will consist of counting the number of respondents falling into each category and calculating the percentage of potential coffee bag users in each category. These findings will identify the most important market segments for coffee bags.

Questionnaire

A four-part questionnaire will be used during the personal interview.

1. Questions will measure the type and amount of coffee consumed and necessary demographic information.
2. Respondents will rate their regular coffee drink on each of the following seven traits. (Figures shown in parentheses are the weights to be given to each rating. The weights are used in the analysis discussed below.)

EXHIBIT 1 *(continued)*

Coffee trait	*Very important* (+3)	*Important* (+2)	*Slightly important* (+1)	*Not important* (0)
Aroma	————	————	————	————
Convenience	————	————	————	————
Flavor/taste	————	————	————	————
Freshness	————	————	————	————
No messy cleanup	————	————	————	————
Price	————	————	————	————
Strength	————	————	————	————

3. Respondents who tried coffee bags will compare them with their regular coffee drink on each of the above seven traits using the five-point scale shown in the following table.

	Coffee bags are definitely better (+2)	*Coffee bags are slightly better* (+1)	*Coffee bags are neither better nor worse* (0)	*Regular drink is slightly better* (−1)	*Regular drink is definitely better* (−2)
Aroma	————	————	————	————	————
Convenience	————	————	————	————	————
Flavor/taste	————	————	————	————	————
Freshness	————	————	————	————	————
No messy cleanup	————	————	————	————	————
Price	————	————	————	————	————
Strength	————	————	————	————	————

4. Respondents will be asked their "intentions to buy" coffee bags on a five-point scale: very likely to buy, likely to buy, don't know, not likely to buy, will not buy.

Analysis

1. *For each of the seven traits* measured in questionnaire items 2 and 3, the following weighting system will be used to determine a "score" for each *respondent* relative to each trait. The respondent's "score" is the figure shown at the intersection of the appropriate row and column.

The respondent indicated in questionnaire item 2 that the trait is	In questionnaire item 3 the respondent rates coffee bags on this trait as:				
	Definitely better (+2)	*Slightly better* (+1)	*Neither* (0)	*Slightly worse* (−1)	*Definitely worse* (−2)
Very important (+3)	+6	+3	0	−3	−6
Important (+2)	+4	+2	0	−2	−4
Slightly important (+1)	+2	+1	0	−1	−2
Not important (0)	0	0	0	0	0

EXHIBIT 1 (*concluded*)

Thus, if a respondent indicates freshness is "very important" in question-naire item 2 (weight of +3) and that coffee bags rate "definitely better" than his/her regular coffee drink (+2), the respondent is given a score of +6 (+3 times +2) on freshness. If aroma is "important" (+2) and the respondent rates coffee bags as "slightly worse" (−1), the respondent is given a score of −2.

2. Respondents will be given a score on each trait. These seven scores will be summed to determine "total score," which will lie somewhere between +42 and −42.

3. The respondent's "total score" and "intention to buy" coffee bags (from questionnaire item 4) will classify her/him as a potential user or not a potential user, according to the following rules.

Potential user	*Not potential user*
a. Total "score" is > + 12 and respondent *answers* "very likely to buy" or "likely to buy" coffee bags.	c. "Score is > + 12 and respondent *does not answer* "very likely to buy" or "likely to buy" coffee bags.
b. Total "score" is between +6 and +12 and respondent *answers* "very likely to buy" coffee bags.	d. "Score" is between +6 and +12 and respondent *does not answer* "very likely to buy" coffee bags.
	e. "Score" is +5 or less.

4. All respondents who tried coffee bags will be classified into one (and only one) of the following cells.

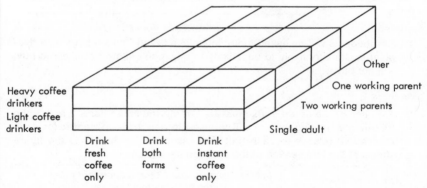

5. Each cell will have a total *number* of respondents and the *percentage* who have been classified as "potential users" of coffee bags. This information will identify the more important market segments which find the new coffee bags appealing.

6. Answers from respondents *in the more important market segments* will then be reanalyzed to identify that aspect, or those aspects, of coffee bags which they find most appealing. This reanalysis will identify the coffee traits which these respondents consider important or very important *and* for which they rated coffee bags as better than their regular coffee drink. Those are the product characteristics which potential users find most appealing.

Should Mr. Brandt accept the proposal in its current state, or is it in need of modification?

If the proposed research is to be rejected: what alternative project should be substituted? (a) Is any research needed? (b) If research is needed, describe the alternative project which should be substituted.

Case 19–2
REGAL FOODS

Jim Slater, the marketing manager for Regal's canned vegetables, fruits and juices, was concerned with the competition which might occur due to the introduction of generic brands by large supermarket chains. In the last year and a half, a number of supermarket chains began to offer generic products —that is, products with no brand name—at prices 20–35 percent below the prices of well-known manufacturers' brands such as Regal and Del Monte, and 10–15 percent below the prices of store brands. However, in spite of the apparent price advantage of generic products, Slater had no evidence that they were taking sales from the Regal line of fruits and vegetables.

Regal Foods sold a wide line of food products and had annual sales in excess of $200 million. The Regal brand of fruits and vegetables accounted for the bulk of the company's sales. Those products were of the highest quality and grade, they used the best ingredients available, and they were well-prepared and packaged. Also, the Regal brand had excellent distribution nationwide, and was given good advertising and promotional support. Slater believed that Regal's past marketing programs had been effective, and that the brand's reputation did not appear to be vulnerable to competition. Even though he felt that Regal was in a strong competitive position, Slater still wondered if the new generic products would prove to be strong competition within a few years.

Generic grocery products were also called no-name or no-brand products because the only printing on the product would be plain black letters on a white label spelling out the product contained inside the package, for example COFFEE or DILL PICKLES. In looking into the matter, Slater found that generics were lower priced primarily because of lower quality. For example, generic fruits and vegetables contained "standard" grade commodities rather than the "fancy" grade used by Regal, and the contents of generic fruits and vegetables were likely to contain broken pieces, rather than whole or nicely cut pieces. Lower quality seemed characteristic of a number of generic products—some generic paper towels were less absorbent than manufacturers' brands and store brands of paper towels, and some generic deodorants had an unpleasant odor. Also, the quality of generic products was uneven—that is, their quality was not consistent over time—and it was not unusual for a given generic product (e.g., cut beets) to be out of stock.

Slater also found other reasons why generic products were lower priced—they were offered only in one size or flavor, they used less expensive packaging, and less was spent on advertising. From the information he could gather, Slater was led to believe that retailers' profit margins on generics were small, and probably quite a bit below the margins on manufacturers' brands and store brands. In spite of these apparent weaknesses, one advertising agency reported that among shoppers who had bought generic products, 43 percent had bought canned vegetables and 20 percent had bought canned fruit.

Although generic products had been popular in Europe for a number of years, the idea had not really caught on in the United States until the last year or so. At first, only a few supermarket chains began offering generic products, but their number had increased. Slater thought that perhaps 15–25 percent of the supermarkets in the country might already be selling some generic products, or were planning to do so in the near future. Furthermore, he saw no evidence indicating that the trend would not continue. As far as he knew, no chain had given up selling generic products, and some were reported to have added still more product types to their line of generic products. Slater believed it was reasonable to assume that more chains would begin to offer generic products, and that more than likely they would include canned fruits and vegetables in their line.

Because generic products were so new, very little was known about their users. The situation was complicated by the fact that, for some types of products, there were already three or four different levels of quality from which a shopper could choose. In most product categories shoppers could also select from a second-level store brand and even a third-level store brand. In effect, generic products would represent a fifth level of quality. Slater wondered if consumers could really distinguish between five different levels of quality. Yet, if consumers were buying generic products, it was reasonable to assume they had switched from some other level of quality, but he didn't know from which.

In looking into the matter further, Slater found a study of people who shopped at a supermarket which offered a full line of generic products. The study found that 60 percent of the shoppers surveyed were aware of the generic products. Of those who were aware, almost half had tried at least one generic product, and a majority of those who had tried generic products said they would probably continue to purchase them. One trade publication reported that generic products were being purchased in place of manufacturers' brands, but one chain executive said that generic products were taking sales away from manufacturers' brand and store brands equally. From this, Slater could only conclude that not much was known about who was purchasing generic products, how satisfied they were with them, and what brands they had purchased previously.

Although generic products had not as yet had an effect on Regal's sales, Slater felt it might be due to the generics being so new. But a lot was at stake, and Slater didn't want to be caught unprepared if generic products became a more serious threat to the Regal line. If the threat from generic products were to increase, Slater wanted to be able to recommend a good marketing plan to offset the threat.

Because there was almost no detailed information regarding generic products, Slater began to identify the information he would need in order to develop a marketing plan which would be effective against generic products. He wanted to identify users of generic products, to find out if they also used generic canned fruits and vegetables and, if so, what their attitudes were toward those generic products in comparison with manufacturers' brand of like products. He also wanted to know the brands of canned fruits and vegetables these people had purchased previously. It seemed likely that some people had tried generic products, including canned fruits and vegetables, but for one reason or another did not continue to purchase them. Slater wanted to find their reasons for not continuing to use generic fruits and vegetables, and to learn of their attitudes toward those generic products. He also wanted to interview users of manufacturers' brands of canned fruit and vegetables, especially of the Regal brand, and to measure their awareness of, trial and usage of, and attitude toward, generic products in general and canned fruits and vegetables in particular.

Recommend a research project for Slater to use.

Design the questionnaire to be used in the study. Show how it will obtain the information that Slater will need.

20

Product research

The single most important strategy of any firm is the development of a product line which meets the needs of certain groups of consumers. No other strategy has greater effect in the long run on the firm's profits and, hence, its survival. Thousands of new products are introduced to the market every year. A majority of the products on supermarket shelves were not in existence ten years ago and the number of new industrial products introduced in recent years is equally impressive. The growth rate of many, if not most, U.S. corporations is tied closely to the success experienced in their new product work. As profit margins decline on their established products, companies must rely on new products to sustain their overall profit margins.

Evidence of management's concern about the dedication to new products is found in the large annual amounts being spent on R&D—tens of billions of dollars.

Only a small proportion of new products is successful. Just how small is not known precisely, but estimates have ranged as low as 20 percent.[1] Further, it takes about 58 new product ideas to find one which can be commercialized.[2] In commenting on the risks involved in new product marketing, Paul Harper reported in 1976 that only eight of the new food products launched over the previous seven years had generated more than $30 million in incremental sales.[3] And there is every indication that new product devel-

[1] Davis S. Hopkins and Carl L. Bailey, "New Product Pressures," *Conference Board Record* (June 1971):16–24.

[2] *Management of New Products* (New York: Booz, Allen, and Hamilton, 1968).

[3] Paul C. Harper, Jr., "New Product Marketing: The Cutting Edge of Corporate Policy," *Journal of Marketing* (April 1976):76–85.

opment will become increasingly difficult in the years ahead due to a maturing of basic technologies, increased government regulation, shorter product life cycles, higher cost of capital, and increasing costs associated with the new product development process.

The essence of any firm's new product policy is the identification of those product opportunities which will generate, over a stated time period, the greatest return on the funds invested in relation to the risk involved *and* which are in harmony with the firm's resources. To attain the above objective, it is necessary to take the following steps.

1. Develop an overall product strategy based on market needs, industry structure, and corporate resources.
2. Develop a flow of new product ideas from a variety of sources.
3. Develop preliminary product screening procedures.
4. Develop procedures for final screening.
5. Develop product specifications with regard to optimum product attributes.
6. Test the product.
7. Test market the product.
8. Commercialization, including supervision of the product through its life cycle and its termination or phase out.

Although the contributions which can be made by marketing research in each of the above steps are significant, the remainder of this chapter places emphasis on the role of marketing research in steps five, six, and seven.

DEVELOPING PRODUCT SPECIFICATIONS

It is necessary to determine that set of product attributes which are optimum for the market segment(s) to which the product will appeal. Since the number of forms that a product can assume is almost unlimited, the determination of the best combination is a difficult undertaking.

As a result of the research conducted in connection with the earlier steps, much information should be available concerning those product attributes which consumers believe should be incorporated in the product. But it is one thing to have verbal expressions about product attributes and quite another to translate them into a specific physical entity. Consumers cannot give precise technical answers about how the product should be made, or even how it will be used. Many consumers provide conflicting views with respect to product attributes; for example, most consumers want high quality and low price.

The difficulty can be minimized by defining as precisely as possible the particular market segment for which the product will be designed. The preferences of this market segment may be more homogeneous than those of a wider group of consumers and, thus, more helpful. Doing marketing research among these people can provide the research and development staff with important leads as to what will constitute a good product design. At the minimum, marketing research should provide a list of those features or attributes which *must* be included in the product as well as a list of those which *must not* be included. Any data on how consumers evaluate or test the product to determine its qualities are useful. It is very likely that consumers will test a product in far different ways from those used by the technical staff.

What attributes are important

One *cannot* obtain a list of important product attributes by asking consumers: "What qualities should such a product have and what is the relative importance of each?" Such questions produce ambiguous answers which are difficult to interpret. In the case of consumer products, many respondents play back the advertising themes to which they have been exposed.

With new products, researchers must find out what consumers want and *then* translate these desires into meaningful technical language. Consumers typically describe what they want in terms of product benefits, functions, and effects. These must be translated into ingredients, design characteristics, performance criteria, and even manufacturing procedures. Such communication problems indicate the necessity for the marketing researchers to work closely with the technical staff while trying to determine what is and what is not acceptable in terms of product attributes.

Research techniques such as focus group interviewing or the projective methods of word association, story telling and sentence completion provide sound ways of obtaining from consumers their real feelings and thoughts about product factors. Using such techniques in a study dealing with detergents, one company found that when consumers said they "liked the suds" they had different product attributes in mind, such as the amount of suds, the heaviness of suds, the time required to generate the suds, the permanency of suds, and the reactivating qualities of suds.

There are three prevailing methods of determining the importance of various product attributes, and experiments have shown they provide different results.[4] The first method is self-reporting, in which respondents define which product attributes are deterministic, that is, which most influences their preferences or purchases.[5] Self-reported information can be obtained by direct and indirect questioning, observation, and experimentation. The direct questioning approach, because of its relative simplicity and ease in use, has been the most popular.[6]

---

[4] Roger M. Huber, Chike Okechuker, and Stan Reid, "Attribute Importance: Contrasting Importance," *Journal of Marketing Research* (February 1979):60–63.

[5] James H. Meyers and Mark Alpert, "Determinant Buying Attitudes: Meaning and Measurement," *Journal of Marketing* (October 1968):13–20.

[6] Mark Alpert, "Identification of Determinant Attributes: A Comparison of Methods," *Journal of Marketing* (May 1971):184–189.

The second method is that which involves having consumers evaluate products as bundles of attributes and provide information about the relative importance or trade-off value of each attribute. Such data are critical to the development of multiattribute models and are typically obtained using a direct questioning approach (for example, having respondents allocate the points contained in a constant sum scale to each attribute, thereby providing a ranking of importance). If conjoint measurement is involved, then an indirect method is used to evaluate alternative products. The process consists of obtaining rank order reactions to products where all their attributes are described or where sets of partial products (incomplete statements of attributes) are judged, two attributes at a time.[7]

The third method consists of an information display board (IDB) which provides in sequence information which consumers might wish to obtain before purchasing a product. The information is revealed until respondents feel they have enough to make a decision. The relative importance of product attributes is determined by this process.[8] It is an inferential technique which is based on direct observation of the respondent's choice behavior.

An experimental study involving electric blenders used all three methods and found that the most reliable method was self-reporting. The researchers involved, however, were not convinced by their own study. They argued that on the face value the IDP findings were better. Their logic was that this technique more closely represents the marketplace since it alone ranked price and brand name as important whereas the two other methods emphasized the rational attributes of product warranty, safety, and quietness. The researchers contended that both self-reporting and conjoint measurement methods were biased to the extent that respondents felt compelled to provide rational "answers." They speculated that the three methods may be measuring different things: self-reporting was a measure of saliency (top of the mind), conjoint was concerned with relative importance, and IDP focused on the attributes which were deterministic.[9]

Relative importance of individual attributes

The preceding discussion anticipated the subject to be covered in this section. Saliency measures of product attributes—both individually and in combinations—are critical to the design of the product, the need to position it properly in the market place, and to estimate demand. Most of the research on this subject is based on the Fishbein attitudinal model which explains attitude or preference towards a given brand as being a function of the importance of its various attributes and the way the brand is perceived in

---

[7] Huber et al., "Attribute Importance," pp. 60–61.

[8] Jacob Jacoby, George J. Szbillo, and Jacqueline Busato-Schach, "Information Acquisition Behavior in Brand Choice Situations," *Journal of Consumer Research* (March 1977):209–16.

[9] Huber et al., "Attribute Importance," p. 63.

terms of these attributes compared to alternative brands. Methods of determining these factors rely heavily on the concepts used to measure brand preferences and the perceptions of the attributes of one brand versus those of another. Since these subjects have been covered at some length in earlier chapters, the discussion here is concerned mainly with the techniques used to measure product attributes both in relative and absolute terms.

The problem of how best to determine the relative importance of an attribute is a difficult one. Usually it is accomplished via scaling, but the "questioning" context within which data are obtained is important. Research has shown that situational factors impact on the ratings accorded to certain product attributes and, if not accounted for, may seriously bias the findings.[10] The following discussion covers three research approaches to the problem of measuring the importance of product attributes.

Concept testing. It is important to distinguish between a product concept and a product idea. The latter is ". . . a possible product, described in objective functional terms, that the company can see itself offering to the market. A *product concept* is a particular subjective consumer meaning that the company tries to build into the product idea."[11] Typically a single product idea can be used to generate many different product concepts.

Over the years large numbers of researchers have used concept testing as a way of determining whether potential customers understood the product idea behind the concept and how they evaluated the product or brand's attributes in light of the benefits claimed. Concept tests can also be used to have consumers evaluate several different product concepts, each of which has a different set of attributes.

Concept testing is a highly flexible research instrument; it is simple to make operational. Such tests can employ a number of means to express the concept, although pictures or drawings are among the more common. Cards which describe the concept are often used to solicit evaluations. Some companies go so far as to use product models, samples, or prototypes as the stimulus to provide the consumer with a more complete understanding of what is being tested. Concept testing lends itself readily to the use of experimental designs.

Concept testing should be used primarily for diagnostic purposes; that is, to help management understand better the dimensions of the product idea, the value of the concept(s) to the end user, and the ways in which the benefits and product attributes are linked. Such tests should not be used to forecast ultimate sales since that is a function of a good many other variables including the marketing mix employed.[12]

---

[10] Russell W. Belk, "An Exploratory Assessment of Situation Effects in Buyer Behavior," *Journal of Marketing Research* (May 1974):156–63.

[11] Philip Kotler, *Marketing Management*, 4th ed. (Englewood Cliffs, N.J.: Prentice-Hall, Inc., 1980), p. 321.

[12] Edward M. Tauber, "Why Concept and Product Tests Fail to Predict New Product Results," *Journal of Marketing* (October 1975):69–71.

Conjoint analysis.   In recent years the technique of conjoint analysis has been used more and more in product concept testing. This is particularly true when the new product is targeted to fit into an existing product class where each brand has to compete on the basis of its perceived uniqueness. Thus, it centers on determining what consumers want in a product. In the discussion of conjoint analysis presented in Chapter 17, this type of new product development application was demonstrated in a study involving three package variations, three brands, three price levels, a money-back guarantee, and a seal of endorsement. The study involved 108 possible combinations of product attributes. The results of the conjoint analysis gave an indication of which product attributes were likely to be more acceptable.

Preference distribution analysis.   Useful data relating to consumer product attribute preferences can be obtained using paired comparison tests, rank orders, rating scales, or statements concerned with likes and dislikes. The latter usually involve using a semantic differential test. Regardless of method employed, the objective is to obtain consumer preference measures for each salient product characteristic as well as for the overall product. The stimulus can range from actual product samples to pictures, drawings, or cards describing the product concept.

Paired comparison tests are typically used when the number of objects involved is small, but when the number of possible pairs is large, rating scales are usually used. Paired comparisons are simple to administer and easily understood by respondents.

Samples of the product with differing characteristics can be made up and tested using either rating scales or paired comparisons. From such tests the percentage of consumers who prefer each "level" of the product attribute is estimated. These preference ratings can be compared with consumer preferences for the company's existing products as well as those of competitors. Thus, such an approach enables management to determine to what extent new products out-perform existing products and to define relevant market segments.

In a study to determine preferences for differing amounts of chocolate flavoring in ice cream, 928 respondents participated in ten coordinated paired comparison tests. The number of "chocolate levels" to be tested was set at five. Test batches were prepared with great care to make certain that all other product attributes were held constant.

> Test items from each of the five batches were grouped with items from each of the other batches to form the ten possible unique pairs of test items. Each pair was tested with a randomly selected unique subsample to avoid bias from learning or fatigue which might occur if the same individuals tested more than one pair. . . .
>
> The results were something of a surprise, since they indicated that the level of chocolate thought to be the most preferred in the general population . . . was not the most popular level in the sampled population (Pennsyl-

vania State University students). Batch 2, with a substantially milder level of chocolate (80 percent of commercial normal) was preferred.[13]

Similarity measures. There are three major techniques which can be used to "sort out" what product attributes are important to consumers. These are similarity scaling, factor analysis, and conjoint anaysis. The latter two were discussed in Chapter 17 so only similarity scaling is discussed here. Similarity scaling involves obtaining the judgments of consumers on the substitutability among various brands. The simplest way is to ask consumers to specify the degree of substitutability between pairs of brands using a rating scale ranging from none to high. The meaning of "substitutabilities" is not made specific.

A more complicated way of evaluating the more important product characteristics uses rating scales, but in addition an overall preference rating is obtained for the company's existing or proposed product. This approach can be used where several product variations are being tested simultaneously, although the following example applies to a single product situation.

Assume a cake mix manufacturer believes a product change might win greater consumer acceptance for the company's brand. Prior research has determined that the main product characteristics are sweetness, spiciness, moistness, texture, and size of cake. A seven-point rating scale ranging from −3 to +3 is set up for each attribute; for example, a +3 rating means "too sweet," "too spicy," "too moist," "too fine in texture," or "too large a cake." A rating of 0 means acceptable sweetness, spiciness, and so on. A −3 rating means "not sweet enough," "not spicy enough," "too dry," "too coarse," or "too small a cake." In addition, an overall preference rating is obtained for the product relative to a competitor or a test product. Such a study was made with the results shown in Table 20–1.[14]

It appears from the above data that the product tested is a bit too sweet, just right in spiciness, not moist enough, too fine in texture, and too large. But more precise information can be provided by relating the product characteristic scores to the overall acceptance. This can be accomplished by

---

TABLE 20–1. Consumer ratings of cake mix characteristics

	−3	−2	−1	0	+1	+2	+3	Average score
1. Sweetness	4%	8%	20%	20%	22%	16%	10%	(0.36)
2. Spiciness	—	—	15	75	10	—	—	(−0.05)
3. Moistness	—	15	30	40	10	5	—	(−0.40)
4. Texture	4	12	12	25	15	12	10	(0.21)
5. Size of cake	5	5	20	35	20	10	5	(0.10)

---

[13] Ralph L. Day, "Systematic Paired Comparisons in Preference Analysis," *Journal of Marketing Research* (November 1965):406–12.

[14] *Product Evaluation: An Examination of Research Procedures* (Chicago: Market Facts, Inc., 1962), pp. 11–18.

determining the relative overall preference for the product among those who rated it (-3) on sweetness as compared to those rating it (-2), (-1), and so on. With respect to sweetness, the results found were those shown in Table 20–2. Similar analyses would be made for each of the characteristics.

TABLE 20–2. Consumers giving tested product indicated ratings on sweetness

	Not sweet enough −3	−2	−1	0	+1	+2	Too sweet +3
Expressed this average degree of preference for product	−0.20	0.01	0.20	0.27	0.41	0.29	0.19

These data show that the average overall preference score for those consumers who said the product was not sweet enough (-3) was -0.20, while those who said the product was a bit too sweet ($+1$) had an average overall preference for the product of 0.41. This relating of overall preference and sweetness suggests that a mix "a little too sweet" may be better than one "exactly right," because the highest average degree of preference for the product (0.41) was obtained from those consumers who gave the mix a ($+1$) on the sweetness rating.

This methodology leaves something to be desired, since it does not provide needed data regarding the optimum set (combination) of values. By dealing in averages the values can be distorted, as would happen in a polarized situation where heavy weights at the extremes produced an average value of approximately zero which would mean "acceptable."

It is desirable to take those who had an overall preference for the product and to get a profile of their average scores for each characteristic. This "profiling" for each of the overall preference groups (that is, the $+3$s, the $+2$s, the $+1$s, the 0s, the -1s, and so on) can be helpful in determining what product attributes (for example, moistness) appeal to a larger market segment.

PRODUCT TESTING

On the basis of the information developed from earlier steps, management is now in position to undertake research which will provide insights into whether they have been successful in developing the desired product. In many ways the types of testing described in the preceding section overlap with the types used to test the product under actual use conditions. The discussion here will center on the research problems encountered when the objective is to test the product under "live use" conditions.

Management will, of course, test the product intensively in the laboratory whenever it is possible to simulate real world usage conditions. This is particularly true for both consumer and industrial mechanical products which can be submitted to a battery of lab tests to determine reliability and performance over time. For some industrial goods, it is feasible to have customers try the product under a set of specified conditions. It must be remembered that real world tests are designed primarily to determine whether the product's physical attributes lead to satisfaction and preference.

Paired comparison placement tests

Paired comparison placement tests are relatively simple in concept, but difficult to implement. Such tests typically involve two variations of the same product, variations which often differ in ways not easily identified by consumers. Consumers who are members of the target market are asked to use both products and then to choose the one they like most. If it is desired to test several different product variations, a number of paired comparison tests must be run. Each variation must be tested against each other variation. Respondents must have only two different products to compare at any one time, but they may have different pairs at different times, or different groups of consumers may be used for different pairs. If respondents are asked to compare several different product designs at one time, the results obtained may be misleading. For example, assume that three product designs, A, B, and C are to be tested. Each respondent tests all three and is asked to pick the one preferred. The replies might be distributed as follows:

	Percent of respondents preferring
Product	
A	40%
B	30
C	30
Total	100%

At first glance it must appear that design A should be the one selected for marketing. But is this conclusion valid? The 30 percent of respondents who voted for B might have preferred C over A if they could not have B. If this were true, 60 percent of the respondents would actually prefer design C over A. This "vote splitting" produces ambiguity which is not found if only paired comparisons are used. With paired comparisons in the above situation, three different tests would have to be run—A with B, A and C, and B with C.

The results of any paired comparison test are difficult to analyze. Assume that 80 percent of the respondents vote for product A and only 20 percent for product B. Does this mean that A should be chosen and that B should be rejected? This situation is similar to the problem of comparing three or more designs discussed earlier. Since the experiment does not reproduce the choices available in the market, it cannot be said with certainty that either A or B should be chosen. It may be that in an actual buying situation with other brands to select from, the persons voting for A would switch to some other brand, while those voting for B would not do so. This is particularly possible if B has a unique feature which differentiates it from all other brands and if A is a composite product with no individually strong attributes.

The simplest type of paired comparison test is that in which the respondents are given the test product in an unidentified package and asked to try it and to compare it with the product they have been using. Such a test is not usually a satisfactory one, because respondents tend to vote in favor of the unknown brand. This may be a result of the respondents' desire to please the researcher or of the respondent's assumptions that the new product must be better. In any case biased results are obtained.

A more common paired comparison test is to have respondents try two "masked" products under similar use conditions for a period of time. The interviewer then returns to get a preference rating and to find out what attributes were liked or disliked in each product.

Staggered comparison tests.   Such tests are similar to the "side-by-side" comparison tests discussed above, but they differ in that respondents use one product first and then, either days or weeks later, try the second product. The identities of the two products are masked. One half of the respondents receive product A first and the other half receive product B first. Such a split is necessary to avoid a "tried last" bias.

Staggered comparison tests have many of the disadvantages of the paired comparison tests, but in theory replicate better the actual market, since customers usually buy one product at a time instead of two different brands of the same product at one time. In practice, however, there is little difference between the two types of tests.

Difficulties in conducting paired comparison tests.   In appraising the paired comparison technique, it is important to keep in mind some basic weaknesses which reduce the confidence one can have in the results. For example, it is difficult to obtain and maintain the cooperation of members of a consumer-use panel; to increase cooperation, incentives such as pay may be used. If respondents are paid, they are more apt to feel some responsibility for completing the test. Even so, the sample may be biased because some people will not participate.

Another difficulty comes from the fact that the test can never simulate precisely the conditions in the marketplace under which buying decisions are made. In a paired comparison test respondents usually have no knowledge of price differentials and must, therefore, assume that no difference exists. It is doubtful if respondent statements as to how much more they would be willing to pay for a given product are very meaningful.

There is the further question of how valid the findings are relative to actual behavior. The typical user of a product does not compare the merits of one product with those of others on a side-by-side basis. Participants in a consumer test realize they are test subjects. They assume that differences exist among the different products and that their job is to find them. In other words, in a test situation differences are apt to be magnified out of proportion to their importance in the "normal" market.

Another difficulty is that consumers are inconsistent in their preference over a number of trial uses. Day reports that choice reversals of 40 percent are not uncommon. Thus, ". . . behavior in preference tests can be viewed as probabilistic rather than deterministic. When so viewed, behavior . . . is predictable only in probabilistic terms."[15] This implies that greater instability will be found when the differences between the test products are slight than when the differences are substantial. This has an obvious effect on sample size.

Order bias in paired comparison tests poses yet another problem. There seems little doubt that preferences are often related to the order in which the two items are tested. Further, there is evidence that the greater the difference between the test units the less important the order bias. Day explains the situation as follows:

> When faced with a choice between two items perceived to be similar the consumer . . . is prone to look for clues of any sort to help him [or her] choose and may react to extraneous factors or very weak stimuli. For example, a group of thirsty people who are presented two similar or identical samples of a cola drink may have a definite tendency to report that the first item was *best*. However, if there are substantial differences on one or more cola attributes such as sweetness, flavor strength, or carbonation the individual can recognize this and is much less likely to be influenced by any weak stimulus associated with the testing order.[16]

Daniels and Lawford conclude much the same based on an evaluation of the results from some 50 paired comparison product tests. Their data indicate a clear bias in favor of the product tried first and especially when the rating of the first item is accomplished prior to testing the second. They conclude there is no easy solution to the problem since juxtapositioning products, undertaking sequential placement tests, introducing a third product to be used as a reference point for the two test items, and use of an experimental design in which products are tested against themselves do not remove the difficulties and in some cases further confound the test situation. They advocate

> . . . controlling the order of trial, but allowing respondents to try both products before committing themselves to any responses. A monadic rating of products after both products have been tried would be free of the "warm-

---

15 Ralph L. Day, "Systematic Paired Comparisons in Preference Analysis," *Journal of Marketing Research* (November 1965):406–12.

16 Adapted from Ralph L. Day, "Position Bias in Paired Product Tests," *Journal of Marketing Research* (February 1969):99.

ing up" phenomenon between first and second trials and would thus allow an estimation of order bias, product preference and interaction. The danger is that, if interaction is identified, one may not be able to interpret any of the data.[17]

Nondirective comparison method. This type of study attempts more nearly to duplicate actual market conditions in the test situation without going as far as a sales test. A specific example will illustrate the method.[18] Respondents were given a "pair" of products which were wrapped in exactly the same fashion. The respondents had no reason to believe any difference existed between the two. Homemakers were asked to use the products, but they were not told that any future interviewing would be done. They had no reason to think that they were participating in any kind of product test. Probably they thought of the products as free samples.

Approximately two weeks after the respondents received the free merchandise, an interviewer called and conducted a nondirective type of interview with the respondents about their experiences, if any, with the products. First, the interviewer ascertained whether both packages had been used. Following this the respondents were given several opportunities to indicate whether any differences had been noted. If no differences were volunteered, direct questions on differences were asked.

The results of the nondirective approach as compared to the paired comparison and the "staggered" techniques were as follows:

	Paired comparisons	Staggered	Nondirective
Not aware of any differences	21%	22%	93%
Aware of differences	79	78	7
Slightly aware of differences	62	60	2
Quite aware of differences	17	18	5

These findings suggest the possibility that the other two techniques provide an exaggerated picture of product differences. Whether this is due to imaginary differences or not is another matter. Some participants may have actually found differences after a careful search that they would not otherwise have noted. In any case the nondirective method points up the possibility that product differences, which may seem very important to management, are noticed by very few people. These minor differences, however, may become very real as advertising claims are made to the consumer or as the product is used over a period of time. Thus, while variations of the paired comparison technique possess characteristics of value to researchers, their failure to reproduce fully the real world is still a severe limitation.

---

[17] Peter Daniels and John Lawford, "The Effect of Order in the Presentation of Samples in Paired Comparison Product Tests," *Journal of the Marketing Research Society* (April 1974):133.

[18] *Product Research Methodology* (Chicago: Market Facts, Inc., n.d.), pp. 24–32.

TEST MARKETING

Test marketing is a procedure by which a company attempts to test on a small basis the commercial viability of the marketing plan for a new or modified product or package. Such a test has a two-fold purpose: It is designed (1) to provide a reasonable estimate of the sales and profit potentials in the new product and (2) to help management identify and correct any problems having to do with the marketing plan and the product before making the final commitment to a full-scale introduction.

It is important to note that test markets are seldom used to test whether a product is acceptable or not acceptable to the consumer. This can be determined more inexpensively through the use of the kinds of tests discussed earlier in this chapter. Companies put into test markets only those products for which there is strong evidence that they will be successful. Even so the percentage of products which are withdrawn during or after a test market is high—probably around 50 percent.[19]

The costs of test marketing are not trivial, ranging from $500,000 to $1.5 million or more. Further, there is the question of how reliable the projected test market results are at the national level. According to one source, there is only about a 50-50 chance that the test results will be within ± 10 percent of the national performance.[20] It is difficult to assume for most test markets that the national scene can be replicated with two to three test markets, especially with respect to competitive reaction over time. And finally, test marketing can be audited by competitors, thereby eroding the time advantage of the innovator.

Pre-test-market research

Given the above, it is understandable why efforts have focused in recent years on the development of low cost alternatives to the more traditional full-scale test market. These alternatives typically involve attempts to simulate a full-scale test market using a small-scale or laboratory approach. All are designed to obtain measures concerned with awareness, trial, and repeat buying over time in an effort to predict sales and market share for the new product. Diagnostic information is obtained concerning the product and the marketing mix.

One laboratory test market facility has operated since the late 1960s. It consists of a simulated supermarket where consumers buy products under controlled conditions and a theater-auditorium where advertisements and

---

[19] See "New Brand or Superbrand," *The Nielsen Researcher* 29, no. 5 (1971):4–10; "The Rebuilding Job at General Foods," *Business Week* (August 25, 1973):48–55; and N. O. Cadbury, "When, Where, and How to Test Market," *Harvard Business Review* (May-June 1975):96–105.

[20] "To Test or Not to Test?" *The Nielsen Researcher* 30, no. 4 (1972):3–8.

other promotional materials can be exposed to consumers. Separate samples of consumers are used if more than one "option" (e.g., different prices or copy treatments) is involved. Respondents in each sample are "representative" of the target audience and participate in the following experiments.

1.   After completing a self-administered questionnaire concerned with their individual demographics and purchase behavior relative to the product class of interest, respondents are exposed to a TV program containing a number of communications about brands in the product class, including one for the brand/option being tested.
2.   Respondents visit the simulated store which is stocked with the brands shown in the commercials and any others of importance. Respondents are provided with a fixed amount of money and told to purchase the brand they choose.
3.   After purchase, small groups of respondents are engaged in focused discussions concerning reasons for their purchase. Following this, the respondents return home.
4.   Sometime later, respondents are reinterviewed by phone to determine reactions to the product purchased, including satisfaction or dissatisfaction, usage data, repurchase, and comparisons with previous brands used.
5.   If an extended usage test is involved, then respondents are given the opportunity to repurchase the test brand which, if requested, is then delivered to them. Step number four is then repeated at a later date.

Silk and Urban have developed a model (ASSESSOR) which involves a system similar to the one described above. As of 1978 some 30 new packaged goods had been studied using ASSESSOR. Of these, nine had completed test markets and their final market shares in the test markets were known. The differences in the predicted and observed shares were small, with the average difference being less than one share point, but higher when expressed as a percentage of the observed share in the test market. Part of the differences can be explained by the fact that somewhat different marketing mixes were used in the test markets than in the pre-test-markets.

From experience gained in using ASSESSOR, it was determined that at least three conditions are necessary for its success. First, the product category involved must be well defined in terms of close substitutes. A new product category poses problems. Second, the usage/purchase rate must be the same for the new brand as for the established ones. And last, consumption and learning must occur quickly enough so that preferences will stabilize in a short time period.[21]

---

21 Alvin S. Silk and Glen L. Urban, "Pre-Test Market Evaluation of New Package Goods: A Model and Measurement Methodology," *Journal of Marketing Research* (May 1978):171–91.

Developing the test market plan and sample designs

The heart of the test market plan is the company's intended national marketing plan for the new product. The nature and extent of the research plan depends to a considerable extent upon how certain management is of its proposed national marketing strategies. For example, if management is not secure regarding its national plan to use sampling instead of couponing as a way of introducing the new product, provisions for testing these alternatives should be built into the test marketing plan.

More and more sellers are conceptualizing their test marketing efforts as controlled experiments during which certain selected marketing variables are tested to determine their effects on sales and profitability. Given an understanding of what management wants to test in order to finalize its national plan, the researcher can develop the proper test design and set up the necessary controls.

The selection of the appropriate test markets (usually cities or metropolitan areas) is a difficult one. The number selected (typically three) is a function of the reliability desired in the projected results and the number of variables being tested. It is reasonable to assume that as the number of markets included in the test increases, the reliability of the results also increases, if only by decreasing the chances of extreme errors.

One way to improve the sample design is to select from pairs of matched marketing areas using one set as the experimental group and the other as the control group. The matching can be accomplished on the basis of similarities in market shares of leading brands, media patterns, population, income, and so on. An increasing volume of data is available for such purposes. The A. C. Nielsen Company provides store audit data on individual markets, thereby simplifying the task of matching on brand shares. In addition, Nielsen provides back data on the test markets selected.

But what about the situation where a totally new product is test marketed? Market-share data cannot be used to match test markets. In such cases the selection of test markets is no easy undertaking. The following criteria are suggested:

1. The markets should not be "over-tested."
2. The markets should be "normal" regarding the historical development of the product class involved.
3. The markets should be typical regarding the competitive advertising situation.
4. No single industry should dominate the markets.
5. The markets should represent different geographical regions (where different conditions might affect sales) so that results can be projected.
6. Markets which contain groups not normal to the product's target should be avoided.
7. The markets should have a media pattern similar to the proposed national media plan.

8. The markets should not be too small to provide meaningful results or so large that the testing becomes unusually expensive.
9. The markets should be relatively self-contained, that is, not too much "waste" circulation going outside the market and no strong outside media present.

A critical problem is estimating the level of sales at which a new product will stabilize. Most such estimates are based on panel data. Since these estimates are derived through the use of a number of estimates, it is difficult to figure the sampling error. One study has reported that these errors may be as large as 20–40 percent of the sales estimate when standard panel sizes are used.[22]

The problem of how to project the test market results to the national level is also difficult. One test used three different projection methods—buying income, sales ratio, and share of market. The formulas were as follows:

1. National sales estimate $= \dfrac{\text{Total U.S. income}}{\text{Test area income}} \times$ Test market sales.

2. National sales estimate $= \dfrac{\text{National sales of related product}}{\text{Test area sales of same product}} \times$ Test market sales.

3. National sales estimate $=$ Share-of-market ratio in the test area $\times$ National sales of the product class.

The share-of-market method provided the most accurate national projection of sales, but this method possesses limitations in that it requires accurate estimates of national sales of the product category involved, it assumes that the test product will not expand the sales of the product class, and it is more expensive to apply because it requires information that necessitates auditing the total product class.[23]

Test market data

Many different kinds of marketing information can be obtained from test markets, including:

1. Sales in units.
2. Market share.
3. Characteristics of consumers who buy the product.

---

[22] Robert Shoemaker and Richard Staelin, "The Effects of Sampling Variation on Sales Forecasts for New Consumer Products," *Journal of Marketing Research* (May 1976):138–43.

[23] See Jack A. Gold, "Testing Test Market Predictions," *Journal of Marketing Research* (August 1964):15–16. For further discussion of Gold's methods see Edwin M. Berdy, "Testing Test Market Predictions," *Journal of Marketing Research* (May 1965): 196–98 and Gold's reply, *Journal of Marketing Research* (May 1965):198–200.

4. Characteristics of consumers who sample the product, but who do not buy it again.
5. Frequency of purchase by different groups of consumers.
6. Ways in which the product is used.
7. Maximum profitability as a result of varying the quantity of such marketing inputs as advertising and couponing.
8. Effectiveness of various coupon and cents-off introductory offers.
9. Effectiveness of the advertising copy in getting certain points about the product across to selected groups.
10. Effectiveness of overall marketing program in obtaining trial and usage at the consumer level.
11. Effectiveness of the overall marketing program in obtaining support from the trade.

Total unit sales and marketing share are usually the first items looked for in test market results. Factory shipments will not suffice for either the sales or market-share data. A substantial part of such shipments goes into dealer stocks and, of course, information about sales of other brands cannot be obtained in this way. It is, therefore, necessary to set up either a consumer panel or a store audit, usually the latter. It may be possible to obtain data from regular services such as A. C. Nielsen Company or National Purchase Diary Panel, Inc. Both of these organizations maintain services which provide data on certain test cities. Some local media maintain store audits and consumer panels that can be used.

Repeat purchasing

A measurement of repeat purchasing is probably the single most important item of information to obtain in a test market, since without it total consumer sales can be misleading. During the introductory period, the advertising and the introductory price offer may succeed in getting people to sample the product. The important question, however, is whether a substantial portion of the people who try it once will become loyal customers. A continuous consumer panel is useful for measuring repeat purchases. With such a panel the purchasing activities of the sampling units can be studied over a period of time, and the extent of brand loyalty or brand switching can be determined.

Current efforts to maximize the value of test-market data center on the development of models for predicting the long-term market share level of a new product from early sales in the test market. The critical measure is concerned with repeat buying. Blattberg and Golanty provide an illustration of such efforts with their TRACKER model.[24]

---

[24] Robert Blattberg and John Golanty, "TRACKER: An Early Test Market Forecasting and Diagnostic Model for New Product Planning," *Journal of Marketing Research* (May 1978):192–202.

This model's objective is to forecast the end of the year sales from early test market results (usually three months). It also provides diagnostic information about the new product's performance. Survey data are used, in contrast to panel data, which help to hold the costs down to about $15,000. The process consists of three waves of 500–1,000 questionnaires, each undertaken every four weeks. Data pertaining to brands purchased, media, price, special distribution problems, and other such data are collected. From these data the model estimates awareness, trial, and repeat buying and projects year-end sales. The results obtained by TRACKER when compared to actual results are impressive.

Consumer reactions. It is important to find out why some consumers only try the new product and do not buy it again. This information may help to determine what, if anything, can be done to convert such consumers into regular users. In analyzing the results of such research, it must be kept in mind that no product can satisfy all people and that the very reasons why some people reject the product may be the same reasons why other people prefer it.

SUMMARY

Marketing research can provide much help in the design of new products. Too often, individual firms fail to provide the proper balance between technical and marketing research.

In determining the attributes of the optimum product, the research must determine what attributes are important and the relative importance of each. The use of conventional questions such as, "What features do you want in this product?" are not likely to uncover a complete listing of important attributes. Research must develop a consumer's language and translate this into a producer's technical language for action. A number of different techniques can be used to obtain the approximate utilities of the various product attributes.

All the major types of consumer use tests have serious shortcomings in that they fail to duplicate actual market conditions. Evidence indicates that there is little difference in the results obtained by paired comparison and staggered comparison tests. In both situations, the fact that respondents know they are participating in a test and that they are expected to find differences can easily lead to the reporting of exaggerated differences.

In recent years, more use has been made of pre-test market research in product research. The techniques, while possessing obvious limitations, are conceptually sound and offer considerable promise. These models offer a more analytical way of approaching the problem of product testing than the more conventional methods.

Test marketing is a method of testing a company's marketing plan for a new product before going national. It is not a test of whether the product is acceptable to the consumer, but rather of the extent of the consumer's response given certain marketing inputs. Marketing research is critical since data on sales, market share, brand loyalty, and consumer reactions must be obtained and evaluated.

Case 20–1
OVALTINE PRODUCTS, INC.

Officials of Ovaltine Products, Inc. were worried about the poor sales record in recent years of the company's Ovaltine product. Ovaltine, a powder-like product made from milk, eggs, barley and malt extract was developed by a Swiss doctor at the turn of this century in response to the need for a nutritive drink which could be easily digested by the seriously ill. When mixed with milk, it became a nutritious drink which could be consumed by itself or with a meal. It gained wide acceptance with the medical profession, and was used during both World Wars as a fortified food supplement at military hospitals as well as included in Red Cross packages sent to the prisoner of war camps.

Ovaltine became a household word during the 1920s, 30s, and 40s, with much of the credit for its widespread use due to its sponsorship of the "Little Orphan Annie" and "Captain Midnight" radio programs, both of which were very popular. European ethnic groups were very fond of the product, as were depression era mothers who found that Ovaltine supplied added nutrients, and thus was an inexpensive way to provide a nutritious, well-balanced diet for their youngsters.

After World War II, parents were economically able to provide well-balanced diets for their children without having to use nutrition supplements. Parents had also become more permissive, tending to let children choose many of their own foods. Such foods were usually selected for taste rather than nutrition. In addition, television replaced radio as the main advertising medium, but Ovaltine's marketing program did not adapt to the new development. The result of these changes was that Ovaltine did not gain new users, although old users tended to be loyal to the product. Competition from chocolate-flavored milk additives like Nestle's Quik and Instant Hershey made inroads into Ovaltine's market, primarily because they were tastier and cheaper. These newer products did not include special nutritional additives, but apparently these weren't as important as taste.

Though aware of their depressed sales, officials of Ovaltine Products, Inc. were reluctant to change the product for three reasons: (1) they were steadfast in their belief that Ovaltine would continue to sell because it possessed nutritive attributes which competitive products did not have; (2) changing the product's flavor would be difficult because of the vacuum drying process used to make Ovaltine; and (3) the company's management was afraid of the effect a flavor change might have on its small core of steady Ovaltine drinkers.

New ownership brought a change to the company. The new owners selected as president Carl Garson, a man with many years of experience in food marketing. Garson commented on what he believed was a major reason for Ovaltine's poor market performance. "Our marketing research told us the kids weren't drinking Ovaltine because they liked the taste of the other products better." What Ovaltine needed was new flavors—"more chocolatey chocolate, less malty malt."

The new president also arranged to buy a milk additive product which was manufactured with a process entirely different from that used on Ovaltine. However, the newly acquired process could be used in the manufacture of Ovaltine with some very favorable results, the most significant being that Ovaltine could be made with new and different flavors. The new manufacturing process would also permit Ovaltine to be made with fewer calories per serving and with better solubility characteristics. This last characteristic would have no effect on either taste or calories, but esthetically the product would appear more attractive after it had been mixed with milk. The new Ovaltine would also be more concentrated, and thus a smaller container would provide an equivalent number of servings as the old product in the old container.

Since the new production process allowed the company to produce a whole range of flavor variations, both chocolate and malt, Garson found himself faced with a series of questions. Among all the flavor variations that could now be produced, which would be "the best?" Which flavor improvement would attract new users without driving away the current users of Ovaltine? Was there a flavor which would both attract new users and cause the old users to consume more of the product?

Garson knew that some marketing research would have to be undertaken in order to answer some of these questions, and so he organized a small team from the company's marketing staff to review the product's situation. This team was to identify the issues likely to be encountered while making the proposed flavor changes, and to make recommendations relative to those issues which could be studied by marketing research. The company's sales manager, Jack Moran, who had been appointed chairman of the committee, called a meeting to discuss the concerns raised by Garson and to evaluate potential marketing research projects. After the conclusion of the meeting, the sales manager recorded the highlights in a memo (see Exhibit 1) which he circulated to Garson and the team members for review prior to the next meeting.

EXHIBIT 1

To: Carl Garson and members of the Marketing Research Committee

From: Jack Moran, Sales Manager

The following is a summary of the highlights of our first meeting concerning the potential marketing research which might be undertaken if one or more new Ovaltine flavors are introduced.

Research program outline

As envisioned, our marketing research could consist of four separate phases, each of which would be distinct and would be begun only after successful completion of the previous phase.

These four phases are:

1. Basic research to develop a variety of new flavors.
2. Taste testing to select the best one or two flavor variations.
3. Store testing to verify the selection choice.
4. Final test marketing of the new product.

Our discussions concerning the purpose and implementation of each of these phases are summarized below.

Phase 1.   Product development

Since a number of flavor variations are possible with the new manufacturing process, the objective of this phase would be to identify and eliminate from further consideration all flavor variations which are not judged to be good or excellent. This screening process could be carried out in a number of ways. For example, it might be conducted in-plant among employees, in-home among employees' families, in local stores with consumers, or even in consumers' homes. If taste comparisons are to be made between the current Ovaltine flavors and potential new flavors, it would be possible to disguise the identity of the different flavors from the participants.

Phase 2.   Taste testing

This component of the research should accomplish three things. First, it should confirm that the one or two new flavors developed in Phase 1 are highly acceptable to consumers. Second, it should measure the acceptability of the new flavor to current Ovaltine users by determining whether their consumption levels would be maintained, increased, or decreased if the new flavor were introduced. This information should be broken down by heavy, moderate and light users. Lastly, the research should determine how the new flavor will appeal to consumers who are currently using alternative milk additive products such as Hershey's Instant or Nestle's Quik.

This phase of the research could be undertaken in a number of different ways. For example, a mobile taste laboratory might be operated at appropriate, randomly selected, shopping center locations. Or, perhaps through a telephone survey we could locate Ovaltine users who would be willing to cooperate in the research, and who then would be sent samples of the new product to taste. This approach would require some type of follow-up interview. Alternatively,

EXHIBIT 1 *(continued)*

we might use a research firm which has a mail panel. The firm could screen their panel members to identify Ovaltine users, users of competing products and non-users of milk additive products. The first two groups could be broken down into heavy and light users, and then all five groups would be asked to participate in the taste testing. Further consideration should be given to how this research should be disguised—perhaps as a usage or consumption test rather than a taste test.

This second phase of the research is very critical in the sense that a "go" decision here on a new flavor will require that we begin to make significant financial commitments as we move into phase 3 of the research. Consequently, it is very important that the research selected for this phase yield information whose reliability and validity will be appropriate relative to the financial commitment associated with moving into phase 3 of the research.

Phase 3.   Store testing of the product, flavor and package

This phase will employ controlled tests in stores to compare the sales performance of the new Ovaltine product, flavor and package with the sales performance of the old Ovaltine product, flavor and package when the two are sold under the same conditions. Since the new flavor is 25 percent more concentrated than the old, either it will have to be packaged in a smaller jar, or we will have to charge a higher price for a jar the same size as the old. Either way, to the public it might look like we are merely trying to disguise a price increase—a situation which must be avoided if the new product is to be compared with the old on its flavor and solubility merits alone. This phase of the research must deal with this "greater product concentration—smaller jar" complication. We discussed the possibility of printing on the new label a notice such as "Improved Flavor, Now Concentrated, Same Nutrition"; possibly two or more label designs for the new flavor could be tested during this phase.

This phase of the research will utilize some type of store test in which all marketing factors are given their "normal" treatment, except that some of the stores will carry only the old Ovaltine while others will carry only the new product. However, a number of questions must be answered before the research designed for this phase can be finalized. For example, how many stores should be selected and what should be the basis for their selection? How should the stores be matched to assure the most valid test of the effect of the new flavor or new flavor-label combination? In how many cities should the test be conducted, or how long should it be run? We must also devise a method which will give us accurate measurements of unit sales, since the performance of the new flavor relative to the old will determine whether, and to what extent, we test market the new Ovaltine.

Phase 4.   Test marketing

In this phase one or more markets will be selected to test a total marketing program including price, promotion and advertising. The design of the test marketing phase of the research cannot reasonably be started at this time because too many facets of the test marketing will be determined by the outcomes of the previous three phases of the research—for example, how the new flavor will be received among current Ovaltine users, among users of compet-

EXHIBIT 1 *(concluded)*

ing brands, and among those who currently do not use milk additive products. However, the extent to which we will want to test market will depend upon the sales results from the store-testing phase of this research program. At this time we can imagine three possible store-testing results which might be observed, each of which could have different implications for test marketing: (1) marginal success (sales of the new flavor exceed those of the old flavor by only 5–10 percent); (2) good success (new flavor sales are 20–40 percent better than old flavor sales); (3) excellent success (new flavor sales exceed old flavor sales by 50 percent or more). Since we may wish to act quickly after seeing the results from phase 3, we should establish a test marketing strategy for each of these possible phase 3 outcomes. At our next meeting we will attempt to develop these three strategies, as well as finalize the planning for the first three phases of the research program.

What program of marketing research should be used on the new Ovaltine?

What specific research designs should be used in each separate project and test?

Show how the entire program fits together into a useful information gathering activity which will help management identify the "best" new flavor and help decide whether or not to go into test marketing.

Case 20–2
ROBLES, INC.

Robles, Inc., owned and operated a chain of 23 fast food units located in and around such areas as Memphis, Tennessee, Little Rock, Arkansas, and Jackson, Mississippi. The company had experienced rapid growth despite strong competition from such well-known franchise operators as McDonald's, Burger King, and Wendy's. While specializing primarily in hamburgers, hot dogs, and french fries, the company had in recent years introduced a number of new food items including a fried chicken sandwich, a roast beef sandwich, and ham on a bun. None of these had been very successful, and none was currently being carried by all units within the chain.

The company's experimental kitchens had recently developed a new fried, breaded catfish sandwich for possible adoption by all operating units. In doing so it was guided by several research studies designed to determine what people wanted in a fried fish sandwich, and by numerous taste tests of different types of sandwiches conducted among such captive groups as Robles employees, church groups, and high school clubs. After several months of work, the project chef had developed three different formulations.

At this point, the company asked a Memphis-based marketing research firm to undertake a study, the objective of which was to evaluate consumer attitudes towards the three different formulations of the fried catfish sandwich. In essence, what was being requested was a taste test among a group of respondents who were similar in demographics to consumers who constituted Robles' target audience.

The research company proposed a three-day central location taste test among prerecruited, qualified respondents in Memphis and Little Rock. The respondents were to be recruited by telephone and upon arrival at the test site were to be screened. All respondents had to meet the following qualifications.

1. Head of household (either male or female).
2. 18–55 years of age.
3. Have purchased food from a fast food restaurant within the past month to eat there or take out.
4. Have eaten fish (of any kind prepared in any form) either at home or while eating out in the past four months.

The sample design called for a random selection of names from the appropriate telephone directories. Ultimately, a total of 300 qualified individuals were to participate in the test. Three matching subsamples were then to be drawn in each city—one for each treatment. Each respondent was to taste and evaluate only one alternative sandwich. The difference between the three alternatives consisted mainly in the type of batter used: plain corn meal, seasoned (herb), and "puff" (egg whites, baking powder and flour). Each alternative would retail at the same price.

The proposed design called for each respondent to taste and evaluate one treatment on a "blind" basis; i.e., without any knowledge of brand or price. Respondents would be given no descriptive statements whatsoever about their sandwiches. After tasting the fried catfish sandwich, respondents were to be asked to rate it on the basis of its overall appeal, appearance, taste, and moistness; shape of sandwich; color, taste, texture, shape, and amount of catfish; amount of breading; overall bun rating; price expected to pay; and unbranded purchase intentions. Respondents would then be told the brand name of their product and the retail price involved, and again asked to state their purchase intentions.

The research company planned to use a series of five-point scales to analyze the different aspects of the test sandwiches. These scales were to deal with purchase intent, overall ratings, and attribute ratings. The scale used for purchase intent ranged from "definitely would buy it" to "definitely would not buy it."

Definitely would buy it 1
Probably would buy it 2
Might or might not buy it 3
Probably would not buy it 4
Definitely would not buy it 5

The basic performance measure computed from this scale was to be the "positive purchase intent;" that is, the percentage of respondents who indicated "definitely" or "probably" would buy it.

A similar five-point scale was to be used to obtain the overall ratings:

> Excellent 1
> Very good 2
> Good 3
> Fair 4
> Poor 5

The primary performance measure to be computed here was the highly positive rating; that is, the percentage of respondents who indicated either an "excellent" or a "very good."

The individual attribute ratings were also to be obtained using a five-point scale. The primary performance measure to be computed for each attribute was the middle rating—"just about right." The ratings on either side of the "just about right" rating were to be analyzed to show respondent tendencies to consider the particular fried catfish sandwich they tasted as having "too much" or "not enough" of a given attribute.

Evaluate the proposed research design. How would you improve it?

21

Advertising research

Advertising is one of the more important decision areas facing the business executive. In 1978 it was estimated that American businesses spent approximately $44 billion on advertising.[1] Given such a large expenditure it is not surprising that a great deal of attention has been given to advertising research. It is likely that more money has been spent on advertising research than on research in any other area of marketing. In recent years more and more applied research in communications has been done by behavioral scientists.

Advertising research is primarily of three types. One is concerned with the setting of advertising objectives. Ideally, one would want to see the "payout" in terms of sales and/or profits—but this is known to be a difficult measure to obtain except under unusual conditions. Since advertising interacts with other marketing inputs as well as with uncontrolled variables, it is not difficult to understand why a measurement of its effect is hard to come by.

After deciding upon the objectives, advertisers must next decide what their message should be. How should they present their message? What copy should they use? What headlines? What pictures? What situations? Many concepts have been developed by the behavioral scientist which are helpful in the construction of advertising copy. In the final analysis, however, it is the effect of the copy on the target segments in the market which counts. Typically, such effect can only be determined via marketing research.

In addition to deciding what to say, advertisers must also choose appropriate vehicles. Should they use newspaper, radio, magazines, television,

---

[1] "In Their Quest for Sure-Fire Ads, Marketers Use Physiological Tests to Find Out What Grabs You," *The Wall Street Journal* (April 12, 1979):40.

billboards—or some combination thereof? If they choose radio or television: What program? What day of the week? What time of the day? The countless alternatives available to advertisers make careful study necessary. Assumptions made relative to the number of people to be reached, the type of people forming the market, the desired frequency of message receipts by selected audiences, the periodicity with which the message should be received, and the context in which the message can best be presented will determine the media schedule—they can all be usefully researched.

Basic marketing research techniques, as discussed in earlier chapters of this text, apply to advertising research, but many ingenious adaptations of these techniques have been made by advertising researchers. It is desirable, therefore, to study in detail some of the various types of advertising research. In addition, a number of specialized research agencies provide information on advertising. The student should be familiar with the more important of these.

This chapter is divided into three major parts which conform essentially to the advertising process. Part one covers advertising objectives and product appeals: What should be said about the product? Part two discusses copy testing: What is the best way to put the appeal into a message? Part three deals with media selection: What media types should be used? What vehicles within media types should be selected? What combinations should be used? The problem of how much to spend on advertising is not considered here because of space limitations.[2]

SETTING ADVERTISING OBJECTIVES

If the firm has specified its target market segments, refined its thinking about target segments in terms of geography, determined the relative importance of each segment, ascertained what product characteristics are important to each segment, developed the optimum product at a competitive price, and set up the "ideal" channels strategy—then a big part of the advertising job is done. Essentially, advertising objectives consist of some measurable output which relates directly to sales and, hence, ultimately to profits. This is tantamount to saying that the advertising objective must relate to consumer behavior.[3]

---

[2] For discussions on this subject, see Russell I. Haley "Sales Effect of Media Weight," *Journal of Advertising Research* (June 1978): 9–20; Paul W. Farris and Robert D. Buzzell, "Why Advertising and Promotion Costs Vary: Some Cross Sectional Analysis," *Journal of Marketing* (Fall 1979): 112–22; Robert C. Blattberg, "The Design of Advertising Experiments Using Statistical Decision Theory," *Journal of Marketing Research* (May 1979):191–203; and Darral G. Clarke, "Econometrics Measurement of the Duration of Advertising Effect on Sales," *Journal of Marketing Research* (November 1976):345–75.

[3] For an informative discussion of the relationships between the behavioral sciences and advertising see Michael L. Ray, "The Present and Potential Linkages Between the Microtheoretical Notions of Behavioral Science and the Problems of Advertising: A Proposal for a Research System," Research paper no. 172 (Stanford, Calif.: Stanford University Graduate School of Business, 1972).

In recent years the use of attitude maintenance or shift as a measure of advertising effectiveness has grown in importance. This has resulted from recent work dealing with product positioning in which product benefits serve as the basis for market segmentation; that is, individuals vary with respect to their evaluation of what attributes they want in a given product as well as their perceptions of the extent to which different brands possess the desired attributes.[4] To achieve any attitudinal change objective, the communication must satisfy several requirements including attracting attention, being understood, and being convincing.

The technical problems associated with attitude measurement were discussed in Chapter 9; therefore, the discussion here centers mainly on measuring the attitudes of target audiences toward products and then attempting to determine the effect of advertising on those attitudes. Actually, more than a single measurement is needed; marketers need to evaluate attitudes toward their product's salient characteristics as well as toward those of competing brands. Such a set of measurements should give some indication of what *specific* attitudinal changes must be effected in order to obtain sales. Thus the goal of advertising can be stated in terms of changing consumer attitudes with respect to selected product characteristics. This approach assumes that attitudes are predictors of behavior and that they can be measured with some reasonable degree of accuracy.

Research on attitude change resulting from advertising exposure shows mixed results. The problem of measurement is an enormous one as is understanding the process by which attitudes change.[5] After evaluating the more relevant articles dealing with the subject one researcher concluded that ". . . unsurprisingly, research suggests that more research is needed. There is neither the certainty that attitude shift does all that its proponents claim for it, nor that it lacks any virtue, as its detractors believe."[6] Despite the inconclusiveness of the research to date the idea of using attitudes as the focus of advertising effort has great appeal because of its presumed link with behavior. Thus, many advertising effectiveness measures implicitly recognize the importance of attitudes and seek indirectly to measure them.

The use of attitudes as research objectives assumes that average consumers have reasonably stable sets of attitudes toward those salient product characteristics pertaining to a product class. With this as a "backdrop," they evaluate one brand against another. Consumers differ with respect to what

---

[4] Situational factors are known to impact on attribute importance and brand preferences. For a discussion on this subject see Kenneth E. Miller and James L. Ginter, "An Investigation of Situational Variation in Brand Choice Behavior and Attitude," *Journal of Marketing Research* (February 1979):111–23.

[5] Thus, for example, one experiment showed not unsurprisingly that past advertising exposure, brand familiarity, and prior attitude are strongly related to attitudinal response to advertising exposure. See Frederick W. Winter, "A Laboratory Experiment of Individual Attitude Response to Advertising Exposure," *Journal of Marketing Research* (May 1973):130–40.

[6] Neil Holbert, "Key Articles in Advertising Research," *Journal of Advertising Research* (October 1972):7.

product characteristics are salient, as well as to how they perceive various brands, thereby giving rise to attitudinal segments. The goal of advertising often centers on attempting to alter the attitudes of consumers toward a specific brand. The messages hopefully generate over time a favorable "image." The acceptance of this brand is then based on its image versus the images of competing brands.

If the more important choice criteria for a dentifrice include such product characteristics as flavor, whitening power, and decay prevention, then consumers who give considerable weight to one of these properties will select that brand which they perceive as being the best in this respect. Thus, the market is segmented in terms of product attributes wanted in a particular brand. Assuming a particular brand wanted to position itself as the "best" decay preventative dentrifice, then the goal of advertising would be to reinforce the positive ratings it has on this characteristic among present users and to improve its ratings among nonusers who want this particular attribute.[7]

In addition, information is needed about the behavior which surrounds the selection, purchase, and use of a product. Among other things this means that the advertiser needs to know the role played by the product with respect to what the user is trying to accomplish, the consumption system employed, the criteria used by the consumer to determine whether the product is performing satisfactorily or not, and how the product is perceived in terms of functional equivalents (substitutes).[8]

The above types of data can be obtained using a variety of research techniques.[9] In recent years attitude and activities research (also referred to as life-style, psychographics, activities, interests, and opinions research) has sought to describe the "kinds" of individuals and households buying certain product classes. Such research . . . "resembles motivation research in that a major aim is to draw recognizable human portraits of consumers. But it also resembles the tougher-minded, more conventional research in that it is amenable to quantification and respectable samples."[10] There is, however, some question regarding the reliability of some psychographic measures.[11]

---

[7] William L. Moore, Edgar A. Pessemier, and Taylor E. Little, "Predicting Brand Purchase Behavior: Marketing Application of the Schönemann and Wang Unfolding Model," *Journal of Marketing Research* (May 1979):203–10.

[8] One study of comparative advertising found that before using such a copy approach the advertiser should consider carefully his particular objectives, competitive situation, and other such variables. See Linda L. Golden, "Consumer Reactions to Explicit Brand Comparisons in Advertising," *Journal of Marketing Research* (November 1979): 517–32.

[9] Allan D. Shocker and V. Srinivasan, "Multiattribute Approaches for Product Concept Evaluation and Generation: A Critical Review," *Journal of Marketing Research* (May 1979):159–80.

[10] See William D. Wells (ed.), *Life-Styles and Psychographics* (Chicago: American Marketing Association, 1974).

[11] Alvin C. Burns and Mary Carolyn Harrison, "A Test of the Reliability of Psychographics," *Journal of Marketing Research* (February 1979):32–38.

COPY TESTING[12]

Copy testing research seeks to evaluate alternative ways for advertisers to present their messages. The use of the word "copy" is perhaps unfortunate, since it seems only to refer to print media and, more specifically, to the headline and text of the advertising message. For this discussion, the word "copy" will refer to an entire advertisement, including the verbal message, pictures, colors, and dramatizations, whether the advertisement appears in print, or on radio, television, or some other medium.[13] This area of research has received considerable criticism in terms of the low validity and reliability associated with the more common copy testing measures. One major problem is that most such techniques attempt to measure the effectiveness of an advertising campaign based on a single exposure of one commercial.[14]

This discussion of copy testing is divided into two major divisions, those tests which are made before the copy is released on a full-run basis and those tests which are applied after the copy is run. The latter are sometimes considered tests of advertising effectiveness rather than copy tests. Actually, all advertising research represents an effort to improve the effectiveness of advertising, although it must be kept in mind that copy testing has a limited role to play given that it comes after decisions have been made regarding what target segments are involved and what product benefits must be stressed.

The basic distinction between "before" and "after" tests is the purpose of the test. If the objective is to make improvements in the advertising copy prior to the full-run release of the advertising, then the test is classified as a "before" test. The distinction is not always clear because some "before" copy testing methods call for the advertising copy to be run in one or several media. The results of such a test might be measured by the number of inquiries received after the test advertisements had appeared. Nevertheless, this would be considered a "before test" since the purpose was to determine which copy was to run eventually in all scheduled media.

---

12 We will not discuss research designed to test the effect of message size, color, position of advertisement within the vehicle, size of vehicle, and similar variables on advertising effectiveness. For a discussion of these subjects see Dennis H. Gensch, "Media Factors: A Review Article," *Journal of Marketing Research* (May 1970):216–25. Also see Alvin J. Silk and Frank P. Geizer, "Advertisement Size and the Relationship Between Product Usage and Advertising Exposure," *Journal of Marketing Research* (February 1972):22–26.

13 In recent years more and more advertisers have become concerned with the rate of information flow, particularly in connection with television commercials given their increasing time costs. One research study found that advertising impact can be enhanced by increasing the flow. See James MacLachlan and Priscilla LaBarbara, "Time-Compressed TV Commercials," *Journal of Advertising Research* (August 1978): 11—18.

14 "Multiple Exposure Test Needed to Evaluate Commercials," *Marketing News* (September 21, 1979):13.

Behind each of the various types of copy testing is an implicit assumption regarding how advertising accomplishes its effect. If it is thought that the ability of advertising to attract attention is directly related to its effectiveness, researchers will then, of course, measure the attention-getting ability and consider the results to be a measure of advertising effectiveness. If it is thought that the fact that an advertising phrase is remembered signifies effectiveness, researchers will use memory measurements as a criterion of performance. If it is believed that advertising has to give pleasure and be liked, researchers may then subject the pleasantries or the aesthetic values to measurement and will interpret a positive result as the proof of the advertising effectiveness. In each case the researchers call upon an implicit assumption about the mechanisms by which advertising achieves its effect.

Measures dealing with recognition, recall, comprehension, believability, persuasion, and attitude change are the more typical measures used to judge advertising effectiveness. All involve assumptions on how advertising works. As noted earlier, one of the basic problems is that pretesting cannot measure the long-term effectiveness of advertising. And yet, we know that many attitudes change very slowly.

"Before" tests

Consumer jury. This is one of the oldest and simplest tests. Such a test provides a "rating" which is given an advertisement by a group of consumers who represent potential buyers of the product. Personal interviews may be used or a group may be assembled and the members asked to vote on the alternatives. The copy may be made up in dummy form or the major theme placed on cards. Respondents are then asked to rank the alternatives as to their preference, interest, or the influence to buy the product. It is assumed that respondents will always like at least one advertisement; in reality, the rating may be on the basis of which advertisement is disliked the least. Paired comparisons or rankings may be used.

A variation of the above is sometimes used to analyze television programs and commercials. The procedure consists of exposing the audience to the program or commercial and having members record at specific intervals whether they liked, disliked, or were indifferent to what they had just heard or seen. This can also be accomplished using an electronic machine known as the program analyzer. The machine has two buttons and the respondents press one when they find the program interesting, the other when the program is uninteresting, and neither when they are indifferent. A recording machine summarizes the data and charts the continuous reactions of the audience. Such machines do not measure the extent of feeling or, of course, reasons for liking or disliking.

Rating scales. This method of copy testing requires the establishment of standards for effective copy and numerical weights for each standard. The weights or values indicate a standard's relative worth in the overall success of the copy. Ads are then "rated" in accordance with the scale values and a numerical score obtained. If the total weight for one item, for example, is 10, analysts might give one ad 8 if they thought it was above average on that item. The total of the individual standard scores provides the numerical rating for an ad. Such ratings are not usually done by consumers, although there is no reason why they could not do so, but rather by advertising agency or advertising department personnel.

The major advantage of a rating scale is that it provides a list against which to check an ad and helps to single out the elements of an ad that are good and bad. The disadvantages are: (1) while the scale items may be well selected, it is difficult to set up relative weights regarding their contribution to the "ideal" ad; (2) different judges will rate the items differently, leaving the question of who is right; and (3) high scores may not be an indication of success, since the ad may have received high scores on most items but low scores on a few.

A variation of the above has been developed by the Leo Burnett agency to quantify the consumer's subjective reaction to a TV commercial. It is called VRP (Viewer Response Profile) and differs from other copy testing methods by seeking to measure a viewer's "experience" with a commercial on several dimensions. Scale items are evaluative statements made by consumers about commercials in general. VRP focuses on the emotional component of communication effects and provides information relative to such questions as "Do viewers empathize with the characters and situations in the commercial?" and "Do viewers see the commercial as confusing, entertaining, or unusual?" The seven dimensions included in the scale are entertainment, confusion, relevancy, brand reinforcement, empathy, familiarity, and alienation.[15]

Portfolio tests. These tests are named after the manner in which the advertisements to be tested are "packaged." A group of ads, usually a mixture of ads to be tested and control ads, is placed in a portfolio. Sometimes the ads are actually placed in dummy copies of newspapers or magazines. Respondents who are thought to be representative of the target audience are given the folio and asked to go through it, reading whatever interests them and taking as much time as they want. After completing this task, the respondents are asked to recall (with the folio closed) the ads that they can remember. Such recall may be on a completely unaided basis, or the interviewer may aid recall by asking about specific ads or ads for specific products. For each recalled ad, the respondent is asked to play back as much of the ad as possible. This information is recorded verbatim. Additional questions may be asked about such things as the believability of the claims in the ad, the general reaction to the ad, and whether the respondent uses the product.

---

[15] Mary Jane Schlinger, "A Profile of Responses to Commercials," *Journal of Advertising Research* (April 1979):37–48.

ASI offers a print advertising service which uses released copies of general distribution magazines as the vehicles to carry both the test and control ads. Such magazines are placed in the home of a sample of readers at which time respondents provide information regarding their demographics and brand usages and preferences. A call-back interview provides measures on recognition/recall, communications impact, persuasive appeal, and the quality of the respondents' perception of the test ad. Thus, it can be argued that such a copy test provides a measure of selective exposure, perception, and retention under natural conditions. But it is likely that such measures are strongly influenced by the respondent's prior knowledge of and interest in the brands and products involved.

Frequently, the portfolio test is used to test the merits of two or more alternative ads. In such cases, an experimental design is used in which two or more sets of folios are prepared. The only difference between folios is that one set contains test ad A, another set contains test ad B, and so on. The nontest ads (control ads) are the same in all folios—and are positioned in the same order. By using small matched samples and comparing recall and playback scores among the various groups, a "winner" is obtained.

In the theater type of test, attitudes towards a set of brands are measured; then a program is presented in which are embedded a number of advertisements, including those to be tested, and attitudes are again measured. This is a before-after experimental design. Such tests are often supplemented by data obtained via the use of focus group interviews with small samples selected from the general theater audience.

Psychological tests.   These tests are somewhat related to the tests already discussed, but they differ in the methods used. Advertisement effectiveness depends on the results which are achieved in the mind of the individual reached by the advertisement. Ideally, one could set up a list of the reactions which might result from a given advertisement, such as self-pity, security, fear, or nostalgia. Alternative advertisements could then be rated as to how readers responded with respect to those reactions.

Psychological tests employ a variety of research techniques, including word association, sentence completion, depth interviewing, and story-telling. Typically, a number of these techniques are employed on the same study. The major objective is to find out what respondents see in various advertisements and what it means to them. Such studies can be undertaken either before or after the copy has run. These are difficult studies to implement since only skilled interviewers can be used. The content needs to be developed by a trained individual, and the results are difficult to interpret. The need for skilled interviewers (expensive) leads to relatively small samples, sometimes as few as 10 to 15 respondents, so the results are subject to wide variation.

Physiological tests.   Measures derived from physiological tests are obtained using special laboratory equipment which records an individual's physiological responses to advertisements. Such tests have prevailed over the years because of their potential for providing objective responses to identifiable stimuli. Two of the older tests are the galvanic skin response and the eye movement. The former uses a device similar to the polygraph machine which is used in lie detection work. Respondents are linked by electrodes to a monitor and are exposed to a number of stimuli in the form of test and control ads. The monitor records the impact of these ads on the nervous system by measuring the amount of perspiration occurring on the hands. Advertising effectiveness is judged on the basis of the "arousal" registered on the monitor. To date this method has not played an important role in copy testing. Aside from the problem of sample size, there is a question of what is being measured, since arousal does not necessarily mean favorable reaction.

The eye camera is a device which records continuously the activity of the eye—both horizontal and vertical—as it reads printed material. By analyzing the route "taken," researchers can determine what part of the advertisement attracted the initial attention, what was interesting in it, and whether there was any part which appeared confusing. Interpretation of the results is difficult since it is impossible to correlate eye action with what readers are thinking; for example, when the eye lingers at one point in the advertisement does this indicate interest or confusion?[16]

One testing aid is a machine which measures pupil dilation. The basis of this test is that the pupil dilates when respondents receive an interesting or pleasant stimulus. Conversely, the pupil contracts when individuals receive uninteresting or unpleasant stimulus.[17] By comparing the changes induced by a message against a base line produced through the use of neutral stimuli, a measure of effectiveness can be obtained.

There is a disagreement however, as to what the pupillometer is measuring. Hess argues that pupillary change reflects an emotional response to a stimulus. Other researchers believe that dilations are the result of any substantial increase in mental activity regardless of whether it is pleasant or unpleasant.[18]

Another device, the tachistoscope, permits researchers to control the amount of time (in fractions of a second) that an advertisement (either in rough or finished form) is exposed to a group—or to an individual. This

---

[16] *Wall Street Journal,* "Quest for Sure-Fire Ads." Unfortunately, there have been no studies done on the interrelationships between various physiological tests. See Paul J. Watson and Robert J. Gatchel, "Autonomic Measures of Advertising," *Journal of Advertising Research* (June 1979):15–26.

[17] Eckhard H. Hess and James M. Polt, "Pupil Size as Related to Interest Value of Usual Stimuli," *Science* (August 1960):349–50.

[18] Roger D. Blackell, James S. Hensel and Brian Sternthal, "Pupil Dilation: What Does it Measure?" *Journal of Advertising Research* (August 1970):15–18.

permits researchers to study perception and comprehension under rigid time conditions. Thus, for example, the ability of outdoor billboard copy to impart a message can be tested under simulated exposure conditions.[19]

Inquiries.   Some advertisements are designed to produce direct results. When these results are inquiries or sales, a basis exists for accurately measuring the advertisement's "worth."

It must be remembered that a large number of inquiries does not mean that the advertising is successful—unless inquiries are the sole advertising objective. If the advertising objective is to help the long-term buildup of a general attitude, the number of inquiries may not necessarily be a sound basis for judging the advertisement's effectiveness. This would be particularly true with a single advertisement that was part of an advertising campaign.

Inquiry tests may be handled in several ways.

1.   The same offer may be placed in different pieces of copy which are placed in different issues of the same medium. The offers are "keyed" so that they can be traced to the specific advertising copy. Assuming that all other factors remain constant between issues—a difficult assumption to make— the difference in the number of inquiries received should indicate the "pulling power" of the different pieces of copy.

2.   The same offer is placed in different advertising copy which appears in different magazines or newspapers. The assumption is that differences between media are either negligible or can be corrected for (say on the basis of circulation), and that the adjusted returns will indicate the best copy.

3.   The same offer is placed in a medium which provides a split-run service. This is a procedure whereby half the copies of the magazine or newspaper contain one piece of copy and half another piece of copy. This is accomplished in a systematic way so that the two pieces of copy reach similar audiences.

Sales tests.   Such tests can be conducted using a variety of experimental designs. They are sometimes done as part of a test marketing program in which case the number of cities is typically small. Despite their appeal, such tests have important limitations: they measure only short term effects; the measuring instruments may not be sufficiently sensitive to detect relatively small differences in sales; they are time consuming; it is hard to hold "all other" factors constant; and they are quite expensive.

Sales tests may be simulated in a variety of ways; for example, consumers are exposed to alternative pieces of copy through point-of-purchase displays or direct mail. In the case of "displays," the need to test two advertisements would require two matched store samples. Product sales would be measured in each store before and after the introduction of the appropriate display.

---

[19] See Jonathan Gutman, "Tachistoscopic Tests of Outdoor Ads," *Journal of Advertising Research* (August 1972):21–27.

The changes in sales between the two periods for the two store samples would be compared and that group with the largest increase would be presumed to have the best copy. Similar experimental design studies can be conducted by mail using coupons.

These simulated sales tests have the advantage of being simpler and less expensive to implement than actual sales tests. Otherwise they suffer essentially the same disadvantages plus the fact that they are artificial. The fact that an advertisement "pulls" better as a point-of-sale piece does not prove it will create more sales when run in a newspaper or magazine, although one is inclined to believe that it would.

Day-after recall tests. Such tests are typically applied to television commercials. They consist of an on-air exposure of a finished commercial in one or more cities following which several hundred viewers are interviewed by phone to determine if they can recall the message. Based on their answers, a recall score is derived which is then compared with a standard or normative score (derived from similar studies) and on this basis the commercial is either accepted or rejected.

The advantage of this test is that it is accomplished in a natural setting and permits the use of proper sampling methodology. Its main weakness lies in the fact that it measures only a part of the commercial's objectives, namely, attention-getting power and the effect on the respondent's ability to play back some part of the advertisement's content. But there is little evidence that recall is correlated with behavior in any predictive sense. There is also the question of the reliability of recall test scores. The evidence is that this technique is relatively insensitive to differences among a majority of commercials. Substantial differences in scores can be "explained" in good part by city variability, education, age, time of exposure, position of commercial in program, brand usage, and program liking.[20]

As a result of the above, the straight recall type test has been modified to provide more discriminating data pertaining to copy effectiveness. The natural setting and timing of the interviews have been retained, but questions other than those dealing with recall have been added. One such version is called Positive Product Response (PPR) which seeks to provide an attitude measure. Based on test-retest experiences it appears that PPR scores are reliable. They also seem to be sufficiently sensitive to discriminate between commercials dealing with the same brand. In addition to being asked about their exposure to the program and test commercial, viewers are asked four questions as follows.

1. Would you describe the commercial?
2. What did this commercial make you think of?
3. What was the main idea the commercial was trying to get across?

---

[20] See Kevin J. Clancy and David M. Kiveskin, "TV Commercial Resale Correlates," *Journal of Advertising Research* (March 1971):18–20.

4.   Which brand of (name product) was being advertised? (If not mentioned earlier.)

PPR is an indirect measure of attitudes about the brand and its "score" depends upon answers to questions 1 and 2. It is

> . . . a favorable response specifically to the advertised product, not just to the commercial. It may be either a mental rehearsal or mental review of favorable experience, but it must be an indication of active personal involvement. It includes statements of intention to buy or try the brand, and statements of favorable attitude toward it as long as the attitude can be assumed to reflect actual experience.[21]

Clearly a rigorous coding procedure is required.

"After" tests

Once an advertisement or a campaign has been "run," it is literally impossible to measure the effects of the message separately since the results are confounded by the frequency of the media schedule, the impact of the medium selected, and other market factors. An "after" test is a test, therefore, of total advertising effectiveness, to a considerable extent.

"After" tests may be designed in a number of ways. All of them, with the exception of inquiry and sales tests, are based on the respondent's memory, and we have noted earlier the limitations of this approach. This raises the question of how soon after the advertisement has run that the measurement should be made.

Recall.   Advertising tends to be forgotten at a rapid rate which explains, in part, why its carryover effects are, on average, relatively short.[22] One study showed that 63 percent of sample respondents recalled a given piece of advertising after receiving 13 successive weekly exposures. Four weeks later, this percentage had dropped by half; and after six weeks, it had dropped by two thirds.[23] But much depends on the frequency with which advertising is received. After analyzing the same data, another researcher reports:

> the . . . rate of forgetting the entire campaign after its completion is slower after 13 exposures spread over a year than after 13 exposures spread over 13 weeks . . . the decrease in recall from 1 to 5 weeks after the last of the 13 ads is 70 percent for the weekly schedule, but only 29 percent for the 4-week schedules. . . . For a given advertising budget and a given campaign time period, a campaign that spreads the exposures as widely as possible over the period produces much more sales impact (as measured in recall-

---

[21] Joseph T. Plummer, "Evaluating T.V. Commercial Tests," *Journal of Advertisement Research* (October 1972):21.

[22] Clarke, "Econometrics Measurement."

[23] Hugh A. Zielske, "The Remembering and Forgetting of Advertising," *Journal of Marketing* (January 1955):239–43.

weeks) than does a pulsed campaign. And the advantage of the spaced campaign is very large in percentage terms.[24]

Greenberg and Suttoni, after reviewing the literature on television commercial wearout, concluded that since ". . . learning generally increases with repeated exposure, copy testing methods predicated on a single viewing will not measure the commercial's maximum performance."[25] Thus, the performance of a given advertising commercial should be measured with repeated studies. Krugman argues that the inability to recall something does not mean that it is forgotten; rather that it is simply put out of the mind. He believes that three exposures of an advertisement are sufficient in most situations.[26]

Recognition tests. These tests are commonly referred to as readership studies. In the print field such ratings are synonymous with "Starch scores." The procedure consists of taking "qualified" readers of a given issue of a magazine and asking them to point out what they saw and read. If an advertisement is reported as having been read, the interviewer asks the respondent to indicate what parts were read.

The validity of readership tests has been questioned by many researchers. W. R. Simmons, for example, found that readership claimed by nonreaders was about as great as that claimed by readers.[27]

The Advertising Research Foundation replicated the data collection methods of the Starch organization using a single issue of *Life* with a probability sample of over 600 readers. The ARF study found that the recognition scores obtained were largely independent of the age, education, and socioeconomic levels of respondents; the amount of time which had elapsed since the issue was released; the amount of reading done in the issue; and the competency of the interviewer.[28] But since such findings do not "make sense," what does the recognition method really measure? It is not memory, as was typically thought by many. Lucas and Britt suggest that the scores really measure interest.[29]

The recognition method suffers from the fact that respondents may confuse specific advertisements with similar or identical ones seen elsewhere, may believe they saw the advertisement because of its being near familiar editorial material, may desire to please the interviewer, and may "cooperate" because of fatigue from the length of the interview.

---

[24] Julian L. Simon, "What Do Zielske's Real Data Really Show about Pulsing," *Journal of Marketing Research* (August 1979):418–19.

[25] Allan Greenberg and Charles Suttoni, "Television Commercial Wearout," *Journal of Advertising Research* (October 1973):47–54.

[26] Herbert E. Krugman, "Why Three Exposures May Be Enough," *Journal of Advertising Research* (December 1972):11–14.

[27] W. R. Simmons, "Controlled Recognition in the Measurement of Advertising Perception," *Public Opinion Quarterly* 25 (Fall 1961):470.

[28] See Darrel B. Lucas, "The ABC's of ARF's PARM," *Journal of Marketing* (July 1960):9–20.

[29] Darrel B. Lucas and Stuart Henderson Britt, *Measuring Advertising Effectiveness* (New York: McGraw-Hill, 1963), p. 57.

MEDIA SELECTION

The goal of the advertiser is to select a media schedule from among the almost infinite number of alternatives which will maximize some combination of reach and frequency, meaning the number of people reached and the frequency with which they are reached. Such a decision presupposes that advertisers have specified the market segments which they want to reach. They must then decide what frequency of message exposure is desired in order to effect a change in behavior which will affect the sales of their brand favorably and the maximum number in the market segment that can be reached with that frequency. The greater the frequency desired, the smaller the reach obtainable with a given budget.

The problem of media selection is complicated because not only is it necessary to choose among major media types, such as newspapers, billboards, magazines, radio, and television, but also specific selections must be made within each general type. If magazines are chosen, specific magazines and even issues must be selected. In radio and television there is not only the question of what networks or stations, but what programs, what day or days of the week, and what time of the day.

While the copy itself is thought to play the primary role in effecting a favorable impression, the media selected affect such things as the recall of the advertising message, the ratings of its sponsors, and coupon return.

A variety of studies have documented the fact that the "character" of media vehicles will influence advertising effectiveness. Thus, Gensch concludes that such factors as editorial climate, product fit, technical capabilities, competitive advertising strategy, target population receptiveness, and product distribution system may affect the degree to which a media vehicle will impact on advertising effectiveness. The problem is how to weigh these factors for alternative vehicles at the time of scheduling the advertising.[30]

The number of readers, viewers, or listeners is basic in selecting a medium, but the characteristics of such persons must also be considered because not all persons are prospective buyers for a particular product. Some persons are better prospects than others because they consume greater quantities of the product type. Thus, an important step in making media comparisons is to distinguish between prospects and nonprospects in the audiences provided by the alternative media. The Advertising Research Foundation suggests that, following the elimination of nonprospects, the media analyst pay attention to the six levels at which the media vehicle operates to contribute to the effectiveness of the advertising message. These are as follows.[31]

---

[30] Gensch, "Media Factors," 216–25.

[31] Advertisement Research Foundation, *Toward Better Media Comparisons* (New York: Advertising Research Foundation, 1961).

1. *Vehicle distribution.*   This refers to the individual medium's circulation—the process by which it becomes available.
2. *Vehicle exposure.*   This deals with the exposure of people to the vehicle, for example, reading a given issue of a magazine or watching a particular television program.
3. *Advertising exposure.*   This is the same as level two above, but it involves the advertisement. It requires that the message physically come within the audience's attention range. It is likely that a sizable percentage of individuals who are classified as television viewers are actually engaged in other activities. Also, television commercials which are integrated in the program receive more attention than do those which are surrounded by other commercials and station breaks.
4. *Advertising perception.*   This requires that the audience have conscious awareness of the advertisement. Perception of print advertising is affected by the size, color, and position of the advertisement as well as the thickness of the vehicle. Measures are also influenced by product interest, past and present usage, and prospect status.
5. *Advertising communication.*   The audience receives the message in a desired context.
6. *Sales response.*

The problem of audience measurement is difficult even at the definitional level of what constitutes a reader, a viewer, a listener. In addition there are other problems including the following:

1. The variations in the composition and size of the audience of a given medium vehicle over time.
2. The variations due to geography, for example, a television show may get a high rating in one area because only two channels are available and a much lower rating in another where five channels are present.
3. The variations due to the rate at which different vehicles accumulate audiences, that is, variations in how many are reached over a period of time as compared with one issue or program.
4. The difficulty of estimating the value of different sizes of message units within and between media—for example, the effectiveness of a 30-second television commercial versus a 60-second television commercial versus a full-page advertisement in a general interest magazine.
5. The actual geographical area covered. This is particularly difficult with electronic media.

Media audiences

With but a few exceptions, media research is concerned with measuring the size and composition of individual vehicle audiences. In the case of print media the audience is typically defined as being comprised of individuals who say they have seen one or more major editorial features. With television and radio the audience can be defined in various ways such as sets tuned to a program or number of people listening or watching. Since there are substantial differences in measuring print versus electronic media audiences, the discussion will deal with each one separately.

Print media.   The Audit Bureau of Circulation (ABC) reports the paid circulation of a medium, the number of home subscriptions, and the number of newsstand sales. For newspapers, circulation is broken by daily and Sunday editions. For magazines, circulation data are shown by census regions and city size groups.

But circulation does not provide information about the number of readers. The problem of so doing for a given publication is a most difficult one. How does one define a reader? The typical method, commonly referred to as recognition, defines readers as individuals who are exposed to any of the editorial contents of a given issue. Respondents are classified on the basis of whether they "claim" to have read any of the editorial contents of the particular issue even though we know that this method yields unreliable data.

There is also the problem of "when" to interview, since exposure is cumulative. Thus, to interview early means some respondents who will read the issue later will be excluded. To interview late means that some who were exposed will forget. This is particularly true with certain magazines that have a long readership life. The usual procedure is simply to interview continuously over a given period of time and, therefore, to provide an "average" readership count. Another problem is what issue to study. Because of the cost involved, only a very few issues are studied in a given year despite the fact that readership of individual issues varies widely.

To confound the problems cited above, the act of reading certain publications (particularly magazines) has a status connotation which affects reported readership substantially. Order effects are also present. Belson reports that when respondents are questioned *first* about monthly magazines, readership figures are 35 percent higher on the average than if they are queried first on weekly magazines and daily newspapers.[32]

Media analysts need information on the duplication among magazines. Since consumer readership of three or more magazines is quite common, the problem of duplication is an important one, but rarely are data available showing the duplication among three or more magazines. An extensive study to determine duplication among all possible combinations of magazines is obviously an expensive, time-consuming activity. Agostini cites a study in France in which duplications were obtained for 30 magazines taken two by two, as well as for all the possible combinations of 15 of the 30 magazines. This resulted in 32,767 possible combinations. He proposes (and validates) the use of a "short-cut" method to estimate the unduplicated audience of combinations of 3, 4, 5, and so on magazines using total

---

[32] Harry Henry, "Belson's Studies in Readership," *Journal of Advertising Research* (June 1962):11.

audience and duplication data of the magazines involved taken two by two.[33] The major drawback to Agostini's method is the need for outside data which requires periodic studies to be kept current.

Radio and television. Radio and television are very different from magazines and newspapers when it comes to measuring the size of their audiences. Such media leave no visible trace that they have been "received." The program and the advertising message are often mixed, and it is difficult to divorce the two. There are four basic ways to measure the size of the audience for any radio and television program. Each of these is discussed briefly below.

Coincidental method. This method is based on a sample of homes, using the telephone to solicit responses as to what radio and television programs are being listened to or viewed. Typically, respondents are called and asked whether anyone in the home is listening to the radio or viewing television and, if so, to what program and station they are tuned. The question is also asked, *What is the name of the sponsor or product being advertised?* Ratings are based on the percentage of radio or television homes tuned to a particular program. This method measures average audience on the assumption that calls are spread evenly throughout the time of the program.

This system has the advantage of speed and economy; however, it has severe limitations. First, the results may not be valid since only homes with telephones are included. Even where network shows are concerned, it is usually not economically feasible to obtain a sample of rural homes. For these reasons, the total size of audience cannot be estimated accurately.

A second difficulty is that such procedures do not produce any continuous information about the audience. One cannot tell how many homes are reached over a period of several programs, that is, what the cumulative audience is. Nor can one tell what the total audience is for a given program at any one time, since no measure of tuning in or out is obtained.

A third major limitation is that calls must be limited to certain hours of the day and night, such as after 8:00 A.M. and before 10:30 P.M. Programs not included in this time span cannot usually be measured using the telephone coincidental method. There may also be a tendency on the part of some respondents to report they are viewing a more socially approved program than they are.

Roster recall. This is a technique which consists of aided recall via personal interviews. The interviewing is done shortly after the particular time period (usually four hours) to be measured has been completed. A list or *roster* of programs by quarter hours is used to aid respondents in remembering what programs were listened to or viewed.

---

[33] See J. M. Agostini, "How to Estimate Unduplicated Audiences," *Journal of Advertising Research* (March 1961):11–14; J. M. Agostini, "Analysis of Magazine Accumulative Audience," *Journal of Advertising Research* (December 1962):24–27; J. M. Agostini, "The Case for Direct Questions on Reading Habits," *Journal of Advertising Research* (June 1964):28–33.

The ratings obtained by the use of the roster-recall method are dependent upon memory and are subject to inflation or deflation as a result of the status, or lack of status, of certain programs. This is the method's biggest limitation, since the less popular shows tend to be discriminated against. Such a method does not provide any continuous information about the nature of the audience, nor does it permit measurement of the cumulative audience. Because respondents are queried about only a short time span, duplication analysis cannot be made. It is not possible to estimate the number of persons who view program A and also program B unless both programs fall within the time span on which the respondent is being interviewed.

The audimeter. This method receives its name from a machine of the same name used by the A. C. Nielsen Company. This machine is an electronic recorder which can be attached to a television set without interfering with its normal operation. It records on a tape when the set is turned on and to what station it is tuned. All of this is keyed to time periods so that a continuous record of the use of the set can be obtained by decoding the tape.

Using the audimeter, the Nielsen Company provides a television service which reports the following facts:

1. Total audience—number and percent of television homes tuned to each network program for a minimum of six minutes.
2. Average audience—equivalent to the number of television homes tuned to the full program (the average number of homes minute by minute).
3. Share of audience

$$= \left[\frac{\text{number of homes watching a specific program}}{\text{number of homes watching any program at that time period}} \right].$$

Since the audimeter sample remains essentially the same from month to month, a measure of the cumulative audience can be obtained and, in addition, elaborate duplication data can be studied, since all programs over a long period of time are covered. Data can be broken down by such household characteristics as region, city size, age of male head, total family income, and presence of children. While this service provides more objective data than any of the other measurement methods in that it relies on mechanical observation, it must be remembered that because a set is "on" does not indicate it is being viewed, nor does it indicate who is viewing. Further, the sample size is not large enough to enable local breakouts.

Diary method. This method obtains estimates of listening or viewing by having respondents record in a specially designed diary their radio listening and/or television viewing. Such an operation assumes that the panel members will cooperate by recording their listening or viewing at the time it occurs and, thus, will do it accurately. If this assumption is valid, then the diary method has an advantage—that of obtaining data on individuals viewing programs. Even so, the diary cannot provide a precise minute-by-minute audience flow as does the audimeter. A continuous panel operation can provide much useful duplication data, not only between radio and television programs, but also between such programs and other media to which the individual was exposed such as magazines and newspapers. The disadvantages of the diary method have been discussed in an earlier chapter.

Arbitron Company is the leading user of the diary method to measure television viewing and radio listening at national, regional, and local levels. The company reports contacting some 2 million households annually to obtain its data. Television metered sets are used in New York, Los Angeles, and Chicago.

Media models

Almost all media models basically seek to maximize some measure of advertising exposure which is assumed to impact on sales. In brief, such models report, for a given advertising schedule, the number of individuals or households exposed and the number of times they are exposed. Since different schedules have different costs, the exposure "output" can be divided by the costs involved in order to obtain an effectiveness ratio.

In recent years there has been considerable interest in trying to obtain measures of the complete frequency distribution of exposure; the percent of the audience who were exposed once, twice, and so on. Such distributions are useful in measuring the value of one media schedule versus that of another.

But even assuming one can predict exposure with reasonable accuracy, not all individuals or households who are "exposed" are of equal value to the advertiser. Some may be heavy buyers of the product class in question and, thus, constitute prime prospects while others may not be prospects at all. Further, how should successive exposures be weighed? Is the second exposure worth more than the third exposure? And if so, how much more? How much time should elapse between exposures? How much forgetting takes place over time and what is the variation in forgetting between different exposures? And, of course, there is the differential effect between media vehicles as well as those related to length of commercial. While most models seek to address the above problems, they are handicapped by a lack of precise input data, especially with regard to current data pertaining to duplication, forgetting, and accumulation.

Some models provide reach (extent of audience) and frequency of exposure for each media schedule. Others stipulate that advertisers state their objectives in terms of reach and frequency by target segments. In the case of the latter, the model output consists of a recommended media schedule by media vehicle, by time period, and by number of units purchased as well as information about the composition and size of the audience reached, the total number of impressions, the distribution of exposure frequencies, and the cost.[34]

Many advertisers obtain media exposure data which can be tied directly to brand usage. Such data clearly facilitate the selection of a media schedule since a target audience can be selected and its exposure to various media vehicles can be determined as well. As Assall and Cannon note, it is far better to match media vehicles directly with target market members (prospective or actual product or brand users) than to match indirectly on the basis of mediating variables such as demographic characteristics of vehicle and target audiences.[35]

In spite of the apparent advantages of media models, they are handicapped by a lack of precise input data, especially with regard to current data pertaining to duplication, forgetting, and accumulation.

SUMMARY

Over the years the field of advertising has received considerable attention from research workers, but still there is no general agreement as to what are the best techniques to use to answer the questions: "What should be said about the product?" "What is the best way to put these appeals into words and pictures?" "What media should be selected?" It is doubtful if any single technique will be developed which will answer these questions satisfactorily.

Copy testing is designed to determine the best way of presenting the selected appeals. There are two major kinds of copy tests—"before" and "after." If the objective is to make improvements in the copy before it is released on a full-scale basis, then the test used is classified as a "before" test. The different kinds of "before" copy tests are (1) consumer jury, (2) rating scales, (3) portfolio tests, (4) psychological tests, (5) physiological tests, (6) inquiries, (7) sales tests and (8) day-after recall. Similar techniques are used in some of these tests so the differences are more a matter of degree than of kind. The two types of "after" tests are (1) recall and (2) recognition.

In selecting media, the objective is to find the most efficient vehicle for carrying the message to potential buyers. This necessitates a determination of both the size of the audiences delivered by alternative media and the characteristics of these audiences. Readership studies are used to obtain such information for printed media. For radio and television programs a number of methods are currently used, including the telephone coincidental, roster recall, audimeter, and diary. If advertisers are using more than one

---

[34] For an excellent discussion of media models see David A. Aaker and John G. Meyers, *Advertising Management* (Englewood Cliffs, N.J.: Prentice-Hall, Inc., 1975), chap. 14.

[35] Henry Assall and Hugh Cannon, "Do Demographics Help in Media Selection," *Journal of Advertising Research* (December 1979):7–12.

medium, they are faced with the problem of duplication. While duplication studies are based primarily on qualitative differences in media, they are still of value in helping to narrow down the alternatives in the media selection program.

Mathematical models to select the "best" media schedule (typically based on number of exposures) have been developed, but are handicapped by the lack of current and accurate data.

Case 21–1
METZGER BREWERY

Metzger was a small, privately owned brewery that sold a hearty, hop-flavored, European-like beer in three midwestern states. Henry Metzger, great grandson of the founder, was quite concerned about the problems of competing with large national firms. A big problem was that, like most small breweries, Metzger couldn't afford to advertise on the same scale as big breweries. They had done some advertising in the past, but that was generally limited to local radio and television spots.

The beer industry had undergone considerable change in the last several decades. In 1933, after prohibition ended, there were 750 breweries in the United States. By the late 1970s, less than 50 remained. There were fewer breweries with each passing year, because the larger ones were able to take market share from the smaller ones through their extensive advertising campaigns and their better distribution.

Another change in the industry was that it was producing a greater variety of beers. Recent trends were towards specialty products like low-calorie beer. For example, the Miller Brewery was the first to successfully market such a beer, but soon thereafter every major brewery had a similar product. European beers, some of which had a hearty taste like Metzger's, were also growing in popularity. If these beers continued to gain in popularity, it could have a favorable impact on sales of Metzger beer.

Metzger believed that many beer drinkers wanted a beer which was more hop-flavored than the well-known domestic beers, all of which tasted about the same, he felt. As a result, they either bought foreign beer, or they drank a brand of domestic beer which they found to be only partially satisfying. Metzger felt that he had to get people to try his beer, so they would know it was a heartier beer than most domestic brands. He wondered if advertisements using comparisons might be effective in stimulating trial.

In looking into the matter, he found there to be some controversy regarding the effectiveness of comparative advertising. Some people felt that comparative advertising worked best, if at all, when a smaller company challenged the industry leader. There was also some feeling that the industry leader should not respond to, or even acknowledge, such advertising when it was employed by a competitor. In addition, some questions had been raised as to whether comparative advertisements were more helpful to their sponsor or to the competitor named, but there was no definite evidence either way.

In order to gain a better understanding of the effectiveness of comparative advertising, Metzger looked at the Pepsi-Cola television advertisements which were directed against Coca-Cola. In these advertisements, which were called "The Pepsi Challenge," people were asked to compare Coca-Cola and Pepsi-Cola in a blind taste test. The advertisement claimed that more than half the Coca-Cola drinkers judged Pepsi-Cola to be the better tasting of the two. This advertising seeemed to have worked extremely well for Pepsi-Cola, which soon thereafter became the leader of all cola brands sold through supermarkets. Rather than ignore the comparative advertisements, Coca-Cola aired a television commercial in which Fresca (a Coca-Cola product) was compared with Pepsi-Cola, and another which claimed that "one sip is not enough" for a good comparison of two soft drinks. Many people in the soft drink industry felt that Coca-Cola did not benefit in any way from responding directly to "The Pepsi Challenge."

Still confused on the issue, Mr. Metzger came across an advertising agency study which attempted to measure the effects of comparative television advertisements that specifically mentioned the names of competing brands. The study attempted to answer two questions: (1) Does comparative advertising help the sponsor of the advertisement or the competitor named? (2) Does comparative advertising help or confuse the consumer? The agency's research design utilized two sets of television advertisements, of which one set was comparative and the other set was noncomparative. The comparative set of advertisements consisted of seven comparative tests commercials, and the noncomparative set consisted of seven noncomparative test commercials. Two different groups of respondents saw commercials for the same seven brands, but one group saw comparative advertisements and the other group saw noncomparative advertisements. Of the seven test advertisements, two were concerned with consumer services, three were concerned with durable goods, and two were concerned with packaged goods.

The results of this study (See Tables 1–4) seemed to be inconclusive and to cloud the issue further. The only thing Metzger could deduce from the tables was that some findings seemed to favor comparative advertising, while some favored noncomparative advertising.

TABLE 1. Percentage of respondents who felt the commercials were believable

	(1) *Saw the* *comparative* *advertisements*	*(2)* *Saw the* *noncomparative* *advertisements*	*(3)* *Difference* *(Col. 1 — Col. 2)*
Consumer service	63%	80%	−17%
Durable goods	62	60	2
Packaged goods	55	63	−8

TABLE 2. Percentage of respondents who felt there were important differences between brands

	(1) Saw the comparative advertisements	(2) Saw the noncomparative advertisements	(3) Difference (Col. 1 — Col. 2)
Consumer service	60%	51%	9%
Durable goods	89	87	2
Packaged goods	46	53	—7

TABLE 3. Percentage of respondents who identified (unaided recall) the brands in the advertisements

	(1) Saw the comparative advertisements	(2) Saw the noncomparative advertisements	(3) Difference (Col. 1 — Col. 2)
Consumer service			
Brand A	83%	81%	2%
Brand B	77	77	0
Durable goods			
Brand A	64	74	—10
Brand B	77	81	—4
Brand C	68	47	21
Packaged goods			
Brand A	85	81	4
Brand B	88	90	—2

TABLE 4. Percentage of respondents who changed their brand preference from pre-exposure to postexposure.*

	(1) Saw the comparative advertisements	(2) Saw the noncomparative advertisements	(3) Difference (Col. 1 — Col. 2)
Consumer service			
Brand A	6%	0%	6%
Brand B	0	1	—1
Durable goods			
Brand A	0	—1	1
Brand B	3	2	1
Brand C	2	0	2
Packaged goods			
Brand A	—2	2	—4
Brand B	1	1	0

* Pre-exposure tested which brand the respondents considered best. Postexposure tested which brand the respondents would be most likely to buy.

After reviewing what he learned about comparative advertising, Metzger was still unsure if it was right for his company. Comparative advertising seemed to have helped Pepsi-Cola gain some ground on Coca-Cola, but the statistics from the comparative advertising study were unclear. Some seemed to favor it, while others did not. The whole issue was very confusing, but Mr. Metzger needed to make a decision soon.

> *Evaluate the study Mr. Metzger found on comparative advertising. What conclusions can you draw relative to the effectiveness of comparative advertising?*
>
> *Is further research needed before Mr. Metzger can make a decision? If so, what kind of research would you recommend?*

Case 21–2
BREWER COMPANY*

The Brewer Company, located in a large city in the Southwest, sold its line of malt beverages in parts of the states of Arizona, New Mexico, and Texas. Since its founding in the 1880s this family-owned business had enjoyed almost continuous success. Although the company was enjoying an accelerating demand for its line of products, the company's general manager, James Brewer, was concerned about a number of problems including what advertising strategy to employ over the next several years for the company's major brand—the Brewer label.

Four leading companies accounted for about two-thirds of the total beer sales in Brewer's marketing area. All but Brewer had lost share over the past four years as follows:

Brand	Estimated present share	Gain or loss past four years
Brewer	23.8	+4.8
Brand A	22.9	−1.7
Brand B	11.2	−5.1
Brand C	8.5	−1.6

A recent market survey among some 500 male beer drinkers in the company's marketing area indicated that Brewer had made its gains primarily at the expense of brand B. Several years earlier, this local brand had been

---

* Adapted from *Stanford Business Cases 1970* with the permission of the publisher, Graduate School of Business, Stanford University, copyright © 1970 by the Board of Trustees of the Leland Stanford Junior University.

purchased by a large national brewer which proceeded to divert the brand's advertising and sales promotion funds to its national brand. The same survey also revealed that, in part, the Brewer success had been due to going in the opposite direction from brand A; that is, letting brand A have the mild, light segment of the market and going after the real beer drinker who wanted taste, tang, hops, malt, quality, and aging.

This same study reported on the effectiveness of Brewer advertising versus other leading brands. The results are shown in Tables 1–9.

TABLE 1. Recall of brand A advertising

	Total	Recall among brand A drinkers
Recall slogan "It's light"	68%	62%
"Pure ingredients"	22	21
Quality	20	22
Saw advertising—television, billboard	11	18
Good flavor, good taste	10	11
Made in Arizona	10	13
Mild, light, smooth	6	10
Cool, refreshing	6	4
Horse show	5	9
Open for tours	5	4
All other positive	4	4
All other negative	2	2
Confused with other brands' advertising	—	—
Don't know	7	6

TABLE 2. Recall of brand B advertising

	Total	Recall among brand B drinkers
Sponsor wrestling	15%	23%
Singing, yodeling	8	5
Saw ad on billboards, television	6	24
Old recipe beer	5	9
German type of beer	5	2
Let's have a brand B	4	7
Sociable, fun, get-together	4	11
Remember German scenes	3	5
Remember little men	2	3
Slow-brewed	2	10
Best quality	2	5
Best flavor, taste	2	2
Light, mild	2	2
All other positive	3	11
Confuse with other brands' advertising	3	2
Don't know	49	31

TABLE 3. Recall of brand C advertising

	Total	Recall among brand C drinkers
"The Beer of the Old Southwest"	24%	36%
Label with spurs (Red, Silver, Gold)	15	20
Aged	13	25
Local beer—made in the Southwest	11	15
Partying, fun	4	5
Dance time	4	10
Sports	4	—
American beer	4	5
Dislike advertising	3	—
People's beer; working people's beer	2	5
Outdoor sports	2	—
Old reliable beer	1	10
Less expensive, better buy	1	5
All other positive	3	10
Don't know	40	15

TABLE 4. Recall of Brewer advertising

	Total	Recall among Brewer drinkers
Remember "Made for over 60 years by experienced craftsmen"	15%	21%
Remember "Made locally"	12	21
Saw advertising on billboards, television	10	12
Quality, best beer	7	7
Show outdoor scenes	5	9
Waterfalls	4	7
Sponsor sports	4	6
"Perfected"	3	3
Refreshing, cool	2	2
Made from old formula	1	2
Good flavor	1	—
Man pouring beer from glass	1	2
Light, mild	1	1
Visit the brewery, tours	3	4
Confuse with other brands' advertising	3	1
All other positive	1	2
All other negative	1	—
Don't know	60	39

TABLE 5. Brand and slogan association*

Largest selling beer		Aged		Does the most advertising	
Brand A	37%	Brand C	55%	Brand A	42%
Brewer	14	Brewer	9	Brand C	28
Brand B	14	Brand A	4	Brewer	6
All others	20	Don't know	32	All others	10
Don't know	19				

Slow-brewed		People like it		Best tap beer	
Brand B	15	Brand C	48	Brewer	22
Brewer	11	Brewer	8	Brand A	18
All others	20	All others	11	Brand B	10
Don't know	43	Don't know	31	All others	5
				Don't know	35

Oldest beer company		Pure pleasure		The best packaged beer	
Brewer	40	Brand A	19	Brand A	19
Brand A	13	Brand C	12	Brewer	12
All others	7	Brewer	7	Brand B	9
Don't know	40	All others	10	Brand C	8
		Don't know	30	All others	7
				Don't know	28

The lady's beer		The sportsman's beer	
Brand A	35	Brand A	12
Brand C	2	Brewer	15
Brand B	2	Brand B	10
All others	2	Brand C	8
Don't know	50	All others	10
		Don't know	23

* Respondents were reminded of slogan and asked what brand came to mind for each.

TABLE 6. When brand tastes best (by favorite brand)*

	Total	Brewer	Brand A	Brand B
When I'm hot	24%	33%	24%	12%
When I'm thirsty for a glass of beer	22	35	15	22
After work	35	46	35	22
When I'm tired	14	17	13	17
In the summer	11	8	14	11
With meals	4	4	4	5
Social occasions	9	2	13	7
Anytime	3	—	5	4
In the evening, after dinner (watching TV)	22	15	23	25
Outdoors	9	2	14	11
When I'm relaxing	9	7	11	10
All others	9	9	6	8

* Respondents were asked the question: "When does your brand of beer taste best?"

TABLE 7. Brands associated with different occupations and types of people*

	Brewer	Brand A	Brand B	Brand C	Don't know
Associate more with Brewer's					
Men	27%	16%	9%	6%	26%
Fishermen	21	16	3	8	28
Mechanics	21	12	7	8	36
Truck drivers	18	11	10	11	30
Hunters	18	11	8	11	30
Boaters	15	12	7	7	38
Associated more with Brand A					
Women	7	46	4	2	25
College students	11	36	5	5	30
Young people	10	35	3	5	30
Retired people	7	28	4	1	39
Waiters	8	27	4	3	38
Athletes	9	20	8	3	49
Sales representatives	11	15	7	4	40
Doctors	6	14	8	1	40
Farmers	12	13	7	7	44
Military officers	9	11	9	4	44

* Figures given in percentages of respondents associating brand with that occupation or type.

TABLE 8. Mean averages of ratings given "ideal" beer compared with ratings given various brands*†

	Ideal Beer	Brand A	Brewer	Brand B	Brand C
Light/dark					
Total beer drinkers	2.0	1.7	2.2	2.3	2.6
Heavy beer drinkers	1.9	1.6	2.2	2.3	2.4
Moderate-light beer drinkers ...	2.0	1.7	2.2	2.3	2.7
Smooth/tangy					
Total beer drinkers	2.7	2.4	3.4	3.2	3.4
Heavy beer drinkers	2.8	2.4	3.5	3.2	3.2
Moderate-light beer drinkers ...	2.5	2.3	3.3	3.3	3.5
Bland/sharp					
Total beer drinkers	2.9	2.5	3.4	3.2	3.4
Heavy beer drinkers	3.0	2.5	3.4	3.1	3.4
Moderate-light beer drinkers ...	2.7	2.5	3.4	3.3	3.4
Light body/full body					
Total beer drinkers	2.9	2.5	3.4	3.4	3.4
Heavy beer drinkers	3.1	2.4	3.5	3.3	3.2
Moderate-light beer drinkers ...	2.7	2.6	3.3	3.4	3.7
Mild flavor/strong flavor					
Total beer drinkers	2.3	2.0	3.0	2.9	3.4
Heavy beer drinkers	2.4	1.9	3.0	2.7	3.3
Moderate-light beer drinkers ...	2.2	2.1	3.1	3.1	3.6
Sweet/hoppy					
Total beer drinkers	3.6	3.2	3.8	3.7	3.7
Heavy beer drinkers	3.7	3.2	3.8	3.7	3.7
Moderate-light beer drinkers ...	3.4	3.2	3.7	3.7	3.7

* In an attempt to determine the importance of various beer characteristics and to evaluate image with these characteristics, respondents were presented with sets of paired values on a five-point rating scale. The "pairs" consisted of matched antonyms. Negative words were avoided and words connoting similar ideas were rotated, thus minimizing bias.

Respondents were asked in the beginning to designate for each "pairing" where they would rate "what they look for" in a beer. For example, respondents were asked to indicate whether they looked for a very light beer, a somewhat light beer, neither a light nor a dark beer, a somewhat dark beer, or a very dark beer. The same procedure was used for five other "pairs" of values. The frequencies for the various traits were averaged to derive comparable means for the different brands and subgroups. The means for "look for" ratings will be referred to, in this report, as the "ideal" beer.

The purpose of this design was to provide a workable benchmark for future reference so that trends can be observed and evaluated. Therefore, statistical variance and standard deviation were determined for every mean average shown. The size of the sample was such that a difference of .02 percent or more in a total column should be considered significant. Lowering the sample size increases the variability, therefore, when evaluating the means in the heavy user, moderate-light user, or other subgroups, they must be at least .04 percent from one another to be statistically significant.

† Figures given are average scores based on a value of one for the first adjective in each pair and five for the second.

TABLE 9. "Ideal" beer ratings of various groups*

	Drink Brewer	Drink brand A	Drink brand B	Drink brand C	Drink other brands
Light/dark	2.1	1.8	1.9	2.0	2.0
Smooth/tangy	2.9	2.4	3.1	2.0	2.5
Bland/sharp	3.1	2.7	3.0	2.8	2.7
Light body/full body	3.3	2.8	2.9	2.7	2.7
Mild/strong	2.6	2.0	2.3	2.5	2.2
Sweet/hoppy	3.7	3.4	3.4	3.6	2.4

	Heavy beer drinkers	Moderate-light beer drinkers	Males	Females
Light/dark	1.9	2.0	2.0	1.8
Smooth/tangy	2.8	2.5	2.7	2.4
Bland/sharp	3.0	2.7	2.9	2.6
Light body/full body	3.1	2.7	3.0	2.8
Mild/strong	2.4	2.2	2.4	2.0
Sweet/hoppy	3.7	3.4	3.7	3.2

* See note on Table 8 for explanation.

Based on your analysis of the data contained in Tables 1–9, what advertising copy strategy would you recommend for Brewer?

What additional analyses of the data would you suggest?

What additional data would you have collected? Why?

22

Market and sales analysis research

Marketing management relies heavily on research in setting marketing policies, in planning marketing operations, and in controlling marketing operations, including the functioning of the sales unit. In its broadest meaning, market and sales analysis research covers the identification and measurement of all those variables which individually and in combination have an effect on sales. Thus, such activities as measurement of market potential, sales forecasting, sales territory evaluation, and measurement of sales representative's performance are included.

Any marketing expenditure (input) assumes some kind of a result (payout). Marketing directors must have enough knowledge of the market and their organization's performance to estimate the impact of their organization's efforts on the market. Market and sales analysis research make up a large portion of the activity of most marketing research departments. Research studies dealing with the development of market potentials, market-share analysis, and sales analysis are among the most common activities undertaken by a marketing research unit. Short-range forecasting, long-range forecasting, and establishment of sales quotas and sales territories are also standard activities.

Since this chapter will discuss primarily market analysis, sales forecasting, and sales analysis, it is desirable to give specific meaning to each. *Market potential analysis* will apply to those studies of individual markets which seek to determine the sales potential(s) within them. *Sales forecasting* will be used to mean the prediction of sales of a particular product, company, branch office, or other unit for a given period of time. *Sales analysis* will include the analysis of a company's sales to ascertain such things as distribution of sales by territories, by type and size of customer, by order size, by product, and by combinations of these classifications.

MARKET POTENTIAL ANALYSIS

Marketing management is interested in obtaining sales potentials for each of the geographic markets it serves. By sales potentials is meant "the maximum possible sales opportunities for all sellers of a good or service."[1] When applied to geographical areas it means simply the maximum sales which will be generated by buyers in that area for some stated time period. Area potentials can be expressed in both absolute and relative terms. In the latter form they can be shown as a percent of the total market (100 percent).

Since most products are similar to a number of others, consumers often engage in considerable substitution; therefore, the degree of substitution, as well as the conditions under which it takes place, must be considered in the development of potentials. The decision as to whether to include or exclude closely related substitutes will often have a pronounced effect on estimated sales potentials. For example, in considering the relative sales potential for canned peas one would have to consider the possible sales of frozen peas, since the two can be viewed as close substitutes for each other.

Market potentials and sales forecasts are not the same thing, although the two are sometimes used interchangeably. Market potentials typically refer to total sales possibilities. Several different potentials may be considered, depending on what conditions are assumed. One potential could have to do with the conditions of use, for example, the amount of toothpaste which would be used if all persons using toothpaste brushed after every meal. Another potential could be one based on brushing only once a day and so on. Thus, the word "potential" has specific meaning only in terms of the assumptions used when making the calculation.

Uses of potentials

Allocation of marketing resources. The primary use of information on market potentials has been in the allocation of marketing resources, especially the allocation of salesmen. It is difficult to estimate a market response function, that is, the way a given group of potential customers will respond to various combinations of marketing inputs. Under ideal conditions, resources will be invested in each market until the incremental returns for each unit of resources invested is equal in each market and until further investment will yield a return smaller than could be obtained by investing elsewhere.

All selling effort—sales force, advertising, and nonadvertising promotion—should be allocated only after a consideration of potentials. In the most simple situation, a market with 10 percent of the total potential should receive 10 percent of the sales effort. If New York has twice as much potential as Chicago, New York should receive twice as much sales effort as Chicago.

---

[1] American Marketing Association, *Marketing Definitions,* p. 5.

Potential not sole criterion for allocating sales effort.   The primary use-fulness of market potentials is to focus attention on the relative worth of individual markets. No firm should, however, rely completely on such rankings as a basis for allocating sales resources. Potentials do *not* reveal the competitive structure of the market and the firm's ability to exploit that market. For example, Los Angeles may represent a high potential to a given firm, but competition may be so strongly entrenched that the expenditures needed to gain a satisfactory brand share would be too great.

Actually, market responsiveness is a function of the potential, the competitive structure, and the firm's input into the market. The later includes managerial ability as well as adequate finances. Thus, the firm must appraise realistically its own abilities—both qualitatively and quantitatively.

The firm needs to augment its potential data with information about the competitive structure of the individual markets. One firm, for example, ascertains the following information about each of its markets:

1.   Number of brands in the market and the brand share of each.
2.   Trend of each major brand's market share over the past several years.
3.   Amount of money spent by the major brands in advertising currently and over the past several years.
4.   Price structure.
5.   Distribution structure with particular reference to the leading retail outlets and exclusive distributor franchises.
6.   Availability of evening local-station television time.

These data are then used in connection with the company's experience in the market plus the data on market potential. These factors form the basis for this firm's allocation of its sales resources to the various markets.

The ultimate objective is to make an optimum allocation of the sales resources among the alternative markets. This cannot be done precisely since it would require exact measurements, both short and long run, of the effect of a given increment of sales effort. However, a careful study of the potential and competitive structure should permit the firm to array the markets in order of their likelihood of response to sales efforts. By matching the available sales resources against the requirements of these markets, it is possible to arrive at a satisfactory distribution of funds. One firm in following this procedure found it best to spend its money in the smaller markets because the competitive structure was more conducive to relatively good sales results despite the lower potentials.

Defining sales territories.   A sales manager typically tries to develop sales territories that are equal in sales potential and in workload so that each salesman has an equal opportunity to make sales. A recent study of the literature in the field found that four territorial characteristics were typically used in defining territories.[2] Market potential was used in every case, while con-

---

    2 Adrian R. Ryans and Charles B. Weinberg, "Territory Sales Response," *Journal of Marketing Research* 16 (November 1979): 453–65.

centration, dispersion, and workload were used to lesser degrees. Potential was found to have a positive effect on sales in almost all instances and concentration, the extent to which potential was concentrated in a few accounts, also tended to have a positive relationship to sales. Geographical dispersion and workload were not found to be strongly related to sales, but this may be partially the result of the fact that only proxy measures were available to measure them.

This study concluded that workload is difficult to define operationally and has an uncertain relationship with sales so that it should not be used in defining sales territories. Furthermore, the study found the relationship between potential and sales has been so clearly determined that it recommended potential be the primary factor used to establish territories.[3]

The sales representative's workload is a function of a number of variables including the number and size of accounts, average order size, account location, travel time between accounts, and nonselling activities required of the sales force. Ultimately, the workload must be defined in terms of the number of clients and call frequencies by type or class of customer. Through experience a company can usually develop such workload measures which, when coupled with the time required to travel and perform other activities (for example, paperwork), can serve as the basis for designing sales territories. At the minimum, the firm should be able to eliminate extreme cases, such as where sales representatives have more potential (for example, many large accounts) than they can exploit properly or have insufficient potential to occupy their time fully. Also, such data are useful in helping the company decide whether to concentrate on high-potential markets in an effort to increase sales while simultaneously reducing expenses.

Setting sales quotas.   Sales quotas should be set after market potentials have been derived and sales territories established. The potential for each territory is then known, but sales quotas must also consider past sales performance, changes to be made in the amount of supporting sales effort during the coming year, and anticipated activities of competitors. Quotas are usually set for each sales territory and for each sales representative. They are ordinarily not the same as potentials or even of the same relative size. One market may have twice the potential of another but may have local competitors that take a large share so that a given firm's quota may be smaller there than in an area with less potential.

Sales quotas set in light of sales potentials furnish a much better basis for measuring the efficiency of sales representatives than do quotas set by the old rule of thumb—last year's sales plus 5 percent. If two sales representatives turn in the same annual sales volume, they are usually paid about the same and are held in equal esteem by the sales manager. If market analysis shows sales representative A to have a territory with far less potential than

---

[3] See also L. M. Lodish, "Sales Territory Alignment to Maximize Profit," *Journal of Marketing Research* 12 (February 1975):30–36.

sales representative B, the sales manager may wonder if representative A may not actually be superior. A shift of the two might lead to an improvement in total sales. The following table illustrates.

	Sales representative A	Sales representative B
Sales last year	500,000	635,000
Territory potential	2,000,000	4,000,000
Percent of potential ....:...	25.0%	15.9%

As noted above, however, market potential and sales representative effectiveness are but two of the basic determinants of sales results in a territory. To measure sales representative performance, it is necessary to take into account some of the other factors which influence sales results. One study of a national sales organization found six factors explained 72 percent of the variation in sales among territories. These factors and the methods of measuring them were the following:[4]

Factor	Method of measurement
1. Market potential	Industry sales (units) in territory
2. Territory workload	Weighted index based on annual purchases and concentration of accounts
3. Experience of sales representative	Length of time employed by company (months)
4. Motivation and effort of sales representative	Aggregate ratings by field sales manager on eight dimensions of performance
5. Company experience	Weighted average of market share past four years Market-share trend same period
6. Company effort	Advertising dollar expenditure in territory

Methods for measuring market potential

Two major methods are available for estimating market potentials. One of these involves the use of direct data, that is, data on the actual product for which one wishes to estimate potentials. The other method involves the use of corollary data—data related to, but different from, the product at hand. Corollary data methods can use single or multiple factors, and the latter can be combined in a variety of ways. The more important variations are discussed in the following pages.

---

[4] David W. Cravens, Robert B. Woodruff, and Joe C. Stamper, "An Analytical Approach for Evaluating Sales Territory Performance," *Journal of Marketing* (January 1972):31–37.

Direct data method.   Total industry sales of a particular type of product can be used as the basis for estimating market potentials for one brand of that product. The usual procedure in using such data is to break down total industry sales by the firm's sales territories (see columns 1, 2, and 3 in Table 22–1). The percentage distribution is used as a measure of the relative potential existing in each of the firm's territories. These percentages can then be applied to the firm's estimate of its total sales to arrive at a potential figure for each territory. Column 4 in Table 22–1 illustrates the resulting potential for a company which has estimated its total potential at $968,000.

TABLE 22–1. Illustration of use of direct data method

Company sales territory	Total industry sales		Company potential*	Actual company sales
	Volume ($000)	Percent of U.S.		
1	$ 104	3.13%	$ 30,300	$ 24,140
2	208	6.25	60,500	56,110
3	156	4.69	45,400	47,300
4	312	9.38	90,800	71,040
5	52	1.56	15,100	19,870
Etc.	—	—	—	—
Total	$3,328	100.00%	$968,000	$1,023,660

* Figures obtained by applying percent of industry sales to firm's total forecasted sales ($968,000).

Comparison of potential sales with actual sales indicates this company is weak in sales territories 1, 2, and 4 and strong in territories 3 and 5. It might be concluded that management should exert itself in the weak areas where the firm has not been able to obtain its "proper" sales. Such a conclusion, however, does not take into account the cost of exploiting these deficit areas. Therefore, it cannot be stated categorically that it will be profitable to attempt to reach potentials in such territories. Local competition may be unusually stiff in some areas. There is disagreement as to whether a company should concentrate its sales effort in its weak or strong territories. An analysis such as the above, however, will highlight those areas which need to be investigated to determine why the company is not obtaining its share of the market. This is the first step in deciding what action, if any, should be taken.

Total industry sales data may be obtained in some cases as a result of licensing or the imposition of taxes. For example, all states impose taxes on liquor and gasoline, and these receipts can be used to estimate the total gasoline and liquor consumption by states. Trade associations frequently compile total industry data by having their members report shipments. An excellent guide to many sources of information useful to firms involved in estimating market potentials is the federal government publication *Measuring Markets.*[5]

The principal advantage of using total industry sales to measure market potential is that actual results (sales) are being used. The method is straightforward and does not require as much clerical work as do some of the other methods.

Several limitations prevent this method from being used by more firms. First, there are very few commodities on which total sales data are available. Even where data are available, they are usually available only at the state level, thereby precluding a breakdown by sales territories that do not follow state lines. Sometimes the data are ambiguous in that they cover several variations of the commodity. For example, manufacturers selling a high-priced item would probably be in error if they used total unit sales as a guide, since the distribution of the higher-priced units may not be the same as for the other units.

The most important limitation to this method is that past sales are used to indicate market potentials; that is, no attention is given to the potentials except as they are revealed through past experience. Past sales were made with the help of certain advertising and sales methods. Changes in these activities, as well as changes in price and product, may shift demand and redistribute total sales.

In the absence of direct data on the sales of individual products by geographical areas, the manager must turn to corollary data.

Corollary data method.   The corollary data method of measuring market potentials is based on the idea that, if a given series of data (such as industry sales) is related to a second series of data (such as the number of employed persons), the distribution of the second series by market areas may be used to indicate the distribution of the first series in the same market areas.

Single factor indexes.   Single factor indexes are the most simple of the corollary data methods of market analysis. A typical example is the use of the sales of one product to indicate the market potential of another. This is more apt to be satisfactory if the two items have a closely related demand —that is, the demand for one is derived from the other or is a complementary demand. Automotive replacement parts offer a good illustration of a derived demand. The demand in any area is closely related to the number of cars of that type in the area. For example, the number of Chevrolet cars can be used as an index of the potential for sales of Chevrolet parts. The procedure involved is essentially the same as for direct data and is illustrated in Table 22–2 which shows the estimation of potential for Chevrolet parts by area when the total U.S. potential is estimated at $2 million.

---

[5] *Measuring Markets: A Guide to the Use of Federal and State Statistical Data* (U.S. Department of Commerce, Industry and Trade Administration, August 1979).

TABLE 22–2. Hypothetical illustration of use of corollary data—single factor method

Company sales territory	Chevrolet cars registered Number (000)	Percent	Potential for Chevrolet parts ($000)
1	331	2.91%	$ 58.2
2	873	7.68	153.6
3	741	6.52	130.4
4	529	4.66	93.2
5	587	5.17	103.4
Etc.	—	—	—
Total U.S.	11,359	100.00%	$2,000.0

Factors other than sales of related products are also used in the corollary data, single factor method. For example, population and household data are frequently used to indicate market potentials. The reasoning back of this use of population data is that sales can be made where people are; therefore, if one area has twice as many people as another, it has twice the sales opportunity. Total retail sales are often used as an index of market potential for specific consumer products. Sales of the types of stores handling the product in question, for example, food stores, are probably a better index if available.

Disposable income is a general index often used to measure general potential for consumer goods. The number of families by income class is often better, especially for products that cater particularly to high or low income groups. Many analysts in developing market potentials for industrial products use the number of production workers in the market industries to measure the relative potential of different areas. Thus, a county employing 1,000 workers in a given industry would be rated as having twice the potential as one employing only 500.

Of course there are many series which can be used as indexes in given cases. All have one general weakness—it is hard to establish the relationship between the index series and the product at hand.

In some cases, this difficulty is overcome by comparing the particular company's sales with various possible index series. The index series most closely resembling the company sales pattern is used. The obvious weakness of this approach is that the net result is to tend to establish sales potentials for various markets in the same relative amounts that company sales have existed in the past—not in proportion to actual potential. This is not entirely true, since a series that matches the sales pattern in general may still point up specific areas that do not match.

If a close relationship does not exist between the index series and the company's sales, then the index series may give a mistaken impression of the relative potentials in various markets. Population, for example, fails to account for differences in buying power and, therefore, may not be a good index for many consumer goods. Retail sales tend to be concentrated in cities and to understate the buying power in rural areas. Sales by store types do not account for sales of "nontype" products; for example, many drug products are sold in grocery stores.

Multiple factor indexes.   All market potential indexes are not developed from a single series; some are combinations of several factors, occasionally as many as 20. Many of these indexes are developed by particular companies or industries to measure market potentials for their products. Others are developed by independent organizations, frequently publishers, as indexes of market potential for consumer products in general.

Special multiple factor indexes are designed to measure the relative potentials of different markets for a particular product. Such indexes have the advantage of taking into account several factors which influence the sales of the given product. When such indexes are constructed for specific products, it seems logical that they should measure potential relatively accurately. They have some pitfalls, however, which make them much less foolproof than they appear. Individuals preparing the index usually use their judgment in selecting the factors to combine. Whether this judgment is sound or not cannot be proven. Furthermore, who is to say how many factors should be used, or, once the factors to use have been determined, how to combine them?

As indicated above, many subjective decisions tend to be made in using the multiple factor procedure. Many such judgments are based on estimates of how close the indexes obtained correspond to actual sales results. If this comparison is used to select an index, one can argue that sales themselves might as well be used as a direct index; that is, if sales data are available for purposes of comparison, they are also available for use as a direct index. They would be superior to the other index if the sign of accuracy in the other index is its similarity to actual sales. A multiple factor index, however, may correspond in general with the sales pattern, but may still show specific areas that do not correspond.

Multiple regression analysis is frequently used to eliminate some of the subjective aspects of the multiple factor method such as determining the relative importance of alternative factors and the weights to be assigned each factor. But since the dependent variable (the geographical sales potential) is not known, it is not possible to obtain an estimate of the regression equation. To overcome this problem analysts frequently resort to company sales as a substitute for sales potentials.

General multiple factor indexes have been developed by a number of organizations. They usually are constructed as indexes of consumer purchasing power and are presumed to be indexes of market potential for consumer goods in general.

The best-known general index of this type is the *Sales Management Buying Power Index.*[6] This index is constructed from three factors—income, retail sales, and population. Income is weighted 5, sales 3, and population 2. For each county in the United States income, retail sales, and population are reduced to percentages of the U.S. total. These percentages are weighted as indicated above, then summed, and the total divided by 10 (the sum of weights). This gives an index for each county as a percent of the U.S. total. General indexes of this type differ from special indexes only in the fact that they are designed for use with many products rather than with one specific product. Presumably, this makes these general indexes more a measure of real market potential instead of merely a measure of a particular firm's past sales distribution.

Comparisons of different general indexes, however, show many significant variations in the potentials for the same markets. How does one pick the index to use in this dilemma? One solution is to compare the indexes with actual sales and to select the one which most closely approximates sales. But in this situation, one is again partially measuring sales potential by past sales.

A major weakness of the general index is that it is general; that is, it is not designed to measure the potential for a specific product. This assumes that the relative market potential in a given area is the same for all consumer products. This, of course, is not true. Air conditioners have a larger potential in hot climates, overcoats in cold; automobiles sell best where income is high, potatoes do not. Thus, while general indexes are available for quick and easy use, they have little else to recommend them over special indexes.

Use of surveys to determine potentials. This procedure consists of projecting sample survey results to the total market through the use of published market data. With industrial products, the Standard Industrial Classification (SIC) system provides a unique and effective way of projecting survey data.

Because the Standard Industrial Classification system (SIC) as developed by the federal government is by far the most widely used system of industrial classification, it is described here in some detail.

The SIC system is intended to cover the entire field of economic activity: agriculture; forestry and fisheries; mining; construction; manufacturing; transportation; communication; electricity, gas, and sanitary services; wholesale and retail trade; finance, insurance, and real estate; services; and government. Reporting units are establishments, *not* legal entities or companies. Each establishment is classified according to its major activity. The SIC distinguishes two broad classes of establishments—operating establishments or economic units which produce goods or services *and* central administrative offices and auxiliary units which manage or provide services

---

[6] "Survey of Buying Power," *Sales and Marketing Management* (July 23, 1979).

for other establishments of the same company. The latter type is only partly measured by the SIC system.

All manufacturing industries are combined into about 20 major groups, 150 subgroups, and 450 industries. The following is an illustration:[7]

Group no. 358—Service industry machines.

Industry no. 3581—Automatic merchandising machines. Includes establishments primarily engaged in manufacturing automatic merchandise units, also referred to as vending machines (excluding music, amusement, or gaming machines) and coin-operated mechanisms for such machines.

Firms which are grouped together in the SIC system have a considerable amount in common. The advantage of using this system is that the government publishes a wide variety of data by such groupings (for example, the Census of Manufactures) and the classification has been kept reasonably current to reflect changes in the American manufacturing scene. But the system is not without its drawbacks.

1. When an establishment produces two or more products, the SIC is based on the *principal* product which is so determined on the basis of sales. Thus, the data on the primary product are "inflated."
2. When an establishment is integrated (produces a component part), it is not shown as part of the industry which produces the component part.
3. When an establishment is part of a company complex which engages in centralized buying, the fact is not taken into account in the SIC data.
4. When a firm makes a specialized product which is not important enough to constitute an industry, it may be grouped with producers of other unrelated types of products in a miscellaneous category (for example, furniture casters are classified in SIC 3429, "Hardware, not otherwise classified").

The need to relate SIC groups to geographical areas can be met through the use of the federal government publication entitled *County Business Patterns,* which contains statistics based on information reported under the Federal Old Age and Survivors Insurance Program. Data are presented by SIC within counties on the number of employees, payrolls, total number of establishments, and number of establishments by employment size. Only for the large counties is the information given for the 150 industry subgroups—otherwise the data are limited to the 20 major industry groups.

---

[7] For a detailed presentation of the SIC system, see the Office of Management and Budget, *Standard Industrial Classification Manual* (Washington, D.C.: U.S. Government Printing Office, 1972).

In the survey procedure researchers use mail, telephone, or personal interviews to obtain information on purchases made by firms which have been identified as belonging to the appropriate SIC categories. This information is then projected to the universe of all firms in those SIC categories.

The following steps illustrate the use of the survey method to determine potentials for an industrial product using the SIC system:

1. From a sample of companies within each of the industry classes that could conceivably buy the product, determine the amount of the product purchased and the number of employees for each company. (See columns 1–4 in Table 22–3.)
2. Using the sample data, compute average purchases per worker for each SIC group. (See column 5 in Table 22–3.)
3. Multiply the average purchases per worker in each SIC group by the total number of workers in that group. This gives an estimate of the national market potential for each SIC group. (See colums 5–7 in Table 22–3.)
4. Allocate the national market potential for each SIC group among the various counties according to the proportion of that SIC group workers in each county. Thus, if Los Angeles County employs 10 percent of all the workers in a given SIC group, Los Angeles will have a potential of 10 percent of the national potential represented by that SIC group.

The same general procedure can be used to estimate market potential in a single market. Separate potentials for each SIC group in the single market can be estimated and then added to give a total potential for the market area. Table 22–4 illustrates this for the Chicago market. The potential for Chicago ($588,663) represents 11.6 percent of the national market.

As might be expected, it is more difficult to use the survey approach to determine market potentials for consumer goods than for industrial goods. Buying intention studies are typically limited to major purchase items for obvious reasons. Even so, their reliability can be questioned because of the assumptions made regarding future conditions under which the purchase will or will not be made.

The procedure for estimating market potentials for consumer goods using the survey method is essentially the same as for industrial goods. Purchase data for the specific item are obtained via a sample and correlated with family characteristics information; for example, it may be determined that families with incomes of less than $15,000 a year buy $112 of the product, families with incomes of between $15,000 and $25,000 buy $128, and families with incomes of over $25,000 buy $142 of the product. Since family income data can be obtained at the county level, the sample results can be easily projected to a national level and, in so doing, the relative worth of each county and major city are also determined.

TABLE 22–3. Example of market potential calculation for product Y using market survey approach for national area, P. A. Whitman Manufacturing Co.

(1)	(2)	(3)	(4) Market survey results	(5)	(6)	(7)
SIC	Effective industries	Product purchases	Number of workers	Average purchases per worker	National market number of workers	Estimated national market potential
3611	Electric measuring	$ 1,600	3,200	$ 0.50	34,913	$ 17,456
3612	Power transformers	50,150	4,616	10.86	42,587	462,494
3621	Motors, generators	28,400	10,896	2.61	119,330	311,451
3622	Electric industrial controls	40,100	4,678	8.57	46,805	401,118
3631	Household cooking equipment	2,600	2,104	1.24	23,502	29,142
3632	Home refrigerators	149,600	5,215	28.69	47,981	1,376,574
3633	Home laundry machines	35,200	3,497	10.07	35,493	357,414
3634	Minor electric appliances	1,200	3,208	0.37	31,218	11,550
3635	Vacuum cleaners	1,875	402	4.66	4,572	21,305
3636	Sewing machines	600	912	0.66	8,182	5,400
3639	Appliances, NEC	225	1,100	0.20	9,029	1,805
3661	Telephone and telegraph equipment	65,500	6,451	10.15	62,345	632,801
3662	Radio and TV equipment	132,100	6,889	19.18	67,137	1,287,687
3693	X ray	14,000	491	28.51	5,725	163,219
	Total	$523,150				$5,079,416

Column
(1), (2) Four-digit SIC industries making up the industrial market for the product.
(3) Dollar value, classified by industries, of purchases of product Y as reported by those plants included in the survey.
(4) Number of production workers as reported by those plants included in the survey.
(5) Average dollar value of product Y purchases per production worker for each effective SIC industry. Computed by dividing column 3 by column 4.
(6) Number of production workers for the entire U.S. industrial market for the given SIC industries. "Basic Marketing Data on Metal-working," *Iron Age* (1957), p. 31.
(7) The resultant estimated national market potential for the total market. Computed by multiplying column 6 by column 5.

Source: Francis E. Hummel, *Market and Sales Potentials* (New York: Ronald Press, 1961), p. 110.

TABLE 22–4. Example of market potential calculation for product Y using market survey approach for Chicago, Illinois area, P. A. Whitman Manufacturing Co.

(1) SIC	(2) Effective industries	(3) Market survey national average purchases per worker	(4) Chicago market number of workers	(5) Estimated Chicago market potential
3611	Electric measuring	$ 0.50	1,168	$ 584
3612	Power transformers	10.86	2,464	26,759
3621	Motors, generators	2.61	3,293	8,594
3622	Electric industrial controls	8.57	6,084	52,139
3631	Household cooking equipment	1.24	2,055	2,548
3632	Home refrigerators	28.69	5,400	154,926
3633	Home laundry machines	10.07	495	4,984
3634	Minor electric appliances	0.37	8,454	3,127
3635	Vacuum cleaners	4.66	760	3,541
3636	Sewing machines	0.66	850	561
3639	Appliances, NEC	0.20	1,639	327
3661	Telephone and telegraph equipment	10.15	27,681	280,962
3662	Radio and television equipment ...	19.18	1,894	36,326
3693	X ray	28.51	466	13,285
	Total			$588,663

Column
(1), (2) Four-digit SIC industries making up the industrial market for the product.
(3)   Average dollar value of product Y purchases per production worker for each effective SIC industry as determined from market survey.
(4)   Number of production workers for Chicago trading area for the given SIC industries. "Basic Marketing Data on Metalworking," *Iron Age* (1957), pp. 58–59.
(5)   The resultant estimated Chicago area market potential. Computed by multiplying column *3* by column *4*.
    Source: Francis E. Hummel, *Market and Sales Potentials* (New York: Ronald Press, 1961), p. 112.

SALES FORECASTING

The sales forecast is the factor around which most business planning centers. Such important areas of decision-making as production and inventory scheduling, planning of plant and equipment investments, manpower requirements, raw material purchases, advertising outlays, sales force expenditures, and cash flow needs are dependent on the sales forecast. It follows that any significant error in the forecast will have far-reaching and serious consequences. For planners in general ". . . the world has never looked as bewildering as it does today. The very uncertainties, from the clouded economic outlook to the energy crisis, that make sophisticated forward planning more vital than ever before, also make accurate planning that much more difficult."[8]

Sales forecasting is a complex subject which uses a variety of concepts

---

[8] "Corporate Planning: Piercing Future Fog in the Executive Suite," *Business Week* (April 28, 1975):46.

and techniques.[9] Because it is important to business planning, and because the traditionally used techniques have been found wanting, researchers have turned to new techniques, most of which are highly sophisticated and require that a great deal of historical data be processed on a computer. Unfortunately, these newer and more complex techniques do not appear to be more successful than the traditional forecasting methods.[10] For this reason, and because the newer techniques are too complex to discuss here, only the more traditional approaches will be described. These can be categorized as being either subjective or objective.

Subjective methods

One of the more simple methods of forecasting sales is to use the judgments or opinions of knowledgeable individuals within the company. Such forecasts can use inputs from a number of different organizational levels, for example, executives, regional managers, and even sales representatives. Probably the most common forecasts in use today are the forecasts made by executives.

Jury of executive opinion. Some firms begin with executive forecasts in what is known as a jury of executive opinion. Each of a number of executives makes an independent forecast of sales for the next period, usually a year. These forecasts are more than just guesses. These executives have considerable factual data available to them, and presumably they possess mature judgment.

Once the various executives have made their estimates, some method of reconciling the differences must be found. The chief executive of the company may consider the various estimates and make a final decision. A better procedure is to bring the group of executives together to discuss their estimates. Discussion may bring out new ideas and lead some individuals to modify their previous estimates. If the group cannot come to general agreement, the chief executive will have to make the decision.

The jury method has the advantage of simplicity and of representing a number of different viewpoints. Its chief disadvantage is that it is based on opinions. The opinions are all apt to be influenced in a similar direction by general business conditions and conditions in the specific company; that is, the executives are apt to become overly optimistic or overly pessimistic together.

One study found that the total forecast error of subjective forecasts resulted from two effects—the error associated with the expertise of the

---

[9] A thorough discussion of these techniques is found in Vithala R. Rao and James E. Cox, Jr., *Sales Forecasting Methods: A Survey of Recent Developments* (Cambridge, Mass.: Marketing Science Institute, 1978).

[10] See the evaluation made by Spyros Makridakis and Steven C. Wheelwright, "Forecasting: Issues and Challenges for Marketing Management," *Journal of Marketing* (October 1977):24–38, but esp. pp. 30–33.

individuals involved and the contagion effect; that is, the tendency of individuals to be systematically biased by factors which influenced all their forecasts.

The study concluded that subjective forecasts should be studied on a trial basis to determine the relative magnitude of the two error sources. If the expertise error is relatively large, then the forecasters can be provided with more information about the individual components of the forecast—for example, trend data on key accounts. If the contagion effect is relatively high then . . . "management should be wary of the use of supplementary information of a general nature. Economic indicators . . . are especially likely to introduce this type of bias if forecasters are urged to consider them."[11]

Sales force estimates.   Another common method of forecasting is by means of sales force estimates. The actual process by which a "final" sales forecast is derived varies substantially among firms. If the process starts with sales representatives they may be asked to state the probabilities of selling various quantities of each product or product group to each present and prospective customer in their territories. It is probable that they will receive inputs designed to help them make better forecasts from a variety of people including sales supervisors, product managers, company economists, and marketing researchers. This help will include projections of the general economic climate, activities of competitors, and the planned activities of the firm.

In some cases sales representatives may be given a forecast for their territories and asked to "adjust it" or they may be given a range within which sales will probably fall and asked to indicate a most likely figure. Branch managers may go over sales representatives' estimates and discuss changes with them or they may simply adjust the forecasts according to their own judgment and pass them "up"—either on an aggregated or disaggregated basis—to higher level management where they are reviewed again and an ultimate decision made as to the forecast to accept.

For short-term forecasts (for example, quarterly), it is likely that sales representatives can do a better job than can be done using more sophisticated objective methods—particularly during times of great change. Sales representatives' knowledge of the probable demand of major accounts for the product over the next several months is about the only basis on which a firm—especially those selling industrial products—can adjust its plans to the dynamics of the marketplace.

Use of the sales force to prepare forecasts has the obvious advantage of involving all sales representatives and making them feel responsible for achieving the sales target. But their estimates also have severe limitations in that the sales representatives are hardly disinterested parties; that is, it is very much to their advantage to be held responsible for conservative sales goals.

---

[11] Richard Staelin and Ronald E. Turner, "Error in Judgmental Sales Forecasts: Theory and Results," *Journal of Marketing Research* (February 1973):15–16.

Objective methods

Objective methods of forecasting are statistical methods which range in complexity from relatively simple trend extrapolations to the use of sophisticated mathematical models. More and more companies are tending toward the use of advanced methods in which the computer correlates a host of relationships.

Trend analysis via extrapolation.   A simple objective method of forecasting is the extrapolation of past sales trends. In this method the assumption is made that sales for the coming time period will be equal to the current level *or* that sales will change to the same degree that sales changed from the prior period to the current period. Such simple predictive models are more reliable than might at first be thought—especially for very short periods of time (a month or a quarter) under stable conditions. This forecasting method assumes that some past pattern in sales can be identified and measured, and that it reflects accurately what will happen in the coming period. Thus, the forecasting task centers on quantifying the trend or tendency in such a way as to "project" it into the future. For example, using historical data on total births per 1,000 and current population statistics, it is possible to forecast the number of births in the coming year. In undertaking any kind of trend analysis, the researcher must keep in mind that each time series is made up of four factors: long-term trend, cyclical variations, seasonal variations, and irregular variations. If the pattern of these factors is at all well developed, each of them can be separated from the other. The first three (trend, cyclical, and seasonal) can then be projected to determine the sales pattern for the future.

Regression analysis.   Regression analysis can be used in sales forecasting to measure the relationship between a company's sales and other economic series. For example, automobile manufacturers may find their sales are related to personal income—when incomes go up their car sales go up and when income goes down their sales drop. To use this relationship in forecasting car sales, the manufacturers must determine the degree of relationship. If income rises 10 percent, do car sales rise 10 percent, 30 percent, 2 percent or what? Regression techniques enable the producers to estimate the relationship between changes in income and changes in car sales.

One may wonder how the discovery of a relationship between sales and one or several other factors helps to forecast sales. The problem is merely shifted from forecasting sales to forecasting the other factors. However, this indirect approach has two advantages. First, a number of other factors such as general economic series and personal income are forecast by many people. A particular company then can take advantage of the forecasts of a number of experts. On the average, this should enable the company to make a better forecast of the related series than it could of sales. Second, in some cases a lead-lag relationship may be found between a series and the company's sales. Income changes may precede changes in auto sales by three months. When such a relationship exists, the correlation with the related series has a direct advantage. A building supply company, for example, has found a high correlation between the sales of its products and building contracts awarded; however, sales seem to lag five months behind building contracts.

Regression analysis has the advantage of being more objective than the previous methods discussed. If sales are related to a widely used series, forecasters have the advantage of many opinions to aid them in forecasting the other series. Another advantage of the method is that it can be done by an office staff or a consultant, thus leaving the executives and sales organization free to carry on their regular operations. In general, regression forecasts are considered highly accurate for short terms such as two years or less.

Survey methods.   This approach to forecasting is the least used because of its expense, the time required (particularly when done by mail), and its problems of reliability. Surveys at the consumer level dealing with intentions to buy have not, as yet, contributed significantly to accurate forecasting. More success has been obtained with the prediction of capital expenditures by business firms through surveys conducted by the U.S. Department of Commerce. Surveys can, however, be used to obtain information which will be useful in making the forecast; for example, the number of households owning and the number not owning a microwave oven may be useful to a microwave oven manufacturer. Similarly, a company may find it useful to survey its customers to determine their buying intentions in the coming period.

SALES ANALYSIS

Sales analysis is a term which is used to mean analysis of actual sales results. Sales analyses usually are made on one or more of four bases—territory, product, customer, and order size. The objective of these analyses is to find the areas of strength and weakness, the products which are producing the greatest and the least volume, the customers who furnish the most productive sales results, and the size of order which accounts for the majority of the firm's business. Such information enables a company to concentrate its sales efforts where they will bring the greatest return.

Each of the four bases for analysis will be considered in turn. The general approach is the same in each case.

Sales analysis by territory

The invoice is usually the basic sales record. It contains the following data which are essential to sales analyses: (1) customer's name, (2) customer's location, (3) products sold, (4) quantity of each item sold, (5) price per unit, (6) total dollar sales per product, and (7) total dollar amount of order. In some cases it may be desirable to add further information about the customer such as size, type of business, user or wholesaler, chain or independent, and so on.

The first step is to decide on what geographical control unit to use. The county is the typical choice because (*a*) counties can be combined to form larger units such as sales territories and (*b*) market potentials are usually developed on a county basis since it is the smallest unit for which many items of data are available. Thus, it will be possible to compare actual sales in a county with the county's market potential.

Both sales and market potential are then tabulated by territorial units. Those territories in which sales fall below potential can then be given special attention. Is competition unusually strong in these areas? Has less selling effort been put there? Is the sales force weak? Studies of these points will help the company bolster its weak areas. Sales efforts can be concentrated where it will do the most good.

Sales analysis by product

Over the years a company's product line tends to become overcrowded unless strong continuing action is taken to eliminate those items which no longer are profitable. By eliminating weak products and concentrating on strong ones a company can often increase its profits substantially. An example is Hunt Foods which over an 11-year period reduced its product lines from 30 items to 3 items and yet increased sales from $15 to $120 million.[12]

As in the analysis of territories, deciding what product units to use in product analysis is a problem. At one extreme a firm might classify products only by such general groupings as industrial and consumer. At the other extreme, a firm might classify separately each product variation by color, size, and so on. Sales of the more general groupings of products may be easier to analyze, but the poor sales performance of certain individual products may go unnoticed due to the combining of a number of products into one group. Analysis by detailed breakdowns is more expensive, but is more apt to show the strong and weak products in a way that will permit constructive action.

A product abandonment decision must take into account such variables as market-share trends, contribution margins, effect of volume on product profitability, and degree of product complementarity with other items in the line. Two analysts have constructed a time-sharing computerized model (PRESS) which takes the above types of data into account. Its goal is to assist management in its product deletion decisions. It does so by dealing with the total product line. Data inputs consist of standard cost accounting and market data while the outputs show the value (typically in the form of ratios) of each product in the line. This model is particularly of value to a

---

[12] Philip Kotler, "Phasing Out Weak Products," *Harvard Business Review* (March–April 1965):109.

multiproduct firm where some degree of complementarity exists between products and where individual products vary substantially in their projected growth rates.[13]

Product analysis may be particularly effective when combined with territory analysis. Such a study may show that while territory A is above quota in total sales, it is very weak in sales of product 2. Combined analysis of this type makes it much easier to spot the places where action should be taken.

Sales analysis by customer

Procedures similar to those described above may be used to analyze sales by customers. Such analyses typically show that a relatively small percentage of customers accounts for a large percentage of sales. Distribution cost accounting should then be applied to determine the smallest customer it is profitable to keep on the books. By dropping customers smaller than this size, the firm can improve its profitability. In many cases, analyses of this sort combined with a study of sales calls will show that as much time is spent on the small accounts as on the large. Shifting some of that sales effort to the larger accounts may well increase sales.

Analysis by customer combined with analysis by territory and product may be particularly helpful in "pinpointing" weak spots in the sales program. Some salesmen may not be developing sales with a certain type of customer or product which has proven profitable in other territories. When this is discovered, remedial action can be taken because the precise point of weakness is known.

Sales analysis by size of order

Sales analysis by size of order may identify orders (and customers) which are not profitable. For example, certain customers may place frequent orders, each for a relatively small quantity. If the customers also require a great deal of service and attention by the sales representatives, the cost of securing and handling each order may be high. If cost accounting data are available, it is possible to identify if such orders are incurring a loss. This analysis may be extended to find territories, products, and customers where small orders are prevalent. This may lead to setting a minimum order size, to training sales representatives to develop larger orders, or to dropping certain territories, products, or customers.

Dunne and Wolk report the application of such an analysis to a small appliance manufacturer, which incurred a loss of $8,695 on sales of almost $3 million.[14] Sales were analyzed by type of product, by geographic region,

---

[13] Paul W. Hamelman and Edward M. Mazze, "Improving Product Abandonment Decisions," *Journal of Marketing* (April 1972):20–26, and James V. Davis, "The Strategic Divestment Decision," *Long Range Planning* (February 1974):15–26.

[14] Patrick M. Dunne and Harry I. Wolk, "Marketing Cost Analysis: A Modularized Approach," *Journal of Marketing* (July 1977):83–94.

by type of customer, and by size of order. The results showed that one product yielded about 50 percent more profit contribution than the company's other product. They also showed that the eastern region yielded about 25 percent more profit contribution than the western region. Most important, however, was that the total four-way analysis (by product, region, customer, and size of order) showed that the company was particularly weak in the sale of one product (blenders) to one type of customer (wholesalers) in one region (western).

Distribution cost analysis

This type of analysis employs various combinations of the sales analyses discussed above. It is used to determine the costs associated with specific marketing activities and to determine the profitability of different market segments, products, and customer classes. The use of this technique can produce dramatic results. In one case profits were increased 300 percent, and in another marketing expenses were cut from 22.8 to 11.5 percent of sales and a net loss of 2.9 percent was turned into a profit of 15 percent. The latter was accomplished by shifting some marketing effort from the 68 percent of the company's accounts that had been unprofitable.[15]

More and more firms are using some form of contribution accounting to determine the profitability of products, channel units, and market segments. Such a method first assigns all variable marketing and production costs to a product. Variable production costs are direct labor and materials. The variable marketing costs are due to credit, shipping, sales commissions, merchandising, and advertising. Some firms go further and allocate certain fixed joint costs, but this should only be done when one can find a logical relationship between the assigned expenditure and the product sales. All questionable costs should be treated as overhead. While overhead must eventually be absorbed, the contribution method makes it more clear what will be gained or lost by adding or dropping a product or a customer.

Ultimately, the objective of any distribution cost analysis and the computation of potentials is to help the marketing manager make better decisions regarding how to allocate the firm's marketing resources. Since the potential in any area is a function of the number and worth of prospective customers, and since the cost analysis relates cost to scale of buying, the logical next step is to undertake a marginal analysis to determine which accounts within which areas represent the most likely units on which to exert additional pressure.

Since the response to marketing effort will vary by customer and by product, marketing managers must decide how their marketing efforts will

---

[15] Charles H. Sevin, "A Rational Approach to Marketing Cost Reduction," *Indiana Business Review* (June 1958):5–6.

be allocated among customers and products. Thus, marketing managers must have knowledge of each major account, including its potential by product. They must also know if they are getting a greater or lesser share of an account's potential, and whether they have been applying increasing or decreasing amounts of marketing effort to the account. Through ex post facto types of analyses—or through experiments—managers can estimate the likely results of applying additional marketing efforts to accounts of certain sizes, given the share of the account's potential which has already been obtained by the firm. For example, one company determined that with accounts representing $100,000 and over annual potential, it was most unlikely that they could obtain better than a 30 percent "share" regardless of the nature and magnitude of the inputs.

Analyses of this type with consumer products are more difficult than with industrial products. However, an example of one approach to distribution cost analysis with a consumer product is shown in Table 22–5. In this table the researcher has attempted to identify marketing costs and profit contributions by market areas. Some explanation is necessary to understand the terminology in the table. The following accounting format was used to determine the "gross margin," and "contribution to earnings" shown at the top of Table 22–5.

Sales		100
Standard variable distribution costs	5	
Standard variable manufacturing costs	40	45
Gross margin		55
Advertising	11	
Sales promotion	10	21
Contribution to earnings		34

Note that the objective is to isolate three important measures: (1) gross margin; (2) the advertising and sales promotion expenditures that caused, or led to, the gross margin; and (3) the contribution to earnings. By isolating these three measures, management can identify the response (the gross margin) of individual markets to the marketing effort (advertising and promotion expenditures) used in those markets. The resulting contribution to earnings can also be identified.

Looking at the data in Table 22–5, management might observe the following:

1. In area A, advertising and promotion expenses of $100,000 produced $260,000 of contribution to earnings while in area E advertising and promotion expenses of $400,000 produced only $280,000.
2. Area A had 4.4 percent of the firm's gross margin and 3.1 percent of the advertising and sales promotion expenses. Area E had 8.4 percent

TABLE 22–5. Distribution cost analysis by market ($000)

	Area A	Area B	Area C	Area D	Area E	F+G....n	U.S. total
Gross margin	$360	$770	$620	$850	$680		$8,210
Advertising	42	203	165	290	276		1,683
Sales promotion	58	172	130	191	124		1,507
Contribution to earnings	$260	$395	$325	$369	$280		$5,020
Financial analysis							
Percent of total gross margin	4.4%	9.4%	7.6%	10.4%	8.4%		100.00%
Percent advertising and sales promotion	3.1%	11.5%	9.2%	15.0%	12.4%		100.00%
Incremental gross margin, this year versus last year (loss)	($53)	($50)	($75)	$115	$25		$744
Incremental advertising and sales promotion, this year versus last year (decrease)	($20)	($85)	$10	$165	$100		$354
Incremental contribution to earnings (decrease)	($33)	$35	($85)	($50)	($75)		$390

	Area A		Area B		Area C		Area D		Area E		U.S. total	
Market research data	This year	Last year	This year	Last year	This year	Last year	This year	Last year	This year	Last year	This year	Last year
Total dollar retail market	$1,790	$1,810	$6,150	$6,175	$2,590	$2,680	$7,525	$7,395	$5,900	$4,950	$54,650	$56,000
Percent share of retail market	50.2%	51.9%	35.6%	36.1%	48.6%	50.3%	38.7%	32.4%	42.9%	46.1%	45.8%	44.6%
Percent distribution	88.3%	88.2%	96.2%	96.2%	97.9%	98.1%	98.1%	97.9%	96.4%	96.6%	96.2%	96.2%

Source: Adapted from Richard A. Feder, "How to Measure Marketing Performance," *Harvard Business Review* 43 (May–June 1965): 137.

of the gross margin and 12.4 percent of the advertising and promotion expenses.

3. Area A had a decrease of $53,000 in gross margin from last year and a decrease of $20,000 in advertising and promotion expenditures. Contribution to earnings dropped $33,000.

4. Area A is a relatively small market (total retail market $1,790,000), in which the firm has a large market share (50.2 percent) which decreased slightly, and has a low distribution (88.3 percent) which increased slightly.

These data indicate that area A's decline in gross margin, earnings contribution and market share occurred along with a period-to-period decrease in area A's marketing expenditures. The data also show that area A makes a large contribution to gross margin (4.4 percent) for only a relatively small portion of total marketing expenditures (3.1 percent). This suggests that area A might profitably use an increase in marketing expenditures rather than a decrease. On the other hand, area E had only a small increase in gross margin, even with a very large increase in marketing expenditures. Area E also is contributing only 8.4 percent of total gross margin, but is receiving 12.4 percent of total marketing expenditures. This suggests that area E should not be given an increase in marketing expenditures, but a decrease.

SUMMARY

Market and sales analysis include market potential analysis, sales forecasting, and sales analysis.

Market potential analysis involves the development of potentials for individual markets. Market potentials are used in establishing sales territories, allocating marketing effort, and setting sales quotas. Market potentials may be estimated in two major ways: (1) through direct sales data or (2) through corollary data.

Sales forecasts are attempts to predict a company's sales of a specific product in a specific market or region during a specific period of time. Sales forecasts are important because they serve as the basic guide for planning within the company. Methods of forecasting vary from estimates made by executives or the sales force to more complex procedures involving trend analysis and regression.

Sales analyses are useful for identifying strong and weak points in the company's sales programs. Typically, sales analyses are performed by comparing the sales and selling costs associated with different territories, products, customers, or order sizes. Sales analyses made on various combinations of territories, products, customers, and order sizes are especially useful, as are sales analyses made in conjunction with a distribution cost analysis.

Case 22–1
MILWAUKEE MACHINE COMPANY (B)*

Milwaukee Machine Company was a long-established, well-known manufacturer of machine tools—primarily turning machines and boring machines. These products were marketed throughout the United States through machinery distributors. The country was divided into 34 sales territories, each of which was assigned to one distributor. Annual sales fluctuated widely with the business cycle, but they averaged about $125 million.

Four different categories of turning machines made up the company line —engine lathes, turret lathes, automatic lathes, and chucking machines. Boring machines were all of one type, but varied in size from machines that would drill holes ¼″ in diameter to machines that bored holes 4″ in diameter. The average selling price per machine was $20,000.

When new management was installed in the company, it established ambitious growth objectives. This led to consideration of the distribution system and particularly to consideration of individual distributors. The company found it had no real basis for judging the quality of the job done by the various distributors. Data on sales by each distributor were available, but there was no information on the market potential in the different sales territories.

After consideration of this problem, the firm decided to conduct a research study to establish basic information about its markets which would enable it to appraise the work of its distributors, to assist the distributors to increase sales, and to provide a base for better marketing planning.

To define market segments by industry, the company checked all its sales for the last five years and classified the buyers by four-digit SIC codes. Industry publications were searched to identify industries conducting milling and boring operations and the *Standard Industrial Classification Manual* was reviewed in detail. All four-digit SICs which were known to be industries that did milling or boring were listed. In this manner, 211 four-digit SIC classifications were identified; they were grouped into 73 three-digit classifications.

Each of these industry segments was studied for its importance to the metal-working industry. This process identified a number of industries that were so small as machine tool customers as to be negligible. The remaining industries were regrouped into three-digit codes and ranked according to Milwaukee Machine's sales to them. The top 13 three-digit industry segments were found to account for 89.12 percent of Milwaukee Machine's sales of turning machines and 89.04 percent of its sales of boring machines.

Bureau of Census data showed a total of 91,702 plants in these industries

---

* Data provided by Management Research and Planning, Inc., Evanston, Ill.

and these plants were identified as the market for study purposes. Those plants with less than 20 employees were classified as small and those with 20 or more employees as large. There were 66,313 small plants (72.3 percent) and 25,389 large plants (27.7). More than two-thirds (69.1 percent) of these plants were manufacturing establishments, 12.6 percent were construction and contracting firms, and 18.3 percent were metal wholesale establishments.

The market for machine tools had two distinct portions—(1) the market for new tools because of the construction of new plants or the expansion of existing plants and (2) the market for replacement tools. Company officers estimated that sales divided about equally between these markets, but they considered this a rough estimate at best.

Census data showed the number of large plants (20 or more employees) in each county for each industry classification. County data were cumulated for sales districts and the percentage of all the large plants in the United States which was in each sales district was calculated. It was then assumed that each sales territory had the same percentage of large and small plants as did the nation as a whole.

With the number of large and small plants in each county established, the company set out to measure the average inventory of installed machines in each industry market on a national basis. A probability sample was selected from a listing of companies maintained by Dun & Bradstreet and a telephone survey was conducted with the sample plants. Six percent of the plants refused to provide information; similar-sized firms from the same industry classification were substituted. The following information was obtained from each plant participating in the survey:

1. Verification of industry and number of employees.
2. Number of turning machines installed in the plant by
    a. Type—engine lathes, turret lathes, automatic lathes, and chucking machines.
    b. Age of machines—5 years or less, 6 to 20 years, over 20 years.
    c. Manufacturer of each machine.
3. Number of boring machines installed in the plant by
    a. Size—under 1″ diameter, 1″–1.99″, 2.00″–2.99″, 3.00″ to 3.99″, and 4.00″ and over.
    b. Age of machine—5 years or less, 6 to 20 years, over 20 years.
    c. Manufacturer of each machine.
4. For the next turning machine the company would buy which manufacturer would be the first choice? For the next boring machine?

For each of the 13 industries the following calculations were made:

1. For large plants, the average number of:
    a. Turning machines.
        1. Total.

　　　2.　0–5 years of age.
　　b.　Boring machines.
　　　　1.　Total.
　　　　2.　0–5 years of age.
2.　For small plants, the average number of:
　　a.　Turning machines.
　　　　1.　Total.
　　　　2.　0–5 years of age.
　　b.　Boring machines.
　　　　1.　Total.
　　　　2.　0–5 years of age.

　　With a national average inventory per large and small plant in each industry and the number of both large and small plants in each territory, it was possible to project the total inventory of each type of machine in each of the two age brackets for each of the 13 industry groups for each territory. The industry totals were then added to give a total inventory of each type of machine by age group for each territory. Sales of each of these product groups were then compared to the inventory with results as shown in Tables 1 and 2.

　　The proportion of inventory of both types of machines combined which was accounted for by each of the 13 SIC industry groups within each sales territory was calculated and is shown in Table 3.

　　Tables 4 and 5 show the distribution of the national inventory of turning machines by type and boring machines by size, respectively, among the SIC groups. Reported brand preferences and distribution of the national inventory by brand were tabulated as in Tables 6 and 7.

TABLE 1. Inventory of all turning machines in use and Milwaukee brand sales of turning machines by age and sales territory

Territory	All turning machines			Turning machines 0–5 years old		
	Territory inventory	Milwaukee sales	Sales as percent of inventory	Territory inventory	Milwaukee sales	Sales as percent of inventory
A	1,500	466	31%	156	46	30%
B	2,828	445	16	374	83	22
C	145	48	33	17	8	47
D	397	109	27	69	27	39
E	822	309	38	56	40	71
F	789	207	26	77	20	26
G	597	207	35	65	23	35
H	3,881	996	26	351	134	38
I	937	215	23	82	29	35
J	179	98	55	21	13	62
K	391	62	16	54	10	19
L	4,785	601	13	489	100	20
M	368	60	16	79	15	19
N	1,808	482	27	196	54	28
O	925	208	23	117	16	14
P	208	33	16	24	9	38

Q	1,033	460	45	154	25	16
R	278	83	30	32	13	41
S	3,145	534	17	248	92	37
T	1,487	134	9	201	16	8
U	3,245	471	15	373	67	18
V	1,305	235	18	129	34	26
W	1,161	142	12	146	32	22
X	383	55	14	49	11	22
Y	227	93	41	21	8	38
Z	628	110	18	70	14	20
AA	735	128*	17	106	23	22
BB	192	236*	123*	20	20*	100*
CC	411	118	29	42	20	48
DD	307	59	19	38	8	21
EE	2,690	313	12	263	45	17
FF	577	52	9	85	14	17
GG	1,062	78	7	177	29	16
HH	371	65	18	42	15	36

* Milwaukee Machine Company sales should not have exceeded the total inventory for the territory, but that is what the data showed.

TABLE 2. Inventory of all boring machines in use and Milwaukee brand sales of boring machines by age and sales territory

Territory	All boring machines			Boring machines 0–5 years old		
	Territory inventory	Milwaukee sales	Sales as percent of inventory	Territory inventory	Milwaukee sales	Sales as percent of inventory
A	1,173	513	31%	151	58	30%
B	2,422	230	10	388	55	14
C	141	48	34	23	13	57
D	370	162	44	76	36	47
E	738	214	29	65	24	37
F	738	102	16	89	14	16
G	460	97	21	68	14	21
H	3,328	513	15	369	120	33
I	757	146	19	91	27	30
J	146	91	62	27	7	26
K	298	24	8	52	9	17
L	4,164	593	14	537	109	20
M	287	64	22	84	22	26
N	1,528	498	33	210	96	46
O	810	137	17	125	20	16
P	145	14	10	23	4	17

Q	779	48	6	162	25	15
R	246	47	19	31	5	16
S	2,469	449	18	307	78	25
T	1,146	150	13	250	45	18
U	2,991	257	9	435	55	13
V	1,020	142	14	144	17	12
W	961	81	8	151	32	21
X	287	40	14	44	6	14
Y	188	106	56	21	12	57
Z	400	65	16	57	6	11
AA	586	70	12	102	17	17
BB	163	233*	142*	20	14	70
CC	317	95	30	43	36	84
DD	237	38	16	41	5	12
EE	2,343	180	8	287	37	13
FF	415	56	14	84	14	17
GG	840	79	9	189	24	13
HH	314	48	15	46	10	22

* Milwaukee Machine Company sales should not have exceeded the total inventory for the territory, but that is what the data showed.

TABLE 3. Percentage distribution of combined turning and boring machine inventory by industry within each territory

Terri-tory	Standard Industrial Classifications													
	176	251	331	344	343	352	354	356	358	361	364	371	509	Total
A	8.5	2.2	3.9	18.9	12.1	4.7	4.7	1.9	5.9	1.3	2.1	2.9	30.9	100%
B	7.7	4.9	2.8	15.9	10.1	7.5	7.6	3.0	9.4	1.0	1.5	5.3	23.3	100
C	12.3	7.6	2.8	13.7	9.0	9.7	9.7	4.1	11.7	2.1	2.8	8.3	6.2	100
D	7.1	—	6.0	24.5	15.6	8.6	8.8	3.5	0.8	1.3	2.0	6.3	5.5	100
E	13.8	4.4	7.8	20.8	13.3	6.7	6.7	2.7	8.3	2.3	3.5	2.2	7.5	100
F	17.6	7.3	2.8	14.7	9.2	3.8	3.8	1.5	4.8	1.6	2.5	3.9	26.5	100
G	19.1	5.2	1.5	11.2	7.0	5.0	5.0	2.0	6.4	1.2	1.8	5.2	29.4	100
H	10.5	7.0	2.8	16.4	10.4	5.1	5.1	2.0	6.3	2.5	4.0	2.6	25.3	100
I	10.7	4.7	3.6	13.1	8.4	7.1	7.3	2.9	9.0	2.2	3.5	2.6	24.9	100
J	29.6	5.0	1.7	12.8	7.8	4.5	4.5	1.7	5.6	1.1	1.7	6.7	17.3	100
K	17.3	5.1	1.8	12.8	8.2	5.4	5.6	2.3	6.9	1.0	1.5	3.3	28.8	100
L	13.3	9.2	2.0	14.0	8.9	3.8	3.8	1.5	4.7	3.6	5.8	2.3	27.1	100
M	21.7	10.3	1.6	6.5	3.8	3.0	3.3	1.4	3.8	1.6	2.7	4.9	35.4	100
N	12.6	6.7	3.6	13.7	8.7	6.6	6.7	2.7	8.2	2.0	3.2	3.4	21.9	100
O	12.3	5.0	3.5	16.4	10.5	5.5	5.5	2.3	6.9	2.2	3.5	5.7	20.7	100
P	32.7	2.9	1.9	13.0	8.2	2.9	2.9	1.0	3.4	0.5	1.0	3.8	26.8	100
Q	25.0	8.1	0.6	10.6	6.8	1.7	1.7	0.7	2.2	1.3	1.9	4.6	34.8	100
R	14.7	6.5	3.2	12.2	7.9	8.6	9.0	3.6	11.2	2.2	3.6	4.7	12.6	100
S	11.7	6.5	2.6	13.5	8.6	3.5	3.5	1.4	4.4	2.0	3.2	3.1	36.0	100
T	28.2	11.6	1.3	7.9	5.0	3.4	3.5	1.4	4.3	1.2	2.0	2.4	27.8	100
U	17.2	8.2	2.2	14.4	9.2	4.0	4.0	1.6	5.0	3.2	5.1	6.5	19.4	100
V	25.1	7.5	2.0	11.1	7.0	3.4	3.4	1.4	4.3	1.8	2.8	3.6	26.6	100
W	18.4	9.4	1.6	12.7	8.1	4.0	4.0	1.6	5.0	1.2	1.9	4.2	27.9	100
X	35.2	6.8	1.8	9.9	6.3	2.9	2.9	1.0	3.4	1.3	1.8	4.4	22.3	100
Y	13.7	1.8	5.7	13.7	8.4	7.0	7.0	2.6	8.8	3.5	5.3	4.4	18.1	100
Z	20.9	2.1	2.4	8.9	5.7	4.5	4.5	1.8	5.4	0.8	1.1	2.7	39.2	100
AA	18.4	4.9	1.6	11.8	7.5	7.1	7.2	2.9	8.8	1.8	2.7	3.4	21.9	100
BB	12.5	6.8	1.0	15.1	9.4	8.9	9.4	3.6	11.5	2.1	2.6	—	16.1	100
CC	21.7	5.4	2.4	10.9	6.8	3.6	3.6	1.5	4.4	1.0	1.7	6.3	30.7	100
DD	18.6	4.2	2.3	13.0	8.1	4.6	4.6	0.3	5.5	1.3	2.0	4.9	30.6	100
EE	10.7	4.8	3.1	17.5	11.1	6.1	6.1	2.4	7.5	3.1	4.9	2.7	20.0	100
FF	30.0	3.8	1.0	10.1	6.4	3.8	3.8	1.6	4.7	0.5	0.9	5.7	27.7	100
GG	23.1	9.0	1.9	12.1	7.7	2.7	2.7	1.1	3.4	1.0	1.6	4.0	29.7	100
HH	23.1	8.9	6.2	17.5	11.0	2.7	2.7	1.1	3.5	0.8	1.1	3.2	18.2	100

TABLE 4. Percentage distribution of turning machine national inventory by industry by type of turning machine

Industry SIC groups	Engine lathes	Turret lathes	Automatic lathes	Chucking machines
176	4.3%	5.4%	—	—
251	27.1	12.5	—	*
331	5.7	5.4	10.7%	*
344	7.7	9.7	14.3	*
343	8.4	8.6	—	—
352	6.4	10.1	25.0	*
354	3.3	1.6	3.6	*
356	3.7	7.0	7.1	—
358	6.0	5.1	—	—
361	4.0	5.4	1.8	—
364	13.4	12.5	1.8	*
371	2.3	6.6	3.6	—
509	7.7	10.1	32.1	*
Total	100%	100%	100%	100%

* For chucking machines the sample size was not large enough to be meaningful. Machines were found in industries marked with an asterisk.

TABLE 5. Percentage distribution of boring machine national inventory by industry by size of boring machine

Industry SIC group	Under 1" diameter	1.0" to 1.9" diameter	2.0" to 2.9" diameter	3.0" and over diameter
176	2.4%	3.7%	0.9%	—
251	34.6	37.8	21.4	—
331	3.1	1.6	8.5	*
344	4.6	7.4	17.9	*
343	8.3	5.9	4.3	*
352	6.4	7.4	14.5	*
354	1.5	0.5	—	—
356	5.5	4.8	1.7	—
358	6.1	3.2	2.6	—
361	0.9	10.1	6.8	*
364	20.5	10.1	11.1	*
371	3.4	4.3	6.8	*
509	2.8	3.2	3.4	*
Total	100%	100%	100%	100%

* For the largest size boring machine the sample size was not large enough to be meaningful. Machines were found in industries marked with an asterisk.

TABLE 6. Maufacturer preferred for next turning and boring machines bought

Manufacturer	Turning machines		Boring machines	
	Number	Percent	Number	Percent
Milwaukee Machine Co.	31	36.0	24	24.5
Victoria	22	25.6	28	28.6
Smith, Oberdig, & Crenshaw	4	4.6	15	15.3
Harrison, Inc.	13	15.1	7	7.1
All others	16	18.6	24	24.5
Total	86	100%	98	100%

TABLE 7. Percentage distribution of turning machine and boring machine national inventories by age of machine and manufacturer

Manufacturer	Turning machines		Boring machines	
	0–5 years old	Over 5 years old	0–5 years old	Over 5 years old
Milwaukee Machine Co.	12.8%	33.6%	12.2%	13.3%
Victoria	35.0	29.0	8.9	7.7
Harris & Waldrup	—	—	44.8	42.8
Smith,Oberdig, & Crenshaw ..	13.9	11.8	—	—
Harrison, Inc	35.1	17.9	—	—
Gary Co.	—	—	24.2	26.1
All others	3.1	7.7	9.8	10.0
Total	100%	100%	100%	100%

Is the procedure for measuring distributor effectiveness sound? How could it have been improved?

How do you account for the results in territory BB?

What conclusions should Milwaukee Machine Company draw about the efficiency of the various distributors?

What marketing plans should result from these data?

Case 22–2

WALD OFFICE SUPPLIES CO.

The Wald Office Supply Company sold a complete line of such products to a variety of accounts in the metropolitan area in which Wald was located. The company sold approximately $1 million of supplies to a number of markets including public and private sectors, contract, over the counter in its retail store, and end user industries (such as manufacturing, financial institutions, and distribution organizations). In the most recent year the company's sales were broken down approximately as follows: (1) state and local governments (38 percent); (2) over-the-counter sales (13 percent); (3) computer supplies (12 percent); (4) contract sales to commercial accounts (11 percent); and (5) all other commercial (26 percent). Total company sales varied annually primarily because of sales made to the state, which depended upon how many contracts the company was successful in capturing on a bid basis.

Company salesmen were responsible for all nongovernment sales. In the most recent year, their total sales were $632,000. The company's sales manager handled the state and local government (city and county) business while also supervising five salespersons. The company also employed an inside support staff of three individuals who handled all phone inquiries and orders. They also did follow up work for the sales force pertaining to orders, backorders, and adjustments.

Salesmen received a commission on all sales except those to state and local governments, and to major accounts assigned to another salesperson. Their compensation was $750 monthly plus $150 for expenses plus 5 percent of their net sales. Total compensation payments to the five salesmen last year were $86,000, with the average being $17,200 and the range being $15,500 to $22,100. The sales manager was paid a salary plus expenses plus a bonus at the end of the year which was based upon the profits earned by the company.

Each salesperson had both "assigned accounts" and a geographical territory. Accounts "assigned" to each salesman had a long history and were considered by company executives and salesmen to be largely "irrevocable." Since accounts assigned to salespersons were not necessarily within their geographical territories, they had to be deducted from each territory before credit for the other sales was given to the various salespersons. On the average, the assigned accounts represented about sixty percent of all sales generated by the sales force.

Both the president and the sales manager had long thought that the present compensation system was not sufficiently motivating, and did not provide standards by which salesmen could be evaluated. According to the president it was "literally impossible to know how good a job each man is doing given the market opportunities which exist." For these reasons, both men began to think of setting up a sales quota system. Both men recognized that such a system could be implemented in many ways, but they wanted a system which would reflect a reasonable picture of the market potential available to each salesperson.

In his investigation of secondary source data, the sales manager found that the National Office Products Association (NOPA) published a report entitled *County Buying Patterns for Office Products* every two or three years. It reported annual U.S. sales of all office supplies at the dealer level (based on office employment) broken down by state, county and standard metropolitan statistical area (SMSA), and showed this demand as a percent of the total

U.S. demand. Such data were available for the previous year and would have to be projected to the current year by using an average annual growth rate and by adjusting the figures for inflation.

The sales manager thought that the state's Department of Commerce could provide reliable estimates of the number of office workers employed in Wald's metropolitan area. If so, he would be able to calculate the average annual sales dollars per office worker at the dealer level for the metropolitan area in which the company was located. The estimate would be based on the following four steps:

1. Estimate the total U.S. sales of all office supplies for the coming year by updating the NOPA data.
2. Determine the number of office workers in the local metropolitan area from the data provided by the state.
3. Since NOPA reported that the local metropolitan area represented 1.2804 percent of total U.S. office supply sales, determine the total dollar sales of all office supplies in the local metropolitan area by applying 1.2804 percent of the total estimated in step one above.
4. Determine annual dealer sales per office worker in the local metropolitan area by dividing the data from step three by the number of office workers in the local metropolitan area (step 2).

Next, the sales manager planned to sit down with each salesperson and make an estimate of the number of office workers employed by each "assigned" account. The salesperson would be asked to obtain the data from the account if an estimate could not be made. By multiplying the sales per office worker (step 4 above) by the number of such workers in a given account, the annual potential per assigned account could be obtained. A sales quota for each account would be set equal to 50 percent of the account's annual potential. If past sales to the account exceeded 50 percent of the account's potential, the larger percentage would be used for the sales quota.

The market potential of "all other" business in a territory would be determined in the following way (using territory A as an example).

1. Determine "all other" territory A sales last year = total territory A sales last year ($109,000) − total territory A "assigned accounts" sales last year ($71,000) = $38,000.
2. For territory A, determine the ratio of "all other" sales/"assigned account" sales = $38,000/$71,000 = 53.5 percent.
3. Total sales quotas for all "assigned accounts" located in territory A (determined in the manner described earlier) = $96,000.
4. Total quota for "all other" sales in territory A = the ratio determined in step two multiplied by the quota shown in step three = 53.5 percent times $96,000 = $51,360.

The total annual sales quota for each salesperson would be the sum of the quota for the salesperson's assigned accounts plus the quota for all other sales in the salesperson's territory. For example, the salesman in territory A would have a sales quota equal to $51,360 plus the sum of the sales quotas established for each of his assigned accounts. Once set, the quotas for each salesperson would be adjusted annually for inflation, share trend, and any shifts in assigned accounts. They would also be adjusted whenever NOPA published a new report on the total office supply sales in Wald's metropolitan area. Presumably, this would be every two or three years.

Critically evaluate the planned procedures for setting quotas for each salesperson. What sources of error may be present in the system?

How could any of the steps be validated?

What changes would you suggest?

Appendixes

APPENDIX A. Percentage of sample means falling between —Z and + Z under the normal curve, and in one tail under the normal curve

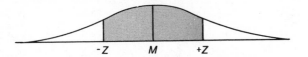

M = True universe mean (or hypothesized universe mean, if appropriate).
$\bar{x}$ = Sample mean.*
s_x = Standard error of the mean.
Z = The *number* of standard errors of the mean between M and $\bar{x}$.

$Z = \dfrac{M - \bar{x}}{s_{\bar{x}}}$	Percent of sample means falling within the —Z to +Z range† (shaded area)	Percent of sample means falling to the right of +Z or to the left of —Z‡
0.8	57.62	21.19
1.0	68.26	15.87
1.2	76.98	11.51
1.4	83.84	8.08
1.6	89.04	5.48
1.8	92.82	3.59
2.0	95.44	2.28
2.1	96.42	1.79
2.2	97.22	1.39
2.3	97.86	1.07
2.4	98.36	.82
2.5	98.76	.62
2.6	99.06	.47
2.7	99.30	.35
2.8	99.48	.26
2.9	99.62	.19
3.0	99.72	.14
3.1	99.80	.10
3.2	99.86	.07
3.3	99.90	.05
3.4	99.94	.03
3.5	99.96	.02

* In the case of a percentage of proportion, p is used instead of $\bar{x}$.
† Percentage of sample means falling outside of —Z to +Z = 100 percent — Column 2.
‡ Column 3 is always (100 percent — Column 2)/2.00.
Source: J. F. Kenney and E. S. Keeping, *Mathematics of Statistics* (New York: D. Van Nostrand Co., 1954). Reprinted by permission of D. Van Nostrand Co.

APPENDIX B. Critical Chi-square values for 90 percent, 95 percent, and 99 percent confidence.

Degrees of freedom	Level of Confidence*		
	90 percent	95 percent	99 percent
1	2.71	3.84	6.63
2	4.61	5.99	9.21
3	6.25	7.81	11.34
4	7.78	9.49	13.28
5	9.24	11.07	15.09
6	10.64	12.59	16.81
7	12.02	14.07	18.48
8	13.36	15.51	20.09
9	14.68	16.92	21.67
10	15.99	18.31	23.21
11	17.28	19.68	24.72
12	18.55	21.03	26.22
13	19.81	22.36	27.69
14	21.06	23.68	29.14
15	22.31	25.00	30.58
16	23.54	26.30	32.00
17	24.77	27.59	33.41
18	25.99	28.87	34.81
19	27.20	30.14	36.19
20	28.41	31.41	37.57
21	29.62	32.67	38.93
22	30.81	33.92	40.29
23	32.01	35.17	41.64
24	33.20	36.42	42.98
25	34.38	37.65	44.31
26	35.56	38.89	45.64
27	36.74	40.11	46.96
28	37.92	41.34	48.28
29	39.09	42.56	49.59
30	40.26	43.77	50.89
40	51.80	55.76	63.69
50	63.17	67.50	76.15
60	74.40	79.08	88.38

* The calculated Chi-square value must exceed the figures shown in the appropriate row of the table in order for researchers to be ——% confident that there is a significant difference between the observed and expected data, that is, that the observed and expected data were not drawn from the same population.

Source: Adapted from E. S. Pearson and H. O. Hartley, eds., *Biometrika Tables for Statisticians,* vol. I, Table 18, pp. 160–63, published for the Biometrika Trustees by Cambridge University, 1954, by permission of Professor Pearson and the Trustees of Biometrika.

APPENDIX C. Critical values* of the F distribution for 95 percent confidence

Degrees of freedom for numerator

Degrees of freedom for denominator	1	2	3	4	5	6	7	8	9	10	12	15	20	24	30	40	60	120	∞
1	161	200	216	225	230	234	237	239	241	242	244	246	248	249	250	251	252	253	254
2	18.5	19.0	19.2	19.2	19.3	19.3	19.4	19.4	19.4	19.4	19.4	19.4	19.4	19.4	19.5	19.5	19.5	19.5	19.5
3	10.1	9.55	9.28	9.12	9.01	8.94	8.89	8.85	8.81	8.79	8.74	8.70	8.66	8.64	8.62	8.59	8.57	8.55	8.53
4	7.71	6.94	6.59	6.39	6.26	6.16	6.09	6.04	6.00	5.96	5.91	5.86	5.80	5.77	5.75	5.72	5.69	5.66	5.63
5	6.61	5.79	5.41	5.19	5.05	4.95	4.88	4.82	4.77	4.74	4.68	4.62	4.56	4.53	4.50	4.46	4.43	4.40	4.37
6	5.99	5.14	4.76	4.53	4.39	4.28	4.21	4.15	4.10	4.06	4.00	3.94	3.87	3.84	3.81	3.77	3.74	3.70	3.67
7	5.59	4.74	4.35	4.12	3.97	3.87	3.79	3.73	3.68	3.64	3.57	3.51	3.44	3.41	3.38	3.34	3.30	3.27	3.23
8	5.32	4.46	4.07	3.84	3.69	3.58	3.50	3.44	3.39	3.35	3.28	3.22	3.15	3.12	3.08	3.04	3.01	2.97	2.93
9	5.12	4.26	3.86	3.63	3.48	3.37	3.29	3.23	3.18	3.14	3.07	3.01	2.94	2.90	2.86	2.83	2.79	2.75	2.71
10	4.96	4.10	3.71	3.48	3.33	3.22	3.14	3.07	3.02	2.98	2.91	2.85	2.77	2.74	2.70	2.66	2.62	2.58	2.54
11	4.84	3.98	3.59	3.36	3.20	3.09	3.01	2.95	2.90	2.85	2.79	2.72	2.65	2.61	2.57	2.53	2.49	2.45	2.40
12	4.75	3.89	3.49	3.26	3.11	3.00	2.91	2.85	2.80	2.75	2.69	2.62	2.54	2.51	2.47	2.43	2.38	2.34	2.30
13	4.67	3.81	3.41	3.18	3.03	2.92	2.83	2.77	2.71	2.67	2.60	2.53	2.46	2.42	2.38	2.34	2.30	2.25	2.21
14	4.60	3.74	3.34	3.11	2.96	2.85	2.76	2.70	2.65	2.60	2.53	2.46	2.39	2.35	2.31	2.27	2.22	2.18	2.13
15	4.54	3.68	3.29	3.06	2.90	2.79	2.71	2.64	2.59	2.54	2.48	2.40	2.33	2.29	2.25	2.20	2.16	2.11	2.07
16	4.49	3.63	3.24	3.01	2.85	2.74	2.66	2.59	2.54	2.49	2.42	2.35	2.28	2.24	2.19	2.15	2.11	2.06	2.01
17	4.45	3.59	3.20	2.96	2.81	2.70	2.61	2.55	2.49	2.45	2.38	2.31	2.23	2.19	2.15	2.10	2.06	2.01	1.96
18	4.41	3.55	3.16	2.93	2.77	2.66	2.58	2.51	2.46	2.41	2.34	2.27	2.19	2.15	2.11	2.06	2.02	1.97	1.92
19	4.38	3.52	3.13	2.90	2.74	2.63	2.54	2.48	2.42	2.38	2.31	2.23	2.16	2.11	2.07	2.03	1.98	1.93	1.88
20	4.35	3.49	3.10	2.87	2.71	2.60	2.51	2.45	2.39	2.35	2.28	2.20	2.12	2.08	2.04	1.99	1.95	1.90	1.84
21	4.32	3.47	3.07	2.84	2.68	2.57	2.49	2.42	2.37	2.32	2.25	2.18	2.10	2.05	2.01	1.96	1.92	1.87	1.81
22	4.30	3.44	3.05	2.82	2.66	2.55	2.46	2.40	2.34	2.30	2.23	2.15	2.07	2.03	1.98	1.94	1.89	1.84	1.78
23	4.28	3.42	3.03	2.80	2.64	2.53	2.44	2.37	2.32	2.27	2.20	2.13	2.05	2.01	1.96	1.91	1.86	1.81	1.76
24	4.26	3.40	3.01	2.78	2.62	2.51	2.42	2.36	2.30	2.25	2.18	2.11	2.03	1.98	1.94	1.89	1.84	1.79	1.73
25	4.24	3.39	2.99	2.76	2.60	2.49	2.40	2.34	2.28	2.24	2.16	2.09	2.01	1.96	1.92	1.87	1.82	1.77	1.71
30	4.17	3.32	2.92	2.69	2.53	2.42	2.33	2.27	2.21	2.16	2.09	2.01	1.93	1.89	1.84	1.79	1.74	1.68	1.62
40	4.08	3.23	2.84	2.61	2.45	2.34	2.25	2.18	2.12	2.08	2.00	1.92	1.84	1.79	1.74	1.69	1.64	1.58	1.51
60	4.00	3.15	2.76	2.53	2.37	2.25	2.17	2.10	2.04	1.99	1.92	1.84	1.75	1.70	1.65	1.59	1.53	1.47	1.39
120	3.92	3.07	2.68	2.45	2.29	2.18	2.09	2.02	1.96	1.91	1.83	1.75	1.66	1.61	1.55	1.50	1.43	1.35	1.25
∞	3.84	3.00	2.60	2.37	2.21	2.10	2.01	1.94	1.88	1.83	1.75	1.67	1.57	1.52	1.46	1.39	1.32	1.22	1.00

* Critical F values for higher levels of confidence are larger than those shown here.
Source: This table is reproduced from M. Merrington and C. M. Thompson, "Tables of Percentage Points of the Inverted Beta (F) Distribution," *Biometrika* 33 (1943), by permission of the Biometrika Trustees.

APPENDIX D. SPSS Computer Program For Univariate and Multivariate Tabulations

Figure D–1 presents a computer program designed to use SPSS (Statistical Package for the Social Sciences) to perform univariate and multivariate tabulations on survey data which have been keypunched onto computer cards. This program can be used for any number of questionnaires, from a few dozen to as many as 500 or more. As shown, the program can be used for questionnaires with as many as 40 questions, including multiple choice and open questions, if the number of response categories per question is ten or fewer. (Even longer questionnaires can be analyzed by following the instructions below.)

It should be noted that this program is not the only way to program SPSS to perform univariate and multivariate tabulations, and that researchers skilled in computer programming are likely to write more sophisticated programs. Researchers inexperienced in the use of the computer to analyze data, however, will be able to create the univariate and multivariate tabulations they desire if they follow the instructions presented here.

Figure D–1 shows the computer cards which constitute the program. *Each line of capitalized print in the Exhibit represents one computer card.* Researchers should keypunch their computer cards to be identical to those

---

FIGURE D–1. SPSS Computer Program For Univariate and Multivariate Tabulations*

```
//ABCDEFGH_JOB_(1423,1,2)BOWEST,MSGLEVEL=1,CLASS=1,TIME=(0,30)
//S1_EXEC_SPSS
RUN_NAME_____DEMOGRAPHICS_OF_COLLEGE_STUDENTS
VARIABLE_LIST__RESPNUM,SEX,HEIGHT,WEIGHT,YEAR
INPUT_MEDIUM___CARD
INPUT_FORMAT___FREEFIELD
N_OF_CASES_____100
VAR_LABELS_____SEX,SEX_OF_THE_RESPONDENT/
               HEIGHT,HEIGHT_OF_THE_RESPONDENT/
               WEIGHT,WEIGHT_OF_THE_RESPONDENT/
               YEAR,RESPONDENTS_YEAR_IN_COLLEGE/
VALUE_LABELS___SEX(1)MALE(2)FEMALE/
               YEAR(1)FRESHMAN(2)SOPHOMORE(3)JUNIOR(4)SENIOR/
READ_INPUT_DATA


        ┌──────────────────────────────────┐
        │  Data cards are inserted here     │
        └──────────────────────────────────┘


FREQUENCIES____GENERAL=SEX,YEAR
STATISTICS_____ALL
CROSSTABS_____TABLES=YEAR_BY_HEIGHT/
                      WEIGHT_BY_HEIGHT/
STATISTICS_____ALL
FINISH
```

* The first two cards in the program (i.e., the first two lines in the figure) are system specific and must be written according to the specifications established at each computer installation. Each underscore (—) shown in the figure represents one column left completely blank.

shown in the Exhibit (except for the name of the researcher, the title of the research or the computer run, and the names of the variables or data being analyzed). Where the exhibit shows a blank space (indicated by an underscore), a comma, a slash, an equal sign, or a parentheses, researchers should do exactly the same.

A hypothetical example is used to illustrate this program. One hundred college students were asked questions about their height in inches, weight in pounds, sex, and year in college. For the purpose of identification, each student (and questionnaire) was given an identification number. Data from each questionnaire were keypunched onto computer cards, one card per questionnaire.

Three types of computer cards are used in the program—(1) data cards, (2) SPSS control cards, and (3) job control cards. (1) The data from each questionnaire are keypunched onto computer cards, which then become part of the program. (2) There are about 20–30 SPSS control cards in a typical program, and these give the computer instructions on how the data are to be tabulated. (3) The first few cards in the program are job control cards (JCL), which are used to identify the researcher, the research job, and the standardized computer program to be used (in this case, SPSS).

One characteristic of JCL cards is that they *must follow specifications established at each computer installation*. This means that JCL cards will differ from installation to installation. Therefore, it is *absolutely necessary* that researchers first determine the JCL standards utilized by the computer installation at which the data analysis will occur, and then follow those standards when keypunching the JCL cards.

This example shows the use of two JCL cards. (In some computer installations only one JCL card may be required, while other computer installations may require the use of three or more JCL cards.) The two JCL cards represented by the first two lines in Figure D–1 are shown only to indicate the presence of some JCL cards in the program. Their purposes are as follows:

//ABCDEFGH JOB.   This JCL card is the JOB card, and it serves to identify the job name (ABCDEFGH), the user's name (BOWEST), the user's account number (1423), an estimate of the maximum amount of computing time needed (TIME = (0,30)), and similar things.

//S1 EXEC SPSS.   This JCL card informs the computer that the researcher would like to execute (that is, use) the SPSS program.

The remaining cards shown in Figure D–1 are SPSS control cards. While these cards will result in a workable computer program in practically all computer installations, it is suggested that researchers ask personnel at their local computer facility to confirm that this is so.

SPSS control cards are used to present control words and operating instructions to the computer. Computer cards have 80 columns, and control words *always begin* in the first column and *cannot extend beyond* the 15th column. Columns 16–80 on SPSS control cards are used for operating instructions, *which must begin* in column 16 (except where noted otherwise). The SPSS control cards shown in Figure D–1 are described below.

RUN NAME.   This card is used to give a title to the research. Any title may be used if it fits into columns 16–80.

VARIABLE LIST.   Each variable, that is, each item of data or question should be given a unique name or identity, limited to 8 characters, of which the first is always a letter and the others are either letters or numbers. For example, the names given to the five variables in the hypothetical study are RESPNUM (for respondent number), SEX, HEIGHT, WEIGHT, YEAR. If the researcher wished, identities such as V1, V2, V3, . . . could have been used instead. This list of names and identities should be presented *in the order they appear on the data cards,* beginning from the left and moving to the right. Each variable name must be followed by a comma, unless it is the last name in the list. If there are many variables and more than one card is needed to identify them, the first card must end with a comma (anywhere up to column 80), and the next name should be keypunched on a second card, *beginning in column 16.*

INPUT MEDIUM.   This is a required control card which should be keypunched exactly as shown.

INPUT FORMAT.   This is a required control card which should be keypunched exactly as shown.

N OF CASES.   Beginning in column 16, keypunch the number of questionnaires which have been transferred onto data cards and will be used in the analysis. In the hypothetical example, 100 is keypunched into columns 16–18 because it represents the number of questionnaires to be analyzed.

VAR LABELS.   These control cards let researchers specify more descriptive titles for the rows and columns of the final tables resulting from the computer program. For example, the second variable on the VARIABLE LIST is SEX. If researchers wish to have tables which use the label, SEX OF THE RESPONDENT, instead of just SEX, they should include a VAR LABEL card like the one shown in the Exhibit. On these cards, beginning in column 16, researchers should keypunch-in the name given to the variable on the VARIABLE LIST card, followed by a comma, followed by the more descriptive title, followed by a slash. The more descriptive title is limited to forty letters and spaces. Note that a separate card should be used for each additional variable which is to be given a descriptive title. However, additional cards need not include the control words. The Exhibit shows such cards for three of the other variables in the example.

VALUE LABELS.   Control cards such as these are needed whenever a variable uses numerical codes to identify a response category. For example, if the questionnaire in the example coded the sex of males with a 1 and females with a 2, the computer must be given that information. On this card, beginning in column 16, researchers should keypunch the variable name, followed by (1), followed by the label associated with 1, namely MALE, followed by (2), followed by the label associated with 2, namely FEMALE, followed by a slash. Similarly, if freshman were identified by a 1, sophomores by a 2, and so on, the computer must also be given that information. (See Figure D–1.) Each of these descriptive labels is limited to 20 letters and spaces. Note that a separate card should be used for each additional variable which uses numerical codes to identify a response category. However, additional cards need not include the control words. Note also that in the example numerical codes were not used to record the height and weight of respondents. Since the height and weight of respondents were recorded in inches and pounds, respectively, value label cards are not needed for those variables. If a variable has a large number of response categories and all of the labels do not fit into columns 16–80 on one card, more than one card will have to be used. In such a case, the first card should end with a complete label, and the second card should begin in column 16 with the value of the label enclosed in parentheses, e.g. (3), and then the next label, e.g. JUNIOR.

READ INPUT DATA.   This control card tells the computer that data cards follow next, and should be read into the computer.

In most surveys there will be one data card for each completed questionnaire. (Longer questionnaires can be accommodated by adding a second data card. In such surveys, researchers should seek advice from computer personnel on how to keypunch the second data card.) On each data card, one or more columns should be reserved for each question on the questionnaire, and this reservation scheme should be identical for all data cards. (See the "keypunching" discussion in Chapter 13.) At least one column should be left completely blank (that is, with no keypunches) after each column assigned to a question. For example, columns 1, 2, and 3 could be used for the respondent's identification number. Column 4 should be left completely blank, Column 5 could be reserved for responses to the first question, column 6 should be left blank, columns 7, 8, and 9 could be reserved for responses to the second question, column 10 should be left blank, and so on. Responses to each question should be coded and keypunched into their appropriate columns. If for some reason a respondent skipped a question, or was not asked a certain question, those responses should be coded with a number that is different from all of the numbers which represent valid responses to the question. For example, if a respondent didn't report his year in college, that could be coded with –1, 0, or 5–9 (see the above discussion on VALUE LABELS). The selected number should be keypunched into the appropriate column.

FREQUENCIES.   This control card follows the last data card. Researchers use this control card to identify the variables on which a univariate tabulation will be made. Columns 16–23 should be keypunched as shown in Figure D–1. Researchers should then insert the names of the variables (see VARIABLE LIST) to be tabulated, using a comma between names. Exhibit 1 shows that the researcher has asked the computer to perform a univariate tabulation on the variables SEX and YEAR. These instructions will result in one frequency distribution of males and females, and another frequency distribution of freshman, sophomores, juniors and seniors. The resulting computer printout will appear much like the data presented in Table 13–7 and in "Approach A" in Table 13–2. If researchers want univariate tabulations of many variables, it may be necessary to use more than one card. In such cases, the first card should end with a comma and the next variable name should be keypunched on the second card, beginning in column 24.

STATISTICS.   This control card should be keypunched exactly as shown. This card requests that all possible statistics associated with the univariate tabulation be printed out. These statistics include the mean, mode, median, and range.

CROSSTABS.   Researchers use this card to identify the variables on which a multivariate tabulation will be made. Columns 16–22 should be keypunched as shown in Figure D–1. Researchers should then insert the names of the variables (see VARIABLE LIST) to be cross tabulated, leaving a space both before and after BY, and placing a slash after the last letter of the second variable name. The program in Figure D–1 requests a multivariate tabulation of YEAR, which will appear as the rows of the resulting table, and HEIGHT, which will appear as the columns of the resulting table. Figure D–1 also requests a multivariate tabulation of WEIGHT BY HEIGHT, which should be keypunched beginning in column 23 of the following card. These instructions will result in tables of a form similar to those shown in Figure 13–2. If other cross tabulations are needed, an additional card should be used for each additional cross tabulation, with the first letter of the first variable being keypunched in column 23.

STATISTICS.   This control card should be keypunched exactly as shown. This control card requests that all possible statistics associated with the multivariate tabulation be printed out. One of these statistics is the ratio of (number of responses in a given cell ÷ total number of responses in all cells) shown as a percentage. Also shown are each cell's percentage of both its row total and its column total.

FINISH. This card tells the computer it has reached the end of the program.

The multivariate tabulations shown in Figure D–1 involve only two variables. It is possible to perform multivariate tabulations involving three or more variables. To illustrate, assume the researcher wishes tabulations of WEIGHT BY HEIGHT for males who are sophomores, juniors, or seniors. This tabulation can be accomplished with the addition of two control cards which should be inserted after the VALUE LABELS cards and before the READ INPUT DATA card. These two control cards are:

SELECT_IF _ _ _ _ _ _ (SEX_EQ_1)
SELECT_IF _ _ _ _ _ _ (YEAR_EQ_2_OR_3_OR_4)

The first letter in SELECT should be keypunched in column 1, with the remainder of the card spaced as shown above. The first of these cards tells the computer to analyze only those data cards on which a 1 has been keypunched in the SEX column. The second of these cards tells the computer to analyze only those data cards on which a 2, 3, or 4 has been keypunched in the YEAR column. The cross tabulations of WEIGHT BY HEIGHT (and YEAR BY HEIGHT) would then be performed for only those respondents who are males in the sophomore, junior or senior years in college.

Index

A

Accuracy
  of observation data, 96–97
  of survey data, 97–98
Administrative process, 7–13
  action phase, 10–11
  goal-setting phase, 7–9
  planning phase, 9–10
  reappraisal phase, 11–13
Advertising data, 149–51
Advertising research, 602–29
  copy testing, 613–22
    "after" tests, 613, 620–21
      recall, 620–21
      recognition, 621
    "before" tests, 613–20
      consumer jury, 614
      day-after recall, 619–20
      inquiries, 618
      physiological, 616–18
      portfolio, 615–16
      psychological, 616
      rating scales, 614–15
      sales, 618–19
  media selection, 622–28
    audience measures, 623–27
      print, 624–25
      radio and television, 625–27
    media models, 627–28
  setting objectives, for, 610–12
    attitude shifts in target audience, 611–12
Advertising Research Foundation, 621
Aided recall, 226–27
Analysis, collected data, 396–416, 424–50, 454–82, 488–535
  categories, ordering data into, 398–415
    editing and coding, 399–405, 408–10
      "don't knows," 408–10
      establishing categories, 402–3
      incomplete answers, 401–2
      incorrect answers, 401
      keypunching, 403–5
      planning, 399–400

Analysis—*Cont.*
  editing and coding—*Cont.*
    preliminary check, 400–401
    tabulation, 405–15
      bivariate and multivariate, 412–15
      computer program for, 415
      manual versus machine, 403–5
      multiple answers, 410–12
      planning, 399–400
      univariate, 408–12
      use of percentages, 406–7
  explaining observed differences, 454–82, 488–506
    automatic interaction detector, 491, 498–506
    comparison of different methods for, 491
    correlation analysis, 456, 462–68
    cross tabulation, 456–62, 491
    linear discriminant analysis, 491–98
    regression analysis, 456, 462–63, 468–82, 491
      multiple linear, 477–80
      simple linear, 469–77
      stepwise multiple linear, 480
  identifying interdependencies, 490–92, 507–35
    cluster analysis, 491, 507–16
    conjoint analysis, 491, 526–34
    factor analysis, 491, 516–26
  significant differences, determining, 424–50
    analysis of variance, 438–50
    chi square analysis, 431–38
    sampling statistics, 425–31
      continuous variables, 429–30
      percentages, 425–29
      small samples, 430–31
  summary statistics, 406
Analysis of variance, 438–50
  estimated variance, 443, 449
  F statistic, 443–44, 449
  one-way, 440–44

This book has been set linotype in 10 and 9 point Times Roman, leaded 2 points. Part numbers are 10 and 42 point Helvetica Semi Bold. Part and chapter titles are 18 point Helvetica, and chapter numbers are 42 point Helvetica Semi Bold. The type page is 27 x 47 picas.